Administrative Law in Context

SECOND EDITION

Edited by

Colleen M. Flood
Faculty of Law, University of Toronto

Lorne Sossin
Osgoode Hall Law School

<adminlawincontext.emp.ca>

2013
EMOND MONTGOMERY PUBLICATIONS
TORONTO, CANADA

Emond Montgomery Publications Limited
60 Shaftesbury Avenue
Toronto ON M4T 1A3
http://www.emp.ca/lawschool

Printed in Canada.
Reprinted January 2013.

We acknowledge the financial support of the Government of Canada through the Canada Book Fund for our publishing activities.

Publisher: Bernard Sandler
Sales and marketing coordinator: Jenna Williams
Marketing manager: Christine Davidson
Supervising editor: Jim Lyons
Copy editors: Paula Pike, Diane Gula
Copy and production editor: Nancy Ennis

Library and Archives Canada Cataloguing in Publication
    Administrative law in context / edited by Colleen M. Flood and Lorne Sossin. — 2nd ed.

Includes index.
ISBN 978-1-55239-471-7

    1. Administrative law—Canada—Textbooks.   I. Flood, Colleen M. (Colleen Marion), 1966-   II. Sossin, Lorne Mitchell, 1964-

KE5015.A845 2012   342.71'06   C2012-904450-4
KF5402.A845 2012

Foreword to the Second Edition

It is a pleasure and honour for me to continue my association with *Administrative Law in Context* by providing these remarks for its second edition. Two factors are especially important behind the appearance of a second edition. One is explained by the organic nature of the law, whether legislative or judicially inspired, in that it develops and changes rapidly and administrative law is no exception. The other factor is that the work in question merits a second edition as judged by the response to the first edition; as such, this second edition is praiseful recognition for the editors and contributors who have toiled to produce this very helpful volume.

The second edition has retained all of the virtues of the first edition that I mentioned in my Foreword and indeed has added special attractions by the inclusion of new chapters on Aboriginal administrative law and on the Federal Court and administrative law. As well, the editors and contributors have reordered many of the chapters, changed many of the titles, as well as updating the commentary that follows, and welcomed some new contributors into their scholarly midst. All of this with no loss in the coverage, calibre, utility, or lucidity of the book. Put another way, the bottles, labelling, and packaging may have changed in some respects, but the wine tastes as good as ever, and some new vintages have been added!

I congratulate the editors and contributors for another excellent effort.

Frank Iacobucci

Foreword to the First Edition

Having spent close to 50 years in the law, I have been a witness to the remarkable growth and development of administrative law in Canada and abroad. In my student days, the administrative law syllabus was rather thin compared with the course topics and materials found in the contemporary administrative law course. There are many reasons for this turn of events, but chief among them is the tremendous proliferation of boards, tribunals, and agencies brought about by the perceived needs and preferences of the modern regulatory state. As a lawyer in the private and public sectors, law professor, member of an administrative tribunal, judge, and now back to being a lawyer, I have been privileged to have an almost front-row seat to view the parade of administrative law developments and growth. It is that perspective which causes me to state that I enthusiastically welcome the arrival of *Administrative Law in Context*. Allow me to explain my enthusiasm.

I agree with the basic premise of this volume that for many years excessive emphasis has been placed on judicial review of administrative tribunals. Indeed, in the beginning years of the subject, and for too long, there was, in my view, far too much attention paid to legal controls of administrative action, as reflected, for example, in the views of A.V. Dicey[1] and Lord Hewart of Bury,[2] and not enough attention to what might be called a realistic approach to the subject, as reflected in the writings of John Willis.[3]

Granted, lawyers must obviously be attuned to judicial review since legal remedies and oversight are part of the tool kit for every lawyer in advising clients. Consequently (and most appropriately), the book includes chapters on remedies, the rule of law, the duty of fairness, and judicial review. But the book goes well beyond those topics to give the reader a better understanding of what tribunals do, the complexities they face, and how they reach decisions and shape policy. Also explored are a number of theoretical issues on the legitimacy of public authority; the interplay among law, regulations, and guidelines; the choice of regulatory instruments; and other topics.

---

[1] A.V. Dicey, *An Introduction to the Study of the Constitution* (London: MacMillan & Co., 1885 and subsequent editions).

[2] Lord Hewart of Bury, *The New Despotism* (London: E. Benn, 1929).

[3] See, for example, John Willis, *Three Approaches to Administrative Law* (1935/36) 1 U.T.L.J. 53; John Willis, 1974 Cecil Wright Memorial Lecture, University of Toronto Faculty of Law (later published as "Canadian Administrative Law in Retrospect" (1974) 24 U.T.L.J. 225); and John Willis, "Administrative Law in Canada" (1961) 39 Can. Bar Rev. 251.

The manner of presentation of the various chapters is also noteworthy. Some 17 scholars from across the country have combined to provide a highly readable text, with a range of diversity reflected in the transnational backgrounds of the authors, and this has resulted in a menu of innovative and instructive commentary.

In short, the collection appropriately takes a broad view of the subject and does so in an informative and well-structured manner. I have no doubt that the book will accomplish the goal of its authors to serve as a primary resource for administrative law students throughout Canada. But the book is also an important scholarly contribution to the field in a variety of topics that will be of great benefit to lawyers and judges. And for all that, I wish to commend and thank the contributors for their efforts.

Frank Iacobucci

Preface

Standing on the shoulders of giants, we were inspired to build on the teaching and scholarship of David Mullan, Hudson Janisch, Dick Risk, and John Evans, who pioneered the first edition of Emond Montgomery's *Administrative Law: Cases and Materials*, in 1981. On behalf of all the contributors to this volume, we express our gratitude to these leaders in administrative law for all they have done in advancing this field, and dedicate this volume in their honour. Building on their legacy, we sought to create a new kind of text for administrative law in order to explore the myriad contexts of administrative decision making. And since the publication of the first edition of this volume in 2008, it has been adopted in administrative law classes across the country, introduced new readers to the field, informed debates among scholars and practitioners, and cited at every level of court proceeding, including the Supreme Court of Canada. The volume has contributed, as we had hoped, to the growing recognition that administrative law happens outside the courtroom—in government departments, agencies, boards, commissions and tribunals—affecting the experience of all those involved in the administrative justice system.

Apart from emphasizing the context of administrative law on the ground, an additional goal was to create an accessible, readable text that reflects the many perspectives in administrative law. We are proud to include in this volume scholars and teachers in administrative law from across Canada, with some of the most experienced voices in the field, as well as some new ones. Because administrative law is ever evolving, a further goal was to create a flexible, living text. To this end, the book is accompanied by a website, at <adminlawincontext .emp.ca>, where both students and teachers can find edited and full-text cases for each chapter; recommendations for additional readings; and important additions, clarifications, and updates to the published text. Although every chapter in the volume has been substantially revised for the second edition (and two new chapters have been added), we have also revamped the website with new cases, commentaries, and resources. We hope this format will continue to do justice to the dynamic nature of the field.

While the contributions to this volume reflect distinctive voices, they also speak to shared themes and concerns. These have been the subject of three lively workshops held at the Faculty of Law, University of Toronto, which included discussions on how best to cover the diverse fields of administrative law and administrative justice. Transforming the rich array of available material into relatively short, accessible chapters is a daunting task, but all our contributors were equal to the challenge. We believe each author has skillfully managed to both survey the field and provide more scholarly punch than is possible in a traditional casebook. This volume has been a truly collaborative project and we thank the contributors for their efforts, which we hope will benefit the new generation of administrative law students.

In addition to the debt we owe to our contributors, we want to acknowledge the unflagging support of the Faculty of Law, University of Toronto, and a number of individuals at Emond Montgomery who have done so much to get this book, and this second edition, to print, particularly Paul Emond, Peggy Buchan, Bernard Sandler, Nancy Ennis, Cindy Fujimoto, and Jim Lyons. We are also grateful for the administrative and research assistance provided by Greg Hinds and Oscar Cabrera (first edition) and Marcelo Rodriguez Ferrere and Ryan MacIsaac (second edition). We also wish to express special thanks to Sujith Xavier and Bryan Thomas (first edition) and Arthur Wilson (second edition), research managers during different phases of this book's development at the Faculty of Law, University of Toronto.

Finally, we would like to thank all our students of administrative law—past, present, and future—who stimulate and engage us, and always hold our feet to the fire.

Colleen M. Flood and Lorne Sossin
July 2012

Table of Contents

Table of Cases

List of Contributors

Geneviève Cartier

Geneviève Cartier is a Professor of Law at the University of Sherbrooke. She holds a Ph.D. from the University of Toronto and an M.A. from Cambridge University. A member of the Consultative Committee of the Law Commission of Canada from 2003 to 2006, she teaches and researches in the areas of public law and jurisprudence. Her work focuses on administrative discretion, the rule of law, and common-law constitutionalism, and she is currently working on the question of prerogative powers. Her recent contributions include the co-ordination of a special issue of the *McGill Law Journal*, dedicated to the celebration of the 50th anniversary of the Supreme Court decision in *Roncarelli v. Duplessis*. In February 2012, she was appointed research director of the Commission of Inquiry into the granting and administration of government contracts in the construction industry, set up by the government of Quebec.

Peter Carver

Peter Carver, M.A. (Toronto), LL.B. (McGill), LL.M. (U.B.C.) is Associate Professor, Faculty of Law and Chairperson of the Board of the Centre for Constitutional Studies at the University of Alberta. Professor Carver teaches and researches in the areas of Canadian constitutional, administrative, immigration, and mental health law. Before coming to the University of Alberta, Professor Carver served as a member of the Immigration and Refugee Board and practised law in British Columbia. Recent publications include "Comparing Aboriginal and Other Duties to Consult in Canadian Law" (Alta. Law Rev., forthcoming 2012); "Canadian Mental Health Law" in *Canadian Health Law and Policy*, 4th ed. (Toronto: LexisNexis, 2011); "Recurring Constitutional Principles" in *Public Law*, 2d ed. (Toronto: Emond Montgomery, 2011); and "Reality Check: On the Uses of Empiricism" (2008) 21 Can. J.L. & Jur. 447.

Jennifer Dolling

Jennifer Dolling is a Toronto-area lawyer who has practised primarily in the area of health law. She holds a B.A. in Criminology with high distinction from the University of Toronto (1996); an LL.B. from Queen's University (1999); and an LL.M. with a specialty in Health Law and Policy from the University of Toronto (2009), for which she was awarded a Canadian Institutes of Health Research Training Program Fellowship. After her call to the Ontario Bar in 2001, Jennifer practised for several years in the areas of medical malpractice, professional negligence and liability, health disciplines defence, insurance defence, and personal injury. She has appeared before administrative tribunals such as the Health Professions Appeal and Review Board. She was a member of the Research Ethics Board at Mount

Sinai Hospital from 2007 to 2012. After completing her LL.M., Jennifer worked as a research associate in the Faculty of Law at the University of Toronto. She most recently held the position of research counsel in the Samuel Lunenfeld Research Institute at Mount Sinai Hospital.

Colleen M. Flood

Colleen M. Flood is a Canada Research Chair at the Faculty of Law, University of Toronto and is cross-appointed to the School of Public Policy and the Institute of Health Policy, Management & Evaluation. From 2006 to 2011 she served as the Scientific Director of the Canadian Institute for Health Services and Policy Research. Her primary areas of scholarship are in administrative law, comparative health care law & policy, public–private financing of health-care systems, health-care reform, and accountability and governance issues more broadly. She is the author and editor of eight books, including editor of *Data, Data, Everywhere: Access and Accountability?* (Montreal: McGill-Queen's University Press, 2011); co-editor of *Canadian Health Law and Policy*, 4th ed. (Markham, ON: Butterworths, 2011); co-editor of *Exploring Social Insurance: Can a Dose of Europe Cure Canadian Health Care Finance?* (Montreal: McGill-Queen's University Press, 2008); editor of *Just Medicare: What's In, What's Out, How We Decide* (Toronto: University of Toronto Press, 2006); co-editor of *Access to Care, Access to Justice: The Legal Debate Over Private Health Insurance in Canada* (Toronto: University of Toronto Press, 2005); and author of *International Health Care Reform: A Legal, Economic and Political Analysis* (London: Routledge, 2000).

Craig Forcese

Craig Forcese is Vice Dean and Associate Professor, Faculty of Law (Common Law Section), at the University of Ottawa. He teaches national security law, public international law, administrative law, and public law/legislation. Much of his current research and writing relates to national security, human rights, and democratic accountability. Craig is the author of *National Security Law: Canadian Practice in International Perspective* (Toronto: Irwin Law, 2007) and co-editor of the *Human Rights and Anti-terrorism* (Toronto: Irwin Law, 2008). He is also co-editor and co-author of *International Law: Doctrine, Practice, and Theory* (Toronto: Irwin Law, 2007); co-managing editor of *Public Law: Cases, Materials, and Commentary*, 2d ed. (Toronto: Emond Montgomery, 2011); and co-author of *The Laws of Government: The Legal Foundations of Canadian Democracy*, 2d ed. (Toronto: Irwin Law, 2010). Before joining the law school faculty, Craig practised law at the Washington, DC office of Hughes Hubbard & Reed LLP, specializing in international trade and commercial law. He has a B.A. from McGill University (1992), an M.A. from the Norman Paterson School of International Affairs, Carleton University (1997), an LL.B. (summa cum laude) from the University of Ottawa (where he shared the gold medal for the best graduating average of his class) (1997), and an LL.M. from Yale University (2001). He is a member in good standing of the bars of Ontario, New York, and the District of Columbia.

Cristie Ford

Cristie Ford is an Assistant Professor at the University of British Columbia Faculty of Law. She writes and teaches in the areas of administrative and public law, securities regulation, and regulatory theory. Her research focuses on the intersection of securities and global financial regulation, on the one hand, and public law theory and regulatory design, on the other. Some of her recent scholarship has examined novel regulatory enforcement strategies, principles-based securities regulation, the regulation of systemic risk, and prospects for "responsive" financial regulation. Professor Ford holds LL.M. and J.S.D. degrees from Columbia Law School, where she also taught in various capacities before joining UBC. She also practised law for six years in Vancouver and New York. In 2012, Professor Ford became an editor of the international, peer-reviewed journal *Regulation & Governance*. She is co-authoring the fifth edition of a leading textbook, *Canadian Securities Regulation* (with David Johnston, O.C., and Kathleen Rockwell) (forthcoming 2013), and is working on a project that considers the relationship between innovation and regulatory design.

Evan Fox-Decent

Evan Fox-Decent is Associate Professor at McGill University, Faculty of Law. He teaches and publishes in legal theory, administrative law, First Nations and the law, immigration law, the law of fiduciaries, and human rights. He has worked on human rights and democratic governance reform in Latin America since 1987, beginning with advocacy and relief work in El Salvador under the auspices of Nobel Peace Prize nominee Medardo Gómez. His recent book, *Sovereignty's Promise: The State as Fiduciary* (Oxford: Oxford University Press, 2011), explores the implications of viewing the state and its institutions as fiduciaries of the people subject to their power. Among these implications is a distinctive interpretation of common-law constitutionalism, called "administrative law as solicitude."

Andrew Green

Andrew Green, B.A. (Hons.) (Queen's University, 1987), M.A. (University of Toronto, 1988), LL.B. (University of Toronto, 1992), LL.M. (University of Chicago, 1994), J.S.D. (University of Chicago, 1997), called to the Bar of Ontario in 1996, is an Assistant Professor at the University of Toronto, Faculty of Law. Before joining the Faculty, Professor Green practised environmental law in Toronto for six years at Davies Ward Phillips & Vineberg LLP; Osler, Hoskin & Harcourt LLP; and Hicks Morley Hamilton Stewart Storie. His practice encompassed both litigation (including prosecutions, administrative appeals, and civil actions) and transactional work. From 2002 to 2004, Professor Green was Senior Research Fellow for Ontario's Panel on the Role of Government, with Professor Michael Trebilcock and Ronald Daniels, former dean of the Faculty of Law, University of Toronto. The panel identified the major challenges that the province faces in areas such as education, health, environment, economic policy, and taxes. Professor Green's research and teaching interests focus on environmental law; international trade; and administrative law, including how international trade rules constrain countries' ability to implement domestic environmental policy, instrument choice in environmental law (including instruments for fostering renewable energy), and the role of law (including administrative law) in fostering individuals' environmental values.

Gerald Heckman

Gerald Heckman is Associate Professor at the Faculty of Law, University of Manitoba. His research and teaching interests focus on public law, including administrative and constitutional law, labour law, human rights law, international human rights law, and refugee law. After receiving his LL.B. from the University of Toronto, he clerked for the Federal Court of

Canada. He obtained an LL.M. in administrative law from Queen's University, where he analyzed the gatekeeping powers of Canadian human rights commissions. After practising labour, employment, and human rights law for several years, he earned his Ph.D. at Osgoode Hall Law School, York University. His dissertation focused on the gap between domestic and international institutional and procedural safeguards in Canadian, American, and Australian refugee protection decision making. He is currently conducting an empirical investigation of the causes of delay in administrative decision making.

Grant Huscroft

Grant Huscroft is Professor of Law at Western University and was formerly a member of the Faculty of Law at the University of Auckland. He is co-director of the Public Law and Legal Philosophy Research group at Western, where his research focuses on constitutional law and judicial review in Canada and the Commonwealth. He is co-author of the treatise *The New Zealand Bill of Rights* (Melbourne: Oxford University Press, 2003) (with Paul Rishworth, Richard Mahoney, and Scott Optican) and has edited or co-edited seven collections of essays, including *The Challenge of Originalism: Theories of Constitutional Interpretation* (New York: Cambridge University Press, 2011) (with Bradley Miller); *Expounding the Constitution: Essays in Constitutional Theory* (New York: Cambridge University Press, 2008); *A Simple Common Lawyer: Essays in Honour of Michael Taggart* (Oxford: Hart Publishing, 2008) (with David Dyzenhaus and Murray Hunt); *Inside and Outside Canadian Administrative Law: Essays in Honour of David Mullan* (Toronto: University of Toronto Press, 2006) (with Michael Taggart); *Constitutionalism in the Charter Era* (Toronto: LexisNexis-Butterworths, 2004) (with Ian Brodie); *Litigating Rights: Perspectives from Domestic and International Law* (Oxford: Hart Publishing, 2002) (with Paul Rishworth); and *Rights and Freedoms* (Wellington, NZ: Brookers, 1995) (with Paul Rishworth).

Laverne Jacobs

Laverne Jacobs is an Associate Professor at the University of Windsor's Faculty of Law. She teaches Judicial Review of Administrative Action, Civil Liberties, Constitutional Law, and an interdisciplinary seminar on Law, Disability & Social Change. Her research interests include the independence and impartiality of administrative actors, access to information and privacy law, human rights law, disability rights, comparative public law, and empirical research methodology. Through her scholarship, Professor Jacobs explores the gap between public law jurisprudence and public law realities through the use of qualitative empirical research. Laverne Jacobs was a Visiting Scholar at Cornell University Law School in 2006 and, in 2005, at the University of Ottawa, Faculty of Law. She holds law degrees in Common Law and Civil Law from McGill University and a doctorate from Osgoode Hall Law School. Upon graduating from McGill, she clerked for Justice Brian Malone at the Federal Court of Appeal. She has worked for the Department of Justice Canada, where she was counsel in the Public Law Policy Sector and, between 2005 and 2010, was a part-time member of the Human Rights Tribunal of Ontario.

Freya Kristjanson

Freya Kristjanson is a partner at Cavalluzzo Hayes Shilton McIntyre & Cornish LLP. Freya has argued judicial review and appeal cases at all levels of court in Canada, including the

Supreme Court of Canada, and before numerous tribunals. She has significant public inquiry experience, including representing Mayor Hazel McCallion at the Mississauga Judicial Inquiry, serving as Lead Counsel to the Military Police Complaints Commission in the Afghanistan detainee hearings, Legal Counsel to Justice O'Connor in the Arar Inquiry Policy Review, Commission Counsel to the Walkerton Inquiry, and counsel to the Rt. Hon. A. Kim Campbell at the Somalia Inquiry. Freya advises numerous public authorities on governance, oversight and accountability, legal ethics, and procedural fairness issues. Freya has taught Administrative Law in the International Business LL.M. Program at Osgoode Professional Development, Osgoode Hall Law School, York University (2012). She served as an Adjunct Professor at the Faculty of Law, University of Toronto from 2007 to 2011, where she taught Administrative Law. Freya serves on the Legal Advisory Committee to the Financial Services Tribunal, is a member of the Board of Directors of the Advocates' Society, and serves as Treasurer of the Sir William Campbell Foundation. Freya is recognized in Lexpert in the field of Public Law—Litigation and in The Best Lawyers in Canada in the field of Administrative and Public Law. She graduated from the Faculty of Law, University of Victoria (J.D., 1987) and from Queen's University (B.A. (Hons.), 1983), clerked to Mr. Justice McIntyre at the Supreme Court of Canada, and was called to the Bar of Ontario in 1989.

Mary Liston

Mary Liston is an Assistant Professor at the Faculty of Law, University of British Columbia, where she teaches administrative law, legal theory, and public law. Before her appointment at UBC, she held a post-doctoral fellowship in Law and Ethics at the Centre for Ethics, University of Toronto. She completed her doctoral work in the Department of Political Science at the University of Toronto, having already received an M.A. in Social and Political Thought at York University, an LL.B. from the Faculty of Law at the University of Toronto, and an Honours B.A. in English Language and Literature at the University of Western Ontario. As a graduate student, she received a number of prestigious awards, including the Peter Russell/Ontario Graduate Scholarship in the Department of Political Science and a Social Sciences and Humanities Research Council of Canada Scholarship for her doctoral work. Her doctoral thesis, "Honest Counsel: Institutional Dialogue and the Canadian Rule of Law," constructed a theoretical model of a democratic rule of law from a close reading of Canadian jurisprudence in public law, with a particular focus on constitutional law and administrative law. Her recent publications include "Witnessing Arbitrariness: Roncarelli v. Duplessis Fifty Years On" (2010) 55 McGill L.J.; "The Rule of Law" in The Encyclopedia of Political Science (Washington, DC: CQ Press, 2010); and "The Rule of Law Through the Looking Glass" (2009) 21(1) Law and Literature.

Audrey Macklin

Audrey Macklin is an Associate Professor at the University of Toronto, Faculty of Law. She holds law degrees from Yale University and the University of Toronto, and a bachelor of science degree from Alberta. After graduating from Toronto, she served as law clerk to Justice Bertha Wilson at the Supreme Court of Canada. She was appointed to the faculty of Dalhousie Law School in 1991, promoted to Associate Professor in 1998, and moved to the University of Toronto in 2000. While teaching at Dalhousie, she also served as a member of the Immigration and Refugee Board. Professor Macklin's teaching areas include criminal law, administrative law, and immigration and refugee law. Her research and writing interests include transnational migration, citizenship, forced migration, feminist and cultural analysis, and human rights. She has published on these subjects in journals such as Refugee and Canadian Woman Studies, and in collections of essays such as *The Security of Freedom: Essays on Canada's Anti-Terrorism Bill* (Ronald J. Daniels, Patrick Macklem, and Kent Roach, eds.) (Toronto: University of Toronto Press, 2001) and *Engendering Forced Migration: Theory and Practice* (Doreen Indra, ed.) (Oxford: Berghahn Books, 1998).

Leslie McIntosh
Leslie McIntosh, B.A. (University of Toronto, 1974), LL.B. (University of Western Ontario, 1977), LL.M. in administrative law (Osgoode Hall Law School, 2003), is Adjunct Professor of Administrative Law at Osgoode Hall Law School. Leslie was called to the Bar of Ontario and started her career with the Ontario Ministry of the Attorney General in 1979. Initially, she was seconded to the Ministry of Community and Social Services, where she appeared before a broad range of administrative tribunals. In 1982, she transferred to the Crown Law Office, Civil, of the Ministry of the Attorney General, where she was subsequently appointed General Counsel. She retired from the public service in 2011. Her practice consisted mainly of appellate work in the Supreme Court of Canada, the Court of Appeal, and the Divisional Court in the areas of civil litigation and administrative law. She was counsel for the Province of Ontario at the Inquiry into the Actions of Canadian Officials in Relation to Maher Arar, and is counsel in the SARS actions. From 2007 to 2011, Leslie was an Adjunct Professor of Administrative Law at the University of Toronto Law School. She is the author of numerous articles and publications, and a regular speaker at Ontario Bar Association and other continuing legal education events.

Alexander Pless
Alexander Pless, B.A. Hon, B.C.L./LL.B. (McGill), M.P.A. (Harvard), is Regional Manager and Senior Counsel in the Department of Justice's Quebec Regional Office, Commercial Litigation Directorate. He practises administrative law, constitutional law, and Crown liability. He teaches Judicial Review of Administrative Action at McGill University. He is a member of the bars of Quebec and New York and has appeared before all levels of court in Canada. He has acted as counsel for the Attorney General of Canada in such cases as same-sex marriage, the *Reference re Securities Commission of Canada*, and a number of judicial reviews related to national security matters (for example, passports and the "no-fly" Specified Persons List).

Janna Promislow
Janna Promislow, B.A. (University of Alberta), LL.B. (University of Victoria), LL.M. (York University), Ph.D. candidate (York University), is an Assistant Professor at Thompson Rivers University Faculty of Law. Before graduate studies, Janna clerked with the Law Courts of Alberta and practised law with Davis & Company in the Northwest Territories. More recently, she worked for the government of Ontario, providing policy advice on consultation with Aboriginal communities. Janna's teaching and research interests encompass constitutional and administrative law, Aboriginal law, colonial legal history, indigenous–settler relations, and legal pluralism. She has published on the historical development of intersocietal law between Indigenous and European fur traders in collections of essays by Lisa Ford and

Tim Rowse, eds., *Between Indigenous and Settler Governance* (London: Routledge, forthcoming 2012), Jeremy Webber and Colin Macleod, eds., *Between Consenting Peoples: Political Community and the Meaning of Consent* (Vancouver: UBC Press, 2010), and Hamar Foster, Benjamin L. Berger, and A.R. Buck, eds., *The Grand Experiment: Law and Legal Culture in British Settler Societies* (Vancouver: UBC Press, 2008).

Lorne Sossin
Lorne Sossin, B.A. (McGill), M.A. (Exeter), Ph.D. (Toronto), LL.B. (Osgoode), LL.M., J.S.D. (Columbia), of the Bar of Ontario, is a Professor and Dean of Osgoode Hall Law School, York University. Before this appointment, Professor Sossin was a Professor with the Faculty of Law at the University of Toronto, where he served as Associate Dean and as the inaugural Director of the Centre for the Legal Profession.

Sheila Wildeman
Sheila Wildeman is an Assistant Professor at Dalhousie University's Schulich School of Law. Before taking up that position, she was a Research Associate at Dalhousie's Health Law Institute, and an articled student at Eberts Symes Street & Corbett in Toronto. Professor Wildeman's teaching areas include public law, administrative law, jurisprudence, and critical approaches to law. Her research and writing interests lie at the intersection of human rights, disability, and administrative law, with particular attention to the human rights imperative to support legal capacity. She has published on these subjects in collections of essays, including *Being Relational: Reflections on Relational Theory and Health Law and Policy* (Jocelyn Downie and Jennifer Llewellyn, eds.) (Vancouver: UBC Press, 2011).

CHAPTER ONE

An Introduction to Administrative Law: Some History and a Few Signposts for a Twisted Path

COLLEEN M. FLOOD
Faculty of Law, University of Toronto

JENNIFER DOLLING*
LL.M., University of Toronto

---

*   We would like to thank Ryan MacIssac, Arthur Wilson, and Marcelo Rodriguez Ferrere for their excellent
    research support.

Administrative boards play an increasingly important role in our society. They regulate many aspects of our life, from beginning to end. Hospital and medical boards regulate the methods and practice of the doctors that bring us into this world. Boards regulate the licensing and the operation of morticians who are concerned with our mortal remains. Marketing boards regulate the farm products we eat; transport boards regulate the means and flow of our travel; energy boards control the price and distribution of the forms of energy we use; planning boards and city councils regulate the location and types of buildings in which we live and work. In Canada, boards are a way of life. Boards and the functions they fulfill are legion.[1]

I. Introduction

If you are a student, you may be somewhat hazy about what administrative law is and its relationship to other areas of law—for example, constitutional law and private law. You may also have little sense of the relevance of administrative law to your future clients or to Canadian society. If you are an expert in your field, but new to administrative law, you may find that familiar words like "fairness" and "reasonableness" take on new and sometimes unfamiliar meanings in the administrative-law context. In this introduction, we hope to give you a framework for approaching administrative law that will guide you through the other chapters of this text, representing a collaboration of leading scholars and teachers across Canada. As the text unfolds, you will see that we stress the importance of administrative decision making in the lives of Canadians, the endless variety of administrative decision making, and the relationship of administrative decision making to public policy. In what follows, we attempt to help guide you in your study of administrative law by:

1. providing a brief history in Canada of both the administrative state and administrative law;

2. highlighting some of the big themes and contests that have arisen over the course of history that have rendered administrative law an area still much in flux;

3. illustrating further the history of administrative law by discussing the role of remedies over time and the constitutional foundation for judicial review on the part of s. 96 courts, which are provincial superior courts that have been found to have inherent jurisdiction to review administrative decision making; and

4. providing a high-level overview of the major parts of this text—namely, procedural and substantive review.

As a student, you may be taking administrative law because it is compulsory or because it is viewed as a core course whose absence from your transcript will be suspicious when you

---

are in the job market. You may not be approaching the course eagerly, having heard, perhaps, that it is dull, complex, and tedious. With respect to complexity, administrative law is guilty as charged, probably because of its relative newness as a field of study compared with, for example, contract and tort law. Much of administrative law—particularly substantive review— is still in flux, which can be frustrating for a student looking for clear-cut answers, not end- less puzzles and riddles. But administrative law is anything but dull and tedious—it is ef- fervescent—and the tensions and puzzles that arise go to the very heart of good governance and how governments, the executive, those empowered to act on the part of government, and courts should function together. Part of the problem with the image of administrative law (or "admin law" as most of you will start calling it) is its name—"administration" sounds bureaucratic and boring. A far better name for this course would be "the citizen and the state," "law for ordinary people," or "public justice." Most people will never see the inside of a court- room, but they will be affected in a multitude of ways by decisions of administrative bodies.

To get a sense of the enormous variety of administrative boards and tribunals and their role in your day-to-day life, take a look at the examples listed in the Appendix to this text and, if possible, see an administrative board or tribunal in action. This will help you get a far better understanding of the world and context of administrative decision making than is possible from reading court judgments alone. Also, be assured that, at a minimum, a grasp of administrative law will immensely broaden the range of topics that you can talk about over dinner—more so than many other courses you may take. This is because, as mentioned above, for most Canadians, administrative law will be much more important in their lives than civil or criminal law. Consider, for example, your grandmother. Few of you will have grandmothers who have sued or been sued or have been charged with or convicted of a criminal offence. However, all of your grandmothers will have come into contact with the administrative state or administrative decision making, whether in the context of immigra- tion; obtaining health care, housing, or medical benefits; or simply obtaining a driver's li- cence or passport. Those of you reading this who are lawyers and admitted to practice with a law society or students and admitted to study at a university are already within the world of administrative law. Whether we know it or not, we all become enmeshed with the admin- istrative state—and thus administrative law—at some point in our lives.

PART 1: THE ORIGINS OF ADMINISTRATIVE LAW

II. In the Beginning

As we mentioned above, some of the complexities and flux we find in administrative law jurisprudence is likely connected to its relative newness as a field of study. Today, "[w]e are only three generations removed from the great British constitutional authority, A.V. Dicey, who could assert that '[t]he words "administrative law" ... are unknown to English judges and counsel, and are in themselves hardly intelligible without further explanation.' "[2] Mike

---

[2]   Law Reform Commission of Canada, Working Paper 25: *Independent Administrative Agencies* (Ottawa: Min- ister of Supply and Services Canada, 1980) at 1, online: <http://www.lareau-legal.ca/LRCWP25.pdf> [LRC, Working Paper 25], citing A.V. Dicey, *An Introduction to the Study of the Law of the Constitution*, 7th ed. (1908) at 330.

Taggart noted that the first book in Britain with the words "administrative law" in the title did not appeared until 1928, and the first comprehensive textbook on the topic was published as late as 1959. In Canada it took longer still.[3] Notwithstanding this late start, Canadian administrative law has come a long way since Dicey uttered those words. To understand administrative law, it is helpful to know something about that history[4]—both the legal context and the "parallel growth of government agencies and independent agencies."[5] So we will start at, or at least near, the beginning to explain the rise of the Canadian administrative state. Note that, in doing so, we are relying heavily on the work of others and synthesizing their interpretation of the primary material.

III. The Constitution

Forsey notes that, by the time of Confederation in 1867, responsible government had been operating in most of what is now central and eastern Canada for almost 20 years.[6] As such, in drafting the Constitution, the fathers of Confederation simply continued the system that was already working.[7] This meant responsible government, with formal executive authority vested in the Queen (and exercisable by her representative, the governor-general), "a cabinet responsible to the House of Commons, and the House of Commons answerable to the people."[8]

The Canadian Constitution today "is a collection of 25 primary documents outlined in the *Constitution Act, 1982*"[9] including, of course, the *Constitution Act, 1867*,[10] which brought Canada into existence.[11] However, the formal written Constitution "is only part of our whole working Constitution, the set of arrangements by which we govern ourselves. It is the skeleton; it is not the whole body."[12] The Constitution does not mention the basic features of Canada's system of government, those being responsible government, the national Cabinet, the bureaucracy, and political parties.[13] "The flesh, the muscles, the sinews, the nerves of our Constitution have been added by legislation, ... by custom, ... by judgments of the courts, ... and by agreements between the federal and provincial govern-

---

3   Michael Taggart, "Prolegomenon to an Intellectual History of Administrative Law in the Twentieth Century: The Case of John Willis and Canadian Administrative Law" (2005) 43 Osgoode Hall L.J. 223 at 228-29 [Taggart, "John Willis and Canadian Administrative Law"].

4   LRC, Working Paper 25, *supra* note 2 at 17.

5   *Ibid.* at 18.

6   Eugene A. Forsey, *How Canadians Govern Themselves*, 7th ed. (Ottawa: Minister of Public Works and Government Services Canada, 2010) at 3, online: <http://www.parl.gc.ca/about/parliament/senatoreugeneforsey/book/assets/pdf/How_Canadians_Govern_Themselves7.pdf> [Forsey].

7   *Ibid.*

8   *Ibid.* at 1.

9   Schedule B to the *Canada Act, 1982* (U.K.) 1982 c. 11; Forsey, *supra* note 6 at 10.

10 *The Constitution Act, 1867*, 30 & 31 Vict., c. 3. (U.K.) (consolidated with amendments).

11 Forsey, *supra* note 6 at 11.

12 *Ibid.* at 10.

13 *Ibid.*

ments."[14] Thus, the Constitution is the latticework on which the vines of the administrative state and administrative law grow. In essence, administrative law concerns the "supervision" (although this word is unduly loaded) by courts of decision making made pursuant to statute or the royal prerogative. Administrative boards and tribunals (such as those listed in the Appendix to this text) and ministers and departmental officials, have no inherent power to make decisions that affect people's lives but for the statute (or royal prerogative) that empowers them to do so. Thus the role of the court in administrative law's outer frame is to make sure, at a minimum, that decision-makers do not step outside the boundaries of what they are legally empowered to do.

If we fast-forward for a moment to 1982 we must also acknowledge the profound impact of the *Canadian Charter of Rights and Freedoms*[15] on administrative decision making through judicial review and vice versa. This topic is fully explored by Evan Fox-Decent and Alexander Pless in Chapter 12, The Charter and Administrative Law: Cross-Fertilization or Inconstancy? For present purposes, the interrelationship between Charter rights and administrative law for the purposes of both procedural and substantive review is a deeply complex one that courts still struggle with.

IV. The Expansion of Government

A. The Early Years: 1850-1913

In the decades preceding and following Confederation, "the federal government and its administrators were preoccupied with the extension and protection of the frontier and the development of a national economy."[16] Then, the need to connect Canada through its nascent railway industry first revealed the requirement for new decision-making structures.[17] Well before Confederation, the *Railway Act* of 1851 was enacted, from which sprang what became known as the Railway Committee of the Privy Council.[18] At this time, the committee was composed of Cabinet ministers, but the early 1870s brought about pressure for change.[19] "In a period of economic recession, many farmers and merchants blamed the railways for charging excessive or discriminatory rates and blamed the government for doing nothing about the problem."[20] These concerns drove calls to establish an independent, apolitical regulatory tribunal—modelled along the lines of the English Railway Commission—with the hope that it would do a better job of setting prices on a non-discriminatory basis.[21]

---

[14] *Ibid.*

[15] Part I of the *Constitution Act, 1982.*

[16] LRC, Working Paper 25, *supra* note 2 at 20-21.

[17] *Ibid.* at 21.

[18] *Ibid.*

[19] Bernard J. Hibbitts, "A Change of Mind: The Supreme Court and the Board of Railway Commissioners, 1903-1929" (1991) 41 U.T.L.J. 60 at 62 [Hibbits].

[20] *Ibid.* note 17.

[21] *Ibid.*

The idea of creating a railway regulatory body or commission *independent* from Cabinet was, however, rejected by the Galt Royal Commission Report of 1888,[22] which felt that the concept of an independent body responsible for decision making was inconsistent with the Canadian system of responsible government and represented "a rejection of the legislature as the locus of the regulatory enterprise"[23] and "a rejection of the common law courts as legitimate arbiters of regulatory issues."[24] As we will see throughout this text, these kinds of concerns are still present in modern-day debates over the legitimacy of administrative decision making. In the late 1800s, "the tradition of patronage in the public service of the day gave rise to fears that designated departmental personnel might have inappropriate backgrounds or lack the technical capacity to deal with the kinds of issues being raised in the context of railway regulation."[25] Nonetheless, the Galt Commission recognized the limitations of Cabinet ministers as regulators—Railway Committee members served part-time only, were based in Ottawa, lacked expertise, and were vulnerable to political pressure.[26]

It would be another decade before serious consideration was given to the concept of a non-elected, full-time body outside any departmental structure to regulate railways.[27] Sir Wilfrid Laurier appointed a one-man commission of inquiry, S.J. McLean, to legitimize the notion of an independent railway board.[28] McLean's reports, tabled in 1902, concluded that the Railway Committee was "over-worked and ill-equipped to deal with its responsibilities"[29] and recommended the appointment of an independent commission to take its place.[30] And so came the *Railway Act*[31] of 1903, which established a new administrative agency, the Board of Railway Commissioners,[32] followed six years later by the International Joint Commission (IJC) with the United States to handle boundary waters issues.[33] By appointing experts to decide rather than merely to advise,[34] the IJC "marked a further important step in establishing a framework for government regulation in Canada."[35] In 1912, "the *Canada Grain Act*[36] established a Board of Grain Commissioners charged with the administration of terminal warehouses and generally all matters related to the inspection, weigh-

---

22   LRC, Working Paper 25, *supra* note 2 at 21.

23   Hibbitts, *supra* note 19.

24   *Ibid.*

25   LRC, Working Paper 25, *supra* note 2 at 22.

26   *Ibid.* at 21.

27   *Ibid.* at 22.

28   Hibbitts, *supra* note 19 at 64.

29   *Ibid.* at 64-65; McLean's two reports were titled Railway Commissions, Railway Rate Grievances, and Regulative Legislation.

30   LRC, Working Paper 25, *supra* note 2 at 22.

31   S.C. 1903, 3 E. VII, c. 58.

32   LRC, Working Paper 25, *supra* note 2 at 23.

33   *Ibid.*

34   *Ibid.* at 24.

35   *Ibid.* at 23.

36   S.C. 1912, c. 27.

ing, trading and storage of grain."[37] Relevant Supreme Court cases at this time focused on issues of jurisdiction—for example, in *Montreal Street Railway v. Montreal Terminal Railway*,[38] the Court upheld a challenge to the jurisdiction of the Board of Railway Commissioners when the board attempted to make orders that contradicted provincial law, and in *Re Canadian Northern Railway*,[39] when the board made a general order regarding the erection of fences to prevent livestock from straying onto the tracks.

Inquiries, the modern versions of which are discussed by Peter Carver in Chapter 16, Getting the Story Out: Accountability and the Law of Public Inquiries, also formed part of Canada's early administrative law history. *An Act respecting inquiries concerning Public Matters*, given Royal Assent in 1868, gave the governor in council the power to summon witnesses to testify under oath and produce whatever documents were requested by the commissioners when the governor in council deemed it "expedient to cause inquiry to be made into and concerning any matter connected with the good government of Canada, or the conduct of any part of the public business thereof."[40] Since 1868, by our count, there have been 291 commissions of inquiry at the federal level alone.[41]

Without a doubt, this early period of administrative action was an exciting period in Canada's history, when major economic and societal changes were occurring.[42] "By 1900, the major economic and political problems that had precipitated Confederation had been resolved—the frontiers had been established and guaranteed, transportation and communication links had been forged, and our national political and legal institutions had been established."[43] The first part of the 20th century saw "intense economic development, stimulated by waves of immigration [and] integration with the American economy."[44] Immigration rose from 49,000 in 1901 to 402,000 in 1913.[45] Then came the First World War.[46]

B. The First World War and the Growth of Government Controls

The commencement of the First World War and Canada's commitment to the war effort brought about increased intervention in the economy by the federal government, including rent and price controls and the prevention of hoarding.[47] As its reach expanded, it became

---

37 LRC, Working Paper 25, *supra* note 2 at 24.

38 [1905] 36 S.C.R. 369.

39 [1909] 42 S.C.R. 443.

40 Law Reform Commission of Canada, Working Paper 17, *Commissions of Inquiry: A New Act* (Law Reform Commission of Canada, Ottawa: 1977) at 7.

41 We calculated this using statistics provided by the Privy Council Office, online: Government of Canada <http://www.pco-bcp.gc.ca/index.asp?lang=eng&page=information&sub=commissions&doc=archives/comm-eng.htm>.

42 LRC, Working Paper 25, *supra* note 2 at 24.

43 *Ibid.*

44 *Ibid.*

45 *Ibid.*

46 *Ibid.*

47 *Ibid.*

logistically impossible for the government to centrally administer all aspects and so arose the advent of administrative agencies such as the Board of Grain Supervisors (succeeded in 1919 by the Canadian Wheat Board), the Food Control Board (later called the Canada Food Board), the Wage Trade Board, and the municipal Fair Price Committees.[48] The government also made major inroads in health and welfare, with a Board of Pension Commissioners established in 1916, the Department of Soldiers Civil Re-establishment in 1918, and the Department of Health in 1919.[49] The rationale for the creation of these new administrative agencies was not clearly articulated, but it was likely a combination of the need for arm's-length decision making and specialized expertise or simply that the volume and complexity of matters before government required separate attention and leadership.

The federal civil service was placed on more of a professional footing[50] with the *Civil Service Act* of 1918,[51] and "the Civil Service Commission assumed responsibility to pass upon the qualifications of candidates for admission to and classification, transfer, and promotion in the civil service."[52] "To finance the expansion of the public sector, direct taxation was introduced [by way of] an excess business profits tax in 1916 and an income tax on individuals and corporations in 1917,"[53] with income tax "providing guaranteed means for [future] bureaucratic growth."[54]

Thus Canada emerged from the First World War in 1918 "profoundly changed";[55] one consequence of the war was a massive expansion of government and a corresponding "increase in the extent of governmental intervention in the daily economic life of [the citizenry]."[56] This new era of government set the stage for subsequent contests of the appropriate role for courts in reviewing delegated decision making, because such decisions were not subject to the sunlight of scrutiny within the House of Commons—a topic we return to below in section V, Administrative Bodies Meet the Law: Conflicts and Tensions in Theories of Administrative Law.

C. The Inter-War Period

In the period following the First World War, until the Depression, the federal government was more preoccupied with war debts and issues related to its absorption of the railways than with expanding its scope of regulatory control.[57] However, with the Depression of the

---

48   *Ibid.* at 24-25.

49   *Ibid.* at 25.

50   *Ibid.*

51   S.C. 1918, c. 12.

52   LRC, Working Paper 25, *supra* note 2 at 25.

53   *Ibid.*

54   *Ibid.*

55   Bernard J. Hibbitts, "A Bridle for Leviathan: The Supreme Court and the Board of Commerce" (1989) 21 Ottawa L. Rev. 65 at 67.

56   *Ibid.*

57   LRC, Working Paper 25, *supra* note 2 at 26-27.

1930s came renewed federal legislative efforts[58] and "massive changes in regulation, both in degree and in kind."[59] The turbulent 1930s witnessed skyrocketing unemployment rates and plummeting international trade. "The federal government intervened with regulatory measures in several fields including agriculture, culture, finance, transportation and social security."[60] "In 1931 the Tariff Board was created as an independent agency to carry out advisory and quasi-judicial functions."[61] The Canadian Broadcasting Corporation was created in 1932,[62] and the Ontario Securities Commission followed a year later.[63] In 1935, the Canadian Wheat Board was given responsibility for marketing wheat in interprovincial and export trade[64] and, in the same year, legislation equivalent to the American "New Deal" was enacted, resulting in a number of new regulatory and adjudicatory agencies.[65] As legal historian Blake Brown notes, the consistent theme of judicial review cases at this time reflected an inseparable intertwining of constitutional and administrative law history in Canada: challenges were against the jurisdiction of these administrative boards on constitutional grounds.[66] They were simple jurisdiction arguments, challenging either on the basis of the strict construction of federal legislation or on the basis of an alleged conflict with the then-named *British North America Act 1867*.[67] For example, in *British Columbia Electric Railway v. Canadian National Railway*,[68] a successful challenge prevented the Board of Railway Commissioners from exercising jurisdiction over a foreign-owned B.C. rail operator (the board's jurisdiction was limited to railways provided for by federal legislation). Similarly, in *Halifax (City) v. Halifax Harbour Commissioners*, the Court prevented a provincial act from taxing federal property and the province from taking action against a federal agency under that act.[69]

---

58 *Ibid.* at 27.

59 R.C.B. Risk, "Lawyers, Courts, and the Rise of the Regulatory State" (1985) 9 Dal L.J. 31 at 39-40 [Risk, "Rise of the Regulatory State."]

60 Jamie Benidickson, "From Empire Ontario to California North: Law and Legal Institutions in Twentieth-Century Ontario" in DeLloyd J. Guth & W. Wesley Pue, *Canada's Legal Inheritances* (Winnipeg: Canadian Legal History Project, 2001) 620 at 636 [Benidickson].

61 LRC, Working Paper 25, *supra* note 2 at 28.

62 *Ibid.*

63 Risk, "Rise of the Regulatory State," *supra* note 59 at 636.

64 LRC, Working Paper 25, *supra* note 2 at 28.

65 *Ibid.* at 27.

66 R. Blake Brown, "The Canadian Legal Realists and Administrative Law Scholarship, 1930-1941" (2000) 9 Dal. J. Leg. Stud. 36 at 38 [Blake Brown].

67 *Supra* note 10.

68 [1932] S.C.R. 161.

69 [1935] S.C.R. 215, applied in *Oatway v. Canada Wheat Board*, [1945] S.C.R. 204.

D. The Second World War and Its Aftermath

During the Second World War, the federal government again took more direct control of the economy.[70] However, unlike most of the agencies created in the First World War, many of the agencies created during the Second World War continued to operate after the war's end[71] and, in the post-war period, governmental organizations proliferated,[72] with specialized bodies such as the Atomic Energy Control Board (1946) set up.[73] It was during this period that welfare programs were developed or significantly expanded; at the federal level, the following all came into effect—the Family Allowances Plan (1944), the Old Age Security Pension (1952), and the Canada Pension Plan (1965).[74] With the proliferation of administrative agencies, "many people [began] to ask if what we [had] planted [was] a garden or a jungle."[75]

Marketing boards also spread across Canada during the economic booms of 1946-1949 and during the Korean War.[76] In 1952, in *P.E.I. Potato Marketing Board v. Willis*,[77] the Supreme Court held "that regulatory power within the jurisdiction of the federal government could validly be delegated to boards created and operated by a provincial government, and vice versa."[78] This, in turn, spurred the establishment of yet more independent administrative agencies.[79]

The 1960s and 1970s witnessed yet further "rapid growth in the public sector and an increasing complexity in the matters dealt with by government."[80] Both accompanying and instigating these changes was "the rise of a large number of semi-independent boards, commissions, agencies, tribunals, and Crown corporations."[81] As we shall see, at this time, some profound changes arose in the approach to administrative law with, for example, the landmark case of *CUPE*[82] and increasing self-reflection on the part of courts as to their appropriate role in reviewing administrative action.

---

[70]   LRC, Working Paper 25, *supra* note 2 at 28.

[71]   *Ibid.* at 29.

[72]   *Ibid.*

[73]   *Ibid.*

[74]   *Ibid.* at 30.

[75]   Robert Reid, "Administrative Tribunals Under Review in Ontario" (1958) 1(4) Can. Bar J. 57.

[76]   LRC, Working Paper 25, *supra* note 2 at 29.

[77]   [1952] 2 S.C.R. 392, 4 D.L.R. (2d) 146.

[78]   LRC, Working Paper 25, *supra* note 2 at 30.

[79]   *Ibid.*

[80]   Law Reform Commission of Canada, Study Paper, *Parliament and Administrative Agencies* (Ottawa: Law Reform Commission of Canada, 1982) at 5.

[81]   *Ibid.*

[82]   *C.U.P.E. v. N.B. Liquor Corporation*, [1979] 2 S.C.R. 227 [*CUPE*].

E. A Closer Look at the Reasons for the Expansion of Government Activity

As we can see from the above, the emergence of a large and complex administrative state in Canada was not created according to a blueprint[83]—it evolved organically in response to problems as they arose over the years.[84] The choice of certain types of bodies to perform particular functions appears to have been ad hoc, with "[t]he selection of a non-departmental rather than a departmental body to regulate, or an administrative tribunal rather than the courts to adjudicate, … hav[ing] been influenced … by the exigencies of the case and existing institutional precedents rather than by an overall plan."[85] But some of the reasons cited for devolving responsibility to independent, arm's-length agencies are still important today and include:[86]

1. the desire to depoliticize certain decisions;

2. the need for greater specialization and technical or subject-matter expertise to make decisions than is possible or feasible to collect and retain within central government; and

3. a reluctance to enmesh courts in matters not suitable to judicial review because of their specific nature or the volume of decisions that have to be made.

Notwithstanding the good and pragmatic reasons for the rise of the administrative state, concern arose about the proliferation of administrative agencies and the legitimacy of their decisions, given the significant impact a decision could have on an individual and the fact that boards and tribunals are not publicly accountable in the same way that government is when, for example, passing legislation in the House of Commons.

V. Administrative Bodies Meet the Law: Conflicts and Tensions in Theories of Administrative Law

In the following section we canvass in broad strokes some of the ideas that shaped administrative law over the 20th century to help us understand how we got to where we are, where these ideas may be taking us, and how the history of these ideas will affect contests within, and the development of, administrative law in the future.[87]

During the late 19th century, English legal thought was the predominant model for Canadian lawyers.[88] English, and consequently Canadian, legal professionals were affected by the rise of legal formalism, a concept characterized by adherence to four principles. First, legal formalists held the "belief that law was composed of 'scientific' legal rules that could be

---

83 LRC, Working Paper 25, *supra* note 2 at 17.

84 *Ibid.*

85 *Ibid.*

86 Law Reform Commission of Canada, *Independent Administrative Agencies*, Report 26 (Ottawa: Law Reform Commission of Canada, 1985) at 5.

87 See Taggart, "John Willis and Canadian Administrative Law," *supra* note 3 at 233.

88 R.C.B. Risk, "Canadian Law Teachers in the 1930s: 'When the World Was Turned Upside Down'" (2004) 27 Dal. L.J. 1 at 8 [Risk, "Canadian Law Teachers in the 1930s"].

discovered by a careful study and application of legal principles."[89] Second, as Blake Brown has identified, they believed that these rules were best discerned by a close examination of previously decided cases.[90] Third, they thought legal documents spoke for themselves, so that judges could interpret the meaning of legal documents by simply looking for the "plain meaning" of the words.[91] Last, judges could all but ignore the policy implications of their impartial rulings.[92] Under legal formalism, "decisions were to be made on the basis of scientific legal doctrines" with little regard for equitable outcomes.[93] The leader of legal formalism was A.V. Dicey, a law professor at the University of Oxford in the late 19th century, who "emphasized individual rights and the role of courts as the upholder of these rights."[94] In Chapter 2, Governments in Miniature: The Rule of Law in the Administrative State, Mary Liston provides a thorough discussion of Dicey and the rule of law and other competing theorists.[95]

The tidal wave of expansion of the welfare state, described earlier, was met with by resistance on the part of the English legal establishment.[96] The best-known opponent in the common-law world of "the pretensions and encroachments of bureaucracy"[97] was Lord Hewart, the Lord Chief Justice of England and Wales, whose 1929 book *The New Despotism* "issued a clarion call to lawyers around the common law world to rise up and protect the rule of law against the executive and the bureaucracy, which were taking liberties with the citizens' liberties."[98] For Lord Hewart, "despotism" meant placing government departments (and the officials that inhabited them) "above the Sovereignty of Parliament and beyond the jurisdiction of the Courts" and he was dismayed at the delegation by Parliament of legislative powers to government departments.[99]

In Canada, the English concept of legal formalism was virtually the only lens through which to review administrative action from the late 19th century to the late 1920s.[100] Although Canadian courts in the late 19th century had interpreted the Constitution to permit the existence of administrative bodies, by the turn of the century, formalism had begun to affect constitutional interpretation such that administrative agencies were increasingly chal-

---

[89] Blake Brown, *supra* note 66 at 39.

[90] *Ibid.*

[91] *Ibid.*

[92] *Ibid.*

[93] *Ibid.*

[94] *Ibid.*

[95] See also *Administrative Law Today: Culture, Ideas, Institutions, Processes, Values: Essays in Honour of John Willis* [special issue] (2005) 55(3) U.T.L.J.

[96] R.C.B. Risk, "My Continuing Legal Education" (2005) 55(3) U.T.L.J. 313 at 324 [Risk, "My Continuing Legal Education"].

[97] Lord Hewart of Bury, *The New Despotism* (London: Ernest Benn, 1929) [Hewart].

[98] Michael Taggart, "From 'Parliamentary Powers' to Privatization: The Chequered History of Delegated Legislation in the Twentieth Century" (2005) 55(3) U.T.L.J. 575 at 576 [Taggart, "Chequered History of Delegated Legislation"].

[99] *Ibid.* at 576, citing Hewart, *supra* note 97 at 14.

[100] Risk, "Canadian Law Teachers in the 1930s," *supra* note 88 at 9.

lenged as being outside the jurisdiction (that is, *ultra vires*) of the federal or provincial legislature that created the agency in question.[101] The underlying theme in these challenges was
a general and substantial concern about the increasing size of the administrative state.[102]
Legal formalists argued that tribunals had the effect of reducing the primacy of courts and
were less likely to protect individual rights because they employed procedures different from
those used in the courts.[103] Formalists also complained that "[t]ribunals were free to disregard precedents and interpreted statutes by explicitly considering policy ramifications."[104]

Challenges to the formalist mode of thinking began in the United States in the late 19th
century and grew stronger early in the 20th century.[105] Shaped by pragmatism, the social sciences, political turmoil, and calls for a new social order, a new group of scholars named the
"Progressives" emerged. Two major figures in this group were Roscoe Pound and Benjamin
Cardozo. Pound argued that "common law reasoning should be instrumental and seek social
welfare,"[106] while Cardozo argued that "[t]he final cause of law is the welfare of society."[107]

Nonetheless, many Canadian lawyers and judges remained unenthused by the new administrative institutions[108] and continued to be "clouded by their reverence for tradition and
their romanticized perception of the English system."[109] Concerned about the erosion of
traditional legal principles, they challenged the growth of government regulation and the
increasing use of administrative bodies to implement new social and economic policies.[110]
In 1934, Chief Justice Muloch described tribunals as "non-judicial bod[ies], often ignorant
of the law, bound by no law, free to disregard the evidence and the law, and practically at
[their] own will, to dispose finally of [the citizen's] rights."[111] Many Canadian lawyers in the
1930s felt that "to deny to the individual his traditional right of access to the Courts, threatens to undermine the achievements of centuries."[112] They felt that "the sacred rights of individuals [were] often entrusted to the whims of officials whose main qualification [was]
political loyalty."[113] Accordingly, the key complaint was that tribunals "recklessly intruded
upon liberty, by mistake or through excessive zeal."[114] However, once it became clear that

---

[101] Blake Brown, *supra* note 66 at 38 and 40.

[102] *Ibid.* at 40.

[103] *Ibid.* at 39.

[104] *Ibid.*

[105] Risk, "Canadian Law Teachers in the 1930s," *supra* note 88 at 10.

[106] *Ibid.*

[107] Benjamin N. Cardozo, *The Nature of Judicial Process* (New Haven, CT: Yale University Press, 1921) at 66, cited
       in Risk, "Canadian Law Teachers in the 1930s," *supra* note 88 at 10.

[108] Benidickson, *supra* note 60 at 633.

[109] C.I. Kyer & J.E. Bickenbach, *The Fiercest Debate: Cecil A. Wright, the Benchers, and Legal Education in Ontario
       1923-1957* (Toronto: Published for the Osgoode Society by University of Toronto Press, 1987) at 272.

[110] Blake Brown, *supra* note 66 at 36.

[111] Rt. Hon. Sir W. Muloch, "Address of the Chief Justice of Ontario" (1934) 12 Can. Bar Rev. 35 at 38.

[112] H.G. Sparling, "Editorial: Views of the Profession" (1937) 2 Sask. Bar Rev. 23 at 29.

[113] *Ibid.*

[114] Risk, "My Continuing Legal Education," *supra* note 96 at 326.

such tribunals were a permanent fixture, lawyers grudgingly adopted a more conciliatory tone: a 1941 special committee of the Canadian Bar Association urged its members to, simply, "under this situation … make the best of [tribunals] that is possible."[115]

As Blake Brown has identified, in the late 1920s and, particularly, the 1930s, several Canadian legal academics attempted to reconceptualize the relationship between state and citizen through questioning commonly held assumptions about the law.[116] As Kerry Rittich explains: "[w]hat was at stake was a choice between a laissez-faire state, whose limits were policed by a judiciary steeped in common law rights, on the one hand, and the newly emerging regulatory state, on the other."[117] These scholars were "in direct opposition to the prevailing orthodoxy of analytical legal positivism, underpinned by the political values of classical liberalism and exemplified in the work of A.V. Dicey."[118] Dicey would have thought that "liberty" imposed a negative obligation on government: not to interfere with individuals and their actions, whereas these new scholars believed that liberty imposed a positive obligation on government: to provide individuals with the basic qualities of human life and thus give them the freedom to reach their potential.[119] They "embraced the [new welfare and regulatory] state and the politics it expressed,"[120] and believed that this new state came about as a result of fundamental change in social values and demands.[121] They viewed delegated legislation as essential to the achievement of the goals of social welfarism.[122] Moreover, they "identified that the Depression was a time of change—a terrifying time, but also a time of experimentation in public law."[123] Canadian scholars Bora Laskin, John Willis, and Cecil "Caesar" Wright chose to reject the past, with respect to both its way of thinking about the law and its politics, and, instead, look for "new ways of thinking about the law that would be … 'functional' and 'realistic,' and that would serve the changing needs of modern society."[124] In doing so, they sought to escape from the basic principle that the courts alone must determine and implement the intent of the legislature.[125]

Although the above gives a taste of changing legal thought in the 1930s, no discussion of administrative law theory from this period would be complete without specific mention of John Willis. In Canada, he was "the most important proponent of the dissenting trad-

---

[115] Benidickson, *supra* note 60 at 633, citing "Report of Special Committee on Administrative Tribunals and Law Reform" (1941) 25 C.B.A. Proceedings 208 at 209.

[116] Blake Brown, *supra* note 66 at 44.

[117] Kerry Rittich, "Functionalism and Formalism: Their Latest Incarnations in Contemporary Development and Governance Debates" (2005) 55(3) U.T.L.J. 853 at 858.

[118] Martin Loughlin, "The Functionalist Style in Public Law" (2005) 55(3) U.T.L.J. 361 at 362.

[119] *Ibid.* at 367.

[120] Risk, "Canadian Law Teachers in the 1930s," *supra* note 88 at 38.

[121] *Ibid.* at 41.

[122] Blake Brown, *supra* note 66 at 69.

[123] *Ibid.* at 72.

[124] Risk, "My Continuing Legal Education," *supra* note 96 at 313.

[125] R.C.B. Risk, "Here Be Cold and Tygers: A Map of Statutory Interpretation in Canada in the 1920s and 1930s" (2000) 63 Sask. L. Rev. 195 at 196.

ition"[126] and a "zealous proponent of the administrative state."[127] He wrote in an era of "continuous and often dramatic expansion of the administrative state,"[128] and was part of the generation of 1930s legal scholars who supported new instruments for achieving the public agenda.[129] Willis believed that "[i]f the state was to look after its subjects from the cradle to the grave—which was the wish of the voters,"[130] then sweeping delegations of parliamentary power to administrative tribunals was both necessary and inevitable for the regulatory or welfare state to operationalize itself.[131] He supported the establishment of commissions or "governments in miniature" (hence the title of Chapter 2 of this text) to hear disputes about policy.[132] He believed that courts and legislatures were "inadequate to perform the tasks required of a government of the twentieth century"[133] and "consigned the courts to the dust heap of history, too old-fashioned and set in their ways to be willing or able to adjust to the new facts of government."[134] He argued that the development of administrative government departments should "be designed and assessed to serve current, concrete social need and not some abstract ideal."[135] Willis was a self-declared "government man,"[136] who invested a lot of energy into arguing against court intervention in administrative action so as to create a "wide discretionary latitude for bureaucrats ... to get things done."[137] Although "Willis recognized the problem of unlimited administrative discretion, [he] believed that the courts were not well suited to considering appeals from tribunals"[138] because then "the amateur is asked to upset the expert."[139] For Willis, judicial review "would always be 'sporadic' and, in any event, the judges' ignorance of policy should disqualify them from a major role."[140] Instead of having courts review administrative decisions, "Willis advocated for the creation of a special administrative review court, which, like the lower tribunal, possessed specialized knowledge of the subject area within its jurisdiction."[141] He believed it important that such

---

126   J.M. Evans, H.N. Janisch, David Mullan, & R.C.B. Risk, *Administrative Law: Cases, Text, and Materials*, 5th ed. (Toronto: Emond Montgomery, 2003) at 30 [Evans et al.].

127   Blake Brown, *supra* note 66 at 45.

128   David Szablowski, "John Willis and the Challenges for Public Law Scholarship in a Neoliberal Globalizing World" (2005) 55(3) U.T.L.J. 869 at 870 [Szablowski].

129   Roderick A. Macdonald, "Call-Centre Government: For the Rule of Law, Press #" (2005) 55(3) U.T.L.J. 449 at 454.

130   Taggart, "Chequered History of Delegated Legislation," *supra* note 98 at 585.

131   *Ibid.*; G. Blaine Baker, "Willis on 'Cultured' Public Authorities" (2005) 55(3) U.T.L.J. 335 at 348 [Baker, "Willis"].

132   Blake Brown, *supra* note 66 at 50.

133   J. Willis, ed., *Canadian Boards at Work* (Toronto: Macmillan, 1941).

134   Taggart, "John Willis and Canadian Administrative Law," *supra* note 3 at 248.

135   Risk, "My Continuing Legal Education," *supra* note 96 at 326.

136   Szablowski, *supra* note 128 at 870.

137   Baker, "Willis," *supra* note 131 at 335.

138   Blake Brown, *supra* note 66 at 50.

139   *Ibid.* at 51.

140   Taggart, "John Willis and Canadian Administrative Law," *supra* note 3 at 247.

141   Blake Brown, *supra* note 66 at 51.

body have experience of the actual exercise of policy and *administrative* decision making, and thus have less of a focus on legal doctrine and *judicial* decision making.

The arguments of the scholars mentioned above represented an important shift in thinking about the administrative state in Canada.[142] Indeed, they "helped undermine the traditional ways of thinking about the administrative state, and, more importantly, about the basic functioning of the law."[143] They quieted many of the fears about the growing administrative state, and in doing so, accomplished a difficult goal: "by convincing Canadian lawyers that discretion existed in administrative and judicial processes, and that policy implications were inherent in any decision, these academics opened the door for future debate and scholarship in administrative law."[144] As we will discover throughout the following chapters, the tension between the appropriate role for governments, administrative agencies, and courts—and which set of decision-makers are accountable to others—is still a strongly contested area in administrative law. We will also see shifting views on the appropriateness of roles, depending on the nature of the case in question with, for example, proponents arguing for a much greater role for administrative action when it comes to progressive distribution of benefits in a welfare state or the resolution of labour disputes, but being far less comfortable with administrative action that seeks to curtail access to the courts for vulnerable individuals—for example, immigrants and refugees.

VI. From a Focus on Remedies to a Focus on Review

We now shift our focus to the question of remedies and their role in the history of administrative law; doing so illustrates not only the importance of the common law of judicial review but also the essentiality of statutory interpretation and reform to this area of law.

This issue of remedies is related to the source of power that courts may have to review. Where do courts get the power to review administrative decision making? There are three sources of review power: original jurisdiction; right of appeal; and, most important for our purposes, courts' inherent judicial review jurisdiction. These are explained, in turn, below.

1. *Original jurisdiction:* The ordinary courts have jurisdiction over the decisions of administrative decision-makers when they are challenged by way of direct actions by a citizen in contract or tort on the ground that the state has infringed an individual's private legal right. For example, in 1995, a court granted a declaration that the Liberal government had breached a contract in cancelling the agreement made by the previous Progressive Conservative government with developers for the renovation and privatization of Pearson International Airport.[145]

2. *Statutory right of appeal:* Many students new to law, but not to television shows, think there is always a right of appeal. In fact, there is no automatic right to appeal the substance of an administrative decision to the courts. A right to appeal must be

---

142   Risk, "Rise of the Regulatory State," *supra* note 59.

143   Blake Brown, *supra* note 66 at 72.

144   *Ibid.*

145   *T1T2 Limited Partnership v. Canada*, [1995] O.J. No. 137 (QL).

provided for in a statute. A critically important first lesson for all students of administrative law is to review the statute establishing the administrative agency and see whether any right of appeal is provided for and on what grounds.

3. *Courts' inherent judicial review jurisdiction:* Third, and most important from our perspective, the superior courts in each province (the judges appointed by the federal government) may review decisions made by institutions and officials with responsibility for administering public programs through the courts' inherent judicial review jurisdiction. The constitutional guarantee of this jurisdiction is discussed below in the context of s. 96 courts.

The words "inherent jurisdiction" refer to the fact that the jurisdiction of the superior courts is broader than whatever may be conferred by statute. Superior courts may hear any matter unless there is a specific statute that says otherwise or grants exclusive jurisdiction to another court or tribunal. As Craig Forcese discusses in Chapter 15, Making a Federal Case Out of It: The Federal Court and Administrative Law, superior courts have greater freedom to craft remedies and grant relief than courts created by statute, such as the federal courts. However, inherent jurisdiction is not jurisdiction for a general appeal; thus, a court cannot simply substitute its own decision for that of an agency's—it is a bit more complicated than that.

The inherent jurisdiction of our superior courts was inherited from the United Kingdom in the 16th and 17th centuries from the Royal Court in Westminster. The Royal Court reviewed the legality of decision making by a whole host of what were then front-running administrative tribunals such as the Bridge Commission, the Poor House Commissions, and the Sewer Commission.[146] Here is where we circle back to the issue of remedies; historically, courts' inherent "supervisory" power over administrative decision-makers had to be exercised through the remedies available—if there was no appropriate remedy, then the administrative action could not be challenged. As Cristie Ford discusses in Chapter 3, Dogs and Tails: Remedies in Administrative Law, the relevant remedies were known as the prerogative writs and were once tremendously important in administrative law. These prerogative writs were certiorari (to quash or set aside a decision), prohibition (to order a tribunal not to proceed), mandamus (to order the performance of a public duty), and habeas corpus (to order the release of the unlawfully imprisoned). These writs were used by the Royal Courts in England, and subsequently by the superior provincial courts in Canada, to ensure that administrative bodies and tribunals did not exceed their legal powers and encroach on powers or matters that were the responsibility or privilege of central government. Before the 1970s, administrative law was about trying to squeeze cases into one or more of the prerogative writs, and courts made fine distinctions about, for example, whether or not a writ would lie. There were thousands of cases dealing with these fine distinctions. Determining whether an issue was a question of *vires* could be critical to the substantive outcome of the case. If an administrative decision was *intra vires*, a reviewing court could only apply one of the writs if the lower decision was so "patently unreasonable" (a term which, as Audrey Macklin and

---

[146]   Jerome J. Hanus, "Certiorari and Policy-Making in English History" (1968) 12 Am. J. Legal Hist. 63, n. 2; S.A. de Smith, *Judicial Review of Administrative Action*, 4th ed. by J. Evans (London: Stevens & Sons, 1980) at 584 (appendix 1) and 596 (appendix 2).

Sheila Wildeman discuss in, respectively, Chapter 9, Standard of Review: Back to the Future?, and Chapter 10, Pas de Deux: Deference and Non-Deference in Action, our Supreme Court has now abandoned, although it still exists in a number of statutes) so as to cause the administrative decision-maker to lose jurisdiction.[147] Conversely, regardless of how reasonable or correct the administrative decision had been, if a decision had been *ultra vires* the administrative decision-maker, the reviewing court could make an order of certiorari, prohibition, or mandamus in favour of the person challenging the decision.[148]

Thus, for the first three-quarters of the 20th century, judicial review of statutory decision-making was very confined.[149] However, "[w]ith greater government intervention in the private sector, increased social programs, and legislative derogation from the traditional jurisdiction of the courts came a rather different attitude on the part of the Canadian courts,"[150] which became "far less hospitable to the advent of many administrative tribunals and, more generally, the new social order."[151] As hinted at in the preceding section, the courts reacted defensively against a government that was giving their jurisdiction away to administrative agencies.[152] The legislatures inserted "privative clauses" into the statutes in an attempt to stop courts from reviewing the decisions of administrative decision-makers, but the courts responded in turn by either ignoring such clauses or interpreting them in a very restrictive way[153] and squeezed as many cases as possible into the old prerogative writs.[154] In so doing, the concept of jurisdictional error became so distorted that the courts were able to review administrative decisions just like they would review a lower court decision.[155] If you did not like an administrative decision, you would argue before the courts that the administrative decision-maker had exceeded its jurisdiction. The words "*ultra vires*" became so common that their original meaning was all but lost. Thankfully, change was on the way.

The McRuer Commission[156] was a watershed moment in the administrative-law revolution that took place during the 1960s and 1970s.[157] It was "set up in 1964 in response to opposition criticism of a [provincial] government bill that would have conferred broad-ranging investigatory powers on the Ontario Police Commission."[158] The McRuer Commission helped to bring about a basic codification of procedures for administrative tribunals in a number of

---

147   See e.g. *Jarvis v. Associated Medical Services, Inc.*, [1964] S.C.R. 497. The contrast between the majority and dissenting reasons in this case is particularly illustrative of the liberties that judges would take with the *vires* approach.

148   *Supra* note 145.

149   Evans et al., *supra* note 126 at 697.

150   *Ibid.*

151   *Ibid.*

152   *Ibid.*

153   *Ibid.* at 698.

154   *Ibid.*

155   I.e. on a "correctness" standard of review: Evans et al., *supra* note 126 at 698.

156   Ontario Royal Commission, *Inquiry Into Civil Rights* (J.C. McRuer Commissioner, 1968) [McRuer Commission].

157   David J. Mullan, "Willis v. McRuer: A Long-Overdue Replay with the Possibility of a Penalty Shoot-Out" (2005) 55(3) U.T.L.J. 535 at 535 [Mullan, "Willis v. McRuer"].

158   *Ibid.*

provinces.[159] For example, in 1966, the *Administrative Procedures Act*[160] was enacted in Alberta[161] and, in 1971, the *Statutory Powers Procedure Act*[162] was enacted in Ontario.[163]

McRuer also made several recommendations with respect to the scope of judicial review.[164] He wanted to extend the availability of judicial review, "in terms of both the grounds on which it [was] available and the ease with which it [could] be sought procedurally."[165] In 1971, Ontario enacted the *Judicial Review Procedure Act*,[166] which established rules for courts reviewing errors of both law and fact. For questions of law, courts could now review the decisions of any statutory authorities that determined rights and interests of an affected party.[167] For questions of fact, courts could now review the decisions of those charged with making a "statutory power of decision" on the basis of the evidence presented and facts of which they could take official notice; this meant most judicial or quasi-judicial bodies.[168] Over the next 30 years, nearly all of the provinces and territories enacted statutes that replaced the old common-law writs (the remedies) with a single application for judicial review.[169] However, the old remedies were mostly subsumed into these acts and were, and in many jurisdictions still remain, "[s]treamlined versions of the old prerogative writs (along with declaratory and injunctive relief)."[170]

As Craig Forcese discusses in Chapter 15, one of the most significant changes was the enactment of the *Federal Court Act*[171] in 1970,[172] which allowed for the almost complete transfer of "remedial jurisdiction over federal statutory decision makers ... from the provincial superior courts to the newly created Federal Court of Canada, a court that replaced the former Exchequer Court of Canada, which had had only very limited judicial review jurisdiction."[173] It was thought that by relocating jurisdiction over judicial review of federal administrative action to a federal court "there would be greater assurance of the development of an appropriate level of judicial expertise respecting the federal administrative process."[174] "Almost contemporaneously, Ontario ... [conferred] most judicial review authority onto a three-judge bench of the then Ontario High Court, the Divisional Court."[175]

---

[159] McRuer Commission, *supra* note 156.

[160] S.A. 1966, c. 1.

[161] Evans et al., *supra* note 126 at 302.

[162] S.O. 1971, c. 47.

[163] Evans et al., *supra* note 126 at 302.

[164] Mullan, "Willis v. McRuer," *supra* note 157 at 550.

[165] *Ibid.*

[166] S.O. 1971, c. 48 (now R.S.O. 1990, c. J.1).

[167] Mullan, "Willis v. McRuer," *supra* note 157 at 556.

[168] *Ibid.*

[169] David Mullan, *Administrative Law* (Toronto: Irwin Law, 2001) at 12, 405 [Mullan, *Administrative Law*].

[170] *Ibid.* at 405-6; see e.g. *Judicial Review Procedure Act, supra* note 166, s. 2(1).

[171] R.S.C. 1970, c. 10 (2d Supp.).

[172] Evans et al., *supra* note 126 at 1135.

[173] Mullan, *Administrative Law, supra* note 169 at 404.

[174] *Ibid.* at 425.

[175] *Ibid.* at 404.

The importance of these new statutes cannot be understated. Previously, judicial review of administrative decisions was defined by the common law—more specifically, by the ancient prerogative writs. Now, in many cases, statutes allowed an application for "judicial review," organized the procedure to be followed, and specified which court would have jurisdiction to review. The content of judicial review of both procedural fairness and substantive error is introduced in the second half of this chapter. To sum up, administrative law moved from a pure common-law regime to a simpler statutory-based regime informed by the common law.[176] But the relationship in the law of judicial review found in statute and the common law is not always an easy one—as we will see when we get to evolutions of the standard-of-review jurisprudence following the Supreme Court's decision in *Dunsmuir*.[177]

VII. Section 96 and the Courts' Constitutional Right to Review Administrative Decisions

We now digress from a linear history of Canada's administrative state and the evolution of administrative law to provide a bit more detail on a topic not otherwise covered in the rest of the text—namely, the nature of s. 96 courts and the constitutional basis for judicial review of administrative action. As we discussed earlier, a privative or preclusive clause is a way in which the legislature attempts to stop the courts from reviewing the decisions of administrative boards or tribunals. As you will see in the jurisprudence, historically, courts have made every effort to largely ignore or otherwise narrowly interpret these kinds of clauses. "For decades such clauses were largely ignored by the courts, despite much critical commentary by academic writers such as the late Chief Justice Laskin, before he was appointed to the bench"[178] and courts did not accept even strongly worded privative clauses as ousting their authority to review administrative decision making for excess of jurisdiction.[179] Why is this?

Because administrative agencies and tribunals have only those powers conferred by legislation, their powers are legally limited. Courts have long seen their role as one of patrolling the borders of those legal limits to make sure that an administrative agency does not step outside its jurisdiction and exercise power that it does not have. Because privative clauses essentially prevent the court from undertaking this role, courts have given such clauses short shrift.

So why do "superior" courts undertake this role of keeping "inferior" administrative boards and tribunals in check, even when the legislature has told them not to? And how tightly should courts police the boundaries of administrative decision making? Part of the answer is that, through their approach to statutory interpretation, courts have wide discretion in how they approach their role —a topic that a number of contributors to this volume

---

176 Evans et al., *supra* note 126 at 1087.

177 *Dunsmuir v. New Brunswick*, 2008 SCC 9, [2008] 1 S.C.R. 190 [*Dunsmuir*].

178 Andrew J. Roman, "The Pendulum Swings Back: Case Comment W.W. Lester (1978) Ltd. v. U.A., Local 740," (1991), 48 Admin. L.R. 274 at 283.

179 *Ibid.* at 284. See also e.g. *Jarvis v. Associated Medical Services Ltd.*, [1964] S.C.R. 497; David Mullan, "Dunsmuir v. New Brunswick, Standard of Review and Procedural Fairness for Public Servants: Let's Try Again!" (2008) 21 Can. J. Admin. L. & Prac. 117 at 128.

discuss, including Mary Liston in Chapter 2 and Sheila Wildeman in Chapter 10. However, the main reason is that there are constitutional grounds for the oversight of administrative decision-makers by superior courts.

The superior courts' role, however, creates a constitutional tension. Can a provincial legislature or the Parliament of Canada have the constitutional capacity to exclude *all* kinds of judicial review of decisions made by an administrative agency? On the one hand, the doctrine of parliamentary supremacy means that there is nothing preventing legislatures from enacting whatever it wishes, including privative clauses. But what happens when those privative clauses step on the toes of the superior courts and their constitutional role? There is nothing *explicitly* said about this in the *Constitution Act, 1867*.[180] However, there is an argument for implying a constitutionally guaranteed right to judicial review of administrative action—one that trumps parliamentary supremacy in this context—and it has centred on the provisions of the *Constitution Act, 1867*, ss. 96-101.

The starting point of this argument is s. 96 of the *Constitution Act*, which provides that the appointment of superior court judges is the sole responsibility of the federal government. Remember from our discussion above that superior courts have an inherent jurisdiction to review administrative decision making. However, another important aspect of the superior courts created under s. 96 is that they themselves are immune from judicial review, because they do not have jurisdiction to judicially review *other* superior courts: they can only review inferior administrative tribunals.

Provinces do not have the jurisdiction to create s. 96 courts. However, for various reasons, they have wanted to give administrative tribunals the same immunity from judicial review that s. 96 courts have. Accordingly, provinces have created de facto s. 96 courts by (conveniently) calling them "administrative tribunals," but inserting privative clauses making them immune from judicial review, just like superior s. 96 courts. "Real" superior courts have not appreciated the provinces' attempts to create unreviewable tribunals and have developed a three-part test to determine whether an administrative tribunal is actually acting like a s. 96 court, and is therefore unconstitutional because the province was without jurisdiction to create it:

1. *Historical inquiry:* Is the administrative decision in question similar to one that, at the time of Confederation, would have been exclusively within the power of a superior, district, or county court to make? (The jurisprudence suggests that this should be interpreted broadly so as to ensure the protection of s. 96 courts.)

2. *Judicial versus legislative or administrative power:* Is the impugned power a "judicial" power as opposed to a legislative or an administrative power? A judicial power is one where there is a private dispute between parties, adjudicated through the application of a recognized body of rules and in a manner consistent with fairness and impartiality.

3. *Contemporary character:* Even if the decision-making power was historically under the jurisdiction of a superior, district, or county court, has the decision-making power in its contemporary institutional setting sufficiently changed its character

---

[180]   *Supra* note 10, reprinted in R.S.C. 1985, App. II, No. 5.

such that it cannot conform to the jurisdiction of a court? For example, it was noted in *Tomko v. Labour Relations Board*,[181] while referring to the Nova Scotia Labour Relations Board, that the adjudicative functions of such a board were part of its broader administrative and policy-making role as administrator of the labour relations legislation. Thus, it was agreed that one could not compare a labour relations board's cease and desist order with the jurisdiction of a superior court to issue mandatory injunctions to halt illegal activities.

The leading case on administrative tribunals masquerading as s. 96 courts is *Crevier*,[182] a Supreme Court of Canada decision from 1981. In this case, Quebec legislation created a Professions Tribunal to hear appeals from discipline committees of most statutory professional bodies in Quebec. The tribunal was composed of provincially appointed judges. The Act included a privative clause stating, in effect, that the tribunal's decisions were final, even those about the reach of the tribunal's own jurisdiction.

The Supreme Court asked the following question: was the Quebec Professions Tribunal acting like a s. 96 court? Chief Justice Laskin, for the Court, noted that a provincial government, in creating an administrative tribunal, could include a privative clause if it allowed superior court jurisdiction to review questions of jurisdiction even if there was limited judicial review of all other kinds of decisions from the tribunal. But, if the wording of a privative clause tried to oust review by courts over even strict jurisdictional questions, as was the case in *Crevier*, then the clause was not constitutionally valid, because the province had de facto created a s. 96 court.[183] The Court concluded that to give a provincial tribunal unlimited jurisdiction to interpret and apply law and then preclude any supervision by provincial superior courts created a s. 96 court.

Crevier is a landmark case for the proposition that there is a constitutionally recognized right to judicial review, at least of questions of jurisdiction that cannot be displaced by a privative clause, no matter how it is worded. For example, following *Crevier*, Beetz J. said in *Bibeault* that "[t]he role of the superior courts in maintaining the rule of law is so important that it is given constitutional protection."[184] The Supreme Court confirmed this proposition in *MacMillan Bloedel Ltd.*[185] At stake here were provisions in federal legislation that attempted to give provincial youth courts the exclusive jurisdiction to try youths for *ex facie* contempt of superior courts. The Supreme Court agreed that, although it was permissible to confer jurisdiction over such matters on courts staffed by provincial appointees, that jurisdiction could not be to the exclusion of the superior courts. A superior court has a constitutionally guaranteed entitlement to try youths for flouting an injunction issued by it. According to Lamer C.J.:

---

181   *Tomko v. Labour Relations Board (N.S.) et al.*, [1977] 1 S.C.R. 112, as referenced in *Re Residential Tenancies Act, 1979*, [1981] 1 S.C.R. 714 at 731-32.

182   *Crevier v. A.G. (Québec) et al.*, [1981] 2 S.C.R. 220 [*Crevier*].

183   This argument was recognized five years earlier by Stephen A. Scott, "The Supreme Court and Civil Liberties" (1976) 14 Alta. L. Rev. 97 at 132: "It is one thing to admit a power to *curtail* the jurisdiction of the superior courts. It is another to admit a power to turn inferior into superior courts" (emphasis in original).

184   *U.E.S., Local 298 v. Bibeault*, [1988] 2 S.C.R. 1048 at 1090, citing *Crevier, supra* note 182.

185   *MacMillan Bloedel Ltd v. Simpson*, [1995] 4 S.C.R. 725, [1996] 2 W.W.R. 1.

The superior courts have a core or inherent jurisdiction which is integral to their operations. The jurisdiction, which forms this core, cannot be removed from the superior courts by either level of government, without amending the Constitution. Without this core jurisdiction, s. 96 could not be said to either ensure uniformity in the judicial system throughout the country or to protect the independence of the judiciary.[186]

To conclude, as recognized in *Crevier*, *Bilbeault*, and *MacMillan Bloedel*, superior courts have a constitutional role and inherent jurisdiction to judicially review administrative decision making, at least with respect to questions of jurisdiction. The way they protect this role is by ignoring provincial legislatures' privative clauses completely excluding judicial review of administrative tribunals as an unconstitutional attempt to create a de facto superior court. A superior court, even in the face of the most strongly worded privative clause, is constitutionally entitled to check the jurisdiction of an administrative board or tribunal.

PART 2: AN INTRODUCTION TO MODERN ADMINISTRATIVE LAW

VIII. Where to Start?

Having considered the constitutional basis by which superior courts may review administrative boards and tribunals, in the second half of this chapter we provide a high-level overview of the various parts of this book (and by extension, administrative law). The context of administrative decision making is extremely important to the resolution of issues in this field, and a variety of sectors and kinds of decisions are examined in this book. However, we must leave the particular valleys and mountains of, for example, immigration law, labour law, and securities law for other texts. Here we concentrate on the general principles of administrative law. Our analysis focuses on how courts review decision making on the part of those delegated power by the legislature, but we also hope to capture to a much greater extent the real world and context of administrative decision making itself.

Historically, as discussed somewhat above, the stance of courts toward administrative agencies has been negative: to limit, to reign in, to supervise, to oversee, and to constrain. As Mary Liston describes in Chapter 2, this historical orientation of the courts toward administrative agencies and tribunals, best captured in the writings of A.V. Dicey on the rule of law, was one that was largely antithetical to the administrative state. As we hinted at earlier, perspectives on the rule of law and the appropriate relationships between courts, Parliament, Cabinet, and delegated decision-makers like boards and tribunals have changed over time. The emphasis has shifted so that courts will tend to be deferential to administrative boards and tribunals where it seems that this was what Parliament intended. However, battles and differences in opinion over the appropriate balance between parliamentary sovereignty and the rule of law continue to play out in the jurisprudence, as do battles between progressive and more libertarian stances toward claims for, for example, social services. There is still no satisfactory resolution of all the various theoretical and political complexities and, in the absence of an agreed on and coherent framework, there is room for courts to obtain (or appear to obtain) the results they prefer.

---

[186] *Ibid.* at para. 15.

Like most administrative law texts, this book looks carefully and critically at how courts review, view, and interact with administrative agencies. In addition, we try to convey a much greater sense of how administrative boards and tribunals work in practice. In Chapter 7, Access to Administrative Justice and Other Worries, for example, Lorne Sossin looks at how people access administrative tribunals and how decisions on budgets, staffing, websites, and translation can make the difference between justice and injustice. In Chapter 16, Peter Carver takes up the challenge of looking at how administrative law works differently in the politically charged context of public inquiries. In Chapter 6, Advocacy Before Administrative Tribunals, Freya Kristjanson and Leslie McIntosh look at administrative law from a hands-on practitioner's perspective, providing useful checklists, tips, and an overview for those starting to practice administrative law. Administrative law scholars and teachers from across Canada have joined together to work on this text to provide multiple voices, perspectives, and approaches to administrative law and to convey a greater sense of the real world of administrative decision making. We leave it to those authors and the chapters that follow to illuminate this world. The remainder of this introduction provides a basic overview of the core features of administrative law to help guide the reader through subsequent chapters.

The core function of judicial review of administrative action is to examine how and why the courts decide to intervene in the administrative process. Administrative law is roughly divided into three parts:

1. *Procedural fairness:* First, is this an issue courts should review and, if so, did the administrative decision-maker use the proper procedures in reaching a decision?

2. *Substantive review:* Regarding the decision itself, did the administrative decision-maker make an error of the kind or magnitude that the court is willing to get involved in?

3. *Remedies and the legitimacy of judicial review:* If there are procedural or substantive defects in the decision, should the court intervene and, if so, how?

Having covered, from a bird's-eye view at least, the issue of remedies and the constitutional basis for judicial review, below we provide a snapshot of review for procedural fairness and substantive review.

IX. Review for Procedural Fairness

Chapters 5, 6, 8, and 12, by Grant Huscroft, Freya Kristjanson and Leslie McIntosh, Laverne Jacobs, and Evan Fox-Decent and Alex Pless, respectively, all deal with aspects of procedural fairness, both in the common law and pursuant to the Charter. When it comes to the common law of procedural fairness or natural justice as required by s. 7 of the Charter, the court, in reviewing the actions of the tribunal, is not interested in the actual decision that the tribunal came to in the end (the substance), but in the *procedures* followed by the tribunal in coming to the decision. As you review this discussion, consider the extent to which ensuring fair procedures is the best way to ensure good decision making and, also, the extent to which courts believe that court-like procedures are "fair," and to what extent this is true.

There are several parts to this focus on procedure: the threshold question, the content of procedural fairness, bias and independence, and institutional decision making. What follows is a simplified summary; the hard work and necessary detail are provided in Chapters 5, 6, 8, and 12.

A. Threshold Question

First, a court should ask itself what is called the "threshold" question: Is this the kind of decision that should attract some kind of procedural right? At this stage, the court is not asking what those rights would encompass, but only the preliminary question of whether there should be any entitlement to procedural fairness at all. To put it another way, the court is asking whether it should review the administrative decision-maker's procedures or whether it is more appropriate to conclude that whatever the decision-maker decides to do by way of procedure is sufficient. Generally, if, as a result of delegation by the legislature of governmental power, a decision is made that affects an individual's rights or interests, there will be some minimum entitlement to procedural fairness, but there are still some exceptions. Grant Huscroft explores them in Chapter 5, From Natural Justice to Fairness: Thresholds, Content, and the Role of Judicial Review. Exceptions include situations where the decision is a legislative or policy decision or preliminary or investigative (and then there are the exceptions to the exceptions). Another issue to consider here is the doctrine of legitimate expectation and in what circumstances, if any, an individual should be entitled to certain procedural rights if a representation of some form has been made that such rights would be forthcoming.

Traditionally, the determination whether this threshold had been passed was carried out at common law. The earliest such example is *Cooper*, an English case from 1863.[187] In *Cooper*, the plaintiff had built a house without giving the requisite notice to the district board. The board was entitled by statute in this situation to demolish the plaintiff's house, which it did. The court unanimously held that the plaintiff should have been given at least some procedural fairness because the board's decision to demolish a house has a huge impact on the person affected. Willes J. in *Cooper* stated that the rule that the threshold can be passed even when the statute does not require fairness is "of universal application, and founded upon the plainest principles of justice."[188] Note that, although the statute was silent about the right to procedural fairness, this was nonetheless read in by the court.

A century later in *Ridge v. Baldwin*,[189] the House of Lords held that a public office holder had a common-law entitlement to reasons and a chance to respond before being dismissed from office. The case involved a police constable who had been charged with but acquitted of several crimes. The relevant statute empowered the Watch Committee[190] with discretion to dismiss the constable, which it did, but did not provide any rights to, for example, a hearing or reasons. The House of Lords held first that the constable was not employed "at pleasure,"

---

187 *Cooper v. Wandsworth Board of Works* (1863), 14 C.B. (N.S.) 180 (Ct. of Common Pleas) [*Cooper v. Wandsworth*].

188 *Ibid.* at 190.

189 *Ridge v. Baldwin (No. 1)*, [1964] A.C. 40, [1963] U.K.H.L. 2.

190 *Municipal Corporations Act 1882*, 1882, c. 50 (Regnal. 45 and 46 Vict.), s. 191(4), cited in *Ridge v. Baldwin, supra* note 189.

nor was he employed in a master–servant relationship, so there had to be some reason against him to fire him. Second, this made the Watch Committee's decision "quasi-judicial," and in discharging a quasi-judicial task, the Committee had to adhere to the principles of natural justice—that is, it owed the constable a duty of fairness and was required to provide him with some reasonable opportunity to be heard.

Fast-forward to 1979 and Canada, where the Supreme Court introduced the duty of fairness owed to public office-holders in a watershed case—*Nicholson*.[191] The *Nicholson* majority, written by Laskin C.J., held that a police constable employed during a probationary period could not be dismissed arbitrarily without being given any reasons. A decade later, the Supreme Court in *Knight*[192] expanded that duty of fairness to include even those office-holders who were employed "at pleasure." Grant Huscroft explains these developments in Chapter 5 and how in *Dunsmuir*[193] the Supreme Court retreated from earlier jurisprudence to find that, in the case of a public employee under contract, the contract itself, rather than the common law of procedural review, determined what if any procedural rights an employee is entitled to. This wrinkle aside, the basic principle remains that a fair process may be required even if it is not specifically provided for in a statute.

In recent years, another component of the threshold discussion has been the *Charter of Rights and Freedoms*.[194] In Chapter 12, Evan Fox-Decent and Alexander Pless explore the kinds of actions or decisions that fall under s. 7 of the Charter. They examine in detail how the guarantee that one is not to be deprived of life, liberty, or security of the person except in accordance with fundamental justice (s. 7) relates to the common law of procedural fairness and the synergistic (and complicated) relationship between the two.

An exciting area in development is the intersection of public administrative law and private law. What happens when the government and an individual have a contract that purports to govern procedural fairness? Some examples include bids for government procurement contracts (see *Irving Shipbuilding*[195]), employment contracts for civil servants (see *Dunsmuir*[196]), and contracts between immigration sponsors and the Department of Immigration (see *Mavi*[197]). Do the terms of the contract trump statutory or common-law duties of fairness? Can a decision be so important to the individual that fairness is required no matter what the contract says? Does it matter whether the terms of the contract flow completely from statute? Moreover, the privatization, corporatization, and outsourcing of government services and programs have raised questions concerning the continued applicability of the principles of administrative law.[198] If a province hands over the operation of juvenile cor-

---

[191]   *Nicholson v. Haldimand-Norfolk Regional Police Commissioners*, [1979] 1 S.C.R. 311.

[192]   *Knight v. Indian Head School Division No. 19*, [1990] 1 S.C.R. 653.

[193]   *Supra* note 177.

[194]   *The Constitution Act, 1982*, being Schedule B to the *Canada Act 1982* (U.K.), 1982, c. 11.

[195]   *Irving Shipbuilding Inc. v. Canada (Attorney General)*, 2009 FCA 116, [2010] 2 F.C.R. 488, 314 D.L.R. (4th) 340, leave to appeal refused, [2009] 3 S.C.R. vii.

[196]   *Dunsumuir, supra* note 177.

[197]   *Canada (Attorney General) v. Mavi*, 2011 SCC 30, [2011] 2 S.C.R. 504.

[198]   Mullan, *Administrative Law, supra* note 169 at 5.

rectional facilities to the private sector, to what extent do the rules of procedural fairness still apply?[199]

As you progress through the cases, you will notice that the division into two separate questions of the threshold and the content of procedures is often rather artificial. It is not easy to separate the questions whether the threshold has been passed and, if so, what procedures are appropriate.

B. The Content of Procedural Fairness

If a court determines that the threshold for some form of procedural fairness has been met, it must then address what those procedures will be. The common law traditionally looked to how much of an impact the administrative decision would have on the affected individual's life. Thus in *Cooper*, the English case from 1863 discussed above, the court held that the plaintiff should have been given notice of the board's decision to demolish his house and an opportunity to respond to that notice.[200] There were many possible excuses why the plaintiff defaulted by failing to tell the board that he planned to build his new house, and he ought to have been given a chance to explain the default.[201]

The Supreme Court of Canada in *Baker*[202] identified the following five factors as relevant in determining the general level of procedural fairness: the nature of the decision and the process followed in making it; the nature of the statutory scheme; the importance of the decision to the individual affected; the legitimate expectations of the parties; and the procedures chosen by the tribunal.

Having determined the general level of procedural fairness, the court will then decide from a range of possibilities what specific procedures are required. There are many possibilities:

- *notice* that the decision is going to made;
- *disclosure* of the information on which the tribunal will base its decision;
- some opportunity to *participate* or make views known;
- a full *hearing* similar to that which occurs in a court;
- an opportunity to give *evidence* and cross examine;
- right to *counsel*; and
- oral or written *reasons* for its decision.

You may notice that many of these possibilities seem to be a way of asking, "To what extent must the administrative decision-maker act like a court?" We also need to think about who is better situated to determine what various procedures the tribunals should follow: the tribunals or the courts? Can courts really understand the day-to-day reality, costs, and impact of requiring different procedures from those that a tribunal would select itself?

If your client asks whether he or she has a right to be represented by legal counsel before an administrative board or tribunal, to where should you turn first? Students often overlook

---

199   *Ibid.*

200   *Cooper v. Wandsworth, supra* note 187.

201   *Ibid.*, Erle C.J.

202   *Baker v. Canada (Minister of Citizenship and Immigration)*, [1999] 2 S.C.R. 817 [*Baker*].

the most important aspect of administrative law—namely, the necessity for closely examining the legislation setting up the board or tribunal, often referred to as the "enabling statute." It is possible that the common law may expand on these, but the first port of call should be the statute itself. Additionally, as discussed above, the 1970s saw the establishment of umbrella statutes that codified administrative procedure. It is important to check whether your province has such an umbrella statute that sets out the types of procedures that must be made available for all or specific types of boards and tribunals—for example, Ontario's *Statutory Powers Procedures Act*,[203] Alberta's *Administrative Procedures and Jurisdiction Act*,[204] and Quebec's *Administrative Justice Act*.[205] In British Columbia, the *Administrative Tribunals Act*[206] focuses on empowering the tribunal to enact its own rules. These Acts are available on the companion website to this text at <adminlawincontext.emp.ca>. It is critical to remember that where a statute—be it umbrella or specific to the tribunal—specifies a certain kind of procedural right or specifically denies a procedural right that would otherwise have been available in the common law, the statute prevails over the common law. Where there is no such specificity, however, the common law may be read in to supplement the provisions of the statute.

In addition to the statutory regime, in practice, it is also important to check the rules pursuant to which the board or tribunal operates (these binding rules or regulations or nonbinding guidelines go beyond the content of the enabling statutes). As Andrew Green discusses in Chapter 4, Regulations and Rule Making: The Dilemma of Delegation, these rules are critical to the day-to-day operation of boards and tribunals and, in reality, the decisions of the hundreds of boards and tribunals across the country have a far greater impact on Canadians than the relatively few decisions that are taken on judicial review to the general courts.[207] For example, the guidelines issued by the minister of immigration set out the basis on which immigration officers are to determine whether an individual deserves humanitarian and compassionate consideration, and these guidelines were central to the resolution of the *Baker* decision, which we discuss below.[208]

C. Bias, Independence, and Institutional Decision Making

Another aspect of the part of this text that focuses on procedures is the idea of bias and the related concepts of independence and institutional decision making, which is more fully explored by Laverne Jacobs in Chapter 8, Caught Between Judicial Paradigms and the Administrative State's Pastiche: "Tribunal" Independence, Impartiality, and Bias. If a decision-maker acts in a biased manner, favouring one party over another, what then? And what do we mean by bias? Do we mean that we have actual evidence that the decision-maker has

---

[203]   R.S.O. 1990, c. S.22.

[204]   R.S.A. 2000, c. A-3.

[205]   R.S.Q., c. J-3.

[206]   S.B.C. 2004, c. 45.

[207]   See Lorne Sossin, Chapter 7, and his reference to McLachlin J.'s passage from *Cooper v. Canada (Human Rights Commission)*, [1996] 3 S.C.R. 854.

[208]   Cited *supra* note 202.

already made up his or her mind or has been bribed to decide in a particular way? Or is it enough that, given all the circumstances, there is an appearance of bias?

Related to the issue of bias is independence, which, as mentioned above, is a key feature of most boards and tribunals and one of the original rationales for their creation (independence being seen as important to ensure non-political, fair decision making). Institutional independence is related to the concept of bias, but is more about the systemic structure of a board or tribunal as opposed to individual decision making. In the context of independence we ask questions such as: Do the members of the tribunal have financial security or do they have security of tenure? A related issue is whether they are so dependent on or connected to the government that, if appointed, they cannot be perceived as being sufficiently able to make an independent decision.

With respect to institutional decision-making we explore the thorny issue of the extent to which boards and tribunals can consult with others to whom the person affected will not have had the opportunity to present his or her case. For example, is it acceptable that, in order to deal with a high caseload, a board has set up a process whereby just one member of the board hears an application or case, but the full board is involved in the final decision? If so, in what circumstances is it acceptable?

X. Substantive Review

Historically, administrative law has focused primarily on procedural review (with the implicit notion that if a sound process is followed, a fair decision will be reached). The second major focus of administrative law is substantive review and, here, the courts look at the decision itself, not just at the procedures that were followed in reaching the decision. Recall from the discussion above of the *intra vires–ultra vires* era that courts were quite eager to assert their influence in the administrative sphere. However, all of this began to change in the revolution that took place in the 1960s and 1970s. The culmination of the changes was the landmark Supreme Court decision *C.U.P.E. v. N.B. Liquor Corporation*,[209] which acknowledged that, often, there was no one right answer in terms of legal interpretation, but a range of different reasonable interpretations, and that the view or choice of an administrative decision-maker may be as legitimate as that of a court's. This case should have ushered in a new era of judicial deference toward administrative tribunals—although, as we shall see, the road toward this goal has been both tentative, twisted, and rocky—often two steps forward and one step back.

Regarding the substance of a decision itself, the courts ask themselves what the standard of review is; in other words, how big an error must the tribunal make before the court will get involved? There are now, following the Supreme Court's decision in *Dunsmuir*,[210] two categorical possibilities:

1. The standard of *correctness*, an exacting standard of review (that is, was it a correct decision, the same decision that the court would have reached?)

---

[209]   *Supra* note 82.

[210]   *Supra* note 177.

2. The standard of *reasonableness*, a more respectful or forgiving standard of review (that is, did the tribunal's decision fall within a range of reasonable alternatives?)

Recall the above discussion on the history of remedies. If these two standards look a little bit like the *intra vires–ultra vires* distinction, it's because they are the legal descendants of the two *vires* standards. Historically, if a decision was *intra vires* the decision-maker, it could be quashed only if the decision was so blatantly unreasonable as to make the decision-maker lose jurisdiction. As the practice of judicial review evolved, "*intra vires*" morphed into the present standard of reasonableness—that is, a reviewing court will only overturn a tribunal's decision if it is unreasonable. Conversely, if in the past a court found a decision to be *ultra vires* the decision-maker, the reviewing court would happily substitute its own judgment. Thus, "*ultra vires*" morphed into the standard of correctness—that is, the court will only overturn a tribunal's decision if it is not what the court itself would have decided.

In Chapters 9 and 10, Audrey Macklin and Sheila Wildeman, respectively, set out in much greater detail the history of the development of the tests for the standard of review and the modern test and all its myriad twists, turns, and agonies. In Chapter 11, Administrative Discretion: Between Exercising Power and Conducting Dialogue, Geneviève Cartier takes the reader through the history and modern tests for review of the exercise of discretion, which historically has been treated differently from other types of decisions; however, relatively recent jurisprudence (*Baker*), brought within the same test for the standard of review and then even more recently (*Dunsmuir*) arguably seeks to treat this area somewhat differently again. The question of which standard of review to apply is often framed in terms of how much "deference" or "respect" the reviewing court should show to the tribunal.[211] If the court decides to be deferential to the tribunal's decision, it applies the reasonableness standard. If the court decides it will not show any deference at all, it applies the correctness standard.

In deciding which standard to apply (that is, how much deference to show) to an administrative decision, the reviewing court follows a new process set out by the Supreme Court in *Dunsmuir*.[212] Audrey Macklin outlines the process in far greater detail in Chapter 9, Standard of Review: Back to the Future? but, in a nutshell, the Supreme Court requires a reviewing court, as a default starting position, to assume a deferential stance vis-à-vis administrative decision making—the default standard of review should thus be "reasonableness" as opposed to "correctness." Correctness may nonetheless still be the standard required when it comes to the following: questions of central importance to the legal system as a whole and outside the adjudicator's specialized area of expertise, constitutional questions, "true" questions of jurisdiction, and questions regarding the jurisdictional lines between two or more competing specialized tribunals. Beyond these guidelines, the Supreme Court tries to aid courts from spending so much jurisprudential energy on fixing the standard of review instead of applying it to the facts by counselling a reviewing court to first see if any past cases have already decided the standard of review to be applied to this type of

---

211   David Dyzenhaus, "The Politics of Deference: Judicial Review and Democracy" in M. Taggart, ed., *The Province of Administrative Law* (1997) 279 at 286 (quoted with approval in *Baker, supra* note 202 at para. 65, L'Heureux-Dubé J.; *Law Society of New Brunswick v. Ryan,* 2003 SCC 20, [2003] 1 S.C.R. 247 at para. 49; *Dunsmuir v. New Brunswick, supra* note 177 at para. 48).

212   *Supra* note 177.

administrative decision. If the case at bar does not fit into one of these precedential categories, only then does the reviewing court move to a more in-depth analysis: the standard of
review analysis (previously called "the pragmatic and functional analysis"). In the standard
of review analysis, the reviewing court weighs four non-exhaustive factors:[213]

1. the presence or absence of a privative clause; ⟶(un/ reasonableness

2. the purpose of the tribunal as determined by interpretation of enabling legislation;

3. the nature of the question at issue; and

4. the expertise of the tribunal.

The standard of review analysis is contextual and does not necessarily involve all of the
listed factors.[214]

Let us look at one of the factors: the existence of a privative clause (also known as a preclusive clause). A privative clause is a provision in the statute setting up the tribunal that
says the tribunal's decision is final and not open to review by the courts. As discussed above
in the history of remedies, the court's historical treatment of such clauses is a twisted one,
beginning with an approach that readily allowed courts to ignore such express clauses (by
arguing that the error made by the board or tribunal went to the very jurisdiction it had to
make the decision, and thus a decision that must be reviewable by the court) to a time where
the existence of a privative or preclusive clause meant that a standard of patent unreasonableness must automatically apply. The modern approach is to treat the existence of a privative or preclusive clause as strongly determinative but not definitive in pointing toward a
standard of reasonableness (now the most deferential standard possible). But, as Sheila
Wildeman fully explores in Chapter 10, what reasonableness *in its application* actually
means is far from cut and dried. It may be that the complexities and tensions that once be-
devilled the setting of the standard of review will now lurk when *applying* the standard once
it is set.

Having determined the standard of review—the level of intensity with which the court
will review a decision—the court then applies it to the decision in question, be it a decision
taken by a minister, a municipality, a board, or a tribunal. Even if a court has determined
that the standard of review must be one that is unforgiving and shows no deference (that is,
correctness), in reviewing the decision it may nonetheless determine that the standard has
been met. In other words, the decision reached by the board or tribunal is the same as that
which would have been reached by the court and thus will not be overturned. Similarly, if
the standard of review is forgiving and deferential (that is, reasonableness), then it does not
necessarily mean the decision will stand; it may be that the court finds that no reasonable
decision-maker could have reached that conclusion because the conclusion did not fall
within a range of reasonable alternative decisions. For example, in the case of *Del Vecchio v.
Canada*,[215] the Federal Court found with respect to decisions on prisoner transfers from the
United States to Canada that the minister of public safety had a high degree of discretion

---

[213]   *Ibid.* at para 64.

[214]   *Ibid.*; *Canada (Citizenship and Immigration) v. Khosa*, 2009 SCC 12, [2009] 1 S.C.R. 339 at para 54.

[215]   *Del Vecchio v. Canada (Public Safety and Emergency Preparedness)*, 2011 FC 1135. At the time of publishing, this
        case had not yet been appealed; the reader should therefore update the status of this case before relying on it.

and was owed deference—the court should apply a standard of reasonableness to test the minister's decision. However, in arbitrarily refusing to allow Mr. Del Vecchio to transfer into a Canadian prison while letting Mr. Del Vecchio's criminal accomplices transfer, the minister's decision was outside the range of reasonable alternatives. The minister's decision was thus unreasonable, and the court set aside the minister's original order and ordered him to make a new, reasonable decision.

Judicial review of substantive error can and does occasionally overlap with that other main branch of administrative law, judicial review of procedural fairness.[216] Recall that an element of procedural fairness is the duty to give reasons. But a failure to give reasons, or a failure to give reasons that sufficiently explain the decision, can also lead to a finding of unreasonableness. To go back to our example of *Del Vecchio v. Canada*,[217] the minister's decision appeared arbitrary to the Court (and to Mr. Del Vecchio) because the minister had failed to explain why Mr. Del Vecchio was being treated differently than his accomplices. The minister had provided some reasons, meaning that procedural fairness was met, but those reasons were inadequate, meaning that the decision was unreasonable. Had the minister paid better attention to procedural fairness—the duty to give reasons—his decision may not have appeared arbitrary and may, in fact, have been reasonable.

It is important to remember that, regardless of the standard of review that a court adopts, judicial review for substantive error in a decision is not the same as an appeal against that decision. An important indicator of this is what the court is allowed to receive and see in evidence. In what is called an "appeal *de novo*," the court essentially repeats the decision-making exercise: it receives oral testimony of witnesses and can hear new evidence that was not before the original decision-maker. In contrast, in judicial review, the court is restricted to the evidential record that was before the decision-maker: witnesses do not testify and the court cannot receive new evidence.[218] "Review" is literally what the court is doing, rather than making a new decision.

It is also relevant to consider the intersection of Charter review and administrative law. For example, the recent Supreme Court decision of *Doré v. Barreau du Québec*[219] changed the approach used to review discretionary decisions involving an alleged Charter infringement stating that the standard of review approach in administrative law for discretionary decisions should be used in place of the usual *Oakes* test employed in Charter challenge reviews.[220] The Supreme Court found that the standard of review in the case of administrative decisions engaging Charter interests and values will be reasonableness with the concept of "proportionality" helping to determine what is in fact reasonable. This requires the ad-

---

[216] Diana Ginn, "New Words for Old Problems: The Dunsmuir Era" (2010) 37 Advocates' Q. 317 at 334-37.

[217] *Supra* note 215.

[218] This is provided for, at the federal level, by r. 317 of the *Federal Courts Rules*, SOR/98-106, which allows a party in judicial review proceedings to request "relevant" material not in its possession. As Teitlebaum J. in *Gagliano v. Gomery* (2006), 49 Admin. L.R. (4th) 261 (F.C.T.D.), aff'd (2007), 57 Admin. L.R. (4th) 1 (F.C.C.A.) explains at para. 50, relevance has always been understood to be limited to material before the decision-maker: "It is trite law that in general only materials that were available to the decision-maker at the time of rendering a decision are considered relevant for the purposes of Rule 317."

[219] 2012 SCC 12.

[220] *Multani v. Commission scolaire Marguerite Bourgeoys*, 2006 SCC 6, [2006] 1 S.C.R. 256.

ministrative decision-maker to consider how best to protect the particular Charter interest or value at stake while achieving the statutory objective and weighing these appropriately. As with many Supreme Court decisions in the field of administrative law attempting to address difficult problems, the *Doré* decision still leaves much unresolved. For example, to what extent does this new approach allow judicial reconsideration and re-weighing of values as part of the "reasonableness" review? And to what extent will the change in the onus of the burden of proof (with the reasonableness test in administrative law the burden lies with those seeking to challenge the decision; in Charter reviews under s. 1 it lies with those seeking to defend the impugned law or decision) have an impact on how well administrative law serves to uphold Charter values?

XI. Applying the Concepts: Baker

This is a continuing battle, a continuing tension in administrative law, which has to be resolved. As mentioned earlier, and as Mary Liston further develops in Chapter 2, historically, the rule of law was usually employed to fetter, limit, and prevent administrative decision making and was thus viewed as inherently conservative. The courts were being called on essentially to impede the development of the welfare state insofar as it affected private property rights. Thus the prevailing sentiment in administrative law scholarship in the 1950s, 1960s, and 1970s was to protect administrative tribunals' decision making from overzealous courts, and this movement eventually caught on in the jurisprudence with growth in notions of deference starting, as Audrey Macklin describes in Chapter 9, most famously in Canada with the *CUPE* decision.[221]

It is interesting to consider to what extent the pendulum has swung from a need to protect administrative agencies from judicial review to further a progressive agenda and toward a need for courts to review administrative decision making to protect, for example, human rights. For example, consider whether in *Baker*[222] the actions of the immigration officer underscore a sense that administrative decision making does have its limits and that courts may have to intervene to ensure fairness and, more generally, to support a larger progressive agenda such as the human rights of children.[223]

One method of learning how to swim is to jump into the deep end. In reality, this method is rarely tried and, when tried, can result in a watery demise. Yet we recommend it (metaphorically) for admin law. To jump into the deep end and to provide an overview in the areas of procedural and substantive review, you may start by reading and analyzing the 1999 Supreme Court of Canada case, *Baker v. Canada (Minister of Citizenship and Immigration)*.[224] This, along with *Dunsmuir*, is one of the two most important Supreme Court decisions on administrative law in the past 20 years. It involved a woman, about to be deported for overstaying, who requested that the minister use his discretionary power to allow her,

---

[221]   *Supra* note 82.

[222]   Cited *supra* note 202.

[223]   Lorne Sossin & Colleen M. Flood, "The Contextual Turn: Iacobucci's Legacy and the Standard of Review in Administrative Law" (2007) 57 U.T.L.J. 581.

[224]   *Supra* note 202.

on humanitarian and compassionate grounds, to remain in Canada with her four Canadian-born children while she applied for permanent residency. Her application was denied. An immigration officer wrote up inflammatory notes about the merits of Ms. Baker's application. Despite the relatively informal nature of these notes, the Supreme Court accepted they were sufficient to act as reasons for the decision. (For a fuller summary of the facts, see Grant Huscroft, Chapter 5.)

Important issues covered in *Baker* that will be the focus of attention throughout this text include what fairness is required in terms of Ms. Baker's procedural rights to participate in the decision-making process—for example, the right to make her case and have an oral hearing); the duty to give reasons and the scope of that duty; bias; and the relevance of international treaties ratified but not yet incorporated in domestic law. In terms of substantive review, the Supreme Court provided a new test for determining the standard of review for discretionary decisions such as those made by the minister of immigration. For administrative law redux, read *Baker* (the full decision is available on the accompanying website at <adminlawincontext.emp.ca>) and then attempt to answer the following questions.

QUESTIONS

SOURCE OF LAW

1. What sources of law did the Supreme Court consider in reaching its decision?

THE SCOPE OF THE APPEAL

2. What are the arguments for and against the Supreme Court's decision to use the certification of "a question of general importance" to be the trigger to review the whole decision? How should the courts approach statutes that preclude an administrative decision-maker being reviewed in the general courts?

PROCEDURAL FAIRNESS

3. Madam Justice L'Heureux-Dubé said that the duty of fairness required that Ms. Baker be accorded more than "minimal" procedural rights even though she was seeking a highly discretionary benefit. How should the principles of procedural fairness be applied to those, like Ms. Baker, seeking a highly discretionary benefit? How does one decide what procedural rights should be available generally? What do you think of the test laid out?

4. What procedural rights was Ms. Baker found to have had? Do you think they were satisfactory? Why or why not? When do you think an oral hearing should be required?

5. Prior to *Baker* there was division of opinion over the requirement of statutory or prerogative decision-makers to provide reasons for their decisions. On what grounds was Ms. Baker found to be entitled to reasons? Why does this illustrate the absence of a bright line between procedural and substantive review? What do you

think is the nature of the relationship between reviewing discretionary decision making and the requirement to give reasons?

6. The notes of Immigration Officer Lorenz were taken to be sufficient reasons for the decisions. On what grounds did the Court decide that this was sufficient? Why is the Court's requirement for reasons such an important finding?

7. One of several factors identified by L'Heureux-Dubé J. as helpful in determining the scope of the duty of fairness is "legitimate expectation."

    a. How did she interpret the doctrine of legitimate expectation in terms of its ramifications for procedural and substantive rights?

    b. The Court found that the federal government signature to the *Convention on the Rights of the Child* should not be viewed as a representation. What would have been the implications if the Court had viewed this as a representation?

    c. Do you think Ms. Baker should have had to know of the existence of the *Convention on the Rights of the Child* in order to make an argument in legitimate expectation?

8. What is the test for establishing bias? At what point does a decision-maker's obvious lack of sympathy give rise to a reasonable apprehension of bias?

SUBSTANTIVE REVIEW AND ABUSE OF DISCRETION

9. *Baker* is an important decision because it is a step toward reconciling the theory on which the courts review decisions for error of law and jurisdiction and the theory on which they review for abuse of discretion. *Baker* resulted in the folding of all questions of review of discretion into the general law of review using a "pragmatic and functional" analysis (which was later modified in *Dunsmuir* to become the "standard of review analysis"[225]). What were the factors relied on in *Baker* to determine what the standard of review should be? What concerns arise in applying these factors to discretionary decisions?

10. With regard to review of discretionary decision making, what three standards of review did the Supreme Court acknowledge? What standard of review did Ms. Baker seek, and what standard was found? How will you know when you should apply one standard as opposed to another?

11. As a result of *Baker*, what advice would you give clients who ask you about the impact of international agreements that Canada has ratified but not incorporated into domestic law? How does this affect discretionary decision making?

---

[225] *Supra* note 177.

XII. Conclusion

Administrative law today cannot be properly understood without knowing at least something about its historical evolution. What began as limited prerogative writs developed over the 20th century into a whole category of law on par with contract or criminal law. Catalysts for this exponential growth included the two world wars, the expansion of the welfare state, and the introduction of the Charter. As the executive branch of government grew more and more powerful, the need for a judicial check on that power grew accordingly. Of course, the courts were probably also concerned that these new things called "administrative tribunals" were getting to wade into their turf and make quasi-judicial decisions or would make decisions that were not subject to the sunlight of scrutiny in the House of Commons.

Today, administrative law is pervasive, not only encompassing judicial review of administrative decision making, but also informing the way decisions are made in the first instance. How courts approach the review of this enormously variable set of administrative decisions depends on the type of administrative agency, the type of decisions being made by the agency, and the impact of those decisions. Some agencies appear more court-like in nature, adjudicating on particular disputes and having a huge impact on particular individuals. These kinds of agencies arguably should be required to act more like courts in terms of the type of processes that they follow in order to ensure the highest possible standard of decision making, although this requirement may have to be balanced against the volume of decisions to be adjudicated on (for example, in the immigration area). However, many agencies and tribunals combine adjudicative-like functions with broad-based policy making where it seems much less appropriate to restrict the agency or tribunal to a court-like process. What is fair in terms of processes in this case?

One thing that has not changed since the beginnings of administrative law is the basic tension in "the constitutional divide between the executive and judicial branches of government."[226] On the one hand, as A.V. Dicey would say, the executive (including tribunals) has to play by the rules of the law just like anyone else. On the other hand, John Willis might retort, the democratically elected executive has to be allowed leeway in order to get things done and look after its citizens. The difficulty often is that, when a court reviews the actions of an administrative tribunal, the court holds the tribunal up to the standard that it expects of other courts and, unsurprisingly, frequently finds that administrative decision-makers fall short of this mark. At the same time, the courts have to be respectful of democratic will. This requires courts to respect the purpose for which administrative tribunals have been established and the fact that these functions have explicitly *not* been delegated to courts for a reason.

Administrative decision making and the courts' responses thereto are critical to the effective implementation of public policy and the smooth operation of public programs. In what follows we hope to convey to you the complexities and challenges in administrative law and the importance of administrative decision making and administrative law in the lives of many Canadians. We hope you find this text useful and easy to follow and that it stimulates

---

226   *Ocean Port Hotel Ltd. v. British Columbia (General Manager, Liquor Control and Licensing Branch)*, 2001 SCC 52, [2001] 2 S.C.R. 781.

an interest in and even a passion for administrative law. We value your feedback and thoughts on improvement for subsequent editions; you can provide feedback on the website that accompanies this text at <adminlawincontext.emp.ca>. Although there may be no salve for the frustration you feel when courts revisit a particular area of administrative law (again) and promulgate yet another test, understand that what underlies these repeated attempts to improve the law are currents of tensions and contests over the appropriate role of courts in relationship to the myriad types of administrative decision making that exist. The last word we leave you with on this is from Justice Scalia of the Supreme Court of the United States—"[a]dministrative law is not for sissies."[227]

SUGGESTED ADDITIONAL READINGS

CASES

Baker v. Canada (Minister of Citizenship and Immigration), [1999] 2 S.C.R. 817.

Crevier v. A.G. (Québec) et al., [1981] 2 S.C.R. 220.

Re Residential Tenancies Act, 1979, [1981] 1 S.C.R. 714.

---

[227] Forsey, *supra* note 6 at 1, citing Scalia, "Judicial Deference to Administrative Interpretations of Law" (1989) Duke L.J. 511. The Forsey paper also provides a brief but useful overview of the English and American approaches to the standard of review, as well as the standard of appellate review of judicial decision making.

CHAPTER TWO

Governments in Miniature: The Rule of Law in the Administrative State

MARY LISTON*

Faculty of Law, University of British Columbia

* I would like to thank Alan Freckelton and Andrew Pilliar for excellent research assistance. I would also like to thank the editors: Colleen Flood, Lorne Sossin, and Arthur Wilson. Lastly, I thank David Duff, Evan Fox-Decent, Zvi Halpern, and Audrey Macklin for their constructive feedback.

I. Introduction

If there is one concept that ties together the seemingly disparate strands of administrative law, it is surely the rule of law. This chapter discusses several attributes of the rule of law and explores their relevance for Canadian administrative law. Although it is unlikely that the rule of law will constitute a direct and complete basis for answering a law exam question, the puzzles that administrative law evokes cannot be understood without recourse to this foundational concept.

Section II presents several of the main features of the rule of law: the rule of law as a foundational legal principle, the rule of law as a political ideal concerning institutional relations and competencies, and the rule of law as a distinctive political morality.[1] Section III assesses the Canadian articulation of the rule of law in the jurisprudence of the Supreme Court of Canada. Section IV focuses on judicial review of administrative action as a key component of the rule of law, the importance of statutory interpretation, and three difficulties for the "deference as respect" model of Canadian administrative law. The conclusion argues that Canadian administrative law is committed to a distinctive form of the rule of law, which simultaneously attempts to ensure rule-of-law accountability and democratic accountability in all parts of government.

II. The Rule of Law in Theory

Certain philosophical concepts—for example, democracy, freedom, autonomy, equality, and the rule of law—do not have a firmly agreed-upon core of meaning and, therefore, can be considered essentially contested.[2] Despite this uncertainty, I will argue that the rule of law can be characterized by three interrelated features: (1) a jurisprudential principle of legality; (2) institutional practices of imposing effective legal restraints on the exercise of public power within the three branches of government; and (3) a distinctive political morality shared by all in the Canadian political community. While this presentation may seem uncontroversial, deeply embedded within any discussion of the rule of law is a debate about the legitimate scope and content of judicial power, particularly in a democratic state.

A. The Purpose of the Rule of Law: The Non-Arbitrary Rule of Men (and Women)

The rule of law initially seems a simple and straightforward idea, concisely articulated by Aristotle in his view that the laws, not men, should rule in a well-ordered political community.

---

[1]   By political morality, I mean principles of justice that are publicly endorsed and justify the use of coercive state power—power that the state claims universal authority to exercise over all members of a political community. As will be discussed further, different political moralities provide different bases to justify the supervisory role of courts and the scope of judicial power in the Canadian legal system.

[2]   For an elucidation of the nature of "essentially contested concepts" with reference to the rule of law, see Jeremy Waldron, "Is the Rule of Law an Essentially Contested Concept (in Florida)?" (2002) 21 Law & Phil. 137. Waldron discusses how disagreements about underlying normative issues—issues such as what values the rule of law is meant to promote or what is the best understanding of the rule of law—are pervasive and predictable. Disagreement can also exist about what the most important features are, or what features are necessary but not sufficient, or how the features work together in a successful realization of the concept.

Though men and women do, of course, wield public power, the rule of law represents a normative standard by which all legal subjects can evaluate and challenge the use of public power. Because the concept stands for the supremacy of law over unconstrained political power, a state committed to the rule of law will go some distance to guarantee that all public officials are both authorized and bound by law in the exercise of their functions and powers. In a legal system governed by the rule of law, all persons will possess formal equality, ensuring that elected officials and high-ranking members of the executive branch of government will be held legally accountable just like any other person. This aspirational prescription for good government has united thinking about the rule of law from the ancients Greeks down to contemporary theorists.

The principle of the rule of law is animated by the need to prevent and constrain arbitrariness within the exercise of public authority by political and legal officials in terms of process, jurisdiction, and substance. Arbitrariness commonly connotes indifference by the decision-maker about the procedures chosen to reach an outcome. Indifference about the procedures used to make a decision makes it more likely that the result will be unjust or unfair. In Canada, it is a generally held belief that all government decisions should be made using processes that put relevant considerations before decision-makers who care about achieving the best possible outcomes. As Binnie J. writes regarding procedural fairness in the *Mavi* decision, "it is certainly not to be presumed that Parliament intended that administrative officials be free to deal unfairly with people subject to their decisions ... [because the] simple overarching requirement is fairness, and this 'central' notion of the 'just exercise of power' ... ."[3]

All branches of government—executive, legislative, judicial, administrative—can behave arbitrarily in relation to other branches of government. For example, if the federal or a provincial government acts in contravention of the constitutional division of powers, it is acting arbitrarily and will be found *ultra vires* its jurisdiction. If one branch of government attempts to monopolize government power, or encroaches on the powers of another branch, the action will offend the doctrine of the separation of powers, which is a principle that authorizes a particular distribution of public power in a state. If a decision-maker in government uses statutory powers outside the purpose of the enabling statute, the decision will be found arbitrary and will be invalidated because it is incorrect or unreasonable in law.

In addition to the examples concerning procedure and jurisdiction, a decision may be found arbitrary in substance because it is biased, illogical, unreasonable, or capricious. In other words, it will offend what appear to be shared standards of reasonableness, rationality, or morality. Such a decision may exhibit a lack of care, concern, or good judgment on the part of the decision-maker toward the affected individual or group. It can, instead of a justified response, show mere opinion, preference, stereotyping, or negative discrimination. Decision-makers act arbitrarily when they treat individuals with a lack of respect, ignore dignity interests, or deny the equal moral worth that we all share as members of the Canadian political community.[4] Arbitrariness can also suggest that a decision-maker possesses

---

3   *Canada (Attorney General) v. Mavi*, [2011] 2 S.C.R. 504 at paras. 39 and 42.

4   The benefits of the rule of law can extend to non-citizens who are present in Canadian territory. Evan Fox-Decent and Alexander Pless, in Chapter 12, The Charter and Administrative Law: Cross-Fertilization or Inconstancy?, discuss how cases involving non-citizens in the immigration context have posed challenges for, and often been the source of extensions to the scope of, procedural fairness in administrative law.

unconstrained discretionary powers, such that he or she alone can decide on how to use these expansive powers; hence, arbitrariness can be associated with a unilateral method of decision making or one that is not sufficiently reciprocal, consultative, or participatory. Historically, this type of arbitrariness has been associated with the type of power wielded by absolute monarchs. Most familiarly, arbitrariness is expressed in the idea of an untrammelled exercise of will, or the uncontrolled power, of a public decision-maker. A decision, for example, may exhibit unilateralness to a degree that becomes oppressive and will therefore be considered an abuse of power. This understanding informs familiar criticisms of majority decision making that infringes minority rights. Finally, arbitrariness seems to suggest the absence of a rule, but it should be remembered that judges or administrators can arbitrarily apply a valid rule.

A recent example of substantive arbitrariness is *Insite*,[5] a case concerning North America's first government-sanctioned safe injection facility, located in Vancouver, which provides medical supervision to intravenous drug users. The federal minister of health decided not to renew the exemption protecting the provincial facility from federal drug laws concerning possession and trafficking in the *Controlled Drugs and Substances Act*.[6] The lack of an exemption meant that the facility would have to close. On review, the Supreme Court of Canada found that the CDSA was a valid federal statute, was applicable to Insite and its activities, and had only an incidental effect on the provincial health care facility. Section 56 of the CDSA gave the minister of health a broad discretionary power to grant exemptions from the application of the Act "if, in the opinion of the Minister, the exemption is necessary for a medical or scientific purpose or is otherwise in the public interest." Relying on this provision, the claimants argued that the CDSA limited their s. 7 rights under the Charter[7] because the effect of the discretionary decision denied injection drug users access to potentially life-saving medical care. The Court held that the CDSA did not violate s. 7, even though liberty and security interests were engaged, because the possibility of an exemption acted as a safety mechanism. Nevertheless, the Court went on to find that it was the minister's actual exercise of discretion in not granting the exemption that violated s. 7 of the Charter and was, therefore, "not in accordance with the principles of fundamental justice because it [was] arbitrary, disproportionate in its effects, and overbroad."[8] The Court considered all of the available evidence before the decision-maker when he made the decision, and concluded that the decision was inconsistent with the statutory objectives of public health and safety found in the CDSA. The discretionary decision to deny the licence was therefore arbitrary in the sense that it did not further the statutory objectives and lacked a real connection on the facts to the statutory purposes—during its eight years of operation, Insite proved to save lives without undermining public health and safety. The Court also

---

5   *Canada (Attorney General) v. PHS Community Services Society*, 2011 SCC 44, [2011] 3 S.C.R. 134 [*Insite*].

6   S.C. 1996, c. 19 [CDSA].

7   *Canadian Charter of Rights and Freedoms* (the Charter), Part I of the *Constitution Act, 1982*, being Schedule B to the *Canada Act 1982* (U.K.), 1982, c. 11. Section 7 guarantees that "Everyone has the right to life, liberty and security of the person and the right not to be deprived thereof except in accordance with the principles of fundamental justice."

8   *Supra* note 5 at para. 127.

concluded that denying the essential services Insite provides was grossly disproportionate to the benefit of having a uniform drug policy. In a surprising move, the Court used the remedy of *mandamus* to order the minister to grant the exemption to Insite.

The ever-present political and legal problem of the arbitrary use of public power profoundly animates rule-of-law attempts to ensure the legality, reasonableness, and fairness of administrative processes and their outcomes so that public authorities do not overreach their authority. Before turning to administrative law, however, this section considers legal and political theory in order to identify several common features of the rule of law.

B. Attributes of the Rule of Law

The rule of law acts as a foundational "metaprinciple"[9] that organizes an open set of related principles such as the principle of legality, the principle of the separation of powers, the principle of responsible government, the principle of judicial independence, the principle of access to justice, the principles of fundamental justice, the principle of the honour of the Crown,[10] and so on. If the rule of law has a core meaning in jurisprudence, it is the principle of legality, which conveys the basic intuition that law should always authorize the use and constrain the risk of the arbitrary use of public power. The principle of legality restrains arbitrary power in three ways: first, it constrains the actions of public officials; second, it regulates the activity of law making; and third, it seeks to minimize harms that may be created by law itself. The views of three prominent legal theorists—Albert V. Dicey, Lon Fuller, and Joseph Raz—illustrate how the principle of legality constrains the misuse of public power in each of these ways. Their views will then be contrasted to Ronald Dworkin's rights-based model of adjudication at the end of this section.

The first model of legality was most famously articulated by Albert V. Dicey in his theory of 19th-century British constitutionalism. In Dicey's view, the rule of law possessed three features: (1) the absence of arbitrary authority in government, but especially in the executive branch and the administrative state; (2) formal legal equality so that every person—including and especially public officials—in the political community is subject to the law; and (3) constitutional law that forms a binding part of the ordinary law of the land.[11]

Common-law courts, in this model, provide the institutional connection between rights and remedies and are the site for the development of the general principles of the common-law constitution. According to Dicey, judge-made law combined with an unwritten constitution represented a better mode of legal constraint than written codes and constitutions

---

9   See Friedrich A. von Hayek, *The Constitution of Liberty* (Chicago: University of Chicago Press, 1978) at 205 [Hayek].

10   In Chapter 13, In Search of Aboriginal Administrative Law, Janna Promislow and Lorne Sossin discuss the rule-of-law dimensions of the honour of the Crown in Aboriginal administrative law and the duty to consult and accommodate Aboriginal interests in decision-making processes. The Supreme Court confirmed the principle of the honour of the Crown and its supporting doctrine of the duty to consult as constitutional limits on executive discretion in *Beckman v. Little Salmon/Carmacks First Nation*, [2010] 3 S.C.R. 103.

11   Ordinary law usually means domestic law, and only international law if it has been incorporated by Parliament. This chapter focuses on domestic law. Gerald Heckman, in Chapter 14, explores the relationship between international human rights norms and administrative law.

because they were less vulnerable to executive attempts to suspend or remove rights. To take away the right to individual freedom in the English Constitution, Dicey wrote, would require "a thorough revolution in the institutions and manners of the nation."[12] In a common-law constitutional system like Britain's, the Constitution is not the source, but the consequence, of the rights of individuals as defined and enforced by the common-law courts. Dicey argued that this particular institutional advantage of the courts meant that they were best placed not only to control the political executive in the name of the rule of law, but also to provide superior protection of fundamental rights, like liberty and property, in the English system.

In the Diceyan model, Parliament was sovereign and supreme. Parliament was the primary source of all ordinary law and ought to be the source of all governmental power. If the use of public power was not authorized by Parliament, or if a decision-maker had acted beyond the powers delegated to it, then this would be considered *ultra vires* by the courts.[13] The justification for judicial intervention rested on a number of grounds, including:

1. the institutional role of the courts as the principal external check on executive and agency powers;
2. the specific task allocated to the courts through administrative law to constrain administrative discretion by ensuring that an administrative body did not overstep the jurisdiction that the legislature had set down in the statute; and
3. the judicial perception that a fundamental role of courts was to protect and vindicate the private autonomy of affected individuals, primarily through common-law rights derived from contract, tort, and property.

One key consequence of the Diceyan model was that administrative bodies were viewed with distrust as almost inherently lawless forms of governance and should be shown no curial deference in the review of their decisions.[14] This perception worsened when it became clear that Parliament could no longer provide proper oversight of administrative agencies in the modern state through regular legislative scrutiny or through political practices like ministerial responsibility.

In contrast to Dicey's common-law model, which offers institutional control on forms of executive discretion through the judiciary, other theories of the rule of law recommend a legal system that aims for a set of formal characteristics that are public and can guide the conduct of all legal subjects, including public officials. A common set of principles has evolved over time and includes those enunciated by Lon Fuller and Joseph Raz: publicity, non-retroactivity, clarity, generality, consistency, stability, capability of being obeyed, and declared rules constraining the administration of law as well as the discretion of public officials such as administrative decision-makers and the police. The presumed virtue of these

---

12   See Albert V. Dicey, *Introduction to the Study of the Law of the Constitution*, 8th ed. (Holmes Beach, FL: Gaunt, 1996) at 197.

13   For a more detailed exposition of the implications of Dicey's *ultra vires* model, see Paul P. Craig, "The Nature and Purpose of Administrative Law" in *Administrative Law*, 5th ed. (London: Sweet & Maxwell, 2003) at 3.

14   See e.g. Hayek's characteristic overstatement: "When the administration interferes with the private sphere of the citizen ... the problem of discretion becomes relevant to us; and the principle of the rule of law, in effect, means that the administrative authorities should have no discretionary powers in this respect." Hayek, *supra* note 9 at 213.

formal requirements rests on the belief that they permit individuals to predict legal responses to their behaviour by state officials, thereby avoiding sanctions and benefiting from a minimum ambit of freedom. Such a presumption is especially important for criminal law.[15] People can also interact with each other secure in the knowledge that they know in advance the rules that will likely apply to their behaviour should a dispute arise between them. Advanced knowledge is, of course, not empirically true and this claim relies on the ability of the law to align with other co-existing normative orders (i.e., shared or general norms, custom, etiquette, workplace, religious, or business relations) in order to be effective. Individuals can also rely on a certain determinacy in the application of law so that like cases will be treated alike. In this minimalist form, the rule of law can be equated with legal formalism because adherence to the rule of law does not mean that the resulting laws are substantively just, only that they are valid and meet the minimum legal conditions considered essential for the realization of procedural justice.

Lon Fuller's "inner morality" of law represents a procedural approach to understanding the principle of legality—in other words, the laws of lawfulness.[16] Fuller conceived of the rule of law as the enterprise of subjecting human conduct to the governance of rules in order to create and sustain a framework for successful social interaction. Compliance occurs, in part, because citizens derive benefits from following the law.[17] Lawmakers, then, have an interest in optimizing the legal conditions necessary for, and conducive to, voluntary compliance and cooperation. Fuller called this relationship between government and the citizen a "kind of reciprocity" that respects people's autonomy because the enterprise of law is not a "one-way projection of authority" onto legal subjects.[18] Fuller's principles of legality aim to guide lawmakers in achieving this end. For example, the principle of publicity guides accountability and transparency in government decision making because secret laws undermine legality and frustrate the citizen's ability to know where he or she stands in relation to a system of rights, benefit distribution, and/or enforcement and punishment. To take another example, the principle of congruency ensures a match between the rules as announced and the rules as applied in order to avoid a legal system composed of arbitrary or ad hoc commands. This last principle deeply informs discretionary decision making in the administrative state. These principles therefore guide law making wherever it is found in the state:

---

15 These principles differ according to the specific area of law. The principle of legality in criminal law, for example, includes the prohibition against retroactive criminalization or *ex post facto* laws as well as the void for vagueness doctrine with respect to provisions within criminal statutes. See *R. v. Grant*, [2009] 2 S.C.R. 353, where the Supreme Court explains the relationship between the principles of the administration of justice and the rule of law in a case concerning improper police conduct and the admission of evidence. On the relationship between the rule of law and vagueness in constitutional law, chiefly in the criminal law area, see Marc Ribeiro, *Limiting Arbitrary Power: The Vagueness Doctrine in Canadian Constitutional Law* (Vancouver: University of British Columbia Press, 2004).

16 See Lon L. Fuller, *The Morality of Law*, rev. ed. (New Haven & London: Yale University Press, 1969) at 33 [Fuller].

17 Hence the rule of law provides one basis for the duty to obey the law and invokes concerns about when it is morally appropriate to disobey the law. For a discussion of the relationship between the duty to obey the law and the rule of law, see *Sauvé v. Canada (Chief Electoral Officer)*, [2002] 3 S.C.R. 519 at paras. 6-64, 90-121.

18 Fuller, *supra* note 16 at 39, 207.

legislative, judicial, and administrative. But, unlike Dicey, Fuller's conception of legality does not assume that administrative bodies are inherently lawless. Rather, if they follow these principles, they may be more likely to engage in lawful activity and reviewing bodies, like the courts, may be obliged to show deference to their decisions.

Joseph Raz provides a third well-regarded interpretation of the rule of law.[19] Though in agreement with several of Fuller's principles, he believes it is possible to reduce the rule of law to one basic idea: law must be capable of guiding the behaviour of its subjects.[20] Raz further claims that most of the requirements we associate with the rule of law can be derived from this one basic idea in which the rule of law as the principle of legality acts as a practical guide for making effective law, thereby constraining the harms created by law itself. Raz's principles aim to guide both the formation and application of law, but he also emphasizes that his theory does not enumerate all of the possible principles associated with the rule of law. His set of principles explicitly includes the principle of judicial independence in order to preserve the rule of law. An additional principle that he proposes is access to justice— though Raz offers no views on how such access should be realized in practice, and whether or not access to the courts constitutes a positive duty on government.[21] Lastly, Raz empha- sizes the necessity for a legal system to provide effective remedies so that affected legal subjects can vindicate their rights.[22]

Because law in part creates the danger of the exercise of arbitrary public power, the rule of law acts to minimize this risk, thereby minimizing harms that the legal system might itself create. For example, overbreadth in a statutory provision is a deficiency that makes it more likely that the law will cause harm by: (1) not adequately constraining the use of power; (2) not providing guidance for individual behaviour; or (3) widening the potential to infringe a specific right, such as individual liberty. Vagueness in statutory language may present similar risks. A lack of generality, on the other hand, may violate legal equality or individual dignity interests because the classification or categorization may disproportionately "single out" a particular segment of the population. A lack of generality may also indicate negative discrimination on the grounds of race, sexual preference, or other enumerated grounds.

According to Raz, the rule of law has an instrumental role as a means to realizing other important ends such as democracy, equality, and human rights.[23] This is because in a society

---

19   See also Andrei Marmor, who claims to hold a position in between those articulated by Fuller and Raz, in "The Rule of Law and Its Limits" (2004) 23 Law & Phil. 1.

20   Joseph Raz, "The Rule of Law and Its Virtue," in *The Authority of Law: Essays on Law and Morality* (Oxford: Clarendon Press, 1979) at 214 [Raz, *The Authority of Law*].

21   He writes: "Long delays or excessive costs may effectively turn the most enlightened law into a dead letter and frustrate one's ability effectively to guide oneself by the law." *Ibid.* at 217. For judicial treatment of undue delay, see Grant Huscroft's discussion of *Blencoe v. British Columbia (Human Rights Commission)*, [2000] 2 S.C.R. 307 in Chapter 5, From Natural Justice to Fairness: Thresholds, Content, and the Role of Judicial Re- view, and Evan Fox-Decent and Alexander Pless's discussion of *Blencoe* in Chapter 12.

22   Cristie Ford, in Chapter 3, Dogs and Tails: Remedies in Administrative Law, describes the variety of admin- istrative law remedies a tribunal might impose as well as those available through judicial review.

23   Raz controversially states that "[a] non-democratic legal system, based on the denial of human rights, on extensive poverty, on racial segregation, sexual inequalities, and religious persecution may, in principle, conform to the requirements of the rule of law better than any of the legal systems of the more enlightened

characterized by deep diversity, we may agree on a common set of values that we hold important, but we will not all or always agree how these fundamental values should be ranked in relation to each other.[24] Because we live in a modern, industrial pluralistic society, we require both democracy and the rule of law and this fact underscores the importance of democratic legislation in responding to different interests, perspectives, subcultures, and continuous social and economic change.[25] Courts and legal culture simply can neither respond as quickly nor as adequately as democratic politics can.

The relative autonomy of law from politics, for which Raz seems to be the strongest advocate, is a central requirement of the rule of law, but one that poses a number of challenges for the administrative state. Though it is impossible to isolate law from politics completely, a complex institutional structure helps guarantee impartiality and fairness in decision making. One way of thinking about this relative autonomy is through the doctrine of the separation of powers and the principle of judicial independence as fundamental constitutional requirements.[26] According to the doctrine of the separation of powers, sovereign power is divided and housed within three different branches of government, each with its own function and staff: the executive, the judiciary, and the legislature. Canada's Westminster system of government, however, cannot be characterized by bright-line distinctions among the three branches—particularly, the executive, Cabinet, and bureaucracy. In parliamentary systems such as Canada's, the executive branch exerts considerable influence in appointing judges as well as in controlling the legislative agenda during a majority government. As the Supreme Court writes in *Wells*:

Western democracies. This does not mean that it will be better than those Western democracies. It will be an immeasurably worse legal system, but it will excel in one respect: in its conformity to the rule of law." Raz, *The Authority of Law*, *supra* note 20 at 211. For Raz, a legal system can be said to exist despite the fact that it does not conform to the principles of the rule of law. He therefore rejects the natural law maxim that "an unjust law is no law at all."

[24] Raz belongs to the philosophical school of moral or value pluralism, which holds that in modern societies, fundamental values may be correct, but will conflict with or be incommensurable with each other and therefore involve tough choices and sacrifices in order to resolve the conflict. Sometimes, a constitution will rank our values for us in terms of importance—consider, for example, how the Charter equally ranks equality and liberty, but explicitly excludes property interests. A statute can indicate this ranking of values—recall, for example, how the statute in the *Insite* case prioritized both medical or scientific purposes as well as public health and safety, though it was up to the judiciary, through interpretation, to resolve the conflict between them. Alternatively, the political process presents the chief forum for us to argue and work out collectively which values we hold most important. These value conflicts inevitably arise in legal decisions, especially in those cases involving dissents and concurrences. Raz and other value pluralists should be distinguished from moral relativists who hold that no objective or universal standards of right and wrong exist and that moral judgments are culturally and temporally dependent on the traditions, convictions, or practices of an individual or a group of people.

[25] Joseph Raz, "The Politics of the Rule of Law" (1990) 3:3 *Ratio Juris* 331 at 335 [Raz, "Politics of the Rule of Law"].

[26] For discussion of the separation of powers in constitutional jurisprudence, see *Newfoundland (Treasury Board) v. N.A.P.E.*, [2004] 3 S.C.R. 38; *Doucet-Boudreau v. Nova Scotia (Minister of Education)*, [2003] 3 S.C.R. 3; *Cooper v. Canada (Human Rights Commission)*, [1996] 3 S.C.R. 854 [*Cooper*]; *Wells v. Newfoundland*, [1999] 3 S.C.R. 199 [*Wells*]; and *Operation Dismantle v. The Queen*, [1985] 1 S.C.R. 441 [*Operation Dismantle*].

The doctrine of separation of powers is an essential feature of our constitution. It maintains a separation of powers between the judiciary and the other two branches, legislature and the executive, and to some extent between the legislature and the executive. ... The separation of powers is not a rigid and absolute structure. The Court should not be blind to the reality of Canadian governance that, except in certain rare cases, the executive frequently and *de facto* controls the legislature.[27]

Nevertheless, the doctrine, when informed by the principle of judicial independence, constitutionally guarantees the separate function of the courts and informs the tradition of independence that our legal profession, police, and civil service share.[28] In Chapter 8, Caught Between Judicial Paradigms and the Administrative State's Pastiche: "Tribunal" Independence, Impartiality, and Bias, Laverne Jacobs further discusses both judicial independence and the independence of administrative bodies such as tribunals.[29] There she describes administrative tribunals as hybrid bodies, or "governments in miniature,"[30] possessing differing combinations of policy making, rule making, and adjudication, which make their purposes and functions difficult to separate. Because administrative tribunals are creatures of statute that "span the constitutional divide between the judiciary and the executive"[31] and have a significant policy-making role, their independence will be much less protected than that of the courts.

The growth of the regulatory state and administrative tribunals, however, underscores the importance of bureaucratic justice and the expectation that one can "conduct one's life without being frustrated by governmental arbitrariness or unpredictability."[32] As Raz argues, implementing the principle of the rule of law in modern government requires an elaborate institutional complex staffed by competent and relatively impartial officials, using predictable and fair procedures in order to make reasoned and public decisions that, if an individual wishes to dispute, can potentially be argued by specially trained legal professionals and reviewed by an independent judiciary.[33]

---

27 *Wells, supra* note 26 at paras. 52, 54.

28 See *Valente v. The Queen*, [1985] 2 S.C.R. 673; *Beauregard v. Canada*, [1986] 2 S.C.R. 56; and *Provincial Court Judges' Assn. of New Brunswick v. New Brunswick (Minister of Justice); Ontario Judges' Assn. v. Ontario (Management Board); Bodner v. Alberta; Conférence des juges du Québec v. Quebec (Attorney General); Minc v. Quebec (Attorney General)*, 2005 SCC 44, [2005] 2 S.C.R. 286.

29 See, in particular, Jacobs's discussion of *McKenzie v. Minister of Public Safety and Solicitor General et al.*, 2006 BCSC 1372, a case concerning procedural fairness, tribunal independence, the rule of law, and the dismissal of a residential tenancy arbitrator for arbitrary reasons.

30 I borrow this phrase from John Willis, an important early Canadian public law scholar. See "Three Approaches to Administrative Law: The Judicial, the Conceptual and the Functional" (1935) 1 U.T.L.J. 53 at 73. See also Mary Liston, "Willis, 'Theology,' and the Rule of Law" (2005) 55 U.T.L.J. 767.

31 *Ocean Port Hotel Ltd. v. British Columbia (General Manager, Liquor Control and Licensing Branch)*, [2001] 2 S.C.R. 781 at para. 24.

32 Raz, "Politics of the Rule of Law," *supra* note 25 at 332.

33 Raz, however, notes that the bureaucratic model of the rule of law may serve the business and legal communities, but it makes the law both financially inaccessible as well as remote and alienating for ordinary people. *Ibid.* at 333.

C. Ruling the Judges

How might each of these theories inform judicial understandings of their role in a rule-of-law order? Returning to the three theorists discussed above, Dicey considered the courts to be the chief rule-of-law check on the executive in a Westminster system of government and, later, the primary means to control delegations of discretion from the executive to the administrative state. The Diceyan model saw the judiciary as guardians of common-law checks—in his words, "regular law"—on the arbitrary power of the executive and its delegates in order to protect individual rights. Such a view meant that courts need not defer to, or show respect for, the decisions made by administrative bodies that implicated common-law rights and interests. In matters of agency interpretation, his theory of the rule of law argues for the primacy of a correctness standard of review in order to scrutinize administrative decisions on their merits. The implications of a Diceyan approach to the standard of review will be discussed more fully in section IV.C.2 of this chapter.

As Colleen Flood and Jennifer Dolling explain in Chapter 1, An Introduction to Administrative Law: Some History and a Few Signposts for a Twisted Path, Canadian courts gradually became aware of the problems of legitimacy when intervening in decisions made by administrative agencies and sought to set some limits to the exercise of their own reviewing powers. Although courts were wary about too overtly substituting their views for those of the agency when they held a different opinion about the merits of the decision, they could still intervene easily through their approach to statutory interpretation. Through their approach to statutory interpretation, courts could argue that intervention was justified when the legislature intended that questions of law or mixed fact and law implicated the jurisdiction of the agency, thereby requiring judicial review.

The approaches articulated by Fuller and Raz are both aware of this dilemma and intend that their common set of principles also control judicial power and judicial exercises of discretion in order to prevent arbitrariness in the courts. The procedural practices available by virtue of the rule of law—rights to representation, cross-examine witnesses, *habeas corpus*, the right to appeal an adverse decision, standing to raise legal issues—ensure that judges play a prominent role in Fuller's theory. Moreover, because Fuller viewed law making as a shared and ideally cooperative institutional enterprise among state actors and institutions, he emphasized the democratic potential of law to ensure accountability in government by facilitating participation of affected individuals in the decision-making process. Nevertheless, Fuller argued that litigation alone is an unsatisfactory method of ensuring access to justice and just outcomes because "haphazard and fluctuating principles concerning this matter [standing] can produce a broken and arbitrary pattern of correspondence between the Constitution and its realization in practice."[34] Serious disadvantages of relying

---

[34] Fuller, *supra* note 16 at 81. In "The Form and Limits of Adjudication," Fuller controversially claimed that many polycentric disputes—disputes involving a large number of affected parties—are inherently unsuitable for adjudication and should therefore be considered non-justiciable in public law. According to Fuller, polycentricity is both pervasive and a matter of degree. Private law disputes, by contrast, take the familiar form of a bipolar encounter between plaintiff and defendant, and will likely have few polycentric elements. The problem Fuller identified is that of knowing when polycentric elements have become so significant that the proper limits of adjudication have been reached such that these disputes should be resolved by the legislature or by the market. (1978) 92 Harv. L. Rev. 353.

solely on the courts as a bulwark against the "lawless administration of the law" include the willingness and financial ability of the affected party to litigate, the inability of the courts to properly constrain police lawlessness, and the ability of courts to make things much worse by departing from principles, not articulating reasonably clear general rules, issuing contradictory rulings, changing direction frequently or suddenly, and aggravating the already vexed problem of interpretation.[35]

Raz's theory gives support to institutional design, such as revised procedures, because he intends the common set of principles to inform the creation of effective statutory purposes, standards, and rules with the overall aim of providing guidance to decision-makers and affected parties. His theory also attempts to reconcile the rule of law with democracy. As discussed earlier, Raz's approach places a great emphasis on the role of legislation in modern societies. Nevertheless, he does not deny a role for the courts in making and developing public law. For him, the rule of law consists of a core idea in the "principled faithful application of the law."[36] Legislatures are directed by, and satisfy, this ideal when they make reasonably clear laws that are coherent and transparent in their purposes. An open and public administrative of justice is directed by and satisfies the ideal when the judiciary and subordinate legal institutions apply statutory and common law faithfully, openly, and in a principled way in order to facilitate legislative purposes. The rule-of-law role of the courts arises out of the ability of the judiciary to ensure coherence in law by bringing legislation into line with legal doctrine.[37] In Raz's model, each institution mutually supports the other: legal institutions will be loyal to democratic legislation through interpreting intent while rejecting inconsistent purposes.[38] Democratic institutions will, in turn, respect civil rights, legal coherence, and long-term interests reflected in existing legal culture.[39]

Section II.A on the legal control of substantive arbitrariness above alluded to the normativity of the legal subject animating individual rights against the state as well as the duties with which the state must comply. This potentially authorizes greater judicial intervention, but not on the same grounds as in Dicey's model. A current and prominent proponent of this approach to adjudication can be found in the legal philosophy of Ronald Dworkin.[40] Dworkin's legal subject is an individual bearer of rights who is entitled to demand the resolution of disputes over the content of these rights through the legal system—specifically through courts, which he calls the "independent forum of principle."[41] Dworkin's theory

---

[35]   Fuller, *supra* note 16 at 82.

[36]   Raz, "Politics of the Rule of Law," *supra* note 25 at 335.

[37]   *Ibid.* at 336.

[38]   Raz distinguishes between conflicting and inconsistent purposes. Conflicting purposes are endemic to pluralistic societies and require compromise. But "no rational society should entertain inconsistent [values]": for example, a society cannot endorse the indissolubility of marriage while, at the same time, permit divorce on demand. Inconsistent purposes and values are a form of conflict that is logical, not political. *Ibid.* at 337.

[39]   Raz acknowledges that his model of the rule of law is anti-majoritarian because it constrains democratic legislatures. Though part of the culture of democracy, the rule of law demands restraint and a willingness to compromise by the majority so as not to disregard the rights and interests of minorities.

[40]   Two significant texts for this argument are Dworkin's *A Matter of Principle* (Cambridge, MA: Harvard University Press, 1985) and *Law's Empire* (Cambridge, MA: Harvard University Press, 1986).

[41]   See *A Matter of Principle, ibid.* at 30-32 and Chapter 2, "The Forum of Principle."

therefore grounds what he calls the "rights conception of the rule of law."[42] For Dworkin, the rule of law necessarily entails the judicial determination of rights through principled interpretation in hard cases where a legal answer must be crafted by judges from existing legal sources (e.g., statutes, regulations, constitutional documents, and case law) and principles of political morality. A principled interpretation must fit the existing positive law but it also must be compatible with select principles from a larger political morality. Government respect for individual freedom and equality, for example, would be principled requirements of this larger political morality. A key consequence of Dworkin's theory is that judges, not legislators, are ultimately charged with guarding the moral integrity of the political order because, as the chief political actors in the form of principle, they possess the knowledge and the skills—honed through their unique access to the interpretation of the law—to be the better articulators of a constitutionalized public morality.[43] Dworkin's theory of adjudication has as its central focus a concept of justice designed to further political principles of autonomy, dignity, equality, and liberty for all individuals in the political community. Politics, on his account, should be held to a higher standard because we ought to prioritize the pursuit of justice in society. Nevertheless, if courts should respect pluralism as a political fact, and ideological pluralism in particular, their job is not to endorse wholeheartedly one particular substantive political morality: that, many critics of Dworkin argue, is typically seen as the role of the legislature.[44]

III. The Supreme Court of Canada on the Rule of Law

Legal and political theories like those canvassed above constitute the often unstated background assumptions that inform judicial understandings of the rule of law and appear either implicitly or explicitly in specific cases. The Supreme Court of Canada has articulated various features of the rule of law, but the Court has not (and perhaps never should) set out a fully articulated conception of the rule of law.[45]

A. The Heart of the Canadian Rule of Law

The marked difference between the formal and substantive approaches to the rule of law can be seen in the case of *Roncarelli v. Duplessis*,[46] which contains several examples of arbitrary

---

[42]   *Ibid.* at 11-12.

[43]   Contrary to Dworkin, the authority of the courts in Raz's model to constrain legislation does not come from their superior wisdom or from their guardianship of superior law. Raz, "Politics of the Rule of Law," *supra* note 25 at 336.

[44]   Many democratic theorists have criticized Dworkin's theory of adjudication and his conception of the rule of law. See e.g. the collection of essays in Allan C. Hutchinson & Patrick Monahan, eds., *The Rule of Law: Ideal or Ideology* (Toronto: Carswell, 1987); Jeremy Waldron, *Law and Disagreement* (Oxford: Oxford University Press, 1999); Christopher Manfredi, *Judicial Power and the Charter: Canada and the Paradox of Liberal Constitutionalism*, 2d ed. (Toronto: Oxford University Press, 2001); and Ran Hirschl, *Towards Juristocracy: The Origins and Consequences of the New Constitutionalism* (Cambridge, MA: Harvard University Press, 2004).

[45]   Perhaps because, as Raz writes, "judges who become philosophically ambitious are bad judges." *Supra* note 25 at 336.

[46]   [1959] S.C.R. 121 [*Roncarelli*].

power: the existence of unlimited discretionary powers in an agency; a decision-maker acting in bad faith; inappropriate responsiveness to an individual situation where important interests were at stake; consideration of irrelevant factors in the decision; disregard of the purpose of a statute; and dictation of the decision by an external and unauthorized person. *Roncarelli* illustrates one of the primary functions of the rule of law: the control of executive arbitrariness.[47]

Frank Roncarelli owned a Montreal restaurant and was a Jehovah's Witness. At that time, the Quebec government and the Catholic Church joined forces to persecute Jehovah's Witnesses, whom they viewed as dangerous to the established order, seditious, and anti-Catholic. Hundreds of Jehovah's Witnesses were jailed for distributing religious pamphlets in violation of municipal bylaws. Roncarelli posted bail for fellow Witnesses. Premier Duplessis publicly warned Roncarelli to stop posting bail, and, when Roncarelli continued, Duplessis ordered that the liquor board cancel Roncarelli's permit to sell alcohol. The cancellation of the liquor licence forced Roncarelli to shut down his restaurant.

The Supreme Court examined the actions of Maurice Duplessis, who acted as both premier and attorney general, and found them invalid. Invoking the unwritten principle of the rule of law, the Court held that no public official is above the law. Duplessis had stepped outside the authorized bounds of his power as attorney general by ordering the revocation of Roncarelli's liquor licence. He also inappropriately exercised the power that was properly given to the chairperson of the Quebec Liquor Commission by the enabling statute, *An Act Respecting Alcoholic Liquor*. Last, regardless of who actually was the decision-maker, the decision offended the rule of law because the substance of the decision was incompatible with the purpose of the statute. Being a Jehovah's Witness was irrelevant to a decision concerning the continuation of a liquor licence for operating a restaurant. The true nature of the decision was to punish Roncarelli for exercising his civil right to post bail.

There are two ways to understand the use of the principle of the rule of law in this judgment: the formal Diceyan model, discussed in section II, above; and a more value-laden substantive constitutionalism, or what David Dyzenhaus calls the unwritten "constitution of legality."[48] On the Diceyan model, the Supreme Court held that Chairman Edouard Archambault of the Quebec Liquor Commission had not made a decision at all because Duplessis had substituted his decision for that of the proper authority, thus exercising his power arbitrarily. The case confirmed that Premier Duplessis had overstepped his jurisdiction as attorney general by, in effect, telling Chairman Archambault to cancel Roncarelli's liquor licence "forever" so that his restaurant would go out of business. Under the terms of the governing statute, however, this power had been delegated to Chairman Archambault, not to the attorney general who, at most, could only provide advice on the matter.[49] The legal wrong committed against the rule of law here was the violation of the legal principle

---

[47] For a detailed exposition of the relation between the rule of law and the administrative state in administrative law, see Gus Van Harten et al., "The Administrative State and the Rule of Law" in *Administrative Law: Cases, Text, and Materials*, 6th ed. (Toronto: Emond Montgomery, 2010) chapter 1.

[48] See David Dyzenhaus, "The Deep Structure of Roncarelli v. Duplessis" (2004) 53 U.N.B.L.J. 111 at 124.

[49] Alternatively, and to paraphrase Don Corleone in *The Godfather*, Duplessis provided "advice," the nature of which Archambault could not refuse.

of validity, which affirms that "every official act must be justified by law" or be found *ultra vires*: the decision was not valid because the power to cancel licences was not given to either the premier or the attorney general.[50] As Dyzenhaus points out, the problem with this line of argument is that had Archambault not consulted Duplessis, his decision would have been found valid, particularly because the enabling statute granted Archambault seemingly un-fettered discretion.[51] Indeed, the relevant provision of the statute, s. 34, simply and broadly stated that the Commission "may refuse to grant any permit." On this basis, only when an administrative authority acts beyond the power given to it by Parliament can the courts legitimately enforce the rule of law or reaffirm the separation of powers.

In contrast, Rand J., writing in a concurring judgment for the majority, stated that public authorities, especially those with broad discretionary powers, are always constrained by the unwritten constitutional principle of the rule of law, even when the legislation contains no explicit or written constraints:

> In public regulation of this sort there is no such thing as absolute and untrammelled "discre-tion," that is that action can be taken on any ground or for any reason that can be suggested to the mind of the administrator; no legislative Act can, without express language, be taken to contemplate an unlimited arbitrary power exercisable for any purpose, however capricious or irrelevant, regardless of the nature or purpose of the statute. ... "Discretion" necessarily implies good faith in discharging public duty; there is always a perspective within which a statute is intended to operate; and any clear departure from its lines or objects is just as objectionable as fraud or corruption.[52]

Even if Archambault had acted on his own in cancelling Roncarelli's licence, he would have used his discretionary powers inappropriately according to Rand J. because his deci-sion contradicted the substantive content of the rule of law:

> That, in the presence of expanding administrative regulation of economic activities, such a step and its consequences are to be suffered by the victim without recourse or remedy, that an ad-ministration according to law is to be superseded by action dictated by and according to the arbitrary likes, dislikes and irrelevant purposes of public officers acting beyond their duty, would signalize the beginning of disintegration of the rule of law as a fundamental postulate of our constitutional structure. An administration of licences on the highest level of fair and im-partial treatment to all may be forced to follow the practice of "first come, first served," which makes the strictest observance of equal responsibility to all of even greater importance.[53]

Conventionally in public law, the rule of law's constraints on government actors seeks to prevent such "[virtual] vocation outlawry" through enforcement of the purpose of the stat-ute and good faith decision making achieved through the use of fair procedures.[54] Rand J.

---

[50] This is the view taken by Peter Hogg, *Constitutional Law of Canada: 2011 Student Edition* (Toronto: Carswell, 2011) at 34-4.

[51] Dyzenhaus, *supra* note 48 at 125.

[52] *Roncarelli, supra* note 46 at 140.

[53] *Ibid.* at 142.

[54] *Ibid.* at 141.

added more content: the administrative tribunal violated Roncarelli's rights as a citizen—freedom of religion, freedom of expression, freedom to pursue his livelihood—thereby damaging the normative relationship between the state and the citizen.[55]

On the formalist account, administrative law concerns the written statutes, rules, and principles that govern public decision-makers. Public decision-makers must not act outside their authority, must not abuse their authority, and must be seen not to do so. Judicial scrutiny within administrative law focuses on the limits on the authority given to decision-makers by statute or prerogative. On the substantive account, such authority is bound by the purpose and terms of the statute, by regulations and guidelines, by the Constitution, and by both written and unwritten legal principles. Formally valid exercises of discretion can offend the rule of law and can subsequently be determined to be a legal wrong as an abuse of power. *Roncarelli* still stands as a paradigmatic example of the deeper principled and purposive approach to understanding how the rule of law animates administrative law.

B. A Foundational Principle, but an "Unwritten" One

Roncarelli was an early implied bill of rights case that relied on the unwritten principle of the rule of law. As a foundational principle, the rule of law is both part of the written and (so-called) unwritten Constitution.[56] As an unwritten principle, the rule of law implicitly appears in the preamble to the *Constitution Act, 1867*, where it states that Canada will have a "Constitution similar in principle to that of the United Kingdom."[57] The rule of law also appears as an explicit principle in the preamble to the *Constitution Act, 1982*: "Whereas Canada is founded upon principles that recognize the supremacy of God and the rule of law."[58] Whether implicit or explicit, then, the principle of the rule of law applies to the entire constitutional order and every part of government. The deepest and broadest articulation of the unwritten principle of the rule of law in the Canadian order appears in two reference cases: the *Manitoba Language Rights Reference*[59] and the *Secession Reference*.[60]

In the *Manitoba Language Rights Reference*, the Supreme Court invoked the rule of law to conclude that the Manitoba government's repeated failure to respect the mandatory requirement of bilingual enactment of provincial laws rendered all subsequent unilingual legislation invalid. By failing to adhere to the terms of the province's constitutional document,

---

55   Dyzenhaus, *supra* note 48.

56   Canada, as a former British colony, not only possesses a written constitution, but has also inherited the "unwritten" British constitution. In Britain, the constitution is said to be unwritten because no single constitutional document defines its constitutional system. Instead, a collection of statutes, decrees, conventions, customs or traditions, and royal prerogatives comprise the constitution. Seen from this perspective, it would be a mistake to think that a single document, even if comprehensive, could ever capture an entire constitution. For most countries, a constitution comprises a mix of written and unwritten sources including customary law, conventions, treaties, and other legal documents.

57   Preamble to the *Constitution Act, 1867* (U.K.), 30 & 31 Vict., c. 3, reprinted in R.S.C. 1985, App. II, No. 5.

58   Preamble to the *Constitution Act, 1982*, being Schedule B to the *Canada Act 1982* (U.K.), 1982, c. 11.

59   *Reference re Language Rights Under s. 23 of Manitoba Act, 1870 and s. 133 of Constitution Act, 1867*, [1985] 1 S.C.R. 721 [*Manitoba Language Rights Reference*].

60   *Reference re Secession of Quebec*, [1998] 2 S.C.R. 217 [*Secession Reference*].

Manitoba had acted without legal authority, had acted arbitrarily, and had allowed its officials to act outside the law. The Court concluded that these actions constituted a complete transgression of the principle of legality—that is, the "manner and form" requirements for provincial law stipulated by the constitution—while the larger normative force of the unwritten principle of the rule of law compelled invalidation of much of the provincial legal order and bilingual enactment of all unilingual provincial laws. In order to avoid creating legal chaos in Manitoba, however, the rule-of-law principle also justified the creation of a new remedy—the delayed declaration of invalidity—which the Court devised to maintain the existence of the unconstitutional legal order, while giving the province time to comply by re-enacting all of the offending legislation. Because of the extraordinary nature of the legal problem, the Court found an opportunity to provide more content to the rule of law, describing it as a "highly textured expression … conveying … a sense of orderliness, of subjection to known legal rules and of executive accountability to legal authority."[61] The Court also recognized the rule of law as a "fundamental postulate of our constitutional structure"[62] whose constitutional status was beyond question.

Throughout the judgment, the Court characterized the rule of law as the principle of legality. This principle was understood in two ways. First, it meant that the law is supreme over government officials as well as private individuals and therefore excludes the influence and operation of arbitrary power.[63]

Second, it meant that law and order are indispensable elements of civilized life within a political community. The rule of law therefore required "the creation and maintenance of an actual order of positive laws which preserves and embodies the more general principle of normative order. Law and order are indispensable elements of civilized life."[64] For the Court, Canada must be thought of as a "society of legal order and normative structure"[65] in which the rule of law was embedded as both an implicit and explicit constitutional principle. As an expression of a commitment to peace, order, and good government over war, anarchy, and arbitrary power, the rule of law, to the Court's mind, represented a "philosophical view of society" that "in the Western tradition is linked with basic democratic notions."[66] Just how the principle of legality is linked to basic democratic notions was not spelled out fully in the *Manitoba Language Rights Reference*. Nevertheless, the Court stated that the Constitution is deeply intertwined with the principle of parliamentary sovereignty, because the Constitution "is a statement of the will of the people to be governed in accordance with certain principles held as fundamental and certain prescriptions restrictive of the powers of legislature and government."[67] In Canada, the people have elected to be governed through a democracy, with its institutional forms, and political ideals. Democracy and parliamentary sovereignty, then, are related but not synonymous principles. The interconnectedness of the principles

---

61 *Manitoba Language Rights Reference, supra* note 59 at para. 62.

62 *Ibid.* at para. 63.

63 *Ibid.* at para. 59.

64 *Ibid.* at para. 60.

65 *Ibid.* at para. 64.

66 *Ibid.* at para. 61.

67 *Ibid.* at para. 48.

of democracy, parliamentary sovereignty, and the rule of law inform our understanding of what good or responsible government means.[68]

In the *Secession Reference*, the Court further articulated the content of the principle of the rule of law in the context of questions about the legal validity of a potential unilateral act of secession from Canada by the province of Quebec. In this judgment, the Court identified four unwritten principles that animate the Canadian constitutional order: federalism, democracy, constitutionalism and the rule of law, and respect for minorities. These principles neither stand alone nor can they be used to trump each other. Instead, according to the Court, they are highly interrelated, permeate every part of the legal order, are the "vital unstated assumptions" that govern the exercise of constitutional authority, constitute the "lifeblood" of the Constitution, and mutually support every part of the Canadian state.[69] Moreover, in addition to their highly persuasive interpretive import, these principles can have *"full legal force"* in certain circumstances.[70] This means that they are binding upon courts, can give rise to substantive legal obligations (both general and specific), and may function as real constraints on government action.[71] It would be impossible, the Court declared, to understand the Canadian constitutional order without these architectonic and organic principles. The principle of the rule of law guarantees the existence of formal conduits and processes in government through which participation can occur, and obliges institutions comprising the legal and political system to realize these substantive constitutional commitments. The Court underscores this point in the *Secession Reference* when it declares that democracy cannot exist without the rule of law:

> To be accorded legitimacy, democratic institutions must rest, ultimately, on a legal foundation. That is, they must allow for the participation of, and accountability to, the people, through public institutions created under the Constitution. Equally, however, a system of government cannot survive through adherence to law alone. A political system must also possess legitimacy, and in our political culture, that requires an interaction between the rule of law and the democratic principle. ... Our law's claim to legitimacy also rests on an appeal to moral values, many of which are embedded in our constitutional structure. It would be a grave mistake to equate legitimacy with the "sovereign will" or majority rule alone, to the exclusion of other constitutional values.[72]

---

68   Democracy—another contested concept—literally means "rule by the people." What distinguishes democracy from other forms of government is the participation of citizens in producing the laws that bind the entire community. Citizens rule themselves as free and equal beings, usually through formal voting equality and political freedoms, rather than being ruled by an internal elite or an external power. Democracy is therefore often strongly associated with majority rule in which the will of the majority is realized through the election of public officials into the legislature. A liberal democracy, on the other hand, will recognize a set of basic liberties such as the *Charter of Rights and Freedoms* that take priority over popular rule. For a helpful overview of the concept of democracy, see Amy Gutmann, "Democracy" in Robert E. Goodin, Philip Pettit, & Thomas Pogge, eds., *A Companion to Contemporary Political Philosophy*, 2d ed. (Malden, MA: Blackwell Publishing, 2007), vol. 2 at 521-31.

69   *Secession Reference, supra* note 60 at paras. 50-51.

70   *Ibid.* at paras. 51-54 (emphasis added).

71   *Ibid.* at para. 54.

72   *Ibid.* at paras. 67, 68.

Canada, then, is a complicated state: it can be described as a democratic, federal, constitutional monarchy. Though all acts of government are done in the name of the Queen—our head of state—the authority for these acts comes from the Canadian people and from the participation of, and accountability to, the people through public institutions created under the Constitution at both the federal and provincial levels of government. The unwritten principle of the rule of law therefore constrains the principle of parliamentary sovereignty from its tendency to define democracy merely as a set of formal institutional arrangements.[73]

Democracy presupposes that we have a process for arriving at binding decisions that take everyone's interests into account. But, though all members may possess equal constitutional rights to participate politically—the s. 3 right to vote in the Charter, for example—the democratic process may not be representing all interests equally as a result of continuing historical exclusions and deep socio-economic biases. Public policy making, for example, may be undermined by active minorities such as interest or lobby groups who can "capture" particular policy areas and legislative outcomes. Andrew Green discusses this problem—commonly labelled the principal–agent problem—in Chapter 4, Regulations and Rule Making: The Dilemma of Delegation. But, as the Supreme Court emphasizes above, the principles of democracy and the rule of law are mutually supportive in the shared goal of minimizing the abuse of public power. They can also, under the right conditions, work in harmony to secure accountability and legitimacy in public institutions. Both democracy and the rule of law justify the creation of institutional mechanisms for citizens and affected persons to prevent or challenge the abuse of power by public officials. As we have seen, the rule of law supports the creation of procedures that treat individuals fairly when their rights, interests, and privileges are affected in public decision making. The rule of law also supports judicial review of administrative decisions on their merits and greater access to the courts through the expansion of standing and intervener status. The hope here is that judicial deliberation will lead to better and more reasonable decision-making processes and policy outcomes. A participatory democracy will create conduits for direct participation in political decision making through, for example, public hearings. The hope here is that greater participation will lead to greater accountability and less abuse of power through public oversight. A deliberative democracy supports the creation of open, deliberative processes for public reasoning and debate on political issues. Rather than continual direct political participation, then, deliberative democracy seeks ongoing accountability about public issues. The hope here is that greater public deliberation will lead to more justifiable public policies. Contemporary governance therefore offers a range of institutional possibilities for public participation on democracy and rule-of-law grounds. These institutional spaces for participation aim to secure legitimacy, justice, and administrative efficiency. Some processes will be open to all, while others may engage only certain stakeholders or interest groups.

---

[73] One crucial institutional arrangement for a democratic state is the design of the electoral system. Citizen participation through the electoral system is called popular sovereignty. When citizens participate directly in the production of law—for example, in referendums—we call this popular democracy. Canada has a system of indirect participation by citizens, called representative democracy, where we elect party members to represent us and work on our behalf to implement law and policy. The principle and practice of responsible government ensures that elected officials who are ministers in Cabinet are collectively answerable to the House of Commons or the provincial legislature.

Participants may simply offer information on paper or take positions, exchange reasons, and influence substantive policy matters. In its most robust form, participation actually authorizes the resulting decision such as with referendums and general elections.

C. The New Minimalist Rule of Law

Perhaps not surprisingly, Supreme Court judges disagree about the scope and content of the principle of the rule of law. In a trilogy of cases—*Imperial Tobacco*,[74] *Charkaoui*,[75] and *Christie*[76]—the Supreme Court has considerably narrowed the scope and effect of this principle within Canadian law. In Canada's constitutional house, the current decor is sleek and spare.

The Supreme Court continues to affirm the unwritten constitutional principle of the rule of law by asserting its status as a foundational principle at the root of our system of governance, implicit in the very concept of a constitution. According to the Court, the rule of law incorporates a number of familiar themes and embraces at least four principles: (1) it is supreme over private individuals as well as over government officials, who are required to exercise their authority non-arbitrarily and according to law; (2) it requires the creation and maintenance of a positive order of laws; (3) it requires the relationship between the state and the individual to be regulated by law; and (4) it is linked to the principle of judicial independence.[77] These four attributes clearly conform to the theoretical discussion of the rule of law presented in section II, above.

Although the rule of law may possess additional principles, there is one key attribute that this principle does not possess: the ability to strike down legislation based on its content.[78] The rule of law, then, does not speak "directly" to the terms of legislation (or provisions of statutes). This does not mean that the rule of law has no normative force at all, says the Court, but simply that the government action it is able to constrain is usually that of the executive and administrative branches. Legislatures are constrained by "manner and form" requirements in the processes of enacting, amending, or repealing legislation.[79] This is because the principles of democracy, constitutionalism, and judicial independence favour the validity of legislation that conforms to the express terms of the Constitution, or those terms that follow as necessary implications from the express terms.[80] Nevertheless, the normative force of the rule of law on this understanding does appear to have been significantly curtailed and the Court has minimized reference to substantive rule-of-law values.

---

[74] *British Columbia v. Imperial Tobacco Canada Ltd.*, [2005] 2 S.C.R. 473 [*Imperial Tobacco*].

[75] *Charkaoui v. Canada (Minister of Citizenship and Immigration)*, 2007 SCC 9 [*Charkaoui*].

[76] *British Columbia (Attorney General) v. Christie*, 2007 SCC 21 [*Christie*].

[77] *Imperial Tobacco, supra* note 74 at para. 58; *Charkaoui, supra* note 75 at para. 134; *Christie, supra* note 76 at para. 20.

[78] *Imperial Tobacco, supra* note 74 at para. 59.

[79] But see *Authorson v. Canada (Attorney General)*, [2003] 2 S.C.R. 40, both for troubling insights into how an executive-controlled government can manipulate and avoid the manner and form requirements of enacting legislation, and for a tragic example of a systemic failure of accountability.

[80] *Imperial Tobacco, supra* note 74 at para. 66.

The Court took its clearest stance concerning the power of and limits on the unwritten principle of the rule of law in *Imperial Tobacco*. *Imperial Tobacco* concerned a statute enacted by the province of British Columbia, the *Tobacco Damages and Health Care Costs Recovery Act*,[81] which allowed the province to sue manufacturers of tobacco products for compensation of tobacco-related health care costs incurred by individuals exposed to tobacco products. The tobacco companies challenged the validity of the statute on three constitutional grounds: extra-territoriality, judicial independence, and the rule of law. Major J., writing for the Court in *Imperial Tobacco*, focused on the debates concerning the meaning of the rule of law and what principles it might incorporate, noting with approval Strayer J.A.'s dictum in *Singh v. Canada (Attorney General)*[82] that: "[a]dvocates tend to read into the principle of the rule of law anything which supports their particular view of what the law should be."[83] The Court affirmed that the rule of law does not require that legislation be prospective (except in criminal law) or general. It also does not prohibit the conferral of special privileges on the government, except where necessary for effective governance.[84] Lastly, it does not ensure a fair civil trial.[85] The Court claimed that to affirm these features constitutionally, as the tobacco companies had argued, would be tantamount to endorsing one particular conception of the rule of law, thereby seriously undermining the legitimacy of judicial review. The written Constitution has primacy, such that the attributes of the rule of law are simply broader versions of the rights already contained in the Charter.[86] Protection from unjust or unfair legislation "properly lies not in the amorphous underlying principles of our Constitution, but in its text and the ballot box."[87] When legislatures use their powers validly but arbitrarily, and the content of such legislation does not engage an express constitutional provision, then citizens must look to other forms of government accountability as well as the democratic process of elections for correction, not to the courts.[88]

The *Charkaoui* decision declared unconstitutional the detention review hearings process set out in the *Immigration and Refugee Protection Act*.[89] The Court held that the statutory scheme violated several Charter provisions, including s. 7 principles of fundamental justice, ss. 9 and 10 guarantees against arbitrary detention, and the protection against cruel and

---

81   S.B.C. 2000, c. 30.

82   [2000] 3 F.C. 185 (C.A.).

83   *Imperial Tobacco, supra* note 74 at para. 33.

84   One effect of the Act was to permit not only the recovery of current and future costs, but also to recover costs retroactively from the past 50 years. The statute also changed rules of civil procedure in order to counter the systemic advantages that tobacco manufacturers enjoy in private law litigation by shifting the onus of proof from the government to the tobacco manufacturers. Tobacco companies had to prove, on a balance of probabilities, that their products did not and do not cause harm to affected persons in British Columbia. The tobacco companies argued that the shift of the evidentiary burden interfered both with the guarantee of a fair trial and the ability of judges to assess and weigh the relevant evidence.

85   *Imperial Tobacco, supra* note 74 at para. 63.

86   *Ibid.* at para. 65.

87   *Ibid.* at para. 66.

88   See *Bacon v. Saskatchewan Crop Insurance Corp.* (1999), 180 Sask. R. 20 at paras. 30, 36 (C.A.).

89   S.C. 2001, c. 27 [IRPA].

unusual treatment in s. 12. The Court, however, could not actually review the reasonableness of security certificates (certificates issued jointly by the ministers of public security and immigration) because they are not subject to review or appeal. The Court held that the use of secret evidence and the likelihood of indefinite detention without meaningful and timely review for non-citizens clearly violated due process rights. To guarantee a fair hearing under the Charter, a different procedure should be created—one that does not so greatly infringe Charter rights. But the rule of law did not support a right to appeal from the Federal Court judge's determination of the reasonableness of the certificate, nor could it prohibit automatic detention or detention on the basis of executive or ministerial decision making[90] and therefore the rule-of-law argument against the certificate provisions in the IRPA was relegated to the margins. While the *Charkaoui* decision should be celebrated for upholding s. 7's requirement of a fair procedure for determining an issue of vital importance to a detainee, the Court's reliance on a formal conception of the rule of law comes at a cost: where s. 7 of the Charter is not triggered, as in administrative proceedings, the reach of the *Charkaoui* decision will be considerably truncated. Incorporation of substantive rule-of-law values, like those found in the *Roncarelli* decision, would provide a toehold for judicial scrutiny of the failure to provide a right of appeal from the reasonableness of a security certificate, as well as the power of detention given to executive actors under the IRPA.[91]

The *Christie* case involved a constitutional challenge brought by Dugald Christie, a lawyer and political activist, who claimed that British Columbia's 7 percent legal service tax made it impossible for many of his low-income clients to retain him to pursue their claims. The Court affirmed that one purpose of the rule of law is to ensure access to justice. The Court noted that, when rights and obligations are at stake, individual access to justice can often only happen through lawyers whose role is to bring citizens' complaints about unlawful or abusive private or state action to courts or administrative tribunals. As a component of the rule of law, access to justice may guarantee a right to legal services, such as a right to counsel in some circumstances (particularly in the criminal context). But the rule of law does not underwrite a general right to legal services, to legal assistance, or to counsel in relation to court and tribunal proceedings.[92] It therefore also cannot constitutionalize a particular type of access to justice, such as a specific institutional form of legal aid.[93] Although the argument against the use of the rule of law in this case does not foreclose the possibility of a circumscribed right to counsel in other circumstances, a general right to counsel could not be found. Once again, the Court emphasized that the principle of the rule of law could not

---

[90]   The Court noted that the Federal Court is a superior court, not an administrative tribunal—such a right could be said to flow from a decision made in the administrative context. The legality of the process, according to the Court, is nevertheless reinforced because the Federal Court of Appeal can circumvent the privative clause where the constitutionality of the legislation is challenged or where the individual alleges bias on the part of the judge. *Charkaoui, supra* note 75 at paras. 136, 137.

[91]   Craig Forcese further analyzes the national security context in more detail in his online chapter at <admin-la0wincontext.emp.ca>.

[92]   *Christie, supra* note 76 at paras. 23-27.

[93]   In an effort to raise awareness about the inadequacy of legal aid across Canada, Christie decided to bicycle across the country, starting in Vancouver. While cycling through Ontario in 2006, Christie was killed when he was hit by a van.

be used to strike down otherwise valid legislation. As Lorne Sossin discusses in Chapter 7, *Access to Administrative Justice and Other Worries*, the relationship between the unwritten principles of the rule of law and "access to justice" remains unclear in Canadian law, although his chapter concretizes several factors that inform the quality of access to justice.

The tensions among the rule of law, fairness, equality, and efficiency remain particularly acute in administrative law because many tribunals were established to provide inexpensive and efficient access for low- and middle-income or otherwise vulnerable individuals; however, these tribunals may fail to do so and, for reasons concerning the separation of powers, recourse to the courts may not provide a remedy. Indeed, in *Toussaint v. Canada*, the Federal Court of Appeal held that in the context of the humanitarian and compassionate grounds contained in s. 25 of the IRPA, the rule of law cannot be used to create an application fee waiver for low-income or indigent persons who are applying for permanent residency under that provision where none exists in the legislation.[94]

Recalling the concepts of the rule of law advanced by the three theorists in section II, above, all suggested some degree of access to the legal system.[95] Each theory therefore comports with the fundamental conviction that individuals should have access to due process when their rights and interests have been affected by government action. Each also supports some measure of access within a rule-of-law state, but again none explicitly argues for effective equal access for all legal subjects. Indeed, of all the theorists considered in this chapter, only Ronald Dworkin explicitly considers access to be a matter of fairness that benefits the least well off and satisfies the demands of legal equality in the rule of law. When government is the wrongdoer, then it is contrary to the rule of law for citizens to be without a remedy, but how and when a legal system permits access to accountability remains problematic.[96]

In the consideration of the jurisprudence after the *Manitoba Language Rights Reference* and *Secession Reference*, it is clear that the Court has become anxious about the risks of its

---

94 *Toussaint v. Canada (Citizenship and Immigration)*, 2011 FCA 146. The Court held that the ability of the minister to waive such fees—$550—for low-income or poor persons is a function that is not analogous to access to the courts because it is limited to providing individuals with an exceptional discretionary benefit. *Ibid.* at para 60. The Supreme Court dismissed leave for appeal. The IRPA has since been amended by the *Balanced Refugee Reform Act*, S.C. 2010, c. 7 to preclude fee waivers under s. 25 of the IRPA. The Supreme Court denied leave to appeal.

95 Access to justice appears in Dicey's conception of the rule of law by necessity in his common-law model, in Fuller's procedural understanding of the rule of law, and explicitly as one of Raz's principles. Yet none of these theories dictates a particular institutional arrangement facilitating or guaranteeing access to justice.

96 This includes the expansion of standing, the limiting of non-justiciability, and the ability of courts to craft and enforce appropriate remedies. See *Reece v. Edmonton (City)*, 2011 ABCA 238 (CanLII), a novel case that considers the circumstances under which citizens or advocacy groups such as Zoocheck Canada and People for the Ethical Treatment of Animals (PETA) may be granted public-interest standing to seek a declaratory judgment that the municipal government has failed to comply with animal welfare laws. Chief Justice Fraser's powerful dissent argued, on rule-of-law grounds, that public-interest standing ought to be granted to advocacy groups representing Lucy, an elephant in the Edmonton Valley Zoo, because this would be the most effective way to hold the executive branch of government accountable and to speak for animals whose voices are not otherwise audible to the law. The City, on the other hand, argued that two regulatory agencies already had the statutory authority and powers to oversee the Zoo's operations and that the appellants were inappropriately using a civil action to circumvent existing procedures and abusing access to the courts. The Supreme Court denied leave to appeal.

own forms of arbitrariness through recourse to unwritten principles and is attempting to constrain the use of these principles by judges, counsel, and litigants. Judges seem to have an interpretive monopoly on unwritten principles, thereby "ousting" interpretations from other branches of government. Robust use of unwritten principles—and ironically the rule of law itself—risks entrenching the rule of judges and opens the door to judicial arbitrariness by permitting courts to unilaterally and anti-democratically substitute their views for that of Parliament's. This has led the Court to move to what Peter Hogg and Cara Zwibel define as the "middle" ground where unwritten principles like the rule of law have no direct legal effect, but are merely influential, interpretive "constitutional values."[97]

D. Lower Court Unruliness?

Though the Supreme Court of Canada has not completely shut down the legal and normative force of the unwritten principle of the rule of law, it has signalled a marked unwillingness to engage in any such "gap-filling" through the use of unwritten principles.[98] Such a conclusion cuts against the grain of earlier jurisprudence concerning unwritten constitutional principles. Those who wish to see robust use of unwritten principles must look to lower-court decisions where the unwritten principle of the rule of law, in conjunction with other unwritten principles, has supplemented the written constitutional text.[99]

Unwritten principles provided the justification for judicial intervention in discretionary decision making. In *Lalonde*, for example, the Ontario Court of Appeal[100] reviewed a discretionary decision made by the Health Services Restructuring Commission to close the sole

---

[97] Peter W. Hogg & Cara F. Zwibel, "The Rule of Law in the Supreme Court of Canada" (2005) 53 U.T.L.J. 716 at 718. Hogg and Zwibel suggest that the claim that the rule of law requires our laws to "respect equality, human dignity, and other good moral values is really just natural law in disguise. The rule of law is not a protection against laws that are bad." Remedies for bad laws are to be found in the written constitution and democratic institutions. *Ibid.* For a sophisticated, contrary argument, see Mark D. Walters, " 'Common Public Law in the Age of Legislation': David Mullan and the Unwritten Constitution" in Grant Huscroft & Michael Taggart, eds., *Inside and Outside Canadian Administrative Law* (Toronto: University of Toronto Press, 2006) at 421.

[98] This seems to be the conclusion despite some tension with McLachlin C.J.'s public remarks: "I will suggest that actually quite a lot is going on, and that it is important. What is going on is the idea that there exist fundamental norms of justice so basic that they form part of the legal structure of governance and must be upheld by the courts, whether or not they find expression in constitutional texts. And the idea is important, going to the core of just governance and how we define the respective roles of Parliament, the executive and the judiciary." "Remarks of the Right Honourable Beverley McLachlin, P.C.," given at the 2005 Lord Cooke Lecture in Wellington, New Zealand, December 1, 2005, online: <http://www.scc-csc.gc.ca/aboutcourt/judges/speeches/UnwrittenPrinciples_e.asp>.

[99] See e.g. the discussion by the majority in the Court of Appeal of British Columbia of the principle of the rule of law in relation to the principle of access to justice. *Christie v. British Columbia*, 2005 BCCA 63. The Supreme Court rejected this line of argument in its decision discussed above.

[100] *Lalonde v. Ontario (Commission de restructuration des services de santé)*, 2001 CanLII 21164 (Ont. C.A.) [*Lalonde*]. In Chapter 12, Evan Fox-Decent and Alexander Pless discuss unwritten principles in the relationship of procedural fairness to legislation. They note that judges have imposed duties to give reasons where an unwritten constitutional principle was at stake and the relevant legislation was silent on the issue. In *Lalonde*, for example, the principle of the protection of minorities led to the imposition of a duty to give reasons.

francophone hospital in Ontario, a decision allegedly made in the public interest. The statute stipulated that a right to receive French language services could be limited only if all reasonable and necessary measures to comply with the statute had been exhausted.[101] Montfort was explicitly designated as a francophone hospital for the Ottawa-Carleton community and the decision to restructure it was a shift in policy for which little explanation was given.[102] While the Commission could exercise discretion to change and even limit the provision of these services, "it cannot simply invoke administrative convenience and vague funding concerns as the reasons for doing so."[103] The Health Services Commission forfeited its entitlement to deference by providing no justificatory policy for impinging on fundamental constitutional values. In this case, the Court of Appeal relied on the Supreme Court of Canada's decision in *Baker*[104] to conclude that "the review of discretionary decisions on the basis of fundamental Canadian constitutional and societal values"[105] is possible and, despite being accorded a large degree of deference, such discretionary decisions are not immune from judicial scrutiny. Because the commission failed to give serious weight to the linguistic and cultural significance of the Montfort Hospital to the Franco-Ontarian minority, it acted in a contrary manner to the normative and legal import of the unwritten constitutional principle of respect for and protection of minorities; the decision was therefore quashed.

In *United States of America v. Khadr*,[106] the Ontario Court of Appeal concluded that national security interests and intelligence objectives cannot trump the rule of law by putting vital human rights interests at risk. In this judgment, Sharpe J.A. concluded that the courts could not permit the extradition of suspected terrorist and Canadian citizen, Abdullah Khadr, to the United States, the very country that participated in human rights violations while he was arbitrarily detained in Pakistan and subjected to executive lawlessness by two countries.

---

[101] The normative force of unwritten constitutional principles therefore animated a large and liberal interpretation of the relevant provincial statute, the *French Language Services Act*, R.S.O. 1990, c. F.32, and motivated the Court's less-deferential attitude toward the commission's decision.

[102] See *Lake v. Canada (Minister of Justice)*, 2008 SCC 23, [2008] 1 S.C.R. 761 [*Lake*], which discusses the adequacy of reasons in the context of a discretionary decision made by a minister. See also the discussion in section IV.C.3.

[103] *Lalonde, supra* note 100 at para. 168.

[104] *Baker v. Canada (Minister of Citizenship and Immigration)*, [1999] 2 S.C.R. 817 [*Baker*].

[105] *Lalonde, supra* note 100 at para. 177.

[106] *Attorney General of Canada on behalf of the United States of America v. Abdullah Khadr*, 2011 ONCA 358 (CanLII). In 2004, the United States paid the Pakistani intelligence agency, the Inter-Services Intelligence (ISI) Directorate, half a million dollars to abduct Abdullah Khadr, who was suspected of supplying weapons to Al Qaeda forces in Pakistan and Afghanistan. Khadr was secretly held in detention for 14 months in Pakistan and abused by the ISI who interrogated him for intelligence purposes. The ISI refused to deal with the Canadian government, but did have contact with a Canadian Security Intelligence Service (CSIS) official. The American authorities discouraged the CSIS official's request that Khadr be granted consular access, and the ISI denied access for three months. The ISI refused to bring Khadr before the Pakistani courts. Once the ISI had exhausted him as a source of anti-terrorism intelligence, it was prepared to release him. The United States, however, insisted that the ISI hold Khadr for a further six months in secret detention so that they could conduct a criminal investigation and start the process for Khadr's possible rendition to the United States. When Khadr was finally repatriated to Canada, the United States sought to have him extradited on terrorism charges.

Invoking the need to maintain respect of the rule of law in times of crisis, Sharpe J.A. affirmed that the appropriate judicial response was to deny the minister of justice's surrender order and affirm the extradition judge's decision because:

> the rule of law must prevail even in the face of the dreadful threat of terrorism. We must adhere to our democratic and legal values, even if that adherence serves in the short term to benefit those who oppose and seek to destroy those values. For if we do not, in the longer term, the enemies of democracy and the rule of law will have succeeded. They will have demonstrated that our faith in our legal order is unable to withstand their threats. In my view, the extradition judge did not err in law or in principle by giving primacy to adherence to the rule of law.[107]

On Sharpe J.A.'s terms, the rule of law is both part of a larger democratic culture and sustains a pervasive culture of legality that we, as Canadians, hold in common.

IV. Administering the Rule of Law

All of the authors in this textbook allude to the lengthy and complex history in relations among the administrative state, democracy, and the rule of law. As discussed earlier, at the beginning of the 20th century the emerging administrative state was often seen as a threat both to parliamentary sovereignty and to the rule of law because delegated powers from the political executive operated outside legislative scrutiny. Not only did these new administrative bodies possess substantial powers to restrict freedom, redistribute property, and make decisions on matters relating to individual rights, but they also handled many more cases than courts did. Governments—and the executive in particular—could control these new bodies through the appointments process and had significant influence over delegated policy areas. The growth of regulatory law also meant an expanded scope of discretion for government officials in interpreting standards and defining goals in various statutory schemes and executive regulations. This development was extremely worrisome for those concerned with accountability, because Parliament, the responsible minister, and the courts together could not provide full oversight, given their lack of specialized policy knowledge and the sheer quantity of cases that the administrative state generated.

As a result of the expansion of the administrative state, and well before the Charter, administrative law had to struggle to construct a relationship with the modern state that respected the expertise and policy choices of various administrative agencies and boards while simultaneously recognizing the legitimacy and effectiveness of parallel bodies of justice such as administrative tribunals. Because so many of these administrative bodies— labour and marketing boards, for example—were created to respond to political pressures and regulatory problems, courts, through administrative law, had to rethink their attitude in relation to them in the post-war era. This attitude was usually characterized by the term "deference." More important, the courts' view of the state had to change as well. The older

---

[107] *Ibid.* at para. 76. The Supreme Court of Canada dismissed the application for leave of appeal.

and classical liberal view of the minimal state no longer matched reality, and courts had to change their institutional practices to acknowledge the legitimacy of the welfare state. McLachlin C.J. draws on this historical context in *Alberta v. Hutterian Brethen* where she writes: "Concern about overextension of regulatory authority is understandable. Governments should not be free to use a broad delegated authority to transform a limited-purpose licensing scheme into a *de facto* universal identification system beyond the reach of legislative oversight. ... [H]ostility to the regulation-making process is out of step with this Court's jurisprudence and with the realities of the modern regulatory state."[108] Finally, administrative law served as an important pre-Charter vehicle to challenge government policy and to secure rule-of-law restraints on discretionary decision making in social and economic policy, a role that contained both positive and negative features, depending on one's political perspective and the particular issue at bar.

A. Deference as Respect: The Canadian Model of Administrative Law

While the rule of law traditionally serves as a bulwark against the executive branch of government and supports judicial oversight of broad statutory grants of discretion, this role becomes more complicated in the modern administrative state. With legislatively delegated powers to different kinds of administrative bodies, the role of courts can be understood in two contrasting ways. On the one hand, courts provide an essential accountability function by policing the exercise of delegated powers to ensure that they are confined to terms and purposes specified by the authorizing statute. On the other hand, courts are conscious of the separation of powers and, given their lack of expertise in determining the merits of certain policy-making exercises, are themselves under rule-of-law constraints to respect legislative and executive branches. The history of the relations between the courts and the other branches of government in administrative law began as a bipolar relationship: courts showed greater deference to executive decision-making and prerogative powers, as well as to legislation, but were highly antagonistic toward decisions made by actual administrative bodies that were not seen as credible or competent decision-makers on questions of law. The history of this bipolar relationship is nowhere better exemplified than in the courts' treatment of statutory delegates with a significant democratic pedigree. Judicial review of municipal bylaws fluctuated between extreme deference on the basis that municipal councils were accountable to their electoral and pointed intervention on the basis that the contested bylaw was patently unreasonable on rule-of-law grounds. Recent jurisprudence holds that, though municipalities are often given broad legislative discretion, their discretion is not unfettered and their decision making must provide reasonable grounds for courts to defer.[109]

---

[108]   *Alberta v. Hutterian Brethren of Wilson Colony*, [2009] 2 S.C.R. 567 at para. 40.

[109]   A recent decision discussing the relationship between the rule of law and democratic government at the municipal level is *Catalyst Paper Corp. v. North Cowichan (District)*, 2012 SCC 2 (CanLII). These considerations will also inform judicial scrutiny of elected school boards and First Nations band council decisions.

The relationship of courts to other branches now aspires to a kind of respectful defer-ence[110] characterized by an "institutional dialogue" as a joint effort in governance.[111] De-spite this new normative underpinning, the relationship between administrative bodies and courts encounters recurring problems arising from the interpretation of privative clauses, broad statutory grants of discretion, and the choice of standard of review.

B. An Example of Deference as Respect: National Corn Growers

Contrasting approaches to the intensity of judicial scrutiny of agency decisions inform the substance of the differing opinions written by Gonthier and Wilson JJ. in *National Corn Growers Assn. v. Canada (Import Tribunal)*.[112] The Canadian Import Tribunal conducted an inquiry into the importation of corn grain from the United States into Canada, an inquiry authorized under s. 42 of the *Special Import Measures Act*,[113] and determined that continued importation of grain had already caused, or in the future would likely cause, injury to Can-adian producers of corn grain. This decision reaffirmed the deputy minister's prior prelim-inary conclusions that material injury existed and, thus, provided support for his decision to impose a provisional duty on American corn in order to protect Canadian corn growers. The *Federal Court Act*,[114] however, allowed for judicial review if a board, commission, or tribunal had, among other grounds, "based its decision or order on an erroneous finding of fact that it made in a *perverse or capricious manner* or *without regard for the material before it*."[115] Because the Tribunal's decision was based on a factual finding of harm informed by its expertise, and because the Act also contained a privative clause (s. 76(1)) stating that "every order or finding of the Tribunal is final and conclusive," this meant that the decision would

---

110   David Dyzenhaus, "Constituting the Rule of Law: Fundamental Values in Administrative Law" (2002) 27 Queen's L.J. 445 at 489-502 ["Constituting Fundamental Values"]. See also David Dyzenhaus, "The Politics of Deference: Judicial Review and Democracy" in Michael Taggart, ed., *The Province of Administrative Law* (Oxford: Oxford University Press, 1997), where the original phrase occurs at 286. Dyzenhaus contrasts the principle of "deference as respect" to the traditional principle of judicial deference. He labels the traditional approach a Diceyan "deference as submission" where judges must submit to the intention of the legislature because of the overriding principle of parliamentary sovereignty. Deference as respect is the opposite of deference as submission.

111   See Geneviève Cartier's conception of discretion as dialogue versus discretion as power in Chapter 11. Note-worthy articles from the voluminous literature on institutional dialogue include T.R.S. Allan, "Constitutional Dialogue and the Justification of Judicial Review" (2003) 23 Oxford J. Legal Stud. 563; Stephen Gardbaum, "The New Commonwealth Model of Constitutionalism" (2001) 49 Am. J. Comp. L. 707; Peter W. Hogg & Allison A. Bushell, "The Charter Dialogue Between Courts and Legislatures (or Perhaps the Charter of Rights Isn't Such a Bad Thing After All)" (1997) 35 Osgoode Hall L.J. 75; Christopher P. Manfredi, "The Life of a Metaphor: Dialogue in the Supreme Court, 1998-2003" (2004) 23 Sup. Ct. L. Rev. (2d) 105; Kent Roach, *The Supreme Court on Trial: Judicial Activism or Democratic Dialogue* (Toronto: Irwin Law, 2001); and Jeremy Waldron, "Some Models of Dialogue Between Judges and Legislatures" (2004) 23 Sup. Ct. L. Rev. (2d) 7.

112   [1990] 2 S.C.R. 1324 [*National Corn Growers*].

113   S.C. 1984, s. 25 [SIMA].

114   R.S.C. 1970, c. 10.

115   *Ibid.*, s. 28.1(c). Emphasis added. Readers will recall that these are familiar expressions connoting arbitrari-ness in decision making.

be assessed on the (now obsolete) standard of patent unreasonableness so that courts could best respect legislative intent.[116] Review turned on whether or not it was patently unreasonable for the tribunal to refer to the *General Agreement on Tariffs and Trade* (GATT)[117] in interpreting the SIMA, whether the tribunal's interpretation of s. 42 in its constitutive legislation was unreasonable, and whether the tribunal reached its decision without any cogent evidence to support its determination of material injury.

In a concurring judgment, Wilson J. evoked the *CUPE* case[118] to caution the majority (and other like-minded judges) about the effects of engaging in a probing examination of a decision. Wilson J. believed that such a detailed examination sanctioned judicial intervention rather than the restraint represented by *CUPE*. *CUPE* was a landmark case that signalled the beginning of the end of the Diceyan model for administrative law in Canada. It concerned a labour relations tribunal, the Public Service Staff Relations Board of New Brunswick, which had to interpret a poorly worded provision in its enabling statute concerning the meaning of the word "employee." The legislation stated that the employer could not replace striking employees with other employees; moreover, other parts of the statute excluded management from the definition of employee. The representative union, the Canadian Union of Public Employees, complained to the Board that the employer was replacing striking employees with management personnel, contrary to the statute. The Board examined the enabling statute, provided an interpretation of the ambiguous provision, and ordered the employer not to use management to replace striking workers. The Board's decisions were protected by a privative clause. On review, the Supreme Court held that deference was owed to the Tribunal based on its expertise, the privative clause, and the reasonableness of its determination. In cases of statutory ambiguity, and where there are multiple interpretations that are reasonable, a reviewing court should defer to the interpretation of the expert tribunal.

According to Wilson J., *CUPE*'s approach to the standard of review, particularly with respect to patent unreasonableness, entailed a relationship between courts and administrative agencies where the courts should recognize that (1) administrative agencies, not courts, bear primary statutory responsibility for their legislative mandate in the area of regulation; (2) administrative agencies possess expertise, experience, and contextual knowledge about which the courts know very little; and (3) statutory provisions, such as those found in *National Corn Growers*, do not admit only one uniquely correct interpretation but, rather, can sustain a variety of reasonable interpretations. Though concurring with the result reached, Wilson J. clearly feared that such a wide-ranging and probing examination of both the agency's interpretation of its enabling statute and the reasonableness of its conclusions

---

[116] See Audrey Macklin's Chapter 9, Standard of Review: Back to the Future?, and Sheila Wildeman's Chapter 10, Pas de Deux: Deference and Non-Deference in Action, on the recent demise of the patent unreasonableness standard of review.

[117] The General Agreement on Tariffs and Trade was an international agreement, originally negotiated in 1947, governing trade in goods. The GATT aimed to increase international trade by reducing tariffs and other trade barriers hindering the free flow of goods across national borders. The GATT was succeeded by the World Trade Organization in 1995.

[118] *C.U.P.E. v. N.B. Liquor Corporation*, [1979] 2 S.C.R. 227 [*CUPE*]. In Chapter 9, Audrey Macklin describes *CUPE*'s "blockbuster" effect on the standard of review in Canadian administrative law.

risked reintroducing the correctness standard under the guise of reasonableness and displacing the patently unreasonable standard.[119] In other words, this approach would likely gut the hard-won jurisprudential ground symbolized by the earlier *CUPE* decision.

Wilson J. underscored what she believed to be the appropriate institutional attitude or posture. In the face of a privative clause, courts must not engage in a wide-ranging review concerning whether or not the tribunal's conclusions are unreasonable. The merits of a tribunal's interpretation of international obligations, such as the GATT, are for the legislature to address by amending the terms of the statute if interpretive disagreement exists between institutions. And, most important, meticulous analysis of a tribunal's reasoning concerning the evidence should not become the norm. As she tersely wrote:

> Faced with the highly charged world of international trade and a clear legislative decision to create a tribunal to dispose of disputes that arise in that context, it is highly inappropriate for courts to take it upon themselves to assess the merits of the Tribunal's conclusions about when the government may respond to another country's use of subsidies. If courts were to take it upon themselves to conduct detailed reviews of these decisions on a regular basis, the Tribunal's effectiveness and authority would soon be effectively undermined.[120]

The conclusions advanced by Wilson J. explicitly rejected the older Diceyan model in which the rule of law provided the justification for judicial control of administrative agencies and their interpretations, to be replaced by a new model where the rule of law buttressed the "pragmatic and functional" methodological approach to determine the appropriate standard of review. Instead of an unreasonable administrative body whose straitjacket laces are ever more tightly pulled by the courts, the modern judicial approach to the administrative state ought to be informed by a more flexible, respectful, and contextualized methodology that recognizes different exercises of legitimate power by competent institutional partners.

The majority decision written by Gonthier J. also concluded that the tribunal was not unreasonable with respect to any of these three matters. To reach this result, Gonthier J. delved deeply into both how the tribunal came to the decision as well as the decision's merits. In the face of criticism from the concurring judgment written by Wilson J., Gonthier J. responded: "With respect, I do not understand how a conclusion can be reached as to the reasonableness of a tribunal's interpretation of its enabling statute without considering the reasoning underlying it, and I would be surprised if that were the effect of this Court's decision in *C.U.P.E.*"[121] Gonthier J., however, did not believe that his more probing approach repudiated *CUPE*; instead, he continued to see his method of review as more respectful and deferential than that found in the traditional Diceyan model. The effect of this more probing inquiry, however, seemed to move the standard of review away from patently unreasonable and closer to correctness.

---

119   This worry surfaces in the discussion of the so-called intermediate standard of review, reasonableness *simpliciter*, as discussed by Audrey Macklin in Chapter 9 and Sheila Wildeman in Chapter 10.

120   *National Corn Growers, supra* note 112 at 1349–50.

121   *Ibid.* at 1383.

National Corn Growers illustrates how different theoretical models of adjudication can help explain how judges understand their institutional role as well as how these models shed light on the underlying rationale behind the judicial choice of the standard of review. In the confines of the case, the fact that the tribunal had not abused its discretion and had exhibited its expertise suggests that Dicey's approach is a non-starter. Fuller's perspective would support the more respectful approach articulated by Wilson J. According to his model of adjudication, where a reasonable range of policy choices exists, or when multiple reasonable interpretations of an ambiguous statutory term are possible, or when a decision involves balancing multiple sets of competing interests, then these functions are best left with the expert tribunal. Raz narrows the reach of the rule of law to correction for the harms created by law itself. His argument for guided discretion, principled decision making, and judicial faithfulness to the legislative intent seems to support Gonthier's approach. Gonthier's judgment underscored the active role of the courts in interpreting the law and in demanding public and principled justifications from the tribunal. Though this approach may present the best way to control harms created by the administrative state, it perhaps may not address as well the risks created by active judicial oversight.

A different case might produce a different alignment. For example and as discussed below, the later creation of the reasonableness standard of review seems to have generated more unanimity on the part of the Supreme Court in the selection of the appropriate standard of review. Indeed, reasonableness closely mirrors the approach that Gonthier J. undertook in *National Corn Growers*—so much so that one could say that his judgment laid out the path for its future development. What remains unclear is, with the elimination of patent unreasonableness, whether Wilson J.'s approach is part, or at the very margins, of reasonableness review. As with so many aspects of administrative law, context matters greatly, though your own tendencies concerning the appropriate ways that the rule of law constrains judges and administrative decision-makers might reflect one approach more than another.

C. Three Interpretive Problems for Deference as Respect: Privative Clauses, the Standard of Review, and the Adequacy of Reasons

In administrative law, legislative intent should constrain judicial interpretation of statutory provisions and purposes. But the principles of the rule of law, democracy, and parliamentary sovereignty imperfectly guide the interpretive process because statutory language is highly ambiguous, conflicting, does not anticipate or provide many issues that come to court, or indicates that some matters never occurred to the legislative mind. Despite the somewhat fictive nature of legislative intent, courts and other interpreters are obliged to construct the meanings and purposes so far as that intention is discoverable from the language of the provision at issue and in the context of the statute as a whole. Where the text is unclear or ambiguous and the ordinary meaning cannot be determined, judges may draw on other materials to assist in the interpretive effort including legal principles, parliamentary debates, ministerial statements regarding statutory purposes, legislative history, agency interpretations, commission reports, policy manuals, international law, and scholarly opinion. After this often in-depth, creative, textual, and contextual exercise, they will then impute the meaning and purpose as legislative intent and analyze intent in relation to the particular facts of the case. This account of statutory interpretation seems at odds with the rule of law if we understand the content of law as "fixed" by the legislature and the judicial task as simply a legal and technical exercise in rule-application within a simplistic or literal conception of language. As Ruth Sullivan argues, the attraction of the more contextual view is that it "openly acknowledges that interpreting statutes is a complex and creative activity that is not reducible to the mechanical application of fixed legal rules. And it raises an important question, namely, whether the persons who are given power to interpret legislation—police officers and bureaucrats as well as members of administrative tribunals and courts—are appropriately chosen and adequately prepared for the task."[122] In order to counteract arbitrariness in interpretation, courts and other interpreters must give effect to rule-of-law constraints such as transparency, predictability, consistency and even-handedness in their judgments and in considering the impact of implementing the legislature's programs and rules on citizens.

In several recent administrative law cases, the Supreme Court has returned to statutory interpretation with renewed vigour to talk about the role of the statute in guiding exercises of interpretation by all legal actors, themselves included.[123] As the Court has set out, the "General Roadmap" for the modern approach to statutory interpretation is contextual and purposive. Words are read in their entire context, in their grammatical and ordinary sense when not defined, and harmoniously with the scheme of the Act, the purpose or object of the Act, and the intention of Parliament. Invoking the democratic principle and the principle of judicial restraint, the Court has affirmed that interpreters cannot ignore the words chosen by Parliament and rewrite legislation according to the interpreter's perspective concerning how the legislative purpose should be better promoted. If the statutory words are precise and unequivocal, then the ordinary meaning dominates. If the words can support more than one reasonable interpretation, then the ordinary sense plays a lesser role but the interpreter must construct an interpretation that best fulfills the purpose(s) of the statute. Finally, some statutes require a broad and liberal reading—human rights legislation, for example—because they deal with fundamental rights or are quasi-constitutional.

The principles of deference and judicial restraint inform statutory interpretation in multiple ways, three examples of which will be considered here. First, interpretative challenges arise when courts encounter privative clauses purporting to limit or oust judicial review. Second, courts have grappled with the principle of deference when considering the standard of review to be applied when a statutory delegate is interpreting its enabling or home statute. And third, in applying the reasonableness standard, courts will often need to scrutinize the adequacy of the reasons that an administrative decision-maker has given for a decision.

1. Privative Clauses

As seen in the *National Corn Growers* case discussed above, privative or ouster clauses historically posed challenges for the rule of law. Several types of privative clauses exist, but the general form is a statutory provision protecting the decisions made by public officials in boards, tribunals, and ministries either from further dispute internally (that is, a finality

---

122   Ruth Sullivan, *Statutory Interpretation* (Toronto: Irwin Law, 1997) at 39.

123   See *Celgene Corp. v. Canada (Attorney General)*, [2011] 1 S.C.R. 3; *Smith v. Alliance Pipeline Ltd.*, [2011] 1 S.C.R. 160; and *Canada (Information Commissioner) v. Canada (Minister of National Defence)*, [2011] 2 S.C.R. 306.

clause) or from external judicial review (that is, an ouster clause).[124] The powers conferred on administrative agencies through privative clauses were often conferred in absolute terms and, therefore, decisions were meant to be final. A particularly strong example of a privative clause might be: "The Board shall exercise exclusive jurisdiction to determine the extent of its jurisdiction under this Act or the regulations, to determine a fact or question of law necessary to establish its jurisdiction, and to determine whether or in what manner it shall exercise its jurisdiction." The conundrum for courts was that the statute prescribed limits on delegated power but, at the same time, authorized officials to act with seemingly unfettered discretion within those broad confines. The risk to the accountability function of the rule of law was that these officials could behave as a law unto themselves because they would be the sole judges of the substantive validity of their own acts. The institutional result of privative clauses was a system of competing and irreconcilable supremacies between the legislative and judicial branches of government. Those who supported the development of the administrative state, meanwhile, worried about the growth of administrative law and the consequent judicial review of administrative decisions, seeing judicial scrutiny as an altogether too constraining legalism that would hinder the flexible regulation needed in a complex industrialized society.[125]

Courts approached the interpretation of privative clauses in several different ways: reading them out of the statute if a jurisdictional error was implicated in the case, deferring to Parliament's intent to oust judicial oversight, and later developing methods of statutory interpretation grounded in the common-law presumption that Parliament always intends to respect procedural fairness, even with respect to statutorily delegated powers with broad scope.[126] This last approach laid the basis for deference as respect, found in the *CUPE* decision, in which the privative clause came to be viewed as a communication from the legislature that courts should recognize the interpretive authority of the tribunal within its area of expertise, but that judges could exercise their rule-of-law powers of oversight on constitutional and jurisdictional matters.

In Binnie J.'s concurring judgment in *Dunsmuir v. New Brunswick*, he argued that a privative clause should not be conclusive with respect to the choice of the standard of review; nevertheless, it is also not just another factor in the standard of review "hopper."[127] On his account, a privative clause presumptively forecloses a judicial finding of unreasonableness on substantive grounds unless the applicant can satisfy the legal burden of demonstrating how a tribunal's interpretation cannot stand.

---

124 For a discussion of privative clauses in administrative law, see Audrey Macklin, Chapter 9, and Sheila Wildeman, Chapter 10. For a detailed analysis of the history, types, and constitutional effects of privative clauses, see David Dyzenhaus, "Disobeying Parliament? Privative Clauses and the Rule of Law" in Richard W. Bauman & Tsvi Kahana, eds., *The Least Examined Branch: The Role of Legislatures in the Constitutional State* (Cambridge: Cambridge University Press, 2006) at 499.

125 As Audrey Macklin points out in Chapter 9, the motive behind privative clauses was not simply to oust judicial meddling, but to direct judicial respect for the relative expertise of the administrative body and to provide efficient resolution of disputes and allocate scarce judicial resources by restricting access to the courts.

126 See Evan Fox-Decent and Alexander Pless, Chapter 12, for their discussion of privative clauses and procedural fairness.

127 [2008] 1 S.C.R. 190 at para. 143 [*Dunsmuir*].

This argument for the robust role that a privative clause can play in statutory interpretation was developed differently by Rothstein J. in his concurring judgment in *Khosa*[128] where he affirmed that reviewing courts must follow the express (or necessarily implied) legislative intent, absent a constitutional challenge, that a privative clause represents. According to Rothstein J., and in contrast to Binnie J.'s majority judgment in *Khosa*, the conceptual and jurisprudential origins of the standard of review are grounded in the privative clause. Rothstein J. argued that the majorities in *Dunsmuir* and in *Khosa* see the judicial review of administrative decisions as automatically entailing a judicial–legislative tension, whereas he believes it only occurs when a privative clause is engaged. Expertise—contrary to the majority—is not a free-standing basis for deference; rather, expertise stands as a basis for deference only when protected by a privative clause signalling legislative intent, especially when a tribunal is considering legal questions. Courts, he wrote, ought not to construct this intent in the absence of a privative clause and without a full interpretive exercise or else risk being arbitrary themselves because express legislative intent and judicially determined expertise may or may not align. For Rothstein J., "privative clauses and tribunal expertise are two sides of the same coin."[129] Where legislative intent is not clear or necessarily implied, Parliament intended correctness standard to apply. The majority, on the other hand, suggested that both the privative clause and expertise as determined by the courts each independently represent legislative intent for the reasonableness standard to apply.

Because of the fundamental nature of this jurisprudential debate—the constitutional basis for deference—administrative agencies play an important interpretive role in the construction of purposes of their home statutes, and they would be wise to demonstrate and emphasize their expertise because they can shape the interpretive direction a reviewing court might take.

2. The Standard of Review

Pre-Charter administrative law was limited to the review of questions of law, jurisdiction, and procedural fairness in order to determine whether or not decision-makers acted in excess of jurisdiction, without authority, or had otherwise abused their discretion on unreasonable grounds. Reviewing courts were not to examine the full merits of the decision, save on exceptional grounds, so that they would be constrained from substituting their preferred outcome for that of authorized decision-makers. Judicial interpretation of the rule of law and other legal principles, such as the separation of powers, animated the level of deference shown to administrative bodies. This deference was most fully exhibited in the choice of the standard of review—correctness and patent unreasonableness (with reasonableness as a post-Charter development)—to be applied in order to analyze a particular administrative decision. The standard of review therefore functioned as a prime rule-of-law constraint on judges in administrative law. As we have seen in *National Corn Growers*, the contemporary approach to the standard of review reflects fundamental concerns about judicial legitimacy within a democratic state.

---

[128]   *Canada (Citizenship and Immigration) v. Khosa*, [2009] 1 S.C.R. 339 [*Khosa*].

[129]   *Ibid.* at para 96.

The tensions among the rule of law, deference, the standard of review, and the administrative state were forcefully made in the *Baker* case,[130] which involved the review of an immigration officer's biased discretionary decision in the context of a humanitarian and compassionate grounds application by an illegal immigrant. Courts usually show a large degree of deference in this policy area, given the expertise of the decision-maker in immigration cases and the discretionary nature of the exercise.[131] Instead, the treatment of one individual at the hands of the administrative state precipitated the expansion of the content of the duty of fairness, a vital component of the rule of law.[132] On this point, L'Heureux-Dubé J. for the majority wrote:

> The pragmatic and functional approach can take into account the fact that the more discretion that is left to a decision-maker, the more reluctant courts should be to interfere with the manner in which decision-makers have made choices among various options. However, though discretionary decisions will generally be given considerable respect, that discretion must be exercised in accordance with the boundaries imposed in the statute, the principles of the rule of law, the principles of administrative law, the fundamental values of Canadian society, and the principles of the Charter.[133]

According to the Court, the discretionary administrative decision in *Baker* displayed arbitrariness: it did not exhibit a mind that was attuned to the humanitarian and compassionate requirements stipulated in the department's own guidelines; it showed a lack of regard for the person affected; and it gave the impression that important factors, such as the best interests of the children, were outweighed by discriminatory biases. The decision therefore did not meet the threshold of reasonableness that could "command respect" from the reviewers. It might be tempting to position *Baker* closer to the Diceyan model with its distrust of administrative discretion, but it is important to remember, as the Supreme Court argued in the subsequent case *Montréal (City) v. Montreal Port Authority*, that

> in a country founded on the rule of law and in a society governed by principles of legality, discretion cannot be equated with arbitrariness. While this discretion does of course exist, it must be exercised within a specific legal framework. Discretionary acts fall within a normative hierarchy .... The statutes and regulations define the scope of discretion and the principles governing the exercise of discretion, and they make it possible to determine whether it has in fact been exercised reasonably.[134]

---

130 *Baker, supra* note 104.

131 On the one hand, the fact-specific nature of the inquiry, the role of a humanitarian and compassionate grounds application within the statutory scheme as an exception, the fact that the decision-maker is the minister, and the considerable discretion evidenced by the statutory language suggest that a large degree of deference would be appropriate. On the other hand, the absence of a privative clause, the explicit contemplation of judicial review by the Federal Court, and the individual rather than polycentric nature of the decision, argued against patent unreasonableness as the proper standard. "Reasonableness," the intermediate standard, was therefore chosen.

132 Grant Huscroft provides a more detailed examination of the facts of the *Baker* case as well as the scope and content of the duty of fairness in Chapter 5. Historically, the duty of fairness was akin to a jurisdictional question and therefore privative clauses could not protect procedural errors.

133 *Baker, supra* note 104 at para. 56.

134 [2010] 1 S.C.R. 427 at para. 33.

Cases like *Baker* and *Montreal Port Authority*, then, continue the jurisprudential lineage originating in *Roncarelli* and judicial review for abuse of discretion.

In the transformative case *Dunsmuir v. New Brunswick*, the Supreme Court invoked rule-of-law values and attributes to justify reducing the standards of review from three to two: correctness and reasonableness, with reasonableness subsuming the most deferential standard of patent unreasonableness.[135] The Court's goal in this judgment was to provide greater guidance for reviewing courts, counsel, litigants, and decision-makers by striving to introduce clarity, fairness, consistency, and simplicity into administrative law. The Court also finalized an earlier jurisprudential line of thought—most clearly articulated by LeBel J. in *Toronto (City) v. C.U.P.E., Local 79*—that patent unreasonableness and reasonableness were not clearly distinguishable. Moreover, patent unreasonableness no longer seemed consistent with the rule of law if it meant that persons could be subjected to a class of decisions that were valid even though they were clearly very irrational interpretations, or that they were valid simply because they failed to reach the level seemingly required by patent unreasonableness.[136] As will be discussed in more detail by Audrey Macklin and Sheila Wildeman in their respective chapters on the standard of review, the Court introduced a new two-step test in which review would proceed first by examining past jurisprudence to see what level of deference was owed. If past jurisprudence did not address the question satisfactorily, then the standard of review analysis would be used to contextually analyze and determine legislative intent regarding the nature and scope of agency jurisdiction and expertise within the home statute. At least four factors guide this analysis: (1) the presence or absence of a privative clause; (2) the purpose of the tribunal from an interpretation of enabling legislation; (3) the nature of the question at issue (fact, law, mixed fact and law); and (4) the expertise of the tribunal. With this re-crafted approach, the Court suggested that it had found a means to reconcile the tension between the rule of law and democracy. Properly performed, the determination and application of the standard of review ensures that all exercises of public authority are lawful, reasonable and fair, but also respects legislative supremacy by recognizing effective limits on judicial discretion and by rejecting a "court-centric" conception of the rule of law.[137]

Correctness, on the other hand, should be limited to: (1) a constitutional issue; (2) a question of general law that is both of central importance to the legal system as a whole *and* outside the specialized area of expertise; (3) drawing jurisdictional lines between two or more competing specialized tribunals; or (4) a "true" question of jurisdiction or *vires*. According to the majority, rule-of-law values such as universality, consistency, uniformity, predictability, stability justify the unique role of the courts in reviewing tribunal decisions

---

135   *Dunsmuir, supra* note 127.

136   *Toronto (City) v. C.U.P.E., Local 79*, [2003] 3 S.C.R. 77. Instead of eliminating the patently unreasonable standard, David Dyzenhaus conversely argues that the Court should have gotten rid of the correctness standard—a move he sees as more consistent with the principle of deference. See David Dyzenhaus, "David Mullan's Theory of the Rule of (Common) Law" in Huscroft & Taggart, eds., *Inside and Outside Canadian Administrative Law, supra* note 97, 448 at 462.

137   *Ibid.* at paras. 27-33.

on a correctness standard as well as underpinning both the lack of deference in the face of judicial expertise and the constitutional basis of judicial review. The principles of universality and equality demand that the same general legal rules are applied to each legal subject equally and in similar situations.

In *Dunsmuir* and subsequent cases, reasonableness appears as the presumptive standard in administrative law when: (1) a specialized or expert tribunal; (2) interpreting its enabling or home statute; (3) on a question of fact or mixed fact and law; (4) or exercising broad statutory discretion; (5) correctly applies all legal principles or tests; (6) to construct an interpretation of its statutory powers that falls within range of possible acceptable interpretations; (7) resulting in a decision that demonstrates justification, transparency, and intelligibility; (8) and produces a reasonable outcome that is defensible in respect of the facts and law. Should the tribunal satisfy all of these conditions, the decision must be found reasonable by the reviewing court. According to the Supreme Court in *Khosa*, review on the reasonableness standard is not "a single, rigid Procrustean standard of decontextualized review"[138] for administrative agencies, but rather encompasses a range of degrees of deference based on the circumstances of the case. The scope of this range includes both approaches in *National Corn Growers*. It may also authorize deference in the face of a Charter violation.[139]

This presumption appears to be borne out in the cases that have followed *Dunsmuir*, but not all rule-of-law concerns have been laid to rest. Though it is still too early to state definitively whether or not *Dunsmuir* has been a success in controlling the unpredictability of judicial review, it is fair to say that the standard of review methodology has gotten simpler with only two standards from which to choose along with the emerging framework and presumptions for guidance.

Never content to let things stand still for long, though, emerging disagreements about the relationship between the home statute, the interpreter, and expertise have appeared that disclose that the constitutional basis for deference remains unsettled. As Deschamps J. questions in her concurring reasons in *Smith v. Alliance Pipeline Ltd.*, a tension continues to exist around the role of the privative clause and expertise in the standard of reasonableness:

> Deference towards administrative bodies raises important issues, both of a political and legal theoretical nature. This Court has not dealt with this topic lightly, sometimes struggling to find a balance between deferring to the expertise or experience of many of these administrative bodies and reviewing the limits to their decision-making authority under the rule of law. A consistent holding of this Court has been, and continues to be, that legislative intent should, within the confines of constitutional principles, ultimately prevail. In the case at bar, the issue of deference is shaped narrowly: Should an administrative decision-maker's interpretation of its "home" statute usually result in a court deferring to that interpretation—through the adoption of a standard of review of reasonableness—based on a presumption that the decision-maker has particular familiarity with its home statute?[140]

---

[138]   *Supra* note 128 at para. 28.

[139]   See e.g. *Lake*, where the Court applied a reasonableness standard to review of a s. 1 Charter limitation extradition decision by the minister of justice. *Lake, supra* note 102.

[140]   *Supra* note 123 at para. 78.

In this case, Deschamps J. raised concerns that according expertise to a decision-maker simply on the basis of the existence of a privative clause, and without further contextual analysis of statutory language indicating a decision-maker with specialized knowledge, pays mere lip service to legislative intent and risks sweeping too many issues into a single standard; the result, she fears, may be arbitrary judicial decisions upholding arbitrary administrative interpretations.

3. The Adequacy of Reasons

On some accounts, *Baker* represents an instance of judicial creativity in the crafting of a context-specific duty to give reasons, particularly in the immigration sphere. Mavis Baker and her counsel were lucky to gain access to the "reasons" for the negative decision in her case—the immigration officer's unofficial notes. In order to control for the arbitrariness of luck, the Court imposed a duty to give reasons on statutory and prerogative decision-makers in certain administrative contexts where important individual interests are at stake. Despite the fact that this is not a general duty for all decision-makers in the state, it nevertheless still stands as a substantive procedural protection. Ideally, the duty to give reasons has the potential to advance both restraint and respect, thereby facilitating rule-of-law concerns and administrative legitimacy. The provision of reason stands as an opportunity for the agency to show both its expertise and the adequacy of concern for affected individuals by observing procedural fairness. Judicial recognition of reasons—that is, acknowledgment that the reasons are justified and justifiable—constrains the ability to re-weigh the factors and affirms specific instances of non-arbitrary decision making. On this account, deference does not occur simply because the statute has a privative clause ordering courts not to intervene; rather, deference is the result of institutional competence, expertise, and mutual respect for the rule of law.

The subsequent trajectory of the duty to give reasons has taken several interesting turns since *Baker*. It is clear that the absence of reasons may constitute a breach of procedural fairness and, if so, will be remedied by the imposition of the duty to give reasons as a common-law requirement. But how should a court treat inadequate or unreasonable reasons? Canadian case law, for some time, remained uncertain whether inadequate reasons were a procedural deficiency to be reviewed on the fairness standard or part of substantive review and reviewed on a reasonableness standard. Recall from *Dunsmuir* that reasons and deference possess a strong interrelationship. Judicial deference to a decision is appropriate where the decision demonstrates justification, transparency, and intelligibility within the decision-making process, and where the outcome falls within a range of possible, acceptable outcomes defensible with respect to the facts and law. Reasons are generally held to serve three functions: (1) they disclose expertise in the subject area of the home statute "using concepts and language often unique to their areas and rendering decision that are often counter-intuitive to a generalist";[141]

---

[141]   *Newfoundland and Labrador Nurses' Union v. Newfoundland and Labrador (Treasury Board)*, 2011 SCC 62 (CanLII) at para. 13 [*Newfoundland Nurses' Union*].

(2) they justify the decision using transparent, intelligible, and reasonable reasoning that all audiences—counsel, affected persons and especially the losing party, reviewing courts, other agencies, and the general public—can understand; and (3) they illustrate that the outcome is also reasonable when, as is often the case in administrative decision making, more than one reasonable result is possible. This means that reasons support the principle of deference because the reviewing court ought to defer to the decision-maker who provides legally valid reasons that support a reasonable outcome even if the court disagrees with the outcome. Reasons therefore hearken back to the import of the *CUPE* decision and its articulation of the principled grounds for deference.

In *Newfoundland Nurses' Union*,[142] the Supreme Court clarified several problems that inadequate reasons raised in the lower courts. First, they confirmed that inadequate reasons are not analyzed under procedural fairness but, rather, reasonableness review. The Court then outlined the analytic framework for determining adequate reasons. If a decision-maker must give reasons, the reasons should justify the decision—that is, show that the decision-maker has considered relevant facts and law, applied legal principles and tests correctly, and is able to explain the decision in a way that both the affected person and the reviewing court can understand. In language that evokes *Baker*, Abella J. wrote that reasons show a mind that is "alive to the question at issue."[143] Reasons must be transparent and show the basis for the reasonable outcome. And, reasons should be reviewed as an organic exercise, not with a forensic or microscopic lens because reasons are not a stand-alone basis for intrusive review. Therefore, reasons do not have to be perfect, do not have to be comprehensive or lengthy, may contain some errors, do not have to be well written, and speed, economy, and informality may take priority given the day-to-day realities administrative officials face. Nevertheless, they still must permit effective review in order to satisfy the principles of legality, accountability, and the rule of law.

But what, then, do inadequate reasons look like and where found imperfect, what would judicial deference look like?[144] The test is functional and purposeful. The reasons must address the substance of the live issues, key arguments, contradictory evidence, and non-obvious inferences. Bare or opaque conclusions with no supporting information or not supported by principles will be found unsatisfactory. Inconsistencies and irrelevant considerations, or when relevant considerations or obvious topics are omitted, will be considered serious flaws. The decision-maker cannot write minimal reasons that effectively provide

---

142 *Ibid.*

143 *Ibid.* at para. 26. In *Newfoundland Nurses' Union*, the Court characterized the "bread and butter" decision made by the labour arbitrator as a simple interpretive exercise in the home statute, involving a decision-making process that is very different from judicial contexts, and in a context with which the decision-maker was highly familiar and expert. The Court found the decision to be reasonable in terms of the form, content, and outcome.

144 Important lower-court judgments that have fleshed out the analytic framework for determining adequate reasons include: Justice Evans's dissent in *Canada Post Corp. v. Public Service Alliance of Canada*, 2010 FCA 56 (CanLII); *Vancouver International Airport Authority v. Public Service Alliance of Canada*, 2010 FCA 158 (CanLII) [*VIAA*]; *Clifford v. Ontario Municipal Employees Retirement System*, 2009 ONCA 670 (CanLII); and *Spinks v. Alberta (Law Enforcement Review Board)*, 2011 ABCA 162 [*Spinks*].

immunization from review and accountability. And, finally, the decision-maker cannot exhibit an attitude of "Trust us, we got it right."[145]

While cases like *Newfoundland Nurses' Union* have provided much guidance and clarification, as well as a strong statement regarding how necessary deference is when reviewing reasons, some matters remain unsettled. Courts will disagree when a more intrusive review is required based on differing assessments of the seriousness of the perceived flaws.[146] In *Newfoundland Nurses' Union*, Abella J. cited with approval the concept of "deference as respect" regarding the function of reasons.[147] She agreed with David Dyzenhaus that even if the reasons do not seem wholly adequate to support the decision, the court must first seek to "supplement them before it seeks to subvert them" and therefore improve on the reasons that the original decision-maker gave.[148] The *Lake* decision provides a thought-provoking example of this kind of deferential review and judicial supplementation of inadequate reasons.[149] This case involved the review of the minister of justice's discretionary decision to permit extradition of a Canadian citizen, and convicted criminal, to the United States for prosecution on criminal charges there. Despite the fact the extradition clearly engaged Charter rights, the Supreme Court reviewed the decision on a standard of reasonableness, rather than correctness, because of the minister's superior expertise in foreign affairs and because he was better placed to weigh the relevant factors. Though the minister's reasons were brief, the Court held that they were not inadequate and could permit them to determine that the minister had applied the proper principles and fairly considered any submissions that provided alternative factors weighing against surrender.

An open question therefore remains whether or not authorizing reviewing courts to substitute reasons is only a superficial form of deference, opens the door too widely for intrusive merits review, or does not have the effect of disciplining administrative decision-makers as a matter of practice because they know that appellate courts will alter or even completely substitute their improved reasons for the original reasons.

D. Constraining the Charter

In Canada's pre-Charter Westminster system of government, the principle of parliamentary sovereignty traditionally meant that Parliament could pass laws on any subject, and that no

---

[145] *VIAA, supra* note 144 at para. 21. Stratas J.A. laid out four overarching purposes governing reasons: (1) the substantive purpose, which allows us to understand why the decision-maker reached this result; (2) the procedural purpose, which permits parties to decide whether or not to have the decision reviewed; (3) the accountability purpose, which enables a supervising court to assess whether the decision-maker met minimum standards of legality; and (4) the justification, transparency, and intelligibility purpose, which facilitates scrutiny by all observers and furthers the public interest because the decision-maker is part of our democratic governance structure. *Ibid.* at para. 16.

[146] As Justice Côté writes in the *Spinks* decision, *supra* note 144 at para. 21: "And where the tribunal stated some unsatisfactory reason, what should the Court of Appeal do to defer? What would a deferential decision by the Court of Appeal look like? 'We can almost understand these reasons'? or 'These reasons are almost rational'? or 'Four of six vital topics were covered, and that is a good enough batting average'?"

[147] *Newfoundland Nurses' Union, supra* note 141 at para. 11.

[148] *Ibid.* at para. 12.

[149] *Supra* note 102.

institution or person could override or strike down these laws. The rule of law required that statutes meet the "manner and form" criteria of enactment—that is, the legislature must be identified as the proper source of law and the proper legislative procedure must be used. Existence of these two factors sufficed in order to recognize a statute as valid or "prescribed by law" by all institutions and persons, including the judiciary. In the pre-Charter world of public law, the authority of legislatures was not constrained by courts, but rather by political sanctions. Political sanctions manifested themselves through regular elections as well as political conventions such as the confidence convention and by ministerial responsibility in which Cabinet ministers faced demands for accountability by way of scrutiny in Question Period in the legislature. The enactment of the Charter has fundamentally constrained the principle of parliamentary sovereignty. Legislatures can theoretically respond to some judicial rulings by using the s. 33 notwithstanding clause to override decisions temporarily.[150] Constitutional rights, however, can be limited subject to the government satisfying the justificatory requirements of s. 1 in the Charter.[151] In this way, Canada continues to endorse the principle of parliamentary sovereignty, but reconciles it with the principle of the rule of law as manifested in judicial review.[152]

The interpretive role of the courts in public law means that they must provide cogent and coherent justifications that explain the nature of the conflict and the appropriateness of the decision in favour of one right or one balance over another, even in the face of grants of broad powers of discretion. The Charter can significantly constrain delegations of broad discretionary powers where Charter rights and freedoms are directly or indirectly implicated, or which may not be sufficiently confined by the terms of the enabling statute. So, while the existence of broad discretionary powers is not suspect in itself, courts can be more demanding in cases that involve broad delegations of power by ensuring that discretion is structured or confined within the parameters of the Charter. In administrative law, this kind

---

[150]   See Jeremy Waldron, "The Core of the Case Against Judicial Review" (2006) 115 Yale L.J. 1346. Although Waldron is discussing the role of the judiciary in the United States, his argument finds purchase in Canada with critics who bemoan the growth of judicial activism and the inability of legislatures to use the notwithstanding clause to advance a different interpretation of a constitutional matter for fear of political backlash. The abeyance of s. 33, they argue, gives judges the *de facto* last word and ensures that the courts remain supreme over other branches of government. The litmus test for this debate is whether or not one believes that in a reasonably democratic society with functioning legislatures, where its citizens disagree about the scope and content of rights, judicial review of legislation constitutes an inappropriate mode of final decision making.

[151]   Citing constitutional scholar Peter Hogg, the Supreme Court describes the constitutional and rule-of-law basis of the "prescribed by law" requirement of s. 1 as: (1) all government action in derogation of rights must be authorized by law or be found arbitrary and discriminatory; and (2) members of the public must have a reasonable opportunity to know what is prohibited by law so that they can regulate their conduct. Moreover, the law must be sufficiently precise in order to provide guidance to those who apply it. See *Greater Vancouver Transportation Authority v. Canadian Federation of Students*, [2009] 2 S.C.R. 295 at para. 50.

[152]   See e.g. Wilson J.'s characterization of s. 1 of the Charter in her dissent in *Operation Dismantle v. The Queen*, [1985] S.C.R. 441 at para. 104: "Section 1, in my opinion, is the uniquely Canadian mechanism through which the courts are to determine the justiciability of particular issues that come before it. It embodies through its reference to a free and democratic society the essential features of our constitution including the separation of powers, responsible government and the rule of law. It obviates the need for a 'political questions' doctrine and permits the Court to deal with what might be termed 'prudential' considerations in a principled way without renouncing its constitutional and mandated responsibility for judicial review."

of activity is particularly controversial if it means judges can, in certain cases and with a constrained approach, "re-weigh" the factors that administrative decision-makers use based on their expertise and experiential knowledge, if such decisions violate constitutional values—as L'Heureux-Dubé J. arguably did in the *Baker* decision. Those who support this conclusion argue that the Charter reinforces the constitutional commitment that all persons—individuals, corporations, groups, and state actors—must adhere to the rule of law and respect fundamental constitutional values. *Baker* therefore represents an important link in the rule-of-law narrative that can be traced back to *Roncarelli*. Like *Roncarelli*, *Baker* discloses that administrative and constitutional law are attuned to underlying fundamental values such as basic concerns for human dignity, the vindication of rights, and the effects of political power on individuals.[153]

The recent *Doré v. Barreau du Québec* decision from the Supreme Court changed the methodological approach used to review discretionary decisions involving Charter interests and values.[154] Overturning the majority approach previously endorsed in the *Multani* decision, the Supreme Court confirmed that the orthodox approach used to review whether or not a *law* justifiably infringes a right or freedom—the *Oakes* test—should not replace administrative law review for discretionary decisions.[155] The standard of review will be reasonableness with "proportionality" serving, in such cases, as the central criterion of reasonableness. Deference will be shown and reasonableness will be recognized when the administrative body has asked itself how the particular Charter value will best be protected while recognizing statutory objectives, and then has properly balanced the severity of the interference in light of these statutory objectives. It seems clear that the primary way to show that proportionality analysis has been properly undertaken is through the provision of adequate reasons. *Doré* seems to align judicial review of discretionary decisions with the *Cooper* dissent, discussed immediately below. Several issues, however, remain unclear including: (1) how exactly will proportionality analysis be constructed in reasonableness review; (2) can administrative law adequately protect Charter interests and values in discretionary decision making; (3) how does the interpretation and weighing of Charter values relate to agency expertise; and (4) does *Doré* endorse judicial re-weighing of the values considered and balanced by the original decision-maker?

Another significant development in the relationship between the Charter and administrative bodies is the judicial finding that an administrative tribunal may have the jurisdiction

---

153   See Mary Liston, "'Alert, Alive and Sensitive': *Baker*, the Duty to Give Reasons and the Ethos of Justification in Canadian Public Law" for this understanding of *Baker* in David Dyzenhaus, ed., *The Unity of Public Law* (Oxford: Hart Publishing, 2004). This collection of essays offers a multiperspectival examination of a public law culture of justification through the lens of *Baker*.

154   *Doré v. Barreau du Québec*, 2012 SCC 12 [*Doré*]. For further discussion of the implications of the *Doré* decision, see Chapter 10 by Sheila Wildeman, Chapter 11 by Geneviève Cartier, and Chapter 12 by Evan Fox-Decent and Alexander Pless.

155   See Deschamps and Abella JJ.'s concurring reasons in *Multani v. Commission scolaire Marguerite-Bourgeoys*, [2006] 1 S.C.R. 256, 2006 SCC 6 [*Multani*]. See also LeBel J.'s dissent in *Blencoe*, *supra* note 21. The Court, therefore, has drawn a jurisprudential distinction between a law (i.e., a norm of general application produced by a legislative body which may also include a regulation and a bylaw) and decisions and orders made by administrative bodies. When a tribunal determines the constitutionality of a law, on the other hand, the standard of review will be correctness.

to consider Charter challenges to its enabling legislation and to award Charter remedies under s. 24(1).[156] This determination represents a major shift in the earlier approach, which allocated the power to determine questions of law to courts, while leaving administrative bodies the power to interpret and apply their enabling legislation. Originally, only administrative tribunals that structurally and purposively mirrored courts possessed the jurisdiction to hear Charter claims. Now, sometimes the enabling legislation will empower an administrative tribunal to interpret and apply all law, including the Charter, while at other times the statutory scheme as a whole will confer an implicit jurisdiction. These changes are grounded in concerns for access to justice and recognition of the competence and capacity of such tribunals as legal bodies to interpret legislation. Jurisdiction to apply the Charter to enabling legislation and to award Charter remedies may be explicitly given by the legislature in the statute. Certain rule-of-law considerations stemming from the separation of powers will flow from this mandate: the particular decision will not be binding authority as precedent for future cases; and, in subsequent judicial review, the decision will be subject to a standard of correctness, ensuring that it receives little or no curial deference.

The ability of administrative agencies to question unconstitutional enabling provisions not only provides an economical and efficient resolution of a rights dispute (avoiding the need to go to court), but also conforms to the "institutional dialogue" and "deference as respect" models. This democratically informed perspective emerged clearly in the dissent written by McLachlin J. (as she then was) and L'Heureux-Dubé J. in the case *Cooper v. Canada (Human Rights Commission)*. This case concerned the fundamental question of whether or not human rights tribunals have the authority to determine the constitutionality of provisions in their enabling statutes. In *Cooper*, they wrote a resounding affirmation:

> The *Charter* is not some holy grail which only judicial initiates of the superior courts may touch. The *Charter* belongs to the people. All law and law-makers that touch the people must conform to it. Tribunals and commissions charged with deciding legal issues are no exception. Many more citizens have their rights determined by these tribunals than by the courts. If the *Charter* is to be meaningful to ordinary people, then it must find its expression in the decisions of these tribunals.[157]

The dissent in *Cooper* expresses a vision of democratic constitutionalism that respects the legitimacy of the administrative state and that has been subsequently affirmed in the *Martin* decision.[158] This vision of Canadian constitutionalism relies on a democratic interpretation of the separation of powers and therefore recognizes the appropriate role of administrative

---

[156] In Chapter 12, Evan Fox-Decent and Alexander Pless discuss the difficulties in the relationship between the Charter and administrative law, including agency jurisdiction over the Charter and the trilogy of cases affirming tribunal authority to consider questions of law. See *R. v. Conway*, [2010] 1 S.C.R. 765 and Cristie Ford in Chapter 3 on the expansion of the ability of tribunals to award Charter remedies. Parliament and provincial legislatures, however, retain the power to make it clear in the enabling legislation that statutory delegates do not have the power to consider the Charter, other constitutional issues, or issue Charter remedies.

[157] *Cooper, supra* note 26 at para. 70.

[158] *Nova Scotia (Workers' Compensation Board) v. Martin; Nova Scotia (Workers' Compensation Board) v. Laseur*, [2003] 2 SCR 504 [*Martin*]. Lorne Sossin in Chapter 7, Access to Administrative Justice and Other Worries, provides a fuller discussion of *Martin* and agency jurisdiction under the Charter.

tribunals—particularly human rights tribunals—in determining the content and scope of fundamental legal norms.[159] The institutional aspiration underlying this vision wishes to create a constitutional democracy that reconciles the formerly competing sovereignties and reinforces institutional competencies. On this account, administrative agencies as constitutional partners do exhibit rule-of-law attributes, have embraced rule-of-law values, and can facilitate access to justice for the benefit of citizens and other affected persons.

E. Other Routes to Accountability in the Administrative State

Judicial review represents an important, but not the sole, route to securing administrative accountability. Courts should be seen as merely one among the many means by which we hold government to account. Moreover, it will be better for the legitimacy of courts if we recognize them as one among a "family" of legitimate routes to securing accountability within a liberal democratic state: public inquiries,[160] task forces, departmental investigations, special legislative officers, and ombudsmen. The rule of law will also inform the various institutional alternatives to judicial review of government action.

V. Conclusion: A Democratic Rule of Law in the Administrative State

This chapter has explained how the concept of the rule of law and its associated legal and political principles are fundamental to understanding the relationship between courts and administrative bodies. The realization of the rule of law within a democratic culture cannot only legitimate the sharing of public power among courts, the executive, legislatures, and administrative bodies, but also facilitate the creation of multiple routes for citizens (and non-citizens) to secure accountability for the use of public power. All parts of and persons in the state participate in the creation and maintenance of the rule of law. This reality points to a conception of the rule of law, which recognizes that all branches of government have a duty to realize a rule-of-law state and that all branches can fail to do so in distinctive ways. The multiplicity of institutional environments, however, means that the rule of law will require different responsibilities and restraints for different institutional actors and practices. Though this makes administrative law a difficult field of study and provides unending complications for judicial review of administrative decision making, one positive reading of such complexity suggests that this is a necessary consequence of the interaction between the rule of law and democracy. The simple system suggested by both legal and political theory, then, is capable of infinite variations and complexity in the design of institutions and their constraints. These permutations must nevertheless continue to adhere to the substance and procedures of legality—a process in which courts play an important role through interpretation of legal principles and oversight of administrative practices.

---

159   For a more expansive argument, see Dyzenhaus, "Constituting Fundamental Values," *supra* note 110 at 453-87.

160   See Peter Carver, Chapter 16, Getting the Story Out: Accountability and the Law of Public Inquiries, for a discussion of administrative law in relation to public inquiries.

How a judge understands the rule of law, and his or her role in upholding it through judicial review, will necessarily shape how he or she approaches the review of decisions made by an administrative tribunal. Judicial temperament is not completely predictable: judges may conceive of themselves as the Diceyan defenders of the rule of law against the administrative state; or they may view themselves the Dworkinian legal guardians of the constitution, committed to upholding the rights conception of the rule of law; or perhaps they may see their role as the Fullerian cooperative partner who recognizes democratic initiatives, but still maintains institutional fidelity to rule-of-law principles; and lastly, they may perceive themselves as the Razian interpreters of guided discretion and judicial faithfulness to coherent legislative purposes. Institutional dialogue and deference as respect stand as distinctive forms of the commitment to judicial restraint in Canadian administrative law—a restraint that simultaneously attempts to ensure judicial accountability and larger democratic accountability. Nevertheless, the modern development of deference and respect for administrative tribunals is both an ongoing and vulnerable achievement.

SUGGESTED ADDITIONAL READINGS

BOOKS AND ARTICLES

Canadian

Huscroft, Grant, & Michael Taggart, eds., *Inside and Outside Canadian Administrative Law* (Toronto: University of Toronto Press, 2006).

McLachlin, Madam Justice Beverley M., "The Role of Administrative Tribunals and Courts in Maintaining the Rule of Law" (1999) 12 Can. J. Admin. L. & Prac. 171.

Sullivan, Ruth, *Statutory Interpretation* (Toronto: Irwin Law, 1997).

Van Harten, Gus, et al., *Administrative Law: Cases, Text, and Materials*, 6th ed. (Toronto: Emond Montgomery, 2010).

International

Allan, T.R.S., Constitutional Justice: A Liberal Theory of the Rule of Law (Oxford: Oxford University Press, 2001).

Bauman, Richard W., & Tsvi Kahana, eds., *The Least Examined Branch: The Role of Legislatures in the Constitutional State* (Cambridge: Cambridge University Press, 2006).

Bellamy, Richard, ed., *The Rule of Law and the Separation of Powers* (Aldershot, UK: Ashgate/Dartmouth, 2005).

Craig, Paul P., *Administrative Law*, 5th ed. (London: Sweet & Maxwell, 2003).

Dworkin, Ronald, *A Matter of Principle* (Cambridge, MA: Harvard University Press, 1985).

Dyzenhaus, David, ed., Recrafting the Rule of Law: The Limits of Legal Order (Oxford: Hart, 1999).

Harlow, Carol, & Richard Rawlings, *Law and Administration*, 3d ed. (Cambridge: Cambridge University Press, 2009).

Shapiro, Ian, ed., *NOMOS XXXVI: The Rule of Law* (New York and London: New York University Press, 1994).

Tamanaha, Brian Z., *On the Rule of Law: History, Politics, Theory* (Cambridge: Cambridge University Press, 2004).

CASES

British Columbia v. Imperial Tobacco Canada Ltd., [2005] 2 S.C.R. 473.

Canada (Attorney General) v. PHS Community Services Society, 2011 SCC 44, [2011] 3 S.C.R. 134.

Canada (Citizenship and Immigration) v. Khosa, [2009] 1 S.C.R. 339.

Cooper v. Canada (Canadian Human Rights Commission), [1996] 3 S.C.R. 85.

Dunsmuir v. New Brunswick, [2008] 1 S.C.R. 190.

National Corn Growers Assn. v. Canada (Import Tribunal), [1990] 2 S.C.R. 1324.

Reference re Language Rights Under s. 23 of Manitoba Act, 1870 and s. 133 of Constitution Act, 1867, [1985] 1 S.C.R. 721.

Reference re Secession of Quebec, [1998] 2 S.C.R. 217.

Roncarelli v. Duplessis, [1959] S.C.R. 121.

CHAPTER THREE

Dogs and Tails: Remedies in Administrative Law

CRISTIE FORD

Faculty of Law, University of British Columbia

I. Introduction

From time to time, one hears the criticism that a particular court judgment has allowed the "tail" of the remedy to "wag the dog" of the substantive case. In traditional treatments of administrative law remedies, the metaphor could potentially be carried even further. One has the sense that the "tail" of what is called "judicial review"—that is, court review of remedies that have been imposed by administrative law agencies and tribunals[1]—has been allowed to "wag the dog" of the discipline's entire approach to remedies, and even administrative law. Some classic textbooks treat administrative law remedies as if they *begin* at the point at which a party to an administrative action seeks judicial review of that action through the courts.

The legal preoccupation with court action derives, to some extent, from law's discomfort with public decision-making bodies that work differently from courts. Law's role vis-à-vis administrative action is often focused on what tools courts have to police and intervene in administrative agencies' actions, to ensure that those agencies observe the rule of law and basic principles of justice. Legal scholars and practitioners (and, of course, judges) do not always trust administrative agencies to the degree they trust courts. Concerns for justice and the rule of law are legitimate. Yet, a tight focus on court action misses the hugely important first step in real-life administrative action: the varied and sometimes creative remedies that the tribunal itself may impose.

If courts and legal scholars sometimes seem to overemphasize the role of judicial review, legislators often simultaneously try to limit its practical use. One of the themes that runs through this chapter, and indeed this book, is the "dialogue" (some might say tug-of-war) that courts and legislators engage in as they try to steer the course of administrative law.[2] Administrative tribunals, although generally quite independent of the political process, are still products of the executive arm of government. Legislative drafters, in crafting tribunals' enabling statutes, may use various tools to limit or circumscribe the available scope of court intervention in tribunals' decision-making processes. One common mechanism is the privative clause.[3] Another technique, relevant in this chapter, is to provide for avenues of appeal of a decision that are internal to the tribunal itself. This limits recourse to judicial review, because the general (court-developed) rule is that recourse to the courts is only available after a party has exhausted all avenues of appeal, including internal appeals and any appeals to the courts provided for in the statute. By providing for appeal mechanisms,

---

1   For simplicity I will use the term "tribunal" throughout to refer to the full range of administrative agencies, commissions, and other bodies. This is an oversimplification, because many administrative decision-makers do not take a tribunal form. Many administrative decisions are made by bureaucrats without a hearing or the court-style structure of a tribunal; administrative agencies also regularly make policy decisions that affect individual and social interests. However, the tribunal is perhaps the prototypical administrative structure for the purpose of understanding the remedies available to a party to tribunal action.

2   See Mary Liston, Chapter 2, Governments in Miniature: The Rule of Law in the Administrative State.

3   On privative clauses and substantive fairness, see Sheila Wildeman, Chapter 10, Pas de Deux: Deference and Non-Deference in Action, and Audrey Macklin, Chapter 9, Standard of Review: Back to the Future?

and in particular for internal appeal mechanisms with their own unique and sometimes uncourtlike structures, the executive is able to maintain a greater degree of control over the statutory scheme that it has constructed to address a particular public issue.

This chapter provides an overview of administrative law remedies as a whole, including not only judicial review but also tribunal decisions, internal and external appeals, enforcement mechanisms, and extralegal strategies. Discussing remedies near the beginning of an administrative law textbook may seem unconventional. We have chosen this approach because understanding the available remedies is an important part of understanding what one is "getting into" in administrative law, and it provides a broad structural framework on which subsequent chapters can build. This chapter is meant to operate almost as a decision tree, to help guide students through the different stages where remedies issues arise. Figure 3.1 sets out the broad outlines of the chapter.

The chapter is divided into five sections, with sections I and V providing an introduction and a conclusion, respectively. Section II, "Remedial Options at the Tribunal Stage," section III, "Enforcing Tribunal Orders Against Parties," and section IV, "Challenging Administrative Action" have not traditionally been located in the "remedies" chapter of administrative law texts (if they appear at all). As we shall see in section II, remedial options available to administrative agencies at the first stage differ from those available to courts and reflect the different composition of tribunals. The remedies available at the administrative stage are both more limited (in terms of the tribunal's statute-derived authority to impose them) and, potentially, more expansive (as a consequence of tribunals' particular expertise and their ability to remain seized of a matter over time). Section III looks at the ability of a party or tribunal to *enforce* a tribunal order against another party, either civilly or criminally. Section IV considers parties' ability to *challenge* tribunal action. This includes internal appeal options, extralegal options, appeal to the courts, and, finally, the classic administrative law remedy of judicial review. In addressing these three aspects in a single chapter, the goal is to provide the reader, in a systematic and chronological fashion, with a conceptual frame of reference that includes the full range of remedial options available to parties before administrative tribunals.

II. Remedial Options at the Tribunal Stage

Administrative tribunals are as varied as the topics on which they adjudicate, and it would be unwise to generalize about the remedial powers available to them. However, two general comments about available remedies can safely be made. First, because a tribunal does not have the general jurisdiction that a court does, the power to impose a particular remedy must be provided for in the tribunal's enabling statute. Second, most tribunals' composition, structure, and mandates are different from courts', and their approach to remedies reflects those differences. For example, certain tribunals' expertise with a more limited subject matter may help them to identify systemic problems or recurring patterns across multiple individual disputes. Their ability to stay involved in (that is, to remain "seized" of) a dispute over a longer period of time is well established, and many tribunals are less constrained by formal rules than courts are in developing remedies. Together, on occasion, these factors allow tribunals to conceptualize and implement novel remedial strategies aimed at addressing the systemic problems they see.

Figure 3.1

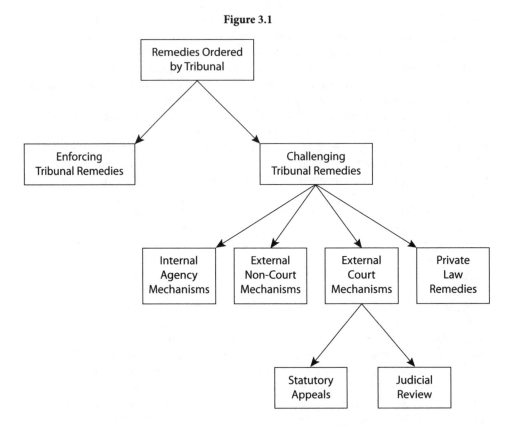

A. Statutory Authority

As a creature of statute, a tribunal cannot make orders that affect individuals' rights or obligations without authority from its enabling statute.[4] Therefore, the first step in determining a tribunal's remedial options is to look at the statute itself. If a tribunal makes orders outside the scope of its enabling statute, it is exceeding its jurisdiction, and those orders will be void.[5]

Many enabling statutes set out express lists of the remedies a tribunal may order. For example, tribunals often have the power to make declaratory orders, to order a party to repair a problem or to mitigate damage, or to order a party to comply with the tribunal's enabling statute. Licensing powers may also be given to tribunals in statutory regimes designed to protect the public (for example, through professional licensing qualifications or requirements for corporations issuing securities to public investors), or to manage natural resources (for

---

[4] *Att. Gen. of Can. v. Inuit Tapirisat et al.*, [1980] 2 S.C.R. 735, [1980] S.C.J. No. 99 (QL) [*Inuit Tapirisat*].

[5] When two tribunals share jurisdiction over a particular statutory provision (e.g. a workers' compensation tribunal and a human rights tribunal considering a statutory provision that concerns them both), a tribunal can also be found to exceed its jurisdiction if it deals with a claim that has already been "appropriately dealt with" by the other relevant tribunal. See *British Columbia (Workers' Compensation Board) v. Figliola*, 2011 SCC 52, [2011] 3 S.C.R. 422.

example, fishing and forestry licences). Some tribunals can appoint conciliators and otherwise assist in settling matters before them.[6] Some enabling statutes empower tribunals to impose significant fines and possible incarceration or provide for more serious quasicriminal offences that must be prosecuted by the Crown.[7]

Other statutes accord their tribunals broad, discretionary power to fashion the remedies they see fit. For example, the Ontario *Human Rights Code* gives the Ontario Human Rights Tribunal the discretion to order a party who has been found to discriminate to "do anything that, in the opinion of the Tribunal, the party ought to do to achieve compliance with this Act, both in respect of the complaint and in respect of future practices."[8]

Even where a tribunal's remedial power is less certain (that is, its enabling statute does not expressly permit a particular remedy and the tribunal has no broad discretionary power), one may try to argue that, as a matter of practical necessity, a tribunal must have the remedial power to do the things its statute requires it to do.[9] However, orders for the payment of money, such as compensation or damages, fines, fees and levies, and costs, can generally only be ordered by tribunals that have the express statutory authority to do so. Tribunals also lack the equitable jurisdiction to order interim injunctions, although they may be given statutory authority to seek an injunction in court to enforce a statute. Finally, whether a tribunal has the power to grant remedies under the *Canadian Charter of Rights and Freedoms* is a separate question. As Evan Fox-Decent and Alexander Pless explain in Chapter 12, The Charter and Administrative Law: Cross-Fertilization or Inconstancy?, the common law prescribes a separate test for determining whether particular administrative tribunals can grant remedies under s. 24(1) of the Charter.[10] Moreover, some provinces have now enacted statutes that explicitly bar at least some tribunals from considering Charter issues.[11]

B. Novel Administrative Remedies

Administrative tribunals and agencies vary widely in their structures and functions, but collectively they also differ from courts in important ways. The particular structures and qualities of administrative tribunals equally affect the kinds of remedies they are inclined, and empowered, to grant. This part of the chapter seeks to set out in broad strokes the kinds of remedies that tribunal-type administrative bodies in particular are likely to grant. The

---

[6]   E.g. *Canadian Human Rights Act*, R.S.C. 1985, c. H-6, ss. 47-48; B.C. *Employment Standards Act*, R.S.B.C. 1996, c. 113, s. 78.

[7]   See e.g. B.C. *Securities Act*, R.S.B.C. 1996, c. 418, ss. 161, 162, 155.

[8]   *Human Rights Code*, R.S.O. 1990, c. H.19, s. 41(1)(a).

[9]   *ATCO Gas & Pipelines Ltd. v. Alberta (Energy & Utilities Board)*, 2006 SCC 4, [2006] 1 S.C.R. 140.

[10] See *R. v. Conway*, 2010 SCC 22, [2010] 1 S.C.R. 765.

[11] See e.g. the B.C. *Administrative Tribunals Act*, 36 S.B.C. 2004, c. 45 [ATA], which provides that the majority of provincial tribunals do not have discretion to consider either constitutional questions generally, or at least constitutional questions relating to the Charter. The statute establishes a mechanism for referring constitutional questions to the courts. Sections 46.1-46.3 of the Act impose similar restrictions on many tribunals' jurisdiction to apply the B.C. *Human Rights Code* to any matter before it on the basis that the Human Rights Tribunal is the more appropriate forum.

kinds of functions performed by tribunal-type administrative bodies—namely, party-on-party dispute resolution, party-versus-agency enforcement and disciplinary proceedings, and other similar forms of hearings and decision making—tend to be the most common ways in which members of the public engage with administrative bodies. These functions also square especially well with the concept of "remedies," defined by *Black's Law Dictionary* as "the field of law dealing with the means of enforcing rights and redressing wrongs."[12]

However, the reader should be aware that tribunal-type administrative agencies are only one version of administrative agency operations. Parties may interact, be answerable to, and seek to influence administrative law agencies in other ways. Agencies' policy-making functions, in particular, are outside the scope of this chapter but should not be outside one's field of vision.[13] Through their statutory drafting choices, legislators regularly delegate detailed policy-making decisions to administrative tribunals. Many larger administrative agencies have formal policy-making departments, which generally operate at some remove from their tribunal departments. Administrative policy instruments can range from formal, binding interpretive releases to relatively informal, non-binding administrative guidance. Policy releases and guidelines have a direct impact on regulated entities. They are publicly available, and regulated entities are expected to know about them. Their release can be preceded by formal public consultation, providing those affected with a chance for input in advance.

Moreover, even when acting in their tribunal capacity, administrative tribunals often do, and should, take a broader perspective on a dispute than courts necessarily will. One way to understand the difference is in terms described by an American scholar, Abram Chayes, in the mid-1970s.[14] Chayes talked about courts, not administrative agencies. Nevertheless, his point illuminates the distinction between the two. Chayes described an emerging dichotomy between traditional conceptions of adjudication and an emerging judicial role in what he described as public law litigation. In traditional adjudication, a suit involves only the private parties before the court. It is self-contained and party-initiated. A dispassionate judge identifies the private right at issue on the basis of doctrinal analysis and retrospective fact inquiry. The judge imposes relief, understood as compensation for the past violation of an identifiable existing right. (This portrayal describes party-on-party dispute resolution, but this sort of rights-based approach also underpins tribunal-on-party regulatory action.) By contrast, in public law litigation, Chayes argued that the debate is more focused on the vindication of broader statutory or constitutional policies. The lawsuit is not self-contained. The judge must manage complex trial situations involving not only the parties to the dispute but also the many and shifting parties not before the court who nevertheless may be affected by the suit's outcome. Fact inquiry is predictive, not retrospective. Through a combination of party negotiation and continuing judicial involvement, the judge fashions relief that is ad

---

12　*Black's Law Dictionary*, 8th ed., s.v. "remedies."

13　See Andrew Green, Chapter 4, Regulations and Rule Making: The Dilemma of Delegation.

14　Abram Chayes, "The Role of the Judge in Public Law Litigation" (1976) 89 Harv. L. Rev. 1281; see also D.M. Gordon, "'Administrative' Tribunals and the Courts" (1933) 49 Law Q. Rev. 94 (defining a judicial function as one that determines "pre-existing" rights and liabilities by reference to a "fixed objective standard," as contrasted to an administrative function, in which rights and liabilities are created by "policy and expediency").

hoc, ongoing, and prospective. On the Chayes model, judges can become change agents under whose management specific cases can have far-reaching effects.

Like Chayes's public law adjudicatory model, administrative agencies—even when acting as tribunals rather than policy-making bodies—may have a broader mandate, and the ability to leverage a broader range of tools than a traditional assertion of rights-based claims provides. Many administrative bodies are explicitly charged with managing complex and often "polycentric" problems in a comprehensive manner. The Supreme Court of Canada has recognized this, pointing out that "while judicial procedure is premised on a bipolar opposition of parties, interests, and factual discovery, some problems [assigned to tribunals by their enabling statutes] require the consideration of numerous interests simultaneously, and the promulgation of solutions which concurrently balance benefits and costs for many different parties."[15] This has a few implications. First, it means that administrative tribunals have stronger theoretical justifications for remaining seized of a case over a longer period of time.[16] Second, it means that administrative tribunals may try to develop remedies that address underlying structural or systemic problems, in a forward-looking rather than retrospective, rights-oriented way. This is not to say that courts do not also craft systemic, forward-looking remedies. Indeed, Chayes's point is that they do.[17] However, relative to courts, administrative tribunals may be especially well placed to develop and implement novel remedies thanks to their subject-specific expertise, their field sensitivity, and their particular statutory mandates.

Just as important, administrative tribunal members are a more diverse group than judges are, especially in terms of their training and expertise. Some tribunals' enabling statutes stipulate that a certain portion of their tribunal members should be laypersons. For example, the federal *Competition Tribunal Act*[18] stipulates that the tribunal shall consist of not more than six members who are Federal Court judges, and not more than eight other "lay" members. The statute goes on to stipulate that the governor in council should establish an advisory council, "to be composed of not more than ten members who are knowledgeable in economics, industry, commerce or public affairs,"[19] to advise the minister of industry with respect to the appointment of lay members. The result is a tribunal with substantial expertise in economics and in commerce.[20] The tribunal's expertise also makes it more likely that its members will devise remedies that reflect their training and perspective and that may be more economic than legal.

---

[15] *Pushpanathan v. Canada (Minister of Citizenship and Immigration)*, [1998] 1 S.C.R. 982, [1998] S.C.J. No. 46 (QL) at para. 36 (S.C.R.) (advising curial deference where the purpose of the enabling statute as a whole and the provision in question present the tribunal with this sort of question).

[16] See e.g. *Ontario (Ministry of Correctional Services) v. Ontario (Human Rights Comm.)* (2001), 39 C.H.R.R. D/308 (Ont. Sup. Ct.), aff'd [2004] O.J. No. 5051 (QL) (C.A.) (holding that the Human Rights Tribunal of Ontario had extensive supervisory jurisdiction over its orders and could remain seized of a matter to recast its orders to deal with ongoing systemic racism at correctional facilities).

[17] *Doucet-Boudreau v. Nova Scotia (Minister of Education)*, 2003 SCC 62, [2003] 3 S.C.R. 3 provides justification for structural injunction-style remedies by courts.

[18] R.S.C. 1985, c. 19 (2d Supp.), s. 3(2).

[19] *Ibid.*, s. 3(3).

[20] *Canada (Director of Investigation and Research) v. Southam Inc.*, [1997] 1 S.C.R. 748.

Sometimes, the composition of tribunal membership reflects an explicit attempt to represent different interest groups, perhaps especially in subject areas where there is a perception that judges historically have been unsympathetic or not alive to some of the issues at stake. A classic example is a tripartite labour board, on which a representative of labour, a representative of management, and a third member must sit. A further example of a tripartite structure is the B.C. Review Board, charged under the *Criminal Code* of Canada with making dispositions with respect to individuals found unfit to stand trial or not criminally responsible on account of mental disorder. The B.C. *Mental Health Act* requires that each panel of the Review Board consist of a doctor, a lawyer, and a person who is *neither* a doctor *nor* a lawyer.[21] The kinds of remedies that such boards devise are likely to reflect the particular priorities and assumptions of its members and may not be limited to the set of strictly legal remedies that spring most easily to the legally trained mind.

Administrative law has also been affected by what is variously called "new public management" theory, neoliberalism, or administrative structures that "span the public–private divide." Effectively, these are mechanisms by which public structures, such as administrative tribunals, retain ultimate accountability for their programs but "outsource" the implementation of those programs to private or third-party actors. For example, hundreds of standards developed by private bodies are incorporated into law and used for enforcement and compliance purposes.[22] Regulators also delegate enforcement and compliance functions to private bodies. For example, the Technical Standards and Safety Association (TSSA) is a delegated administrative authority for Ontario safety regulation covering elevating devices, amusement rides, boilers, and other products. The various provincial securities commissions also delegate the regulation of investment dealers and mutual fund dealers to their respective self-regulated organizations, the Investment Industry Regulatory Organization of Canada (IIROC) and the Mutual Fund Dealers Association (MFDA). Many professionals, including doctors and lawyers, are regulated in Canada by their self-governing professional bodies, which are not government agencies.

These are deeply embedded features of Canadian law, especially in fields where there are highly technical product or process issues to be regulated. They are also controversial, particularly as their use becomes more widespread and it becomes clear that "technical" standards are not so easily divorced from larger social and policy considerations. Proponents of "new governance"–style approaches argue that delegated implementation is the best way forward for administrative agencies that are otherwise at risk of being ineffective and out of touch; that it allocates action to those bodies best equipped and with the greatest information to perform tasks effectively; that public–private partnerships are capable of accomplishing public ends more efficiently than the public sector could acting alone; and that such

---

21 R.S.B.C. 1996, c. 288, s. 24.1(3). Additional guidelines on qualifications for part-time members of the board can be found in "Recruitment, Screening and Appointment Procedures" (Vancouver: British Columbia Review Board, 2004), online: British Columbia Review Board <http://www.bcrb.bc.ca/BCRB%20Recruitment%20 ProceduresFinal.pdf>.

22 For example, since 1927, the Canadian Standards Association's Canadian Electrical Code, Canadian Standards Association Standard C22.1-06, has provided the standards for addressing shock and fire hazards of electrical products in Canada. It has been incorporated by reference into provincial regulations across the country: see e.g. *Electrical Safety Regulation*, B.C. Reg. 100/2004, s. 20.

partnerships do not eliminate the public state, but rather "save" it from its own bureaucratic flaws.[23] Those opposed argue that these mechanisms are privatization by another name; that they reduce accountability and the public sector's responsibility for what should be publicly provided goods and services; and that they "hollow out" the state in potentially irretrievable ways.[24] We must leave this important debate for another day. At a practical level, though, parties to administrative actions should be aware that a constellation of ostensibly private actors may play more or less formal roles in real-life public administration.

A combination of these factors—ongoing seizin, a broad mandate, different expertise, and the trend toward crossing the public–private divide—have led some tribunals to create innovative remedies. One cluster of innovations incorporates an independent third party in trying to develop and implement remedial measures within a subject organization or corporation where systemic problems seem to be significant. These remedies try to effectuate meaningful systemic change within the organization through sustained engagement with the problem by an impartial outsider. They have become fairly common among securities regulators in particular, in both Canada and the United States.[25] An important function of the third party in this context is to facilitate a deliberative process within the organization itself—that is, to help the troubled organization confront and work through its problems internally. Some scholars argue that transparent, accountable, and broadly participatory dialogue of this nature, potentially facilitated by such third parties, is the most legitimate and most effective mechanism for making decisions in complex organizational structures.[26]

One effort at creating such a deliberative, third-party facilitated process took place within Ontario's Ministry of Correctional Services, as a response to a long-standing human

---

[23] Jody Freeman, "Private Parties, Public Functions, and the New Administrative Law" (2000) 52 Admin. L. Rev. 813; Richard Stewart, "Administrative Law in the Twenty-First Century" (2003) 78 N.Y.U. L. Rev. 437.

[24] See e.g. Harry Arthurs, "Public Law in a Neoliberal Globalized World: The Administrative State Goes to Market (and Cries 'Wee, Wee, Wee' All the Way Home)" (2005) 55 U.T.L.J. 797.

[25] Canadian examples include Settlement Agreement, Mackie Research Capital Corporation, 2010 BCSECCOM 646 (22 November 2010), online: <http://www.bcsc.bc.ca/comdoc.nsf/0/599572db2a73de48882577ed00618 775/$FILE/2010%20BCSECCOM%20646.pdf>; Settlement Agreement, *In the Matter of Union Securities Ltd. and John P. Thompson* (18 April 2006), online: <http://docs.iiroc.ca/DisplayDocument.aspx?Document ID=71522FD9816A452F8246B58D8776B613&Language=fr>; Order, *In the Matter of Agnico-Eagle Mines Limited* (28 April 2005), online: Ontario Securities Commission <http://www.osc.gov.on.ca/en/10499.htm>. In the United States, corporate monitorships have been imposed on dozens of corporations under the terms of deferred criminal prosecution agreements or regulatory enforcement settlements. On the effectiveness of corporate monitorships in that context, see Cristie Ford & David Hess, "Corporate Monitorships and New Governance Regulation: In Theory, in Practice, and in Context" (2011) 33:4 Law & Pol'y 509-541. The Australian Competition and Consumer Commission was a pioneer in developing what are known there as "enforceable undertakings": Christine Parker, "Restorative Justice in Business Regulation? The Australian Competition and Consumer Commissions Use of Enforceable Undertakings" (2004) 67 Mod. L. Rev. 209-246.

[26] See e.g. Amy Gutmann & Dennis Thompson, *Why Deliberative Democracy?* (Princeton, NJ: Princeton University Press, 2004); Michael C. Dorf, "Legal Indeterminacy and Institutional Design" (2003) 78 N.Y.U.L. Rev. 875; Lisa Blomgren Bingham, Tina Nabatchi, & Rosemary O'Leary, "The New Governance: Practices and Processes for Stakeholder and Citizen Participation in the Work of Government" (2005) 65 Pub. Admin. Rev. 547. But see César A. Rodríguez-Garavito, "Global Governance and Labor Rights: Codes of Conduct and Anti-Sweatshop Struggles in Global Apparel Factories in Mexico and Guatemala" (2005) *Politics & Society* 203.

rights complaint by an employee of the ministry.[27] The complainant in that case, Michael McKinnon, was a person of native Canadian ancestry and a correctional officer with the Ministry of Correctional Services. In 1998, the Human Rights Tribunal of Ontario (then the Board of Inquiry) found that Mr. McKinnon suffered discrimination and harassment at his workplace, the Toronto East Detention Centre, because of his race, ancestry, and ethnic origin. The tribunal ordered a number of systemic remedies to address a "poisoned atmosphere." Among other things, the tribunal ordered that certain individual respondents be relocated, that the tribunal's order be publicized among Corrections employees, and that a human rights training program be established. The tribunal reconvened the hearing in 2002 because of Mr. McKinnon's allegations that the poisoned work environment had not improved. The issue for the tribunal was not whether the existing systemic remedies had been implemented in a strict sense, but whether they had been carried out in good faith.

After dealing with the question whether it could remain seized of the matter—finding that it could, as affirmed later by the Ontario Court of Appeal[28]—the tribunal ordered an additional range of remedies, including training for ministry and facility management; establishing a roster of external mediators to deal with discrimination complaints; and appointing, at the ministry's expense, an independent third-party consultant nominated by the Ontario Human Rights Commission (OHRC) to develop and oversee the delivery of training programs ordered. The third-party consultant was to be nominated by the OHRC, to be paid for by the ministry, and to report to the tribunal. What makes these remedies interesting is that they are so different in character from traditional legal remedies, such as damages (in the civil context) or quashing of ministry or facility decisions (in the administrative law context). This looks like Chayes's public law litigation model: these remedies are prospective, open-ended, and subject to ongoing revision and elaboration. The tribunal's remedial orders—the emphasis on training, and bringing in the expertise of external human rights consultants to work with the ministry in developing that training—seem geared less toward redressing the wrongs against Mr. McKinnon in particular, and more toward effecting wide-ranging, permanent, *systemic* change to institutional culture.

The *McKinnon* case became the longest-running human rights case in Canada but, ultimately, it had a happy ending. In May 2005, the parties were still arguing over the scope of the third-party consultant's responsibilities, with the consultant alleging that the ministry was attempting to gain control over the process. The process of defining the consultant's mandate seemed itself to have become an adversarial contest that did not bode well for the consultant's ability to catalyze the hoped-for meaningful dialogue within the ministry.[29] By 2007, the tribunal found that the ministry had not been implementing the tribunal's previous orders in good faith,[30] and in February 2011 the tribunal found that a *prima facie* case

---

27   *McKinnon and Ontario Human Rights Commission v. Ontario (Ministry of Correctional Services) et al.*, [2002] O.H.R.B.I.D. No. 22 (22 November 2002), online: <http://www.opseu.org/legal/MichaelMcKinnonDecision .pdf>.

28   *Ontario v. McKinnon*, [2004] O.J. No. 5051 (QL), [2004] CarswellOnt 5191 (C.A.).

29   Human Rights Tribunal of Ontario, Interim Decisions and Rulings, *Ontario Human Rights Commission and Michael McKinnon and Ontario Ministry of Correctional Services et al.*, 2005 HRTO 15 (CanLII) (19 May 2005), online: <http://www.canlii.org/en/on/onhrt/doc/2005/2005hrto15/2005hrto15.html>.

30   *McKinnon v. Ontario (Minister of Correctional Services)*, 2007 HRTO 4.

had been made out that the deputy minister was in contempt for failing to implement the earlier orders. The tribunal exercised its discretion to state a case for contempt to the Ontario Divisional Court.[31] Before that could be heard, however, and after 23 years of litigation, Michael McKinnon and the ministry finally reached a settlement. Under the August 2011 settlement agreement, the OHRC, the Ministry of Community Safety and Correctional Services, and the Ministry of Government Services all signed on to a three-year Human Rights Project, which appears promising in its scope and structure. It establishes what looks like a meaningful training program, imposes high-level responsibility for adhering to human rights obligations, and includes all-important accountability mechanisms.[32]

The *McKinnon* settlement is cause for optimism, perhaps even celebration, but a good result for Mr. McKinnon was not a foregone conclusion. It might not have happened in the absence of a factor external to the tribunal process—the appointment of a new deputy minister of corrections with a mandate to professionalize the service and improve its record.[33] Nor is a 23-year-long litigation action an unalloyed victory, no matter what its outcome. In spite of its resolution, *McKinnon* raised and still leaves us with some challenging questions: is it possible to effect real, substantive "good faith" compliance in a truly recalcitrant employer like Corrections seemed to be (prior to the appointment of a new deputy minister)? Is it appropriate to use law to simultaneously enforce rights, redress wrongs, and "cure" systemic problems? Is it appropriate for a tribunal to continue crafting new orders in an effort to achieve an optimal outcome? Can external third parties really change culture and create meaningful dialogue? If not, what legal options do we have left—through tribunal remedies or otherwise?

As a final note, both tribunal-side and policy-side administrative functions have been affected by globalization. The effects of globalization mean that domestic administrative tribunals no longer act entirely free of international and transnational agreements, organizations, standard-setting bodies, and national commitments. Some of the most notable international examples come out of the European Union, whose policy and harmonization directives and court decisions have had a direct impact on European nation states' domestic administrative law. In Canada, as well, international obligations have had an impact on federal labour policies and their subsequent administration through a variety of public bodies,[34] and international

---

[31] *McKinnon v. Ontario (Correctional Services)*, 2011 HRTO 263.

[32] The Human Rights Project Charter that forms the backbone of the settlement is available online: Ontario Human Rights Commission <http://www.ontla.on.ca/library/repository/mon/25008/312240.pdf>.

[33] Note that the Toronto East Detention Centre is not the only facility at which correctional officers have alleged that they suffer discrimination and harassment based on their race or ancestry. In February 2012, a correctional officer at Toronto's Don Jail named Leroy Cox filed a complaint with the Ontario Human Rights Tribunal, alleging a campaign of hate mail directed at African-Canadian correctional officers going back to 2004. Mr. Cox claims that the mail is coming from fellow correctional officers. Like Mr. McKinnon, Mr. Cox alleges that his employer has not taken adequate affirmative steps to respond to the problem, and that the majority of Don Jail correctional officers do not participate in its ostensibly mandatory human rights training program. He also alleges, *inter alia*, that the Ontario Public Service Employees Union actively undermined an earlier investigation into the incidents. See http://www.cbc.ca/news/pdf/Affidavit-LeroyCox.pdf.

[34] Canada, Commission on Labour Standards Review, *Fairness at Work: Federal Labour Standards for the 21st Century* (Gatineau: Human Resources and Skills Development Canada, 2006) at 51-52, online: <http://www.hrsdc.gc.ca/eng/labour/employment_standards/fls/pdf/final_report.pdf>.

human rights norms have influenced the substantive review of administrative decisions.[35] Relevant international or transnational standards are sometimes set by governments acting together (such as the North American Free Trade Agreement [NAFTA] and its associated side agreements) and sometimes by independent, private, or non-governmental bodies filling lacunae in international law (as is the case with forest practices certification).[36] Looking at these developments, some scholars have even begun to herald the birth of a "global administrative law."[37]

The conversation about proper tribunal action spans multiple disciplines—law, public policy, and organizational and political theory—and it is taking place at the levels of practice and theory, both within tribunals and with respect to them. The forces that influence tribunals produce remedies that can be more dynamic and varied than the ones we are accustomed to seeing in the courts. Court review of tribunal remedies by means of judicial review serves a valuable "sober second thought" function, based on important rule-of-law values, but court action is only one facet of administrative law.

III. Enforcing Tribunal Orders Against Parties

After a tribunal makes a decision and imposes an order, assuming no one challenges that decision,[38] another set of administrative law remedies becomes available: the enforcement powers. These may be invoked where a tribunal needs to enforce its order against a party that is not complying with the order. This is not uncommon among self-regulatory organizations such as professional licensing bodies, where the tribunal acts against particular individuals rather than adjudicating disputes between parties. Alternatively, a party to a multiparty dispute before a tribunal may want to enforce the tribunal's order against another party on which the order was imposed. Criminal prosecution is also a possibility. Of course, regardless of any broader social patterns or systemic factors operating, tribunal orders can only be enforced against the parties on which they are imposed.

A. The Tribunal Seeks to Enforce Its Order

Rarely, a tribunal may enforce its own orders. One tribunal that has the power to enforce its own orders—for example, an order for civil contempt—is the federal Competition Tribunal.[39] Some other tribunals are also given the authority to enforce monetary obligations,

---

35   See Gerald Heckman, Chapter 14, The Role of International Human Rights Norms in Administrative Law.

36   Errol Meidinger, "The Administrative Law of Global Private–Public Regulation: The Case of Forestry" (2006) 17 E.J.I.L. 47.

37   Benedict Kingsbury, Nico Krisch & Richard B. Stewart, "The Emergence of Global Administrative Law" (2005) 68 Law & Contemp. Probs. 15.

38   See section IV.

39   *Competition Tribunal Act*, R.S.C. 1985, c. 19 (2d Supp.), s. 8(1). See *Chrysler Canada Ltd. v. Canada (Competition Tribunal)*, [1992] 2 S.C.R. 394, [1992] S.C.J. No. 64 (QL), 92 D.L.R. (4th) 609 [*Chrysler Canada*] (holding that clear and unambiguous statutory language can override the common-law rule that only superior courts have the power to punish for contempt and that the wording of the *Competition Tribunal Act*, s. 8(1) (as it then was), which conferred on the tribunal jurisdiction "to hear and determine all applications made under Part VIII of the *Competition Act* and any matters related thereto," constituted such clear and unambiguous statutory language).

such as requiring unpaid wages or family maintenance to be paid, imposing liens, making garnishment orders, seizing assets, or even suspending driving privileges.[40] However, any enforcement powers a tribunal has must be granted to the tribunal in its enabling statute, and that delegation of enforcement power must pass constitutional scrutiny. For example, a provincially created tribunal cannot have criminal (and therefore federal) enforcement powers.[41]

In British Columbia, certain sections of the *Administrative Tribunals Act* (ATA)[42] are intended to assist tribunals in obtaining compliance with their orders. For example, s. 18 permits certain tribunals to schedule a hearing, make a decision, or dismiss an application if a party fails to comply with an order (presumably, an order to appear). Section 31(1)(e) permits some tribunals to dismiss an application if the applicant fails to comply with a tribunal order. Section 47, which permits some tribunals to make orders for payment of costs, also allows some tribunals, under s. 47(1)(c), to require a party to pay the *tribunal's* actual costs "if the tribunal considers the conduct of a party has been improper, vexatious, frivolous or abusive." Orders for costs, on being filed in the court registry, have the same effect as a court order for the recovery of a debt (s. 47(2)).

More commonly, the tribunal must make an application in court to enforce any order it makes. Where a party has disobeyed a tribunal order, the statute provides that the tribunal may apply to court for an order requiring the person to comply.[43] The tribunal's order is presumed to be valid and correct if the party disobeying it failed to file an appeal (if one is available) or if the party appealed and lost.[44] Other statutes allow tribunal orders to be registered with the court, sometimes only with leave.[45] In Quebec, a distinct procedure known as homologation gives courts the authority to compel individuals to fulfill tribunal orders. Courts can only access homologation if it is expressly provided for in the tribunal's enabling statute.[46] The omnibus *Statutory Powers Procedure Act* in Ontario allows tribunals to state a case for contempt to the Ontario Divisional Court, as happened in the *McKinnon* case in 2011.

Once a tribunal has successfully converted its order into a court order through one of the mechanisms above, the order can be enforced in the same manner as a court judgment. Among other things, this means that the court can initiate contempt proceedings if the party

---

[40] E.g. *Employment Standards Act*, R.S.B.C. 1996, c. 113, ss. 87-101; *Maintenance Enforcement Act*, S.N.S. 1994-95, c. 6, ss. 19, 27-30.

[41] *MacMillan Bloedel Ltd. v. Simpson*, [1995] 4 S.C.R. 725, [1996] 2 W.W.R. 1; *United Nurses of Alberta v. Alberta (Attorney General)*, [1992] 1 S.C.R. 901, [1992] S.C.J. No. 37 (QL), 89 D.L.R. (4th) 609.

[42] ATA, *supra* note 11.

[43] See e.g. *Statutory Powers Procedure Act*, R.S.O. 1990, c. S.22, ss. 13 and 19, respectively.

[44] *British Columbia (Provincial Agricultural Land Commission) v. Pickell*, 1980 CanLII 509 (1980), 109 D.L.R. (3d) 465 at 473 (B.C.S.C.); *Estevan Coal Corp. v. Estevan (Rural Municipality No. 5)*, [2000] 8 W.W.R. 474, (2000), 199 Sask. R. 57 (C.A.).

[45] See e.g. ATA, *supra* note 11, ss. 47, 54.

[46] See e.g. *Regulation respecting the conciliation and arbitration procedure for the accounts of members of the Corporation professionnelle des physiothérapeutes du Québec*, R.R.Q., c. C-26, r. 141.1. For a more in-depth discussion on homologation, see René Dussault & Louis Borgeat, *Administrative Law: A Treatise*, 2d ed., vol. 2, trans. by Murray Rankin (Toronto: Carswell, 1985) at 283.

continues to disregard the order.[47] Contempt proceedings may be available if a party fails to abide by a tribunal's procedural order (for example, by failing to appear as a witness or to produce documents) or a tribunal's final substantive order.[48] Contempt can be civil or, where the conduct constitutes an intentional public act of defiance of the court, criminal.[49] In a contempt proceeding, the judge does not inquire into the validity of the tribunal's underlying order. However, only violations of "clear and unambiguous" tribunal orders will form the basis of a contempt order.[50] A court can also refuse to hold a party in contempt until an appeal or judicial review application (discussed in section IV below) is completed, although parties can be required to pay moneys into court in the meantime.[51]

Note that legislators seem content to house tribunal order enforcement powers in the courts, even while using privative clauses to try to limit the availability of judicial review from administrative tribunals. For the legislative drafter, then, recourse to courts to *enforce* tribunal orders seems to be acceptable, although recourse to courts to *challenge* tribunal orders is less so. There is history at work here, along with separation of powers concerns and the legislator's appreciation for courts' existing enforcement powers. Arguably, this drafting choice also signals that legislators may be most concerned about conserving scarce judicial resources when those judicial resources might be deployed to undermine, rather than buttress and reinforce, the authority of the tribunals the legislation creates.

B. A Party Seeks to Enforce a Tribunal's Order

A party to an administrative action may also bring an action against another party in court to enforce the tribunal's order. For example, a group of teachers may seek to enforce an arbitrator's order that a school board annually set aside certain funds for teachers' professional development.[52] Sara Blake has suggested that the party's success "may depend on whether the tribunal order is of a type that a court would enforce, and whether the court believes it should enforce the tribunal order in the absence of any statutory procedure for obtaining court assistance."[53] In other words, courts may be more likely to grant a private application

---

47   Tribunals themselves may have the power to make orders for *in facie* contempt (contempt "in the face of" the court during the proceedings) because this power is implicit in the designation of a tribunal as a court of record. If a tribunal is not designated as such, then the power to punish for *in facie* contempt, like the power to punish for *ex facie* contempt (contempt outside the proceedings), must be explicitly conferred by the enabling statute. *Chrysler Canada, supra* note 39.

48   See e.g. *Statutory Powers Procedure Act, supra* note 43, s. 13.

49   *United Nurses of Alberta v. Alberta (Attorney General)*, [1992] 1 S.C.R. 901, [1992] S.C.J. No. 37 (QL), 89 D.L.R. (4th) 609.

50   *Chrysler Canada, supra* note 39; *United Food & Commercial Workers, Local 1252 v. Western Star*, [1995] N.J. No. 334 (QL), 130 D.L.R. (4th) 538 (S.C.(T.D)); *Toronto Transit Commission v. Ryan*, [1998] O.J. No. 51 (QL), 37 O.R. (3d) 266 (Gen. Div.).

51   *Boucher v. Logistik Unicorp Inc.*, [2001] J.Q. No. 64 (QL) (C.A.), leave to appeal to S.C.C. refused [2001] C.S.C.R. No. 115; *Sodema Inc. v. Sarafian*, [2006] J.Q. No. 5460 (QL) (C.A.).

52   *Melia v. Moose Jaw Roman Catholic Separate School District No. 22*, [1979] S.J. No. 568 (QL), 108 D.L.R. (3d) 113 (C.A.); *Twentieth Century-Fox Corp. Ltd. v. Broadway Theatres Ltd.*, [1951] 3 D.L.R. 105 (Sask. C.A.).

53   Sara Blake, *Administrative Law in Canada*, 4th ed. (Markham, ON: LexisNexis Butterworths, 2006) at 226.

to enforce a tribunal order where the court recognizes the tribunal's order as similar to the kind of order that a court might make. However, the private applicant will first have the difficult task of convincing the court that it should intervene in this way, even though there may be no statutory provision explicitly empowering it to do so.

C. Criminal Prosecution

Many statutes provide for quasi-criminal prosecution of persons who disobey tribunal orders. Quasi-criminal offences are prosecuted by the federal or provincial Crown, as appropriate, and they carry penalties that include fines and imprisonment. For example, a person who commits an offence under s. 155 of the B.C. *Securities Act*[54] is liable to a fine of not more than $3 million, to imprisonment for not more than three years, or both. Indictable offences under the federal *Fisheries Act* may attract, at their upper end, fines of up to $500,000 or imprisonment for up two years, or both.[55]

In the absence of other provisions, it is a criminal offence to disobey a lawful order of a federal or provincial tribunal. The federal *Criminal Code* states:

> 127(1) Every one who, without lawful excuse, disobeys a lawful order made by a court of justice *or by a person or body of persons authorized by any Act to make or give the order*, other than an order for the payment of money, is, *unless a punishment or other mode of proceeding is expressly provided by law*, guilty of
>> (a) an indictable offence and liable to imprisonment for a term not exceeding two years;
> or
>> (b) an offence punishable on summary conviction.[56]

The *Criminal Code* provision is only available where no other penalty is expressly provided by law. What does this mean? Superior courts' own contempt powers do not count as an "other mode of proceeding" for purposes of this section.[57] Most administrative tribunals do not have the ability to make contempt orders on their own. Therefore, the *Criminal Code* provisions should apply where no "punishment or other mode of proceeding" is explicitly set out in the *tribunal's enabling statute*. This has been held not to violate the constitutional separation of powers, even when dealing with provincial tribunals, on the basis that the provincial tribunal is still making orders that are non-criminal. Parliament, acting within its sphere, is the one that has decided that breach of those provincial provisions is a criminal offence.[58]

---

54   *Supra* note 7.

55   R.S.C. 1985, c. F-14, s. 78(b).

56   R.S.C. 1985, c. C-46, s. 127(1) (emphasis added).

57   Unless the court's contempt powers are laid out comprehensively in the Rules of Court: *R. v. Clement*, [1981] 2 S.C.R. 468, [1981] S.C.J. No. 93 (QL); *R. v. Mulhall*, [2001] O.J. No. 5237 (QL) (Ct. J.). But see *Telus Communications Inc. v. Telecommunications Workers Union*, [2007] B.C.A. 413, 2007 Carswell BC 1851.

58   *United Nurses of Alberta v. Alberta (Attorney General)*, [1992] 1 S.C.R. 901.

IV. Challenging Administrative Action

A party to an administrative action may also decide to challenge that administrative action directly. The possible bases for a party's challenge are described in other chapters in this text. For example, a party may challenge the tribunal's jurisdiction, its procedure, its impartiality, its exercise of discretion, or the substance of its final decision. Each of these usually amounts to a direct or indirect challenge to the remedies or orders the tribunal imposes. Sometimes, these challenges are made through applications for judicial review. However, judicial review is only one method of challenging administrative action. Applications for judicial review, like litigation generally, can be expensive and drawn-out affairs. Moreover, it is important to be realistic about what can be achieved through judicial review. In order to bring a successful judicial review application, a challenger must be aware of the specific remedial mechanisms available and how those mechanisms will help him or her achieve the result that he or she wants. For example, a motion to quash a tribunal decision for lack of procedural fairness, if successful, will likely lead to the court sending the matter back to the original tribunal for rehearing.[59] This result may not satisfy the challenger. Even assuming that procedural fairness is observed the second time, there is no guarantee that the party will receive the substantive outcome he or she seeks.

For these reasons, parties seeking to challenge administrative action should consider their options carefully. This part of the chapter outlines the various mechanisms available, including both non-court mechanisms and court-based mechanisms. We begin first with mechanisms that are internal to the administrative apparatus itself, then move to mechanisms that exist externally to both the administrative agency and courts (for example, ombudspersons), finally turning to court-based mechanisms. Here we distinguish between appeals and judicial review and discuss private law remedies that may exist against tribunals.

A. Internal Tribunal Mechanisms

A party considering a challenge to tribunal action will need to understand the particular tribunal's structure and capacity, as established by its enabling statute. All tribunals can fix certain things, such as clerical errors or factual errors due to mistake or dishonesty, without express statutory authority. This is sometimes called the "slip rule."[60] Tribunals can also "change their minds" until the time a final decision is made. Therefore, what constitutes a "final decision" is important. For example, if a statute provides that final decisions must be in writing, then only written decisions will constitute final decisions. Preliminary rulings can also be changed until the final decision on a matter has been made.[61]

---

[59] See Grant Huscroft, Chapter 5, From Natural Justice to Fairness: Thresholds, Content, and the Role of Judicial Review.

[60] See e.g. *Chandler v. Alberta Association of Architects*, [1989] 2 S.C.R. 848 at 861 [*Chandler*]; *Muscillo Transport Ltd. v. Ontario (Licence Suspension Appeal Board)* (1997), 149 D.L.R. (4th) 545 at 553 (Ont. Gen. Div.), aff'd [1998] O.J. No. 1488 (QL) (C.A.).

[61] *Comeau's Sea Foods Limited v. Canada (Minister of Fisheries and Oceans)*, [1997] 1 S.C.R. 12.

Some enabling statutes specifically provide tribunals with the ability to reconsider and rehear decisions they have made. This is most common where a particular tribunal has ongoing regulatory responsibility over a particular domain, such as public utilities regulation or employer–employee relations. For example, the *Public Service Labour Relations Act* provides, "[s]ubject to subsection (2) [prohibiting retroactive effect of any rights acquired], the Board may review, rescind or amend any of its orders or decisions, or may re-hear any application before making an order in respect of the application."[62] Absent such express statutory authority, however, for policy reasons that favour finality of proceedings, a tribunal cannot reconsider or alter a final decision made within its jurisdiction. Once it has made a final decision, the tribunal is *functus officio*.[63]

Some administrative tribunals are part of multitiered administrative agencies. Those tribunals' enabling statutes may provide for appeals internal to the administrative agency itself. For example, parties appearing before Canada's Immigration and Refugee Board Immigration Division may appeal to its Immigration Appeal Division.[64] Similarly, provincial securities acts across the country provide that persons directly affected by decisions made by Securities Commission staff may appeal to (or, in some statutes, seek "review" from) the commission itself, to which staff reports.[65] Again, parties should be aware that internal appellate structures may not look much like courts.

These internal review proceedings do not preclude subsequent appeals to the courts. Indeed, the various provincial Securities Acts mentioned above provide for appeals under limited conditions from their internal appellate bodies to the courts. These are called "statutory appeals." Where the statute does not provide for an appeal to the courts, the parties' only access to the courts is by means of judicial review. However, as discussed in more detail below, where a statute provides for reconsideration or appeals, a challenger should generally exhaust those avenues before making an application for judicial review.

One of the more interesting innovations in internal administrative appeals was created in 1996, with the passage of Quebec's *Administrative Justice Act*.[66] The statute creates the Tribunal administratif du Québec (TAQ), a supertribunal that hears "proceedings" brought against almost all administrative tribunals and public bodies in the province, including government departments, boards, commissions, municipalities, and healthcare bodies.[67] As a practical matter, this means that there is now one main appellate/review

---

62 *Public Service Labour Relations Act*, S.C. 2003, c. 22, s. 43.

63 *Chandler, supra* note 60. Because rights of appeal from tribunals tend to be more limited than from courts, the *functus officio* doctrine should be more flexible and less formulistic for such tribunals.

64 *Immigration and Refugee Protection Act*, S.C. 2001, c. 27, ss. 62-71, 174-175. Recourse to the courts is only available with leave of the Federal Court: *ibid.*, s. 72.

65 See e.g. Ontario *Securities Act*, R.S.O. 1990, c. S.5, s. 8(2); Alberta *Securities Act*, R.S.A. 2000, c. S-4, s. 35(1); British Columbia *Securities Act, supra* note 7, ss. 165(3), 167(1).

66 R.S.Q., c. J-3.

67 *Ibid.*, s. 14. The use of the word "proceedings" rather than "appeal" or "review" indicates that the tribunal can hear appeals in the traditional sense, but it can also hear various demands that look more or less like review or *révision*. The scope and nature of the available proceedings depend on the wording of each tribunal's enabling statute.

body for administrative matters in the province. According to the Act, the tribunal's purpose is "to affirm the specific character of administrative justice, to ensure its quality, promptness and accessibility and to safeguard the fundamental rights of citizens."[68] It is an administrative (that is, executive branch) institution, not a judicial one, but its remedial powers include judicial review-style options and, surprisingly, the ability to substitute its decision for an original tribunal's: "[i]n the case of the contestation of a decision, the Tribunal may confirm, vary or quash the contested decision and, if appropriate, make the decision which, in its opinion, should have been made initially."[69] Where the TAQ has jurisdiction to consider a proceeding, claimants should exhaust the remedies available from it rather than trying to circumvent the administrative process.[70] Avenues of appeal from the TAQ to the Superior Court of Quebec are limited.[71]

B. External Non-Court Mechanisms

A party considering a challenge to administrative action should not overlook non-legal avenues. For example, ombudspersons or similar positions exist by statute in every Canadian province. There is no overarching federal ombudsperson, but some federal departments and subject areas have their own specialized ombudspersons. For example, in 2007 and 2008, respectively, the federal government created a Federal Ombudsman for Victims of Crime and a Taxpayers' Ombudsman.[72] Generally, the mandate of an ombudsperson is to provide a forum for citizens to bring their complaints regarding the way that government departments and agencies have dealt with them. There is no charge to make a complaint to an ombudsperson. Ombudspersons have discretion as to whether or not they will investigate a complaint.

An ongoing issue has been the degree to which an ombudsperson can assert jurisdiction with respect to administrative tribunal decisions and processes (as opposed to the general run of government departments and ministries—that is, public servants not possessing the statutorily created decision-making structure that tribunals have). Most legislation defines the ombudsperson's jurisdiction as being over "matters of administration," and courts have tended to define "administration" expansively as involving generic administrative processes,

---

68 *Ibid.*, s. 1.

69 *Ibid.*, s. 15.

70 *Okwuobi et al. v. Lester B. Pearson School Board; Casimir v. Quebec (Attorney General); Zorrilla v. Quebec (Attorney General)*, 2005 SCC 16, [2005] 1 S.C.R. 257.

71 The tribunal is composed of four divisions (social affairs, immovable property, territory and environment, and economic affairs), but, per s. 159 of the Act, an appeal to the court is only available from the immovable property division and from decisions regarding the preservation of agricultural land. This tracks the appeals that were available from those tribunals before the TAQ was created; the TAQ replaced a plethora of administrative appeal bodies, but was not intended to increase the number of available appeals to the courts.

72 Their respective websites are online: Federal Ombudsman for Victims of Crime <http://www.victimsfirst .gc.ca/index.html> and Taxpayers' Ombudsman <http://www.oto-boc.gc.ca/menu-eng.html>. The gender-neutral term "ombudsperson" seems to have become the standard term in Canada, although the word "ombudsman" is an old Scandinavian word, not a gender-specific English word. Other gender-neutral terms include "ombuds office" and simply "ombuds."

not simply as the antonym of "judicial" processes.[73] Among the tribunals themselves, the range of bodies subject to an ombudsperson's investigatory powers can be quite broad. In Ontario, for example, the courts have held that even largely independent bodies can be subject to ombuds review if the government pays its members' wages.[74] However, most ombuds statutes provide that an ombudsperson is not authorized to investigate a tribunal's decision until after any right of appeal or review on the merits has been exercised or until after the time limit for doing so has expired.[75]

Several other public officials similar to ombudspersons also exist, including freedom of information and privacy commissioners, the auditor general, provincial auditors, and human rights commissioners. While harder for individuals to instigate, public inquiries are another mechanism for challenging government conduct.[76]

C. Using the Courts: Statutory Appeals

The ability to challenge administrative action in the courts is a mixed, but necessary, blessing. On the downside, courts may be reluctant to embrace novel, non-courtlike, yet potentially effective remedies devised by specialized tribunals. The richness and creativity that characterize administrative law remedies could be stifled by overjudicialized, overly interventionist court scrutiny. This is one reason that the internal appeal mechanisms described above make sense. On the other hand, there are times—for example, during national emergencies—when executive action unquestionably needs to be subject to the rule of law, as applied by independent courts.[77] As with so many things in administrative law, context matters in thinking about the legitimacy of each alternative. There may be times when it makes sense to maintain the integrity of the administrative regime through all internal appeal stages. There may also be times when what is required is faster and unapologetic recourse to the courts—for example, allowing a party to "leapfrog" the internal appeals and proceed directly to judicial review.

There are two main ways by which a party to a tribunal action can access the courts to challenge that action: appeal and judicial review. Appeal mechanisms—either to internal

---

73 For example, in *British Columbia Development Corporation v. Friedmann (Ombudsman)*, [1984] 2 S.C.R. 447, the Supreme Court ruled that policy-making activities of provincial Crown corporations were "matters of administration" for the purposes of the *Ombudsman Act*. The Ontario Court of Appeal has interpreted the ombudsperson's jurisdiction over "administration of a government agency" to include investigations into matters determined by administrative tribunals: *Ombudsman of Ontario v. Ontario (Labour Relations Board)* (1986), 44 D.L.R. (4th) 312 (Ont. C.A.).

74 *Ontario (Ombudsman) v. Ontario (Health Disciplines Board)* (1979), 104 D.L.R. (3d) 597 (Ont. C.A.).

75 See e.g. the Yukon *Ombudsman Act*, R.S.Y. 2002, c. 163, s. 12. The Manitoba *Ombudsman Act*, C.C.S.M. c. O45, s. 18(d) and the Saskatchewan *Ombudsman and Children's Advocate Act*, R.S.S. 1978, c. O-4, s. 15(1)(d) provide that rights of appeal or review preclude an ombudsperson's intervention "unless the Ombudsman is satisfied that in the particular case it would have been unreasonable to expect the complainant to resort to the tribunal or court," although the time limitation for appeal or review must still have run.

76 See Peter Carver, Chapter 16, Getting the Story Out: Accountability and the Law of Public Inquiries.

77 See Mary Liston, Chapter 2, Governments in Miniature: The Rule of Law in the Administrative State. The national security context is also treated differently: consider *Canada (Prime Minister) v. Khadr*, 2010 SCC 3, [2010] 1 S.C.R. 44 [*Khadr*].

administrative appellate bodies or to courts—are the norm. Judicial review is the exception.[78] Significantly, judicial review is also discretionary. The scope of a possible appeal is confined to what the statute expressly provides. This means that, even though courts struggle sometimes with knotty issues in taking appeals from administrative tribunals, relative to judicial review it is easier to predict the availability and likely outcome of an appeal. By contrast, judicial review doctrine is the product of decades of contentious court battles, modified from time to time by statute, directly pitting "legal" values of justice and the rule of law against "democratic" values and legislative intent, as well as "bureaucratic" values such as efficiency and expertise. Even the seemingly basic questions of whether judicial review is available in a particular situation and what remedies are available through judicial review have been shaped by this debate.

1. Is an Appeal Available?

Below are the major questions a party must ask to determine whether an appeal from a tribunal to the courts is available to him or her.

a. Does the Tribunal's Enabling Statute Provide for a Right of Appeal?

Courts have no inherent appellate jurisdiction over administrative tribunals.[79] A right to appeal must be provided for in a tribunal's enabling statute. If a statute does not so provide, a dissatisfied party will have to access the courts by way of judicial review. Moreover, parties generally may not appeal interlocutory rulings (for example, on jurisdiction, procedural or evidentiary issues, or bias).[80] To be appealable, the tribunal's decision must decide the merits of the matter or otherwise be a final disposition of it.[81]

Usually, a tribunal's enabling statute will also set out the court to which tribunal orders may be appealed. For federal tribunals, appeals are usually taken to the Federal Court or the Federal Court of Appeal.[82] Appeals from provincially constituted tribunals may be taken to the province's trial court of general jurisdiction,[83] to a divisional court,[84] or to the court of

---

[78] David J. Mullan, *Administrative Law* (Toronto: Irwin Law, 2001) at 462.

[79] *Medora v. Dental Society*, [1984] N.B.J. No. 236 (QL), 56 N.B.R. (2d) 145 at 147 (C.A.).

[80] *Mary & David Goodine Diary Farm v. New Brunswick (Milk Marketing Board)*, [2002] N.B.J. No. 177 (QL), 217 D.L.R. (4th) 708 (C.A.); *Roosma v. Ford Motor Co. of Canada Ltd.* (1988), 66 O.R. (2d) 18 (Div. Ct.); *Newfoundland Transport Ltd. v. Newfoundland (Public Utilities Board)*, [1983] N.J. No. 92 (QL), 45 Nfld. & P.E.I.R. 76 at 78 (C.A.); *contra, Fox v. Registered Nurses' Assn.*, [2002] N.S.J. No. 376 (QL), 207 N.S.R. (2d) 330 (C.A.).

[81] *Ontario (Human Rights Commission) v. Ontario Teachers' Federation*, [1994] O.J. No. 1585 (QL), 19 O.R. (3d) 371 (Gen. Div.); *Prince Albert (City) v. Riocan Holding Inc.*, [2004] S.J. No. 337 (QL), 241 D.L.R. (4th) 308 (C.A.).

[82] Respectively, see e.g. *Trade-marks Act*, R.S.C. 1985, c. T-13, s. 56; and *Competition Tribunal Act, supra* note 39, s. 13.

[83] See e.g. Nunavut's *Travel and Tourism Act*, R.S.N.W.T. 1988, c. T-7, s. 8.

[84] See e.g. Ontario's *Expropriations Act*, R.S.O. 1990, c. E.26, s. 31.

appeal.[85] Rarely, a statute will provide a right (seldom exercised) to appeal a tribunal decision to Cabinet itself.[86]

b. What Is the Scope of Available Appeal?

Just as the enabling statute determines whether a statutory appeal is available in the first place, the enabling statute entirely determines its scope. That scope varies enormously from tribunal to tribunal. Some statutes permit complete *de novo* review of a tribunal's decision, while others will be limited to issues of law based entirely on the record. In other words, an appellate court's jurisdiction in reviewing *tribunal* decisions may be different in scope from an appellate court's jurisdiction in reviewing lower *court* decisions. Appellate courts generally review trial court decisions for error of law or, more rarely, for palpable and overriding error in a finding of fact. By contrast, a court that has been designated to take appeals from a tribunal's decision must look to the tribunal's enabling statute to determine the breadth and scope of its appellate powers.

Arguably, the scope of an available appeal is determined by how closely the tribunal's subject matter, and its expertise, mirror the mandate and expertise of general courts. Statutes are more likely to provide a right of appeal to the courts where the tribunal has the power to affect individuals' common-law rights (for example, human rights tribunals, land-use planning tribunals, and professional licensing). Labour relations and employment-related matters, which have long been adjudicated by tripartite boards with specialized expertise and which involve claims by organized labour to which courts were historically perceived to be hostile, cannot generally be appealed to the courts.[87] The same considerations affect the scope of available appeal. For example, statutes generally provide for a broad power to appeal from certain professional disciplinary tribunals on questions of fact and law, where professionals risk losing their ability to practise their profession,[88] and from human rights tribunals adjudicating on violations of human rights codes.[89] Yet even where the appeal rights are broad, courts will show some deference to a tribunal's findings of fact on the assumption that the tribunal had the evidence before it and was in a better position to make those findings.[90] Unlike judicial review, however, at least where there is a broadly worded statutory right of appeal, courts are not expected to defer to tribunals "because of the mere fact that the *legislature designated them*—and not the courts—as the decision-makers of first instance.[91]

---

85   See e.g. Newfoundland and Labrador's *Law Society Act, 1999*, S.N.L. 1999, c. L-9.1, s. 55.

86   See e.g. *Broadcasting Act*, S.C. 1991, c. 11, s. 28.

87   David J. Mullan et al., *Administrative Law: Cases, Text, and Materials*, 5th ed. (Toronto: Emond Montgomery, 2003) at 23.

88   See e.g. *Ontario College of Teachers Act, 1996*, S.O. 1996, c. 12, s. 35(4). See also *Reddall v. College of Nurses of Ontario* (1983), 149 D.L.R. (3d) 60 (Ont. C.A.). Ontario statutes in particular tend to provide explicitly for appeal from various tribunals "on questions of law or fact or both."

89   See e.g. Ontario *Human Rights Code, supra* note 8, s. 42(3); also *Zurich Insurance Co. v. Ontario (Human Rights Commission)*, [1992] 2 S.C.R. 321 at 336-38 [*Zurich*].

90   *Zurich, ibid.*

91   *Smith v. Alliance Pipeline Ltd.*, 2011 SCC 7, [2011] 1 S.C.R. 160 at para. 108 [emphasis added].

c. Is an Appeal Available as of Right, or Is Leave Required? If Leave Is Required, Who May Grant It?

Appeals can be as of right or require leave. Where leave must be obtained, it can be the leave either of the original decision-maker or, more frequently, of the appellate body (that is, the court). For example, British Columbia's *Forest Practices Code* provides for an appeal as of right from the Forest Appeals Commission to the B.C. Supreme Court on questions of law or jurisdiction. By contrast, a person affected by a decision of the B.C. Securities Commission may appeal to the B.C. Court of Appeal only with leave of a justice of that court.[92] Sometimes, additional statutory criteria must also be met before such leave will be granted.[93]

d. Is a Stay of Proceedings Automatic, or Must One Apply for It?

The rules governing stays of proceedings vary between jurisdictions and even tribunals. Specific enabling statutes may expressly empower their tribunals or the appellate bodies (internal or court) to which they appeal to stay enforcement of the tribunal order pending appeal.[94] The Ontario *Statutory Powers Procedure Act* establishes a default rule that an appeal operates as a stay of a tribunal's proceedings.[95] The B.C. *Administrative Tribunals Act*, by contrast, provides that "the commencement of an appeal does not operate as a stay or suspend the operation of the decision being appealed unless the tribunal orders otherwise."[96] In the Federal Court, as well, stays of proceedings are usually discretionary.[97] Unless a statute specifically excludes it, as B.C.'s ATA does, the superior court that is the tribunal's designated appellate court has the inherent authority to grant a stay.[98]

Like the legislative decision to permit appeals as of right or only with leave, a legislative decision to make a stay automatic or not says something about how the legislature views the tribunals in question. Requiring potential appellants to apply for leave to appeal places an

---

92   Compare *Forest Practices Code of British Columbia Act*, R.S.B.C. 1996, c. 159, s. 141 with *Securities Act, supra* note 7, s. 167.

93   For example, an appeal to the Federal Court of Appeal from judicial review by the Federal Court on immigration matters may be made only if the Federal Court judge certifies that "a serious question of general importance" is involved. *Immigration and Refugee Protection Act, supra* note 64, s. 74.

94   See e.g. *Re Hampton Court Resources Inc.*, 2006 ABASC 1447 (June 13, 2006) (holding that, taken together, s. 38(5) of the Alberta *Securities Act* and the provisions of the Alberta Rules of Court require that a stay of a commission decision be sought in the first instance from the commission).

95   *Statutory Powers Procedure Act, supra* note 43, s. 25.

96   ATA, *supra* note 11, s. 25.

97   *Federal Courts Act*, R.S.C. 1985, c. F-7, s. 50(1); but see s. 50.1 concerning mandatory stays of claims against the Crown under certain conditions. In a case in which the minister of citizenship and immigration was seeking to stay an order that a potential refugee be released from detention on the basis that the refugee represented a danger to the public, the Court noted that the granting of a stay requires (1) a serious issue to be tried; (2) that irreparable harm would be suffered if no stay were granted; and (3) that the balance of convenience favour granting the order. The Court also noted that the serious issue threshold "cannot automatically be met simply by formulating a ground of judicial review which, on its face, appears to be arguable." *Cardoza Quinteros v. Canada (Citizenship and Immigration)*, 2008 FC 643 at paras. 10, 13.

98   *Kooner v. College of Physicians and Surgeons of Ontario* (2002), 213 D.L.R. (4th) 707 (Ont. Div. Ct.).

additional hurdle before them. Automatically staying a tribunal's decision holds its powers in abeyance while a court checks the tribunal's decision. Where the legislature decides that stays will not be automatic, the legislature may choose to allocate the power to order a stay either to the tribunal or to a court. These statutory drafting decisions reflect the legislature's assessment of the proper balancing of "due process" and efficiency concerns, the balance between tribunal expertise and judicial oversight, and the legislature's comfort with granting broad autonomy to the relevant tribunal.

D. Using the Courts: Judicial Review

Now, finally, we discuss the tail of judicial review that sometimes wags the dog of administrative law remedies. Judicial review has long been the fixation of administrative law, at the expense of tribunal-based and extralegal mechanisms and statutory appeals—not to mention the hugely important arena of administrative rulemaking—in part because administrative law is created primarily by judges, lawyers, and legal scholars. The legal training these individuals receive is, understandably, preoccupied with legal mechanisms and, in particular, with courts and the common law.

Having situated judicial review in its broader context, it nonetheless deserves careful attention. Judicial review can be conceptually and logistically complex, and it differs from a straightforward appeal. As we shall see throughout this volume, the basic nature of judicial review is different from statutory or internal tribunal appeals because, at its root, judicial review is about the inherent jurisdiction of courts to oversee and check administrative (that is, executive) action in the interest of the rule of law. This makes it a potentially sweeping remedy. Unlike appeals from tribunals, which are statutorily created, judicial review is the review of executive action *beyond* what the legislature provided for. Thus, only on judicial review will courts investigate a tribunal's procedural fairness or the alleged bias of its members.

1. Discretionary Bases for Refusing a Remedy

A court's decision whether to grant judicial review is intimately bound up with the core tension that underlies all of administrative law—what the Supreme Court recently called "an underlying tension between the rule of law and the foundational democratic principle, which finds an expression in the initiatives of Parliament and legislatures to create various administrative bodies and endow them with broad powers."[99] Courts are the indispensable guardians of the rule of law, but they still need to operate within their sphere of authority. This means respecting the fact that, through enabling statutes, legislatures grant authority over certain things to administrative tribunals, *and not to the courts themselves*. A lot of administrative law jurisprudence is devoted to trying to negotiate a path through the difficult territory on the borders of the branches' spheres of authority. What concerns us here is the threshold question of whether to grant judicial review at all—before considering the merits of the case, before figuring out the standard of review, and before determining the degree of procedural fairness a party is entitled to. Judicial review is fundamentally discretionary in a

---

[99]   *Dunsmuir v. New Brunswick*, 2008 SCC 9, [2008] 1 S.C.R. 190 at para. 27 [*Dunsmuir*].

way that appeals are not. A court has the discretion to refuse to grant a remedy even where one seems clearly warranted by the facts of a case.[100]

Interestingly, courts' handling of courts' *own* discretion in granting judicial review is following a different trajectory than the case law dealing with administrative tribunals' exercises of *their* discretion, conferred on them via statute. As Geneviève Cartier discusses in Chapter 11, Administrative Discretion: Between Exercising Power and Conducting Dialogue, there was a time when statutorily conferred administrative discretion was understood to be "beyond law." Its exercise could be subject to judicial review only if it amounted to an abuse of discretion. A number of specific heads of "abuse of discretion" existed, and getting judicial relief depended on falling into one of them. Anything short of the abuse-of-discretion threshold would not attract review, even if the administrative decision was seriously flawed, because the legislature had conferred discretion on the administrative decision-maker. This changed with the *Baker* case,[101] which rejected the conceptual distinction between discretion and law. That case held that reviewing courts should subject exercises of administrative discretion to the same evaluative process—what we now call the "standard of review analysis"—to which they subject *non*-discretionary administrative decisions. This shifted the approach from review based on a series of specific "abuse of discretion" grounds, to review based on a more flexible, context-sensitive array of factors.

When it comes to courts' *own* discretionary decision to grant judicial review, recent cases from the Supreme Court of Canada seem to be doing something quite different. Put frankly, the Court seems to be moving away from an institutional dialogue-based view of the rule of law toward something more court-centred. It is affirming courts' own power (as opposed to the power of legislatures) to establish the terms on which it will grant judicial review, while also trying to corral lower courts' discretion into the kinds of discrete categories that the *Baker* case moved away from with respect to administrative discretion. In the process, the Court is reaffirming the courts' mantle as guardians of the rule of law, validating the concept of the rule of law, and holding lower courts more closely to it. The Court seems to be moving away from a real humility about the rule of law and the role of the courts in defining it, which characterized some of the jurisprudence from the 1990s. The evolution can be discussed in terms of three broad stages.

The original set of discretionary grounds for refusing relief derive from common law and equity and survived the statutory reform of judicial review. They are reminiscent of similar equity-based grounds in civil procedure, such as laches, and (with the possible exception of point one below) are fairly intuitive in the same way that laches is:

1. The most important basis for refusing to grant a remedy in judicial review is discussed above: that *adequate alternative remedies are available*. Parties should exhaust all prescribed avenues of appeal before proceeding to the "last resort" of judicial review.

2. Judicial review applications that are brought before tribunal proceedings have been concluded are usually dismissed as being *premature*. This includes challenges to the

---

100   *Immeubles Port Louis Ltée v. Lafontaine (Village)*, [1991] 1 S.C.R. 326.

101   *Baker v. Canada (Minister of Citizenship and Immigration)*, [1999] 2 S.C.R. 817.

tribunal's interim procedural and evidentiary rulings. The policy rationales that underlie dismissals for prematurity include: (a) that administrative action is meant to be more cost-effective than court proceedings, and interim judicial review fragments and protracts those proceedings; (b) that preliminary complaints may become moot as the proceedings progress; and (c) that the court will be in a better position to assess the situation once a full and complete record of tribunal proceedings exists.[102] To obtain judicial review of a tribunal's preliminary or interim ruling, an applicant must show special circumstances, which mean one cannot wait until the conclusion of the proceeding. A challenge to the legality of the tribunal itself, a clear question of law about the tribunal's jurisdiction, or the absence of an appropriate remedy at the end of the proceedings may constitute special or exceptional circumstances.[103]

3. Even if statutory time limits for filing a judicial review application have been met, parties must be aware that *delay and acquiescence* may be grounds for a reviewing court to refuse a remedy.[104] Parties should object promptly to any perceived impropriety on the part of the tribunal. Similarly, choosing not to attend a hearing could waive any right to judicial review.

4. A remedy in judicial review will not be granted where the issues are *moot*. This may be the case where a dispute is over or has not yet arisen, where a tribunal's order has expired or no longer affects the applicant, or where the litigant no longer actually wants the remedy that the tribunal might have granted had it not erred.[105] The court may also refuse to provide the remedy the tribunal would have granted if present circumstances make doing so impossible, or if the court believes the tribunal's error did not affect its overall conclusion.[106]

5. The court will use its discretion to refuse to grant a remedy on judicial review where the party making the judicial review application *does not come with clean hands.* This could include seeking a remedy to facilitate illegal conduct or to obtain an unfair advantage, or flouting the law or making misrepresentations.[107]

By the 1990s, these long-standing grounds for refusing relief came to be overlayered with a different vision of judicial review that reflects a new sensitivity to separation of powers issues and increased deference toward administrative tribunals. The overarching principle of curial deference toward administrative decision making percolated throughout the judicial

---

[102] See e.g. *Sherman v. Canada (Canada Customs and Revenue Agency)*, [2006] F.C.J. No. 912 (QL); *Zündel v. Canada (Human Rights Commission)*, [2000] 4 F.C. 255 (C.A.); *Quebec (Procureur general) v. Boulaine*, [2004] J.Q. No. 4883 (QL) (C.A.), leave to S.C.C. refused [2004] C.S.C.R. No. 290 (QL).

[103] *Secord v. Saint John (City) Board of Police Commissioners*, [2006] N.B.J. No. 84 (QL) (Q.B.); *Howe v. Institute of Chartered Accountants of Ontario* (1994), 19 O.R. (3d) 483 (C.A.).

[104] *Immeubles Port Louis, supra* note 100.

[105] *Borowski v. Canada (Attorney General)*, [1989] 1 S.C.R. 342 at 353; *Bago v. Canada (Minister of Citizenship and Immigration)*, [2004] F.C.J. No. 1565 (QL).

[106] *Moose Jaw Central Bingo Assn. Inc. v. Saskatchewan (Liquor & Gaming Authority)* (1994), 123 Sask. R. 47 (C.A.); *Mobil Oil Canada Ltd. v. Canada-Nfld. Offshore Petroleum Board*, [1994] 1 S.C.R. 202.

[107] *Cosman Realty Ltd. v. Winnipeg (City)* (2001), 157 Man. R. (2d) 117 (Q.B.); aff'd (2001), 160 Man. R. (2d) 32 (C.A.); *Jaouadi v. Canada (Minister of Citizenship and Immigration)* (2003), 257 F.T.R. 161.

review process, reaching the discretionary grounds for granting relief in the first place. In other words, even where the five original grounds above were not present, courts began to recognize that it may be appropriate to refuse to grant judicial review out of deference to tribunals' unique institutional roles. Perhaps the most forceful statement about the contingent nature of judicial review remedies from this era comes from *Domtar Inc. v. Quebec*.[108] In deciding not to intervene to resolve a conflict in legal interpretation between two tribunals construing the same statutory language, the Supreme Court of Canada stated, "[t]he advisability of judicial intervention in the event of conflicting decisions among administrative tribunals, even when serious and unquestionable, cannot, in these circumstances, be determined solely by the 'triumph' of the rule of law."[109] The Court goes on, in what amounts to a striking acknowledgment that even the most deeply cherished legal values will not always point the way to the only, or perhaps even the most appropriate, response to a problem in administrative law:

> [C]ertainty of the law and decision-making consistency are chiefly notable for their relativity. Like the rules of natural justice, these objectives cannot be absolute in nature regardless of the context. The value represented by the decision-making independence and autonomy of the members of administrative tribunals goes hand in hand here with the principle that their decisions should be effective. In light of these considerations we must conclude that, *for purposes of judicial review, the principle of the rule of law must be qualified.* This is consistent with the continuing evolution of administrative law itself.[110]

Consistent with this, in 1999, Chief Justice McLachlin set forth a vision of a "new rule of law," which would

> [make] it possible for institutions other than courts to play key roles in maintaining it. It opens the door to the idea that courts do not necessarily have a monopoly on the values of reasons and fairness ... [C]ontrary to Dicey's view that the courts' primary role is to constrain, limit and, if possible eliminate administrative power, the new Rule of Law allows courts to respect and advance the roles of administrative tribunals. The courts' role shifts from being a brute guardian of an artificial and restrictive Rule of Law to that of a partner.[111]

Over the past few years, the doctrine seems to have undergone another shift. Beginning in 2008 with *Dunsmuir*, the leading case concerning when courts can review administrative decisions on their merits,[112] the Supreme Court began to reassert the importance of the courts' role in upholding the (not-"new") rule of law, while avoiding "undue interference"

---

[108] *Domtar Inc. v. Quebec (Commission d'appel en matière de lésions professionnelles)*, [1993] 2 S.C.R. 756.

[109] *Ibid.* at 795.

[110] *Ibid.* at 799-800 (emphasis added).

[111] Beverley McLachlin, "The Roles of Administrative Tribunals and Courts in Maintaining the Rule of Law" (1998-1999) 12 C.J.A.L.P. 171-89 at 175. This article is also an early statement of the chief justice's concept of the "ethos of justification" that underlies the rule of law, and this concept continues to be a vital part of contemporary jurisprudence.

[112] See Sheila Wildeman, Chapter 10, Pas de Deux: Deference and Non-Deference in Action, and Audrey Macklin, Chapter 9, Standard of Review: Back to the Future?

with administrative powers.[113] The shift was clear by the time of the Court's decision in *Khosa*.[114] The *Dunsmuir* and *Khosa* cases are discussed in detail later in this textbook. For present purposes, it is enough to say that the *Khosa* case stated that the discretion to grant or withhold judicial review "must be exercised judicially and in accordance with proper principles."[115] In setting out those proper principles, the Court identifies the normal standard of review principles that govern administrative law, plus "other factors such as an applicant's delay, failure to exhaust adequate alternate remedies, mootness, prematurity, bad faith and so forth."[116] Deference to tribunals is understood to be part of normal judicial review analysis, not some freestanding basis for refusing to grant judicial review in the first place. It is difficult to imagine the majority in *Khosa* endorsing the *Domtar* court's equivocal language about the rule of law. The majority makes it clear that *courts* (not legislatures) are the ones with the power to decide whether and when to engage in judicial review and on what grounds, even though in exercising that power they will observe the necessary deference to administrative decision making, and will operate within the bounds of clear reasons and the rule of law.

In the 1990s, courts moved past the five limited, original grounds for refusing to exercise discretion to grant judicial review. They did so in the service of a more respectful relationship with the other branches of government, and particularly with administrative tribunals. But to the extent that this shift introduced some "X factor" into the decision-making process, it exempted courts from the very ethos of justification that the Supreme Court of Canada said that tribunals had to observe. Respecting, protecting, and adhering to the rule of law implies that judges should rest their discretionary decisions on identifiable reasons. A restrained approach to judicial intervention in administrative law matters suggests that judges should, perhaps, hew more closely to the traditional, discrete grounds for refusing relief identified above. This does seem to be where the Supreme Court is going. In fact, the *Khosa* majority seemed to suggest that the threshold question we are discussing here—the purely discretionary decision whether to grant judicial review at all—had largely disappeared, but for the old common-law/equitable bases for refusing relief.[117] In other words, the fact that judicial review is discretionary does not mean that courts should refuse to grant judicial review solely on the basis of some notion of partnership with administrative tribunals, or a relative and qualified rule-of-law value.

The overall result of recent cases such as *Dunsmuir* and *Khosa* has been a resurgence of the original common-law bases for refusing relief, accompanied by a willingness to consider other, analogous and clearly defined, grounds. In *MiningWatch* (per coram with Rothstein J.

---

[113] See esp. *Dunsmuir, supra* note 99 at paras. 20-24.

[114] *Canada (Citizenship and Immigration) v. Khosa*, 2009 SCC 12, [2009] 1 S.C.R. 339 [*Khosa*].

[115] *Ibid.* at para. 40.

[116] *Ibid.* at para. 51.

[117] The majority said it would "presume the existence of a discretion to grant or withhold relief based on the *Dunsmuir* teaching of restraint in judicial intervention in administrative matters (as well as other factors such as an applicant's delay, failure to exhaust adequate alternate remedies, mootness, prematurity, bad faith and so forth)." *Khosa, supra* note 114 at para. 51. As Rothstein J points out in a strongly worded set of concurring reasons, doing so conflates the standard of review analysis with the granting of relief in the first place. *Khosa, ibid.* at para. 134.

writing), the Court added another consideration to the original five mentioned above. It is one that has been rising in salience since *Khosa*: the balance of convenience to the various parties.[118] In that case, the balance of convenience justified reducing the impact of the remedy granted, from relief in the order of certiorari and mandamus to a declaration. (The specific forms of relief are discussed below.) In an interesting juxtaposition to the *Domtar* language, which had proposed that the rule of law must sometimes be qualified, the Court now tells us that, because the discretionary power to refuse judicial review "may make inroads upon the rule of law, it must be exercised with the greatest care."[119] It seems that now, the concern is that *courts themselves* not undercut the rule of law in exercising their discretion to grant, or not to grant, judicial review. The shift may be designed, in part to simplify and clarify judicial review doctrine and, if it sticks, it may succeed in that. But, as with many other shifts taking place right now in administrative law, it remains to be seen whether these reforms will produce more, or less, deference toward the kinds of administrative tribunal decision making we saw at work in the *McKinnon* case.

This chapter suggests, above, that the traditional court-centric approach has perpetuated a somewhat limited understanding of administrative law focused on judicial review at the expense of attention to tribunal-level practices. This is the first way in which the tail of judicial review can be seen to have wagged the administrative law dog. But there is a second way, which we turn to now: it turns out that the historical development of the remedies available through judicial review, and especially their limitations, has actively shaped the possibilities and potential of judicial review itself. In spite of statutory reform and evolving case law, the ancient prerogative writs that were the original forms of judicial review continue to haunt its present forms. Keep each of these effects in mind as you read the sections below, which consider whether and when judicial review is available, the roots of judicial review in the prerogative writs, more recent statutory reform efforts, and the private law remedies that have sprung up around judicial review.

2. Is Judicial Review Available?

Leaving to one side what *Domtar* and *MiningWatch* have said about the discretionary nature of judicial review writ large, the differences in the history, purpose, and function of judicial review also mean that whether it will be available as a remedy in any particular situation depends on a set of considerations unique to administrative law.

One of the key threshold questions is whether the tribunal whose actions are being challenged is, in fact, a public body. Judicial review is available to check executive action. Therefore, only public bodies can be subject to judicial review.[120] While this may sound straightforward, some organizations in Canadian society operate at considerable remove from government, yet exercise some degree of "public" function. Others seem private, but

---

[118] *MiningWatch Canada v. Canada (Fisheries and Oceans)*, 2010 SCC 2 at para. 52, 2010 CarswellNat 55 at para. 52 [*MiningWatch*]; see also *Khosa, supra* note 114 at paras. 36, 133-35.

[119] *MiningWatch* at para. 52.

[120] Private actors may also owe a duty of fairness that can be enforced through the private law remedies of declaration and injunction; however, these remedies are outside the scope of this chapter.

have some connection to public authority. For example, stock exchanges regulate the conduct of their members and issue and revoke licences, and their operations clearly go to the protection of the public. However, their authority to act as they do derives from a compact with their members rather than from any statutory grant of authority. What about corporations incorporated under the *Canada Business Corporations Act* (CBCA)? Corporations are the prototypical "private" institution, yet CBCA companies only come into existence by virtue of government action under that statute. Similarly, one should distinguish between government action qua government, and government action qua private contracting party. As a general matter, a private party will have difficulty seeking judicial review of a government board's decision not to award it a particular contract.[121]

Various factors go into determining whether a particular tribunal is a private body or a public one. Relevant considerations include the tribunal's functions and duties and the sources of its power and funding, whether the government directly or indirectly controls the body, and whether government would have to "occupy the field" if the body were not already performing the functions it does. A body or tribunal will be subject to public law, and therefore judicial review, if it is "part of the machinery of government."[122]

In addition to determining whether a tribunal is a sufficiently "public" body, a party seeking to challenge administrative action should determine whether he or she has *standing* to challenge a tribunal decision. The answer will be straightforward for individuals who are actual parties to an administrative action, but other persons may have a collateral interest in the same matter and may want to challenge a tribunal order that does not directly affect them.[123] The question of standing, including "public interest" standing, is discussed by Lorne Sossin in Chapter 7, Access to Administrative Justice and Other Worries.

Third, a party seeking to challenge administrative action should determine to which court he or she should apply for judicial review. Both the provincial superior courts and the Federal Courts have judicial review jurisdiction. Although a tribunal's enabling statute will generally set out which court has jurisdiction to hear a statutory *appeal*, this is not the case for judicial review. (This makes sense, because judicial review is an extraordinary remedy that does not come out of the enabling statute in the first place.) Typically, the choice of courts is determined by whether the source of the impugned authority's power is provincial or federal.[124] Some overarching provincial statutes, such as Ontario's *Judicial Review Procedure*

---

121 But consider the improper purpose doctrine: *Shell Canada Products Ltd. v. Vancouver (City)*, [1994] 1 S.C.R. 231.

122 *McDonald v. Anishinabek Police Service et al.* (2006), 83 O.R. (3d) 132 (Div. Ct.).

123 See e.g. *Globalive Wireless Management Corp. v. Public Mobile Inc.*, 2011 FCA 194.

124 There are some exceptions. Provincial superior courts have concurrent or exclusive jurisdiction over some specific aspects of federal statutory regimes, as a result of both the *Constitution Act, 1982*, being Schedule B to the *Canada Act 1982* (U.K.), 1982, c. 11, and the *Federal Courts Act*, *supra* note 95. In particular, provincial superior courts have concurrent jurisdiction where Charter issues are raised in attacks on federal legislative regimes (*Reza v. Canada*, [1994] 2 S.C.R. 394) and—although this is private law, not judicial review—over damages actions in which relief is sought against the federal Crown (*Canada (Attorney General) v. TeleZone Inc.*, 2010 SCC 62, [2010] 3 S.C.R. 585 [*TeleZone*]).

Act, stipulate the particular provincial court to which judicial review applications should be brought.[125]

Fourth, a party should ensure that he or she has not missed any deadlines. Some statutes impose time limits within which a party must file an application for judicial review. For example, the *Federal Courts Act* states that a judicial review application from a federal tribunal to the Federal Court must be made within 30 days of the time the underlying decision or order is first communicated.[126] In Alberta, the rules impose a six-month time limit on all applications for judicial review, except habeas corpus applications.[127] Nova Scotia precludes all applications for judicial review after the earlier of six months following the decision, or 25 days after the decision is communicated to the person.[128] In British Columbia, the general time limit is 60 days.[129] Parties should therefore check all applicable statutes, including the tribunal's enabling statutes, global procedural and judicial review acts, and rules of court, for time limits affecting judicial review. However, courts are often statutorily empowered to extend the time limit for making a judicial review application—for example, where there is a reasonable explanation for the delay, where no substantial prejudice or hardship would result from such an extension, or where the party can demonstrate prima facie grounds for relief.[130]

The final threshold matter that a party must establish before gaining access to judicial review is that he or she has exhausted all other adequate means of recourse for challenging the tribunal's actions.[131] Depending on the tribunal's enabling statute, this may include almost any of the remedies above: reconsideration by the same tribunal, appeals to internal appellate tribunals and other intra-agency mechanisms such as grievance arbitration, and appeals to a court. However, some factors may render an alternative form of review inadequate. For example, appeal mechanisms provided for by statute will be inadequate where:

1. the appellate tribunal lacks statutory authority over, or is not willing to address, the issues the appellant raises;[132]

---

125   Ontario *Judicial Review Procedure Act* (JRPA), R.S.O. 1990, c. J.1, s. 6 says that judicial review applications shall be made to the Divisional Court, unless "the case is one of urgency and ... the delay required for an application to the Divisional Court is likely to involve a failure of justice," in which case an application may be made to the Superior Court of Justice.

126   *Federal Courts Act*, *supra* note 97, s. 18.1(2).

127   Rule 3.15 of the *Alberta Rules of Court* (Alta. Reg. 124/2010) imposes this time limit where the relief sought is the setting aside of a decision or act.

128   Rule 7.05(1), *Nova Scotia Civil Procedure Rules*, 2008, imposes the time limit on applications for relief in the nature of certiorari, online: <http://www.courts.ns.ca/rules/cpr_consolidated_11_03_11/cpr_consolidated_rules_11_03_11.pdf>.

129   B.C. ATA, *supra* note 11, s. 57(1).

130   E.g. Ontario *Judicial Review Procedure Act*, *supra* note 125, s. 5; B.C. ATA, *supra* note 11, s. 57(2). The *Federal Courts Act*, *supra* note 97, does not set out the conditions that must be met in order for the court to grant an extension of time: s. 18.1(2).

131   *Harelkin v. University of Regina*, [1979] 2 S.C.R 561, 96 D.L.R. (3d) 14.

132   *Canadian Pacific Ltd. v. Matsqui Indian Band*, [1995] 1 S.C.R. 3, [1995] S.C.J. No. 1 (QL) (per La Forest and Major JJ.) [*Matsqui*]; *Violette v. Dental Society*, [2004] 267 N.B.R. (2d) 205 (C.A.); *Kingsbury v. Heighton* (2003), 230 D.L.R. (4th) 654 (C.A.).

2. the appellate tribunal does not have statutory authority to grant the remedy the appellant requests;[133]
3. the appeal must be based on the record before the original tribunal, but that record does not include evidence relevant to the applicant,[134] or includes evidentiary errors that the appellate tribunal lacks authority to correct;[135] or
4. the alternative procedure is too inefficient or costly.[136]

Courts will not find existing non-court appeal mechanisms to be inadequate based only on unproven allegations that an appellate tribunal will suffer from the same errors[137] or biases[138] as the original tribunal. Nor can challengers circumvent available appeals in favour of judicial review by consent, or simply by raising apparent issues with the original tribunal's procedure or jurisdiction.[139] Also, at least in the context of Aboriginal self-government in the taxation field, the fact that appellate tribunal members lack indicia of institutional independence—that is, they may not be paid, they lack security of tenure, and they are appointed by the people whose claims they have to adjudicate—will not make that appellate body "inadequate" without concrete evidence that independence is lacking in practice.[140]

Parliament and several provinces have also legislated in this area. For example, the *Federal Courts Act* prohibits *judicial review* by the Federal Court where an available appeal of a tribunal's decision to the Federal Court exists. Quebec's *Code of Civil Procedure* also prohibits a superior court from applying Quebec's version of certiorari to a tribunal decision where an appeal is available, unless the tribunal lacked or exceeded its statutory authority. On the other hand, Ontario's *Judicial Review Procedure Act* and Prince Edward Island's *Judicial Review Act* both permit judicial review notwithstanding any right of appeal.[141] Of course,

---

[133]   *Evershed v. Ontario* (1985), 50 O.R. (2d) 198 at 200 (C.A.).

[134]   *V.S.R. Investments Ltd. v. Laczko* (1983), 41 O.R. (2d) 62 (Div Ct.).

[135]   *Cimolai v. Children's and Women's Health Centre* (2003), 228 D.L.R. (4th) 420 at 443-46 (B.C.C.A.) [*Cimolai*].

[136]   *Violette v. Dental Society, supra* note 132.

[137]   *Harelkin, supra* note 131; but see, *contra, Cimolai, supra* note 135.

[138]   *Turnbull v. Canadian Institute of Actuaries* (1995), 129 D.L.R. (4th) 42 (C.A.); but see, *contra, Batorski v. Moody* (1983), 42 O.R. (2d) 647 (Div. Ct.).

[139]   *Canada (Border Services Agency) v. C.B. Powell Limited*, [2010] F.C.A. 61 at para. 33 ("Concerns about procedural fairness or bias, the presence of an important legal or constitutional issue, or the fact that all parties have consented to early recourse to the courts are not exceptional circumstances allowing parties to bypass an administrative process, as long as that process allows the issues to be raised and an effective remedy to be granted ... [T]he presence of so-called jurisdictional issues is not an exceptional circumstance justifying early recourse to courts."). See also *Bayne (Rural Municipality No. 371) v. Saskatchewan Water Corp.* (1990), 46 Admin. L.R. 23 (Sask. C.A.); *Delmas v. Vancouver Stock Exchange* (1994), 27 Admin. L.R. (2d) 294 (S.C.); aff'd (1995), 15 B.C.L.R. (3d) 136 (C.A.).

[140]   *Matsqui, supra* note 132.

[141]   See, respectively, the *Federal Courts Act, supra* note 97, s. 185; *Code of Civil Procedure*, R.S.Q., c. C-25, art. 846; Ontario *Judicial Review Procedure Act, supra* note 121, s. 2(1); and *Judicial Review Act* (P.E.I. JRA), R.S.P.E.I. 1988, c. J-3, s. 4(2).

the fact that a court *may* grant judicial review, even where a right of appeal exists, does not mean that it *will* do so. As we might expect, courts are reluctant to do so.[142]

E. Remedies on Judicial Review

The remedies available on judicial review have their roots in the ancient prerogative writs, discussed further below. Over time, those became unwieldy. In many provinces they were modified by statute to redress problems arising from the writs' extreme technicality and unjustified narrowness. However, it is still necessary to understand the ancient writs to understand the scope and range of remedies available through judicial review. For example, neither the old writs nor the reform statutes, which are based on the old writs, permit a court on judicial review to substitute its views on the substance of a matter for the tribunal's views. The old writs also continue to operate in some provinces, albeit in a more limited way.[143]

A party contemplating judicial review should also be aware that, unlike an appeal, an application for judicial review usually does *not* automatically stay the enforcement of the underlying tribunal order, although the tribunal or the court or both may have the power to stay the tribunal's order on application.[144] The legislative decision to make stays automatic for many appeals but not for judicial review applications is consistent with the "last resort" nature of judicial review. The rules regarding stays vary from jurisdiction to jurisdiction and from tribunal to tribunal, so parties seeking a stay should be sure to review the relevant enabling statute, as well as the rules of court and any omnibus statutes governing procedure or judicial review.

The following sections introduce the prerogative writs and subsequent statutory reform. Because judicial review remains a fundamentally discretionary power, the bases on which courts have refused to grant a remedy are also discussed.

---

[142]   *Odufowora v. Ontario (Board of Inquiry)* (1994), 76 O.A.C. 385 (Div. Ct.); *McKenna's Furniture Store v. Prince Edward Island (Fire Marshall)*, [1997] 152 Nfld. & P.E.I.R. 212 (P.E.I.S.C.(T.D.)).

[143]   For example, the "direct action in nullity" is a judicial review remedy that predates the Quebec *Code of Civil Procedure*, R.S.Q. 1977, c. C-25, and is not referred to in it, yet it continues to operate: *Immeubles Port Louis Ltée v. Lafontaine (Village), supra* note 100. In New Brunswick, one cannot apply specifically for the traditional prerogative writs of certiorari, mandamus, or prohibition, which are now available simply as judicial review. However, a range of "alternative" remedies echoing the old prerogative writs continues to exist. See e.g. *Sullivan v. Greater Moncton Planning District Commission* (1993), 132 N.B.R. (2d) 285 (T.D.). Manitoba's Court of Queen's Bench Rules, Man. Reg. 553/88, Rule 68.01 states only that "[a] Judge on application may grant an order of mandamus, prohibition, certiorari or quo warranto." Yukon Territory has not enacted any statutory changes to the common-law writs.

[144]   See e.g. Ontario *Statutory Powers Procedure Act, supra* note 43, s. 25 (an appeal acts as a stay, but judicial review is not an appeal for that purpose); New Brunswick *Energy and Utilities Board Act*, S.N.B. 2006, c. E-9.18, s. 52(2) (judicial review does not automatically stay an order, but the board itself or the Court of Appeal may stay it). Indeed, one federal statute that establishes securities clearing houses and banking and payment systems stipulates that *no* stay shall be granted for a judicial review application related to the government's administration of those systems. *Canadian Payments Act*, R.S.C. 1985, c. C-21, s. 46.

1. Introduction to the Prerogative Writs

Certiorari is the most commonly used prerogative remedy, both historically and today. Certiorari ("cause to be certified") is a special proceeding by which a superior court requires some inferior tribunal, board, or judicial officer to provide it with the record of its proceedings for review for excess of jurisdiction. It was the established method by which the Court of King's Bench in England, from earliest times, checked the jurisdiction of inferior courts and maintained the supremacy of the royal courts. In the United States, the vast majority of applications to the U.S. Supreme Court are still made by way of a petition for certiorari. A successful certiorari application results in the "quashing" (effectively, the invalidating) of a tribunal's order or decision. It is an *ex post facto* remedy. Note, however, that generally the court cannot substitute its decision for the decision of a tribunal that the court finds had erred, because the court has not been granted the statutory decision-making authority and does not have the expertise that the tribunal has.[145]

The related writ of *prohibition* is another special proceeding, issued by an appellate court to prevent a lower court from exceeding its jurisdiction, or to prevent a non-judicial officer or entity from exercising a power. Prohibition is a kind of common-law injunction to prevent an unlawful assumption of jurisdiction. Unlike certiorari, which provides relief after a decision is made, prohibition is used to obtain relief pre-emptively. It arrests the proceedings of any tribunal, board, or person exercising judicial functions in a manner or by means not within its jurisdiction or discretion.

Mandamus (literally, "we command") is a writ issued by a superior court to compel a lower court or a government agency to perform a duty it is mandated to perform. In practice, it is often combined with an application for certiorari. Certiorari would be used to quash a decision—for example, for a lack of procedural fairness—while mandamus would be used to force the tribunal to reconsider the matter in a procedurally fair manner. A variation on mandamus gives the court the ability to send a matter back to a tribunal for reconsideration with directions. Superior courts have the inherent power to order reconsideration with directions, and several provincial statutes and rules of court, as well as the *Federal Courts Act*, also grant this power. If the court issues directions, it must clearly state what the original panel is to do or what it must refrain from doing. These directions may only protect against unfair procedures or excess of power and cannot tell the tribunal how it must decide. In particular, the general rule is that mandamus cannot be sought to compel the exercise of discretion in a particular way, although exercises of discretion must always conform to the Charter.[146]

---

[145] In exceptional circumstances, a court will nevertheless make the decision that it finds the original tribunal ought to have made. See e.g. *Renaud v. Québec (Commission des affaires sociales)*, [1999] 3 S.C.R. 855, [1999] S.C.J. No. 70 (QL), 184 D.L.R. (4th) 441; *Corp. of the Canadian Civil Liberties Assn. v. Ontario (Civilian Commission on Police Services)* (2002), 61 O.R. (3d) 649 (C.A.); *Allman v. Amacon Property Management Services Inc.*, [2007] B.C.J. No. 1144 (QL) (C.A.).

[146] In the special circumstances of the so-called *Insite* case, which concerned a safe drug injection site in Vancouver's Downtown Eastside neighbourhood, the Supreme Court of Canada held that the minister of health had not exercised his discretion consistent with the Charter when he refused to exempt Insite from certain criminal law provisions. The Court found that sending the matter back to the minister for reconsideration would

A *declaration* is a judgment of a court that determines and states the legal position of the parties, or the law that applies to them. There are two kinds of declarations: the public law variety, used to declare some government action *ultra vires*, and the private law variety, used to clarify the law or declare a private party's rights under a statute. The public law variety is the main concern of administrative law. Declarations are not enforceable, and they cannot require anyone to take or refrain from taking any action. Historically, this made declarations useful in actions against the Crown itself because the traditional common-law position was that relief in the nature of mandamus was not available against the Crown. It was not thought appropriate for a court to order enforcement against the Crown because the Crown was the source of its own authority. (These prohibitions on remedies against the Crown itself were substantially, though not completely, relaxed over the course of the 20th century.) The non-coercive nature of the remedy has not often proven to be a problem, because court declarations against government bodies in particular tend to be respected.[147] Where a declaration does not produce a government response, however, as happened in the *Khadr* case,[148] the declaration may look like a distinctly second-rate remedy relative to mandamus. At least where the Crown prerogative over foreign affairs is concerned, an aggrieved party may find himself or herself having a right without a remedy—or, more accurately, having a right for which a meaningful remedy exists only in the political, and not the legal, arena.

Less common these days are the writs of habeas corpus and quo warranto. *Habeas corpus* (literally, "produce the body") is a writ employed to bring a person before a court, most frequently to ensure that the person's imprisonment or detention is not illegal. Like certiorari, habeas corpus continues to live an active life in the United States, where it is the primary mechanism for challenging state death penalty sentences in federal court. In Canada, habeas corpus applications are rare. Most are brought by prisoners detained in correctional institutions and by police, immigration, child welfare, and mental health detainees. *Quo warranto* ("by what warrant?" or "by what authority?") is a writ used to inquire into what authority existed to justify acts by or powers claimed by a public office. It is rarely used today, and

---

be inadequate in view of the attendant risks and delays. It therefore took the rare step of issuing an order in the nature of mandamus, *compelling* the minister to exercise his discretion so as to issue an exemption to Insite. *Canada (Attorney General) v. PHS Community Services Society*, 2011 SCC 44, [2011] 3 S.C.R. 134.

[147] *Lount Corp. v. Canada (Attorney General)*, [1984] 1 F.C. 332 at 365 (T.D.) (noting that "by long tradition, the executive abides by declarations of the Court even though not formally or specifically directed to do so"); aff'd *sub nom. Canada (Attorney General) v. Lount Corp.*, [1985] 2 F.C. 185 (C.A.).

[148] *Khadr, supra* note 77. In 2008 the Supreme Court of Canada determined that Omar Khadr had been deprived of his s. 7 Charter rights by Canadian officials operating at the Guantanamo Bay detention facility, who shared transcripts of their interviews of Mr. Khadr with U.S. authorities. The Court ordered that the Canadian authorities produce those transcripts to Mr. Khadr, which they did, but the prime minister refused requests to seek his repatriation from the United States to Canada. In its 2010 decision, the Supreme Court of Canada held that, notwithstanding the violation of Mr. Khadr's s. 7 Charter rights, it would not order the Canadian government to request his repatriation. In light of the Crown prerogative over foreign affairs, the Court concluded that the appropriate remedy was a declaration that Canada had infringed Mr. Khadr's s. 7 rights, leaving it to the government to decide how best to respond. The government did not seek Mr. Khadr's repatriation.

some provinces have abolished it by statute.[149] However, quo warranto is still used in Quebec and New Brunswick to challenge the authority of municipal councillors on the basis of a prohibited conflict of interest.[150]

2. Statutory Reform

Over time, each of the prerogative writs above came to be characterized by technical complexity and arcane rules. Potentially meritorious applications were dismissed because the applicant had petitioned for the wrong writ, or because his or her claim was barred by some technical limitation. For example, although court decisions later re-expanded the writ's scope, a number of cases in Canada in the 1960s and 1970s held that certiorari and prohibition were only available to address "judicial" or "quasi-judicial" final decisions that affected the rights of citizens. As the case law became more arcane and the practical injustices more obvious, policy reasons for maintaining the distinction between the various writs eroded.

The result, in many provinces and at the Federal Court,[151] was statutory reform. Some provinces enacted omnibus statutes governing judicial review or statutory/civil procedure,[152] while others used their rules of court to enact changes.[153] Only Yukon Territory seems to have left the common law untouched. The details vary from one statutory scheme to another, but key statutes that may apply are the *Federal Courts Act*, the Ontario and B.C. *Judicial Review Procedure Acts* (JRPAs), the Ontario *Statutory Powers Procedure Act*, the B.C. *Administrative Tribunals Act*, the P.E.I. *Judicial Review Act*, Quebec's *Code of Civil Procedure*, and the rules of court in other provinces and territories. These important statutes have sought to clarify procedure surrounding judicial review. Some have also sought to change the substantive shape of judicial review itself. Therefore, parties considering challenging a tribunal order must be aware of the relevant statutes' provisions, in addition to the provisions of the tribunal's own enabling statutes. Statutory reforms commonly provide for the following:

1. Simplified application procedures. For example, a statute may state that applications for orders "in the nature of" mandamus, prohibition, or certiorari shall be deemed

---

[149] E.g. P.E.I. JRA, *supra* note 141, s. 11; B.C. *Judicial Review Procedure Act* (B.C. JRPA), R.S.B.C. 1996, c. 241, s. 18. These statutes provide that certain remedies for what would have been an information in the nature of quo warranto are still available.

[150] See e.g. *R. v. Wheeler*, [1979] 2 S.C.R. 650.

[151] *Federal Courts Act*, *supra* note 97, s. 18(1) provides that the Federal Court has exclusive original jurisdiction "to issue an injunction, writ of certiorari, writ of prohibition, writ of mandamus, or writ of quo warranto, or grant declaratory relief, against any federal board, commission or other tribunal."

[152] Ontario JRPA, *supra* note 125, B.C. JRPA, *supra* note 149, P.E.I. JRA, *supra* note 141, Quebec *Code of Civil Procedure*, R.S.Q., c. C-25. Ontario and British Columbia have enacted the most comprehensive reforms. Be aware that, apart from habeas corpus, terminology in Quebec is different. For example, prohibition and certiorari are codified under "evocation" and "revision" in s. 846 of the *Civil Code*. Remedies equivalent to quo warranto and mandamus are codified under ss. 838 and 844ff, respectively, and the terms "quo warranto" and "mandamus" are used in practice, but they do not appear in the Code. There also exists the "declaratory judgment in motion," codified at s. 453, which allows a party to have his or her rights "declared."

[153] Alberta, Manitoba, New Brunswick, Newfoundland, Northwest Territories, Nova Scotia, Nunavut, and Saskatchewan.

to be applications for judicial review, to be brought by way of an originating notice or petition. The new judicial review application combines, and in the process supersedes, the old writs of certiorari, prohibition, mandamus, public law declaration, and injunction. (Some statutes include quo warranto and habeas corpus within the ambit of the statute; some abolish quo warranto; some provinces have a dedicated *Habeas Corpus Act*.) It is sufficient for a party to set out the grounds on which relief is sought and the nature of the relief sought, without having to specify under which particular writ he or she might have proceeded at common law.

2. Simplified remedies, including, for example, the power to set aside a decision or direct the tribunal to reconsider its decision, with or without directions. Some statutes also expressly give courts the authority to ignore technical irregularities or defects in form if the court finds no substantial wrong or miscarriage of justice has occurred.

3. Greater clarity as to who may be parties to a hearing—for example, decision-makers whose exercise of statutory authority is being questioned. Generally, judicial review statutes also provide that notice must be given to the attorney general, who is entitled as of right to be heard on the application.

4. A right of appeal. Judicial review applications are generally made to provincial superior courts, and the statutes provide for a subsequent right of appeal to the provincial Court of Appeal.

5. Judicial review mechanisms to challenge interlocutory orders and to resolve interim issues. At common law, certiorari was only available with respect to "decisions"— that is, final orders. However, the B.C. and Ontario *Judicial Review Procedure Acts* use the words "exercise of statutory power," rather than the word "decision," thereby expanding the range of judicial review to include any exercise of statutory power.[154] Other statutes permit a tribunal itself to refer a "stated case" to the courts for determination of a question of law, after which the case can go back to the original tribunal for determination of the ultimate issues.[155] For example, B.C. tribunals that do not have jurisdiction over constitutional questions under the *Administrative Tribunals Act* can issue a stay and refer a constitutional question to a court of competent jurisdiction.[156] Enabling statutes must authorize stated cases.

F. Private Law Remedies

Private law remedies available to parties, as against administrative agencies, are outside the scope of administrative action and judicial review. At the same time, increasingly frequent attempts to obtain private law remedies from public bodies have put pressure on judicial review doctrine. In some circumstances, unhappy parties would likely prefer monetary relief to any remedy they could receive under judicial review. The key issue is that neither the

---

[154] B.C. JRPA, *supra* note 149, s. 3; Ontario JRPA, *supra* note 125, s. 2.

[155] E.g. *Federal Courts Act*, *supra* note 97, s. 18.3; B.C. ATA, *supra* note 11, s. 43.

[156] B.C. ATA, *ibid.*, ss. 44, 45.

old prerogative writs, nor the new statutory remedy of judicial review, allow a party to obtain monetary relief through judicial review.

The Crown and its servants can be liable to private parties for monetary relief,[157] although some statutes limit individual administrative tribunal members' liability.[158] However, to seek monetary relief, an aggrieved party must initiate a separate civil action for restitution or damages alongside, or in lieu of, a judicial review application. The fact that many parties *do* want money damages as a remedy is putting considerable momentum behind the development of the law in this area. It points, again, to how the tail of remedies sometimes wags the dog of legal doctrine.

Government agencies can be sued, for example for breach of contract, for the tort of negligence, or the special tort of misfeasance in (or abuse of) public office. The last one in particular has attracted a lot of attention lately. To succeed in an action for tort of misfeasance in public office, the plaintiff must establish, in addition to the basic elements of negligence, (1) deliberate and unlawful conduct by someone in public office, and (2) the public officer's subjective knowledge that the conduct was unlawful and likely to harm the plaintiff. Because this tort alleges bad faith on the part of a public official, "clear proof commensurate with the seriousness of the wrong" is required.[159] The underlying purpose of the tort is to protect each citizen's reasonable expectation that public officials will not intentionally injure members of the public through deliberate and unlawful conduct in the exercise of public functions.[160]

The leading case on the tort of misfeasance in public office, *Odhavji*, involved an action for damages against police officers and the chief of the Metropolitan Toronto Police by the estate of an individual shot by the police. The plaintiffs alleged that the police officers involved in the shooting did not promptly or fully comply with their statutory duty to cooperate with an ensuing investigation, and that the chief of police did not adequately compel them to cooperate. The case made its way to the Supreme Court of Canada on the defendant's motion to dismiss the plaintiff's claim, where the Court determined that the plaintiff had made out a cause of action and that the matter should be allowed to proceed. In other words, the Court held that there was such a thing as the tort of misfeasance in public office. Since *Odhavji*, only a few cases have succeeded on a claim of tort of misfeasance in public office. *McMaster v. The Queen*[161] is one of them. There, a prisoner with large feet requested

---

[157] The Federal Court has concurrent original jurisdiction over all actions for damages against the federal Crown. Individual servants of the Crown, including ministers, are also liable for breaches of private law duties on the same basis as other individuals. *Federal Courts Act, supra* note 97, s. 17; *Peter G. White Management Ltd. v. Canada (Minister of Canadian Heritage)*, [2007] 2 F.C.R. 475 (C.A.).

[158] E.g. B.C. ATA, *supra* note 11, s. 56.

[159] *Powder Mountain Resorts Ltd. v. British Columbia* (2001), 94 B.C.L.R. (3d) 14 at para. 8 (C.A.).

[160] *Odhavji Estate v. Woodhouse*, 2003 SCC 69, [2003] 3 S.C.R. 263. On the tort's value as a practical tool for enhancing state accountability, notwithstanding its rather poor fit with the conceptual underpinnings of modern tort law, see John Murphy, "Misfeasance in a Public Office: A Tort Law Misfit?" Oxford J. Legal Stud. (forthcoming), online: Oxford Journal of Legal Studies <http://ojls.oxfordjournals.org/content/early/2011/09/21/ojls.gqr018.full.pdf+html>.

[161] *McMaster v. The Queen* (2009), F.C. 937, F.C.J. No. 1071 (QL).

a new pair of properly fitting shoes when his old shoes became worn out. A long and apparently intentional delay followed in getting him new shoes and, while waiting, he injured his knee exercising in his old shoes. Correctional Services of Canada and prison staff were found liable in tort for misfeasance in public office, for unlawfully delaying Mr. McMaster's new shoe request when they should have known he was at risk of injury.

As these cases make clear, some torts overlap with a potential judicial review application while others do not. Judicial review was not a possibility in *Odhavji* or *McMaster*, because no administrative decision was being challenged in those cases. In other cases, a tribunal's conduct may be precisely what is being challenged. The precise relationship and potential overlap between private rights of action and judicial review applications was a cause for concern for a number of years. Then, in 2010, in a case concerning private law claims for breach of contract, negligence, and unjust enrichment, the Supreme Court of Canada made it clear that parties do not need to seek judicial review *before* they can bring a private law action for damages, and the private law action does not violate the rule against collateral attacks.[162] If a party has a fundamentally private law claim arising from an administrative decision, and primarily wants monetary damages, that party may proceed by way of private action. As Binnie J. points out, though, "no amount of artful pleading in a damages case will succeed in setting aside the order said to have harmed the claimant or enjoin its enforcement. ... The claimant must ... be content to take its money (if successful) and walk away leaving the order standing."[163]

V. Conclusion

A goal of this chapter has been to put judicial review in context, both chronologically and conceptually. Administrative law remedies are the product of multiple forces and priorities, often acting in tension with each other. They need to be considered in light of the tug-of-war between courts and legislators as demonstrated by, for example, legislators' creation of internal appeal mechanisms and courts' periodic circumvention of those internal appeals in favour of immediate judicial review. Another recurring theme is the tug-of-war between tribunals and the courts that oversee them, in terms of courts' willingness to recognize and give effect to potentially creative and uncourtlike tribunal remedies. These tensions are emblematic of a deeper contest between deeply held values around the rule of law on the one hand, and administrative expertise, efficiency, and democratic accountability on the other.

Administrative law remedies are also path-dependent, meaning that they have been shaped by their historical origins in the prerogative writs and by subsequent, sometimes piecemeal, attempts to modify judicial review. If we were to design a set of remedies out of whole cloth today, it is not obvious that we would decide to set up two separate mechanisms for accessing the courts (that is, statutory appeals and judicial review). We might create an

---

[162] *TeleZone, supra* note 124. The courts retain the residual discretion to stay a damages action if the claim being made is actually "in its essential character" an application for judicial review. *TeleZone, ibid.* at para. 78; see also *Manuge v. Canada*, 2010 SCC 67, another of the five companion cases released alongside *TeleZone*.

[163] *TeleZone, supra* note 124 at para. 75.

overarching administrative review tribunal like Quebec's instead—and then, unlike Quebec, we might make it a judicial body rather than an administrative one. The point here is that remedies have been influenced by their historical roots, and remedies in turn have influenced the development of administrative law as a whole.

In part as a corrective to the heavy conventional emphasis on judicial review and its idiosyncrasies, this chapter tries to situate judicial review remedies within a larger context. Myriad other remedies are available at different stages of administrative action. Rich debate exists concerning appropriate tribunal functioning and the proper scope of tribunal action. Tribunals develop remedies that are novel, by court standards, because they are differently constituted than courts are. It is in part the heterogeneity and depth of this experience that underlies the modern instinct that courts should show some respectful deference in exercising judicial review of tribunal decisions. This chapter also counsels respect for that difference. A conversation about administrative law remedies illustrates the larger point that animates much of this volume: judicial review and court-centred processes, which make up the bulk of this book, are nevertheless the tail of administrative law and practice. That tail, fascinating though it is, should not limit our appreciation of, and approach to, the complex and varied species of dog that administrative action represents.

SUGGESTED ADDITIONAL READINGS

CASES

Canada (Attorney General) v. PHS Community Services Society, [2011] 3 S.C.R. 134 ("the Insite case").

Canada (Attorney General) v. TeleZone Inc., [2010] 3 S.C.R. 585.

Canada (Prime Minister) v. Khadr, [2010] 1 S.C.R. 44.

Domtar v. Quebec (Commission d'appel en matière de lésions professionnelles), [1993] 2 S.C.R. 756.

Harelkin v. University of Regina, [1979] 2 S.C.R. 561.

McDonald v. Anishinabek Police Service et al. (2006), 83 O.R. (3d) 132 (Div. Ct.).

McKinnon v. Ontario, [2003] O.J. No. 893 (QL) (Div. Ct.).

STATUTES

Federal Courts Act, R.S.C., 1985, c. F-7.

Students should also be familiar with any omnibus statutes or rules of court governing judicial review in their provinces. See section IV.E.2, Statutory Reform, above.

CHAPTER FOUR

Regulations and Rule Making: The Dilemma of Delegation

ANDREW GREEN

Faculty of Law and School of Public Policy and Governance, University of Toronto

I. The Spread of Regulations, Rules, and Soft Law

The *Environmental Protection Act* is Ontario's main statute for addressing environmental issues. One of its principal provisions concerning air pollution prohibits the discharge of a contaminant into the natural environment in excess of limits set in regulations under the Act. The Act provides that the lieutenant governor in council (the provincial Cabinet) "may make regulations" about, among other things, the emission of contaminants.[1] When the Ontario government decided that it needed to get tougher on air pollution, the Ministry of the Environment began developing new air pollution standards to be included in a regulation. The ministry undertook a long process of consultation with the public and with industry to try to set limits on the amount of certain pollutants that could be emitted to the air. At the end of this process, the lieutenant governor in council made a regulation based on a draft prepared by the ministry. The regulation specified how much of various pollutants could be emitted into the air over a given time period, how these pollutants were to be measured, and the manner in which contraventions were to be reported.

---

[1] *Environmental Protection Act*, R.S.O. 1990, c. E.19, s. 28(9).

Regulations are a form of law developed by the executive branch of government that typically do not set general government policy as statutes do, but rather explain how statutes will actually work.[2] Regulations are binding on all those who are made subject to them by the relevant statute or in the particular regulation. Because these environmental regulations were complicated, the Ministry also released numerous non-binding guidelines about how these regulations were to be interpreted.

This pattern of the legislature enacting broad legislation and delegating to the executive the power to fill in the details underlies much of the Canadian regulatory structure. The legislature delegates these powers to different members of the executive such as Cabinet, an individual minister, or a particular decision-making body such as the Ontario Securities Commission. These detailed rules or guidelines govern much of our daily lives at home and at work, from the safety of the food we eat and the music we can listen to on the radio to the safety of where we work.

These rules or guidelines can be broken into two broad categories: (1) regulations and rules, and (2) soft law. Regulations and rules, as noted above, are legally binding requirements and, as such, the power to make them must be expressly granted under a statute.[3] The number of regulations and rules has increased dramatically in recent years. They cover such diverse issues as permissible levels of pollution, the required content of a prospectus, working conditions in mines, and record-keeping requirements for beekeepers.[4] Because they are similar, binding regulations or rules are called "rules" in this chapter. Soft law, on the other hand, while also developed by the executive, is not legally binding. The power to make soft law (such as guidelines about procedures) does not have to be expressly provided in a statute. However, as we will see, soft law plays an important role in how decision-makers make decisions, both procedurally and substantively.[5]

This chapter examines the reliance by Canadian legislators on the delegation of the power to make detailed policy decisions. It focuses primarily on the power to make legally binding rules. However, the general principles also apply to soft law, and some issues relating to soft law are discussed. Section II discusses why we may want such delegation and, in particular, the desire to take advantage of the expertise and experience of different decision-makers. Section III turns to the risk that the party delegating the power loses some control over the actual rules or soft law that are put in place. Section IV examines methods used in Canada and elsewhere to limit the risks that arise from delegating the power to make rules and soft law. These methods include the structuring of the grant of discretion, legislative

---

2   See W.A. Bogart, "The Tools of the Administrative State and the Regulatory Mix" online at <adminlawincontext .emp.ca> [Bogart, "Tools of the Administrative State"].

3   Both regulations and rules are legally binding and arise from a statutory power. The federal *Statutory Instruments Act*, R.S.C. 1985, c. S-22, includes both in the term "statutory instruments." The term "regulation" is generally used in statutes where there is a delegation of the power to fill in detailed requirements.

4   See Bogart, "Tools of the Administrative State," *supra* note 2.

5   See e.g. Lorne Sossin & Charles Smith, "Hard Choices and Soft Law: Ethical Codes, Policy Guidelines, and the Role of Law in Regulating Government" (2003) 40 Alta. L. Rev. 867; and France Houle & Lorne Sossin, "Tribunals and Guidelines: Exploring the Relationship Between Fairness and Legitimacy in Administrative Decision-Making" (2006) 46 Can. Pub. Admin. 283.

review, judicial review, and public participation. Finally, section V briefly discusses the on-going struggle to find a balance between the desire to rely on expertise and the need to control those who are making the rules and guidelines.

II. Why Delegate?

When you examine the range of issues that are covered by rules or soft law, it becomes im-mediately apparent how important they are to our lives.[6] Yet these detailed prescriptions about our lives are not made by the legislature but by members of the executive and some-times by what are essentially private parties. Why is it that we rely so heavily on this struc-ture of our elected officials enacting legislation that sets out broad principles and delegates to others the power to actually fill in what is required? Why would legislators give others the power to make such important policy decisions?[7]

The primary reason for such delegation is *expertise*. Expertise is an important concept in administrative law. As Grant Huscroft discusses in Chapter 5, From Natural Justice to Fair-ness: Thresholds, Content, and the Role of Judicial Review, expertise underlies the tests related to procedural fairness and, as Audrey Macklin discusses in Chapter 9, Standard of Review: Back to the Future?, it is also central to the determination of the standard of review courts use when reviewing the substance of administrative decisions. Expertise is also central to the need to delegate responsibility for detailed requirements in the form of rules and soft law. It is impossible for legislators to have sufficient expertise to understand and evaluate all the various, detailed requirements in the vast range of areas that comprise the regulatory and welfare state. Such expertise requires education and training as well as experience in dealing with a particular issue. For example, developing the appropriate procedures for an immigration hearing may require the expertise of individuals who have been involved in many such hearings. Developing air pollution standards requires an understanding of science as well as the manner in which industries use and dispose of various pollutants. Developing rules for a securities market requires knowledge of how these markets function, the role of the consumer, and the manner in which corporations make decisions. Although individual legislators may have some information on these issues, the concern is that legislators would be unable to make optimal rules because of their lack of expertise. The argument, therefore, is that legislators should delegate the power to make these rules to individuals or groups who do have the expertise.

There is, however, a related reason for delegation of the power to make rules and soft law. Even if they had the expertise, legislators lack the *time and information* to make all the deci-sions necessary for the functioning of the current regulatory and welfare state. The legislature

---

6 Taggart states that "[i]t is trite to observe that delegated legislation ... often has more impact on the lives of ordinary citizens than do most full-blown Acts of Parliament." Michael Taggart, "From 'Parliamentary Pow-ers' to Privatization: The Chequered History of Delegated Legislation in the Twentieth Century" (2005) 55 U.T.L.J. 575 [Taggart, "From 'Parliamentary Powers' to Privatization"].

7 Such shifting of responsibility raised concerns about the constitutionality of delegated powers when it be-came increasingly common in the early part of the 20th century. See Taggart, *ibid.*, for a discussion of the history of the delegated legislation.

lacks the time to think through all the different ways in which specific provisions should be structured, relate to other provisions, and may apply in particular circumstances. For example, in regulating professions such as optometry, the legislators may enact a broad provision that a member of the College of Optometry may be found guilty of professional misconduct if he or she contravenes a requirement specified in regulations. Even if it were possible to do so, legislators do not have the time to consider all the potential ways in which an optometrist might act in a manner that should be considered professional misconduct.

However, the lack of time raises the related point that, even with time and expertise, legislators never have complete information about the future. They cannot possibly know all the different ways in which optometrists may act unprofessionally, or all the different pollutants that may be released into the atmosphere, or the different types of securities that may be developed. Legislation is therefore necessarily and unavoidably incomplete. Because legislation can be difficult and time-consuming to alter, the power to make requirements may be delegated in order to increase flexibility—to allow the requirements to be changed as new information arises. This flexibility represents another rationale for legislation. It is particularly important in rapidly changing areas such as environmental and securities regulation.

The issues of expertise, time, and information arise for both rules and soft law. While not legally binding, soft law such as policies and guidelines can have significant impacts on people's lives. For example, guidelines were central to *Baker v. Canada (Minister of Citizenship and Immigration)*.[8] In that case, Ms. Baker was an overstayer in Canada and had been ordered deported. She applied to the immigration minister to exercise his discretion under the *Immigration Act* to grant humanitarian and compassionate exemptions. She was seeking to stay in Canada pending determination of her application for permanent residency.[9] As a practical matter, immigration officers (not the minister) exercised the humanitarian and compassionate power in individual cases. However, there were minister-issued guidelines setting out the bases on which immigration officers should decide whether the individual deserved humanitarian and compassionate consideration. Although these guidelines were not legally binding, the Supreme Court of Canada took them into account in deciding that the officer had not acted reasonably in exercising the humanitarian and compassionate power in favour of Ms. Baker. These guidelines were therefore important to the Court in deciding the limits on the discretion to be exercised under the *Immigration Act*.

Soft law has some advantages over rules. Both provide a greater measure of certainty to those who come before regulatory decision-makers. Indeed, an administrative decision-maker may choose to use its power to make rules or soft law precisely because, in many cases, it is unwilling to allow the issue to be decided piecemeal through administrative hearings.[10] However, soft law is much more easily adaptable to changing circumstances because making soft law, as opposed to rules, is less likely to involve time-consuming and costly procedural

---

8   [1999] 2 S.C.R. 817.

9   For a discussion of the facts of *Baker*, see Grant Huscroft, Chapter 5, From Natural Justice to Fairness: Thresholds, Content, and the Role of Judicial Review.

10   An administrative decision-maker may, for example, consider the five criteria discussed by Bogart, "Tools of the Administrative State," *supra* note 2, when deciding whether to issue a guideline or rule on an issue rather than allow it to be decided through adjudication.

steps. Regulation making involves mandatory procedures (such as pre-publication), whereas guidelines come in a variety of forms and result from a range of different types of processes, some of which are informal and non-public.[11] As the Federal Court of Canada stated:

> Effective decision-making by administrative agencies often involves striking a balance between general rules and the exercise of ad hoc discretion or, to put it another way, between the benefits of certainty and consistency on the one hand, and of flexibility and fact-specific solutions on the other. Legislative instruments (including such non-legally binding "soft law" documents as policy statements, guidelines, manuals and handbooks) can assist members of the public to predict how an agency is likely to exercise its statutory discretion and to arrange their affairs accordingly, and enable an agency to deal with a problem comprehensively and proactively, rather than incrementally and reactively on a case by case basis. ... Because "soft law" instruments may be put in place relatively easily and adjusted in the light of day-to-day experience, they may be preferable to formal rules requiring external approval and, possibly, drafting appropriate for legislation.[12]

Although soft law may have some advantages from an efficiency perspective, it raises questions from a democratic legitimacy perspective, given the differences in how regulations and guidelines are made. The legislature may therefore want to set out broad policy decisions in legislation. These decisions are left necessarily incomplete, either because legislators lack the expertise to make the decisions or because they lack the time and information needed to make the requirements at the time of enactment. Legislators delegate the power to make rules and soft law in order to allow others to fill in the gaps left in the legislation.

III. The Risks of Delegation

While there are benefits to the delegation of the power to make requirements, it is not without its risks, nor is it necessarily as benign as the above picture implies. Such delegation raises the risk that those who are making the rules or soft law are not following the wishes or expectations of those who delegated the power (and as a consequence, at least in theory, the wishes of the electorate). This risk arises because of a *principal–agent problem* inherent in such delegation.[13] This principal–agent problem has two dimensions. First, the party making the rules or soft law (who, as we will see, can be termed "the agent") is not following the wishes of the legislature (which can be described as the "the principal"). Second, there is a further, underlying principal–agent concern because the legislature or the party making the rules or soft law (either of which could be termed the agent) may not be respecting the wishes of the ultimate principal—the public.

---

[11] For the federal process for regulation making, see *Cabinet Directive on Streamlining Regulation* (April 2007), online: Treasury Board of Canada Secretariat <http://www.tbs-sct.gc.ca/ri-qr/directive/directive00-eng.asp>.

[12] *Canada (Minister of Citizenship and Immigration) v. Thamotharem*, 2007 FCA 198 at paras. 55-56. For a discussion of this decision, see Lorne Sossin, Chapter 7, Access to Administrative Justice and Other Worries.

[13] For a good discussion of the principal–agent problem and its relationship to administrative law, see Matthew D. McCubbins, Roger G. Noll, & Barry R. Weingast, "Administrative Procedures as Instruments of Political Control" (1987) 3 J.L. Econ. & Org. 243 [McCubbins, Noll, & Weingast, "Administrative Procedures as Instruments"].

The principal–agent problem arises when one party (the principal) gives another party (the agent) the power to undertake some task on the principal's behalf. Principal–agent relationships arise all the time in everyday life. You ask a doctor to examine and treat you because you have fallen and hurt your ankle. You contract with a real estate agent to help you sell your house. You, as the shareholder of a company, empower management to act on your behalf in running the company. In each case, you, as the principal, are seeking to have the agent (the doctor, the real estate agent, and the manager, respectively) do something to benefit you. Similarly, a lawyer is the agent for many different principals who come to the lawyer with their problems and empower him or her to take action on their behalf.

These relationships arise for a number of reasons. It could be that the agent has some special expertise that the principal does not have, and so the principal cannot perform the task as effectively as the agent (or at all), as in the case of the doctor or the lawyer. The agent may also have information necessary for the task that the principal does not have—for example, in the case of a real estate agent, information about the housing market and the prices received for similar houses in the area. Further, even if the principal has the time and the expertise, the agent may have more time than the principal. For example, I may hire a plumber to fix my sink even though I could do it myself, simply because I would rather be doing other things with my time (playing with my children or working at my job). There is therefore real value in principal–agent relationships because the agent receives compensation for doing something that the principal cannot or does not want to do himself or herself.

However, there are also real risks that arise from the same features that make principals want to have agents undertake the task for them. If you have no medical expertise, it is hard (if not impossible) to know whether the doctor has taken the appropriate level of care and attention in attending to your ankle. The doctor has the relevant expertise, and you place a large degree of trust in the doctor when you have him or her treat you. The real estate agent has the information about the housing market and you are relying on him or her to use that information to get you the best price possible for your house. The plumber has the time to take apart your sink, fix it, and put it back together. If you are not watching the plumber, you are relying on him or her to do a good job on all aspects of the work.

The principal's lack of expertise, information, or time means that the principal has difficulty ensuring that the agent is actually acting in the principal's best interests in carrying out the task. This is the principal–agent problem. The doctor may be incompetent or may want to see as many patients as possible in the day and may therefore not use as much care as warranted in the circumstances. The real estate agent may not devote much time to your house because he has other, higher-valued houses that would generate more money from a sale. The plumber may use cheap materials or take short cuts in fixing your sink in order to save time or money on the work.

This principal–agent problem also arises where legislators delegate the power to make rules or soft law. Legislators delegate power because they lack the expertise, time, and information to make the decisions but, at the same time, they have difficulty monitoring how this power is exercised because they lack the expertise, time, and information, which means that expertise, time, and information represent both the reasons to delegate and the causes that hinder monitoring. On a more general level, the public has delegated to legislators the power to make decisions on its behalf and has difficulty monitoring what the legislators are doing and even more difficulty monitoring the parties who make the detailed rules or soft law.

There are two risks from delegating the power to make rules or soft law. First, the agent (the party making the rules or soft law) may follow its own views and values rather than the principal's views or values in making the rules or soft law. Because legislators enact legislation setting out broad directions, the ministry or agency making regulations under such legislation has considerable scope to determine the content of the detailed rules. The rule-maker may, for example, have very different views from the legislators of what constitutes the appropriate rule or guideline in particular cases.[14] The legislator often does not have the expertise, time, or information to monitor the content of particular rules or guidelines. The agent may be attempting to further the public interest but is doing so in the way it (as opposed to the legislature) believes is best.

Second, the agent may not even be attempting to further the public interest; it may, instead, be seeking to further its own interest. For example, if regulated parties (such as a particular industry group) offer some form of inducement to the agents (such as future job opportunities or, in the case of elected officials, funds for future election campaigns), the agents may be influenced in how they make rules or soft law. These agents may in some cases simply not want to expend the effort to regulate in a particular area.

Similarly, legislators may delegate in order to further their own interests, such as where broad legislation with delegated rule-making powers is used as a form of blame avoidance or credit attraction by legislators or Cabinet members. The legislature could, for example, enact very broad, tough-sounding pollution control legislation and then delegate the details to Cabinet to work out. Cabinet could then exempt or "grandfather" certain parties, such as particularly powerful industry groups. The legislators seek credit for enacting strong legislation but are also able to satisfy politically powerful parties.[15]

This principal–agent problem arises in any delegation of power where it is difficult for the principal to monitor the actions of the agent. The extent of the problem will vary depending on the relationship between the principal and the agent. As discussed below, the close connection between ministers and their ministries at least provides some (though at times weak) accountability to legislators for those making rules in ministries. The problem may become worse as the power to make rules is delegated to parties more independent of government. As Taggart notes, one of the trends of most concern in delegated legislation is the involvement of private parties (including regulated parties) in making rules. For example, governments in recent years have contracted out public services to private actors, giving rise to questions about the accountability of and control by legislators over these actors.[16]

---

14 As discussed below in the section on structural approaches to controlling delegated legislation, the impact of such a divergence in views will depend in part on the institutional structures in place. For example, in a Westminster system, the legislature and the executive are to some extent connected. Cabinet decides in large part how much detail is provided in legislation and how much is delegated to others to fill in. The minister is then responsible to Parliament for the resulting regulation. Although this system may provide a more direct connection and different dynamic between the rule-maker and the legislatures than the stricter separation of power in the United States, the lack of time, expertise, and information affect legislators' ability to monitor and control rule-makers in both systems.

15 See e.g. Matthew C. Stephenson, "Legislative Allocation of Delegated Power: Uncertainty, Risk, and the Choice Between Agencies and Courts" (2006) 119 Harv. L. Rev. 1035 [Stephenson, "Legislative Allocation of Delegated Power"].

16 Taggart, "From 'Parliamentary Powers' to Privatization," *supra* note 6.

IV. Controlling the Risks

Delegated legislation therefore gives rise to a principal–agent problem. The problem occurs either between the legislature and the executive (the body making the rules or soft law) or between the public and the legislature/executive. The breadth of delegation will depend on a number of factors, such as the capacity of the legislature to make detailed statutory rules.[17] If the members of the legislature have the time, resources, and expertise to make particular rules, they will be more likely to set out detailed requirements in legislation. The willingness of the legislature to delegate powers will also depend on its confidence that there are controls on the exercise of discretion. We focus on four main approaches to controlling delegated legislation:

- *Structuring the discretion:* The breadth of discretion will depend in part on how much the legislators can trust the agent to follow the legislators' policy preferences. Can legislators either choose particular agents or structure the agents in particular ways to influence the resulting rules?

- *Legislative oversight:* To what extent can the legislature exercise some form of direct control over the actual decisions made in the exercise of discretion?

- *Substantive judicial review:* What role do the courts play in supervising the substantive content of the rules? What role should they play?

- *Process requirements:* Do process requirements (such as requiring a certain degree of public involvement in the creation of rules) aid in balancing the benefits and risks of delegated legislation?[18]

We will discuss each of these approaches in turn.

A. Structural Approaches

A legislature will be more likely to delegate broad powers to make rules the more it trusts the agent making the rules to follow the legislature's policy preferences. This trust will vary according to such factors as the level of control the legislators have over those making the policy. For example, in Canada, legislators may delegate rule-making powers in broad terms because Cabinet (whose members are generally part of both the legislature and the executive) may have some control over the ministry or other body making the rules. This element of trust, however, raises the second type of principal–agent problem: trust between the public and elected officials. The ability of Cabinet to both set the scope of discretion and

---

17   See e.g. John D. Huber, Charles R. Shipan, & Madelaine Pfahler, "Legislatures and Statutory Control of Bureaucracy" (2001) 45 Am. J. Pol. Sci. 330 [Huber, Shipan & Pfahler, "Legislature and Statutory Control of Bureaucracy"] (discussing some of the factors influencing the degree of discretion granted by legislatures, including bargaining costs, legislative capacity, and the availability of non-statutory means of control).

18   See e.g. David Mullan, *Administrative Law* (Toronto: Irwin Law, 2001) [Mullan, *Administrative Law*] (discussing three main methods of control of delegated legislation: legislative scrutiny, public consultation, and judicial review); Huber, Shipan, & Pfahler, "Legislature and Statutory Control of Bureaucracy," *supra* note 17 (discussing various means of control of bureaucracy); and David B. Spence, "Managing Delegation Ex Ante: Using Law to Steer Administrative Agencies" (1999) 28 J. Legal Stud. 413 [Spence, "Managing Delegation Ex Ante"].

control the exercise of that discretion provides significant ability to the party in power to steer the details of policy at the expense of other elected members of the legislature.[19] How much power the legislature delegates may therefore depend on whether there is a majority or minority government. In a minority government, for example, the opposition parties have greater bargaining power and, thus, are less likely to be willing to grant broad discretion to ministries controlled by the ruling party.[20]

Legislatures may also attempt to indirectly control the exercise of discretion through, *inter alia*, the choice of body that will exercise the discretion or the resources provided to that body.[21] For example, the rules establishing environmental constraints on rights to log a particular area may be different depending on whether the decision is delegated to an environment ministry, a natural resources ministry, or an agency composed of a majority of members of the forestry industry. Each of these bodies may have the expertise to make the rules or soft law, but their actual policy preferences may differ depending on their mission or composition. These powers may even be delegated to an arm's-length body such as the Canadian Human Rights Commission, which has the power to make binding rules regarding the interpretation of its legislation.[22] Further, for any particular agent, the legislature may constrain the use of a delegated power by limiting the resources to the body that is granted the power.

B. Legislative Review

Instead of indirectly attempting to ensure that the power it delegates conforms to its views, the legislature could directly control the discretion by reviewing the resulting rules or soft law. The legislature itself, or more likely a committee, could examine the rules or soft law and decide whether to approve, disapprove, or amend them. Such legislative committees have been used at both the federal and the provincial level in Canada to examine regulations. For example, at the federal level, there is a joint committee of the Senate and House of Commons that reviews regulations, although the intent is to review the form of the regulation and not the underlying reasons for it.[23] Further, there may be review by Cabinet or

---

19 Mullan, *Administrative Law, supra* note 18, and Taggart, "From 'Parliamentary Powers' to Privatization," *supra* note 6.

20 An example is the *Kyoto Protocol Implementation Act* (S.C. 2007, c. 30), which was a federal, private member's bill aimed at reducing the discretion of the executive in the area of climate change, ostensibly by requiring the government to develop and implement a plan to meet Canada's emission-reduction commitments under the Kyoto Protocol. The Federal Court, however, held these requirements to be non-justiciable: *Friends of the Earth v. Canada (Minister of Environment)*, 2008 FC 1183.

21 Spence, "Managing Delegation Ex Ante," *supra* note 18.

22 These rules also bind the Canadian Human Rights Tribunal. The Supreme Court of Canada has upheld the legitimacy of such delegation of rule making. See *Bell Canada v. Canadian Telephone Employees Association*, 2003 SCC 36, [2003] 1 S.C.R. 884.

23 *Statutory Instruments Act*, R.S.C. 1985, c. S-22, s. 19. See Mullan, *Administrative Law, supra* note 18, describing the federal and provincial committees that have been set up to review regulations. Taggart, "From 'Parliamentary Powers' to Privatization," *supra* note 6 at 624 notes that the second half of the 20th century "was dominated by the attempt to enhance parliamentary safeguards against potential and actual 'abuses' of these delegated powers."

members of Cabinet. For example, the Daniels commission into the Ontario Securities Commission's (OSC's) rule-making powers recommended that an OSC rule should come into effect when made, unless Cabinet disapproves.[24] However, the legislative reforms following the committee's report instead require the OSC to deliver to the minister of finance a copy of the rule, any public comments on the proposed rule, and all material relied on by the OSC. The minister then has 60 days to approve the rule, reject the rule, or return the rule to the OSC for reconsideration.[25] Although legislative committees may review rules and regulations, there is generally no legislative oversight of soft law.

However, the use of legislative committees (or Cabinet or Cabinet ministers) to review regulations only goes part of the way to solving the principal–agent problem. As a committee, it may have some time to examine regulations that are made but, absent a significant allocation of resources, still less time than the agency or ministry, particularly if there is a desire to review not only formal regulations but all rules and even soft law. Further, it exacerbates the problem of time in some ways because it creates a system where regulations go back and forth between the legislators and the agency or rule-making authority. This oversight causes delay in implementation. More important, however, legislative review does not solve the problems concerning expertise and information. Members of the legislature are unlikely to have enough information or expertise to adequately review the regulations. This lack of expertise and information is often one of the main reasons for delegation in the first place. Legislators are likely either to largely defer to the rule-making authority, in which case the purpose of review is lost, or to take a hard look and be willing to substitute their own views, in which case the potential for errors increases significantly. Finally, legislative review does little to aid in the principal–agent problem between the public and the legislature/ executive.

C. Judicial Review of Substance

The courts are an obvious candidate for oversight of rules and soft law. In theory, they are an independent third party that can monitor or review the substance of the rules that are made. Such monitoring may keep the agent within the bounds of the power delegated to it and control the agent where it makes mistakes, substitutes its own views of the public good, or acts in its own self-interest.[26] Such review is similar to the review of other executive decisions discussed in other chapters of this book.

One of the seminal cases in Canada is *Thorne's Hardware Ltd. v. The Queen*.[27] In that case, the federal governor in council (Cabinet) made an order in council under the *National*

---

[24] See Hudson Janisch, "Further Developments with Respect to Rulemaking by Administrative Agencies" (1995) 9 Can. J. Admin. L. & Prac. 1 [Janisch, "Further Developments re Rulemaking by Administrative Agencies"] for a discussion of the background to the Daniels commission's report on OSC rule making.

[25] *Securities Act*, R.S.O. 1990, c. S.5, s. 143.3.

[26] Courts can also review the rule-making procedures to ensure that there is adequate participation in the process. Such review is considered in the next section and more generally by Grant Huscroft in Chapter 5, From Natural Justice to Fairness: Thresholds, Content, and the Role of Judicial Review.

[27] [1983] 1 S.C.R. 106 [*Thorne's Hardware*].

Harbours Board Act extending the boundaries of the Port of Saint John, New Brunswick. The applicant challenged the order in council on the basis that it was made in bad faith. It argued that Cabinet extended the boundaries in order to increase the revenues of the National Harbour Board and that such a purpose was not within the scope of Cabinet's powers under the Act. The Act provided that the boundaries of the Saint John harbour were those set out in a schedule "or as may be determined from time to time by order of the Governor in Council."[28]

The Supreme Court, however, held that while it was possible to strike down an order in council on "jurisdictional or other compelling grounds," "it would take an egregious case to warrant such action. This is not such a case."[29] It refused to examine the evidence of bad faith that the applicant provided, stating that "the government's reasons for expanding the harbour are in the end unknown. Governments do not publish reasons for their decisions; governments may be moved by any number of political, economic, social or partisan considerations."[30] As a result, the Court found against the applicant, stating that the harbour extension was an issue of "economic policy and politics" for which Cabinet "quite obviously believed [it] had reasonable grounds" and the Court "cannot enquire into the validity of those beliefs."[31]

The Court in *Thorne's Hardware* therefore took a strong position against examining the actions of Cabinet in making orders in council (a form of delegated rule making). However, as discussed by Audrey Macklin in Chapter 9, Standard of Review: Back to the Future?, the courts do review the substance of rules made by other agents under judicial review powers similar to the powers used to review other decisions of the executive. For example, *Enbridge and Union Gas v. Ontario Energy Board* involved a rule made by the Ontario Energy Board.[32] Section 44 of the *Ontario Energy Board Act* gave the board the power to make rules "governing the conduct of a gas distributer as such conduct relates to any person, (i) selling or offering to sell gas to a consumer."[33] The board made a rule—the gas distribution access rule (GDAR)—permitting gas vendors (who buy and sell the actual gas for distribution to consumers) to determine who will bill consumers for the gas they buy and for the transportation of the gas to the consumer. The vendor could choose whether both the vendor and

---

28 *National Harbours Board Act*, R.S.C. 1970, c. N-8, s. 7(2).

29 *Thorne's Hardware, supra* note 27 at 111.

30 *Ibid.* at 112-13.

31 *Ibid.* at 115. The Supreme Court applied the principle in *Thorne's Hardware* in refusing to allow an applicant to examine members of a city council to determine their motives in creating a board of inquiry: *Consortium Development (Clearwater) Ltd. v. Sarnia (City of)*, [1998] 3 S.C.R. 3. But see *Catalyst Paper Corp. v. North Cowichan (District)*, 2012 SCC 2 at para. 14 ("this attempt to maintain a clear distinction between policy and legality has not prevailed.").

32 (2005), 74 O.R. (3d) 147 (C.A.) [*Enbridge*]. See also *Canada (Wheat Board) v. Canada (Attorney General)*, 2009 FCA 214 (examining whether the governor in council's Canadian Wheat Board Direction Order limiting the Canadian Wheat Board's use of funds was within the scope of powers delegated under the *Canadian Wheat Board Act*) and *Globalive Wireless Management Corp. and AG (Canada) v. Public Mobile Inc.*, 2011 FCA 194 (discussing the ability of courts to review orders in council).

33 S.O. 1998, c. 15, Sch. B, s. 44(1)(b)(i).

the gas distributor (such as Enbridge Gas, which transports the gas through pipes to the consumer) issue separate bills; the vendor issues a bill for the vendor and the gas distributor; or the gas distributor issues a bill for both the vendor and the gas distributor. The Act contained a statutory right of appeal, which the gas distributors used to challenge the rule. They appeared to be concerned that the rule potentially interfered with their relationships with the consumer.

As with substantive review generally, the Ontario Court of Appeal in *Enbridge* first considered the standard of review. It held that the standard of review should be correctness whether the matter was viewed in the more traditional *ultra vires* framework (that is, as a question whether the board had jurisdiction to make the rule) or the more recent pragmatic and functional approach.[34] The gas distributors attempted to read s. 44 narrowly as only applying where there is a "business relationship" between the gas distributor and the vendor. However, the Court found that there was nothing in the Act that narrowed the interpretation in this manner and, in fact, that this interpretation was inconsistent with the broad purposes of the Act to regulate all aspects of the gas distribution business. It emphasized that the gas distribution business was regulated and that there was no common-law right to engage in it.

Courts therefore will review the substance of rules (including regulations) for whether (as in *Enbridge*) the regulation is within the grant of power. They will also review rules for other reasons, including whether the regulation violates the *Canadian Charter of Rights and Freedoms*.[35] However, they have in many cases been reluctant to do so, in part because the discretion is often granted in such broad terms that review is difficult.[36] Courts have been even more reluctant to review soft law.[37] One exception to this reluctance to review soft law is a review of "fettering." Fettering occurs where a guideline or policy, because of its language or practical effect, is in effect mandatory or binding on a decision-maker, or treated as such, thus taking away the discretion that has been granted to him or her.[38]

Yet even if courts were willing to review rules or soft law substantively, is this something we should want them to do? There are three principal reasons why we may not. First, the

---

[34] In Chapter 9, Standard of Review: Back to the Future?, Audrey Macklin discusses *ultra vires* review and the pragmatic and functional approach. Note that the Enbridge decision was decided prior to *Dunsmuir v. New Brunswick*, 2008 SCC 9, which changed the analysis for determining the appropriate standard of review.

[35] Part I of the *Constitution Act, 1982*, being Schedule B to the *Canada Act 1982* (U.K.), 1982, c. 11 [Charter]. For a discussion of some of the grounds of review, see Mullan, *Administrative Law, supra* note 18, Chapter 7 (including that the party making the rule must act in good faith, for a proper purpose, and on relevant considerations). On the Charter and regulations, see *Eldridge v. B.C. (Attorney General)*, [1997] 3 S.C.R. 624.

[36] See Taggart, "From 'Parliamentary Powers' to Privatization," *supra* note 6, and Mullan, *Administrative Law, supra* note 18.

[37] For a discussion of soft law and the Charter, see e.g. *Little Sisters Book and Art Emporium v. Canada (Minister of Justice)*, [2000] 2 S.C.R. 1120, and Lorne Sossin, "Discretion Unbound: Reconciling Soft Law and the Charter" (2002) 45 Can. Pub. Pol'y 465.

[38] See e.g. *Canada (Minister of Citizenship and Immigration) v. Thamotharem*, 2007 FCA 198 (finding a guideline specifying reverse-order questioning for refugee protection hearings did not constitute an unlawful fetter because it expressly directed panel members to consider the particular facts of each case to determine whether there should be an exception to this order of questioning).

process of judicial review tends, at best, to be random and, at worst, biased in favour of certain interest groups. Judicial review can be time-consuming and expensive. In some cases there are only a few parties who bear the costs from a new rule, while the benefits are spread across many people. For example, if the Ontario Ministry of the Environment makes a rule limiting sulphur dioxide emissions, the rule may impose significant costs on a few industries or firms but provide benefits (in terms of lower levels of air pollution or acid rain) to a large number of people (both within and potentially outside the province). In such a case, the industries or firms affected may have the incentive to challenge the rule in court (and be willing and able to expend the resources to do so), while those who benefit individually receive too little benefit to take on the expense of becoming involved in the application. The government agency that created the rule would have to represent the interests of those who the rule benefits. Conversely, if the costs are spread over a large number of people (for example, a rule imposing a tariff on an imported consumer product), there may be no one person who is sufficiently harmed to bear the costs of challenging the government decision. As a result, this check on government rules depends, in part, on such factors as how many parties benefit or bear costs and the resources of those parties.

The second concern with substantive judicial review is that, even if the "appropriate" challenges come before the courts, the courts often do not have the expertise to review the rules. There is therefore a large potential error cost from substantive judicial review—that is, courts might be less likely than the administrative decision-maker to determine the "right" answer.[39] Generalist courts that are "compulsorily ignorant" may not have the knowledge, experience, or technical expertise to review the, often, very detailed, technical rules.[40] For example, in *Enbridge*, how can a court determine the appropriateness of a rule concerning the billing of consumers or even the appropriate interpretation of the purposes of the legislation? The expertise of the Ontario Energy Board in issues relating to gas would aid in making these determinations. A court could defer to the decisions of the rule-maker, in which case there is no real check on the principal–agent concern. Alternatively, the court could take a hard look (potentially substituting its own view of the appropriate policy), in which case there is an increased risk that the wrong rule will be chosen. As with legislative review, the check on the principal–agent concern comes at the cost of loss of expertise.

Finally, even if the courts have the expertise to review administrative rules, this discussion of the courts' role in reviewing administrative rules has implicitly assumed that courts are attempting to determine the best possible interpretation of legislative power and the appropriateness of the challenged rule. However, judges also have their own policy preferences.[41] Judicial review, therefore, gives rise to a concern that judges' discretion over policy

---

[39] Stephenson, "Legislative Allocation of Delegated Power," *supra* note 15.

[40] See Taggart, "From 'Parliamentary Powers' to Privatization," *supra* note 6 at 589 (discussing the distaste of administrative law scholar John Willis for judicial review).

[41] See, generally, Jeffrey A. Segal & Harold J. Spaeth, *The Supreme Court and the Attitudinal Model Revisited* (Cambridge: Cambridge University Press, 2002) and Thomas J. Miles & Cass R. Sunstein, "Do Judges Make Regulatory Policy? An Empirical Investigation of Chevron" (2006) 73 U. Chicago L. Rev. 823. For an application of the attitudinal model of judicial decision-making in the Canadian context, see e.g. Benjamin Alarie & Andrew Green, "Policy Preference Change and Appointments to the Supreme Court of Canada" (2009) 47(1) Osgoode Hall L.J. 1.

outcomes (the content of rules) creates a further principal–agent problem as judges seek to implement their own views of appropriate policy.[42]

The issue of the extent of desirable substantive review by courts of administrative decisions has long vexed courts, legislators, and legal scholars. This issue is more fully addressed in other chapters in this book. However, there is an interesting connection between judicial review and the discussion above of structural approaches to controlling delegated decision making. In order to increase the likelihood that rules will align with their preferences, legislators may wish a particular agency, rather than courts, to interpret legislative provisions in making rules.[43] For example, legislators who are favourable to unions or workers may believe that a Ministry of Labour interpretation of a rule-making power is more likely to favour unions or workers than a court's interpretation. Thus, in such cases, they may seek to limit judicial review. In other cases, the legislators may believe that courts' interpretations are more likely to be in accordance with their preferences and seek to expand judicial review. Such limitation or expansion of judicial review could come, for example, through a privative clause or a right to appeal, or through other cues as to who the legislature wishes to set policy. However, given the lack of clarity in how the courts interpret their "expertise" relative to that of administrative decision-makers, legislators can never be sure that their choice of delegate (either administrative decision-maker or court) will prevail over time.[44]

D. Process Requirements

A final manner in which the actions of the agent could be controlled is through the process it must follow to make the rules. There is a wide range of processes that a body creating rules could follow. At one extreme, it could make the decision based on no external information and no consultation with any other group. At the other, the body could hold a full hearing on the rule, taking submissions from different groups and engaging in consultations over draft rules. Actual decision-making processes generally fall somewhere between these extremes.

One of the key features of these process requirements is the extent of public participation. Why might we want to have a process that includes public participation? The principal reason is that it may result in better decisions. First, process requirements may ensure that those making the rules have all the relevant information. This information may, for example, be about the costs and the benefits of the particular rule, such as how much it would cost regulated parties to comply with the rule (for example, the cost of putting safety equipment on all machines to protect workers) or how the regulated activity affects the general

---

[42]   See e.g. Stephenson, "Legislative Allocation of Delegated Power," *supra* note 15 (discussing the possible differences in policy preferences between legislatures, agencies, and courts).

[43]   See e.g. *ibid.* (arguing that legislators may wish to delegate the power to interpret legislation to agencies, if they wish to produce consistent interpretation across issues, or to the courts, if they wish to produce consistent interpretation across time—that is, even when other legislators are in power).

[44]   Adrian Vermeule, "The Delegation Lottery" (2006) 119 Harv. L. Rev. 105 (arguing that the choice of who interprets legislation is as much of a "lottery" for legislators as is the ultimate rule or decision that a delegate makes on the basis of broad legislative provisions). See also Chapters 9 and 10 in this book discussing the Supreme Court's approach to determining the standard of review.

public (such as the impact of noise pollution on their daily activities). It may also provide information on how the public and the regulated party value the changes proposed under the rule. Consider a rule limiting greenhouse gas emissions. Public consultation may provide the party making the rule with a better understanding of the extent to which the public cares about and is willing to bear costs of addressing climate change. This additional information may reduce the mistakes made by the party making the regulation about either the extent of the problem or the values of the public regarding the issue.

Second, instead of merely gathering information, such processes may promote deliberation. Deliberation involves individuals debating issues and exchanging ideas. Such debate may lead not only to better understanding of the issues but also to the growth of shared values and goals. For example, deliberation on the rules about public schools in Alberta may lead to new shared values or goals for education for citizens of the province. Some jurisdictions, such as British Columbia, have experimented with "citizen juries" for developing policies. These juries are made up of a number of citizens who are given information on an issue (or set of issues) and time to debate. The hope is that the exchange of ideas will lead to a better, more considered decision on the policy.

More formal processes for making rules therefore potentially lead to better decisions through increased information for the rule-makers or more thoughtful deliberation by citizens. Better information and deliberation may reduce the probability of mistakes by rule-makers. Further, the involvement of the public increases the openness of the process to scrutiny, which may reduce the probability that those making the rules act on their own view of the public interest (as opposed to that of the legislators or the public). It may also reduce the ability of interest groups to pressure those making the rules to decide in their favour (and against the interests of the public more generally).[45]

However, more formal processes are not without their risks. First, formal process can be costly and time-consuming. Making proposals and holding hearings or consultations to obtain public input can be expensive. Perhaps more important, public consultation can considerably lengthen the time it takes to make a rule. Formal processes have been blamed, in part, for the inflexibility and slow-changing nature of the U.S. regulatory system. An example of the time that consultations can add to rule making is the air pollution standards process in Ontario. In the 1970s, the Ontario government made standards setting out permissible levels of emissions of particular substances. The Ministry of the Environment decided to revise those standards in the late 1980s. It engaged in public consultations from 1987 to 1990, but was unable to obtain agreement and stopped the process. It began again in 2001 and went through a series of proposals and different efforts at getting public comments. This process continued over four years before new standards were in force.[46]

Second, while formal processes may provide transparency that reduces interest-group power, the processes at the same time provide another avenue through which interest groups can pressure those making the rules. It is important to consider who is using the process and the nature of that group's involvement. Is a particular group able to use its resources to

---

[45]   See e.g. Richard Stewart, "The Reformation of American Administrative Law" (1975) 88 Harv. L. Rev. 1669.

[46]   Environmental Commissioner of Ontario, *Annual Report 2004-2005* at 55-58, online: Environmental Commissioner of Ontario <http://www.eco.on.ca/english/publicat/ar2004.pdf>.

dominate the process? Little work has been done on this issue in Canada. Third, and relatedly, those making the rules may not actually attend to the public participation. They may simply go through the motions in the process and not substantively change their views.

Finally, public participation may be detrimental if the public itself makes mistakes. Many of the issues that are addressed through rules are highly technical or based on complex science. Individual members of the public may make mistakes in understanding and expressing opinions about an issue. These mistakes can lead individuals to believe that a risk is greater than it actually is. For example, individuals tend to perceive the risk of a car accident to be greater if they have seen a car accident recently. Individuals may also perceive risks to be less than they actually are. For example, individuals tend to be overly optimistic about their risks of accident. Most believe they have above-average skills and are less likely than average to have a workplace accident. Further, many of these mistakes concern the types of issues that involve regulatory choices that are difficult for individuals to understand. Individuals have difficulty, for example, understanding very small probabilities of catastrophic harm, such as a catastrophic shift in climate. They tend to ignore these very small probability risks even though they should be taken into account.[47]

A related concept is that individuals often do not invest the time or cost necessary to become informed on an issue. Instead, they may base their decisions on decisions of others. If some individuals believe, for example, that the use of a hormone in the production of meat is carcinogenic (even though there is no evidence to that effect), other people may adopt the same position, purely on the basis that the first individuals believed it. More may come to the same belief on the basis of the now greater number of people who believe that hormones are harmful. These "information cascades," where people come to believe something on the basis that others believe it, can lead to dramatic shifts in public opinion on issues.[48]

So some mistakes may make the public believe that a risk is greater than it actually is, and some that it is less than it actually is. Some risks may be ignored entirely, and others may attract significant public concern on the basis of very little information. Formal public participation processes are open to individuals who express concern on the basis of such mistaken beliefs. The possibility of such mistakes has led to different types of proposals for structuring decision making. Some commentators have called for the isolation of regulatory decision-makers from the public because of these mistakes—that is, they argue that decisions should be made largely by experts as opposed to through "deliberation," which is likely to be based on mistaken understandings.[49] Others claim that any such isolation is inherently undemocratic and that the mistakes can be reduced through an appropriately deliberative process.[50]

Given these benefits and costs to procedures for making rules, what have we done in Canada to address these issues? Just as the courts have reviewed the substance of rules, you

---

[47] Richard Posner, *Catastrophe: Risk and Response* (Oxford: Oxford University Press, 2004).

[48] Cass Sunstein, *Risk and Reason* (Cambridge: Cambridge University Press, 2002).

[49] Cass Sunstein, *Law of Fear* (Cambridge: Cambridge University Press, 2005).

[50] See Dan Kahan, "Fear of Democracy: A Cultural Evaluation of Sunstein on Risk" (2006) 119 Harv. L. Rev. 1071.

could imagine courts reviewing how the rules were developed and creating a common-law set of procedures that must be followed when making rules under delegated powers. However, as Grant Huscroft explains in Chapter 5, From Natural Justice to Fairness: Thresholds, Content, and the Role of Judicial Review, there is no common-law requirement of procedural fairness where a decision is of a "legislative and general" nature.[51] Because rules are typically general (that is, apply to many parties), they tend to fall under this exception to procedural fairness. "Legislative" in this context does not necessarily mean "by the legislature." In *Att. Gen. of Can. v. Inuit Tapirisat et al.*,[52] the Inuit Tapirisat challenged a rate increase for telephone services supplied by Bell Canada. The Canadian Radio-television and Telecommunications Commission (CRTC) implemented the rate increase following hearings in which the Inuit Tapirisat had participated. The CRTC approved the rate increase without the conditions that the Inuit Tapirisat had requested. The Inuit Tapirisat appealed to the federal Cabinet under provisions of the *National Transportation Act* to have the CRTC decision set aside. As part of this appeal, the CRTC made submissions to Cabinet through the Department of Communications. The Inuit Tapirisat was not allowed to review or respond to the CRTC submission. Cabinet rejected the appeal.

The Inuit Tapirisat sought judicial review, claiming it had been denied procedural fairness in its appeal because the CRTC had made submissions to which it did not have access. The Supreme Court of Canada, however, found that Cabinet did not owe the Inuit Tapirisat procedural fairness in this case. Among other things, Estey J. found that making rates was "legislative action in its purest form" because it affected many Bell subscribers.[53] He pointed to, among other things, the fact that the legislation created procedural rules for the CRTC but not for Cabinet appeals. In the end, he found that there was no obligation on Cabinet to provide procedural fairness, such as notice, a hearing, or reasons.

Inuit Tapirisat shows that for a decision to be "legislative" in nature, the body making the decision does not have to be the legislature. The decision itself must have this "legislative and general" character. Although this legislative and general category is not self-evident, it appears to exclude rules aimed at a single party. For example, *Homex Realty v. Wyoming*[54] involved a dispute between a municipality and a developer over who should pay the costs of installing services for a new subdivision. After extended and bitter negotiations, the municipality used its powers to make bylaws to designate the developer's subdivision plan not to be a "registered plan." It did so without notice to the developer. If the bylaw was valid, the developer would have to obtain permission from the municipality to sell parts of the development and, before providing consent, the municipality would impose conditions (such as installing services). The developer challenged the bylaw on the ground that the municipality did not act fairly in enacting the bylaw. Estey J. held that the bylaw was not general in

---

51   *Knight v. Indian Head School Division No. 19*, [1990] 1 S.C.R. 653.

52   [1980] 2 S.C.R. 735 [*Inuit Tapirisat*]. See also *Denby v. Dairy Farmers of Ontario*, 2009 CarswellOnt 6924 (S.C.J. (Div. Ct.)) (no procedural fairness due for creation of new dairy quota policy by the Dairy Farmers of Ontario because the decision was of a legislative nature).

53   *Inuit Tapirisat, supra* note 52 at 754.

54   [1980] 2 S.C.R. 1011.

nature, but was aimed at resolving a dispute with one party—the developer. The municipality therefore owed a duty of fairness in such situations. Dickson J., in dissent, also agreed that there was duty on the municipality to provide procedural fairness. He stated, "[w]hat we have here is not a by-law of wide and general application which was to apply to all citizens of the municipality equally. Rather, it was a by-law aimed deliberately at limiting the rights of one individual."[55]

The Federal Court more recently considered the issue of the scope for procedural review of regulations in *Canadian Society of Immigration Consultants v. Canada (Citizenship and Immigration)*.[56] The Court found that a decision to terminate the mandate of the existing body regulating immigration consultants and replace it with a new body was "essentially a 'legislative' action (whether it results from an Act of Parliament or from a regulation made by the Executive branch)."[57] The fact that the regulation was aimed at one particular body (the Canadian Society of Immigration Consultants) did not make it an "individual" decision so as to make it non-legislative in nature. As a result, the duty of fairness did not apply to the regulation-making process at issue. The Court did open the door to the possibility of the application of the doctrine of legitimate expectations to the regulation-making process, but found that, even so, there was no breach of the Society's legitimate expectations.

As a result, the general approach of courts in Canada has not been to impose common-law procedural requirements on the making of rules. There are, however, a range of statutory provisions and policies that set out the required procedures. Unlike the approach in the United States, where there is a principal statute (the *Administrative Procedures Act*) that sets out a set of fundamental procedures for rule making, the Canadian approach has tended to be more piecemeal. There are, for example, some procedures at the federal level concerning formal regulations, such as procedures under the *Statutory Instruments Act* for publication of draft regulations.[58] More recently, a federal Cabinet directive on streamlining regulation came into effect on April 1, 2007, replacing the former Government of Canada Regulatory Policy. The Cabinet directive emphasizes the importance of identifying interested and affected persons when making regulations and providing them with meaningful opportunities and information for participation.[59]

---

[55]   *Ibid.* at 1052. The majority and the dissent, therefore, agreed that the developer was owed a duty of fairness because the bylaw was not "legislative" or general. They differed on whether they should, in their discretion, grant the remedy requested by the developer. The majority held that the Court should not grant the remedy because of the actions of the developer during the negotiations and litigation.

[56]   2011 FC 1435.

[57]   *Ibid.* at para 113.

[58]   R.S.C. 1985, c. S-22. Since the mid-1980s, the publication of proposed regulations in the *Canada Gazette* has been accompanied by a regulatory impact-analysis statement. The statement sets out the rationale for the regulation and attempts to measure the costs and benefits of the regulation. There is a more general statute in Quebec. See Janisch, "Further Developments re Rulemaking by Administrative Agencies," *supra* note 24, for a general discussion of rule making in Canada.

[59]   The Cabinet directive also sets out process requirements, such as analysis of the costs and benefits of proposed regulations. See Cabinet Directive on Streamlining Regulation (April 2007), online: Treasury Board of Canada Secretariat <http://www.tbs-sct.gc.ca/ri-qr/directive/directive00-eng.asp>.

There are also more specific procedures in particular substantive areas of law at both the federal and the provincial levels. For example, following a court challenge to policy guidelines of the OSC, the Ontario government struck a committee to reform the rule-making process of the OSC.[60] The legislation that grew out of this committee's work requires the OSC, in making a rule, to publish a notice of the proposed rule, including the rule itself; a statement of the purpose of the rule; a discussion of the alternatives considered and the reasons for not adopting them; a reference to any unpublished material relied on; and a description of the anticipated costs and benefits.[61] The OSC is also required to provide an opportunity to interested parties to comment on the proposed rule. If, after publication and consideration, the OSC wishes to make material changes to the draft rule, it must provide further notice of and opportunity to comment on these proposed changes. The OSC cannot make the rule until it has provided the required opportunity for comments and considered all representations made in the process.

Ontario has enacted similar rules in other areas. For example, the Ontario *Environmental Bill of Rights*[62] creates procedural rights surrounding government decisions in the environmental area, including the making of rules. The Bill provides for the creation of an electronic registry on the Internet of all proposed rules and instruments (including regulations, formal rules, policies, orders, and approvals). There are different notice and comment procedures for different types of decisions (with, for example, longer comment periods for decisions that may have a greater impact on the environment). The minister of the environment is to "take every reasonable step to ensure that all comments relevant to the proposal that are received as part of the public participation process ... are considered when decisions about the proposal are made."[63]

The government can be taken to court for failure to fulfill statutory procedural requirements. For example, in the *Enbridge* case,[64] Enbridge and Union Gas claimed that the Ontario Energy Board did not comply with the notice and comment requirements set out in the *Ontario Energy Board Act*. The notice and comment provisions were similar to those in the *Securities Act*, with a requirement to give notice of the proposed rule, including a description of the anticipated costs and benefits. If the board then decides to make a material change to the proposed rule, it must publish the proposed change and the anticipated costs and benefits. In this case, the Ontario Energy Board proposed the new rule, took comments, and twice gave notice of a proposed change and took further comments. However, in the judicial review, Enbridge and Union Gas argued that the board only provided anticipated costs and benefits for the proposal as a whole and did not break out the costs and benefits of the different billing arrangements. They argued that this was insufficient because the purpose

---

[60]   See Janisch, "Further Developments re Rulemaking by Administrative Agencies," *supra* note 24, and Mullan, *Administrative Law*, *supra* note 18, for a discussion of the history behind the procedural rules for the OSC.

[61]   *Securities Act*, *supra* note 25, s. 143.2.

[62]   S.O. 1993, c. 28.

[63]   *Ibid.*, s. 35.

[64]   *Supra* note 32. See also *Hanna v. Ontario (AG)*, 2011 ONSC 609 (Court reviewing wind power regulations under the *Environmental Protection Act* to determine whether statutorily required process followed).

of the notice and comment requirements was to impose a discipline on the board and allow the parties to make full representations.

The Ontario Court of Appeal rejected this argument. It noted that a cost–benefit analysis was not required for each provision of the proposed rule. It held that the purpose of the rule was not to impose discipline on the Ontario Energy Board and that, if the legislature was concerned that the board engaged in "thoughtless rulemaking, it would surely have imposed a requirement to give reasons for rulemaking, if indeed it left the Board with any rulemaking at all."[65] The court stated that the purpose of the requirement was merely to give interested parties the opportunity to make written submissions on the change and that the parties had ample opportunity to do so. The court therefore seems to limit the usefulness of these provisions to reduce certain principal–agent risks—in particular, the risk of making mistakes in rule making.

Much of the public participation in rule making in Canada therefore consists of the provision of notice of the proposed rule and the opportunity for the public to comment on the proposal. How do such "notice and comment" requirements fit with our discussion of the benefits and risks of process? They are beneficial in that they ensure that the public has some information about the proposed rule and the regulators potentially receive information from the public on the costs and benefits of and trade-offs in making the rule. Further, the cost of these requirements is relatively low. However, notice and comment requirements have a number of drawbacks. First, they can cause delay because those making the rules need to give notice of and time to comment on any proposed material change to a rule. Second, while notice and comment rules potentially open the rule-making process up to a greater range of parties, it is not clear who can participate. It may be that the comment process is dominated by certain parties (including, potentially, the regulated parties). Certain groups may be able to make more detailed and effective comments if they have resources and are willing to invest in the process. As was noted above, if significant costs may be imposed on relatively few parties, they have greater incentive to invest resources to oppose the rule than if the benefits (or costs) are spread over a larger number of parties. Finally, notice and comment rules do not provide scope for deliberation. The comments of each individual are provided to the government, but there is no exchange of ideas between those making the comments.[66]

The process of making rules can therefore aid in controlling the actions of the "agent." It can potentially reduce mistakes in rule making by increasing the flow of information to rule-makers. It can also provide some transparency that may reduce the rule-makers' ability to make rules following not the interests of legislators but either their own idiosyncratic view of the public good or their own self-interest (such as where they seek to favour certain parties because of the rewards those parties can provide to them). Legislators may even be able to use the process to aid in ensuring that rules have a particular substantive content by

---

[65] *Ibid.* at 160.

[66] See Andrew Green, "Creating Environmentalists: Environmental Law, Identity and Commitment" (2006) 17 J. Envtl. L. & Prac. 1 for a discussion of administrative law, deliberation, and the formation of shared values or identities.

altering procedures to favour certain parties.[67] For example, procedures that favour or encourage submissions by environmental groups may lead to rules that tend to favour their interests.

However, there is no necessary connection between these processes and results, or a reduction in interest-group power. As noted above, much depends on the relative resources of the parties and the willingness of parties to become involved in the rule making. It also depends on the willingness of the rule-maker to take the comments of interested parties into account. Interestingly, there may be a connection between these process requirements and substantive review by the courts. If a rule-maker follows expansive procedures (including public participation), courts may be more willing to defer to the resulting decisions (rules) because, for example, the use of the procedures is a signal of better-quality decisions.[68] It is difficult, however, to ensure that the quality of decisions actually is improved and that the rule-makers actually do take public comments into account. Courts have difficulty determining whether a rule-maker actually considered particular comments because there are so many potential reasons for a decision (recall the comments of the Supreme Court in *Thorne's Hardware*[69]). Part of the answer may be to require the rule-maker to provide reasons in the hope that it will be held accountable, either by the public or by legislators. However, as discussed, such accountability can be a weak constraint where time, expertise, and information costs hinder monitoring.

V. The Ongoing Struggle

Legislators thus take a risk when they delegate the power to make rules to other parties. They gain the use of the expertise of these other parties. Further, they expand the reach of their regulatory powers because they would not otherwise have the time to make rules in all the areas that are encompassed by a modern welfare and regulatory state. However, at the same time, they are giving a significant amount of power to parties they cannot fully monitor because of the information and time costs of such monitoring. This difficulty in monitoring creates a principal–agent problem.

Governments continue to search for better ways of overcoming this principal–agent problem. Various solutions have been proposed, such as creating administrative law courts (courts specializing in the general issues related to administrative law or to substantive areas of law in particular, such as labour law or environmental law); having electronic "billboards" for comments on rules so that everyone can review comments submitted by others (thereby, it is hoped, increasing deliberation in notice and comment processes); and increasing the resources for and power of legislative committees that review regulations. There is, however, no perfect solution. The struggle is to address the principal–agent problem while retaining the significant benefits that come with delegation. This struggle will become increasingly

---

[67]   McCubbins, Noll, & Weingast, "Administrative Procedures as Instruments," *supra* note 13.

[68]   Matthew Stephenson, "The Strategic Substitution Effect: Textual Plausibility, Procedural Formality, and Judicial Review of Agency Statutory Interpretations" (2006) 120 Harv. L. Rev. 528.

[69]   *Supra* note 27.

important as governments continue to experiment with new forms of regulation, including greater use of private markets and private parties. These new forms of regulation do not mean fewer rules. Instead, they have led to "more delegated legislation, increased delegation of governmental functions to the private sector, and more quasi-legislation (rules)"[70] and, whether or not these new forms of regulation are otherwise beneficial, to increased principal–agent concerns.

SUGGESTED ADDITIONAL READINGS

CASES

Canada (Minister of Citizenship and Immigration) v. Thamotharem, 2007 FCA 198.

Canada (Wheat Board) v. Canada (Attorney General), 2009 FCA 214.

Canadian Society of Immigration Consultants v. Canada (Citizenship and Immigration), 2011 FC 1435.

Enbridge and Union Gas v. Ontario Energy Board, [2005] O.J. No. 33 (QL) (C.A.).

Thorne's Hardware Ltd. v. Canada, [1983] 1 S.C.R 106.

SECONDARY SOURCES

Croley, Steven P., *Regulation and Public Interests: The Possibility of GOOD Regulatory Government* (Princeton, NJ: Princeton University Press, 2008), part I.

Mullan, David, *Administrative Law* (Toronto: Irwin Law, 2001), chapter 7.

Taggart, Michael, "From 'Parliamentary Powers' to Privatization: The Chequered History of Delegated Legislation in the Twentieth Century" (2005) 55 U.T.L.J. 575.

---

70   Taggart, "From 'Parliamentary Powers' to Privatization," *supra* note 6 at 627.

From Natural Justice to Fairness: Thresholds, Content, and the Role of Judicial Review

GRANT HUSCROFT*

Faculty of Law, University of Western Ontario

*   Thanks to the editors and to Matthew Groves (Monash) and Dean Knight (Victoria University of Wellington) for helpful comments and suggestions on an earlier draft, and to Brandon Duewel (J.D. 2013) and Danilo Popadic (J.D. 2013) for research assistance.

I. Introduction

People are affected by a wide variety of decisions made on a daily basis by public authorities—from Cabinet ministers to bureaucrats, tribunals, agencies, boards, commissions, and other public authorities. The one thing these decisions have in common is that, in general, they must be made pursuant to a fair procedure.

The development of a "duty of fairness" is one of the great achievements of modern administrative law. It promotes a better-informed decision-making process, leading to better public policy outcomes, and helps to ensure that individuals are treated with respect in the administrative process. As we will see, the duty is context-specific: its content is articulated having regard to the circumstances surrounding the relevant decision and can be tailored to suit the wide variety of decision-making contexts to which it applies.

This chapter traces the development of the duty, considers the threshold for its application, and fleshes out the contents of the duty. The most common means to attack an adverse administrative decision is to impugn the procedure pursuant to which the decision was made, and the chapter concludes with a consideration of judicial oversight of the duty and the consequences of an unfair procedure. Some practical implications flowing from the duty are discussed by Freya Kristjanson and Leslie McIntosh in Chapter 6, Advocacy Before Administrative Tribunals.

II. From Natural Justice to Fairness

The availability of procedural protection in administrative law once depended on the way in which a decision was characterized. "Judicial" and "quasi-judicial" decisions were required to be made in accordance with the rules of natural justice: *audi alteram partem*, which requires a decision-maker to "hear the other side" in a dispute before deciding, and *nemo judex in sua causa*, which precludes a man from being a "judge in his own cause."[1]

---

[1]   See, generally, William Wade & Christopher Forsyth, *Administrative Law*, 10th ed. (Oxford: Oxford University Press, 2009), chapters 13-14.

So-called administrative decisions—virtually any decision other than a judicial or quasi-judicial decision—could be made without any procedural impediments. The dichotomy between judicial and administrative decisions made administrative law "formalistic"[2] in nature, and judicial review proceedings focused on the nature of the power exercised rather than the impact of its exercise. To obtain procedural protection, an applicant had to convince a court that a particular decision could properly be characterized as judicial or quasi-judicial. A successful applicant would receive the full range of natural justice protection. An unsuccessful applicant would receive no procedural protection at all.

The growth of the modern regulatory state—and with it the number of important administrative decisions made by everyone from bureaucrats to administrative tribunals and ministers of the Crown—made change inevitable. It was indefensible that important decisions could be made without any procedural protection being afforded simply because they were classified as administrative in nature. Following the lead of the House of Lords in *Ridge v. Baldwin*,[3] the Supreme Court of Canada abandoned the all-or-nothing approach to the provision of procedural protection in *Nicholson v. Haldimand-Norfolk (Regional) Police Commissioners*.[4] *Nicholson* concerned the summary dismissal of a probationary police constable some 15 months into his term of service. He was not given a reason for his dismissal, nor was he given notice or allowed to make any representations prior to his dismissal. Regulations made under provincial legislation provided that police officers could not be penalized without a hearing and right of appeal, but added that the Board of Commissioners of Police had authority "to dispense with the services of any constable within eighteen months of his becoming a constable."[5]

Under the traditional common-law approach that would have been the end of the matter; Nicholson was not entitled to a hearing before his dismissal, nor could his dismissal be characterized as the sort of "judicial or quasi-judicial" decision to which natural justice protection applied. It was an administrative matter and, as such, Nicholson would not have been entitled to any protection at all. In these circumstances, a 5:4 majority of the Supreme Court held that a general duty of "procedural fairness" applies to administrative decisions. Writing for a majority of the Court, Chief Justice Laskin justified the new duty as follows:

> [T]he classification of statutory functions as judicial, quasi-judicial or administrative is often very difficult, to say the least; and to endow some with procedural protection while denying others any at all would work injustice when the results of statutory decisions raise the same serious consequences for those adversely affected, regardless of the classification of the function in question.[6]

---

2 Frederick Schauer discusses some of the vices, and virtues, of formalism in *Thinking Like a Lawyer: A New Introduction to Legal Reasoning* (Cambridge, MA: Harvard University Press, 2009) at 29-35.

3 [1964] A.C. 40 (H.L.) (dismissal of chief constable of Borough of Brighton without notice or right to be heard at meeting of watch committee).

4 [1979] 1 S.C.R. 311 [*Nicholson*].

5 *Ibid.* at para. 5, citing the *Police Act*, R.S.O. 1970, c. 351, Reg. 680, s. 27(b).

6 *Ibid.* at para. 23.

On this approach, the ability of the board to dismiss Nicholson for any reason (or none at all) was irrelevant. Plainly, Nicholson could not claim the procedural protection the regulations afforded to those with 18 months of service (that is, an oral hearing with a right of appeal) but, according to Laskin C.J., it did not follow that he must be denied any protection at all. Nicholson was entitled to be treated fairly, not arbitrarily; he was entitled to be told why he was being dismissed and given an opportunity to make submissions—orally or in writing, at the board's discretion—before he was dismissed.

Laskin C.J. did not reject the distinction between administrative and judicial or quasi-judicial decisions in *Nicholson*. Instead, he accepted as a common-law principle the notion that "in the sphere of the so-called quasi-judicial the rules of natural justice run, and that in the administrative or executive field there is a general duty of fairness."[7] However, in subsequent cases the "duty of fairness" came to replace natural justice as the organizing principle in administrative law and, as a result, there is no longer any reason to differentiate between the two concepts or the spheres in which they operate.[8] The duty of fairness applies across the spectrum of decisions that public authorities may make and the requirements of the duty vary in accordance with the relevant circumstances.

"Fairness" has become short form for procedural fairness, but it is important not to lose sight of the essentially procedural character of the duty. The duty of fairness is concerned with ensuring that public authorities act fairly in the course of *making* decisions, not with the fairness of the actual decisions they *make*. The duty of fairness has nothing to say about the outcome of particular decisions, and in particular does not require that the decisions of public authorities be considered "fair"—a subjective and contestable concept that Canadian administrative law eschews.[9]

The duty of fairness promotes sound public administration and the accountability of public decision-makers by ensuring that decisions are made with input from those affected by them; well-informed decisions are likely to be better decisions, and decisions made pursuant to transparent, participatory processes promote important rule-of-law values. Fairness is,

---

7   *Ibid.* at para. 22, citing *Bates v. Lord Hailsham*, [1972] 1 W.L.R. 1373 at 1378 (Ch. D.).

8   This is not a uniquely Canadian development. In *Kioa v. West* (1985), 159 C.L.R. 550, Mason J. summed up English and Australian law as follows:

> It has been said on many occasions that natural justice and fairness are to be equated … . And it has been recognized that in the context of administrative decision-making it is more appropriate to speak of a duty to act fairly or to accord procedural fairness. This is because the expression "natural justice" has been associated, perhaps too closely associated, with procedures followed by courts of law (at para. 30).

> Nevertheless, the language of natural justice survives in most jurisdictions and is often used interchangeably with fairness terminology. In New Zealand, for example, the *New Zealand Bill of Rights Act 1990* includes a right to natural justice (s. 27), but the right is understood as a codification of the duty of fairness. See P. Rishworth, G. Huscroft, R. Mahoney, & S. Optican, *The New Zealand Bill of Rights* (Melbourne: Oxford University Press, 2003), chapter 27.

9   Under the approach set out by the Supreme Court of Canada in *Dunsmuir v. New Brunswick*, 2008 SCC 9, [2008] 1 S.C.R. 190 [*Dunsmuir*], substantive decisions may be reviewed for legal correctness in some cases or reasonableness in others. Even in this context, however, judicial review is not concerned with the substantive "fairness" of a decision.

in this sense, a means to an end. But the importance of the duty transcends its instrumental purpose. The duty of fairness is important in its own right, for it ensures that people are allowed to participate meaningfully in decision-making processes that affect them. In other words, the duty protects dignitary interests by requiring that people be treated with respect. As we will see, both rationales support the Court's strict remedial approach in cases where the duty is breached: procedurally unfair decisions are quashed and remitted to be made in accordance with the required procedural protection.[10]

In general, the duty of fairness requires two things, both of which are modern restatements of venerable natural justice protections: (1) the right to be heard, and (2) the right to an independent and impartial hearing.[11] Fairness is a common-law concept and, subject only to compliance with the *Canadian Charter of Rights and Freedoms* (the Charter), may be limited or even ousted by ordinary legislation. Such is its importance, however, that courts will require specific legislative direction before concluding that this has occurred. In *Kane v. Bd. of Governors of U.B.C.*, Justice Dickson put the point this way: "To abrogate the rules of natural justice, express language or necessary implication must be found in the statutory instrument."[12] This is justified on the basis that courts presume that the legislature intended procedural protection to apply, even if nothing is said. As Justice Byles stated in *Cooper v. Board of Works for Wandsworth District*, "[A]lthough there are no positive words in a statute requiring that the party shall be heard, yet the justice of the common law will supply the omission of the legislature."[13] On this approach, the courts acknowledge the supremacy of the legislature and at the same time confer heightened, quasi-constitutional protection upon the common-law duty of fairness.[14]

The duty of fairness is codified to varying degrees in Canadian legislation. At the federal level, the *Canadian Bill of Rights* protects a "right to a fair hearing in accordance with the

---

[10] *Cardinal v. Director of Kent Institution*, [1985] 2 S.C.R. 643 at para. 23 [*Cardinal*], discussed in the text below.

[11] The right to an independent and impartial hearing is discussed by Laverne Jacobs in Chapter 8, Caught Between Judicial Paradigms and the Administrative State's Pastiche: "Tribunal" Independence, Impartiality, and Bias.

[12] [1980] 1 S.C.R. 1105 at 1113. For its part, the High Court of Australia has rendered it difficult, if not virtually impossible, for legislation to limit or oust procedural protection, outlining a presumption that it is "highly improbable that Parliament would overthrow fundamental principles or depart from the general system of law, without expressing its intention with *irresistible clearness.*" See *Saeed v. Minister for Immigration and Citizenship*, [2010] H.C.A. 23 (23 June 2010) at para. 15 (emphasis added).

[13] (1863), 14 C.B. (N.S.) 180 at 194. In *Daganayasi v. Minister of Immigration*, [1980] 2 N.Z.L.R. 130 at 141, Cooke J. (as he then was) stated that the availability of fairness protection depends "either on what is to be inferred or presumed in interpreting the particular Act ... or on judicial supplementation of the Act when this is necessary to achieve justice without frustrating the apparent purpose of the legislation" (internal citations omitted).

[14] This point was put strongly by the High Court of Australia in *Electrolux Home Products Pty. Ltd. v. Australian Workers' Union* (2004), 221 C.L.R. 309 at 329: "The presumption is not merely a common sense guide to what a Parliament in a liberal democracy is likely to have intended; it is a working hypothesis, the existence of which is known both to Parliament and the courts, upon which statutory language will be interpreted. The hypothesis is an aspect of the rule of law."

principles of fundamental justice for the determination of his rights and obligations."[15] Procedural protection has been codified more specifically in provincial legislation in Alberta,[16] British Columbia,[17] Ontario,[18] and Quebec.[19] In addition, it is important to note that federal and provincial legislation may establish procedural requirements, short of a complete code, that apply in particular contexts. It is not unusual for legislation or regulations to particularize, for example, notice requirements and rights to make submissions for particular tribunals. The common-law duty of fairness supplements existing statutory duties and fills the gap where none exist. Section 7 of the Charter provides a constitutional backstop for procedural protection, but, as we will see, this right applies in a narrower range of circumstances than the duty of fairness.[20]

Given the wide range of decisions to which the duty of fairness applies, the protection afforded by the duty is necessarily flexible rather than fixed. Although the language of the duty of fairness speaks of the right to a "hearing," this does not mean that formal, oral hearings are required. Oral hearings will sometimes be required by the duty of fairness, but they are not the norm. The modern state could not function if an oral hearing were required every time an administrative decision of some sort were made—a problem not only for the state but also for those who benefit from, or are subject to, the burden of administrative decisions. In practice, the content of the duty is informed by the context in which a particular decision is made and varies in accordance with a number of factors. In other words, the duty may be satisfied by different protection in different decision-making contexts. Thus, to say that the duty of fairness applies to a particular decision-making process is to say little. Everything depends on what the duty is understood as requiring in the circumstances, and this has a normative dimension: fairness requires the procedural protection the courts think *ought* to be required before a decision is made in particular circumstances. An oral hearing

---

[15] S.C. 1960, c. 44, s. 2(e). In *Duke v. The Queen*, [1972] S.C.R. 917 at 923, Justice Fauteux discussed this provision as follows: "Without attempting to formulate any final definition of those words, I would take them to mean, generally, that the tribunal which adjudicates upon his rights must act fairly, in good faith, without bias, and in a judicial temper, and must give to him the opportunity adequately to state his case." In *Re B.C. Motor Vehicle Act*, [1985] 2 S.C.R. 486 at para. 58 [*Re B.C. Motor Vehicle Act*], Justice Lamer noted that the principles of fundamental justice in the *Bill of Rights* were contextually limited to procedural matters because of their qualification of the right to a fair hearing. He proffered a more expansive definition of fundamental justice in s. 7 of the *Canadian Charter of Rights and Freedoms*, among other things because s. 7 is set out in the context of deprivations of life, liberty, and security of the person, which he considered more fundamental rights. Evan Fox-Decent and Alexander Pless discuss the relevance of Charter protection in greater depth in Chapter 12, The Charter and Administrative Law: Cross-Fertilization or Inconstancy?

[16] *Administrative Procedures and Jurisdiction Act*, R.S.A. 2000, c. A-3.

[17] *Administrative Tribunals Act*, S.B.C. 2004, c. 45.

[18] *Statutory Powers Procedure Act*, R.S.O. 1990, c. S.22.

[19] Quebec has codified procedures in several statutes. The *Civil Code of Quebec*, R.S.Q., c. C-1991; the *Charter of Human Rights and Freedoms*, R.S.Q., c. C-12; *Administrative Justice Act*, R.S.Q., c. J-3; and the *Code of Civil Procedure*, R.S.Q., c. C-25 are discussed in Denis Lemieux, "The Codification of Administrative Law in Quebec" in Grant Huscroft & Michael Taggart, eds., *Inside and Outside Canadian Administrative Law* (Toronto: University of Toronto Press, 2006).

[20] The impact of the Charter on administrative law is discussed by Evan Fox-Decent and Alexander Pless in Chapter 12, The Charter and Administrative Law: Cross-Fertilization or Inconstancy?

might be required in some cases, involving processes similar to those used in the judicial system. In other contexts, however, the requirement to provide a hearing may be satisfied by as little as an exchange of written correspondence prior to a decision being made.

Two questions arise when judicial review proceedings are brought alleging a breach of the duty of fairness. First, has the threshold for the application of the duty been met? Second, what does the duty of fairness require in the relevant circumstances? It is important to emphasize that courts require decisions about threshold and content of the duty of fairness to be made correctly. If they are not, the substantive decision made in a particular matter will be quashed and remitted to be remade in accordance with the appropriate procedures.

An order quashing a decision for a breach of the duty of fairness does not, in theory, affect the substantive decision that might be made subsequently; it means only that the decision must be remade in accordance with the appropriate procedures. In practice, however, it may be difficult for a decision-maker to reach the same substantive decision on a rehearing. Fair procedures may make it easier to argue in support of particular substantive outcomes on a rehearing; moreover, there may be impediments—practical or political—to reaching the same decision on a rehearing. Thus, success on an application for judicial review on fairness grounds may have the indirect effect of helping an applicant to secure a preferred substantive outcome. At the very least, it will give the applicant another chance to obtain that outcome, and ensures that the substantive decision will be made on a well-informed basis in any event. Even if the same substantive decision is reached following a rehearing, it will have a greater claim to legitimacy.

III. The Threshold Test: When Is Fairness Required?

A. Rights, Privileges, and Interests

Subject to some exceptions, discussed below, it is well established that the duty of fairness applies to the decisions of public authorities—for example, executive actors, tribunals, and officials acting pursuant to statutory authority—that affect an individual's *rights*, *privileges*, or *interests*.[21] There is little dispute about the meaning of these terms because they are not meant to limit the availability of fairness protection. On the contrary, their purpose is to expand the range of decisions subject to the fairness duty beyond the narrower range of decisions traditionally required to be made in accordance with natural justice protection.

Taken as a whole, the concepts of rights, privileges, and interests are sufficiently broad in scope to cover most decisions made by public authorities that affect or have the potential to affect an individual in important ways, even in the absence of any sort of substantive entitlement. So, for example, although prison inmates may have no right to early release, once the

---

[21] Justice Le Dain summed up the Court's case law in this way in *Cardinal, supra* note 10 at para. 14:

[T]here is, as a general common law principle, a duty of procedural fairness lying on every public authority making an administrative decision which is not of a legislative nature and which affects the rights, privileges or interests of an individual.

Thus, we will not be concerned with procedural entitlements that may arise in a variety of private contexts—for example, decisions made by private clubs that may affect the rights of their members. In these contexts, entitlements are likely to arise out of contractual terms, express or implied, rather than public law.

state establishes a parole system of some sort, they are entitled to procedural fairness in its operation.

B. Constitutional Protection[22]

When, and to what extent, does the Charter require the provision of procedural protection?[23] Section 7 of the Charter provides as follows:

> Everyone has the right to life, liberty and security of the person and the right not to be deprived thereof except in accordance with the principles of fundamental justice.

Despite the conjunctive nature of its language, it is well established that s. 7 protects a single right: the right not to be deprived of life, liberty, or security of the person except in accordance with the principles of fundamental justice. The Supreme Court of Canada has held that the principles of fundamental justice subsume procedural fairness protection,[24] but the right does not constitutionalize the duty of fairness per se. Section 7 applies only in the context of deprivations of life, liberty, and security of the person, and this establishes a higher threshold than simply demonstrating that a right, privilege, or interest is affected.

For example, an application to renew a taxi licence may give rise to an entitlement to fairness protection at common law, but it does not give rise to Charter protection because the denial of a licence does not constitute a deprivation of life, liberty, or security of the person. Licensing is, in this context, an economic matter, and the Court has not interpreted s. 7 of the Charter as including economic rights.[25] Thus, ordinary legislation could limit or even oust the application of the duty of fairness to the licensing scheme without infringing the Charter.

In the event that a deprivation of life, liberty, or security of the person is found not to be in accordance with the principles of fundamental justice, it is highly unlikely that it will be considered justified under s. 1 of the Charter. The Court has held that infringement of s. 7 may be considered justified only in "extraordinary circumstances where concerns are grave and the challenges complex."[26]

---

[22] The development of duty to consult in the context of Aboriginal rights and its link to the duty of fairness is discussed in David Mullan, "The Supreme Court and the Duty to Consult Aboriginal Peoples: A Lifting of the Fog?" (2012) C.J.A.L.P. 233 at 241-45. See also the discussion by Janna Promislow and Lorne Sossin in Chapter 13, In Search of Aboriginal Administrative Law.

[23] The impact of the Charter on administrative law is discussed by Evan Fox-Decent and Alexander Pless in Chapter 12, The Charter and Administrative Law: Cross-Fertilization or Inconstancy?

[24] *Re B.C. Motor Vehicle Act, supra* note 15. More controversially, the Court held that the principles of fundamental justice include a substantive component, despite the apparent intention of the framers to limit the right to matters of procedure. See Peter Hogg, *Constitutional Law of Canada*, looseleaf (Scarborough, ON: Carswell, 1997) at para. 44.10(a).

[25] *Gosselin v. Quebec (Attorney General)*, [2002] 4 S.C.R. 429 at paras. 80-82. However, the Court left open the possibility that s. 7 might be interpreted to include positive obligations in future cases. See the discussion in Grant Huscroft, "A Constitutional 'Work in Progress'? The Charter and the Limits of Progressive Interpretation" in Grant Huscroft & Ian Brodie, eds., *Constitutionalism in the Charter Era* (Toronto: LexisNexis, 2004).

[26] See *Charkaoui v. Canada (Citizenship and Immigration)*, [2007] 1 S.C.R. 350 at para. 66, citing *Re B.C. Motor Vehicle Act, supra* note 15 at para. 85, per Lamer J. (listing "exceptional conditions such as natural disasters, the outbreak of war, epidemics, and the like").

IV. Limitations on the Application of the Duty of Fairness

Although the duty of fairness applies to a broad range of decision-making contexts, there are limitations on the reach of the duty, both inherent in the concept and imposed on the concept by the courts. Significant limitations on the duty are discussed below.

A. The Duty Applies to Decisions

The duty of fairness governs decision-making processes, which is another way of saying that the duty applies only in contexts in which *decisions* may be made. In principle, it does not apply to investigations or advisory processes that may occur prior to the commencement of a formal decision-making process.[27] This is so because the imposition of fairness duties at a preliminary stage may well compromise the relevant processes. To take an obvious example, it would be absurd to require officials charged with responsibility for investigating breaches of the law to provide notice before commencing their investigations. In any case, the exclusion of fairness prior to the commencement of a formal decision-making process will normally be mitigated by the requirement to observe the duty at the formal decision-making stage.

Nevertheless, investigations and advisory processes may have a considerable impact on affected persons. For example, the reputation of anyone caught up in a public investigation may be adversely affected and the need for fairness protection will be clear.[28] Public inquiries may have significant consequences for those required to be involved and fairness protection will be provided here as well, often pursuant to legislation codifying the duty.[29] Fairness protection may be required for ostensibly preliminary decisions, where a formal determination is made subsequently, if the preliminary decision has de facto finality. For example, invariable acceptance by the ultimate decision-maker of the results of an investigation or advice from a preliminary decision-maker suggests that the real decision is being made at the preliminary stage, and in order for the duty of fairness to do its work, it should apply here.

---

[27] This limitation is reflected in the Ontario *Statutory Powers Procedure Act*, *supra* note 18, s. 3(2)(g): procedural requirements do not apply to "one or more persons required to make an investigation and to make a report, with or without recommendations, where the report is for the information or advice of the person to whom it is made and does not in any way legally bind or limit that person in any decision he or she may have power to make."

[28] Human rights investigations are a good example. Where a commission has an investigative function and the authority to refer a matter to a tribunal for a formal hearing, fairness may be required at the investigative stage. See e.g. *Blencoe v. British Columbia (Human Rights Commission*, 2000 SCC 44, [2000] 2 S.C.R. 307 [*Blencoe*].

[29] The Supreme Court discussed the basic fairness principles relevant to public inquiries in *Canada (Attorney General) v. Canada (Commission of Inquiry on the Blood System in Canada—Krever Commission)*, [1997] 3 S.C.R. 440. Peter Carver discusses the law of public inquiries in Chapter 16, Getting the Story Out: Accountability and the Law of Public Inquiries, and see, generally, Allan Manson & David Mullan, eds., *Commissions of Inquiry: Praise or Reappraise?* (Toronto: Irwin Law, 2003).

B. The Duty Does Not Apply to Legislative Decisions

The Supreme Court of Canada has long insisted that the duty of fairness does not apply to legislative decisions or functions.[30] In *Re Canada Assistance Plan (B.C.)*, the Court expressed the point categorically: "[T]he rules governing procedural fairness do not apply to a body exercising purely legislative functions."[31]

The Court has never explained what it means by "legislative" functions, but it is clear that primary legislation, whether passed by Parliament or a provincial legislature, is not subject to the duty of fairness. It is not exempt because it has no impact on rights, privileges, or interests. On the contrary, legislation is likely to have a profound impact for large numbers of people because it applies generally. It is exempt from the duty of fairness because any meaningful conception of a separation of powers between the legislature and the courts demands it. In *Reference re Resolution to Amend the Constitution*, the Court essayed the relationship between the legislature and the courts as follows:

> How Houses of Parliament proceed, how a provincial legislative assembly proceeds is in either case a matter of self definition, subject to any overriding constitutional or self-imposed statutory or indoor prescription. It is unnecessary here to embark on any historical review of the "court" aspect of Parliament and the immunity of its procedures from judicial review. Courts come into the picture when legislation is enacted and not before (unless references are made to them for their opinion on a bill or a proposed enactment). It would be incompatible with the self regulating—"inherent" is as apt a word—authority of Houses of Parliament to deny their capacity to pass any kind of resolution. Reference may appropriately be made to art. 9 of the *Bill of Rights* of 1689, undoubtedly in force as part of the law of Canada, which provides that "Proceedings in Parliament ought not to be impeached or questioned in any Court or Place out of Parliament."[32]

This rationale for exempting legislative functions from the duty of fairness was reiterated in *Wells v. Newfoundland*. In that case, the Newfoundland Legislature passed legislation abolishing a quasi-judicial position to which Wells had been appointed. Wells's argument that he should have been accorded procedural fairness was rejected summarily by the Court, which stated as follows:

> [L]egislative decision making is not subject to any known duty of fairness. Legislatures are subject to constitutional requirements for valid law-making, but within their constitutional boundaries, they can do as they see fit. The wisdom and value of legislative decisions are subject only to review by the electorate.[33]

There is no guarantee that political accountability will be meaningful, of course, but this is no concern of the courts. No one has the right to prevail in the political process, no matter

---

30 *Attorney General of Canada v. Inuit Tapirisat*, [1980] 2 S.C.R. 735 at 757 [*Inuit Tapirisat*], citing *Bates v. Lord Hailsham*, [1972] 3 All E.R. 1019 (Ch. D.).

31 [1991] 2 S.C.R. 525 at para. 60.

32 [1981] 1 S.C.R. 753 at 785.

33 [1999] 3 S.C.R. 199 at para. 59. However, Wells succeeded in a contract suit against the Crown, the Court holding that the legislation abolishing his position had not abrogated his right to seek damages against the Crown for breach of his contract of employment.

how sympathetic his or her cause may seem, as *Authorson v. Canada (Attorney General)*[34] demonstrates. In that case, Parliament passed legislation retrospectively limiting the amount of money owed to disabled war veterans—decades of interest on pension and benefit funds—to whom the Crown owed fiduciary duties. The law affected thousands of veterans, none of whom was given notice of the proposed change to the law. In class action proceedings, Authorson argued that the legislation infringed the right not to be deprived of the enjoyment of property except by due process of law under the *Canadian Bill of Rights* (s. 1(a)), as well as the right to a fair hearing in accordance with the principles of fundamental justice for the determination of one's rights and obligations (s. 2(e)).

This argument succeeded at trial and in the Ontario Court of Appeal, but was given short shrift in the Supreme Court of Canada. The Court emphatically rejected the notion that the *Canadian Bill of Rights* established due process procedures with regard to the passage of legislation, and reiterated that the common law had nothing to add:

> The respondent claimed a right to notice and hearing to contest the passage of s. 5.1(4) of the *Department of Veterans Affairs Act*. However, in 1960, and today, no such right exists. Long-standing parliamentary tradition makes it clear that the only procedure due any citizen of Canada is that proposed legislation receive three readings in the Senate and House of Commons and that it receive Royal Assent. Once that process is completed, legislation within Parliament's competence is unassailable.[35]

If the rationale for the exemption of legislative functions is clear, however, the idea of exemption by category is problematic, because it recalls the long-discredited distinction between administrative and judicial or quasi-judicial decisions. It invites argument over the meaning of the term "legislative" and makes for all-or-nothing outcomes. If an applicant for judicial review succeeds in convincing a court that a decision is subject to the duty of fairness, the court will determine the required procedure and quash the decision if there has been a failure to observe it. But if the public authority succeeds in convincing the court that its actions are legislative in nature, then the duty of fairness will not apply and the court will have nothing to say about any procedures adopted or their adequacy.

The categorical exemption of legislative functions becomes especially problematic as it extends beyond primary legislation to include secondary legislation and policy decisions, both of which are discussed below.

1. Are Cabinet and Ministerial Decisions Covered by the Legislative Exemption?

Cabinet and ministerial decisions are not subject to the legislative exemption per se, but it will often be easy to characterize Cabinet and ministerial decisions as legislative in nature and, as a result, they will be exempted from the duty.

---

34 2003 SCC 39, [2003] 2 S.C.R. 40 [*Authorson*].

35 *Ibid.* at para. 37. The Court held that the protection of s. 2(e) is limited to "the application of law to individual circumstances in a proceeding before a court, tribunal or similar body" (para. 61).

Attorney General of Canada v. Inuit Tapirisat provides a good example. In that case, the federal Cabinet rejected an appeal from a decision made by the Canadian Radio-television and Telecommunications Commission (CRTC) without allowing the petitioning group to be heard. The Cabinet heard from the utility and the CRTC and took advice from minister-ial officials, but the petitioning group was essentially left out of the proceedings. Justice Estey considered the Cabinet's power to be legislative in nature, in part because the legisla-tion authorized Cabinet to overturn a decision of the CRTC on its own motion. This, he said, was "legislative action in its purest form."[36] Estey J. buttressed this position by accen-tuating the practical difficulties inherent in extending the duty of fairness. He did not want to burden the Cabinet with hearing requirements and expressed concern about undermin-ing the Cabinet's public policy-making role.

Inuit Tapirisat has been subject to extensive criticism on the basis that it overstates the difficulties inherent in applying the duty of fairness to Cabinet decisions. After all, the duty is flexible and its content could be tailored to address some of the concerns raised by Estey J.[37] (To take an obvious example, it is difficult to conceive of circumstances in which the Cabinet would be required to hold an oral hearing.) Moreover, the case for exempting Cabinet decisions from the duty of fairness may be thought weaker than the case for ex-empting primary legislation, because Cabinet decision making is not subject to political scrutiny in the same way. Nevertheless, it is not surprising to find the courts wary of scruti-nizing the decisions of the executive branch of government, even for limited procedural purposes. The potential for conflict between the courts and the executive is great.

In other contexts, the Court has emphasized the unique role and responsibilities of the executive branch as a reason for not extending the duty of fairness to ministerial decisions. In *Idziak v. Canada (Minister of Justice)*, Justice Cory discussed the minister of justice's exercise of discretionary authority to issue a warrant of surrender in an extradition case as follows:

> Parliament chose to give discretionary authority to the Minister of Justice. It is the Minister who must consider the good faith and honour of this country in its relations with other states. It is the Minister who has the expert knowledge of the political ramifications of an extradition decision. In administrative law terms, the Minister's review should be characterized as being at the extreme legislative end of the *continuum* of administrative decision-making.[38]

Decisions involving particular individuals are most likely to give rise to the application of the duty of fairness to Cabinet and ministerial decisions, but, as *Idziak* demonstrates, even in this context the Court may be reluctant to impose procedural requirements for a variety of reasons.

---

[36] *Supra* note 30 at 754.

[37] See e.g. *Minister for Arts, Heritage and Environment v. Peko-Wallsend Ltd.* (1987), 75 A.L.R. 218 (Fed. Ct., Aust.) (assuming that Cabinet decisions are subject to the duty of fairness, the ability to make a written sub-mission to the responsible minister suffices). I am grateful to Matthew Groves for this reference.

[38] [1992] 3 S.C.R. 631 at 659 (emphasis in original).

2. Is Subordinate Legislation Covered by the Legislative Exemption?

Political self-interest often ensures that consultation occurs prior to the passage of legislation, even where there is no formal requirement for it. There will, however, be times when it is not in the political interest to consult before legislating and the argument for fairness protection in these contexts may seem strong, especially with regard to subordinate legislation.[39]

Arguably, there is less reason to be concerned about judicial interference in the political process where subordinate legislation is concerned because subordinate legislation is made pursuant to executive authority and democratic accountability may be minimal. American experience with "notice and comment" requirements demonstrates that procedural requirements are not unworkable.[40] Nevertheless, as Andrew Green explains in greater detail in Chapter 4, Regulations and Rule Making: The Dilemma of Delegation, in general the courts have not imposed procedural requirements on the subordinate law-making function. Such requirements as exist in particular contexts have been established by legislation.

However, there are exceptions. For example, in the unique circumstances of *Homex Realty and Development Co. v. Wyoming (Village)*,[41] the Supreme Court of Canada concluded that passage of a municipal bylaw was subject to the duty of fairness. It did so because it was clear that the village's motivation for passing the bylaw was an ongoing dispute it had with a particular developer. In these circumstances, the Court held that the village was not allowed

---

[39] Geneviève Cartier, "Procedural Fairness in Legislative Functions: The End of Judicial Abstinence?" (2003) 53 U.T.L.J. 217.

[40] *Administrative Procedures Act*, 5 U.S.C. § 553 provides as follows:

> (a) This section applies, according to the provisions thereof, except to the extent that there is involved—
> (1) a military or foreign affairs function of the United States; or
> (2) a matter relating to agency management or personnel or to public property, loans, grants, benefits, or contracts.
> (b) General notice of proposed rule making shall be published in the Federal Register, unless persons subject thereto are named and either personally served or otherwise have actual notice thereof in accordance with law. The notice shall include—
> (1) a statement of the time, place, and nature of public rule making proceedings;
> (2) reference to the legal authority under which the rule is proposed; and
> (3) either the terms or substance of the proposed rule or a description of the subjects and issues involved.
> Except when notice or hearing is required by statute, this subsection does not apply—
> > (A) to interpretative rules, general statements of policy, or rules of agency organization, procedure, or practice; or
> > (B) when the agency for good cause finds (and incorporates the finding and a brief statement of reasons therefor in the rules issued) that notice and public procedure thereon are impracticable, unnecessary, or contrary to the public interest.
> (c) After notice required by this section, the agency shall give interested persons an opportunity to participate in the rule making through submission of written data, views, or arguments with or without opportunity for oral presentation._After consideration of the relevant matter presented, the agency shall incorporate in the rules adopted a concise general statement of their basis and purpose … .

> See, generally, Peter L. Strauss, *Administrative Justice in the United States*, 2d ed. (Durham, N.C.: Carolina Academy Press, 2002) at 220-22.

[41] [1980] 2 S.C.R. 1011 [*Homex Realty*].

to couch its actions in a form designed to oust the application of the duty of fairness.[42] This makes the point that substance is more important than form where the legislative exemption is concerned.

3. Are Policy Decisions Covered by the Legislative Exemption?

The legislative exemption includes decisions that may be described as "policy" decisions as well as decisions that are general in nature. In *Martineau v. Matsqui Institution Disciplinary Board*, Justice Dickson observed that "[a] purely ministerial decision, on broad grounds of public policy, will typically afford the individual no procedural protection."[43] In *Knight v. Indian Head School Division No. 19*, Justice L'Heureux-Dubé noted that many administrative bodies have been required to assume duties traditionally performed by legislatures, and distinguished "decisions of a legislative and general nature" from "acts of a more administrative and specific nature."[44]

The rationale for exempting policy decisions from the duty is similar to that of formal legislative decisions. Both are inherently political in nature and are, in principle, subject to political accountability. Thus, in *Imperial Oil Ltd. v. Quebec (Minister of the Environment)*, the Supreme Court held that in exercising discretionary power to require an oil company to undertake site decontamination measures (at its own expense), Quebec's environment minister was performing a political role in choosing from among the policy options allowed under provincial environmental protection legislation and was not subject to fairness obliga-

---

42   The majority of the Court characterized the bylaw as quasi-judicial rather than legislative in substance. Justice Dickson (dissenting on the remedial point) put the case for procedural fairness protection more simply, *ibid.* at 1052-53:

> What we have here is not a by-law of wide and general application which was to apply to all citizens of the municipality equally. Rather, it was a by-law aimed deliberately at limiting the rights of one individual, the appellant Homex. In these circumstances, I would hold that Homex was entitled to some procedural safeguards. This does not mean that the municipality was under a duty to observe the procedures appropriate to a court of law. But, at a minimum, it was under a duty to give Homex notice of the proposed by-law and the opportunity to be heard.

> In *Catalyst Paper Corp. v. North Cowichan (District)*, 2012 SCC 2, the Court asserted that the requirements of procedural fairness and legislation governing a municipality "may require that the municipality comply with certain procedural requirements, such as notice or voting requirements" (para. 12) and did not mention *Homex*. However, the Court went on to say that municipalities make quasi-judicial as well as legislative decisions and that the two are treated differently:

> Formal reasons may be required for decisions that involve quasi-judicial adjudication by a municipality. But that does not apply to the process of passing municipal bylaws. ... The reasons for a municipal bylaw are traditionally deduced from the debate, deliberations and the statements of policy that give rise to the bylaw. ... [T]he municipality is [not] required to formally explain the basis of a bylaw. (paras. 29-30)

43   [1980] 1 S.C.R. 602 at 628, cited with approval in *Re Canada Assistance Plan (B.C.)*, [1991] 2 S.C.R. 525 at para. 60.

44   [1990] 1 S.C.R. 653 at para. 26 [*Indian Head School*].

tions beyond those in the Act.[45] Governments are elected to make policy decisions and must be allowed to do so, provided that they comply with relevant constitutional requirements.

But acceptance of the political rationale does not resolve the difficulties surrounding the exemption of policy decisions. Although legislative functions may be identified by the formalities that surround the legislative process, it can be considerably more difficult to identify a policy decision. Moreover, given different judicial perceptions about institutional roles, accountability, and legitimacy, we should expect to find inconsistent decisions. In truth, it is easy for a court to characterize a decision as a policy decision if it simply does not want to interfere in a particular case.

C. The Duty Does Not Apply to Public Office Holders Employed Under Contracts

Although the duty of fairness developed in the context of public office holders in cases such as *Nicholson* and *Indian Head School*, in *Dunsmuir v. New Brunswick*[46] the Court overruled its earlier approach and held that the law will no longer draw a distinction between public office holders and other employees in dismissal cases. If the terms of an individual's employment are governed by contract, then ordinary private law contractual remedies will apply in the event of his or her dismissal, regardless of the public nature of the employment concerned. By abandoning the distinction between public office holders and contractual employees, the Court hoped to simplify the application of the law, obviating the need for litigation concerning the nature of an individual's employment.[47]

Following *Dunsmuir*, it will be assumed that a contract of employment addresses procedural fairness issues. If it does not, the normal common- or civil-law principles will govern. In either event, protection from wrongful dismissal will be governed by private law contract principles. The Court conceived of two exceptions. First, employees not protected by employment contracts, or subject to employment at pleasure, will still be protected by the duty of fairness. Second, the duty of fairness may arise by necessary implication in some statutory contexts.

---

45 [2003] 2 S.C.R. 624, [2003] 2 S.C.R. 624 [*Imperial Oil*]. The *Environment Quality Act*, R.S.Q., c. Q-2, s. 31.42 provided procedural protection, including a requirement that notice be given to interested persons and that reasons for the decision be given. The Court's remarks concerning the nature of the minister's decision were made in the context of an argument that the minister was not impartial, and as a result, was in breach of the bias rule of the duty of fairness.

46 *Supra* note 9.

47 Nevertheless, *Dunsmuir* necessarily limits the protection of public employees to some extent. It will no longer be possible for public office holders to be restored to their positions, because that remedy is not available for breach of contract. The Court acknowledges as much, but argues that the duty of fairness did not include a reinstatement remedy, given that public office holders could be dismissed provided only that the proper procedures were followed. There is no doubt, however, that reinstatement to a position following a breach of the duty of fairness—even on an ostensibly temporary basis while a new decision is waiting to be made—was a considerable motivation for bringing judicial review proceedings.

D. The Duty May Be Suspended or Abridged in the Event of an Emergency

The duty of fairness establishes duties that must be observed *before* a decision can be made. There will, however, sometimes be circumstances in which procedural requirements cannot be met without risking harm of one sort or another.

In an emergency situation, compliance with the duty of fairness may be suspended until after the required decision has been made. For example, in *Cardinal v. Director of Kent Institution*, the Court held that although the duty of fairness applied to the imposition of isolation or segregation of prison inmates in "apparently" urgent or emergency circumstances (the inmates alleged to have been involved in a hostage taking were transferred to another institution and placed in isolation to secure prison order), "there could be no requirement of prior notice and an opportunity to be heard before the decision. ... [T]he process of prison administration, because of its special nature and exigencies, should not be unduly burdened or obstructed by the imposition of unreasonable or inappropriate procedural requirements."[48] However, once a recommendation to end the segregation of prisoners had been made by the review body, the duty of fairness required that the prison director inform the inmates of his intended decision to reject the recommendation, provide reasons, and afford them an opportunity to contest his intended decision. The Court regarded this as a minimal amount of fairness that would not undermine the administration of the prison.

To what extent will a court defer to a decision-maker as to the existence of circumstances justifying the suspension or abridgment of fairness? Deference to the government in regard to national security matters is to be expected, but care must be taken to ensure that public authorities are not overzealous in apprehending urgent or emergency circumstances. There should be few cases in which minimal fairness procedures cannot be provided before a decision is made.

V. The Content of the Duty of Fairness

As we have seen, the extension of the duty of fairness to a wide range of administrative decisions in *Nicholson* was facilitated by the decision to make the content of duty flexible and context-specific. Thus, fairness requires compliance with some, but not necessarily all, of the requirements of natural justice.[49] Fairness is a *minimum* duty that must be met—a floor for procedural protection rather than a ceiling. In determining whether the duty of fairness has been met, courts ask whether the procedural protection provided in particular circumstances was adequate, not ideal.[50]

Consider the position of those involved in the following three scenarios and the scope of the procedural protection that is appropriate in each.

---

48   *Supra* note 10 at paras. 16, 22.

49   *Martineau v. Matsqui Inmate Disciplinary Board*, [1980] 1 S.C.R. 602 at 630.

50   As Justice Evans put it in *Waycobah First Nation v. Attorney General of Canada*, 2011 FCA 191 at para. 32, "[T]he duty of fairness affords individuals an adequate, not the optimum, opportunity to inform the decision-maker of their case."

1. *Criminal law prosecution.* The criminal law provides a good point of comparison for procedural fairness in administrative law. The stakes for a person charged with a criminal offence are high. Accused persons are at risk of losing their liberty and are subject to significant consequences, both direct and indirect, as a result of the charges they face. In these circumstances, nothing less than full procedural protection will do: an accused person is entitled to a formal, oral hearing before an independent and impartial judge. This protection has long been afforded and is now codified in the Charter (s. 11(d)), which also includes the following protection:

- the right to be informed of the offence (11(a)),
- the right to be tried within a reasonable time (11(b)),
- disclosure of the evidence and case to be met,[51]
- the right to counsel (10(b)),
- the right to call evidence and cross-examine witnesses,
- the presumption of innocence (10(d)), and
- a written decision with reasons.[52]

None of these protections is controversial in the context of criminal law, but some have little relevance in the context of administrative proceedings. Administrative proceedings are typically informal, do not involve oral hearings, and do not take place before judges. Although some administrative proceedings have much in common with a criminal proceeding (for example, disciplinary hearings in professional contexts), in general, a lower standard of protection will usually suffice.

2. *Human rights adjudication.* Human rights legislation is designed to be remedial rather than punitive, so, in principle, the stakes for a respondent to a human rights complaint are lower than for an accused person facing a criminal charge. But the consequences may nevertheless be significant: consider the possible harm to reputation a respondent may suffer by being accused of an act of discrimination; the costs in terms of time and money of defending a complaint; and the damages the respondent may ultimately be ordered to pay by a human rights tribunal. Given these possible repercussions, the respondent will want to test the evidence against him or her, and in order to do so, an oral hearing with many of the protections available in the context of criminal prosecution is required. But some of those protections will apply in attenuated form. For example, human rights litigation usually takes place before tribunals whose members may be part-time or fixed-term appointees who do not enjoy the high level of independence that judges do,[53] and the proceedings are less formal in nature. But the essence of the matter will be the same: the respondent to a human rights complaint is entitled to be represented by counsel and has the right, for example, to call evidence, cross-examine witnesses, and make

---

51   *R. v. Stinchcombe*, [1991] 3 S.C.R. 326 [*Stinchcombe*].

52   *R. v. REM*, 2008 SCC 51, [2008] 3 S.C.R. 3.

53   See the indicia of independence set out in *Valente v. The Queen*, [1985] 2 S.C.R. 673, including security of tenure, financial security, and institutional independence.

and reply to arguments. Such procedures may be set out in the legislation or accompanying rules or regulations, but to the extent that they are not, they will be governed by the duty of fairness.

3. *Licensing regulation.* Consider a regulated industry in which possession of a licence is required in order to work. Those in the industry have an important interest in obtaining and maintaining their licences, but it does not follow that they are entitled to an oral hearing on all licensing matters. The importance of the matter is a consideration, but the needs of the state must also be considered. Oral hearings are expensive and time-consuming, and will not ordinarily be necessary to deal fairly with a licence application. Indeed, in a straightforward case it will ordinarily be enough to allow an applicant to apply for a licence by completing an application form and providing the required information, following which a decision can be made based on consideration of the relevant criteria.

It is not difficult to imagine circumstances in which greater fairness might be required. Suppose, for example, that a licensing authority has information that raises concerns about an applicant's fitness to be granted, or to continue to hold, a licence, and that the authority proposes to rely on that information to deny the applicant's licence application or to revoke an existing licence. In these circumstances, the licensing authority should at least inform the applicant of the information and invite submissions in reply. Depending on the nature of the information, additional procedural protection may be required.

Duty of fairness concerns are least likely to arise in the context of tribunals required to provide oral hearings, because the procedure for those hearings is usually clear. Some tribunals operate pursuant to detailed legislation that establishes procedural requirements; others are empowered to establish their own procedures in secondary legislation. The Ontario Labour Relations Board is a good example of the latter approach. The chair of the Board has rule-making authority and the Board has developed its own procedural code.[54] The Canadian Transportation Agency is another example of a tribunal that has the authority to control its processes and make its own procedural rules.[55] Still other tribunals may operate pursuant to general statutory mandates such as that established by the Ontario *Statutory Powers Procedure Act*,[56] which establishes minimum default procedural provisions for Ontario tribunals required to provide oral hearings.

For a large range of administrative decision-makers, however, common-law considerations govern the scope and content of the duty of fairness. The leading case, *Baker*, is discussed below.

---

[54] *Labour Relations Act*, S.O. 1995, c. 1, Sch. A, s. 110(17).

[55] *Canada Transportation Act*, S.C. 1996, c. 10, s. 17.

[56] R.S.O. 1990, c. S.22.

A. Baker v. Canada (Minister of Citizenship and Immigration)[57]

Mavis Baker was a visitor from Jamaica who remained in Canada as an illegal immigrant. She was employed as a live-in domestic worker for 11 years and during that time had four children, all of whom acquired Canadian citizenship by birth. In 1992 she was ordered to be deported. Immigration legislation required applicants for permanent residence to apply from outside Canada, meaning that Ms. Baker would have to apply from Jamaica. She applied for an exemption from this requirement pursuant to regulations that provided as follows:

> The Minister is hereby authorized to exempt any person from any regulation made under subsection 114(1) of the Act or otherwise facilitate the admission to Canada of any person where the Minister is satisfied that the person should be exempted from that regulation or that person's admission should be facilitated owing to the existence of compassionate or humanitarian considerations.[58]

Baker argued she had psychiatric problems that might worsen if she were forced to return to Jamaica. Moreover, two of her Canadian-born children depended on her for their care, and she was in regular contact with the other two. They, and she, would suffer emotional hardship if she were forced to return to Jamaica.

The discretionary power involved in assessing compassionate and humanitarian considerations was exercised in the name of the minister by an immigration officer. That officer denied Baker's request for an exemption on the advice of another officer, Officer Lorenzo, whose written memorandum was provided to Baker and is set out below:

> PC is unemployed—on Welfare. No income shown—no assets. Has four Cdn.-born children—four other children in Jamaica—HAS A TOTAL OF EIGHT CHILDREN.
>
> Says only two children are in her "direct custody." (No info on who has ghe [sic] other two.)
>
> There is nothing for her in Jamaica—hasn't been there in a long time—no longer close to her children there—no jobs there—she has no skills other than as a domestic—children would suffer—can't take them with her and can't leave them with anyone here. Says has suffered from a mental disorder since '81—is now an outpatient and is improving. If sent back will have a relapse.
>
> Letter from Children's Aid—they say PC has been diagnosed as a paranoid schizophrenic.—children would suffer if returned—
>
> Letter of Aug. '93 from psychiatrist from Ont. Govm't.
>
> Says PC had post-partum psychosis and had a brief episode of psychosis in Jam. when was 25 yrs. old. Is now an out-patient and is doing relatively well—deportation would be an extremely stressful experience.
>
> Lawyer says PS [sic] is sole caregiver and single parent of two Cdn. born children. PC's mental condition would suffer a setback if she is deported etc.
>
> This case is a catastrophy [sic]. It is also an indictment of our "system" that the client came as a visitor in Aug. '81, was not ordered deported until Dec. '92 and in APRIL '94 IS STILL HERE!

---

57 [1999] 2 S.C.R. 817 [*Baker*].

58 *Immigration Regulations, 1978*, SOR/78-172, as am. by SOR/93-44.

The PC is a paranoid schizophrenic and on welfare. She has no qualifications other than as a domestic. She has FOUR CHILDREN IN JAMAICA AND ANOTHER FOUR BORN HERE. She will, of course, be a tremendous strain on our social welfare systems for (probably) the rest of her life. There are no H&C factors other than her FOUR CANADIAN-BORN CHILDREN. Do we let her stay because of that? I am of the opinion that Canada can no longer afford this type of generosity. However, because of the circumstances involved, there is a potential for adverse publicity. I recommend refusal but you may wish to clear this with someone at Region.

There is also a potential for violence—see charge of "assault with a weapon." [Capitalization in original.]

Baker sought judicial review of the minister's decision, arguing among other things that the minister failed to observe the requirements of the duty of fairness. She argued that she should have been granted an oral interview before the decision-maker; that her children and their fathers should have been given notice of the interview; that they should have been allowed to make submissions at the interview; and that the fathers of her children should have been given permission to attend the interview with counsel. She argued, in addition, that she was entitled to reasons for the minister's decision and that the immigration officer's notes gave rise to a reasonable apprehension of bias. The decision to deny Baker's application was upheld in the Federal Court and she appealed to the Supreme Court of Canada.

The Supreme Court of Canada held that Baker was entitled procedural fairness protection, but the content of the duty was minimal in the circumstances. An oral hearing was not required. It was enough that she was permitted to submit complete written documentation and that reasons for the minister's decision were provided—albeit that the Court accepted the immigration officer's memorandum to another officer fulfilled the reasons requirement.[59]

For present purposes, the important point is that the Court used *Baker* as the occasion to reiterate the purpose of the duty of fairness and set out a number of criteria relevant to determining its content. Justice L'Heureux-Dubé described the purpose of the duty of fairness as follows:

[T]he purpose of the participatory rights contained within the duty of procedural fairness is to ensure that administrative decisions are made using a fair and open procedure, appropriate to the decision being made and its statutory, institutional, and social context, with an opportunity for those affected by the decision to put forward their views and evidence fully and have them considered by the decision-maker.[60]

Baker follows on from L'Heureux-Dubé J.'s decision in *Indian Head School Division*, in which she argued that the duty of fairness was "entrenched in the principles governing our

---

59 Officer Lorenz's notes were provided in response to Baker's counsel's request for reasons, and in the absence of any other record, the Court treated them as the reasons for the decisions. The conclusion that the notes revealed bias was enough to quash the decision, but the Court went on to hold that the minister's discretionary decision was subject to review for reasonableness, and was not reasonable because it paid insufficient attention to the interests and needs of the children and the hardship that a return to Jamaica might cause Ms. Baker. The decision was also quashed on this basis and remitted for reconsideration.

60 *Baker, supra* note 57 at para. 22.

legal system."[61] At the same time, however, she emphasized the importance of respecting the needs of administrative decision-makers:

> It must not be forgotten that every administrative body is the master of its own procedure and need not assume the trappings of a court. The object is not to import into administrative proceedings the rigidity of all the requirements of natural justice that must be observed by a court, but rather to allow administrative bodies to work out a system that is flexible, adapted to their needs and fair. As pointed out by de Smith, the aim is not to create "procedural perfection" but to achieve a certain balance between the need for fairness, efficiency and predictability of outcome.[62]

The criteria set out in *Baker* are designed to give effect to these aims.

B. The Baker Synthesis

L'Heureux-Dubé J. enumerated five criteria relevant to determining the content of the duty of fairness in particular circumstances:

1. the nature of the decision being made and the process followed in making it;

2. the nature of the statutory scheme and the terms of the statute pursuant to which the body operates;

3. the importance of the decision to the individual or individuals affected;

4. the legitimate expectations of the person challenging the decision; and

5. the choices of procedure made by the agency itself.[63]

L'Heureux-Dubé J. did not intend these criteria to be exhaustive and the Court has recently reiterated as much. In *Canada (Attorney-General) v. Mavi*, Justice Binnie noted:

> [T]he obvious point is that the requirements of the duty in particular cases are driven by their particular circumstances. The simple overarching requirement is fairness, and this "central" notion of the "just exercise of power" should not be diluted or obscured by jurisprudential lists developed to be helpful but *not* exhaustive.[64]

It is important to note, too, that none of the *Baker* criteria is, in theory, more important than any other. It is not unusual for courts to conclude that some criteria support a high degree of procedural protection in particular circumstances while others suggest that a lower degree of protection suffices. In every case, courts must determine the requirements of the duty of fairness protection by making an overall appraisal of the circumstances.

Each of the criteria set out in *Baker* is addressed below.

---

61   *Indian Head School, supra* note 44 at para. 46.

62   *Ibid.* at para. 49 (internal citation omitted).

63   *Baker, supra* note 57 at paras. 23-27.

64   2011 SCC 30, [2011] 2 S.C.R. 504 para. 42 (emphasis in original).

1. The Nature of the Decision Being Made and the Process Followed in Making It

Although the classification of decisions as judicial, quasi-judicial, or administrative is no longer important in determining the threshold question—*whether* procedural protection must be provided—decisions that are considered judicial or quasi-judicial in nature are likely to demand more extensive procedural protection than administrative decisions. L'Heureux-Dubé J. put the point this way: "The more the process provided for, the function of the tribunal, the nature of the decision-making body, and the determinations that must be made to reach a decision resemble judicial decision making, the more likely it is that procedural protections closer to the trial model will be required by the duty of fairness."[65]

Given that the development of the duty of fairness was predicated on the irrelevance of the nature of the decision in question, it may seem odd that the nature of the decision remains relevant to determining the content of the duty. However, the nature of the decision is only one of several considerations and it will often be uncontroversial. For example, greater procedural protection is likely to be required in an adjudicative context than a regulatory one.

2. The Nature of the Statutory Scheme and the Terms of the Statute Pursuant to Which the Body Operates

It is important to pay close attention to the legislation that authorizes a particular decision to be made. The requirements of fairness may be minimal in the context of steps that are preliminary to a formal decision-making process. For example, as noted above, investigatory procedures are not normally subject to the duty of fairness even though they might give rise to proceedings in which fairness protection will be required. Greater fairness protection will usually be required if a final decision must be made, but a decision need not be final in order to attract a high degree of fairness protection. Enhanced procedural protection may be required if a second level of proceedings is envisaged, in order to allow meaningful participation in those proceedings. For example, the existence of a right of appeal is an important consideration in deciding whether and to what extent reasons for a first-level decision are required.

3. The Importance of the Decision to the Individual or Individuals Affected

The content of the duty of fairness increases in proportion to the importance of the particular decision to the person it affects. L'Heureux-Dubé J. referred to the context of employment in making this point, citing Justice Dickson's observation in *Kane v. Bd. of Governors of U.B.C.* that "[a] high standard of justice is required when the right to continue in one's

---

[65]   *Baker, supra* note 57 at para. 23.

[66]   [1980] 1 S.C.R. 1105 at 1113.

profession or employment is at stake."[66] However, many things short of adverse impact on one's career or livelihood may support claims for greater procedural protection.

4. The Legitimate Expectations of the Person Challenging the Relevant Decision

The doctrine of legitimate expectation may extend the content of the duty of fairness on the basis of the conduct of public authorities in particular circumstances. For example, a person might be led to understand that he or she will be afforded particular procedural protection, such as an oral hearing before a particular decision is made, even though that level of protection would not otherwise be required. In these circumstances, the person may have a legitimate expectation that an oral hearing will be held and, if this is so, the public authority will be required to hold an oral hearing before the relevant decision can be made.

Legitimate expectation began as a threshold inquiry—a means of extending the applicability of the duty of fairness—but in *Baker* the Court subsumed the concept within the considerations relevant to determining the content of the duty.[67] Legitimate expectations of procedural protection may arise out of conduct such as representations, promises, or undertakings or past practice or current policy of a decision-maker. The Court summarized the concept in this way in *Canada (Attorney General) v. Mavi*:

> Where a government official makes representations within the scope of his or her authority to an individual about an administrative process that the government will follow, and the representations said to give rise to the legitimate expectation are clear, unambiguous and unqualified, the government may be held to its word, provided the representations are procedural in nature and do not conflict with the decision maker's statutory duty. Proof of reliance is not a requisite.[68]

More controversially, a legitimate expectation may also arise if a person is led to expect a particular *outcome* from a decision-making process. A public authority might have policies that suggest such an outcome, or perhaps an official may give an undertaking that a particular decision will be made. For example, an undertaking that a licence will be granted may give rise to a legitimate expectation that a person will receive a licence.

However, a legitimate expectation that a particular decision will be made, as opposed to an expectation that a particular procedure will be followed in making a decision, raises different concerns. Fundamentally, public authorities must be entitled to change their minds; indeed, they may sometimes be required to do so to protect the public interest. As a result,

---

[67] *Supra* note 57 at para. 26. The inspiration for the legitimate expectation argument in *Baker* came from the controversial decision of the High Court of Australia in *Minister for Immigration and Ethnic Affairs v. Teoh* (1995), 183 C.L.R. 273, in which a majority of that Court held that Australia's ratification of the International Convention on the Rights of the Child gave rise to a legitimate expectation that the best interests of the child would be a primary consideration for the minister in making discretionary decisions on deportation. However, *Teoh* is not mentioned in the Court's decision in *Baker*.

[68] [2011] 2 S.C.R. 504 at para. 68 [*Mavi*].

the doctrine of legitimate expectation does not require that expectations of particular sub-stantive outcomes must be fulfilled. In the example above, there is no entitlement to the grant of the licence. However, before a legitimate expectation of receiving a licence can be dashed, the person given the undertaking will be entitled to enhanced procedural fairness protection. For example, he or she may be entitled to notice of the intention not to grant the licence and a right to make submissions before the decision to deny the licence is made.

The concept of legitimate expectation is akin to promissory estoppel, an equitable doc-trine that offers relief from reliance on promises that do not give rise to enforceable con-tracts,[69] but there are important differences.[70] The Supreme Court of Canada has on several occasions reiterated that a legitimate expectation affords only procedural protection, where-as a successful claim of estoppel may result in the enforcement of substantive promises.[71]

5. The Choices of Procedure made by the Agency Itself

The content of the duty of fairness affects more than just the person whose rights, privileges, or interests are at stake in a particular case. It also affects the decision-maker, who may be required to make decisions in hundreds, if not thousands, of additional cases and all those whose rights, privileges, or interests will be affected by those decisions. If the Court is to estab-lish a workable standard, the procedural choices made by the decision-maker must be taken into account in determining the requirements of the duty of fairness. After all, the decision-maker will have superior knowledge of not only its needs but also the needs of the community it serves, and its procedural choices are worthy of respect as a result. As the Court noted in *Baker*:

> [T]he analysis of what procedures the duty of fairness requires should also take into account and respect the choices of procedure made by the agency itself, particularly when the statute leaves to the decision-maker the ability to choose its own procedures, or when the agency has an expertise in determining what procedures are appropriate in the circumstances. While this,

---

69   See, generally, Stephen M. Waddams, *The Law of Contracts*, 6th ed. (Aurora, ON: Canada Law Book, 2010) at paras. 195-206. Estoppel is understood as a defensive concept—a "shield" rather than a "sword"—and, in general, does not result in the enforcement of non-contractual promises.

70   Justice Binnie discusses the differences between estoppel, which he suggests may rarely be available in public law contexts, and legitimate expectation in his concurring opinion in *Mount Sinai Hospital Center v. Quebec (Minister of Health and Social Services)*, 2001 SCC 41, [2001] 2 S.C.R. 281.

71   Note that English law has taken a different path. English courts have come to allow substantive expectations to be protected by the doctrine, rather than simply procedural expectations, and the process–substance distinction has become blurred. The leading case is *R. v. North and East Devon Health Authority, ex p. Cough-lan*, [2001] Q.B. 213 (C.A.). Timothy Endicott argues that *Coughlan* is not an unusual or problematic deci-sion. On his account, legitimate expectation must embrace substantive protection, and the substantive protection afforded by the doctrine can be explained as an example of *Wednesbury* unreasonableness—i.e., no reasonable public authority can exercise discretionary power to disappoint a legitimate expectation be-cause to do so would be to abuse its power. At the same time, however, he recognizes that the protection af-forded by the doctrine must be tempered with comity toward administrative authorities and that judges should defer to good reasons for disappointing a legitimate expectation. See Endicott, *Administrative Law*, 2d ed. (Oxford: Oxford University Press, 2011) 289-95.

of course, is not determinative, important weight must be given to the choice of procedures made by the agency itself and its institutional constraints.[72]

Thus, one of the important tasks for decision-makers in responding to applications for judicial review is to educate the court as to the needs of their processes, which may reflect compromises necessary to allow decisions to be made within a reasonable time frame and at a reasonable cost.

It is not clear how significant the procedural choices of decision-makers will turn out to be in determining the content of procedural fairness protection. L'Heureux-Dubé J. stated that "important weight" must be given to the decision-maker's choice of procedure, but this provides little meaningful guidance, especially if the other criteria support claims to greater procedural protection.

C. Specific Components of the Duty of Fairness

Although most of the procedural rights protected by the duty of fairness are well established, their parameters are open to argument in particular contexts. Some of the most important aspects of the duty of fairness are discussed below.

1. Notice

Notice is the most basic aspect of the duty of fairness. It is the starting point for participation in any decision-making process and involves consideration of the following questions:

Who is proposing to make a decision?
What is the nature of the decision to be made?
When will the decision be made?
Where will the decision be made?
Why is the decision being made?
How is the decision to be made?

The requirements of notice are often prescribed in a tribunal's rules of procedure or in legislation governing hearing procedures. Where they are not, litigation may arise over questions concerning the timeliness and sufficiency of notice. Was it timely, in the sense that it provided adequate time to allow the recipient to respond? Did it provide sufficient information to allow the recipient to make an informed response? The overarching requirement of the duty of fairness is the idea of reasonableness. Thus, the general rule has aptly been stated as follows: "[N]otice must be adequate in all circumstances in order to afford to those concerned a reasonable opportunity to present proofs and arguments, and to respond to those presented in opposition."[73]

The requirement to provide notice should be understood as an ongoing duty: it arises prior to the making of a decision and continues throughout the course of a decision-making

---

72 *Baker, supra* note 57 at para. 27 (internal citations omitted).

73 Donald J.M. Brown & John M. Evans, *Judicial Review of Administrative Action in Canada*, looseleaf (Toronto: Canvasback, 1998), vol. 2 at 1200 [Brown & Evans].

process. A party whose rights, privileges, or interests are at stake is entitled to participate meaningfully in the decision-making process, and in order to do so must be kept apprised of any relevant issues that arise during the course of a hearing.

2. Disclosure

Must information held by a decision-maker be disclosed in order to ensure a fair decision-making process? If so, how much?

The concept of disclosure is well known in the context of the criminal law. In *R. v. Stinchcombe*, the Supreme Court of Canada held that the Crown must disclose "all relevant material" to the defence in a criminal prosecution.[74] This decision flowed from the nature of the prosecution process and, in particular, the notion that the role of the prosecution is not to secure conviction, but, instead, to put all the relevant evidence before the court to ensure that there is a fair trial. As Justice Sopinka put it, "the fruits of the investigation which are in the possession of counsel for the Crown are not the property of the Crown for use in securing a conviction but the property of the public to be used to ensure that justice is done. In contrast, the defence has no obligation to assist the prosecution and is entitled to assume a purely adversarial role toward the prosecution."[75]

Proponents of administrative justice soon argued that the *Stinchcombe* disclosure principle ought to apply in administrative law, but this was rejected by the Court in *May v. Ferndale Institution*:

> It is important to bear in mind that the *Stinchcombe* principles were enunciated in the particular context of criminal proceedings where the innocence of the accused was at stake. Given the severity of the potential consequences the appropriate level of disclosure was quite high. In these cases, the impugned decisions are purely administrative. These cases do not involve a criminal trial and innocence is not at stake. The *Stinchcombe* principles do not apply in the administrative context.[76]

Although this appears to be a categorical rejection of the *Stinchcombe* principle in administrative law, the Court made clear that "the duty of procedural fairness generally requires that the decision-maker discloses the information he or she relied upon. The requirement is that the individual must know the case he or she has to meet."[77] Thus, the question is not *whether* disclosure is required in administrative proceedings, but *how much* disclosure is required in particular proceedings?[78]

---

[74]   *Supra* note 51.

[75]   *Ibid.* at para. 12.

[76]   2005 SCC 82, [2005] 3 S.C.R. 809 at para. 91, per LeBel and Fish JJ.

[77]   *Ibid.* at para. 92.

[78]   Disclosure of information held by the public authority may be distinguished from the concept of discovery, which refers to information held by an opposing party involved in litigation. As Freya Kristjanson and Leslie McIntosh note, discovery is unusual in the context of administrative proceedings and gives rise to a number of concerns for counsel in arguing a case. See the discussion by Freya Kristjanson and Leslie McIntosh in Chapter 6, Advocacy Before Administrative Tribunals.

Tribunals required to hold oral hearings are likely to have disclosure obligations spelled out in rules that govern their procedures or in generic procedural statutes such as Ontario's *Statutory Powers Procedure Act*. But there is considerable scope for the duty of fairness to require disclosure on an ad hoc basis, and courts have held that some circumstances, such as professional discipline and the possibility of a loss of livelihood, require a high level of disclosure.[79]

It is often argued that disclosure obligations must be tempered or limited by the needs of the authorities in particular circumstances or the rights of other persons. For example, in parole hearings or prison discipline cases, there may be concerns about the personal safety of informants and a need to keep their identity secret. Criminal investigative material—for example, wiretap and search warrant information[80] and sensitive national security information[81]—may also need to be kept confidential.

How is fairness to be maintained in these circumstances? The answer is that the disclosure duty can be tailored to the needs of particular circumstances. Information can be vetted by a court to determine its materiality and relevance and may be disclosed only to counsel, with instructions limiting its further dissemination. Disclosure after the fact, along with judicial review and rights of appeal, may mitigate any fairness concerns, as the Court suggested in *Ruby v. Canada (Solicitor General)*.[82] Ultimately, the duty of fairness is satisfied if a party has sufficient information to make informed submissions in regard to a particular matter.

3. Oral Hearings

Oral hearings are often demanded, but seldom required. They are not usually necessary to reach an informed decision on an administrative matter and there are good reasons for not granting them, including the expense and delay they occasion. The administrative process would grind to a halt if the duty of fairness required an oral hearing before any decision could be made.

In what circumstances will the common law require that an oral hearing be provided, as opposed to a hearing "on the papers"? The short answer is that it depends on the relevant circumstances. Nevertheless, some of the circumstances in which an oral hearing will be required are well settled. For example, an oral hearing will be required where a decision depends on findings of witness credibility. This was the basis for the Supreme Court's decision in *Singh v. Minister of Employment and Immigration*,[83] in which the Court held that a person claiming Convention refugee status was entitled to an oral hearing. That was because refugee status depended on whether claimants had a "well-founded fear of persecution" in their homeland, and this was not something that could be sorted out on the basis of a paper

---

79 See e.g. *Sherriff and Attorney General for Canada*, 2006 FCA 139.

80 *Ruby v. Canada (Solicitor General)*, 2002 SCC 75, [2002] 4 S.C.R. 3 [*Ruby*].

81 See e.g. *Charkaoui v. Canada (Citizenship and Immigration)*, 2007 SCC 9, [2007] 1 S.C.R. 350 and *Charkaoui v. Canada (Citizenship and Immigration)*, 2008 SCC 38, [2008] 2 S.C.R. 326.

82 *Supra* note 80.

83 [1985] 1 S.C.R. 177.

hearing. Claimants had to be given the opportunity to provide evidence in person—to tell their story—not simply because of the importance of the matter to them, but also because the decision-making authorities could not determine factually disputed evidence without seeing and hearing from the claimant.

Singh was decided under both s. 7 of the Charter and s. 2(e) of the *Canadian Bill of Rights*, because the legislation in question specifically denied an oral hearing. Where legislation does not preclude an oral hearing, however, recourse to constitutional and quasi-constitutional remedies will not be necessary. The common law may require that an oral hearing be held.[84]

4. Right to Counsel

There is no right to counsel in the context of administrative proceedings. Although the right to counsel is constitutionally protected by s. 10(b) the Charter, the protection of that right is limited to circumstances of "arrest or detention." In *British Columbia (Attorney General) v. Christie*, the Court noted that the right to counsel was understood historically as relevant only in the context of the criminal law, rather than something required by the rule of law itself, and concluded that there was no general constitutional right to counsel. The Court reasoned that such a right would render the specific protection afforded by the Charter redundant:

> We conclude that the text of the Constitution, the jurisprudence and the historical understand-
> ing of the rule of law do not foreclose the possibility that a right to counsel may be recognized
> in specific and varied situations. But at the same time, they do not support the conclusion that
> there is a general constitutional right to counsel in proceedings before courts and tribunals
> dealing with rights and obligations.[85]

In proceedings that are determined without an oral hearing, it is uncontroversial that a party may be represented by counsel—that is, there will be no cause for a decision-maker to refuse to deal with a party through his or her counsel. Representation by counsel is usual in the context of oral hearings, and the right to be represented by counsel is often set out in legislation. The right may extend beyond counsel to representation by a lay representative, depending on the nature of the proceedings and their sophistication.

At the same time, the right to counsel should not be understood in all or nothing terms. Even where there is a right to counsel, the right may be subject to limits. There will often be good reasons to limit the role of counsel in particular proceedings: although counsel may be of considerable benefit to the represented party, the involvement of counsel in administrative proceedings is likely to occasion additional cost, delay, and related problems for the administrative decision-maker, in addition to other parties to the proceedings.

Of course, it is one thing to have a right to be represented by counsel and another to be able to exercise that right: legal counsel is expensive, and as a practical matter may be beyond

---

84   See e.g. *Khan v. University of Ottawa* (1997), 34 O.R. (3d) 535 (C.A.), requiring that an oral hearing be held in the circumstances of an improbable factual claim made in the context of a grade appeal.

85   2007 SCC 21, [2007] 1 S.C.R. 873 at para. 27.

the reach of many in the administrative process. The Court acknowledged as much in re-jecting the existence of a general right to counsel and considered cost to be a primary reason for denying the existence of such a constitutional right:

> This general right to be represented by a lawyer in a court or tribunal proceedings where legal rights or obligations are at stake is a broad right. It would cover almost all—if not all—cases that come before courts or tribunals where individuals are involved. Arguably, corporate rights and obligations would be included since corporations function as vehicles for individual inter-ests. Moreover, it would cover not only actual court proceedings, but also related legal advice, services and disbursements. ... [T]he logical result would be a constitutionally mandated legal aid scheme for virtually all legal proceedings, except where the state could show this is not ne-cessary for effective access to justice.[86]

The Court has held, however, that where a deprivation of life, liberty, or security of the person is at stake, the principles of fundamental justice may in some cases require the pro-vision of counsel in the administrative process.[87]

5. Right to Call Evidence and Cross-Examine Witnesses

The right to call and cross-examine witnesses is normally part of the right to an oral hearing. The right is not absolute, however; administrative actors control their own procedures and may limit the exercise of the right.[88] The guiding principle is that parties must be afforded a reasonable opportunity to present their cases. In *Innisfil (Township) v. Vespra (Township)*, Justice Estey emphasized that the right of cross-examination is not to be withheld on the basis of a judgment by the tribunal that it is of limited utility: "The decision to exercise the right is solely that of the holder of the right. He, of course, must exercise it at his peril as is the case in any other administrative or judicial proceeding where such a right arises."[89]

6. Timeliness and Delay

Administrative decision-makers are not usually under specific statutory timelines for holding hearings or making decisions. Nor is there a Charter right to have an administrative matter heard or determined within a reasonable time—no equivalent to the right to a trial within a reasonable time (s. 11(b)), which applies only to persons charged with an *offence*.

It was inevitable that the question of delay would arise in the context of the administra-tive proceedings, for despite the relative advantages administrative tribunals are presumed

---

86 *Ibid.* at para. 13.

87 *New Brunswick (Minister of Health and Community Services) v. G.(J.)*, [1999] 3 S.C.R. 46 (applicant at risk of losing custody of children in proceedings brought by the state).

88 This is reflected in procedural legislation such as Ontario's *Statutory Powers Procedure Act, supra* note 18, s. 3(2) and British Columbia's *Administrative Tribunals Act, supra* note 17, s. 38(2), both of which provide rights to cross-examination while permitting tribunals to limit examination and cross-examination to what they consider sufficient in the circumstances.

89 [1981] 2 S.C.R. 145 at 171.

to enjoy over courts—their ability to provide more efficient, less formal, and less expensive justice—administrative tribunal processes are often anything but speedy. It is not unusual for litigation before administrative tribunals to take longer than a criminal law prosecution involving the most serious offences. Many hearing days may be required to address a matter, and the need to balance the schedules of counsel and tribunal members—many of whom may be part-time members—can exacerbate the problem. Hearing days may be spread over many months and decisions may not be made for many months following the conclusion of a hearing.

Delay in the administrative process can have significant consequences, as the facts of *Blencoe v. British Columbia (Human Rights Commission)*[90] demonstrate. In that case, a former minister in a British Columbia government sought an order staying human rights tribunal proceedings in complaints against him, over 30 months after the date the complaints were filed. During that time his political career came to an end: he was dismissed from Cabinet, expelled from his caucus, and suffered from depression. The majority of the Supreme Court concluded that, in some circumstances, delay in the administrative process might rise to the level of a deprivation of liberty or security of the person under s. 7 of the Charter, which would violate the right if not in accordance with the principles of fundamental justice. In addition, the majority concluded that "undue" delay in an administrative proceeding might impair the fairness of a hearing, and could result in an abuse of process even if the fairness of a hearing were not compromised. However, the majority of the Court concluded that the delay did not infringe either s. 7 of the Charter or the duty of fairness in Blencoe's case.

The minority of the Court chose to deal with the matter solely on administrative law grounds and set out three considerations that had to be balanced in considering complaints of administrative delay:

(1) *the time taken compared to the inherent time requirements* of the matter before the particular administrative body, which would encompass legal complexities (including the presence of any especially complex systemic issues) and factual complexities (including the need to gather large amounts of information or technical data), as well as reasonable periods of time for procedural safeguards that protect parties or the public;

(2) *the causes of delay beyond the inherent time requirements of the matter,* which would include consideration of such elements as whether the affected individual contributed to or waived parts of the delay and whether the administrative body used as efficiently as possible those resources it had available; and

(3) *the impact of the delay,* considered as encompassing both prejudice in an evidentiary sense and other harms to the lives of real people impacted by the ongoing delay. This may also include a consideration of the efforts by various parties to minimize negative impacts by providing information or interim solutions.[91]

---

[90] *Supra* note 28. See also the discussion of *Blencoe* by Evan Fox-Decent and Alexander Pless in Chapter 12, The Charter and Administrative Law: Cross-Fertilization or Inconstancy?

[91] *Blencoe, supra* note 28 at para. 160 (italicized portions underlined in original).

The minority emphasized the importance of a contextual inquiry into the problem, eschewing the sorts of time limits or guidelines that caused so much difficulty in the context of the criminal law.[92] In the context of administrative proceedings, there were important interests, apart from those of persons complaining of delay, that had to be considered—in Blencoe's case, the interests of the women who complained of sexual harassment. The state was not Blencoe's antagonist, and staying the ability of the human rights tribunal to hold the hearing would deny the complainants their right to have their complaints heard. Thus, although they considered that the delay in Blencoe's case constituted an abuse of process, the minority of the Court considered that a stay of proceedings was inappropriate and would have made an order to expedite the proceedings instead.

Following *Blencoe*, it is clear that delay in providing a hearing—or, presumably, in rendering a decision[93]—may breach the duty of fairness and may even rise to the level of a Charter breach. But the normal remedy for delay is likely to be an order in the nature of mandamus, requiring the tribunal to perform its duty expeditiously.

7. The Duty to Give Reasons

Historically, there was no duty on administrative decision-makers to give reasons. That changed in *Baker*, when Justice L'Heureux-Dubé stated simply:

> In my opinion, it is now appropriate to recognize that, in certain circumstances, the duty of procedural fairness will require the provision of a written explanation for a decision. The strong arguments demonstrating the advantages of written reasons suggest that, in cases such as this where the decision has important significance for the individual, when there is a statutory right of appeal, or in other circumstances, some form of reasons should be required.[94]

The scope of the duty established in *Baker* is limited, at least in principle. Reasons are not required for all decisions; rather, they are required in "certain circumstances." L'Heureux-Dubé J. spelled out two such circumstances, and these reflect the dignitary and instrumental rationales that underlie the duty of fairness itself. Reasons are required if a particular decision has "important significance" for an individual, because public actors demonstrate respect for those affected by their decisions by justifying the decisions they make. Reasons are also required if a statutory appeal process exists to facilitate the workings of that process. It is difficult, if not impossible, to determine whether to appeal a particular decision and which sorts of arguments to make on appeal if no explanation is provided for that decision.

---

[92]   The Charter right to trial within a reasonable time has given rise to the extreme remedy of having charges stayed, most controversially in *R. v. Askov*, [1990] 2 S.C.R. 1199, which resulted in tens of thousands of charges being stayed or withdrawn. The Court revisited the decision in *Askov* in *R. v. Morin*, [1992] 1 S.C.R. 771 and tightened things considerably.

[93]   For an Australian example, see *NAIS v. Minister for Immigration and Multicultural and Indigenous Affairs* (2005), 228 C.L.R. 470 (hearing spread over several years, culminating in a decision by the Refugee Review Tribunal five years following the commencement of the claim violates fairness). For a New Zealand example, see *Ngunguru Coastal Investments Ltd. v. Maori Land Court*, [2011] N.Z.A.R. 354 (three-year delay in rendering a reserve decision by land court violates fairness).

[94]   *Baker, supra* note 57 at para. 43.

Baker left open a potentially large residual discretion for courts to require reasons: reasons may be required in "other circumstances." Moreover, *Baker* contemplates flexibility in complying with the duty to give reasons. The requirement is to provide "some form of reasons" and, as a result, reasons may vary in length and formality in different circumstances. This reflects the wide variety of decision-makers covered by the duty and their relative abilities. Not all decisions are made by lawyers nor are they made on the basis of sophisticated submissions that help guide the decision-maker, and these considerations must be taken into account in determining the nature and scope of the duty to provide reasons. This is typified by the facts of *Baker* itself: the Court accepted that informal notes prepared by one immigration officer for the advice of another satisfied the duty.[95]

Two main concerns are likely to arise with regard to the duty to provide reasons. First, there may be a failure to provide reasons in circumstances in which a court concludes that reasons were required.[96] Second, questions may arise as to the adequacy of reasons proffered in particular circumstances, and it may be argued that inadequate reasons are tantamount to no reasons at all, and hence a violation of the duty.[97] As this argument suggests, there may be considerable overlap between the question *whether* reasons have been given and questions concerning the quality of reasons proffered in a particular case—the latter being a matter for substantive rather than procedural review.

The Court rejected a bifurcated approach to procedural and substantive questions about the duty to provide reasons in *Newfoundland and Labrador Nurses' Union v. Newfoundland and Labrador (Treasury Board)*.[98] The Court emphasized that reasons need not be provided in all cases and asserted that *Baker* does not establish that the quality of the reasons proffered in a particular case is a question of procedural fairness. On the contrary, as Justice Abella pointed out, the threshold for satisfying the requirement to provide reasons is very low:

> It strikes me as an unhelpful elaboration on *Baker* to suggest that alleged deficiencies or flaws in the reasons fall under the category of a breach of the duty of fairness and that they are subject to a correctness review. ... [If] there *are* reasons, there is no such breach. Any challenge to the reasoning/result of the decision should therefore be made within the reasonableness analysis.[99]

This seems clear enough, but Abella J. went on to endorse an observation made by David Dyzenhaus that the concept of deference to a decision requires "respectful attention to the

---

[95]   The concession of counsel that these were in fact the reasons for the minister's decision facilitated the Court's decision—the notes were proffered in response to the request of Baker's counsel for reasons.

[96]   See e.g. *Congrégation des témoins de Jéhovah de St-Jérôme-Lafontaine v. Lafontaine (Village)*, 2004 SCC 48, [2004] 2 S.C.R. 650 at para. 13 (reasons for municipal council's refusal of rezoning application "serves the values of fair and transparent decision-making, reduces the chance of arbitrary or capricious decisions, and cultivates the confidence of citizens in public officials"). Cf. *Catalyst Paper Corp. v. North Cowichan (District)*, 2012 SCC 2 (reasons not required for passing municipal bylaws, as opposed to municipal decisions involving quasi-judicial adjudication).

[97]   See e.g. *Clifford v. Ontario Municipal Employees Retirement System* (2009), 312 D.L.R. (4th) 70 (Ont. C.A.); *Sussman v. College of Alberta Psychologists* (2010), 490 A.R. 304 (Alta. C.A.).

[98]   2011 SCC 62, [2011] 3 S.C.R. 708 [*Newfoundland Nurses' Union*].

[99]   *Ibid.*, at paras. 21-22. Remarkably, the Court did not discuss the conflicting authority in provincial appellate courts, *supra* note 97.

reasons offered *or which could be offered* in support of a decision."[100] Dyzenhaus was not concerned with cases in which no reasons were provided; he was addressing a situation in which the reasons provided were "in some respects *defective*."[101] It would be more apt to have said "deficient," for Dyzenhaus was concerned with the situation in which reasons were insufficient rather than problematic. This was the context in which he argued that a court could "supplement" the reasons for a decision.[102]

Given that one reason for deferring to the decisions of administrative actors is to respect the decision of the legislature to confer decision-making authority on them, the extent to which a generalist court can legitimately "supplement" the reasons for decisions they make is surely contestable. This is supported by the more limited reading the majority of the Court gives to the concept of "reasons which could be offered" in *Alberta (Information and Privacy Commissioner) v. Alberta Teachers' Association*.[103] In that case, Justice Rothstein described the concept as "apposite when the decision concerns an issue that was not raised before the decision maker," and emphasized that courts are not to reformulate a tribunal's reasons in order to render them reasonable.[104] On his account, the concept is useful mainly as a means of precluding the parties from misleading a tribunal by failing to raise a matter—in effect, causing the failure to provide reasons that is subsequently challenged on judicial review. Thus, Rothstein J.'s decision contemplates that it may sometimes be necessary to return a decision in order to allow a decision-maker to provide reasons on a particular matter, thereby allowing the Court to defer on an informed basis if the decision is reviewed subsequently.

All of this is to say that much requires clarification in future cases. At least this much is clear: a wholesale failure to provide reasons will constitute a breach of the duty of fairness. Following *Newfoundland Nurses' Union*, however, the Court will not be concerned with the adequacy or sufficiency of reasons in determining whether the duty to provide reasons has been met. The focus will be on the substantive question: do the reasons, such as they are,

---

[100] David Dyzenhaus, "The Politics of Deference: Judicial Review and Democracy" in Michael Taggart, ed., *The Province of Administrative Law* (Oxford: Hart, 1997) 279 at 286 [Dyzenhaus] (emphasis added). Dyzenhaus's observation was made prior to the establishment of a duty to give reasons in *Baker, supra* note 57, in the context of elaborating his "deference as respect" concept. Ironically, Dyzenhaus professed to being "undecided on the important topic of whether my argument entails the claim that there is a common law duty on tribunals to give reasons" (Dyzenhaus, *ibid.*, at n. 63), and went on to refer with apparent approval to the then common criticism that "a reason-giving requirement invites both judicial activism and distortion of the administrative process."

[101] Dyzenhaus, *ibid.* at 304.

[102] "[E]ven if the reasons in fact given do not seem wholly adequate to support the decision, the court must first seek to supplement them before it seeks to subvert them." Dyzenhaus, *ibid.*

[103] 2011 SCC 61, [2011] 3 S.C.R. 654. This case was released one day prior to the decision in *Newfoundland Nurses' Union, supra* note 98, but is not mentioned in that judgment.

[104] Justice Rothstein refers with approval to *Petro-Canada v. British Columbia (Workers' Compensation Board)*, 2009 BCCA 396 at paras. 53, 56, where the Court stated that respectful attention to the reasons "which could be offered in support of a decision" is not "carte blanche to reformulate a tribunal's decision in a way that casts aside an unreasonable chain of analysis in favour of the court's own rationale for the result."

"allow the reviewing court to understand why the tribunal made its decision and permit it to determine whether the conclusion is within the range of acceptable outcomes"?[105]

VI. Judicial Review of the Duty of Fairness

It is well established that the requirements of the duty of fairness are independent of the merits of the substantive matter in issue and that breach of the duty voids a decision. The Supreme Court of Canada expressed the point categorically in *Cardinal*:

> [T]he denial of a right to a fair hearing must always render a decision invalid, whether or not it may appear to a reviewing court that the hearing would likely have resulted in a different decision. The right to a fair hearing must be regarded as an independent, unqualified right which finds its essential justification in the sense of procedural justice which any person affected by an administrative decision is entitled to have. It is not for a court to deny that right and sense of justice on the basis of speculation as to what the result might have been had there been a hearing.[106]

This statement of the law finds considerable support in English law and its rationale is best set out in the oft-quoted remarks of Justice Megarry:

> It may be that there are some who would decry the importance which the courts attach to the observance of the rules of natural justice. "When something is obvious," they may say, "why force everybody to go through the tiresome waste of time involved in framing charges and giving an opportunity to be heard? The result is obvious from the start." Those who take this view do not, I think, do themselves justice. As everybody who has anything to do with the law well knows, the path of the law is strewn with examples of open and shut cases which, somehow, were not; of unanswerable charges which, in the event, were completely answered; of inexplicable conduct which was fully explained; of fixed and unalterable determinations that, by discussion, suffered a change. Nor are those with any knowledge of human nature who pause to think for a moment likely to underestimate the feelings of resentment of those who find that a decision against them has been made without their being afforded any opportunity to influence the course of events.[107]

However, in *Mobil Oil Canada Ltd. v. Canada-Newfoundland Offshore Petroleum Board*,[108] the Court endorsed the view expressed by Sir William Wade that "[a] distinction might perhaps be made according to the nature of the decision. In the case of a tribunal which must decide according to law, it may be justifiable to disregard a breach of natural justice where the demerits of the claim are such that it would in any case be hopeless."[109] The

---

105   The concept of reasonableness is addressed by Sheila Wildeman in Chapter 10, Pas de Deux: Deference and Non-Deference in Action.

106   *Cardinal, supra* note 10 at para. 23.

107   *John v. Rees*, [1970] Ch. 345 at 402.

108   [1994] 1 S.C.R. 202 [*Mobil Oil*].

109   William Wade, *Administrative Law*, 6th ed. (Oxford: Oxford University Press, 1988) at 535. This is repeated in H.W.R. Wade & C.F. Forsyth, *Administrative Law*, 10th ed. (Oxford: Oxford University Press, 2009) at 424.

Court refused to quash a decision in the face of a breach of procedural fairness in *Mobil Oil*, but did so on the basis that it would be "impractical" and "nonsensical" to do so, because, as a result of a cross-appeal, the tribunal would have no alternative but to reject the application in question. The Court described these circumstances as "exceptional," and reiterated that it "would not wish to apply it [the exception] broadly." Thus, *Cardinal* remains good law and the *Mobil Oil* exception should be rare.[110]

It is important to emphasize that although judicial review is concerned with deciding what the duty of fairness requires in the circumstances of a particular decision, the reviewing court's decision is made *after* the decision is made, and is made in the knowledge that a finding that the duty of fairness was breached will result in the relevant decision being quashed.

The retrospective nature of fairness determinations brings to mind Jeremy Bentham's complaint about the common law.[111] The problem is mitigated by the sort of institutional knowledge that builds up over time. Still, there may be a tendency for risk-averse administrators to provide more than the duty of fairness might otherwise be held to require in order to ensure that their decisions can withstand judicial review.

Judicial review of a decision on procedural grounds must be differentiated from judicial review on substantive grounds. The Supreme Court of Canada subjects substantive decisions to review on either a correctness or a reasonableness standard, pursuant to which the Court may defer to the decisions of an administrative agency.[112] No similar approach is taken with regard to the duty of fairness. Historically, compliance with the duty of fairness has been regarded as a jurisdictional question and, as such, a question that must be answered correctly. If it is not, then jurisdiction will be lost, the relevant decision will be quashed, and the decision-maker will be required to make a fresh decision in accordance with the correct procedure.

---

[110] Nevertheless, some courts appear to have assumed the existence of a broader discretion to refuse to quash a decision where the duty of fairness has been breached. In *Veillette v. International Association of Machinists and Aerospace Workers*, 2011 FCA 32 at para. 16, the Federal Court of Appeal put the point this way: "Even a breach of the principles of natural justice or procedural fairness does not automatically invalidate the decision." In addition to *Mobil Oil*, *supra* note 108, the Court cited *Canada (Minister of Human Resources Development) v. Hogervorst*, 2007 FCA 41; *Halifax Employers Ass. Inc. v. Council of ILA Locals for the Port of Halifax*, 2006 FCA 82; *Société des arrimeurs de Québec v. Canadian Union of Public Employees, Local 3810*, 2008 FCA 237; *Palonek v. Canada (Minister of National Revenue—M.N.R.)*, 2007 FCA 281; and *Cartier v. Canada (Attorney General)*, 2002 FCA 384. Cf. *Persaud v. Canada (Citizenship and Immigration)*, 2011 FC 31 at para. 19, in which Justice Hughes of the trial division reads the *Mobil Oil* exception much more narrowly: "The point being made by the Supreme Court is that where a breach of natural justice or procedural fairness has been found the Court cannot refuse to send it back because it supposes that the case would be found to be futile. A rare exception exists where the remedy sought would not be relevant in the context of the matter presently before the Court."

[111] Jeremy Bentham, *The Works of Jeremy Bentham*, ed. by John Bowring, vol. 5 (Edinburgh: W. Tait, 1843) at 235: "It is the judges (as we have seen) that make the common law. Do you know how they make it? Just as a man makes laws for his dog. When your dog does anything you want to break him of, you wait till he does it, and then beat him for it. This is the way you make laws for your dog: and this is the way the judges make law for you and me." (First published in 1792 as "Truth Versus Ashurst; or, Law as It Is, Contrasted with what It Is Said to Be.")

[112] *Dunsmuir, supra* note 9.

As we have seen, there is some room for deference when it comes to determining the content of the duty of fairness, because the procedural choices made by the decision-maker are one of the considerations courts must take into account. However, once the content of the duty in a particular context has been determined, the question for the court is simply whether the duty of fairness has been met on the facts of the case—a question that will yield a yes or no answer.

Violation of the duty of fairness will not result in the imposition of a substantive outcome by the court. The role of the court is to supervise the decision-making *process*—to ensure that the relevant decision has been made properly, not that the "proper" decision has been made. Although a successful application for judicial review on fairness grounds will result in an order quashing a decision and requiring it to be made anew, nothing necessarily prevents the decision-maker from reaching the same substantive decision. Nevertheless, as *Baker* demonstrates, a new hearing may well lead to a different outcome. Mavis Baker was subsequently granted the humanitarian and compassionate exception she sought and was allowed to stay in Canada.

Whether or not a different result obtains on a rehearing, the consequences of a breach of the duty of fairness may be significant. Administrative proceedings can take months—even years—and be hugely expensive for all those involved.[113] An order quashing a decision may cause great inconvenience not only to those involved but also to the public interest, by requiring that proceedings be repeated, with all the associated cost and delay. Strict adherence to the automatic quashing remedy may result in problems from time to time. Moreover, the automatic nature of the remedy may turn out to be counterproductive to the protection of the right. It is possible that, in close cases, courts might err on the side of finding that the duty has been met, given the far-reaching consequences an order quashing a particular decision may have. As long as quashing is the usual remedy for a breach of fairness, courts may be circumspect in expanding the scope and content of the duty of fairness.

SUGGESTED ADDITIONAL READINGS

BOOKS AND ARTICLES

Canadian

Blake, Sara, *Administrative Law*, 5th ed. (Toronto: LexisNexis, 2011).

Brown, Donald, & John M. Evans, *Judicial Review of Administrative Action in Canada*, looseleaf (Toronto: Canvasback, 1998).

Huscroft, Grant, & Michael Taggart, eds., *Inside and Outside Canadian Administrative Law: Essays in Honour of David Mullan* (Toronto: University of Toronto Press, 2006).

Jones, David P., & Anne S. de Villars, *Principles of Administrative Law*, 5th ed. (Toronto: Thomson Carswell, 2009).

---

113   See e.g. *Canada (Attorney General) v. Canada (Commission of Inquiry on the Blood System)*, *supra* note 29 (judicial review of commission of inquiry [the Krever commission] that held hearings over a two-year period).

Kristjanson, Freya, "Procedural Fairness at the McLachlin Court" in Adam Dodek & David A. Wright, eds., *Public Law at the McLachlin Court: the First Decade* (Toronto: Irwin Law, 2011).

Macaulay, Robert W., & James L.H. Sprague, *Hearings Before Administrative Tribunals*, 4th ed. (Toronto: Carswell, 2010).

Mullan, David J., *Administrative Law* (Toronto: Irwin Law, 2001), chapter 8.

Mullan, David J., Gus Van Harten, & Gerald Heckman, *Administrative Law: Cases, Text, and Materials*, 6th ed. (Toronto: Emond Montgomery, 2010).

Régimbald, Guy, *Canadian Administrative Law* (Toronto: LexisNexis, 2008).

Sossin, Lorne, "The Promise of Procedural Justice" in Adam Dodek & David A. Wright, eds., *Public Law at the McLachlin Court: the First Decade* (Toronto: Irwin Law, 2011).

International

Aronson, Mark, Bruce D. Dyer, & Matthew Groves, *Judicial Review of Administrative Action*, 4th ed. (Thomson Reuters Australia, 2008).

Craig, Paul, *Administrative Law*, 6th ed. (London: Sweet & Maxwell, 2008).

Endicott, Timothy, *Administrative Law*, 2d ed. (Oxford: Oxford University Press, 2011).

Joseph, Philip A., *Constitutional and Administrative Law in New Zealand*, 3d ed. (Wellington: Thomson-Brookers, 2007).

Wade, William & Christopher Forsyth, *Administrative Law*, 10th ed. (Oxford: Oxford University Press 2009).

Woolf, Rt. Hon. Lord, Jeffrey Jowell, Andrew Le Sueur, & Catherine M. Donnelly, *De Smith's Judicial Review*, 6th ed. (London: Sweet & Maxwell, 2007).

CASES

Alberta (Information and Privacy Commissioner) v. Alberta Teachers' Association, 2011 SCC 61, [2011] 3 S.C.R. 654.

Att. Gen. of Can. v. Inuit Tapirisat et al., [1980] 2 S.C.R. 735.

Authorson v. Canada (Attorney General), 2003 SCC 39, [2003] 2 S.C.R. 40.

Baker v. Canada (Minister of Citizenship and Immigration), [1999] 2 S.C.R. 817.

Blencoe v. British Columbia (Human Rights Commission), 2000 SCC 44, [2000] 2 S.C.R. 307.

Canada (Attorney General) v. Canada (Commission of Inquiry on the Blood System), [1997] 3 S.C.R. 440 (Krever Commission).

Canada (Attorney General) v. Mavi, 2011 SCC 30, [2011] 2 S.C.R. 504.

Cardinal v. Director of Kent Institution, [1985] 2 S.C.R. 643.

Charkaoui v. Canada (Citizenship and Immigration), 2007 SCC 9, [2007] 1 S.C.R. 350.

Charkaoui v. Canada (Citizenship and Immigration), 2008 SCC 38, [2008] 2 S.C.R. 326.

Congrégation des témoins de Jéhovah de St-Jérôme-Lafontaine v. Lafontaine (Village), 2004 SCC 48, [2004] 2 S.C.R. 650.

C.U.P.E. v. Ontario (Minister of Labour), 2003 SCC 29, [2003] 1 S.C.R. 539.

Dunsmuir v. New Brunswick, 2008 SCC 9, [2008] 1 S.C.R. 190.

Homex Realty and Development Co. v. Wyoming (Village), [1980] 2 S.C.R. 1011.

Idziak v. Canada (Minister of Justice), [1992] 3 S.C.R. 631.

Imperial Oil Ltd. v. Quebec (Minister of the Environment), 2003 SCC 58, [2003] 2 S.C.R. 624.

Kane v. Bd. of Governors of U.B.C., [1980] 1 S.C.R. 1105.

Knight v. Indian Head School Division No. 19, [1990] 1 S.C.R. 653.

May v. Ferndale Institution, 2005 SCC 82, [2005] 3 S.C.R. 809.

Mount Sinai Hospital Center v. Quebec (Minister of Health and Social Services), 2001 SCC 41, [2001] 2 S.C.R. 281.

Newfoundland and Labrador Nurses Union v. Newfoundland and Labrador (Treasury Board), 2011 SCC 62, [2011] 3 S.C.R. 708.

Nicholson v. Haldimand-Norfolk (Regional) Police Commissioners, [1979] 1 S.C.R. 311.

Re Canada Assistance Plan, [1991] 2 S.C.R. 525.

Ruby v. Canada (Solicitor General), 2002 SCC 75, [2002] 4 S.C.R. 3.

Singh v. Minister of Employment and Immigration, [1985] 1 S.C.R. 177.

Wells v. Newfoundland, [1999] 3 S.C.R. 199.

CHAPTER SIX

Advocacy Before Administrative Tribunals

FREYA KRISTJANSON
Cavallozzo Hayes Shilton McIntyre & Cornish LLP

LESLIE McINTOSH
Osgoode Hall Law School

I. Introduction

Advocacy is the art of persuasion. Does the art of persuasion before administrative tribunals differ from advocacy in civil and criminal courts? Does it vary from tribunal to tribunal? While there are obvious similarities, the answer to both questions is "yes."

This book aims to situate administrative law in context. The earlier chapters illustrate that appreciating the different contexts in which various tribunals operate is the key to understanding many administrative law concepts. For example, the content of the duty of fairness varies depending on a number of factors, including the nature of the tribunal.[1] Differences between administrative tribunals and courts, as well as among administrative tribunals, also dictate different techniques of advocacy. The cardinal rule of advocacy before administrative tribunals is, therefore, know the tribunal. The focus of this chapter is on adjudicative tribunals, which decide cases in which two or more parties appear before the tribunal. In adjudicative tribunal settings, a party may be represented by counsel, a law student with a legal clinic, a paralegal, or may be unrepresented. Each of these present different challenges for lawyers. A more complete discussion of these issues is set out by Lorne Sossin in Chapter 7, Access to Administrative Justice and Other Worries. Administrative advocates may also make submissions before a range of other kinds of tribunals—for example, ministers, public inquiries, or advisory councils. Advocacy techniques must be adapted accordingly.

Rather than discussing substantive administrative law principles, this chapter aims to provide a practical review of what advocates need to know and should consider when presenting a case. In a sense, we are building on the substantive principles you will learn from the rest of the textbook and demonstrating how to apply substantive administrative law principles in the practice of law. The chapter is divided into three parts: first, the sources of administrative law that are essential to the presentation of a case; second, pre-hearing issues; and third, advocacy at administrative hearings, including ethics, civility, and professionalism in the practice of administrative law.

---

1   Grand Huscroft's Chapter 5, From Natural Justice to Fairness: Thresholds, Content, and the Role of Judicial Review, and Laverne Jacobs's Chapter 8, Caught Between Judicial Paradigms and the Administrative State's Pastiche: "Tribunal" Independence, Impartiality, and Bias, contain a thorough discussion on the contextual aspects of procedural fairness.

II. Sources of Administrative Law

In any administrative law proceeding, the advocate will have to consider which of the following sources of law apply, and how each of these will affect the nature of the advocacy:

- the governing statutes, regulations, and the general regulatory context;
- tribunal rules, policies, and guidelines;
- statutory procedural codes such as the *Statutory Powers Procedure Act* (SPPA)[2] (Ontario) or the *Administrative Tribunals Act* (ATA)[3] (British Columbia);
- common-law principles of procedural fairness;
- *Canadian Charter of Rights and Freedoms*[4] and other constitutional law principles; and
- other applicable laws, particularly the rules of evidence.

A. Governing Statutes and Regulations

It is critical to start with the tribunal's governing statute or statutes. It is important to remember that the statute that establishes the administrative decision-maker may not be the same statute pursuant to which the particular proceeding arises. For example, in Ontario, most administrative pension proceedings arise under the *Pension Benefits Act*.[5] However, the tribunal that hears those matters—namely, the Financial Services Tribunal—is established under a separate statute—that is, the *Financial Services Commission of Ontario Act*.[6]

The governing statutes and accompanying regulations should be examined not only for provisions that create unique procedural requirements but also to *characterize* the tribunal. Is it primarily adjudicative, deciding disputes between two parties? Is it a regulatory tribunal governing an area of activity? Is it a licensing tribunal deciding whether persons can engage in particular livelihoods? Does it review government decisions with respect to various benefits? The characterization of the administrative decision-maker will often dictate the type of advocacy that will be required, as well as procedural protections that may be available at common law.

The regulatory context is a key factor in advocacy before administrative tribunals. An administrative case is generally argued in the context of a particular statute, before a statutory decision-maker with statutory jurisdiction. In addition to legal constraints, these statutes (often supplemented by tribunal rules and guidelines) reflect normative policy choices—for example, providing income for injured workers, protecting investors and the stability of capital markets, encouraging competition, and protecting the public. The good advocate

---

2   R.S.O. 1990, c. S.22 [SPPA]; in the discussion below, reference is made to the SPPA as an example of general legislation conferring procedural powers on tribunals.

3   S.B.C. 2004, c. 45 [ATA].

4   Part I of the *Constitution Act, 1982*, being Schedule B to the *Canada Act 1982* (U.K.), 1982, c. 11.

5   R.S.O. 1990, c. P.8.

6   S.O. 1997, c. 28.

will discern these normative policy choices and use them to support all of his or her advocacy choices in the context of a specific administrative setting.

A good advocate will reread the tribunal's constituent statute and the statute under which the particular proceeding arises each time a new file is opened. Rereading the statute or statutes and regulations in the context of a specific file can shed new light on what may seem to be familiar provisions.

It is important to be familiar with all the sections that are relevant, because the statutory decision-maker must make a decision in accordance with his or her statutory mandate. The burden is on the advocate to ensure that all statutory preconditions are met and that the appropriate evidence is called to establish what the statute requires. As part of this, the advocate should take time to think about the purpose of the statute. Perhaps one of the fundamental distinctions between criminal and civil advocacy, on the one hand, and administrative advocacy, on the other, is the importance of the purpose of the statutory scheme. A good advocate will present a case that the decision-maker will think is just and in accordance with the purpose of the statute.

The statutory context, including the purpose of the statute, also provides a theme within which the case will be argued. For example, the *Workplace Safety and Insurance Act, 1997*,[7] an income replacement system for injured workers, has a purpose clause that reads:

> 1. The purpose of this Act is to accomplish the following in a financially responsible and accountable manner:
>
>   1. To promote health and safety in workplaces.
>
>   2. To facilitate the return to work and recovery of workers who sustain personal injury arising out of and in the course of employment or who suffer from an occupational disease.
>
>   3. To facilitate the re-entry into the labour market of workers and spouses of deceased workers.
>
>   4. To provide compensation and other benefits to workers and to the survivors of deceased workers.

Advocacy literature teaches that cases are built around the development of a "theme." In administrative law, it is important to use the statute to develop a theme that will resonate with the administrative decision-maker. The purpose clause in the *Workplace Safety and Insurance Act, 1997*, set out above, provides the advocate with a significant set of themes that should be used to develop the case from inception to conclusion. In a dispute between the worker and the employer over whether, when, and how return to work should take place after an accident, each side could use these themes to structure their presentation. From the employer's perspective, the theme could be "financially responsible" decision making—for example, the injured worker is asking for too much. From the injured workers' perspective, emphasis might be placed on the importance of accountability for "facilitating re-entry" into the labour market.

---

7   S.O. 1997, c. 16, Sch. A, s. 1.

B. Tribunal Rules, Policies, and Guidelines

Statutes, regulations, and statutory procedural codes are the obvious sources of a tribunal's authority.[8] These are "rules" that have been imposed on administrative tribunals from the outside—that is, the common law by courts and statutes and regulations by the legislature and the executive, respectively.

There may also be rules promulgated by tribunals themselves.[9] Although it was initially not without controversy, there is now general agreement that rule making by tribunals is a good thing. Rule making is advantageous for the same reason that it is appropriate to have different statutory provisions for different tribunals—that is because of the diversity of administrative tribunals.

Even the most informal of tribunals has likely engaged in rule making in a number of areas. Tribunal rules typically deal with such basic topics as the circumstances in which the tribunal will grant an adjournment, service of documents, motions, and prerequisites for reconsideration of decisions. Because the tribunal will be intimately familiar with its own rules, it is crucial that the advocate have the same degree of familiarity. Failure to comply with a tribunal's rules may cause delay and expense for the client and will erode the patience of the tribunal.

Tribunals also have various other sources of internal law, set out in policies, directives, guidelines, precedents, procedural orders, or notices of hearing.[10] Often, such materials may be found only at the tribunal's offices. The registrars or secretaries of tribunals and their in-house counsel are good sources of information about the tribunal's internal laws.

Externally, administrative tribunals are accountable to a ministry or department of government. Their constituent statutes are administered by a ministry or department of the government. Tribunals may be overseen by various means, such as memoranda of understanding or ministerial policy statements. The statute creating the government ministry or department may also shed some light on the context in which the tribunal operates. A good advocate will understand the policy behind the creation of the tribunal and the role it is intended to fulfill in the broader scheme.

C. Statutory Procedural Codes

Some provinces have statutory procedural codes that establish procedural requirements for administrative proceedings—for example, the Ontario SPPA,[11] the Alberta *Administrative Procedures and Jurisdiction Act*,[12] the Quebec *Administrative Justice Act*,[13] and the B.C.

---

8 See the discussion of substantive issues regarding rules by Andrew Green in Chapter 4, Regulations and Rule Making: The Dilemma of Delegation.

9 See *ibid.* Many statutes or procedural codes provide tribunals with rule-making authority. See e.g. SPPA, *supra* note 2, s. 25.1.

10 See the discussion of "soft law" by Andrew Green in Chapter 4, Regulations and Rule Making: The Dilemma of Delegation.

11 *Supra* note 2.

12 R.S.A. 2000, c. A-3.

13 R.S.Q., c. J-3.

Administrative Tribunal Act.[14] Of note, the federal system does not have a statutory procedural code. These procedural codes are important in administrative law.

Alberta's procedural code does not contain a provision that provides for its general applicability. Instead, the tribunals that are subject to it are designated by regulation. Its provisions are not comprehensive. In contrast, Quebec's procedural code is detailed. There are different procedural requirements for "adjudicative" and "administrative" tribunals.

The approach of British Columbia's procedural code is to empower tribunals to make their own rules. There are few procedural requirements prescribed by the ATA. Reference must be had to the tribunal's enabling statute or statutes to ascertain which, if any, of the procedural provisions of the ATA apply.

Ontario's procedural code also recognizes the differences among administrative tribunals. It does not adopt a one-size-fits-all approach. The SPPA was a compromise between inserting detailed procedural provisions into each statute under which a hearing is required and having one set of procedural rules for all tribunals[15] The former approach was too unwieldy. The latter was too inflexible to take into account the differences among tribunals. The SPPA applies to the exercise of a "statutory power of decision" where a hearing is required by or under a statute or "otherwise by law."[16]

Specific procedural provisions are often set out in a tribunal's enabling legislation. It is important to note that a tribunal may be established under one statute, but its proceedings may be governed by another, and that there may be applicable procedural provisions in both.[17]

Different procedural codes relate to the procedural provisions in enabling statutes in different ways. Alberta's procedural code says that it does "not relieve an authority from complying with any procedure to be followed by it under any other Act relating to the exercise of its statutory power."[18] In Ontario, if the procedural provisions in a tribunal's enabling legislation conflict with the SPPA, the SPPA prevails unless it is expressly provided in the other statute that "its provisions and regulations, rules or by-laws made under it apply despite anything in the [SPPA]."[19] However, the SPPA itself continues or restores the primacy of the tribunal's enabling legislation in certain cases.

What is the relationship between procedural codes and the common law? Because the procedural codes represent "minimum rules," the common law may operate to require greater procedural protections than those set out in the procedural codes.

---

14 *Supra* note 3.

15 *Royal Commission Inquiry into Civil Rights Report* (McRuer J.C., Chair) (1971), vol. 1, c. 14, at 209-10.

16 SPPA, *supra* note 2, s. 3(1); exceptions are listed in s. 3(2).

17 For example, in Ontario, the Social Benefits Tribunal is established under the *Ontario Works Act, 1997*, S.O. 1997, c. 25, Sch. B, but it conducts hearings under the *Ontario Disability Support Program Act, 1997*, S.O. 1997, c. 25, Sch. B.

18 *Supra* note 12, s. 2(8).

19 SPPA, *supra* note 2, s. 32.

D. Common-Law Principles of Procedural Fairness

In any administrative proceeding, the types of procedural protections to which one is entitled vary widely depending on the context. Does procedural fairness require a full oral hearing, or is the nature of the decision such that the affected party's rights are protected by the ability to make written submissions? What level of disclosure is required? Has the administrative body created "legitimate expectations"? Does "the right to state one's case" require cross-examination and representation by counsel? None of these questions can be answered in the abstract. They all require a careful examination of the type of interest at stake, the regulatory context, and the impact of the decision. One of the chief duties of an administrative advocate is to consider what level of procedural protections should be sought pursuant to common-law principles of procedural fairness.

The Supreme Court of Canada's decision in *Baker v. Canada (Minister of Citizenship and Immigration)*[20] established the modern common-law approach to the duty of fairness. This case is the subject of extensive commentary in this book.[21] One of *Baker*'s legacies is that administrative decision making is now seen as falling somewhere on a spectrum between quasi-judicial and legislative decision making, with procedural entitlements varying according to placement on the spectrum. Once an individual's "rights, privileges or interests" are at stake, the duty of fairness applies and the question then becomes one of degree.[22]

The five *Baker* factors attempt to balance the need to give effect to legislative intention in crafting administrative processes, which include accessibility, efficiency, informality and cost, with the need to ensure that those processes protect individual interests. In any administrative proceeding, the advocate must be prepared to argue about the procedural protections being sought on the basis of the five *Baker* principles, making reference to fundamental principles of administrative law.

The question who may be a party to a proceeding is a good example of the interaction among enabling statutes, statutory procedural codes, and the common law.[23] The starting point, as always, should be the statute or statutes governing the tribunal. The different functions of tribunals often dictate different provisions with respect to who may be a party. For example, in professional discipline cases, the statute may provide that, in addition to the governing body and the professional, the complainant may be a party. In environmental or planning cases, the tribunals may have the statutory authority to admit interveners in the public interest.

If the statute expressly sets out who may be a party and does not provide authority to add others as parties, it appears that the tribunal has no authority to do so.[24] However, many statutes provide that persons who are "interested" or "affected" by the proceeding may be

---

[20]   [1999] 2 S.C.R. 817 [*Baker*].

[21]   See, in particular, Grant Huscroft's Chapter 5, From Natural Justice to Fairness: Thresholds, Content, and the Role of Judicial Review.

[22]   *Baker, supra* note 20 at para. 20.

[23]   See the discussion on standing by Lorne Sossin in Chapter 7, Access to Administrative Justice and Other Worries.

[24]   *Re Ontario (Royal Commission on the Northern Environment)*, [1983] O.J. No. 994 (QL), 144 D.L.R. (3d) 416 at 419 (Div. Ct.).

parties. The SPPA provides that any person "entitled by law" may be a party, thereby incorporating the common law. Depending on the nature of the decision and the statutory
decision-maker, the common law of procedural fairness provides that a person seeking
party status demonstrate that "the subject-matter of the inquiry may seriously affect" him
or her. Therefore, the good administrative advocate must consider whether his or her client
is or should be a party, whether other parties should be added or provided with notice of a
hearing, and whether he or she should oppose the addition of parties in a proceeding. It is
important to recognize that clear legislative restrictions will oust the procedural protections
that would typically be afforded at common law. In such circumstances, only the Charter or
constitutional rights can override legislative restrictions.[25] In other words, if a tribunal's
enabling statute expressly disavows any right to a hearing, the common law does not override express statutory language and no hearing will be required. However, courts tend to
narrowly interpret rights-limiting statutory provisions.

E. Charter of Rights and Freedoms and Constitutional Law

It is important to consider whether there are any Charter or constitutional rights in issue
and, if so, whether the tribunal has jurisdiction to entertain a Charter or constitutional
argument or whether it must be brought before a court.[26] Many tribunals now have jurisdiction over Charter and constitutional questions, following the Supreme Court of Canada's
decisions in *R. v. Conway*[27] and *Nova Scotia (Worker's Compensation Board) v. Martin).*[28] In
British Columbia and Alberta, however, the ATA and the *Administrative Procedures and
Jurisdiction* Act, respectively, expressly distinguish those tribunals with jurisdiction to decide constitutional questions from those that do not. The tribunal's constituent statute may
also address whether it can hear Charter issues.[29] If the constitutional validity or applicability of an Act is raised in an administrative hearing, notice, generally, must be provided to
the appropriate attorneys general.[30]

If both the tribunal and the court have jurisdiction, counsel is no longer required to
make a strategic decision as to which ought to be asked to decide the question. Rather, the
tribunal is obliged to exercise its jurisdiction. However, the advocate must ensure that the
remedy sought is within the tribunal's jurisdiction, because courts retain jurisdiction over
certain remedies.[31]

---

25   *Ocean Port Hotel Ltd. v. British Columbia (General Manager, Liquor Control and Licensing Branch)*, 2001 SCC
      52, [2001] 2 S.C.R. 781.

26   See the discussion on administrative law issues and the Charter by Evan Fox-Decent and Alexander Pless in
      Chapter 12, The Charter and Administrative Law: Cross-Fertilization or Inconstancy?

27   2010 SCC 22, [2010] 1 S.C.R. 765 [*Conway*].

28   [2003] 2 S.C.R. 504; see also *Paul v. British Columbia (Forest Appeals Commission)*, [2003] 2 S.C.R. 585 and
      Tranchemontagne v. Ontario (Director, Disability Support Program), [2006] 1 S.C.R. 513.

29   See e.g. *Ontario Disability Support Program Act*, S.O. 1997, c. 25, Sch. B [ODSPA].

30   See e.g. *Courts of Justice Act*, R.S.O. 1990, c. C.43, s. 109.

31   See Cristie Ford's Chapter 3, Dogs and Tails: Remedies in Administrative Law; on Charter remedies, more
      generally, see *R. v. Conway, supra* note 27.

III. Pre-Hearing Issues

While the law underlying the duty of fairness is discussed by Grant Huscroft in Chapter 5, *From Natural Justice to Fairness: Thresholds, Content, and the Role of Judicial Review*, each aspect of this legal standard gives rise to important questions of advocacy. We discuss a number of aspects of procedural fairness below, together with the strategic questions they raise for the advocate. The decisions at each step will be a product of judgment and the strategic assessment of the case.

A. Notice

The proceeding has presumably been commenced by the client's receipt of a notice of a hearing or another administrative decision. The fundamental question is whether the notice is sufficient. Does it comply with the requirements of the tribunal's enabling statutes and rules, if any, and the requirements of any procedural code? It must also comply with the common-law requirement to provide sufficient detail to enable the party to know what is at stake in the hearing. The proper parties must be identified and the notice must have been properly delivered.

Failure to provide the necessary notice may give rise to a pre-hearing motion, a challenge to the tribunal's jurisdiction, or a judicial review or appeal. However, the advocate should consider what can be accomplished by an objection to the sufficiency of the notice. If the client is genuinely prejudiced, then an objection at the outset of the hearing is necessary and appropriate and the proper remedy is a deferral of the decision or an adjournment of the hearing pending the delivery of notice adequate to permit the client to respond.

B. Disclosure

Disclosure is an increasingly complex issue in administrative hearings. The word "disclosure" is used here as a generic term and includes the obligation of one party to provide particulars or to produce documents or witness statements, the mutual exchange of particular documents and witness statements, and the oral or written examination of a party prior to the hearing.

It is incumbent on an administrative advocate to turn his or her mind to the myriad issues involved in disclosure. The starting point is the constituent statute and the statutory procedural code. However, it is rare for statutes and procedural codes to address disclosure, except to provide that the tribunal may issue orders to control its own process or that the tribunal may make rules governing disclosure.[32] This has resulted in some questions about the jurisdiction of tribunals to make disclosure orders.[33]

---

32   SPPA, *supra* note 2, ss. 23(1) and 5.4.

33   See *Canadian Pacific Airlines Ltd. v. Canadian Air Line Pilots Association,* [1993] 3 S.C.R. 724; but see also *Ontario (Human Rights Commission) v. Ontario (Board of Inquiry into Northwestern General Hospital)* (1993), 115 D.L.R. (4th) 279 (Ont. Div. Ct.).

Tribunals commonly make rules governing the exchange of documents by the parties, the exchange of witness statements, the provision of expert reports, and the provision of particulars. Some tribunals have rules providing for interrogatories, or establishing discovery-like pre-hearing procedures. However, rules do not generally address all of the issues regarding disclosure—for example, issues about investigative files containing informant information and redactions to notes and files. If there are third-party records at issue, an *O'Connor*[34] application may be required.

In addition to the tribunal's rules, the extent of the disclosure obligation is governed by the common law. At common law, the degree of disclosure required varies depending on the nature of the tribunal and the nature of the interest affected.[35]

In the case of licensing or regulatory tribunals, a representative of the regulator acts as a "prosecutor." Because such decisions may result in a "loss of livelihood and damage to professional reputation," the duty of disclosure may be similar to the duty placed on Crown prosecutors in the criminal context.[36] This standard, described by the Supreme Court of Canada in *R. v. Stinchcombe*,[37] requires disclosure of "all evidence that may assist the accused, even if the prosecution did not plan to adduce it." The evolution of disclosure obligations in the professional discipline context is in contrast to the more traditional administrative law test, which is disclosure of the case to be met. The advocate must therefore characterize the tribunal and the nature of the interest affected in order to make the case for a higher degree of disclosure.

There are other ways of obtaining information that may be helpful to the case. Increasingly, advocates are using freedom of information requests to obtain documents that may be relevant to a case. Even if the statutes or rules do not provide for it, a simple request for disclosure may suffice. It is the advocate's responsibility to consider all of these avenues to obtain information relevant to the case.

If the disclosure is insufficient, the advocate should consider bringing a pre-hearing motion before the tribunal. Again, if the client is genuinely prejudiced, then a motion is necessary and appropriate and the proper remedy is a deferral of the decision or an adjournment of the hearing pending proper disclosure.

C. Oral or Written Hearing

Generally, the tribunal's constituent statute will simply state that a party is "entitled to a hearing." Procedural codes like the SPPA contain general provisions to the effect that a party is entitled to present evidence and make submissions.[38] However, the right to a hearing or to present evidence does not necessarily include the right to an oral hearing. The statutes, procedural code, or rules governing a tribunal may also permit hearings to be held electronically or in writing. The factors governing the determination of which form of hearing

---

[34]   *R. v. O'Connor*, [1995] 4 S.C.R. 411.

[35]   *May v. Ferndale Institution*, 2005 SCC 82, [2005] 3 S.C.R. 809.

[36]   *Sheriff v. Canada (Attorney General)*, 2006 FCA 139, [2006] F.C.J. No. 580 (QL); see also *Waxman v. Ontario (Racing Commission)*, [2006] O.J. No. 4226 (Div. Ct.) (QL).

[37]   [1991] 3 S.C.R. 326.

[38]   See e.g. s. 10.1 of the SPPA, *supra* note 2.

is required may or may not be listed or may be expressed in general terms only. For example, the SPPA provides that a tribunal "shall not hold a written hearing if a party satisfies the tribunal that there is a good reason for not doing so."[39] In that case, whether an oral hearing will be required (if requested) is determined by the common law. Whether an oral hearing is required at common law depends on the application of the five *Baker* factors.

The advocate must always consider whether to request an oral hearing—that is, whether an oral hearing is necessary or desirable in the circumstances of the particular case. The case law suggests that whether an oral hearing is required at common law depends on the seriousness of the interest at stake and whether there is a significant credibility issue.[40] Administrative law principles requiring the balancing of fairness and efficiency inform this issue. An oral hearing is a burden on an administrative decision-maker. There may also be other competing interests apart from the interest of the party requesting the oral hearing—for example, the protection of alleged victims in a harassment or discrimination case.[41]

From an advocacy perspective, the considerations also include the relative strengths and weaknesses of the various witnesses, whether the public interest that may be generated by an oral hearing would be helpful to the client's cause, and the expense and time required for an oral hearing.

Finally, a tribunal may impose conditions when adding a party, restricting the party's evidence and argument to the party's specific interest. Faced with a request from a person to be added as a party, the advocate for another party should consider whether to seek such an order.

D. Agreed Statement of Facts

Many tribunals expect parties to cooperate in preparing an agreed statement of facts as well as an agreed book of documents. This will expedite the hearing process, reflecting administrative law values of efficiency and expeditiousness. This exercise also forces the advocate to think about those issues that are truly contentious and deserve to be argued and those that are not. It is good discipline, and helps in case planning, to turn one's mind to an agreed statement of facts. It will help to build a reputation as a good counsel and save the client time and money. However, the advocate cannot agree to any facts unless he or she has conducted a complete factual and legal examination of the case. Even if an agreed statement of facts is not achieved, the effort will not be wasted. The draft agreed statement of facts will serve as the advocate's own chronology of the events. Often, much is revealed about a case by a review of a chronology—for example, whether there is a cause-and-effect relationship between certain events.

---

[39]   *Ibid.* s. 5.1(2). See also s. 5.2(2), which states that a "tribunal shall not hold an electronic hearing if a party satisfies the tribunal that holding an electronic hearing rather than an oral hearing is likely to cause the party significant prejudice."

[40]   *Khan v. University of Ottawa* (1997), 34 O.R. (3d) 535 (C.A.).

[41]   *Masters v. Ontario* (1994), 18 O.R. (3d) 551 (Div. Ct.).

E. Witnesses

Regarding witnesses, two important issues need to be considered in advance of the hearing: which witnesses to call and how to secure their attendance. In some circumstances, witnesses may be represented by counsel, which may complicate the hearing.[42] The decision whether to call a witness relates to the determination of what must be proved at the hearing. Is this witness essential? The good advocate must ruthlessly consider whether the witness has undesirable information or qualities. If so, don't call the witness. Seek an agreed statement of facts, so that the weak witness does not have to be called, or find an alternative source for the evidence. There are ethical issues involved in the evidence that an advocate may call. For example, an advocate must not make reckless suggestions to a witness or suggestions that he or she knows to be false, dissuade a material witness from giving evidence, or advise such a witness to be absent.[43]

Particularly before more sophisticated administrative tribunals, the advocate must turn his or her mind to whether expert evidence is required. If an expert is required, one must locate the best expert possible, retain and instruct him or her properly and ethically, and tender his or her evidence in accordance with tribunal rules and practice. Most tribunals require expert reports to be circulated well in advance of a scheduled hearing.

Generally, tribunals have the ability to summons witnesses to appear before them. Although procedures differ, often counsel is expected to obtain the executed summons from the hearing officer in advance of the hearing and serve the summons together with the necessary fees and allowances.

F. General Conduct

Once the advocate has attended to all procedural and substantive issues that he or she anticipates will arise in the case, is there anything else to do before the case is argued before the tribunal? A good advocate will observe a tribunal in action before his or her first appearance before it. At an attendance to observe a proceeding, the advocate learns basic things— for example, whether counsel slips are required, whether it is the practice to rise when the tribunal enters the hearing room, whether the tribunal makes preliminary remarks, whether opening statements from counsel are expected, and even where to sit. Lack of familiarity with a tribunal's practices betrays an advocate as a novice in the forum and can impair the confidence of both the client and the tribunal in the advocate's abilities.

This is not to say that the advocate should adhere to the tribunal's practices when it is not in the client's interest to do so. For example, if the hearing is open to the public and the matter is a contentious one that has attracted media attention, it may be in the client's interest to make an opening statement so that the client's position is set out at the earliest possible opportunity, even if it is not the tribunal's practice to entertain one. In that case, counsel should acknowledge that it is not the tribunal's practice, but ask for permission to do so.

---

42   SPPA, *supra* note 2, ss. 11 and 14(1).

43   See e.g. Canadian Bar Association, Code of Professional Conduct, c. IX, commentary 2(g) and (i), online: Canadian Bar Association <http://www.cba.org/cba/activities/pdf/codeofconduct06.pdf> [CBA].

This forestalls the inevitable response that it is not the tribunal's practice and signals to the tribunal that counsel has considered the tribunal's practice, but is asking the tribunal to make an exception.

IV. Advocacy at the Tribunal Hearing

The advocate must now present the case. He or she must build a persuasive case on the basis of relevant and admissible evidence. The advocate will have developed a theory of the case clearly tied to the statute under consideration, will have ensured that the remedy sought is within the statutory decision-maker's mandate, and be prepared to argue general principles of administrative law in the course of the hearing. Particular issues involved in advocacy are discussed below—for example, motions, opening and closing statements, and evidentiary issues. We begin, however, with the overarching theme of ethical advocacy, because, at every stage, the good advocate will consider ethics, professionalism, and civility in the conduct of his or her case.

A. Ethical Advocacy

The good advocate is civil and professional in his or her advocacy, which means engaging in ethical advocacy, in accordance with rules of professional conduct and canons of civility and professionalism. Canadian lawyers are regulated by the law societies of the provinces and territories, all of which have rules of professional conduct that address ethical advocacy issues, as well as commentaries on the rules that give more concrete guidance on specific issues.[44] The Canadian Bar Association's *Code of Professional Conduct* is also a good guide to ethical behaviour, although in a conflict between the Code and provincial law society rules, the latter prevail.[45]

The rules of professional conduct govern the conduct of lawyers as advocates, situated within the general duties of lawyers. The Law Society of British Columbia, for example, has established canons of legal ethics, which state that "it is a lawyer's duty to promote the interests of the state, serve the cause of justice, maintain the authority and dignity of the courts, be faithful to clients, be candid and courteous in relations with other lawyers and demonstrate personal integrity."[46] This statement captures the three main areas of focus for advocates: duties to the state and the tribunal or court, duties to the client, and duties to other lawyers. In all aspects of an administrative law case, the good advocate will ensure that he or she discharges these duties.

Law society rules specifically govern the conduct of lawyers as advocates. The B.C. Law Society Rules, for example, state:

---

[44]   Web links to provincial and territorial Rules of Professional Conduct can be found online: Federation of Law Societies <http://www.flsc.ca/en/law-society-codes-of-conduct>.

[45]   See CBA, *supra* note 43.

[46]   Law Society of British Columbia, *Professional Conduct Handbook*, c. 1, online: Law Society of British Columbia <http://www.lawsociety.bc.ca/page.cfm?cid=1027&t=Professional-Conduct-Handbook-Chapter-1-Canons -of-Legal-Ethics>.

1. A lawyer must not:

(a)   abuse the process of a court or tribunal by instituting or prosecuting proceedings that, although legal in themselves, are clearly motivated by malice on the part of the client and are brought solely for the purpose of injuring another party,

(b)   knowingly assist the client to do anything or acquiesce in the client doing anything dishonest or dishonourable,

(c)   appear before a judicial officer when the lawyer, the lawyer's associates or the client have business or personal relationships with the officer that may reasonably be perceived to affect the officer's impartiality,

(d)   attempt or acquiesce in anyone else attempting, directly or indirectly, to influence the decision or actions of a court or tribunal or any of its officials by any means except open persuasion as an advocate,

(e)   knowingly assert something for which there is no reasonable basis in evidence, or the admissibility of which must first be established,

(e.1) make suggestions to a witness recklessly or that the lawyer knows to be false,

(f)   deliberately refrain from informing the court or tribunal of any pertinent authority directly on point that has not been mentioned by an opponent,

(g)   dissuade a material witness from giving evidence, or advise such a witness to be absent,

(h)   knowingly permit a party or a witness to be presented in a false way, or to impersonate another person, or

(i)   appear before a court or tribunal while impaired by alcohol or a drug.[47]

B. Misleading the Tribunal on the Facts or the Law

Misleading the tribunal on the facts or the law is improper. It is also bad advocacy. A lawyer who misleads a tribunal will not be trusted again, on any matter, by the tribunal member who heard the case and likely by the tribunal as a whole. Tribunal members start from the proposition that advocates will conduct themselves ethically and professionally. Once an advocate engages in sharp practice, particularly by misleading a tribunal, his or her reputation will be compromised forever. Tribunal members and judges discuss the advocates who appear before them—and they remember those who skirt the ethical line.

It may be difficult for a client to appreciate that an advocate's duties to the tribunal and the administration of justice may seem to prevail over the client's individual interest in winning a case by any means necessary. However, it is important for an advocate to understand *how* the lawyer's duty to the tribunal or court supersedes what the client wants. As stated by Lord Reid in *Rondel v. Worsley*:

> Every counsel has a duty to his client fearlessly to raise every issue, advance every argument, and ask every question, however distasteful, which he thinks will help his client's case. But, as an officer of the court concerned in the administration of justice, he has an overriding duty to

---

47   *Ibid.*, c. 8, online: Law Society of British Columbia <http://www.lawsociety.bc.ca/page.cfm?cid=1037&t =Professional-Conduct-Handbook-Chapter-8-The-Lawyer-as-Advocate> (footnote omitted).

the court, to the standards of his profession, and to the public, which may and often does lead to a conflict with the client's wishes or with what the client thinks are his personal interests. Counsel must not mislead the court, he must not lend himself to casting aspersions on the other party or witnesses for which there is no sufficient basis in the information in his possession, he must not withhold authorities or documents which may tell against his clients but which the law or the standards of his profession require him to produce.[48]

The good advocate recognizes ethical issues as they arise and deals with them squarely. This includes explaining to clients why, for example, you insist on producing a "smoking gun" document where the rules of disclosure so require. It is not the easiest path, but it is an essential one. Advocates should also understand the law society rules governing the duty to withdraw. Generally, if a client wishes to adopt a course that would involve a breach of the rules of professional conduct, the lawyer must withdraw or seek leave to withdraw.

C. Public Statements About Proceedings

As advocates we are frequently called on to comment publicly about cases in which we are involved; in fact, many advocates are attracted to administrative law because of the way in which administrative proceedings affect the lives of the most vulnerable. Advocates must be mindful of the ethical issues involved in making public statements about proceedings in which they are involved and be careful to avoid commenting improperly on such matters. While law society rules differ, a good example is rule 6.06 of the Rules of the Law Society of Upper Canada, which states: "Provided that there is no infringement of the lawyer's obligations to the client, the profession, the courts, or the administration of justice, a lawyer may communicate information to the media and may make public appearances and statements."[49]

The commentary provided under this rule follows:

> Lawyers in their public appearances and public statements should conduct themselves in the same manner as with their clients, their fellow legal practitioners, and tribunals. Dealings with the media are simply an extension of the lawyer's conduct in a professional capacity. The mere fact that a lawyer's appearance is outside of a courtroom, a tribunal, or the lawyer's office does not excuse conduct that would otherwise be considered improper.
>
> A lawyer's duty to the client demands that, before making a public statement concerning the client's affairs, the lawyer must first be satisfied that any communication is in the best interests of the client and within the scope of the retainer.
>
> Public communications about a client's affairs should not be used for the purpose of publicizing the lawyer and should be free from any suggestion that the lawyer's real purpose is self-promotion or self-aggrandizement.[50]

---

48 [1967] 3 All E.R. 993 (H.L.) per Lord Reid at 998.

49 Law Society of Upper Canada, *Rules of Professional Conduct*, rule 6.06(1), online: Law Society of Upper Canada <http://www.lsuc.on.ca/with.aspx?id=671>.

50 *Ibid.*

Advocates must also be careful to avoid the *sub judice* rule, which also applies to tribunal proceedings, and to ensure that their comments are not calculated to influence the course of justice or prejudice a fair hearing. The Law Society of Alberta commentary on this issue, which is detailed, provides:

> A lawyer having any contact with the media is subject to the *sub judice* rule and should be aware of it. Per David M. Brown, What Can Lawyers Say in Public?, *Canadian Bar Review*, Vol. 78, p. 283 at p. 316:
>
> > Designed to ensure the fairness of the trial process to the parties involved, the *sub judice* rule makes it a contempt of court to publish statement [*sic*] before or during a trial which may tend to prejudice a fair trial or influence the course of justice ... . For contempt to be found, it is necessary for a court to be satisfied, beyond a reasonable doubt, that the words published were calculated to interfere with the course of justice in the sense of being apt, or having a tendency, to do so. The *mens rea* necessary for the offence is not an intention to commit a criminal contempt, but to knowingly and intentionally publish the material, irrespective of the absence of an intention or bad faith with respect to the question of criminal contempt itself.
>
> It will be a question of fact in each case whether the words published "were calculated to interfere with the course of justice in the sense of being apt or having a tendency to do so," but because the media frequently publishes lawyers' comments, lawyers should be particularly careful when dealing with members of the media.[51]

D. An Advocate's Duty to Opposing Counsel

Law society rules also address the advocates' obligation to opposing counsel. The Law Society of Manitoba, for example, provides, in part:

> 6.02(1) A lawyer must be courteous and civil and act in good faith with all persons with whom the lawyer has dealings in the course of his or her practice.[52]

The commentary to Manitoba rule 6.02(1) provides:

> The public interest demands that matters entrusted to a lawyer be dealt with effectively and expeditiously, and fair and courteous dealing on the part of each lawyer engaged in a matter will contribute materially to this end. The lawyer who behaves otherwise does a disservice to the client, and neglect of the rule will impair the ability of lawyers to perform their functions properly.
>
> Any ill feeling that may exist or be engendered between clients, particularly during litigation, should never be allowed to influence lawyers in their conduct and demeanour toward

---

[51] Law Society of Alberta, *Code of Professional Conduct*, c. 5, rule 8, Commentary 8, online: Law Society of Alberta <http://www.lawsociety.ab.ca/files/regulations/Code.pdf>.

[52] Law Society of Manitoba, *Code of Professional Conduct*, rule 6.02(1), online: Law Society of Manitoba <http://www.lawsociety.mb.ca/lawyer-regulation/code-of-professional-conduct/documents/english-version/code_of_conduct.pdf>.

each other or the parties. The presence of personal animosity between lawyers involved in a matter may cause their judgment to be clouded by emotional factors and hinder the proper resolution of the matter. Personal remarks or personally abusive tactics interfere with the orderly administration of justice and have no place in our legal system. ...

A lawyer should agree to reasonable requests concerning trial dates, adjournments, the waiver of procedural formalities and similar matters that do not prejudice the rights of the client.[53]

One of the most rewarding aspects of the practice of law is coming to know and respect lawyers who appear on the other side of a case. The good advocate remembers that he or she is appearing on behalf of a client, is discharging an important role in the administration of justice, and that professionalism in all relationships with counsel is of the utmost importance.

E. Dealing with Unrepresented Parties

Dealing with unrepresented parties can pose particular challenges for counsel. The rules of professional conduct address some aspects of dealing with unrepresented parties. The Law Society of Alberta Code, for example, provides that:

5. When negotiating with an opposing party who is not represented by counsel, a lawyer must:

   (a) advise the party that the lawyer is acting only for the lawyer's client and is not representing that party; and

   (b) advise the party to retain independent counsel.[54]

More generally, as discussed by Lorne Sossin in Chapter 7, Access to Administrative Justice and Other Worries, an increasing number of litigants are unrepresented, and advocates and adjudicators both recognize that this affects the conduct of cases. For example, it may be more difficult for an unrepresented party to appreciate the importance of evidence that could be elicited on cross-examination. While we recommend that advocates maintain standards of professionalism and civility with all persons, it is essential to remember that an advocate's primary duty is to his or her client, a duty that cannot be sacrificed to assist another party. In other words, an advocate cannot assist the unrepresented party by suggesting a line of cross-examination. At the same time, as long as it does not compromise the administration of justice and the advocate's duty to his or her client, advocates should consider ways in which they can enhance accessibility to justice for unrepresented parties. Thus, for example, when seeking disclosure, rather than simply reciting the applicable rule, advocates can write a letter in plain English, identifying documents with reasonable specificity. Advocates contemplating bringing a motion to dismiss for a failure to comply with the tribunal's rules, could write a clear letter to the unrepresented party identifying the issue, the relevant rules, the possible consequences, and the deadline for compliance.

---

53   *Ibid.*, commentary.

54   Law Society of Alberta, *Code of Professional Conduct*, *supra* note 51, c. 11, rule 5.

F. Preliminary Motions at the Hearing

There are some types of serious preliminary motions that are generally argued at the commencement of a hearing. These include challenges to the jurisdiction of the tribunal, as well as challenges based on bias or tribunal independence.[55] There are two aspects of bias: impartiality and independence. Impartiality refers to the state of mind of the decision-maker. Independence refers to the relationship of the decision-maker to others. Both impartiality and independence may operate at either an individual or institutional level.[56] Objecting to a member of a tribunal on the ground of bias is a difficult judgment call even for an experienced advocate. The test is whether there is a reasonable apprehension of bias. What is "reasonable" varies greatly depending on the nature of the tribunal. For example, behaviour that would disqualify a member of an adjudicative tribunal may be perfectly acceptable in a member of a tribunal whose decisions are policy-based or whose functions approach the legislative end of the spectrum.[57] It is clear that an objection on the ground of bias must be made when it comes to the party's attention, failing which it will be deemed to have been waived.[58] It is important to inform the hearing officer of these motions in advance, so that the tribunal is prepared to deal with such challenges.

A common mistake is the overuse of preliminary motions at the hearing itself. A good advocate thinks carefully about the usefulness and the timing of a contemplated motion. For example, tribunals generally prefer to deal with motions for production of documents before the hearing, to avoid adjournments. Even if a tribunal does not have rules governing pre-hearing disclosure of documents, a good advocate will contact counsel for the opposite party before the hearing, offer to share the documents on which he or she intends to rely, and ask for the same courtesy from opposing counsel. If there is a real issue and no opportunity for a pre-hearing motion or case conference, at a minimum counsel should advise the hearing officer well in advance of the hearing that a disclosure motion will be brought that may necessitate an adjournment.

G. Opening Statements

There are both similarities and differences between an opening statement before an administrative tribunal and an opening statement at a trial. As is the case in a trial, the purpose of an opening statement is not to make legal arguments. Rather, its chief purpose is to set out the theory of the case, to identify the issue from the perspective of the client, and to offer a simple solution. The opening statement is also an opportunity to "seize the moral high ground" of the case. A secondary purpose is to provide a road map for the tribunal as to

---

55   Independence and impartiality are discussed by Laverne Jacobs in Chapter 8, Caught Between Judicial Paradigms and the Administrative State's Pastiche: "Tribunal" Independence, Impartiality, and Bias.

56   *Canadian Pacific Ltd. v. Matsqui Indian Band*, [1995] 1 S.C.R. 3, [1995] S.C.J. No. 1 (QL), 122 D.L.R. (4th) 12.

57   *Newfoundland Telephone Co. v. Newfoundland (Board of Commissioners of Public Utilities)*, [1992] 1 S.C.R. 623, [1992] S.C.J. No. 21 (QL), 89 D.L.R. (4th) 289.

58   *Canada (Human Rights Commission) v. Taylor*, [1990] 3 S.C.R. 892, [1990] S.C.J. No. 129 (QL), 75 D.L.R. (4th) 577.

how the case will unfold—that is, to identify the chief witnesses and the purposes for which they will be called. This aspect of the opening statement is generally briefer and less-detailed than at a trial, unless the tribunal has court-like procedures or is dealing with a number of complex issues. It is important that the opening statement be flexible enough to take into account the inevitable vagaries of the evidence. It is crucial that the advocate not promise anything in an opening statement that cannot be delivered. Even if the tribunal does not remind the advocate of the promise, opposing counsel will. Many tribunals make opening statements of their own, have a checklist of questions they are expected to ask, or otherwise start the proceeding. Some may even question witnesses themselves.

H. Evidence

As a general rule, tribunals are not bound by the strict rules of evidence. A good example is s. 15 of the SPPA, which states:

> 15(1) Subject to subsection (2) and (3), a tribunal may admit evidence at a hearing, wheth-
> er or not given or proven under oath or affirmation or admissible as evidence in a court,
>> (a) any oral testimony; and
>> (b) any document or thing,
> relevant to the subject matter of the proceeding and may act on such evidence, but the tribunal
> may exclude anything unduly repetitious.
>> (2) Nothing is admissible in evidence at a hearing,
>>> (a) that would be inadmissible in a court by reason of any privilege under the law of
>> evidence; or
>>> (b) that is inadmissible by the statute under which the proceeding arises or any other
>> statute.[59]

For each piece of evidence the advocate proposes to introduce, he or she should ask:

1. What facts will be established with this evidence?
2. How are the facts relevant to the issues in the hearing?

Is there any exclusionary rule that would prohibit calling the evidence—for example, privilege? General privileges in the law of evidence continue to apply in administrative proceedings.[60]

Is there a better source? Although hearsay evidence is admissible, the common-law concern about hearsay was based on fairness. Highly adjudicative tribunals dealing with serious matters involving the livelihood of an individual or behaviour that would amount to criminal conduct often do not admit hearsay evidence.[61] However, it is not an invariable rule that the more serious the subject matter of the proceeding, the less acceptable is hearsay evidence. For example, hearsay evidence is specifically permitted in child welfare proceedings in light

---

[59]   SPPA, *supra* note 2, s. 15.

[60]   *Pritchard v. Ontario (Human Rights Commission)*, 2004 SCC 31, [2004] 1 S.C.R. 809; SPPA, *supra* note 2, s. 15(2).

[61]   *Bernstein v. College of Physicians & Surgeons* (1977), 15 O.R. (2d) 477 (Div. Ct.).

of the need to have all available information before the decision-maker, and in social welfare cases in light of the need for expedition and informality. The lesson is: know the tribunal.

Are there any rules that govern the admissibility of the evidence—for example, are there notice requirements? Tribunal rules often require that expert reports be produced in advance.

If another party objects to the admissibility of the evidence, is there an answer to those objections? In particular, what response is there to arguments about weight?

Some of these issues are discussed below in more detail.

I. Relevance

Tribunals do not have the jurisdiction to hear evidence that is not relevant to the proceedings. The type of evidence that a tribunal can consider relates directly to natural justice concerns. The tribunal cannot take into account entirely irrelevant facts, or decide on the basis of facts for which there is no evidence. Relevant evidence means evidence having any tendency to make the existence of any fact that is of consequence to the determination of the matter more probable or less probable than it would be without the evidence.[62]

On the importance of presenting relevant evidence to support each component of a decision, see *Trinity Western University v. British Columbia College of Teachers*.[63] Trinity Western, a Christian university, was seeking accreditation to sponsor a teacher-training degree. The university's community-standards document prohibited "biblically condemned" practices. From this the College inferred that the outlook of graduates would have a detrimental effect on the learning environment in schools where they taught. The College of Teachers denied the University the ability to sponsor a teacher-training program. The Supreme Court held that the College of Teachers erred in considering the beliefs of the institution, but not the actual impact of their beliefs on the teaching environment. The Court specifically held:

> For the BCCT to have properly denied accreditation to TWU, *it should have based its concerns on specific evidence*. It could have asked for reports on student teachers, or opinions of school principals and superintendents. It could have examined discipline files involving TWU graduates and other teachers affiliated with a Christian school of that nature. Any concerns should go to risk, not general perceptions.[64]

J. Weight

In addition to deciding whether evidence is relevant, a decision-maker must also decide how much weight to give to the tendered evidence. For example, an unsigned, undated letter regarding a fact in question may be relevant, but afford little weight because its statements cannot be verified. The more reliable the evidence is, the more weight should be accorded to it. The rules of evidence were developed by courts to prevent unfairness. Before an administrative tribunal, be prepared to argue issues as to weight from first principles—that is,

---

62 *Canada (Attorney General) v. Gentles Inquest (Coroner of)* (1998), 116 O.A.C. 70 (Div. Ct.).

63 2001 SCC 31, [2001] 1 S.C.R. 772.

64 *Ibid.* at para. 38 (emphasis added).

natural justice, procedural fairness, quality of administrative decision making, relevance given the purpose of the statute, and what is at stake for the individual.

K. Admissibility

Look to the tribunal's statutory provisions and to procedural codes like the SPPA to assist with admissibility issues. First, the statute may contain specific provisions on how evidence is to be dealt with. Second, the statute may describe the mandate of the tribunal and the scheme it administers in terms that suggest which considerations and priorities should weigh heavily on the tribunal in making decisions—for example, whether the tribunal should favour protection of the public or some other value. If there is some question about the admissibility of evidence, reference to the values and mandate of the tribunal may assist in resolving it.

L. Standard of Proof

There is a single standard of proof—that is, the balance of probabilities—for all civil cases, including administrative cases. The evidence must be "sufficiently clear, convincing and cogent" to meet the balance of probabilities test.[65] The advocate must recognize the differences among administrative tribunals in assessing the nature of evidence required. In order to meet this exacting standard, the advocate should make efforts to call the best evidence available.

M. Judicial Notice

Expert tribunals may take notice of generally recognized facts within their specialized knowledge. For example, discipline panels in medical cases may make certain findings of fact based on their own knowledge of human anatomy.[66] Section 16 of the SPPA provides that a tribunal may take notice of facts that may be judicially noticed, and take notice of any generally recognized scientific or technical facts, information or opinions within its scientific or specialized knowledge.

N. Examination-in-Chief

The usual rules of direct examination apply to most administrative hearings. However, a tribunal that is at the inquisitorial, as opposed to the adjudicative, end of the spectrum of administrative decision-makers may elect to question a party first.[67] The advocate must know what kind of tribunal is involved and what its practice is with respect to direct examination.

Perhaps surprisingly, examination-in-chief is a significantly more important skill than cross-examination. In case preparation, the focus should be on presenting a good case.

---

65   *F.H. v. McDougall*, 2008 SCC 53, [2008] 3 S.C.R. 41 at para. 46.

66   *Reddall v. College of Nurses* (1983), 149 D.L.R. (3d) 60 at 65 (Ont. C.A.); *Ringrose v. College of Physicians & Surgeons (No. 2)* (1978), 83 D.L.R. (3d) 680 at 695-96 (Alta. C.A.).

67   *Thamotharem v. Canada (Minister of Citizenship and Immigration)*, 2007 FCA 198, [2008] 1 F.C.R. 385.

More cases are won on direct examination than on cross-examination, because the advocate can (more or less) control direct examination. The most important thing to remember about examination-in-chief is that counsel is trying to assist the witness to tell the story in his or her own words. Counsel's job is to make it seem that the evidence comes out effortlessly and persuasively. The advocate's work in structuring the questions will help the witness tell the story.

As discussed above, the strict civil and criminal rules of evidence do not apply. In practice, however, this may not make much of a difference, because the rules of evidence formally set out what is often a common-sense approach to developing evidence and also govern the expectations of most tribunals about the calling of evidence. For example, although, in theory, there may be more latitude to lead witnesses in an administrative tribunal, it is bad practice and bad advocacy to lead too much.

As also discussed above, the case should have a persuasive theme, consistent with the purpose of the statute, which is designed to take into account the normative policy choices reflected in the regulatory context. The evidence of each witness should advance the theme. What questions will do so? What facts should be highlighted?

Examinations-in-chief should be structured with headlines. Statements such as "The next group of questions is about your health after the operation" and "Turning to questions about your income before the accident ..." help both the witness and the tribunal understand where counsel is going—that is, they flag transitions in the evidence.

Any general advocacy textbook will summarize the rules of advocacy on direct examination. The most important rules include:

- Use open-ended questions—for example, who, what, where, when, why, how, describe, and what happened next?

- Elicit short bits of information through targeted questions—that is, avoid approaches such as "tell us about your complaint."

- Be prepared to introduce and use documents in the course of the examination-in-chief. Practice introducing exhibits and taking the witness through the documents in advance.

O. Cross-Examination

Cross-examination in administrative proceedings may differ substantially from those in court proceedings. Counsel should be aware that statutory procedural codes may limit cross-examination rights. The ATA requires cross-examination only where the party "will not have a fair opportunity" to contradict the allegations against him or her without it. The SPPA permits a tribunal to "reasonably limit cross-examination." What is reasonable is determined by reference to the common law. Refusal to permit cross-examination altogether does not always amount to a denial of fairness at common law. For example, in multi-party hearings involving policy issues, cross-examination may be refused.[68] Similarly, it may not

---

[68]   *Unicity Taxi Ltd. v. Manitoba (Taxicab Board)*, [1992] M.J. No. 381 (QL), aff'd [1992] M.J. No. 608 (C.A.) (QL).

be appropriate to permit cross-examination in a hearing that is intended to be informal and expeditious.[69]

The primary purpose of cross-examination is to test the credibility of the witness. If the proceeding does not involve matters of credibility, cross-examination may not be necessary or appropriate.

Most proceedings will not have any type of examination for discovery, so cross-examination in tribunal hearings is often more fun (with greater opportunity for surprises, both good and bad) than civil trials. That being said, in cross-examining a witness, the traditional techniques of advocacy apply:

- Control the witness.

- Avoid short questions—include only one fact per question.

- Avoid open-ended questions—for example, questions beginning with why or how.

- Impeachment on the basis of a prior inconsistent statement is an effective cross-examination tool. Make sure that the fact is material, helps the case, and that there is a genuine contradiction, before attempting impeachment.

- Have a reason behind every area of questioning—that is, know where the question will lead and think about how to get there with minimal damage. Bad answers count against the client's case.

P. Tribunal Precedents

It is important to understand the composition of the tribunal. Mature tribunals, like the Ontario Labour Relations Board or the Ontario Municipal Board, have well-established jurisprudence. Although tribunals are not bound to follow their previous decisions,[70] it is a bold step for an advocate to ask a tribunal to depart from established precedent. Occasionally, however, a precedent requires re-examination. In such a case, it is best to acknowledge the existence of and the policy reasons for the tribunal's line of authority and argue that a modification of the jurisprudence is necessary to give continuing effect to the policies identified by the tribunal. Many tribunals are concerned with ensuring the consistency of tribunal decisions, particularly busy tribunals with a number of decision-makers. Where an advocate raises a novel or significant issue, particularly where it represents a departure from existing jurisprudence, tribunal members may wish to consult with colleagues who are not on the hearing panel for the purpose of obtaining their advice, input, or expertise. In *Consolidated-Bathurst*, the Supreme Court of Canada confirmed that convening meetings of an entire tribunal is a practical means of consulting the experience and expertise of all tribunal members when making an important policy decision and obviates the possibility that different panels might inadvertently render inconsistent decisions.[71]

---

[69]   *MacInnis v. Canada (Attorney General)*, [1996] F.C.J. No. 1117 (QL), 139 D.L.R. (4th) 72 (C.A.).

[70]   *Domtar Inc. v. Quebec (Commission d'appel en matiere de lesions professionelles)*, [1993] 2 S.C.R. 756.

[71]   See *IWA v. Consolidated-Bathurst Packaging Ltd.*, [1990] 1 S.C.R. 282 [*Consolidated-Bathurst*]; see also *Ellis-Don Limited v. Ontario (Labour Relations Board)*, 2001 SCC 4, [2001] 1 S.C.R. 211.

Q. Closing Argument

Put bluntly, the purpose of a closing argument is to persuade the tribunal that the client should win. In the closing argument, make submissions on the facts and law that establish the client's case and cast doubt on any other interpretation. The closing argument is the opportunity to summarize the evidence in a persuasive manner; argue about the evidence, challenging the other side's case directly; persuade the tribunal to make findings of fact that favour the client's case; argue about the application of the law to the facts of the case; and persuade the tribunal that the client's case is just and in accordance with the facts and the law.

Where there are factual disputes, be prepared to argue issues such as:

- the conclusion or inferences;
- circumstantial evidence;
- analogies;
- credibility and motive;
- the weight of evidence;
- application of the law or justice;
- which witnesses can be trusted, or who should be believed, and why;
- the reasonableness of witness testimony, especially in light of other evidence in the case;
- the importance of documents; and
- which expert is to be preferred, and why.

Written submissions can be effective if it is the practice of the tribunal to reserve its decisions. Know the tribunal. If the case involves complex legal issues, it may also be helpful to the tribunal to have written submissions. However, if the case is one in which the tribunal is being asked to depart from or to expand on a line of authority, it may be preferable to have oral argument or at least a combination of oral and written argument to facilitate a full explanation of the issue and an opportunity for questions from the tribunal. If the opportunity for written submissions is offered to one party, it should be offered to all parties.[72]

Sometimes it may be advisable to request an opportunity to divide up the submissions. For example, in a professional discipline case, it is more effective to make submissions on penalty only after there have been submissions on and a finding of misconduct.[73]

R. Reasons, Reconsiderations, and Reviews

It is not uncommon for enabling statutes to require the decision-maker to provide reasons for decision. The procedural codes have varying provisions. The ATA requires reasons where

---

[72] *Communications, Energy and Paperworkers Union, Powell River Local 76 v. British Columbia (Power Engineers and Boiler and Pressure Vessel Safety Appeal Board)*, [2001] B.C.J. No. 2764 (QL), 209 D.L.R. (4th) 208 (C.A.).

[73] *Brock-Berry v. Registered Nurses' Association*, [1995] B.C.J. No. 1876 (QL), 127 D.L.R. (4th) 674 (C.A.); *College of Physicians and Surgeons v. Petrie*, [1989] O.J. No. 187 (QL), 68 O.R. (2d) 100 (Div. Ct.).

the decision of the authority "adversely affects the rights of a party."[74] Quebec's procedural code requires that every decision of an adjudicative tribunal be accompanied by reasons. In contrast, the SPPA requires that written reasons be provided "if requested by a party."[75] However, as noted above, the common law may require that reasons be provided even if the enabling legislation or the procedural code does not.[76]

Unlike courts, many administrative tribunals have the power to reconsider or review their decisions, under either their enabling legislation or the applicable procedural code. The decision whether to request reconsideration must be made strategically. It may not result in the remedy sought by the client. Rather, it can have the unintended effect of permitting the tribunal to correct or explain a deficiency in the original decision that may have been a ground for appeal or judicial review.[77]

V. Conclusion

It is worth repeating the cardinal rule of advocacy before administrative tribunals: know your tribunal. Advocacy is concerned with how certain disputes reach tribunals (or courts on appeals or applications for judicial review) and how administrative law is advanced in those settings. The different contexts in which administrative tribunals operate is the key to understanding many administrative law concepts. For most of the concepts discussed in this text, there is no more important context than advocacy. Without clients who are willing (and able) to challenge administrative decision making, and advocates arguing for new approaches to existing doctrines, or tribunal members and judges articulating their understanding of administrative law, the rest of this book would not be possible.

SUGGESTED ADDITIONAL READINGS

To prepare for objections at a hearing, bring a textbook or evidence summary with you. Having a textbook handy helps you frame objections you may have and respond to objections. If you have a lot of space, bring:

BOOKS AND ARTICLES

Bryant, Alan W., Sidney N. Lederman, & Michelle K. Fuerst, *Sopinka, Lederman & Bryant—The Law of Evidence in Canada*, 3d ed. (Markham, ON: LexisNexis Canada, 2009).

Paciocco, David M., & Lee Stuesser, *The Law of Evidence*, 6th ed. (Toronto: Irwin Law, 2011).

---

[74] ATA, *supra* note 3.

[75] SPPA, *supra* note 2.

[76] *Baker, supra*, note 20, at para. 43.

[77] See the Ontario Labour Relations Board's reconsideration decision referred to in *Consolidated-Bathurst, supra*, note 71.

If space is limited, bring a slimmer, but useful, text:

Morton, James, *Ontario Litigator's Pocket Guide to Evidence*, 5th ed. (Markham, ON: LexisNexis Canada, 2010).

Another excellent source is the following short article, which requires some updating, but succinctly lists objections and exceptions:

Perrell, Paul, "An Evidence Cheat Sheet" (2007) 33 Adv. Q. 490.

Little is written about tribunal advocacy; however, traditional trial advocacy textbooks are useful for understanding the basics of advocacy. Two useful textbooks are:

Lubet, Steven, *Modern Trial Advocacy: Canadian Edition*, 3d ed., eds. Sheila Block & Cynthia Tape (Boulder, CO: National Institute for Trial Advocacy).

Mauet, Thomas A., Donald G. Casswell, & Gordon P. Macdonald, *Fundamentals of Trial Techniques*, 2nd Canadian ed. (Greenwood Village: Aspen Publishers, 1995).

Other sources include:

Adair, Geoffrey, *On Trial: Advocacy Skills Law and Practice*, 2d ed. (Markham, ON: LexisNexis Butterworths, 2004).

Bennett, D., & W. Cascaden, *Procedural Strategies for Litigators in British Columbia*, 2d ed. (Markham, ON: LexisNexis, 2010).

Cromwell, T., *Effective Written Advocacy* (Aurora, ON: Canada Law Book, 2008).

CASES

Baker v. Canada (Minister of Citizenship and Immigration), [1999] 2 S.C.R. 817.

IWA v. Consolidated-Bathurst Packaging Ltd., [1990] 1 S.C.R. 282.

Nova Scotia (Workers' Compensation Board) v. Martin, [2003] 2 S.C.R. 504.

R. v. Conway, 2010 SCC 22, [2010] 1 S.C.R. 765.

R. v. Stinchcombe, [1991] 3 S.C.R. 326.

STATUTES

Administrative Justice Act, R.S.Q., c. J-3. (Québec).

Administrative Procedures and Jurisdiction Act, R.S.A. 2000, c. A-3 (Alberta).

Administrative Tribunals Act, S.B.C. 2004, c. 45 (British Columbia).

Provincial and Territorial Rules of Professional Conduct, online: Federation of Law Societies of Canada <http://www.flsc.ca/en/law-society-codes-of-conduct>.

Statutory Powers Procedure Act, R.S.O. 1990, c. S.22 (Ontario).

Access to Administrative Justice and Other Worries

LORNE SOSSIN*

Osgoode Hall Law School, York University

I. Introduction

Remarkably, until recently, texts on administrative law rarely canvassed questions of access to administrative justice. Although rule-of-law concerns and the idea of one's "day in court" have come to characterize "access to justice," it is less clear what this means in the diverse variety of settings where vulnerable people come before administrative decision-makers. As LeBel J. observed in *Blencoe v. British Columbia (Human Rights Commission)*:

---

* I am grateful to various contributors to this volume for their helpful comments at a roundtable held on January 27, 2012, especially Colleen Flood and Arthur Wilson.

[N]ot all administrative bodies are the same. Indeed, this is an understatement. At first glance, labour boards, police commissions, and milk control boards may seem to have about as much in common as assembly lines, cops, and cows! Administrative bodies do, of course, have some common features, but the diversity of their powers, mandate and structure is such that to apply particular standards from one context to another might well be entirely inappropriate.[1]

Rights and important interests are often at stake in administrative justice, whether before a human rights tribunal, an immigration board, or a securities commission. Access to a decision-maker may make the difference between justice and injustice. The rule of law is no less significant in an administrative hearing room or decision-making process than in a courtroom, and, arguably, as I discuss below, it may be more so.

For the community at large, generally, and for vulnerable communities, specifically, it is far more likely that a person's rights and important interests will be at stake in an administrative proceeding than in a judicial one. As the Chief Justice of Canada has observed, "[m]any more citizens have their rights determined by these tribunals than by the courts."[2] This chapter builds on a key theme of this volume, which is that administrative law is concerned with the everyday practice of administrative justice, not simply the judicial review of administrative decision making. How tribunals make policy, how tribunal members are appointed, the resources available for parties before tribunals, and the fairness and quality of administrative justice provided by those tribunals all form part of the core concern of administrative law. Although these issues could arise in a myriad of administrative settings, the analysis below is concerned primarily with adjudicative tribunals.[3]

What does access to justice mean in the context of administrative tribunals? There is no one definition expressly developed by administrative law, and the analogy of administrative tribunals to courts sometimes obscures more than it reveals. In this chapter, I canvass the issue of access to justice before administrative decision-makers from the perspective of those affected by administrative decisions. This perspective requires attention be paid not just to the statutory provisions that empower tribunals, or the court decisions that interpret those provisions, but also to the everyday practice before the tribunal. Although I do not suggest that this list is exhaustive, it is possible to approach the question of access to administrative justice from at least three distinct perspectives:[4]

---

[1]   2000 SCC 44, [2000] 2 S.C.R. 307 at para. 158.

[2]   *Cooper v. Canada (Human Rights Commission)*, [1996] 3 S.C.R. 854 at 899-900, McLachlin J. (as she then was), dissenting.

[3]   By "adjudicative tribunals," I refer broadly to tribunals whose primary purpose is the impartial resolution of disputes, such as labour boards, human rights tribunals and worker compensation appeal boards. I do not mean to suggest there are no access concerns for other kinds of agencies, boards, and commissions, but I believe the issues of access are strongest where the subject matter of a tribunal is primarily adjudicative. For a discussion on classifying tribunals, see Ed Ratushny, ed., Report of the Canadian Bar Association Task Force, *The Independence of Federal Administrative Tribunals and Agencies in Canada* (Ottawa: Canadian Bar Association, 1990) at 46-47.

[4]   For a helpful conceptual review of "access to justice," see Rod McDonald, "Access to Justice in 2003: Scope, Scale and Ambitions" in J. Bass, W.A. Bogart & F.H. Zemans, eds., *Access to Justice for a New Century: The Way Forward* (Toronto: Irwin, 2005). McDonald sets out that "commentators identify a broad inventory of

1. *Access to the tribunal.* How do parties find the tribunal? Is it accessible in person through an office open to the public? If so, is the tribunal housed in a single office or in multiple offices in a range of communities? Is videoconferencing available for those unable or unwilling to travel to attend a hearing? Is the tribunal accessible through telephone or Internet services and, if so, are these points of contact made available in the languages spoken by users of the tribunal?

2. *Access to legal or other knowledge necessary to obtain tribunal services.* How do parties learn what they need to know to be able to contribute to the proceedings and to support their claims? Are the relevant legislative provisions and regulations setting out the powers of a tribunal publicized to parties? Are the prior decisions of the tribunal available and accessible? Have guidelines been developed to set out the standards by which decisions will be reached and, if so, have those guidelines been made available to the public? Is tribunal staff available to assist with filling out forms or preparing a party's submissions? Again, are guidelines or tribunal staff available in languages spoken by users of the tribunal?

3. *Access to resources needed to navigate tribunal system.* How do people present their positions before the tribunal? Is there a right to state-funded legal representation? Do fees create barriers and, if so, is there a procedure for waiving fees? Are previous decisions of the tribunal available and, if so, are they in a form that can be searched and sorted by self-represented parties? Is there access to mediation, dispute resolution, or settlement services? Are interpreters available?

In the following analysis, I explore each of these ways of addressing access to administrative justice.

II. Access to Administrative Justice: The Tribunal

When we think of the mandate of a tribunal, we often mean its powers, its jurisdiction, and its statutory purposes. We rarely think of this mandate in terms of the things that matter most to those who come before the tribunal—for example, how do I find the tribunal; where is it located; can I initiate proceedings and, if so, how is this done; how much will it cost? will I have a hearing, and, if so, what will I have to say; is it accessible to people living with physical or mental disabilities; who will help me if I get confused or cannot understand what is expected of me; and what I can expect of others in the process?

Although the governing statute of a tribunal typically sets out its powers, it is often left to the tribunal itself to decide what face to present to the public. There are two aspects to

---

features that would characterize an accessible justice system: (1) just results, (2) fair treatment, (3) reasonable cost, (4) reasonable speed, (5) understandable to users, (6) responsive to needs, (7) certain, and (8) effective, adequately resourced and well-organized. But, as the experiences of the last four decades illustrate, these are not features of an accessible justice system; [these] are merely features of an accessible dispute-resolution system. These experiences point to two main organizing themes of a comprehensive access to justice strategy: the strategy must be multi-dimensional; and it must take a pluralistic approach to the institutions of law and justice" at 23-24.

this perspective: first, the issue of standing before a tribunal, and second, the issue whether a tribunal will hold oral or written hearings and, if oral, whether those hearings are in person or through technological means.

A. Standing

The first aspect of this perspective on access is standing. Who serves as the gatekeeper for administrative justice? This question may have several answers, depending on one's perspective.

For administrative law, the first sense in which standing is understood is the standing to access the tribunal. Tribunals, unlike courts, have no inherent jurisdiction. The standing to bring a matter to a tribunal must be found in the tribunal's governing statute (or some other statutory authority).

As Robert Macaulay and James Sprague have noted, "[t]here are a number of cases on standing before administrative agencies in Canada, but each of them relies so specifically on the mandating legislation of that agency, or at least upon the interpretation of some judicially-oriented chairperson, that they are not really very helpful as a general guide."[5] For example, the *Ontario Residential Tenancies Act, 2006*, establishing the Landlord Tenant Board, sets out that "[t]he parties to an application are the landlord and any tenants or other persons directly affected by the application."[6] Ontario also has a general procedural statute for administrative proceedings, the *Statutory Power Procedures Act* (SPPA), which provides:

> The parties to a proceeding shall be the persons specified as parties by or under the statute under which the proceeding arises or, if not so specified, persons entitled by law to be parties to the proceeding.[7]

The Alberta *Administrative Procedures and Jurisdiction Act*[8] does not address standing, but a report of the Alberta Law Reform Institute, entitled "Powers and Procedures of Administrative Tribunals,"[9] recommended the following standing provision:

> *Parties*
>   (1) A tribunal must grant standing in proceedings before it to the following:
>   (a) persons who have standing under the enabling enactment;
>   (b) persons whose rights or obligations will be directly varied or affected by the tribunal's determination of the matter before it.

With respect to who is entitled by law to be parties to a proceeding before a tribunal, David Mullan has observed that the issue of standing before tribunals has become more

5   R. Macaulay & J. Sprague, *Practice and Procedure Before Administrative Tribunals*, looseleaf (Toronto: Carswell, 2001) at 9.7(b).

6   Ontario *Residential Tenancies Act, 2006*, S.O. 2006, c. 17, s. 187(1).

7   *Statutory Power Procedures Act*, R.S.O. 1990, c. S.22, s. 5 [SPPA].

8   R.S.A. 2000, c. A-3.

9   Consultation Memorandum No. 13 (2008), online: <http://www.law.ualberta.ca/alri/docs/cm013.pdf>.

important as the duty of fairness has been interpreted more expansively in the wake of cases such as *Nicholson v. Haldimand Norfolk (Regional) Police Commissioners*.[10] One might imagine even more pressure for generous approaches to standing now that the scope of fairness continues to expand,[11] and tribunal jurisdiction over the *Canadian Charter of Rights and Freedoms* has also been approached more generously.[12] However, the point of departure for who is entitled to fairness remains the tribunal's governing statute, as indicated by the SPPA. Returning to the Ontario Landlord and Tenant Board, for example, the Act provides:

> The Board shall adopt the most expeditious method of determining the questions arising in a proceeding that affords to all persons directly affected by the proceeding an adequate opportunity to know the issues and be heard on the matter.[13]

Historically, the kinds of tribunals where standing has been an issue were either regulatory tribunals—for example, an energy board or competition tribunal—or tribunals whose decisions touched many people indirectly—for example, a municipal planning board—or labour tribunals, where the rights of some employees may have an impact on a much wider group of employees. In regulatory cases, boards typically work out representative compromises, whereby a ratepayers association or citizens group is granted standing to represent the interests of those indirectly affected by board decisions (these groups are sometimes referred to as interveners). This practice may raise accountability questions because the tribunal rarely inquires into the representative character of public-interest groups.

In the labour board setting, standing issues often involve third-party employees who are affected by another employee's grievance—for example, where an incumbent employee potentially would be displaced following a successful grievance. Should the incumbent employee be given the opportunity to participate in the grievance to protect his or her rights? The answer appears to be "no, except in limited circumstances."[14] As one labour arbitrator observed:

> If the rights of individual employees who are directly or indirectly affected by the outcome of arbitration proceedings were granted standing in all cases where their individual rights were affected, the numbers of potentially affected employees would be quite large, arbitration hearings would become lengthy and more expensive, and employees would come to feel some obligation to be separately represented.[15]

---

[10] [1979] 1 S.C.R. 311; see Gus Van Harten et al., *Administrative Law: Cases, Text, and Materials*, 6th ed. (Toronto: Emond Montgomery, 2010) at 1135-39.

[11] See e.g. *Baker v. Canada (Minister of Citizenship and Immigration)*, [1999] 2 S.C.R. 817.

[12] See *Martin v. Nova Scotia (Workers' Compensation Board)*, [2003] 2 S.C.R. 504; *Paul v. British Columbia (Forest Appeals Commission)*, [2003] 2 S.C.R. 585; and *R. v. Conway*, [2010] 1 S.C.R. 765. See also Evan Fox-Decent and Alexander Pless's Chapter 12, The Charter and Administrative Law: Cross-Fertilization or Inconstancy?

[13] *Supra* note 6, s. 183; see also Grant Huscroft's Chapter 5, From Natural Justice to Fairness: Thresholds, Content, and the Role of Judicial Review.

[14] See *C.U.P.W. v. Canada Post Corp. (Hall Grievance)* (2006), 149 L.A.C. (4th) 306.

[15] *Re Royal Victoria Hospital and O.N.A. (O'Dwyer)* (1993), 30 C.L.A.S. 355.

The second sense in which standing arises in administrative law is the question of a party's standing to challenge an administrative decision in court.[16] Under the historical regime of prerogative writs, discussed in further detail by Cristie Ford in Chapter 3, Dogs and Tails: Remedies in Administrative Law, standing was limited to those directly affected by state action. To the extent that state action concerned the public interest, remedial authority lay with the attorney general. This approach is also captured in the *Federal Courts Act*, which provides standing to the attorney general or to any party "directly affected" by state action.[17]

It remains the case that not every citizen is entitled, as of right, to challenge administrative action. Judicial review of administrative action is reserved for those who are found to have a sufficient legally recognized interest in the matter to justify the judicial review application. It is said that the test for standing is whether the applicant is a "person aggrieved" by the administrative decision. It has been said that a person aggrieved is one who will suffer some "peculiar grievance of their own beyond some grievance suffered by them in common with the rest of the public."[18]

These limits on standing are said to promote the efficiency of administrative action by keeping the administration free from artificial or academic challenges to administrative action. They also, however, serve to respect the rights of third parties. In many cases, where the applicant for judicial review cannot show that he or she is directly affected or aggrieved by the challenged administrative act, there will, in fact, be third parties in the community who are directly affected or aggrieved. The general policy of the court is not to decide issues in the absence of the parties whose rights are most directly affected by the court's decision. In other words, if those who are most directly affected by the administrative decision are content to "live with it," the court will not permit curious busybodies to bring applications for judicial review in their stead. If, on the other hand, those most directly affected or "aggrieved" wish to challenge the administrative action, they should be able to do so free from interference.[19] While an aggrieved party may wish to challenge an administrative decision in the courts, few have the financial resources to launch a judicial review. For this reason, one of the most significant developments in Canadian public law is the concept of discretionary public-interest standing, which may allow a "test" applicant or NGO to launch a judicial review on behalf of a broader group.

The concept of discretionary public-interest standing has also been applied to challenge the decision making of administrative bodies in court. The leading case in this area remains *Finlay v. Canada (Minister of Finance)*.[20] In granting public-interest standing to a claimant challenging a decision by the federal government not to impose penalties on Manitoba for

---

[16] See e.g. D. Mullan, *Administrative Law* (Toronto: Irwin, 2001), chapter 18.

[17] *Federal Courts Act*, R.S.C. 1985, c. F-7, ss. 18(1) and 28(2). See Craig Forcese's Chapter 15, Making a Federal Case Out of It: The Federal Court and Administrative Law.

[18] See e.g. *Friends of the Oldman River Society v. Association of Professional Engineers, Geologists and Geophysicists of Alberta* (1997), [1998] 5 W.W.R. 179, rev'd on other grounds 2001 ABCA 107. See also T.A. Cromwell, *Locus Standi: A Commentary on the Law of Standing in Canada* (Toronto: Carswell, 1986) at 106-8.

[19] For discussion, see *Alberta Liquor Store Assn. v. Alberta (Gaming and Liquor Commission)*, 2006 ABQB 904 at paras. 10-11.

[20] [1986] 2 S.C.R. 607.

garnishing the benefits of a social welfare recipient in apparent breach of the Canada Assistance Plan (CAP) provisions, the Supreme Court accepted that this form of standing would be available to challenge administrative action and not simply legislation.

Under public-interest standing, the test to be applied is threefold:

1. Is the matter serious and justiciable?
2. Is the party seeking standing genuinely interested in the matter?
3. Is there any other reasonable and effective way for the matter to be adjudicated?[21]

In *Finlay*, the Court applied this test to grant standing to a recipient of social benefits to challenge the conduct of the federal government toward the province of Manitoba under the then Canada Assistance Plan. The applicant raised a serious issue with respect to the legality of the government's action (or, in this case, its inaction in failing to penalize a province for breaching the conditions of the Plan) and, as a recipient of the benefit in question, was clearly genuinely interested. Because neither the federal government nor the provinces had an interest in compelling a penalty from the federal government, the Court also concluded that there was no reasonable alternative by which the challenge would reach court.

The Court has elsewhere affirmed that the purpose of granting status is to "prevent the immunization of legislation or public acts from any challenge,"[22] and that public-interest standing is available in the context of challenges that arise out of administrative tribunals,[23] but there is some suggestion that the scope of such challenges may be limited to legislative provisions and public acts of a legislative character, which would exclude most tribunal decision making.[24]

On access grounds, tribunals have also sought standing before courts where their decisions are judicially reviewed. In *Children's Lawyer for Ontario v. Goodis*,[25] the Ontario Court of Appeal considered a case where the information and privacy commissioner responded to a judicial review application by the Office of the Children's Lawyer of Ontario, because the successful requestor chose not to participate in the judicial review proceedings. As Goudge J.A. observed, s. 9(2) of the *Judicial Review Procedure Act* entitles the administrative tribunal to be a party to the proceedings, but leaves to the court's discretion the scope of its standing. The Court found that context is central to the exercise of this discretion, and settings where a party is unable or unwilling to participate in a judicial review, as in the *Children's Lawyer* setting, emphasize the need for tribunal standing to ensure that the court has the legal and factual basis on which to make an impartial and reasoned decision.[26]

---

21 *Ibid.* at 651. This test was developed in a trilogy of public-interest standing cases that preceded *Finlay*: see *Thorson v. Canada (Attorney General)*, [1975] 1 S.C.R. 138; *Nova Scotia Board of Censors v. McNeil*, [1976] 2 S.C.R. 265; *Canada (Minister of Justice) v. Borowski*, [1981] 2 S.C.R. 575.

22 *Canadian Council of Churches v. Canada (Minister of Employment and Immigration)*, [1992] 1 S.C.R. 236 at para. 252.

23 See *Vriend v. Alberta*, [1998] 1 S.C.R. 493 at 528.

24 See *Canadian Bar Assn. v. British Columbia*, 2006 BCSC 1342 at paras. 41 and 42; see further "The Justice of Access: Who Should Have Standing to Challenge the Constitutional Adequacy of Legal Aid?" (2007) 40 U.B.C. Law Rev. 727.

25 (2005) 75 O,R, (3d) 309 (C.A.).

26 See *ibid.* at para. 48.

As these examples illustrate, and as explored by Grant Huscroft in Chapter 5, From Natural Justice to Fairness: Thresholds, Content, and the Role of Judicial Review, the tension between fairness and efficiency is an enduring theme in settings of access to administrative justice. Fairness bounds efficiency concerns in the context of standing and may have the effect of expanding the scope of standing. For example, by extending the scope of those in a tribunal process entitled to fairness, the courts have altered the scope of access.

B. Hearings

The second aspect of the perspective on physical access to administrative justice is how parties will interact with the tribunal. Will the tribunal conduct its process entirely in writing or will there be an opportunity for a hearing of some kind? The types of tribunal proceedings and the discretion available between them is normally set out in a tribunal's empowering statute.[27]

Administrative tribunals, like courts, need to be accessible to all. Various pieces of federal and provincial legislation mandate that tribunals and regulatory bodies comply with a series of uniform standards.[28] Accessibility may mean a ramp to the hearing room and wheelchair accessible washrooms, while in other cases it will mean access to materials to those with visual disabilities or sign language interpretation for the hearing impaired during a proceeding. Accessibility standards also apply to digital materials and proceedings. Various human rights codes also apply to ensure a standard for accommodation and an enforcement mechanism.[29]

While accessibility for parties with physical disabilities is a pressing concern, increasingly, accessibility for parties living with mental or cognitive disabilities is an emerging concern as well. These accessibility issues typically are more difficult to identify and more challenging to accommodate.[30] Tribunals are responding with enhanced training and education for members and staff, dedicated accessibility officers, and accessibility plans. Some tribunals permit parties to bring support persons with them, while others emphasize their flexibility as between written, electronic, and in-person hearings to accommodate different kinds of special needs.

Other approaches to accessibility emphasize access to parties in remote areas or where physical presence in a hearing room would be prohibitively expensive. The Ontario Landlord and Tenant Board, among other province-wide bodies, has instituted videoconferencing as a substitute for in-person hearings. On the one hand, this measure provides much greater access to hearings, without the long travel time and dislocation previously associated

---

27   For further discussion on the fairness requirement of hearings in administrative law, see Grant Huscroft's Chapter 5, From Natural Justice to Fairness: Thresholds, Content, and the Role of Judicial Review.

28   E.g. the *Accessibility for Ontarians with Disabilities Act, 2005*, S.O. 2005, c. 11, mandates a series of customer service standards, which are being developed on a sector-by-sector basis.

29   See e.g. B.C. *Human Rights Code*, R.S.B.C. 1996, c. 210, s. 8.

30   See L. Sossin, "Mental Health and Administrative Justice," paper presented at the Canadian Institute for the Administration of Justice, "Mental Health and the Justice System: Barriers and Solutions," Toronto (26 September 2011) [unpublished, on file with author].

with attending hearings in person; on the other hand, many report disadvantages of a hearing by video, some of which may go to the fairness of the proceeding.[31] For this reason, rule 5.2(2) SPPA, states that a tribunal *shall not* hold an electronic hearing if a party satisfies the tribunal that holding an electronic rather than an oral hearing is likely to cause the party significant prejudice.[32]

In addition to the location of hearings, tribunals also face other questions of how to provide access to the public. Is it important that a tribunal have a physical presence at all or will a "virtual" tribunal, accessible through the Internet be sufficient? Is a centralized tribunal with all of its functions in one location preferable to a decentralized tribunal?

These issues arise not as an abstract question of fairness but as a concrete trade-off involving resources. Videoconferencing, for example, is far less expensive than maintaining an office in remote centres or obtaining facilities for in-person hearings. Of course, a hearing by teleconference would be even less expensive. The question is when efficiency or cost-cutting measures begin to erode the fairness of a decision-making process.

If access turns, as it must, on resources, then the question will be what, if any, legal considerations constrain the government from reducing the resources available to tribunals. Further, where the legislation, government policies, or funding practices create barriers to access, is it the role of the tribunal to raise this issue? If so, what would be the appropriate venue in which to do so—in its annual report to the legislature; in a tribunal's decisions; in a confidential or public dialogue with government? These questions are explored further below.

III. Access to Administrative Justice: Information and Knowledge

Some would argue that accessing a tribunal itself is far less difficult than accessing the legal expertise necessary to succeed at a tribunal. The way in which a tribunal communicates the information and knowledge necessary to access its services or remedies varies and is rarely set out in an empowering statute. The wave of accountability-related legislative initiatives has, in some parts of the country, led to greater transparency requirements for tribunals. For example, the Ontario *Adjudicative Tribunals Accountability, Governance and Appointments Act, 2009*,[33] requires that tribunals publish "public accountability documents" that include, among other things, consultation policies, service standards to the public, and conflict-of-interest guidelines. Although such common informational templates may assist with accountability, they offer little in the way of relevant information to the individual party seeking a remedy before the tribunal. In this, as in so many areas affecting access to administrative justice, it is the policies of the tribunal itself, not those of the government, that are determinative.

---

[31]   For discussion, see L. Sossin & Z. Yetnikoff, "I Can See Clearly Now: Videoconference Hearings and the Legal Limit on How Tribunals Allocate Resources" (2006) [unpublished].

[32]   SPPA, *supra* note 7, r. 5.2(2).

[33]   See online: ServiceOntario <http://www.e-laws.gov.on.ca/html/source/regs/english/2011/elaws_src_regs_r11010_e.htm>.

A. Guidelines

As discussed by Andrew Green in Chapter 4, Regulations and Rule Making: The Dilemma of Delegation, many tribunals develop guidelines to ensure consistency and structure discretion.[34] Transparency with respect to the standards of decision making represents an emerging aspect of access to administrative justice. For this reason, it is important that guidelines be developed that set out these standards and, where this occurs, it is equally important that these guidelines be made publicly available. One interesting question is should it be a requirement of fairness that a tribunal with significant discretion structure that discretion in some fashion? To date, the farthest a court has been willing to go is to state that, where guidelines are in place, it may by a breach of fairness for the decision-making body to ignore those guidelines without justification.[35]

Because tribunals are bound only by statutory provisions, it is not open to a tribunal to develop binding guidelines of its own initiative.[36] This issue has arisen in the context of the Immigration and Refugee Board (IRB).

The IRB issued Guideline 7 in accordance with the legislative authority conferred on the chair of the IRB by s. 159 of the *Immigration and Refugee Protection Act*.[37] Guideline 7: Concerning Preparation and Conduct of a Hearing in the Refugee Protection Division circumscribes inquiry powers of IRB members so that they can limit the scope of the inquiry and, as such, be in position to control the conduct of the hearing in order to ensure efficient and speedy determinations of claims. Guideline 7 "changes the order of questioning by having the Refugee Protection Division (RPD) leading the inquiry in the hearing room. The purpose of this change is to allow the RPD to make the best use of its expertise as a specialist tribunal by focusing on the issues which it has identified as determinative."[38]

In *Thamotharem v. Canada (Minister of Citizenship and Immigration)*,[39] Guideline 7 was challenged as a breach of procedural fairness and on the grounds that it fettered the discretion

---

[34]   See F. Houle & L. Sossin, "Tribunals and Guidelines: Exploring the Relationships Between Fairness and Legitimacy in Administrative Decision-Making" (2006) 46 Canadian Public Administration 282 at 294-300; see also Andrew Green's Chapter 4, Regulations and Rule Making: The Dilemma of Delegation.

[35]   *Bezaire v. Windsor Roman Catholic Separate School Board* (1992), 9 O.R. (3d) 737 (Div. Ct).

[36]   See *Little Sisters Book and Art Emporium v. Canada (Minister of Justice)*, 2000 SCC 69, [2000] 2 S.C.R. 1120 at para. 85. Because they are not considered binding as law, guidelines are not subject to Charter scrutiny. For discussion, see L. Sossin, "Discretion Unbound: Reconciling the Charter and Soft Law" (2003) 45 Canadian Public Administration 465.

[37]   S.C. 2001, c. 27, s. 159:

   (1) The Chairperson is, by virtue of holding that office, a member of each Division of the board and is the chief executive officer of the Board. In that capacity, the Chairperson ...

   (h) may issue guidelines in writing to members of the Board and identify decisions of the Board as jurisprudential guides.

[38]   Immigration and Refugee Board, Guideline 7: Concerning Preparation and Conduct of a Hearing in the Refugee Protection Division at paras. 19-23, online: Immigration and Refugee Board of Canada <http://www.irb-cisr.gc.ca/Eng/brdcom/references/pol/guidir/Pages/preparation.aspx>.

[39]   2007 F.C.A. 198; see also *Benitez v. Canada (Minister of Citizenship and Immigration)* , 2007 F.C.A. 199.

of board members to decide the order of questioning appropriate to a particular claim. It was raised in the context of a refugee application involving a Tamil student claiming persecution if returned to Sri Lanka. The Federal Court held that Guideline 7 does not violate the board's duty of fairness, but is an unlawful fetter on the exercise of discretion because board members often operate as if they are bound by it. The denial of Mr. Thamotharem's refugee status was quashed on this basis. The Federal Court of Appeal affirmed the court's finding with regard to Guideline 7 and the duty of fairness, but reversed the aspect of the decision dealing with administrative discretion. It dismissed Thamotharem's application for judicial review on the basis that Guideline 7 expressly directs members to consider the facts of the particular case before them in order to determine whether there are circumstances warranting a deviation from the standard order of questioning. Also, it was not evident that board members generally disregarded this aspect of Guideline 7 and unthinkingly adhered to the standard order of questioning. Thus, although transparency calls for tribunals to develop and publicize guidelines on which parties before a tribunal may rely, the principles of administrative law may limit the effectiveness of that reliance by requiring that a tribunal not treat its own guidelines as binding.

Although guidelines may not be binding, tribunals often have the authority to issue rules of practice. B.C.'s *Administrative Tribunals Act* (ATA) provides authority for tribunals to make rules and issue practice directions (for example, on the time period for completing an application) as long as these are made public.[40] In Ontario, the SPPA provides that "a tribunal may make rules governing the practice and procedure before it" and also stipulates that, where a tribunal does so, it must make those rules available to the public.[41] By these rules, tribunals exercise significant discretion with respect to access, limited only by the requirement that rules of practice be consistent with a tribunal's enabling statute and, where applicable, general procedural statutes such as the SPPA. Rules of practice will, as a practical matter, determine whether the tribunal is easy or difficult to access. These rules set out the applicable time limits for filing material; the extent of material and disclosure provided; and whether hearings will be in writing, in person, or by electronic means.

B. Simplification

Another important aspect of access to information is simplification. Being provided with forms that are unduly complex or with guidelines that are inscrutable is equivalent to closing the doors to the tribunal. According to the Council of Canadian Administrative Tribunal's report, *Literacy and Access to Administrative Justice*, the following approach should be adopted by tribunals to address the question of access:

> Administrative tribunals, like other courts, have to follow the standards set in case law. We can
> - make sure, as much as is possible, that our clients understand all the proceedings;
> - examine how we deal with low literacy clients and how this can affect fair administration of justice;

---

40   S.B.C. 2004, c. 45, ss. 11-13 [ATA].

41   SPPA, *supra* note 7, s. 25.1.

- follow the lead of many organizations and use "plain language" in all our communications, written, visual, and spoken.[42]

Most tribunals are committed to simple and user-friendly forms. Some are going further, investigating services that provide assistance to individuals on how to complete forms and understand the basic process requirements of the tribunal.[43]

C. Language

Just as "plain language" may facilitate access, so may the capacity of tribunals to provide services and adjudication in the language spoken by those seeking out the tribunal.

Since *R. v. Tran*,[44] the Court has adopted a contextual approach to s. 14 of the Charter, which provides:

> A party or witness in any proceedings who does not understand or speak the language in which the proceedings are conducted or who is deaf has the right to the assistance of an interpreter.[45]

The Court noted that this Charter right is closely linked to the common-law right to a fair hearing. The right to be heard, in other words, implies a right to understand the case to be met, which in some circumstances will not be possible unless interpretation and translation services are available.

As Lamer C.J. held, writing for the Court:

> Importantly, the underlying principle behind all of the interests protected by the right to interpreter assistance under s. 14 is that of linguistic understanding. The centrality of this principle is evident not only from the general jurisprudence dealing with interpreters, but also more directly from the language of s. 14 itself, which refers to "not understanding or speak[ing] the language in which the proceedings are conducted." The level of understanding protected by s. 14 will, therefore, necessarily be high. Indeed, it has been suggested that a party must have the same basic opportunity to understand and be understood as if he or she were conversant in the language of the court.[46]

Even in the criminal context, however, it is clear that the right to an interpreter is not absolute. To establish a violation of s. 14 of the Charter, the claimant of the right must prove on a balance of probabilities not only that he or she was in need of assistance, but also that the interpretation received fell below the basic, guaranteed standard and did so in the course

---

42 Council of Canadian Administrative Tribunals, *Literacy and Access to Administrative Justice: The Promotion of Plain Language* (2005) <http://www.ccat-ctac.org/en/pdfs/literacy/Literacyandjustice.pdf> at 12.

43 Often, this role will fall to the registrar or other front-line staff or tribunals, but, in 2006, Pro Bono Students Canada established an "administrative justice" initiative under which law students are recruited to work with tribunals on providing such services.

44 [1994] 2 S.C.R. 951 [*Tran*].

45 *Canadian Charter of Rights and Freedoms*, Part I of the *Constitution Act, 1982*, being Schedule B to the *Canada Act 1982* (U.K.), 1982, c. 11, s. 14.

46 *Tran, supra* note 44 at 977-78.

of the case being advanced. Unless the Crown is able to show on a balance of probabilities that there was a valid and effective waiver of the right that accounts for the lack of or lapse in interpretation, a violation of the right to interpreter assistance guaranteed by s. 14 of the Charter will have been made out. In terms of the guaranteed standard, it is not one of "perfection," but rather one of continuity, precision, impartiality, competency, and contemporaneousness.

In *Tran*, the Court makes it clear that not every error of translation or interpretation in the context of an accused will constitute a violation of the Charter. Further, the Court holds that the error must be one that goes to the "vital interests" of the accused. Thus, even a serious problem with translation on a minor point—for example, a scheduling motion—will not constitute a violation.

It is clear that the standards developed in *Tran* would have to be modified to the contexts of administrative proceedings and that a spectrum of interpretation and translation rights might be more appropriate to these contexts. In *Tran*, the Court specifically noted:

> I leave open for future consideration the possibility that different rules may have to be developed and applied to other situations which properly arise under s. 14 of the Charter—for instance, where the proceedings in question are civil or administrative in nature.[47]

The right to an interpreter (and, by extension, to translation of relevant material) in the administrative context was considered in *Figueira v. Garfield Container Transport Inc.*[48] In that case, the Canadian Human Rights Tribunal considered its own obligation to provide an interpreter to a complainant alleging discrimination in the workplace. The tribunal noted that the complainant had a bilingual agent assisting with his case. Although this mitigated the complainant's need and it was acknowledged that the ruling would have an impact on scarce resources, the tribunal nonetheless ordered that fairness required that the complainant be provided with an interpreter (for at least part of the hearing).

A judicial review application of the tribunal's decision in *Figueira* was dismissed.[49] In upholding the aspect of *Figueira* dealing with the right to an interpreter, Hughes J. concluded:

> Thus, both the complainant and Respondent/employer, while parties before the Tribunal, are players in a larger endeavour, that of seeking the removal of discrimination. It is within the discretion of the Tribunal to determine whether such an objective can be fairly achieved in the absence of providing, in whole or during part of the process, translation services into a language other than an official language, at taxpayer's expense, to one or more of the parties.[50]

Figueira is an example of the principles in *Tran* being applied flexibly to the realm of administrative adjudication. Although the case law answers the question, in part, as to the legal requirements of interpretation and translation services, it raises a host of others—for example, should tribunals, legal aid, the government, or some other service providers be responsible for interpreter and translation services, and into which languages for which

---

47 *Ibid.* at 961.

48 November 18, 2005, 2005 CHRT 44, File No. T952/7204.

49 2006 F.C. 785.

50 *Ibid.* at para. 38.

tribunals? Should a government-sponsored or administered roster of approved interpreters and translators be established? Some tribunals have undertaken initiatives to translate brochures into languages used by user groups,[51] but linguistic access remains a significant hurdle for almost all tribunals. The exception to this observation is access to one of Canada's official languages—in other words, access to French language tribunal services in English communities, and vice versa, is governed by an additional layer of statutory and, in some cases, constitutional entitlement.[52]

D. Prior Decisions

One of the most controversial aspects of access is how parties can learn about previous decisions of the tribunal. Although privacy concerns make it difficult for some administrative bodies to publish their decisions,[53] in most cases, making the tribunal's past decisions available is seen as a key aspect of its public-interest function. In this sense, it is analogous to the rule that, absent circumstances justifying confidentiality, all tribunal proceedings should be open to the public, and documents used in those proceedings should be available to the public.[54] The practice with respect to publishing decisions is uneven. Some tribunals publish all of their decisions in an easily searchable form.[55] Still others publish anonymized versions of only those previous decisions determined to be of general significance.[56] Some tribunals also charge a fee to access earlier decisions, which appears to impose a financial burden and, in some circumstances, a barrier to the process of learning the standards applied by a tribunal.

Unlike a court, tribunals are not bound by their earlier decisions. In practice, however, many tribunals aim for consistency and will treat previous decisions as strongly influential over similar disputes. For this reason, making prior decisions available could plausibly be seen as an element of fairness and as part of the requirement that parties before the tribunal should know the "case to meet."

For all these reasons, access to administrative justice includes access to sufficient legal and institutional knowledge.

---

51   The Ontario Landlord and Tenant Tribunal e.g. translates its brochures into Arabic, Chinese, Farsi, Korean, Punjabi, Spanish, Urdu, Tamil, Russian and Vietnamese; see Guide to the RTA in Multiple Languages, online: Landlord and Tenant Board <http://www.ltb.gov.on.ca/en/Key_Information/157371.html>.

52   For discussion, see *Caron v. Alberta (Chief Commissioner of Human Rights and Citizenship Commission)*, 2007 ABQB 525.

53   The Canadian Human Rights Commission, for example, cites privacy concerns as the reason it does not publish its past decisions. See online: Canadian Human Rights Commission <http://www.chrc-ccdp.ca/media_room/caselaw_info_jurisprudence-en.asp>.

54   See e.g. ss. 41 and 42 of B.C.'s *Administrative Tribunals Act, supra* note 40; see also the discussion of this legislation by Cristie Ford in Chapter 3, Dogs and Tails: Remedies in Administrative Law.

55   See e.g. the Alberta Labour Relations Board online: <http://www.alrb.gov.ab.ca/decisions.html> or the Ontario Information and Privacy Commission online: <http://www.ipc.on.ca/index.asp?navid=62>, which allows for the public to search prior decisions both by subject and by name.

56   See e.g. online: Ontario's Social Benefits Tribunal <http://www.sbt.gov.on.ca/site4.aspx>.

IV. Access to Resources Needed to Navigate the Tribunal System

Access to administrative justice is not just a matter of obtaining the necessary information, of course; as noted above, access is also a matter of resources. This attention to financial barriers is particularly important in the context of vulnerable parties lacking other access to representation or advocacy services. There are several ways in which an absence of re-sources can create barriers to access. Below, I address three potential barriers: legal repre-sentation, fees and costs, and the budgeting and staffing of tribunals.

A. Legal Representation

The first and most significant impact of resources is the availability of adequate legal repre-sentation. Freya Kristjanson and Leslie McIntosh in Chapter 6, Advocacy Before Adminis-trative Tribunals, highlight the importance of legal representation.

In the criminal justice sphere, a right to state-funded legal representation has long been recognized. In *New Brunswick (Minister of Health and Community Services) v. G.(J.)*,[57] the Supreme Court of Canada affirmed that the constitutional right to legal assistance extends beyond settings where the jeopardy of an individual is concerned. In that case, the New Brunswick minister of health and community services was seeking an extension of custody of a mother's three children for a six-month period. The mother was poor and receiving social assistance. She applied for legal aid, but was turned down because, at the time, cus-tody applications were not covered under the legal aid guidelines in New Brunswick. The Court recognized a constitutional obligation on the New Brunswick government to provide state-funded counsel in the particular circumstances of that case.

Although the principle in *G.(J.)* has potential application in the context of administrative tribunals, at least where Charter rights are at stake, the reach of constitutionally mandated legal aid may be modest. That said, many provincial legal aid statutes fund legal representa-tion before administrative tribunals. For example, in Ontario, those committed to psychiat-ric facilities who appear before the Ontario Review Board to argue for release are covered by legal aid certificates, while specialty clinics provide limited representation for eligible claimants before the Social Benefits Tribunal, the Landlord and Tenant Board, and other administrative bodies.

Access to justice, however, does not always depend on access to lawyers. The availability of paralegal assistance and the development of self-help support networks and resources may all play a role in the administrative justice sphere. For example, a pro bono initiative involving Pro Bono Students Canada and the Medico-Legal Society of Toronto, enables law students to provide limited legal services to unrepresented parties appearing before the Health Professions Appeal and Review Board in Ontario.[58] While paralegal and student

---

57   [1999] 3 S.C.R. 46 [*G.(J.)*].

58   See online: University of Toronto Faculty of Law <http://www.law.utoronto.ca/visitors_content.asp?itemPath=5/12/0/0/0&contentId=2177>.

groups may enhance access, they also may give rise to challenges with respect to oversight and the protection of clients. For example, although paralegal advocates have been regulated by the Law Society in Ontario since 2007, they remain unregulated in other parts of the country.

B. Fees and Costs

The second way in which resources may affect access is through user fees or other costs associated with a tribunal's process.

1. Fees

Tribunals are funded in a variety of ways. Regulatory tribunals are sometimes self-funded, whereby the tribunal levies an assessment on regulated individuals or organizations and funds its adjudicative operations from these levies. Consider the example of energy boards. The National Energy Board receives 90 percent of its funding from industry levies, with the remaining 10 percent coming from the federal government. In Alberta, the government pays for close to 50 percent of the Alberta Energy and Utilities Board's operations, while industry levies pay the rest. In British Columbia and Ontario, energy boards are entirely self-funded.[59]

Although most adjudicative tribunals are free to the parties, the practice of charging fees is attracting increasing attention. These fees can range from the $25.00 per complaint filing fee charged by the Ontario Assessment Review Board to the $50,000 per merger notification filing fee charged by the federal Competition Bureau. B.C.'s ATA provides the government with the power to make regulations setting out the fees associated with filing applications before tribunals.[60]

Fees of any size have the potential to pose a barrier to access to justice. This is even more relevant in the field of administrative justice because low-income individuals are more likely to have interactions with administrative decision-makers than with courts. In *Polewsky v. Home Hardware Stores Ltd.*,[61] the Ontario Divisional Court recognized that the constitutional principle of access to justice required that small claims court fees be waived in the context of an individual who otherwise would not be able to bring a case to court. Similarly, in *Pearson v. Canada*,[62] the Federal Court held that the provision of the *Federal Courts Act* that, in special circumstances, allows the Court to disregard its rules,[63] should be interpreted so as to allow the court to exempt impecunious parties from having to pay filing fees. In so doing, Muldoon J. observed:

---

[59]   See Elenchus Research Associates Inc., Survey of Regulatory Cost Measures (September 2006), online: Ontario Energy Board <http://www.ontarioenergyboard.ca/documents/aboutheoeb/corpinfo_reports/rcm_surveyreport-elenchus_120906.pdf>.

[60]   ATA, *supra* note 40, s. 60(c).

[61]   [2003] O.J. No. 2908 (QL), 109 C.R.R. (2d) 189 (Div. Ct.).

[62]   (2000), 12 C.P.C. (5th) 284, [2000] 195 F.T.R. 31 [*Pearson*].

[63]   *Federal Courts Act*, R.S.C., 1985, c. F-7, s. 55.

The rule of law is a feature of the law, of at least the common-law parts of Canada, and has been such since long before the adoption of the Charter, as demonstrated in part by Prof. Dicey's learned writings. So, indeed, is that precept of the rule of law—the equality of civil rights among all who claim the benefit of the sovereign's peace, in truth all the inhabitants, whether citizens or not. That which is by law reserved for poor folk—taking Court proceedings "in forma pauperis"— is a civil right and therefore available to the plaintiff herein, on even the bare evidence which he has provided in order to qualify for taking his court proceedings "in forma pauperis."[64]

Although administrative tribunals do not necessarily give rise to these same common-law civil rights, the Court's approach of interpreting its statutory rules so as to provide discretion to ensure that fees do not bar access would likely be applied in an analogous fashion to the rules or enabling statute of a tribunal.[65] Consider, for example, the Ontario Landlord and Tenant Board, which charges filing fees but does not offer fee waivers.[66]

The unwritten constitutional principle of "access to justice" was described by Dickson C.J. in *British Columbia Government Employees' Union v. British Columbia (Attorney General)*[67] (a case concerning the constitutional validity of a court-issued injunction to clear the courthouse steps of picketers during a public service strike) in the following terms:

> Let us turn then to s. 52(1) of the *Constitution Act, 1982* which states that the Constitution of Canada is the supreme law of Canada and any law that is inconsistent with the provisions of the Constitution is, to the extent of the inconsistency, of no force or effect. Earlier sections of the Charter assure, in clear and specific terms, certain fundamental freedoms, democratic rights, mobility rights, legal rights and equality rights of utmost importance to each and every Canadian. .... . Of what value are the rights and freedoms guaranteed by the Charter if a person is denied or delayed access to a court of competent jurisdiction in order to vindicate them? How can the courts independently maintain the rule of law and effectively discharge the duties imposed by the Charter if court access is hindered, impeded or denied? The Charter protections would become merely illusory, the entire Charter undermined.
>
> There cannot be a rule of law without access, otherwise the rule of law is replaced by a rule of men and women who decide who shall and who shall not have access to justice.[68]

Access to justice is no less imperative in tribunals than in courts. Unlike judicial independence, which is an unwritten constitutional principle applying uniquely to courts,[69]

---

64 *Pearson, supra* note 62 at para. 14. The principle in *Pearson* recently received positive treatment in both *Spatling v. Canada (Solicitor General)*, [2003] F.C.J. No. 620 (QL), and *Pieters v. Canada (Attorney General)*, 2004 F.C. 1418.

65 In *McKenzie v. Minister of Public Safety and Solicitor General et al.*, 2006 BCSC 1372, for example, the rule-of-law concept developed in the context of civil courts was applied to the setting of a reappointment to an administrative tribunal (note that this decision is under appeal).

66 "Landlord and Tenant Fees," online: Landlord and Tenant Board <http://www.ltb.gov.on.ca/en/Key_Information/STEL02_111530.html>.

67 [1988] 2 S.C.R. 214.

68 *Ibid.* at 229-30.

69 See *Ocean Port Hotel Ltd. v. British Columbia (General Manager, Liquor Control and Licensing Branch)*, [2001] S.C.R. 781 at para. 24.

access to justice has broader application to all adjudicative proceedings in which rights and interests are at stake, and especially to those with jurisdiction over the Charter.

In *Christie v. British Columbia*,[70] it was argued that a tax on legal services, like pickets on the courthouse steps, prevents people from accessing the courts and tribunals and thus violates the right to access justice. The trial judge held that access to justice is a fundamental constitutional right and that taxation on a fundamental right denies service to low-income persons unjustifiably and violates s. 7 of the Charter. The Court of Appeal affirmed this decision and, in fact, went further, holding that, because the right to access justice is held by all, the tax should not be levied on *any* legal services that determine rights and obligations, whether before courts or tribunals, and should be struck down for *all* citizens, not just the less affluent.[71]

The provincial attorney general successfully appealed this decision to the Supreme Court,[72] which held that not every limit on access is unconstitutional. The Constitution does not mandate a *general* right to legal representation as an aspect of, or precondition to, the rule of law. Rather, the right to counsel is limited to instances where life, liberty, and security of the person are affected, as is demonstrated by ss. 7 and 10(b) of the Charter.[73] The decisions of the lower courts were reversed and, as a consequence, the scope of access to justice with respect to non-criminal proceedings remains unsettled.

2. Costs

In addition to the question of fees, there has also been growing concern over the issue of costs in the context of tribunal adjudication and the effect of costs on access to administrative justice. Where the tribunal is deciding a dispute between two or more parties, should the winning parties be able to claim costs against the losing parties as they can in civil courts? Should the tribunal itself ever be in a position to recover costs? What should the consequences be when a party is unable to pay costs?

The B.C. ATA expressly provides for tribunals to develop their own costs regimes:

Power to award costs

47(1) Subject to the regulations, the tribunal may make orders for payment as follows:

(a) requiring a party to pay part of the costs of another party or an intervener in connection with the application;

(b) requiring an intervener to pay part of the costs of a party or another intervener in connection with the application;

(c) if the tribunal considers the conduct of a party has been improper, vexatious, frivolous or abusive, requiring the party to pay part of the actual costs and expenses of the tribunal in connection with the application.

---

[70] 2005 BCSC 122.

[71] 2005 BCCA 631 (2005), 262 D.L.R. (4th) 51.

[72] *British Columbia (Attorney General) v. Christie*, 2007 SCC 21, [2007] 1 S.C.R. 873 at para. 17.

[73] Section 10(b) of the Charter provides that everyone has the right to retain and instruct counsel, and to be informed of that right "on arrest or detention."

(2) An order under subsection (1), after filing in the court registry, has the same effect as an order of the court for the recovery of a debt in the amount stated in the order against the person named in it, and all proceedings may be taken on it as if it were an order of the court.[74]

One of the first decisions of a tribunal considering a costs regime developed pursuant to ATA s. 47 was *BC Vegetable Greenhouse I, L.P. v. BC Vegetable Marketing Commission*.[75] This case concerned an application to the B.C. Farm Industry Review Board (FIRB) by the B.C. Vegetable Marketing Commission ("the Commission") and B.C. Hot House Foods Inc. ("B.C. Hot House") for an order that B.C. Vegetable Greenhouse I, L.P. ("B.C. Vegetable") pay the costs incurred during B.C. Vegetable's appeal of a commission order that required B.C. Vegetable to remit to the commission $376,642 in outstanding levies. Some of B.C. Vegetable's grounds of appeal were unsuccessful or abandoned during the proceeding, and the tribunal generally found the conduct of the company to have rendered the proceeding more costly than it should have been. The FIRB panel ordered B.C. Vegetable to pay the costs of the other parties (but not the FIRB's, although that option would have been open to the Board as well). This decision suggests that, where costs are available, unless otherwise circumscribed by a tribunal's enabling legislation, the applicable principles will be similar to those developed in the civil courts, with the exception of the potential for liability on the part of losing parties to pay costs directly to the tribunal. What remains undeveloped is whether the availability of costs will discourage parties from bringing disputes to tribunals or dilute the notion of the public interest jurisdiction underlying all administrative tribunal mandates.

C. Budget and Staffing

The third area where resources play a role concerns the tribunal's budget and staff allocation. This is a controversial area for administrative law because budgetary issues are usually seen under the rubric of public administration rather than within the sphere of administrative law. Could a court ever compel the government against its will to fund or organize a tribunal differently? The notion seems paradoxical. After all, tribunals are established as a matter of government policy through empowering legislation. There is nothing preventing a government from changing the mandate of a tribunal or repealing it altogether. How, then, could it be unlawful for the government to decide its level of funding or staffing?

Although government may not be under a legal obligation to create tribunals, once it has chosen to do so, it may well be under a legal obligation to provide adequate funding to ensure fairness, the rule of law, and access to justice before these tribunals. For example, in *Khan v. University of Ottawa*,[76] the Ontario Court of Appeal held that an oral hearing was required in the context of a university proceeding to determine whether a student would fail a course. The Court found that, where a decision affecting significant interests of an individual turns on credibility, fairness requires that the individual have an opportunity to put

---

74   ATA, *supra* note 40; see also s. 17.1 of the SPPA, *supra* note 7.

75   Farm Industry Review Board (2005 May 20), online: <http://www.firb.gov.bc.ca/appeals/vegetable/bc_veg_03-23_costs_dec_may20_05.pdf>.

76   (1997), 148 D.L.R. (4th) 577, 34 O.R. (3d) 535 (C.A.).

forward his or her case before the decision-maker in person. What if the body in question is not a university, however, but a province-wide licensing body located in the capital city and the person affected lives in a remote rural community? What if an oral hearing is simply not practicable in the context of a high-volume tribunal? As discussed by Grant Huscroft in Chapter 5, From Natural Justice to Fairness: Thresholds, Content, and the Role of Judicial Review, the standard of procedural fairness required in a particular case will vary, but the standards recognized by administrative law justifying a lesser degree of fairness do not expressly include questions of resources.[77]

Although tribunals are creatures of public policy, once established, and once the rights and interests of people depend on the fairness and reasonableness of that body's decision making, then the duty of fairness clearly imposes constraints on government, as discussed above in the context of the requirement to hold an oral hearing in *Khan*. Perhaps the best known example of this dynamic is *Singh v. Canada*,[78] in which the duty of fairness was held to require that the federal government provide oral hearings for refugee claimants. This decision resulted in significant expenditures for government and the reorganization of the entire refugee determination process. In *2747-3174 Québec Inc. v. Quebec (Régie des permis d'alcool)*,[79] the Court contemplated ordering the government of Quebec to reorganize a liquor board on independence grounds. In *Suresh v. Canada (Minister of Citizenship and Immigration)*,[80] dealing with security certificates, fairness obligations were said to constrain the ability of the government to shield disclosure of national security documents. All of these constraints may implicitly impose resource obligations on government. Courts have yet to consider the corollary issue of whether fairness could be compromised by a tribunal that is provided inadequate funding to fulfill its statutory mandate or to provide fair proceedings.

Some years ago, during research on how administrative independence is experienced by decision-makers in the field of humanitarian and compassionate exemptions under the *Immigration and Refugee Protection Act*, I learned that, from the perspective of decision-makers, independence could be compromised by the requirement that a certain number of cases be "cleared" each week. This clearance rate was a product of the volume of applications and the limited number of staff assigned to these units within Citizenship and Immigration Canada. The result, these decision-makers asserted, was to limit their ability to conduct interviews, to research a file, and to consider and deliberate on the evidence provided.[81]

This focus on the lived experience of decision-makers also raises the broader issue of how decision-makers are selected—whether on a merit principle, by political appointment, or by some hybrid of the two. Is access to a tribunal compromised where decision-makers

---

77 See the discussion of *Baker* by Grant Huscroft in Chapter 5, From Natural Justice to Fairness: Thresholds, Content, and the Role of Judicial Review: in *Baker*, the Supreme Court held that the content of procedural fairness will vary depending on the nature of the decision being made, nature of the statutory scheme, importance of the decision to the people affected, legitimate expectations, and the agency's choice of procedures.

78 [1985] 1 S.C.R. 177.

79 [1996] 3 S.C.R. 919.

80 2002 SCC 1, [2002] 1 S.C.R. 3.

81 For a discussion of this research and its findings, see L. Sossin, "From Neutrality to Compassion: The Place of Civil Service Values and Legal Norms in the Exercise of Administrative Discretion" (2005) 55 U.T.L.J. 427.

are viewed as extensions of the government of the day; is it enhanced where a tribunal is representative—that is, the demographic makeup of members and staff reflects the community or user groups of the tribunal?

The line between public administration and administrative law is clearly blurring. It is no longer possible (or desirable) to exclude significant government discretion over how administrative bodies are designed, funded, and governed from the purview of administrative law principles. Where these dynamics can be tied to the fairness of a decision-making process or the reasonableness of a decision, they cease to be matters of policy preference alone.

V. Conclusions

Administrative tribunals are established for a variety of purposes, but most include the following rationale:

- to resolve disputes or reach decisions on the basis of specialized expertise;
- to resolve disputes or reach decisions in a more informal and expeditious fashion than is possible in the courts, thereby reducing costs to the parties; and
- to resolve disputes in a fashion at arm's length from the government while advancing the policy mandates set out in the applicable legislation.

Accessibility is consistent with all of these purposes. Accessibility may challenge another key consideration, however, and that is the scarce resources of government. Accessibility, whether in the form of more and better facilities, information for parties, or representation services, requires resources and, given the high volume of some tribunals, the resource implications may be quite substantial.

In addition to resources, access may also depend on how a tribunal accommodates unequal power and resources between parties. Consider a social benefits tribunal, where often unrepresented welfare recipients face ministry representatives. How can a decision-maker remain impartial, on the one hand, while ensuring a sufficiently level playing field on the other? This is a challenge familiar to courts as well, particularly in areas such as family law, where power imbalances and self-represented litigants are common. An aspect of this balancing exercise unique to administrative tribunals is the added feature that many tribunals are established precisely to empower vulnerable individuals. In the case of social benefits tribunals, for example, the whole purpose of these tribunals would be undermined if those whose benefits are wrongfully taken away cannot, in practice, access the tribunal.

Access also involves the balance between fairness and efficiency. It might be optimal for a high-volume tribunal such as a landlord and tenant tribunal to have facilities in every major population centre. It will be more efficient, of course, to maintain fewer facilities but invest in new technologies such as videoconferencing, which allow for far greater numbers to have access to dispute resolution. At what point does the pursuit of efficiency erode the fairness of the proceeding? This is precisely the question that administrative law will increasingly have to address.

As important as access is to the parties in administrative justice, it is largely uncharted territory for administrative law. The duty of fairness, for example, typically has not included a concern for the simplicity of forms, the transparency of guidelines, or the adequacy of a tribunal's database of prior decisions. The logic of fairness, however, is that it must be viewed from the standpoint of those affected by decision making and, from this perspective, accessibility and fairness are inextricably linked.

Finally, the analysis thus far has assumed access relates to process. Access to justice, however, not only includes being able to understand, navigate, and participate in a tribunal's decision making, but also presupposes that the tribunal will deliver administrative justice of high quality. In this sense, access to administrative justice extends not only to standing, guidelines, fees, and representation, but also to whether decisions are well reasoned and delivered in a timely fashion. Access in this sense may also extend to whether decision-makers are appointed under a competitive merit-based process and whether decision-makers are able to access appropriate training and education (because substantive expertise in subject areas of a tribunal may not include expertise in the conduct of a hearing or vice versa).

The purpose of this chapter has been to introduce issues of access to administrative justice and to show how integrated such questions are with the broader principles of administrative law, on the one hand, and the everyday practice of diverse tribunals, on the other hand. Ultimately, this analysis leads to a challenge for administrative law, to do justice to questions of access both as part of traditional fairness determinations and as an emerging, independent aspect of the legal framework within which tribunals are established and operate. The many implications of this new focus on access to administrative justice remain to be elaborated.

SUGGESTED ADDITIONAL READINGS

BOOKS

Bass, J., W.A. Bogart, & F.H. Zemans, eds., *Access to Justic for a New Century: The Way Forward* (Toronto: Irwin, 2005).

Trebilcock, M., A. Duggan, & L. Sossin, *Middle Income Access to Justice* (Toronto: University of Toronto Press, 2012).

CASES

BC Vegetable Greenhouse I, L.P. v. BC Vegetable Marketing Commission, Farm Industry Review Board (2005 May 20), online: <http://www.firb.gov.bc.ca/appeals/vegetable/bc_veg_03-23_costs_dec_may20_05.pdf>.

Filgueira v. Garfield Container Transport Inc., 2005 CHRT 44, File No. T952/7204.

Finlay v. Canada (Minister of Finance), [1986] 2 S.C.R. 607.

CHAPTER EIGHT

Caught Between Judicial Paradigms and the Administrative State's Pastiche: "Tribunal" Independence, Impartiality, and Bias

LAVERNE JACOBS*

Faculty of Law, University of Windsor

*   I am grateful to the co-contributors and editors of this volume for their feedback on this chapter. Thanks also to Maria Mavrikkou (J.D. 2012) for her editorial assistance and the Law Foundation of Ontario for its support.

I. Introduction

This chapter addresses the controversial issues of tribunal[1] independence, impartiality, and bias. It is useful at the outset to define the relationship between these three concepts, although this relationship is discussed in greater detail below. Put simply, independence, impartiality, and bias all centre on the notion of fairness in the administrative decision-making process. A key characteristic of a fair proceeding before an administrative body is that the decision-maker and the decision-making process not grant undue preferential treatment or be driven by preconceived notions. This characteristic is vital not only to the litigants before the tribunal, but also to the public's confidence in the administration of justice. Most certainly, the general public would lose faith in public decision-makers if it perceived that their decisions were based on irrelevant considerations such as relationships with the litigants before them, prejudice, or undue pressure from government. As a result, our legal tradition has gone to great lengths to protect this fundamental tenet of fairness. Consequently, regardless of what the reality may be in any given administrative decision-making process, the mere perception of partiality toward a particular outcome, or *bias*, provided that the perception is reasonable, is enough to have a decision overturned.

If bias is the evil that we are trying to avoid, *impartiality* refers to the ideal state of the decision-maker or decision-making institution. An impartial decision-maker is one who is able to make judgments with an open mind—that is, one who comes to the decision-making table without his or her "mind already made up" or without connections that improperly influence the decision-making process. Finally, *independence* is said to be a means of achieving impartiality. For example, by ensuring through legislation that an administrative tribunal is not too dependent on government for the necessities of its day-to-day functioning, it is theoretically less likely that government officials can pull decision-making strings.

Canadian administrative law jurisprudence shows a continual ebb and flow that oscillates between allowing deference to the nature of administrative bodies and legislative choices, on the one hand, and asserting judicial paradigms as ideal forms for resolving issues of administrative independence, impartiality, and bias, on the other hand. This chapter argues that, when it comes to the administrative state, the process of developing appropriate juristic tools such as "guarantees of independence" and "the rule against bias" requires a perspective that is always situated between a court-derived model and the wide variety of administrative actors that exist.

II. Sources of the Guarantee of an Independent and Impartial Tribunal

The guarantee of a proceeding before an independent and impartial tribunal stems from common law, and from constitutional or quasi-constitutional principles. This chapter thus develops on the concepts of procedural fairness discussed by Grant Huscroft in Chapter 5,

---

[1]   The term "tribunal" is a contested one by some decision-making bodies within the administrative justice system, but it is used here generically to encompass all statutory decision-making bodies (variously termed, for example, agencies, boards, or commissions), not simply those that are adjudicative in a court-like sense or those that render binding decisions.

From Natural Justice to Fairness: Thresholds, Content, and the Role of Judicial Review, and is a prelude to Fox-Evan Decent and Alexander Pless's Chapter 12, The Charter and Administrative Law: Cross-Fertilization or Inconstancy? At common law, the principles of natural justice are encapsulated in two central ideas. The first idea is that a decision-maker should neither judge his or her own cause nor have any interest in the outcome of a case before him or her. This idea is generally known as the rule against bias and is often summarized in a Latin maxim: *nemo judex in sua causa debet esse* (no one is fit to be the judge in his or her own counsel). The second idea requires the decision-maker to hear and listen to both sides of the case before making a decision. This requirement has been summarized by the maxim *audi alteram partem* (hear the other side). Both the *nemo judex* and the *audi alteram partem* principles inform the right to an independent and impartial proceeding. The *nemo judex* rule aims to avoid circumstances in which the decision-maker acts as both prosecutor and judge in the same matter or decides for personal gain or benefit. Similarly, by requiring the decision-maker to listen to all sides of a dispute, the *audi alteram partem* rule seeks, in part, to encourage the decision-maker to focus his or her decision on the facts of the dispute and the relevant law and not on extraneous, or irrelevant, considerations.[2]

In addition to these common-law principles, some have argued, with limited success, that the promise of an independent and impartial administrative tribunal is also guaranteed by unwritten constitutional principles and the rule of law.[3] What is more certain is that a determination by an independent and impartial tribunal is guaranteed in some cases through the *Canadian Charter of Rights and Freedoms*.[4] The table on page 236 indicates the wording of the guarantees provided by these various enactments.

The most striking features of this comparative table are the differences in wording, the seeming variation in the rights protected, and the collection of standards employed to protect them in the various enactments. For example, although the Canadian *Bill of Rights* and the *Alberta Bill of Rights* make "due process of law" the decisive factor for determining whether one has been legally or illegally deprived of his or her rights, s. 7 of the Canadian Charter speaks of "principles of fundamental justice." To what extent are the two expressions coterminous? Is one concept broader than the other? And how do concepts such as "due process of law," and "fundamental justice" relate, if at all, to the common-law principle of natural justice? These are all questions with which the courts, lawyers, academics, and students have grappled.[5]

---

[2] I discuss the interplay of these ideas in Laverne A. Jacobs, "Tribunal Independence and Impartiality: Rethinking the Theory After Bell and Ocean Port Hotel—A Call for Empirical Analysis" in Laverne A. Jacobs & Anne L. Mactavish., eds., *Dialogue Between Courts and Tribunals: Essays in Administrative Law and Justice (2001-2007)* (Montreal: Les Éditions Thémis, 2008) [Jacobs & Mactavish].

[3] *Ocean Port Hotel v. British Columbia (General Manager, Liquor Control and Licensing Branch)*, 2001 SCC 52, [2001] 2 S.C.R. 781 [*Ocean Port Hotel*] and *McKenzie v. Minister of Public Safety and Solicitor General et al.*, 2006 BCSC 1372, 61 B.C.L.R. (4th) 57; (2007), 71 B.C.L.R. (4th) 1 (C.A.); [2007] S.C.C.A. No. 601 (QL), appeal to the Supreme Court of Canada dismissed without reasons after the B.C. Court of Appeal determined the issue to be moot because of legislative amendment [*McKenzie*]. Both cases are discussed below.

[4] Part I of the *Constitution Act, 1982*, being Schedule B to the *Canada Act 1982* (U.K.), 1982, c. 11 [Charter].

[5] See e.g. *Singh v. Minister of Employment and Immigration*, [1985] 1 S.C.R. 177 [*Singh*], an immigration case in which the Supreme Court of Canada held that, at a minimum, "fundamental justice" included the notion of procedural fairness.

Statute	Section(s)	Guarantee provided
Canadian Charter of Rights and Freedoms	s. 7	Everyone has the right to life, liberty and security of the person and the right not to be deprived thereof except in accordance with the principles of fundamental justice
Canadian Charter of Rights and Freedoms	s. 11(d)	Any person charged with an offence has the right … to be presumed innocent until proven guilty according to law in a fair and public hearing by an independent and impartial tribunal
Quebec Charter of Human Rights and Freedoms[6]	s. 23	Every person has a right to a full and equal, public and fair hearing by an independent and impartial tribunal, for the determination of his rights and obligations or of the merits of any charge brought against him.
Canadian Bill of Rights[7]	ss. 1(a), 2(e)	1(a) the right of the individual to life, liberty, security of the person and enjoyment of property, and the right not to be deprived thereof except by due process of law; 2(e) [N]o law of Canada shall be construed or applied so as to … deprive a person of the right to a fair hearing in accordance with the principles of fundamental justice for the determination of his rights and obligations
Alberta Bill of Rights[8]	s. 1(a)	the right of the individual to liberty, security of the person and enjoyment of property, and the right not to be deprived thereof except by due process of law

Moreover, it is clear from the table that many situations trigger the right to what we might call globally "an independent and impartial proceeding." What is not always clear is how smoothly these situations translate to the various instances of socioeconomic regulation that are addressed by administrative actors in the administrative state. For example, s. 11(d) of the Canadian Charter has been held to require penal consequences before it can be applied outside the context of courts.[9] And while s. 23 of the Quebec Charter seems all-encompassing

---

6   R.S.Q., c. C-12 [Quebec Charter].

7   S.C. 1960, c. 44, C-12.3.

8   R.S.A. 2000, c. A-14.

9   See *Alex Couture Inc. et al. v. Canada (Attorney General)* (1991), 83 D.L.R. (4th) 577 (Que. C.A.); leave to appeal denied [1992] 2 S.C.R. v, at 91 D.L.R. (4th) vii; *Chrysler Canada Ltd. v. Canada (Competition Tribunal)*, [1992] 2 S.C.R. 394. Section 7 of the Charter seems to offer more fertile ground and has been used with some success

insofar as it allows for a fair hearing by an independent and impartial tribunal for the mere determination of the individual's rights and obligations, this seemingly low threshold is elevated by a legislated definition of "tribunal." The Quebec Charter defines "tribunals" as being adjudicative bodies only.[10] The acceptable degree of independence and the way in which impartiality is understood may be quite different for hearings before a body in Quebec that is established to set prices and develop policy in the natural resources sector than for hearings before a human rights tribunal.

Generally, these variations, whether they stem from legislative enactments, the common law, or from judicial interpretations of both, indicate a context-driven and, at times, uneven promise of independence and impartiality. To predict the degree of independence that any administrative body should exhibit and the ways in which impartiality and bias should be understood within the context of that body's functioning, it is important to have a thorough understanding of not only the law but also the nature, purpose, and practical ways that the administrative body in question operates.

III. What Is "Tribunal Independence" and Why Is It Important?

Challenging administrative tribunals for lack of independence has become one of the most litigated issues in administrative law. Indeed, since the advent of the Canadian Charter, some see this new preoccupation with independent decision making as providing "a more extensive basis for challenging adjudicators and statutory regimes than has been envisaged under traditional common law conceptions of bias."[11] Because independence has attracted such attention as a means of challenging administrative regimes, this chapter focuses first on arguments regarding lack of independence as a reason for alleging reasonable apprehension of bias on the part of individual administrative decision-makers or of administrative decision-making institutions.

The notion of tribunal independence raises several questions. To what extent should tribunals and other administrative bodies be independent of the branches of government that have created them? How can a tribunal (and its members) best fulfill the often competing functions for which it has been created while maintaining an appropriate distance from government, litigants, and other stakeholders? And how do we define "appropriate" in this context? We explore the various relationships that affect the independence of tribunals and their individual decision-makers, and the ways that independence may be, or perceived to

---

in deportation matters (see *Charkaoui v. Canada (Citizenship and Immigration)*, 2007 SCC 9, [2007] 1 S.C.R. 350, but see also *Suresh v. Canada (Minister of Citizenship and Immigration)*, 2002 SCC 1, [2002] 1 S.C.R. 3.

10   Section 56 of the Quebec Charter reads:

    56(1) In sections 9, 23, 30, 31, 34 and 38, in Chapter III of Part II and in Part IV, the word "tribunal" includes a coroner, a fire investigation commissioner, an inquiry commission, and any person or agency exercising quasi judicial functions.

11   See Gus Van Harten, Gerald Heckman & David J. Mullan, *Administrative Law: Cases, Text, and Materials*, 6th ed. (Toronto: Emond Montgomery, 2010) at 444.

be, compromised. These relationships are examined critically from both the perspective of jurisprudential debates and the practical realities of daily tribunal operations. Specific tensions include the appointments process, removal of members, tribunals as a function of policy making, internal interactions among tribunal members and staff, and the vexing question of the extent to which explicit and implicit constitutional, structural guarantees of independence do or should apply to tribunals.

By design, administrative decision-making bodies have been created in a way that leaves them connected to government. Most have a link with the executive branch of government through a minister of Cabinet. Generally, under their enabling statutes, tribunals, or at least their chairs, are required to maintain some contact with this minister. At the very least, they are obliged to file annual reports to this minister.[12] They may also have additional statutory obligations that force them to interact with the minister and his or her department. For example, they may be asked to provide advice to the minister or additional information on developments in the regulation of the industry or sector under their supervision.[13] Finally, the minister will certainly be involved in the process of appointing and removing members of the tribunal. In Ontario, with the enactment of the *Adjudicative Tribunals Accountability, Governance and Appointments Act, 2009* (ATAGAA), the chair of an adjudicative tribunal must interact with the minister responsible for the tribunal or with the executive branch of government in order to recommend the appointment or reappointment of tribunal members.[14] The design of the Canadian administrative state differs markedly from that of some jurisdictions. For example, in the United Kingdom, recent tribunal reform has resulted in all administrative tribunals reporting to an executive agency called Tribunal Service, instead of to host departments.[15]

Given the political nature of the executive branch of government and, in particular, its responsibility to create and promote the government's policies, one can easily see how members of the general public may be wary that inappropriate interference may stem from the regular interactions between government departments and tribunals. For instance, users of the tribunal might be concerned that the minister might use these opportunities to dictate, whether explicitly or implicitly, how particular files should be decided. This concern can be particularly acute in situations where the government is frequently an opposing party before the tribunal—for example, in immigration matters or disputes relating to social benefits.

---

[12] A typical provision imposing the obligation to file an annual report to the minister can be found in the *Residential Tenancies Act, 2006*, S.O. 2006, c. 17, s. 180. The *Adjudicative Tribunals Accountability, Governance and Appointments Act, 2009*, S.O. 2009, c. 33, Sch. 5 [ATAGAA], requires adjudicative tribunals in Ontario to report to their responsible ministers on a wide array of matters relating to tribunal internal governance. These matters include the development and maintenance of consultation policies, ethics plans, and codes of conduct. ATAGAA is discussed in greater detail below. See *infra* note 14 and accompanying text.

[13] See e.g. *Alcohol and Gaming Regulation and Public Protection Act*, S.O. 1996, s. 3(4).

[14] ATAGAA, *supra* note 12. See, generally, L. Jacobs, "A Wavering Commitment?: Administrative Independence and Collaborative Governance in Ontario's Adjudicative Tribunals Accountability Legislation" (2010) 28(2) Windsor Y.B. Access to Just. 285.

[15] Although one must be careful in making sweeping comparisons because the terminology in different jurisdictions varies according to what exactly an administrative tribunal does.

These introductory paragraphs point us in the direction of an initial understanding of the concept of tribunal independence and why it is important. When we speak of "independence," we are referring to the tribunal's ability to decide matters free of inappropriate interference or influence. The executive branch of government may be one source of interference in the administrative law context, but several other sources—for example, litigants, other tribunal members, and staff—may also exist. As in the case of judicial decisions made in the criminal law context or in civil matters, the independence of the administrative decision-maker is valued as an aspect of the rule of law. In theory, when decision-makers are in an insulated zone, the public has greater confidence that the decision being made is based on only relevant considerations, such as the facts of the case and the law. In the context of the administrative state, however, the difficulty arises in determining what constitutes "relevant" considerations or "inappropriate" interference.[16] Some of the most interesting tensions in administrative law arise in the clash between the day-to-day realities of the work of administrative tribunals and judicial understandings of how the administrative state should work. This chapter argues that the law on tribunal independence is no exception. Arguably, it is one of the richest areas in which to explore these tensions. By focusing primarily on judicial review of administrative action, administrative law has, to date, given privilege to judicial conceptions of independence while failing to adequately integrate judicial understandings with on-the-ground tribunal realities.

The following discussion provides an overview of the historical development of the law on tribunal independence and the relationship between independence and the concept of impartiality. It explores administrative law's understandings of independence and impartiality from both judicial and tribunal perspectives, using the appointment and removal of members as an example.

We then take a solid look at the concept of bias and, at the end of the chapter, return to highlight the connections between adjudicative independence, bias, and the common institutional practices used to promote consistency and policy making, employed in the multi-functional context of many administrative bodies.

IV. The Development of the Law of Tribunal Independence in Canada

The jurisprudence on tribunal independence in Canada is easiest understood as having developed through a series of three waves. The first wave of jurisprudence used the independence of the judiciary as a foundation on which to mould the concept of administrative tribunal independence. The second wave, marked by the decision in *Ocean Port Hotel*,[17] affirmed the hybrid nature of tribunals and maintained that there is no general constitutional guarantee of independence where tribunals are concerned. The third wave served as a retrenchment:

---

16   The fact that the enabling legislation may sometimes provide a role for government to play in the decision-making process as a party—for example, in citizen–state contexts such as immigration, radio broadcasting, or social benefits litigation—sometimes also contributes to rendering complex the question of what constitutes relevant or irrelevant considerations.

17   *Supra* note 3.

litigants once again pushed to have judicial declarations that administrative tribunal independence is guaranteed by the Constitution.

A. Laying the Groundwork: The Theory of Judicial Independence

A discussion about the independence of administrative bodies is best started with an overview of the theory of judicial independence. At its core, judicial independence is a means of ensuring that judges act free from any interference or influence. In Australia, Sir Guy Green has described judicial independence as the capacity of the courts "to perform their constitutional function free from actual or apparent dependence upon, any persons or institutions."[18] Chief Justice Dickson, speaking for the majority of the Supreme Court in *Beauregard v. Canada*, offered this useful definition:

> Historically, the generally accepted core of the principle of judicial independence has been the complete liberty of individual judges to hear and decide the cases that come before them: *no outsider—be it government, pressure group, individual or even another judge—should interfere in fact, or attempt to interfere, with the way in which a judge conducts his or her case and makes his or her decision.* This core continues to be central to the principle of judicial independence.[19]

How is this "complete liberty" to be ascertained? Although it is certainly impossible to monitor all the contacts and communications of every judge, when it comes to assuring independence from government (the first of the outside interferences noted by Dickson C.J.), three objective structural conditions have been identified as necessary to guarantee independence: security of tenure, financial security, and administrative (or institutional) control. These three conditions serve to reassure the public that the possibility of interference in judicial decision making by the executive and legislative branches of government has been reduced, if not eliminated.

With respect to security of tenure, the type of interference targeted is the ability of the government to remove a judge for such things as rendering decisions that do not meet the government's approval. As a result, the condition that a judge's tenure be secure mandates that a judge be removed only for cause. Security of tenure is guaranteed by the Constitution, which provides that judges of the superior courts shall hold office during good behaviour or until they reach the age of 75.[20] Moreover, before removal, judges must be provided with an opportunity to respond to the allegations against them.[21] Consequently, "at pleasure"

---

18   Sir Guy Green, "The Rationale and Some Aspects of Judicial Independence" (1985) 20 A.L.R. 135. Sir Guy Green's formulation of the concept of judicial independence was endorsed by the Supreme Court of Canada in *Valente v. The Queen*, [1985] 2 S.C.R. 673 at para. 18, LeDain J.

19   [1986] 2 S.C.R. 56 at para. 21 (emphasis added) [*Beauregard*].

20   See *Constitution Act, 1867* (U.K.), 30 & 31 Vict., c. 3, s. 99.

21   An example of this is found in the federal *Judges Act*, R.S.C. 1985, c. J-1, s. 64; see also online: Canadian Judicial Council <http://www.cjc-ccm.gc.ca>, which outlines the complaints procedure and inquiry process for the investigation of federally appointed judges. For a recent example of the judicial inquiry process in action see *Ruffo (Re)*, [2005] Q.J. No. 17953 (C.A.) (QL).

appointments, which allow judges to be removed at the request of Cabinet, without pre-specified cause and without necessarily allowing the judge to be heard, have been rendered invalid.

"Financial security" aims to satisfy two goals. The first is a guarantee that, although the government is responsible for the remuneration of judges, it will not alter their pay for arbitrary reasons such as discontent with decisions rendered. To accomplish this goal, judges are guaranteed a fixed salary under the Constitution.[22] As well, more recently, compensation commissions have been set up to help facilitate negotiations in judges' pay and pay-related matters, such as pensions.[23] The second goal is a promise that the amount that judges are paid will be sufficient to keep them from seeking alternative means of supplementing their income. Security of tenure and financial security have historical roots dating back to 13th-century England.[24] The concepts evolved from experiences in which the King manipulated the judiciary in order to ensure that the bench was sympathetic toward him, and from the problem of bribery caused by the underpayment of court officials, including judges.

Administrative or institutional control is the third objective guarantee of independence. Institutional control deals with the manner in which the affairs of the court are administered—from budgetary allocations for buildings and equipment to the assignment of cases. It addresses how responsibility for such administration should be divided between the judiciary and the other branches of government. Although questions about, for example, the allocation of court cases have clearly been determined to fall properly within the ambit of the chief justice of the court,[25] other matters, such as obtaining budgetary allocations for equipment, are more problematic.[26] For example, allowing judges to obtain their own funding for resources, instead of asking them to go through a Cabinet minister such as the attorney general, might appear to be an approach that fosters the independence of the judiciary; however, this method could result in judges soliciting funds from the government or others, which is unseemly from the perception of administrative control. For the Supreme Court, the Federal Courts, and the Tax Court, issues of institutional control that rely on a government allocation of resources have been addressed through the use of a negotiating office called the Federal Commissioner of Judicial Affairs.[27] The problem of balancing judicial independence and judicial administration is particularly acute at the provincial and territorial level where, as a result of our constitutional division of powers, the administration of the court system requires some involvement by the provincial legislature and executive.[28]

---

[22] See *Constitution Act, 1867, supra* note 20, s. 100.

[23] See e.g. *Provincial Court Judges' Assn. of New Brunswick v. New Brunswick (Minister of Justice); Ontario Judges' Assn. v. Ontario (Management Board); Bodner v. Alberta; Conférence des juges du Québec v. Quebec (Attorney General); Minc v. Quebec (Attorney General),* 2005 SCC 44, [2005] 2 S.C.R. 286.

[24] See W.R. Lederman, "The Independence of the Judiciary" (1956) 34 Can. Bar Rev. 769, 1139.

[25] See *Valente v. The Queen,* [1985] 2 S.C.R. 673.

[26] See Martin Friedland, *A Place Apart: Judicial Independence and Accountability in Canada* (Ottawa: Canadian Judicial Council, 1995); see also Jules Deschênes and Carl Baar, *Masters in Their Own House* (Ottawa: Canadian Judicial Council, 1981).

[27] Established under Part III of the *Judges Act, supra* note 21.

[28] See *Constitution Act, 1867, supra* note 20, s. 92(14).

As with security of tenure and financial security, administrative control is concerned with making sure that judges are not put in compromising situations where they might choose to make decisions to protect their own employment and interests, rather than for the sake of rendering decisions solely on the basis of their legal judgment. However, unlike the first two guarantees of independence, the nature of administrative control is primarily institutional as opposed to individual. Although there may be implications that affect an individual judge, it is not the individual judge and his or her relationship with the government that is at issue, but the relationship between the government and the court as an institution.

Finally, the jurisprudence has come to recognize another type of independence—that is, independence from interference in deliberations, commonly known as adjudicative independence. Referenced briefly in the Supreme Court's decision in *Beauregard*,[29] the concept of adjudicative independence embodies the ability of a decision-maker to decide, free of inappropriate interference by other decision-makers. Such inappropriate interference may include, for example, pressure to decide a certain way or substitution of another's decision for one's own. Unlike security of tenure, financial security, and administrative control, adjudicative independence is not structural in nature. It does not relate to the design of the institution by the government. Adjudicative independence deals with relational matters and the internal process of deliberation by individual decision-makers. Adjudicative independence is one guarantee of independence that is frequently called into question in the administrative state, especially as a result of institutional practices used to develop policy and consistency. We examine adjudicative independence in greater detail when we discuss institutional bias.

As alluded to in the introduction, the purpose of judicial independence is to help boost public confidence in the justice system. Judicial independence has the protection of the public in mind, not the protection of the judges. The mere appearance of inappropriate interference with the decision-making process is enough to engender a loss of public confidence in the decision-making mechanisms of the state.[30] On a micro level, whether the duty of fairness has been breached in any given proceeding is generally foremost on the minds of particular litigants. Some would argue that a reasonable perception of interference may threaten public acceptance of the law itself. In this light, independence is not a goal in and of itself; rather, judicial independence serves as a cornerstone to protect other values that are considered important within our system of justice. Most commonly, independence is said to be maintained in order to provide an appearance of impartiality in the decision-making process. Providing guarantees of independence aims to assure the public that decision-makers are in a position to make decisions impartially. Similarly, the independence of administrative tribunals seeks to achieve the same goal.

B. From Judicial Independence to Tribunal Independence

Over time, the criteria guaranteeing independence of the judiciary have served as a foundation from which courts have determined whether administrative tribunals are also sufficiently

---

29   See *Beauregard*, *supra* note 19 and accompanying text.

30   See *R. v. Sussex Justices, ex parte McCarthy*, [1924] 1 K.B. 256.

independent. *Valente v. The Queen*[31] was the first Supreme Court case in Canada to suggest the idea that the guarantees for judicial independence could also be applied to a variety of tribunals.[32] Since that time, litigants have pushed for tribunals to be held to the same degree of independence as the courts. These litigants have argued that various constitutional safeguards (namely, ss. 7 and 11(d) of the Canadian Charter as well as the unwritten constitutional principle of judicial independence) and quasi-constitutional provisions (such as, s. 23 of the Quebec Charter and the Canadian *Bill of Rights*) guarantee tribunal independence.[33]

The test for adequate tribunal independence is whether a reasonable, well-informed person having thought the matter through would conclude that an administrative decision-maker is sufficiently free of factors that could interfere with his or her ability to make impartial judgments.[34] The standard for tribunal independence is not as strict as it is for judicial independence. Administrative tribunals do not have to meet the same degree of independence as the courts do. The methodological approach taken by the courts when the independence of an administrative tribunal is challenged consists of applying the guarantees of tribunal independence in a flexible way to account for the functions performed by the tribunal under scrutiny. This method was stated concisely in *Canadian Pacific Ltd. v. Matsqui Indian Band*[35] by Lamer C.J.:

> [W]hile administrative tribunals are subject to the *Valente* principles, the test for institutional independence must be applied in light of the functions being performed by the particular tribunal at issue. The requisite level of institutional independence (i.e., security of tenure, financial security and administrative control) will depend on the nature of the tribunal, the interests at stake, and other indices of independence such as oaths of office.[36]

Reference to the operational context of the tribunal takes place not only through an examination of the tribunal's functions as declared in its enabling legislation, but also

---

[31] [1985] 2 S.C.R. 673 [*Valente*].

[32] *Valente* was the first Supreme Court case to deal with the question of judicial independence in Canada. The question at issue was whether a provincial court judge, appointed under the *Provincial Courts Act*, R.S.O. 1980, c. 398 and sitting as the Ontario Provincial Court (Criminal Division), could be considered an independent tribunal under s. 11(d) of the Charter.

[33] See e.g. with respect to the Charter, s. 7, *Singh, supra* note 5 and, with respect to s. 11(d) of the Charter, *R. v. Généreux*, [1992] 1 S.C.R. 259; *Ruffo v. Quebec (Conseil de la magistrature)*, [1991] A.Q. No. 1101 (QL) (Sup. Ct.)—the argument relating to s. 11(d) of the Charter was abandoned at the higher levels of court; *Alex Couture Inc. et al. v. Canada (Attorney General)* (1991), 83 D.L.R. (4th) 577 (Que. C.A.); leave to appeal denied [1992] 2 S.C.R. v, at 91 D.L.R. (4th) vii; in relation to the unwritten constitutional principles stemming from the preamble of the Constitution, see *Ocean Port Hotel, supra* note 3, and *McKenzie* (Sup. Ct.), *supra* note 3, decision on appeal; as regards s. 23 of the Quebec Charter, see *2747-3174 Québec Inc. v. Quebec (Régie des permis d'alcool)*, [1996] 3 S.C.R. 919 [*Régie*], and *Montambeault v. Brazeau*, [1996] A.Q. No. 4187 (Que. C.A.) (QL).

[34] This test, generally referred to as the "reasonable apprehension of bias" test, has many purposes. It is used to determine whether a reasonable apprehension exists that an administrative decision-maker has acted partially or exhibited bias. Moreover, it has been applied to evaluate administrative bodies as a whole in order to determine whether the institution can be said to exhibit a lack of independence or impartiality in a substantial number of cases. The test is discussed below in section V, Reasonable Apprehension of Bias.

[35] [1995] 1 S.C.R. 3 [*Matsqui*].

[36] *Ibid.* at para. 83.

through an appreciation of the tribunal as it functions in practice. In *Matsqui*, the need to see the tribunal in practice was a point of division between the majority and minority decisions. While all the judges who addressed the issue agreed with the theoretical approach set out by Lamer C.J., outlined above, the majority opinion on this issue maintained that the test should be deferred until the tribunals had actually been up and running in order to have the benefit of knowing how they operated in practice.[37]

The principles developed in *Matsqui* were applied in *2747-3174 Québec Inc. v. Quebec (Régie des permis d'alcool)*,[38] a case argued under s. 23 of the Quebec Charter. In *Régie*, it was held that the directors of Quebec's liquor licensing board possessed sufficient security of tenure despite the fact that their terms of office were limited. The Supreme Court of Canada held that the requirements of tribunal independence do not necessitate that administrative actors, like judges, hold office for life. The Court reasoned that what must be avoided, however, is that adjudicators face the possibility of being simply dismissed at the pleasure of the executive branch of government. The fixed-term appointments in *Régie* were acceptable because they provided expressly that the decision-makers (called "directors" in *Régie*) could be dismissed only for specific reasons. The directors could also contest any dismissals in court. Sanctions were therefore available for any arbitrary interference by the executive in a director's term of office. The respondent in *Régie* also challenged the board's administrative control. It argued that there were so many points of contact between the liquor board and the minister responsible for the board's enabling legislation that the board's institutional independence was threatened. However, the Court held that administrative control was also sufficient. The Court reasoned that it was not unusual for a minister to have many points of contact with a tribunal under its responsibility. The Court noted further that no evidence had been provided to show that the minister could affect the decision-making process.[39]

It is easy to state the test for tribunal independence and to give illustrations of how the test has been applied in the jurisprudence. It is more challenging, however, to explain why flexibility is needed when applying the criteria for judicial independence to tribunals. Standard explanations point to the wide range of tribunal structures, the various ways that tribunals are connected to government, the great divergence in the nature and work of administrative bodies, and the many functions that any one administrative body may be asked to perform in tandem. These standard explanations also emphasize that the test for independence is often a way of investigating whether a reasonable apprehension of bias exists in a particular administrative context. Although such explanations take us to a certain point, they do not explain why tribunals ought not to have the same guarantees of structural independence—

---

[37] *Ibid.* at paras. 116-17.

[38] *Régie, supra* note 33.

[39] Nevertheless, the Supreme Court of Canada held that the liquor licensing board lacked the requisite degree of impartiality to meet the requirements of s. 23 of the Quebec Charter. This is because it was possible for one single employee to participate at every stage of the process leading up to the cancellation of a liquor permit, from investigation to adjudication. The possibility that an employee who had made submissions to the directors might then advise them in respect of the same matter was held to be problematic as it puts the same individual into conflicting roles within the institution. There was also no evidence of on-the-ground measures being put in place to prevent a single employee from playing multiple and possibly conflicting roles; see also *Brosseau v. Alberta Securities Commission*, [1989] 1 S.C.R. 301.

security of tenure, financial security, administrative control—as a court. Perhaps the best judicial attempt to explain normatively why the objective guarantees of judicial independence need not apply to administrative tribunals comes from the Supreme Court of Canada's decision in *Ocean Port Hotel*,[40] discussed in the next section.

In many cases, the objective guarantees of independence for the judiciary do not meet anything near a complete match for tribunals. With regard to administrative control, similar to courts, most tribunal chairs, like chief justices, are responsible for distributing their own caseload and for tribunal management. As well, the tribunal chair usually has the authority to allocate budgetary resources as effectively as possible. However, things differ considerably from the judiciary when it comes to financial security and security of tenure. Although the pay for a tribunal member is normally set by legislation, for part-time members in particular, the pay is often disproportionate to the skill contributed. Generally, tribunal service is seen as a type of public service, done more for honour than for glory or riches.[41] In the administrative tribunal context, security of tenure shows a similar marked difference from the judiciary. Tribunal members can be appointed for a variety of terms. Some statutes provide for fixed-term appointments, varying from months to years. In some cases, appointments are renewable; in others, the statute gives no mention of renewal; and in others still, appointments are not renewable at all.

One type of appointment, termed an "at pleasure" appointment because it allows the government to appoint a member for as long as the government deems fit, has generated significant controversy in administrative law jurisprudence. In essence, "at pleasure" appointments, theoretically, enable the government to remove a decision-maker whose decisions are not in line with its expectations. Given that tribunals are to be independent or "at arm's length" from government, "at pleasure" appointments open the door to the possibility of governmental interference with tribunal decision making. The issue of whether "at pleasure" appointments fail to provide adequate guarantees of independence from arbitrary interference from the executive branch of government was addressed in *Ocean Port Hotel*. The issues surrounding "at pleasure" appointments were not resolved, however, as the more recent case of *Keen v. Canada (Attorney General)*[42] demonstrates. For more than one reason, *Ocean Port Hotel* forms a turning point in the jurisprudence on the independence of administrative tribunals. It constitutes the second wave of jurisprudence in this area. We address it next, along with the practical risks of "at pleasure" appointments, illustrated by the later case of *Keen*.

1. *Ocean Port Hotel and Keen: Parliamentary Supremacy Versus Warding Off Interference*

a. Ocean Port Hotel

In its narrowest sense, the Supreme Court of Canada decision in *Ocean Port Hotel* is significant because it attempted to lay to rest the controversial issue of whether "at pleasure" appointments provide a satisfactory degree of independence for decision-makers sitting on

---

40 *Ocean Port Hotel*, *supra* note 3.

41 See online: Ontario Public Appointments Secretariat <http://www.pas.gov.on.ca/scripts/en/home.asp>.

42 2009 FC 353, [2009] 3 F.C.R. D-16 [*Keen*].

tribunals that impose penalties. This was the Supreme Court's first opportunity to address the crucial question of whether "at pleasure" appointments, which were clearly not as secure as fixed-term appointments, could provide an adequate image of independence from government. From a broader perspective, *Ocean Port Hotel* is an important administrative law case because it offers definitive opinions regarding the constitutional nature of courts and tribunals and the distinction between the two. On both levels, the Court's dicta offers reasons why administrative tribunals should not need the same degree of independence as courts.

The B.C. Liquor Appeal Board was a liquor-licensing body that could impose sanctions and remove licences upon finding that a licensee had contravened the province's *Liquor Control and Licensing Act*.[43] The Royal Canadian Mounted Police (RCMP) had reported that Ocean Port Hotel was responsible for five incidents that violated the Act, the regulations enacted under the statute, and the terms of its liquor licence. The Liquor Control and Licensing Branch, a regulatory branch established under the Act, consequently imposed a two-day suspension on Ocean Port's liquor licence. The Liquor Appeal Board held a hearing *de novo* and confirmed the suspension, finding that the evidence supported four of the five alleged infractions.

On appeal to the B.C. Court of Appeal, Ocean Port argued that the Liquor Appeal Board lacked sufficient independence to render a fair hearing. It submitted that the Board's decision was therefore invalid. The hotel took issue with the terms of appointment of the members of the Liquor Appeal Board. The Act indicated that the chair and the members of the Board were to serve "at the pleasure of the Lieutenant Governor in Council."

In analyzing the question, the B.C. Court of Appeal in *Ocean Port Hotel* focused on the similarities between the B.C. Liquor Appeal Board and its sister institution in Quebec. This comparison could be made easily, given that the Supreme Court of Canada decision in *Régie* had just come down. Gonthier J. in *Régie* had determined that the fixed-term appointments held by the directors of the *Régie des permis d'alcool* would not have been valid had they allowed the directors to be removed without cause—that is, at the pleasure of the executive branch of government. Because *Régie* was a judgment dealing with a body mandated to control the same industry and with adjudicative tasks similar to those of the B.C. Liquor Appeal Board, the Court of Appeal held that the Liquor Appeal Board members must also require more security of tenure than what was offered through "at pleasure" appointments. In its decision, the B.C. Court of Appeal stated that the decision to suspend a licence closely resembles a judicial decision and that the penalty was one of serious economic consequence. The B.C. Court of Appeal also took into account that the same contraventions of the *Liquor Control and Licensing Act* could have been prosecuted in the Provincial Court, where a greater level of independence would have been guaranteed. Moreover, the statute provided a lesser penalty for offences prosecuted in the Provincial Court.

On appeal to the Supreme Court of Canada, Ocean Port Hotel added a new argument. It submitted that, as an administrative tribunal exercising adjudicative functions, the Liquor Appeal Board required the same degree of independence guaranteed to the courts. The independence of the superior courts of inherent jurisdiction is enshrined in the Constitution.

---

43   R.S.B.C. 1996, c. 267.

Ocean Port relied on *Reference re Remuneration of Judges of the Prov. Court of P.E.I.*; *Ref re Independence and Impartiality of Judges of the Prov. Court of P.E.I.*[44] There, the Supreme Court of Canada held that judicial independence is an unwritten constitutional principle that applies not only to the superior courts of inherent jurisdiction but also extends to the Provincial Court of summary jurisdiction. In the *P.E.I. Reference*, Lamer C.J. held further that this unwritten constitutional principle is affirmed by the preamble of the Constitution, which indicates that Canada's Constitution is "similar in Principle to that of the United Kingdom."[45] Ocean Port argued that this unwritten, constitutional principle guaranteeing judicial independence should be interpreted to extend to administrative tribunals as well.

The Supreme Court of Canada disagreed. The Supreme Court asserted that there is no freestanding constitutional guarantee of administrative tribunal independence. The Court held that the enshrined constitutional protection of judicial independence could not be translated to the context of administrative decision-making bodies. In its reasons, the Court emphasized that judicial independence has historically developed to protect the judiciary from interference from the executive branch of government. By contrast, administrative tribunals are not separate from the executive. In the Court's words, administrative tribunals may be seen as "spanning the constitutional divide between the executive and judicial branches of government."[46] Tribunals are created precisely for the purpose of implementing the policies of the executive branch of government. In so doing, they may be required to make quasi-judicial decisions. However, their primary function as policy-makers and their status as extensions of the executive branch of government, make the degree of their independence a question most appropriately determined by Parliament or a provincial legislature. It is up to Parliament or the legislature to determine the structure, responsibilities, and degree of independence required of any particular tribunal. In this way, the Supreme Court in *Ocean Port Hotel* asserted that the will of the legislature should prevail in determining how much independence any given tribunal should have.

Furthermore, the Court reminded us that tribunal independence is a common-law principle of natural justice. As with all principles of natural justice, the degree of independence required at common law could be ousted by express statutory language or necessary statutory implication, so long as the statute is constitutionally valid. As a general rule, administrative tribunals do not attract Charter or quasi-constitutional requirements of independence. However, by virtue of the nature of their work, some tribunals may be subject to these protections. This was the characteristic that distinguished the liquor board in *Régie* from the one in *Ocean Port Hotel*. In Quebec, adjudicative bodies had all been made subject to the Quebec Charter's quasi-constitutional guarantee of independence, which ultimately required them to possess a greater guarantee of independence than tribunals in British Columbia. Finally, the Court pointed out that the *P.E.I. Reference* made no assertions that the unwritten constitutional guarantees of judicial independence were to apply to administrative tribunals as well. In sum, *Ocean Port Hotel* affirmed no general constitutional guarantee of

---

44 [1997] 3 S.C.R. 3 [*P.E.I. Reference*].

45 The British *Act of Settlement* of 1701 was the historical inspiration for the judicature provisions of our Constitution.

46 *Ocean Port Hotel*, *supra* note 3 at para. 24.

independence for administrative tribunals. The only way that constitutional or constitution-like protections can be afforded to a tribunal is if the actions of the particular tribunal trigger the protections offered by the Canadian Charter or by one of the provincial or federal quasi-constitutional statutes.[47]

On a theoretical level, it is up to the legislature or Parliament to create enabling statutes that foster independent decision making when legislating for a variety of different tribunals. *Ocean Port Hotel* affirms this and implicitly encourages legislative policy-makers to consider the specificities of various tribunals, to retain and promote factors that foster independence, and to eliminate those that do not. In some circumstances, use of the judicial conditions of independence may be useful. But, policy-makers should be open to considering factors that actually affect the independence of administrative decision-makers in various contexts. In particular, one wonders whether it may be useful to examine different types of tribunals according to their statutory nature. For example, in the case of parliamentary officers—access-to-information and privacy commissioners and ombudsmen—these bodies have a more direct link to the legislature than to an executive government department. This can lead to the absence or presence of particular challenges with respect to independence that are specific to them. As well, the perception of what a tribunal does and to whom it owes its allegiance may also affect its independence. This may be best reflected in the culture of the institution itself. Empirical exploration of these issues would undoubtedly prove fruitful.

Even as early as *Valente*, the first Supreme Court decision to deal with the issue of judicial independence, the Court noted that the three criteria identified to guarantee independence were not fixed or exhaustive and may evolve over time. *Ocean Port Hotel* seems to have opened the door to allowing us to determine more genuine criteria of independence for administrative tribunals.

b. Keen v. Canada

Although *Ocean Port Hotel* represented the first time that the Supreme Court addressed the question of whether there is a constitutional guarantee of tribunal independence that could guarantee security of tenure to the same degree as their judicial counterparts, it was not the first time that inherent problems with "at pleasure" tribunal appointments had been raised. Several cases prior to *Ocean Port* had addressed the question tangentially.[48] In these cases, the main issue had been whether compensation was owed to appointees whose terms had been terminated early because of restructuring of government tribunals. In determining that compensation was owed, some lower courts had admonished the government for interfering with terms that had been set through order in council.[49] These decisions stressed that the appearance of independence would be undermined if the government could freely change

---

[47]   See the chart and accompanying discussion in section II, Sources of the Guarantee of an Independent and Impartial Tribunal.

[48]   See e.g. *Hewat v. Ontario* (1997), 32 O.R. (3d) 622 (Div. Ct.); varied (1998), 37 O.R. (3d) 161 (C.A.) [*Hewat*]; *Dewar v. Ontario* (1996), 30 O.R. (3d) 334 (Div. Ct.); (1998), 37 O.R. (3d) 170 (C.A.); *Wells v. Newfoundland*, [1999] 3 S.C.R. 199; *Preston v. British Columbia* (1994), 92 B.C.L.R. (2d) 298.

[49]   See, in particular, *Hewat* (C.A.), *supra* note 48.

terms of appointments. Yet, neither *Ocean Port Hotel* nor the prior lower-court decisions addressed the main underlying fundamental problem with "at pleasure" appointments— that the government *is not legally prevented* from removing appointees for the decisions they make. No clearer example of this exists than the case of Linda Keen.

Uproar ensued when Canada's Nuclear Safety Commission President Linda Keen was removed from her job over a decision to keep a nuclear power plant closed for its failure to meet safety standards. The Canada Nuclear Safety Commission regulates all nuclear facilities and activities in Canada to ensure their compliance with health, safety, security, and environmental standards as well as with Canada's international obligations. It does not have jurisdiction over the medical health care of Canadians. The commission reports to Parliament through the minister of natural resources.[50] In 2007, the commission decided to keep closed a nuclear power plant that had been temporarily shut down for routine maintenance because of its failure to meet safety standards. This nuclear reactor, however, was also a primary source for the production of medical isotopes used in health care in the country and around the world.

Natural Resources Minister Gary Lunn was concerned that the commission had not reopened the nuclear power plant in question. The closure had caused a severe shortage of the medical isotopes necessary for the critical health care of many Canadians and people around the world. The minister participated in conference calls with the president of the commission, members of the commission, and the licence holder, at which he requested that a hearing be convened immediately in order to approve the restart of the reactor. Minister Lunn then took advantage of the statutory directive power under the *Nuclear Safety and Control Act*[51] to require the commission to take into account, in its decision making, "the health of Canadians who, for medical purposes, depend on nuclear substances produced by nuclear reactors." Yet, the directive power allows only for directives of "general application on broad policy matters" to be issued to the commission.[52] Finally, the minister brought about the emergency enactment of a piece of legislation (a step that is always open to governments to do) that forced the reactor to remain open for a period of time.[53]

---

[50]   More information about the work of the Nuclear Safety Commission can be found online: Canadian Nuclear Safety Commission <http://www.nuclearsafety.gc.ca/eng>.

[51]   S.C. 1997, c. 9.

[52]   With respect to directives from Cabinet to the Canadian Nuclear Safety Commission, s. 19 of the *Nuclear Safety and Control Act, ibid.*, is the relevant provision. It reads:

DIRECTIVES
      19(1) The Governor in Council may, by order, issue to the Commission directives of general application on broad policy matters with respect to the objects of the Commission.
      (2) An order made under this section is binding on the Commission.
      (3) A copy of each order made under this section shall be
            (a) published in the Canada Gazette; and
            (b) laid before each House of Parliament.

[53]   *An Act to permit the resumption and continuation of the operation of the National Research Universal Reactor at Chalk River*, S.C. 2007, c. 31 (12 December 2007), online: Department of Justice Canada <http://laws-lois .justice.gc.ca/eng/N-15.8/page-1.html>.

About two weeks after these events had occurred, the minister wrote to the president of the commission, asking her to explain why certain evidence had not been taken into account in the commission's decision making and why the directive issued by his office had been ignored. In his letter,[54] Mr. Lunn questioned Ms. Keen's judgment and whether she was duly executing the requirements of the position. In his opinion, her decision demonstrated a grave inability to manage risk to the health of Canadians. Minister Lunn indicated that he was considering asking the governor in council to remove Ms. Keen from her position as president, and asked for her comments.

Ms. Keen responded to Minister Lunn's letter, refuting his assertions. Ms. Keen was also scheduled to appear before a parliamentary committee to explain her position on the matter. However, at 10 p.m. the night before the parliamentary hearing, her position as president was officially terminated. The order in council that removed Ms. Keen stated that the governor in council had considered her letter, but found that she had failed to demonstrate the necessary leadership to address the isotope crisis in a timely way. It stated further that the governor in council had lost confidence in her. The termination cut short Ms. Keen's second five-year term of appointment as president. Ms. Keen was removed as president and relegated to an ordinary member of the commission, but she resigned from the commission several months later.

Ms. Keen applied to the Federal Court for judicial review.[55] At issue was whether she received adequate procedural fairness in the manner of her dismissal. The Court held that the circumstances of her termination were sufficient to satisfy the requirements of fairness for an "at pleasure" appointment (which is how her appointment as president was characterized). The governor in council's dismissal was therefore upheld.

How should the messages from *Ocean Port Hotel* and *Keen* be reconciled? *Ocean Port Hotel* affirmed that a variety of tribunal appointments can satisfy the requirement of security of tenure so long as there are no constitutional standards at play and the terms of the appointment derive from constitutionally valid legislation. However, cases such as *Keen* show that, as a practical reality, governments still can, and do, interfere with administrative decision making because of improper understandings about tribunal accountability. In particular, there is a strong argument that the minister misunderstood the nature of the relationship between the executive and the commission. The commission was not accountable to the minister for the decisions rendered in individual cases. Individual cases are not subject to ministerial oversight, and their outcomes are not meant to be dependent on ministerial input or, worse, ministerial pressure. Legislative design would have been necessary to support such ministerial intervention. One might argue that the "at pleasure" appointment facilitated Ms. Keen's removal.

The Federal Court decision also presents challenges. The Federal Court was faithful to the Supreme Court's guidance in *Dunsmuir*,[56] which provided that a lower level of procedural fairness is required on termination of an "at pleasure" appointee than by the dismissal

---

54 At one point, the letters between Linda Keen and Gary Lunn were posted on the Internet.

55 *Keen, supra* note 42, Hughes J.

56 See *Dunsmuir v. New Brunswick*, 2008 SCC 9, [2008] 1 S.C.R. 190.

of an appointee instated on terms of good behaviour. *Dunsmuir* had specified that, with respect to "at pleasure" appointments, procedural fairness is needed "to ensure that public power is not exercised capriciously."[57] In this vein, the Federal Court held that Ms. Keen had been provided with adequate procedural fairness. It was enough that the minister had written to Ms. Keen advising her that he was contemplating recommending to the governor in council that her position as president be terminated, that he had provided her with the reasons for his concern, and had offered her an opportunity to respond. The Federal Court also noted that the order in council terminating Keen's appointment stated that the governor in council had "carefully considered [her] submission."[58] However, can one genuinely say that the exchange of correspondence and the inclusion of the wording in the order in council served to ensure that the Crown had not acted capriciously? Moreover, this is a situation in which a requirement to provide reasons could be beneficial. One would expect that someone in the position of Ms. Keen, who has suffered a significant impact from the loss of her livelihood, could, practically, benefit from knowing the final reason for her termination. At the very least it would allow her to use that knowledge on further review. The loss of livelihood is a factual element that also seems to fit well with *Baker*'s requirement for a higher duty of procedural fairness.

In the 2000s, some provincial jurisdictions reinforced their legislative enactments to ensure that tribunal members have fixed terms of appointment. An example of this is found in British Columbia. The B.C. *Administrative Tribunals Act* (ATA)[59] was created to provide guiding principles and uniformity to various aspects of the administrative justice system in the province. Section 3 of the ATA suggests that tribunal members be appointed for an initial term of two to four years with reappointment for additional terms of up to five years. An even more profound example is found in Quebec. In 2005, the enabling statute of the Administrative Tribunal of Quebec (ATQ) was modified so that members would hold tenure during good behaviour. Essentially an appointment for life, tenure on the ATQ is at the highest level of tenure possible and comparable to that of the judges of the courts of inherent jurisdiction.[60] Recent jurisprudence in Quebec has also shown success in extending similar permanency of tenure to another adjudicative body, the Commission des lésions professionnelles.[61] Outside Canada, the United Kingdom enacted legislation in 2007 that grants administrative tribunal decision-makers the same guarantees of structural independence as judges and aims to bring tribunals within the realm of the judiciary.[62] Finally, some

---

57   *Ibid.* at para. 115.

58   *Keen, supra* note 42 at para. 54.

59   S.B.C. 2004, c. 45 [ATA].

60   See the *Administrative Justice Act*, R.S.Q., c. J-3, s. 38, as am. 1996, c. 54, s. 38; 2005, c. 17, s. 2.

61   See *Association des juges administratifs de la Commission des lésions professionnelles c. Québec (Procureur général)*, 2011 QCCS 1614 (decision on appeal). See, generally, on the independence of the ATQ, *Barreau de Montréal v. Québec (Procureure générale)*, [2001] J.Q. No. 3882 (C.A.) (QL).

62   See the *Tribunals, Courts and Enforcement Act 2007*, c. 15 [TCEA], s. 1. See also Lord Justice Carnwath, "Tribunals and the Courts—the UK Model" (2011) 24 Can. J. Admin. L. & Prac. 5.

authors have raised the question whether administrative independence in Canada meets international law standards.[63]

C. Reasserting the Push for Independence: Unwritten Constitutional Principles, Tribunal Independence, and the Rule of Law

The Supreme Court of Canada in *Ocean Port Hotel* clearly indicated that there is no free-standing constitutional guarantee of independence for administrative tribunals.[64] As noted above, this is because administrative tribunals form part of the executive branch of government. The Court held that because constitutional guarantees of independence serve primarily to protect the judiciary from interference by the executive, they cannot work to protect tribunals from the branch of government of which they are a part. At the same time, Supreme Court and other Canadian jurisprudence has shown a willingness to expand the notion of "court" to allow litigants before some lesser judicial entities the benefits of constitutional guarantees of independence. The third wave of tribunal independence jurisprudence is marked by litigants reasserting a push for tribunals to have the same independence as courts. Despite the holding in *Ocean Port Hotel*, advocates maintain that this independence can be guaranteed by the unwritten constitutional principles that protect our courts of inherent jurisdiction—principles that stem from the U.K. *Act of Settlement, 1701*.

In the 2006 B.C. Supreme Court decision in *McKenzie*,[65] the petitioner argued that the unwritten constitutional guarantees of independence should be expanded to apply to residential tenancy arbitrators. Her arguments asserted that such arbitrators were at the high end of the adjudicative spectrum. Decided shortly after *Ocean Port Hotel*, *Bell Canada v. Canadian Telephone Employees Association*[66] had suggested a spectrum of decision-making types in which highly adjudicative tribunals endowed with court-like powers and procedures could require more stringent requirements of procedural fairness, including a higher degree of independence.[67] The petitioner in *McKenzie* argued that, because several other courts seemingly on the outer edge of the judiciary had been deemed to attract unwritten constitutional guarantees of independence, residential tenancy arbitrators, because of the nature of their work, should also attract such guarantees. The petitioner, a residential tenancy arbitrator who had had her appointment rescinded mid-term, also argued that it would be a clear violation of the rule of law if such guarantees were not given to administrative bodies at the high end of the adjudicative spectrum—for example, residential tenancy arbitrators.[68]

---

[63]   See Gerald Heckman & Lorne Sossin, "How Do Canadian Administrative Law Protections Live Up to International Human Rights Standards? The Case of Independence" (2005) 50 McGill L.J. 193.

[64]   *Ocean Port Hotel, supra* note 3 at paras. 20-24.

[65]   *Supra* note 3.

[66]   2003 SCC 36, [2003] 1 S.C.R. 884 [*Bell Canada*].

[67]   By contrast, the Court held that tribunals falling at the other end of the spectrum that dealt primarily with developing or supervising the implementation of particular government policies may not need to offer as high a degree of procedural protection and require less independence from the executive.

[68]   The concept of the rule of law is discussed by Mary Liston in Chapter 2, Governments in Miniature: The Rule of Law in the Administrative State.

The respondents contended that a provision of the provincial *Public Sector Employers Act*[69] allowed for this rescission. The Court addressed two main issues in *McKenzie*: (1) a narrow question interpreting the *Public Sector Employers Act*, and (2) a much broader question determining whether the position of residential tenancy arbitrators was protected from interference by constitutional guarantees, including guarantees of their security of tenure.[70]

The B.C. Supreme Court agreed with the petitioner's argument. McEwan J. first set out the principles laid down in the *P.E.I. Reference*, which held that judicial independence not only stemmed from specific provisions of the Charter—namely, ss. 7 and 11(d))—but also derived from unwritten constitutional principles dating back to the U.K. *Act of Settlement, 1701*. That these principles applied in Canada was evident from the preamble to the Constitution, which referred to "a Constitution similar in principle to that of the United Kingdom."[71] Second, the B.C. Supreme Court noted that the Supreme Court of Canada, in *Alberta v. Ell*,[72] had determined that these unwritten constitutional principles serve to protect the judicial independence of justices of the peace, a class of decision-makers for whom the issue of independence had been debatable for some time. McEwan J. also noted that in Ontario, the Court of Appeal had found that deputy judges in the small claims court also attracted such constitutional guarantees.[73] In light of the extension of the principles of independence to classes of adjudicators other than superior and provincial court judges, the B.C. Supreme Court found that judicial independence should apply to residential tenancy arbitrators as well. Moreover, the jurisdiction of residential tenancy arbitrators had been taken directly from the courts of civil jurisdiction. Justice McEwan reasoned that the rule of law required this result because the same matter would have been decided by decision-makers endowed with greater independence if landlord and tenant cases had not been carved out of the courts.

One wonders about other implications that flow from *McKenzie*. For example, the success of the case lay partly in the fact that residential tenancy arbitrators are similar to courts in most of the work that they do. Although some argue for judicial independence for "purely adjudicative" administrative decision-making bodies,[74] what about administrative bodies endowed with both adjudicative and policy-making functions? Would it be possible for constitutional guarantees to attach solely to the adjudicative functions of a multifunctional tribunal? Moreover, in light of the holding in *Ocean Port Hotel*, can any tribunal be said to be purely adjudicative? Through their decision making, all tribunals are said to create policy.

---

[69]   R.S.B.C. 1996, c. 384.

[70]   Indeed, one wonders whether the Court needed to address this broader constitutional question at all. From the way that it framed the issues, it might have been sufficient, once it had determined that the statute did not allow for the rescission, to end its judicial analysis at that point. See the B.C.S.C. decision in *McKenzie, supra* note 3 at para. 5.

[71]   See *P.E.I. Reference, supra* note 44; see also preamble to *Constitution Act, 1867, supra* note 20.

[72]   2003 SCC 35, [2003] S.C.R. 857.

[73]   See *Ontario Deputy Judges' Association v. Ontario (Attorney General)* (2006), 210 O.A.C. 94, 80 O.R. (3d) 481 (C.A.).

[74]   See e.g. S. Ronald Ellis, "The Justicizing of Quasi-Judicial Tribunals (Part I)" (2006) 19 Can. J. Admin. L. & Prac. 303.

Was the Supreme Court in *Ocean Port* correct in this assertion? If so, does this policy making not alter the concept of a purely adjudicative tribunal?

McKenzie raises several interesting questions in the debate on tribunal independence. As part of its reasoning, the Court maintained that the rule of law, through the affirmation of the principles of judicial independence in this case, will serve to keep the legislature from inappropriately vesting tribunals with diminished forms of natural justice if budgetary or other pressures make it convenient to do so. Is the court's decision one of judicial functionalism, as McEwan J. seems to assert, or does his reasoning imply an interference by the courts with the operation of the legislature? The Court's reasoning also raises a much wider question of judicial activism that is often seen in judicial review matters. This is the question of who, as between the legislature in creating the tribunal and the judiciary in reviewing its functioning, is in the best position to dictate the normative aspects of the administrative justice system.

D. The Appointment and Removal Process: Institutions, Ideologies, and Institutional Culture

This section has presented some of the most pressing issues of independence and impartiality currently relating to tribunals. As suggested by the cases discussed, some of the most controversial and contested issues relating to the independence of administrative decision-making bodies are those dealing with appointments, removal, and the guarantee of security of tenure. Whether as a member of the legal community or the tribunal community, one hears concerns expressed about partisan political appointments, the loss of livelihood as a result of short fixed-term appointments, and the removal of members. However, with respect to the appointment process, to what extent is it acceptable for a tribunal to reflect a particular ideology? Can ideology ever play a positive role in relation to tribunal member selection and retention? Although there is often controversy over appointees possibly reflecting the ideology of a political party, what about the ideology that comes from the culture of the institutional workplace of the tribunal members? Is it acceptable for a chair to seek members who will contribute to the values of the tribunal? And when, if ever, is it feasible for a government to appoint members who reflect certain political values?[75] Looking at this question from the opposite perspective brings it into sharper focus—namely, is it ever possible to make appointments that completely evade political thought or ideology?

Tribunals are distinct from courts. They are institutions in which tribunal members and staff work together within a broad framework of regulatory governance aimed at managing a particular sector or industry through their expertise. Tribunals may be statutorily designed so that their members reflect the diversity of interests prevalent within the sector or industry that they are managing.[76] Institutional culture can play an important part in achieving the

---

[75] On the issue of the validity of a change of government resulting in an overt change of tribunal of leadership, see *Saskatchewan Federation of Labour v. Saskatchewan (Attorney General, Department of Advanced Education, Employment and Labour)*, 2010 SKCA 27.

[76] For example, labour boards are often designed so that they maintain a tripartite representation of labour, management, and a neutral perspective on panels.

often multifunctional goals of an administrative tribunal.[77] Having a workplace culture in which all members feel comfortable airing their diverse opinions on how the law should be furthered may be more constructive than having several members who each staunchly put diverse views in their decisions. In light of this, with respect to the removal process, is it legitimate to remove members who are disruptive to the workplace culture?

In summary, it is noteworthy that although security of tenure, financial security, and administrative control may figure within the independence issues discussed, they do not form the main organizing axes of the challenges to independence and impartiality that arise in the everyday work of tribunals. Appointments, adjudicative independence, and managing necessary interactions with the executive branch of government are among the central independence-related concerns in a tribunal's regular operational context. This is one example of how elements of the judicial paradigm may not reconcile easily with the daily operational context of administrative tribunals. A second broad example can be found in the nature of bias in the administrative state. As we will see in the next section of this chapter, determining when disqualifying bias exists in the administrative state also (like independence) requires the consideration of several contextual factors, including the nature and functioning of the particular administrative body under scrutiny.

V. Reasonable Apprehension of Bias

Challenges for reasonable apprehension of bias arise from a variety of administrative law situations. These situations relate to perceived partiality either on the part of an individual decision-maker or on an institutional level. Traditional concerns about bias—for example, the decision-maker has a direct, pecuniary interest in the outcome—stem from easy-to-understand occurrences that would be fatal to any decision-making system, including the judiciary. Others stem from the very nature of the administrative state, which itself comprises a wide range of administrative actors, from government ministers to adjudicative bodies, with very different natures and purposes. Included in the list of situations that have been attacked for reasonable apprehension of bias are the appearance of perceived attitudinal bias in the decision-making process and concern about the practices used by administrative bodies to promote consistency and efficiency within their work. Two such administrative practices that have prompted challenges for reasonable apprehension of bias in the jurisprudence are full-board meetings and the use of "lead cases," discussed in section V.B.2 below.

A. The Rule Against Bias

As discussed at the beginning of this chapter, the *nemo judex* rule aims to maintain public confidence in the administration of justice. The rule against bias contributes to this function by ensuring that decision-makers are not reasonably perceived to be deciding matters that

---

77   See, generally, on the importance of understanding the on-the-ground values of government administration, Lorne Sossin, "From Neutrality to Compassion: The Place of Civil Service Values and Legal Norms in the Exercise of Administrative Discretion" (2005) 55 U.T.L.J. 427. On the importance of institutional culture to the development of consistency, see K. Whitaker, M. Gottheil & M. Uhlmann, "Consistency in Tribunal Decision Making: What Really Goes on Behind Closed Doors …" in Jacobs & Mactavish, *supra* note 2.

will benefit them or those with whom they have significant relationships. The rule seeks equally to avoid decision-making partiality that will result in negative treatment of a party occurring as a result of a decision-maker's interests and relationships. Finally, the rule against bias serves generally to prevent decision-makers from making decisions based on factors that are irrelevant to the decision-making process. The concern regards the decision-maker's current or prior knowledge, relationships, actions, or practices. Allegations of reasonable apprehension of bias exist in two major forms in administrative law: (1) *perceptions of individual bias*, which deal with the impartiality of individual decision-makers; and (2) *perceptions of institutional bias*, which deal with whether reasonable perceptions of partiality regarding the decision-making body as a whole can be raised in a substantial number of cases.

Like independence, the rule against bias aims to preserve the appearance of impartiality in the decision-making process. There have been close to 400 challenges stemming from perceived bias brought before administrative boards and tribunals in the past five years.[78] The rule against bias is one of the oldest common-law doctrines. Yet, reasonable apprehension of bias is clearly still a common challenge raised in the current practice of administrative law. All administrative actors required to meet the standards of procedural fairness—including administrative tribunals, ministers, and other public officials—are subject to the rule against bias. An allegation of perceived bias must be brought to the decision-maker by the party alleging it on the first available occasion. If the claim is successful, its effect will be to quash any decisions made and have the proceedings reheard by a newly constituted panel.

In this section, we consider the common-law test (and its variations) for determining whether disqualifying bias exists in an administrative decision-making process. We examine the most common situations in which a reasonable apprehension of bias has been found to arise. We also discuss various practices of tribunals and other administrative actors that have incited allegations of reasonable apprehension of bias. Throughout this section, we consider the issue of bias from the perspective of both actors within the administrative state and the courts.

B. The Reasonable Apprehension of Bias Test

The test for bias relies on perception. Whether bias *actually* exists in a decision-making context is not the question; to have a decision quashed, it is sufficient that a reasonable person with an informed understanding of how the tribunal functions perceives that the decision making is biased. The classic test was formulated in *Committee for Justice and Liberty v. National Energy Board*,[79] a case in which the chair of a panel of the National Energy Board was responsible for receiving applications and issuing certificates for a pipeline. The chair, Mr. Crowe, had previously been involved in a study group that had put in an application for consideration. The majority of the Supreme Court of Canada held that there was a reasonable apprehension of bias with respect to Crowe's participation as chair.

---

[78]   A search on Quicklaw of decisions by all boards and tribunals across the country between January 2007 and January 2012 produced 368 cases responding to allegations of reasonable apprehension of bias.

[79]   [1978] 1 S.C.R. 369 [*Committee for Justice and Liberty*].

The test for determining reasonable apprehension of bias was formulated in the dissenting opinion of Justice DeGrandpré. However, it has been used consistently by the Supreme Court and lower courts since that time. DeGrandpré J. articulated the test in the following way:

> [T]he apprehension of bias must be a reasonable one held by reasonable and right minded persons, applying themselves to the question and obtaining thereon the required information. In the words of the Court of Appeal, that test is "what would an informed person, viewing the matter realistically and practically—and having thought the matter through—conclude. Would he think that it is more likely than not that Mr. Crowe, whether consciously or unconsciously, would not decide fairly?"[80]

Moreover, the grounds for the apprehension of bias must be substantial. A real likelihood or probability of bias should be demonstrated. Mere suspicion of bias is insufficient for the test to be met. The courts often talk of demonstrating the likelihood of bias on a balance of probabilities. The reasonable, well-informed person is also not one who is overly sensitive.[81] The application of the test has broadened to encompass not only individual decision-makers but also decision-making institutions. The institutional aspect of bias was first recognized in *Lippé*, where the test was identified as determining whether there could be "a reasonable apprehension of bias in the mind of a fully informed person *in a substantial number of cases*."[82]

The standard for bias varies, depending on context. What will give rise to a reasonable apprehension of bias in one administrative decision-making context may not do so in another. For example, although both cases dealt with a decision-maker's prior involvement with a particular matter, the Supreme Court of Canada held that the involvement of the National Energy Board's chair caused a reasonable apprehension of bias in *Committee for Justice and Liberty*, discussed above, but did not so find when the Quebec minister of the environment ordered a company to prepare a site characterization study and decontamination measures in *Imperial Oil Ltd. v. Quebec (Minister of the Environment)*.[83] The difference is explained by the central idea animating procedural fairness in administrative law: the nature and context of the decision-making process drives the content of procedural fairness, including what constitutes impartiality. Primarily because of the quasi-judicial nature of the National Energy Board's functions in determining applications, the Court in *Committee for Justice and Liberty* found that Mr. Crowe's involvement in the decisions leading up to one party's application to the board was enough to suggest that he might make a biased appraisal in his adjudicative capacity. By contrast, the nature of the work done by the minister in *Imperial Oil* did not require him to act in a truly adjudicative capacity. His work was of a political nature and in the public interest. In this way, the minister's prior involvement in

---

80   *Ibid.* at 394.

81   See, generally, on the test for reasonable apprehension of bias and the standard that must be met, *Committee for Justice and Liberty*, *supra* note 79 at 394-95; *Bell Canada*, *supra* note 66 at para. 50; *R. v. S. (R.D.)*, [1997] 3 S.C.R. 484 at paras. 31 and 112.

82   See *R. v. Lippé*, [1991] 2 S.C.R. 114 at para. 59 (emphasis added). See also *Matsqui*, *supra* note 35, where the Court confirmed the test for the administrative context.

83   2003 SCC 58, [2003] 2 S.C.R. 624 [*Imperial Oil*].

decontaminating a site over which lawsuits had been brought against him did not cause him to be in a conflict of interest when he later exercised statutory authority to order a company to remedy the contamination.[84] Determining which procedural safeguards, including the degree of independence and impartiality, are needed in any particular administrative context is a matter of balancing several factors including the nature of the decision being made, the nature of the statutory scheme, and the agency's choice of procedures.[85]

Allegations of reasonable apprehension of bias exist in two major forms in administrative law—individual bias and institutional bias. In the following sections, we examine each of these forms of disqualifying bias and explore the variations in the standard used to determine the existence of a reasonable apprehension of bias in different contexts.

1. Perceptions of Individual Bias

Administrative law jurisprudence has established four situations in which a reasonable apprehension of bias may arise vis-à-vis an individual decision-maker. These are situations in which the decision-maker may reasonably be perceived to have:

1. a pecuniary or material interest in the outcome of the matter being decided;
2. personal relationships with those involved in the dispute;
3. prior knowledge or information about the matter in dispute; or
4. an attitudinal predisposition toward an outcome.

Each of these is discussed in turn. An allegation can be brought on more than one ground—for example, prior involvement and attitudinal bias, or personal relationship and material interest.

a. Pecuniary or Material Interest in the Outcome

i. Pecuniary Interest

The existence of a decision-maker's direct pecuniary interest in the outcome of a case is one of the clearest circumstances giving rise to disqualification for reasonable apprehension of bias. The *nemo judex* maxim is designed to prohibit an administrative actor from making decisions that advance his or her own cause. Standing to receive a monetary gain fits the notion of advancing one's cause in an archetypical way. The seminal case setting out the common law's strict stance against pecuniary interest is *Dimes v. Grand Junction Canal Co.*,[86]

---

84   *Ibid.*

85   The Supreme Court presented a non-exhaustive list of factors in *Baker v. Canada (Minister of Citizenship and Immigration)*, [1999] 2 S.C.R. 817. These factors include (1) the nature of the decision being made and the process followed in making it; (2) the nature of the statutory scheme and the terms of the statute pursuant to which the body operates; (3) the importance of the decision to the individual or individuals affected; (4) the legitimate expectations of the person challenging the decision; and (5) the choices of procedure made by the agency itself. For a broader discussion of these factors see Grant Huscroft's Chapter 5, From Natural Justice to Fairness: Thresholds, Content, and the Role of Judicial Review, and *IWA v. Consolidated-Bathurst Packaging Ltd.*, [1990] 1 S.C.R. 282 [*Consolidated-Bathurst*].

86   [1852] Eng. R. 789, 10 E.R. 301, 3 H.L.C. 759.

in which a decision of the Lord Chancellor of England was set aside because of his shareholder interest in a company that was a party to the proceedings.

Although the common law may be unequivocal when it comes to disqualifying a decision-maker who has a direct pecuniary interest, it becomes more flexible when dealing with cases in which the financial interest is indirect, as opposed to direct. Consider the example of *Energy Probe v. Canada (Atomic Energy Control Board)*.[87] There, the Atomic Energy Control Board renewed the operating licence of a nuclear generating station run by Ontario Hydro. A part-time member of the panel was also the president of a company that supplied cables to nuclear power plants. This member had also been a past director and shareholder of the company. The company had supplied cables to Ontario Hydro in the past after having successfully completed a competitive tender process. Energy Probe contested the decision to renew Ontario Hydro's licence, arguing that the decision should be quashed because of the member's participation. The majority of the Federal Court of Appeal was of the opinion that a reasonable apprehension of bias had not been established. They adopted the reasons of Justice Reed, who, at first instance, had held that a pecuniary interest must be direct and certain in order to give rise to a reasonable apprehension of bias. On the date of the hearing relating to the licences, the part-time member in question did not have a contract with Ontario Hydro or one that would take effect during the life of the new licence. He also was not a shareholder at the time of the hearings. Justice Reed held that his interest was therefore not direct. Moreover, there was no certainty that the part-time member would sell cables to Ontario Hydro in the future. The contracts that the company had held in the past had been contingent on success in a tendering process. *Energy Probe* therefore stands for the proposition that only direct and certain financial interest can constitute pecuniary bias. However, Justice Heald, for a minority of the Federal Court of Appeal, would have held that instead of focusing on directness and certainty, a more rational test would have determined whether the benefits in question stemmed from the decision to be rendered, and whether the benefits would be so sufficiently likely to occur that they would "colour" the case in the eyes of the decision-maker.

In some cases, pecuniary interest may be held not to give rise to a reasonable apprehension of bias if the decision-maker's gain is no more than that of the average person in a widespread group of benefit recipients.[88] Last, we know that, as a general principle, the common law must cede to legislative will. The law relating to pecuniary interest in reasonable apprehension of bias is no different. Statutory authorization that allows for indirect pecuniary benefit has prevailed over the common-law rule against bias in contexts such as the regulation of egg marketing[89] and for some self-regulated discipline committees.[90] In these contexts, the legislation usually requires that members be drawn from the professional community and the courts generally find that the prospect of such members deciding in a manner that

---

[87]   [1985] 1 F.C. 563, 15 D.L.R. (4th) 48.

[88]   Exclusions from the general rule have been created by legislation and at common law. See e.g. *Municipal Government Act*, R.S.A. 2000, c. M-26, s. 170(3)(i) and *R. v. Justices of Sunderland*, [1901] 2 K.B. 357 (Eng. C.A.).

[89]   *Burnbrae Farms v. Canadian Egg Marketing Agency*, [1976] 2 F.C. 217 (C.A.).

[90]   *Pearlman v. Manitoba Law Society Judicial Committee*, [1991] 2 S.C.R. 869.

would undermine competition for their own self-interest to be too speculative and remote to incite a reasonable apprehension of bias.[91]

ii. Non-Pecuniary Material Interest

Although monetary interest is the classic personal interest giving rise to a reasonable apprehension of bias, other forms of material interest have also led to disqualification. For example, a decision of a band council to evict a band member so that his house could be given to a larger family was set aside because an intended resident of the home was one of the councillors.[92] The case of *Service Employees International Union, Local 204 v. Johnson*,[93] a case discussed in detail below in relation to prior knowledge, presents a more involved example. There, the members of the Ontario Labour Relations Board had a potential interest in a case before them dealing with the circumstances in which the government could terminate their appointments.

b. Personal Relationships with Those Involved in the Dispute

When we speak of the personal relationships of decision-makers giving rise to a reasonable apprehension of bias, it is not only their relationships with the parties that can be disqualifying. Significant relationships between administrative actors and others involved in the matter—for example, counsel and witnesses[94]—must also be considered. Key factors to consider are whether the relationship presents a significant enough interest to affect the impartiality of the decision-maker and the amount of time that has passed—that is, whether the relationship is current enough to reasonably pose a significant threat to impartiality.

Although it is outside the administrative law context, a basic example of a personal relationship giving rise to reasonable apprehension of bias is found in the House of Lords' decision in *In re Pinochet*.[95] The *Pinochet* application asked the House of Lords to determine whether former Chilean head of state Pinochet was protected by a continued immunity or could he be extradited to stand trial for crimes against humanity committed in Chile. Pinochet was in England at the time for medical treatment. At the proceedings, Amnesty International, a major intervener, argued in support of Pinochet's extradition. Unbeknown to

---

91 See also *Matsqui, supra* note 35, where this idea was most explicitly stated by Lamer C.J. Municipal law is another area in which pecuniary interests are legislatively addressed. See e.g. the Alberta *Municipal Government Act, supra.* note 88.

92 *Obichon v. Heart Lake First Nation No. 176*, [1988] F.C.J. No. 307 (QL), 21 F.T.R. 1 (T.D.).

93 (1997), 35 O.R. (3d) 345 (Gen. Div.), CanLII 12280 (Ont. Sup. Ct.) [*SEIU*]. This case is discussed in detail below because it relates to reasonable apprehension of bias arising from prior knowledge.

94 For two interesting and contrasting cases concerning expert witnesses before tribunals who were subsequently appointed to the tribunals before the tribunal's decision was rendered, see *Li v. College of Physicians & Surgeons (Ontario)* (2004), 21 Admin. L.R. (4th) 270 (Ont. Div. Ct.) and *Stetler v. Ontario (Agriculture, Food & Rural Affairs Appeal Tribunal)* (2005), 76 O.R. (3d) 321 at paras. 90-97 (C.A.). In these cases, the issue at hand was whether the tribunal would give more weight to the testimony of the expert witnesses because of their elevation to the position of tribunal member.

95 [1999] U.K.H.L. 52.

Pinochet, a member of the House of Lords, Lord Hoffman, had connections with Amnesty International at the time of the hearing. Lord Hoffman was not only a director and chair of Amnesty International Charity Limited, his wife also did administrative work for Amnesty International's press and publications department. The matter was quashed for reasonable apprehension of bias and a new hearing was held. The House of Lords held that, although he was not technically a party to the matter before the Law Lords, Lord Hoffman's involvement with an affiliated charity that was mandated to promote the same goals as the intervener was sufficient to show a relationship between the two, even giving rise to reasonable apprehension of bias. Because Lord Hoffman's connections were sufficiently disqualifying, the Law Lords did not need to examine whether Lady Hoffman's connections with Amnesty International would also be disqualifying.[96]

How far can arguments for reasonable apprehension of bias regarding personal relationships be stretched? A recent case from the B.C. Human Rights Tribunal illustrates an attempt to push the idea of a personal connection in a novel way. In *Brar v. College of Veterinarians of British Columbia*,[97] the appointment of the adjudicator assigned to the case expired before the end of the hearing. By that time, over 200 days of hearings had already taken place and an estimated additional year and a half would be required for hearing completion and a decision to be rendered. Only three weeks before her appointment ended, the adjudicator received notice that her appointment would not be renewed. The adjudicator therefore adjourned the proceedings for the balance of the month, asked that the parties maintain the hearing dates already scheduled for later that year, and that they await further notice from the tribunal. She stated that her decision was based on the uncertainty of the situation and reasoned that it would be inappropriate and unfair for the parties to continue to spend resources to continue the hearing at the time. She was concerned, for example, that if the parties raised interim applications before the expiry of her appointment, she might not be able to fully adjudicate them during the short time remaining. She also indicated that she had asked the Ministry of the Attorney General about reappointment approximately nine months before the expiry date, with repeated follow-up inquiries sent by the tribunal chair.

Shortly thereafter, the complainants sent a letter to each of the tribunal chair and the ministry, requesting the tribunal member's reappointment for another term or, at the very least, her appointment for enough time to complete the decision.[98] The complainants alleged government interference with the decision-making independence of the tribunal member. The respondents sent a reply letter to each of the tribunal chair and the ministry and submitted an application for reasonable apprehension of bias before the tribunal. With respect to reasonable apprehension of bias, they argued that counsel for the complainants had taken up the cause of the tribunal member concerning her reappointment. They therefore argued that the tribunal member should not now be reappointed to continue hearing the matter because she could be perceived to be indebted to counsel to the complainant. The tribunal, and the Superior Court on judicial review, found that no reasonable apprehension

---

96 See also *Poitras et al. v. Bellegarde*, 2011 FCA 317.

97 2010 BCHRT 308; aff'd. 2011 BCSC 486.

98 The ATA, *supra* note 59, allows for such extensions under ss. 6 and 7.

of bias had been established. Despite the respondents' argument that the complainants' decision to champion the tribunal member's reappointment had been incited by the tribunal member's comments when she adjourned, the respondents had submitted no evidence in support of their assertion.

Given that the reasonable apprehension test requires the strong likelihood of an informed person seeing a reasonable risk of partiality, what type of evidence could be brought by respondents in a situation like *Brar*? The common law maintains a strong presumption of impartiality for adjudicators, offers immunity for tribunal members, and protects deliberative secrecy. In light of these tenets of administrative law, it may be a formidable task, even with significant supporting evidence, to launch a successful challenge along the lines of that of the respondents in *Brar*.

As emphasized throughout this book, appreciating context in administrative law is vital; it is equally so in determining disqualifying bias. As Lord Steyn stated about reasonable appearances of bias in *Man O'War Station Ltd. v. Auckland City Council (Judgment No. 1)*: "This is a corner of the law in which the context, and the particular circumstances, are of supreme importance."[99] Lord Steyn's observation is reflected in the fact that there are a myriad of circumstances that may give rise to the reasonable apprehension of bias, especially in the Canadian administrative state where there is a diversity of decision-making bodies. The nature of the tribunal itself can sometimes have an impact on whether an allegation of bias is reasonable. For example, labour arbitration panels traditionally comprise three members, two representing each of labour and management and one neutral chair. Connections between practising lawyers in the field and members from labour or management are almost inevitable.[100] Moreover, nominees are chosen because of their sympathy to the interests of the party that nominated them. Nevertheless, determining whether a reasonable apprehension of bias exists within the tripartite labour context is a matter of balancing a legislated desire to have representative experts populate decision-making panels and the Supreme Court's firm counsel that nominated arbitrators "are to exercise their function not as the advocates of the parties nominating them, and *a fortiori* of one party when they are agreed upon by all, but with as free, independent and impartial minds as the circumstances permit."[101]

Finally, there are additional contextual factors that may diminish an apprehension of bias. The amount of time that has passed between the member's active association with the person involved in the dispute and the member's appointment to the tribunal is one such

---

99   [2002] 3 N.Z.L.R. 577, [2002] U.K.P.C. 28 at para. 11.

100   See "Nominee Bias" in M.R. Gorsky et al., *Evidence and Procedure in Canadian Labour Arbitration* (Scarborough, ON: Carswell, 1991). A critique of the approach of the courts is offered by T.S. Kuttner, "Is the Doctrine of Bias Compatible with the Tri-Partite Labour Tribunal?" (1986) 19 Admin. L.R. 81-98.

101   *Szilard v. Szasz*, [1955] S.C.R. 3. See also *Black & McDonald Ltd. v. Construction Labour Relations Association of British Columbia* (1986), 19 Admin. L.R. 73 (B.C.C.A.); *U.F.C.W., Local 1252 v. Prince Edward Island (Labour Relations Board)* (1998), 31 Admin. L.R. 196 (P.E.I.C.A.) (debating whether indirect interest can avoid disqualifying bias for labour tribunal members with connections to parties). For a recent case illustrating the bias issues relating to tripartite arbitration boards and how they may be handled on the ground by the labour arbitrator at first instance, see *Fredericton (City) v. International Assn. of Fire Fighters, Local 1053 (Collective Agreement Grievance)*, [2008] N.B.L.A.A. No. 17 (QL), M.J. Veniot.

factor. In *Marques v. Dylex*,[102] a labour board member who had previously been a lawyer with the firm acting for an earlier iteration of the union appearing before his panel was not disqualified for appearance of bias. The Divisional Court noted that over a year had passed since the member had been involved with the law firm and had had anything to do with the predecessor of the union. Necessity can also be a relevant factor.[103] Last, keep in mind that, although Canadian common law is grounded in an Anglo-European notion of impartiality in which decisions are considered fair when made by those who are at a distance from the parties and the matter at interest, other conceptions of justice also exist. Some Aboriginal communities, for example, consider decisions to be fair when rendered by non-strangers whom they know and trust. This idea is addressed in more detail by Janna Promislow and Lorne Sossin in Chapter 13, In Search of Aboriginal Administrative Law.

c. Prior Knowledge or Information About the Matter in Dispute

Generally speaking, in deciding whether a reasonable apprehension of bias exists because of a decision-maker's prior involvement with a matter, tribunals, and courts on review, will focus on the nature and extent of the decision-maker's previous involvement. This general principle has been articulated most forcefully by the Supreme Court in the 2003 decision of *Wewaykum Indian Band v. Canada*.[104] The general principles from *Wewaykum* serve as a foundation for deciding reasonable apprehension of bias claims for both judicial and administrative actors with prior knowledge of a matter. *Wewaykum* was a property dispute involving two First Nations bands. In *Wewaykum*, Mr. Justice Binnie's previous employment as associate deputy minister of justice from 1982 to 1986 was challenged as giving rise to reasonable apprehension of bias. During that time, he had been responsible for almost all litigation against the government of Canada and had supervisory authority over thousands of cases. An access to information request showed that in late 1985 and early 1986, he had participated in a meeting at which the current case was discussed and had received some information about one of the bands' claims. The bands sought to set aside the Court's unanimous judgment in the matter, which had been made some nine months earlier.[105]

The parties argued that the memoranda demonstrated that Binnie J. had been involved in developing the Crown's litigation strategy against them.[106] The Supreme Court carefully examined the 14 memoranda that had been revealed by the access request. There were pieces of correspondence in which Binnie J. was involved, either directly or indirectly. After

---

[102] (1977), 81 D.L.R. (3rd) 554 (Ont. Div. Ct.).

[103] See e.g. *Calina v. Directors of Chiropractic*, [1981] O.J. No. 3219 (Div. Ct.) (QL) [*Calina*].

[104] 2003 SCC 45, [2003] 2 S.C.R. 259 [*Wewaykum*]. Of course, the classic case on the matter is *Committee for Justice and Liberty, supra* note 79.

[105] *Wewaykum Indian Band v. Canada*, 2002 SCC 79, [2002] 4 S.C.R. 245.

[106] In further support of their allegation of a reasonable apprehension of bias, the parties had also pointed to Binnie J.'s long-standing interest in First Nations matters and to prior decisions that he had made. The Court held, however, that all that was relevant to deciding whether a reasonable apprehension of bias existed was Binnie J.'s involvement in the file at issue as the head of litigation at the Department of Justice.

this examination, the Court held that, although his connection to the file might have been greater than simply pro forma management, he was never counsel of record and played no active role in the dispute after the claim was filed. The Court also noted that the file was transferred to the Vancouver regional office to be handled by a lawyer located there. The Court therefore found the parties' argument that Binnie J. had been involved in the litigation in a material way to be unsubstantiated.

In the context of the administrative state, reasonable apprehension of bias arising from prior knowledge has sometimes led to severe consequences. For example, in *SEIU*,[107] the entire Ontario Labour Relations Board was found to be disqualified to hear a case before it because of information received earlier at a plenary meeting of the vice chairs. The members of the board were prevented by oath of office from revealing what they knew, but indicated that the information that was received contradicted one or more of the parties' representations. In Ontario, the *Public Officers Act*[108] allows for the Divisional Court to appoint a disinterested person to adjudicate a matter in circumstances where the public officer empowered to perform the functions is disqualified.[109] That was the outcome in *SEIU*.[110] More often, issues surrounding prior knowledge arise when a tribunal adjudicator is asked to hear an appeal or a subsequent proceeding of an original matter.[111] The common-law concept of mediation privilege, which precludes a tribunal member from adjudicating a case that he or she has mediated is an attempt to avoid the reasonable apprehension of bias issue that may come with prior knowledge. Mediation privilege may be directed by statute,[112] but, even where statutes do not explicitly provide for mediation privilege, some administrative bodies will ensure through their formal or informal practice that mediators do not sit in further deliberation of a matter with which they have dealt.[113] Sometimes a statute will authorize a

---

[107] *Supra* note 93. See also *Jogendra v. Ontario (Human Rights Tribunal)*, [2011] O.J. No. 2518 (S.C.J.) (QL).

[108] R.S.O. 1990, c. P.45.

[109] Section 16, *ibid.*, indicates that the person being replaced must be disqualified "by interest" from acting and there must be no other person empowered to perform the function. This compares to the situation in which there is an absence of legislation governing the complete disqualification of all tribunal members. In such cases, necessity may require an impugned tribunal member to serve. See e.g. *Calina*, *supra* note 103.

[110] Although the court is not altogether clear in its reasoning. On the one hand, because the matter before the board also dealt with the government's ability to terminate appointments mid-term, the court structured its analysis around the interest of the vice chairs. In other words, the Divisional Court reasoned that the vice-chairs had an interest in the outcome of the matter as it might have affected their security of tenure. However, through the course of the decision, that reason was supplanted by the court's focus on the prior knowledge of the board and how that prior knowledge disqualified the entire board from hearing the matter. See *SEIU*, *supra* note 93 at paras. 29-57.

[111] See e.g. the debate between the majority and dissenting judges in *Law Society of Upper Canada v. French*, [1975] 2 S.C.R. 767, in which members of the discipline committee for the law society also sat on appeals by convocation. The majority decision did not find disqualifying bias. However, the *Law Society Act* was modified in 1998, removing the adjudicative role of convocation and splitting the body so that there is no overlap between the original disciplinary committees and those hearing appeals.

[112] See e.g. *Health Insurance Act*, R.S.O. 1990, c. H.6, s. 23.

[113] An example is the Office of the Information and Privacy Commissioner of Ontario, which separates mediators and adjudicators through informal but strict practice.

multiplicity of functions that may countenance an administrative actor's prior knowledge from his or her involvement in an earlier stage of the process. We examine multiplicity of functions when we discuss institutional bias.

d. Attitudinal Predisposition Toward an Outcome

Predispositions giving rise to a reasonable apprehension of bias have been gleaned from decision-makers' comments and attitudes in both the course of the hearing and outside the proceedings. During the hearing, antagonism toward litigants, *ex parte* communications, and irrelevant or vexatious comments as well as the adjudicator or any other member of the tribunal taking an unauthorized role as an advocate to the proceeding before it, have all given rise to a reasonable apprehension of bias.

A recent on-the-ground example comes from *Law Society of Upper Canada v. Cengarle*.[114] The original hearing panel in this disciplinary matter had been particularly interventionist. As the appeal panel asserted in *Cengarle* in summarizing the current state of the law, "[t]he effect of interventions by a tribunal on the appearance of fairness in any given case must be assessed in relation to the unique facts and circumstances of the particular hearing."[115] The appeal panel held that the sheer volume of interventions was not the marker of whether the process had been tainted by a reasonable apprehension of bias. However, they examined all the interjections made by the first instance panel and found that 16 of the 56 interventions gave a cumulative appearance of reasonable apprehension of bias. These interventions showed the first instance panel to have descended into the arena and assumed the role of a prosecuting advocate. More specifically, the appeal panel found that the chair of the original hearing had intervened excessively during the examination-in-chief of certain witnesses and had done so in a manner that, to a reasonable person, appeared to cross-examine them.[116]

Cases such as *Cengarle* raise the issue of how to draw the line between valid, non-adversarial or "inquisitorial" processes (sometimes called "active adjudication") and, seemingly, partisan interference by the tribunal. Compare, for example, the concerns in *Cengarle* with the Federal Court of Appeal holding in *Thamotharem*,[117] where a guideline set out by the chair of the Immigration and Refugee Board directed refugee protection officers or, in their absence, a member of the Board to begin the questioning at a hearing.[118] Guideline 7 prompted litigious controversy over the fairness of the procedure. Ultimately, the Federal Court of Appeal held that this process—an inquisitorial one—showed no transgression of the duty of fairness owed by the decision-maker. Although "relatively unfamiliar to common lawyers" who are steeped in the adversarial tradition, an inquisitorial process in and of itself presents

---

[114] [2010] L.S.D.D. No. 61 (QL) [*Cengarle*].

[115] *Ibid.* at para. 21.

[116] An older case that illustrates similar issues of a tribunal descending into the role of advocate is *Golomb and College of Physicians and Surgeons of Ontario* (1976), 12 O.R. (2d) 73 (Div. Ct.) [*Golomb*].

[117] *Thamotharem v. Canada (Minister of Citizenship and Immigration)*, 2006 FC 16, [2006] 3 F.C.R. 168, 2007 FCA 198, [2008] 1 F.C.R. 385.

[118] See also the discussion of *Thamotharem* by Lorne Sossin in Chapter 7, Access to Administrative Justice and Other Worries.

no challenges to notions of fairness. Equally important, the Board's choice of an inquisitorial method fit comfortably within the structure that Parliament had designed for it under the *Immigration and Refugee Protection Act*.[119] Is Guideline 7 simply another instance of statutory authorization permitting divergence from a judicial common-law standard? Or is it greater recognition that administrative decision-making is not always best suited to a traditional common-law adversarial context?[120]

Other situations in which decision-maker's comments have given rise to reasonable apprehension of bias include *ex parte* communications (that is, where the decision-maker chooses to speak privately with one party)[121] and cases in which sexist, condescending, or other irrelevant comments have been made.[122] Although decisions made by the decision-maker in previous unrelated cases will generally not give rise to a reasonable apprehension of bias, comments in a decision showing a predisposition toward an outcome in a specific case before the decision-maker have been held to give rise to reasonable apprehension of bias.[123] At the same time, it is important to note that it is possible for comments made by a decision-maker to show understanding of or to take judicial notice of the broader social context without necessarily giving rise to a reasonable apprehension of bias.[124]

A decision-maker's alleged attitude or predisposition to the outcome of a case has also been said to arise through comments expressed outside the hearing room about the ongoing case. In these cases, the administrative law jurisprudence has held that the standard for determining whether disqualifying bias exists should be whether the adjudicator has a closed mind. In other words, what is central is whether the decision-maker is amenable to persuasion or whether his or her comments indicate "a mind so closed that any submission [by the parties] would be futile."[125] The test has led to permissible variation in the degree to which a decision-maker may be wedded to a position held prior to making a decision on the outcome. The degree to which a prior, fixed view will be accepted by the court is determined by the nature and function of the decision-making process. For example, in *Old St. Boniface Residents Assn. Inc. v. Winnipeg (City)*, the Supreme Court of Canada held that, because of the nature of municipal governance, it is to be expected that municipal councillors would have advocated a position during election time or before different committees prior to sitting

---

[119]   S.C. 2001, c. 27.

[120]   See, generally, Laverne Jacobs & Sasha Baglay, eds., *The Nature of Inquisitorial Processes in Administrative Regimes: Global Perspectives* (Toronto: University of Toronto Press [forthcoming in 2012]).

[121]   See e.g. *Law Society of Alberta v. Merchant*, [2011] L.S.D.D. No. 29 (QL).

[122]   *Yusuf v. Canada (Minister of Employment and Immigration)*, [1992] 1 F.C. 629; see also, generally, *Sawridge Band v. Canada (C.A.)*, [1997] 3 F.C. 580.

[123]   *Alberta Teachers' Association v. Alberta (Information and Privacy Commissioner)*, 2011 ABQB 19. This case is related to the Supreme Court of Canada decision that held that the Commissioner's implied decision to extend the timeline that the office would follow in rendering its decision was subject to and met the *Dunsmuir* standard of reasonableness: see *Alberta (Information and Privacy Commissioner) v. Alberta Teachers' Association*, 2011 SCC 61, [2011] 3 S.C.R. 654.

[124]   *R. v. S. (R.D.)*, *supra* note 81.

[125]   See *Newfoundland Telephone Co. v. Newfoundland (Board of Commissioners of Public Utilities)*, [1992] 1 S.C.R. 623 [*Newfoundland Telephone*].

on municipal council in the final decision of the same issue.[126] The Court held that the reasonable apprehension of bias standard could not apply to a situation of municipal government such as the one in *Old St. Boniface*. Instead, the Supreme Court held that a more appropriate test in light of the nature and function of municipal council is that a councillor be disqualified for bias only if it can be established *in fact* that a councillor has such a closed mind on a matter that any representations made would be futile.[127] In a related case, decided on the same day and reaching the same result, judges for the minority expressed concern that the standard articulated by the Court could lead to posturing on the part of municipal decision-makers.[128]

In the later case of *Newfoundland Telephone*,[129] the Court indicated that a multifunctional administrative body may have varying standards depending on the function being performed. Administrative bodies that perform investigations, policy making, and adjudication, for example, may be afforded more freedom to hold a fixed view during an investigative or policy-making stage than at an adjudicative stage, so long as there are no constitutional contraventions. Despite this general principle, however, the jurisprudence is not always straightforward as to when the reasonable apprehension of bias test should apply and when the closed-mind test should apply. For example, in *Chrétien v. Canada (Ex-Commissioner, Commission of Inquiry into the Sponsorship Program and Advertising Activities)* ,[130] a reasonable apprehension of bias standard was used to evaluate comments made to the media by the commissioner of a public inquiry. The applicant, former Prime Minister Jean Chrétien, was successful in having the factual findings in the public inquiry set aside because the commissioner's media comments made during the inquiry showed prejudgment of the matter. This was surprising because public inquiries aim to determine the facts and do not have binding, enforceable impact. On the basis of Supreme Court jurisprudence, one would have expected the investigatory nature to require a closed-mind test.

In light of these cases, one is left wondering about the conceptual framework that can be used to understand when and why the different tests for disqualifying bias should be applied. First, the Supreme Court cases regarding municipal councillors such as *Old Saint Boniface* suggest that legislative functions will not attract a high degree of scrutiny from the perspective of procedural fairness. Similarly, cases such as *Newfoundland Telephone* seem to reassert a traditional common-law idea that investigative work does not attract the highest degree of procedural fairness because the impact on the individual is not binding. Whereas the first approach may gain purchase from constitutional doctrines relating to the separation of powers, the latter idea is more questionable. Impact on the individual should be measured in ways that extend past the existence or absence of a binding order. If this were done, it may be seen that in some circumstances, such as public inquiries where the impact

---

[126] See *Old St. Boniface Residents Assn. Inc. v. Winnipeg (City)*, [1990] 3 S.C.R. 1170 [*Old St. Boniface*] at para. 45.

[127] *Ibid.* at para. 57.

[128] See *Save Richmond Farmland Society v. Richmond (Township)*, [1990] 3 S.C.R. 1213.

[129] *Supra* note 125.

[130] 2008 FC 802, [2009] 2 F.C.R. 417, aff'd 2010 FCA 283.

on one's reputation can be quite significant, reasonable apprehension of bias may be more appropriate because of its more objective and possibly easier evidentiary standard to meet.

Should public advocacy, such as academic publications, which take a specific view on an issue or area of law, be held to give rise to a reasonable apprehension of bias? The question arose in the case of *Great Atlantic & Pacific Co. of Canada v. Ontario (Human Rights Commission)*,[131] when a professor who had written extensively against gender discrimination was appointed as a board of inquiry to adjudicate human rights applications. Because there was also a distinct, more immediate factor present that had the potential to cause disqualifying bias, the Court held that the issue of the professor's advocacy did not need to be determined. As such, the question has remained outstanding in our jurisprudence. Given that administrative tribunals are designed to be expert tribunals, it is natural that members will be chosen from realms in which their expertise has been shown, such as academia, practice, or otherwise. Having part-time members who are also active in the field through academic writing or as practitioners can be useful so long as they are not engaged as counsel, parties, interveners, etc., and decision-makers in any given case.[132]

In conclusion, whereas the reasonable apprehension of bias test has been held to apply in individual bias cases, the closed-mind test, which supports a different evidentiary burden, is generally used in conjunction with policy-making and investigatory functions. What is interesting about these tests is not only the variation in standards themselves, but the conceptual rationale underpinning their application.

2. Perceptions of Institutional Bias

The need for institutional policy making, collaboration, and consistency is an element that distinguishes administrative tribunals from courts. This section takes a look at the ways in which apprehensions of bias have arisen in response to institutional practices developed by tribunals for these purposes. As you read this section, consider the connection between institutional bias and adjudicative independence.

a. Bias, Adjudicative Independence, and Policy Making (and Whose Policies Are They Anyway?)

Policy making is generally accepted as being central to tribunal existence. This function of administrative tribunals has attracted a significant increase in attention since MacLachlin C.J.'s postulate in *Ocean Port Hotel* that every tribunal, no matter how adjudicative it appears, has some role in implementing a government policy.[133] Tribunals create policy in their day-to-day work in several ways. Focusing primarily on adjudicative bodies, Houle & Sossin identify three modes of policy making by administrative tribunals: decision making; informal rule making through the use of such soft law as guidelines, bulletins, and manuals;

---

131   13 O.R. (3d) 824 [*A&P*].

132   See *ibid.*

133   See *Ocean Port Hotel, supra* note 3 at para. 24.

and formal rule making through delegated legislation.[134] Generally, the policies that administrative bodies make, whether primarily adjudicative or otherwise, serve to further the law under the statute that the tribunal has been mandated to administer, to promote consistency in the decisions rendered by the tribunal's various members, and to render the tribunal more efficient in its decision-making process. Although it can be argued that courts also further the policy of legislation simply by rendering decisions under a statute, the methods used to create policy and the function of policy making itself are distinctive characteristics of administrative bodies. In the context of the administrative state, policy making relates to the expertise (in the subject matter or in managing the subject matter) possessed by the tribunals that administer and further the law under a particular statute.

Tensions arise, however, when the methods used by tribunals in their policy-making activities appear to infringe on the adjudicative independence of any individual tribunal decision-maker. Adjudicative independence is one guarantee of independence that is frequently called into question in the administrative context. Referenced briefly in the Supreme Court's decision in *Beauregard*,[135] the concept of adjudicative independence embodies the ability of a decision-maker to decide free of inappropriate interference by other decision-makers. Such inappropriate interference may include, for example, pressure to decide a certain way or substitution of another's decision for one's own. Of all the guarantees of independence, adjudicative independence is a value that is particularly delicate in the administrative law context. There is often tension between the need for tribunal members to collaborate to further the law as an institution and the need to give each decision-maker space to render his or her rightful decisions. This tension has shown up most frequently with respect to the use of full-board meetings to promote consistency in tribunal decision making. Nevertheless, policy making practices have come up against adjudicative independence more recently in other key ways. In addition to full-board meetings, two additional tribunal practices discussed in this section are using lead cases to promote adjudicative efficiency and consistency, and assisting the executive branch of government to develop its policy.

b. Full-Board Meetings

In administrative law, the methods used to promote consistency in decision making across tribunals as institutions have given rise to allegations of reasonable apprehension of bias. At the heart of the debate over consistency is whether the adjudicative independence of any individual member has been compromised. The tools used to promote consistency often involve the input of tribunal members other than those charged with determining a specific claim. As a consequence, allegations of reasonable apprehension of bias have been made by litigants concerned that the adjudicators deciding their claims have based their decisions on considerations that they themselves did not come across in the course of their adjudications.

---

[134]   See France Houle & Lorne Sossin, "Tribunals and Policy Making" in Jacobs & Mactavish, *supra* note 2. Rule making is also discussed by Andrew Green in Chapter 4, Regulations and Rule Making: The Dilemma of Delegation.

[135]   See *Beauregard*, *supra* note 19 and accompanying text.

The challenge of fostering coherence has become all the more important with the proliferation of larger boards across the country. Such boards have several members, sometimes in the hundreds, in various parts of the country who may each have distinct views on how the law under the legislation should be developed. Similar decisions in similar cases show the general public how a tribunal has chosen to apply its statutes in various factual situations. The "policy" that consistent decisions develop is a form of non-binding guideline that tribunal users can refer to in deciding how to manage their affairs in the industry or sector regulated by the tribunal. It can help them determine, for example, whether to bring a matter before the tribunal or to settle. If tribunals were without the means of promoting consistency, the general public using the tribunal services would be at a disadvantage in regulating their affairs. In a trilogy of cases (*IWA v. Consolidated-Bathurst Packaging Ltd.*,[136] *Tremblay v. Quebec (Commission des affaires sociales)*,[137] and *Ellis-Don Ltd. v. Ontario (Labour Relations Board)*[138]), the Supreme Court of Canada set out the guidelines that tribunals should follow so that members can collaborate within their institution to promote consistency of outcome without compromising the adjudicative independence of any one decision-maker (or fairness to the parties).

In *Consolidated-Bathurst*, the Ontario Labour Relations Board held a meeting of the full labour board to discuss the draft reasons of one of its three-member panels. The purposes of such meetings are to facilitate understanding and appreciation throughout the board of policy developments and to evaluate the practical consequences of proposed policy initiatives on provincial labour relations and the economy. The decision discussed in this particular meeting dealt with whether a particular legal test the board had established through its jurisprudence should be replaced by another. At issue before the Supreme Court was whether full-board meetings constitute a breach of the natural justice principle "he who hears must decide," by placing the decision-makers in a situation where they can be influenced by others who have not heard the evidence or arguments. It was also argued that such meetings are unacceptable because they do not provide the parties with adequate opportunity to answer issues that may be voiced by board members who have not heard the case. The appellant's arguments were therefore cast as a matter of improper encroachment on the adjudicative independence of the decision-makers and of lack of opportunity to know the full case to be met.

The Supreme Court acknowledged the need for full-board meetings. In the majority's opinion, such meetings allowed the members of a large board[139] with a heavy case load[140] to benefit from the acquired expertise of the collective. As well, consultation was useful in achieving the board's mandate. The structure of the board was conducive to exchanges of opinions between management and union (as evidenced by its tripartite nature) in order to use its combined expertise to regulate labour relations in a prompt and final manner.[141] The

---

[136]   *Consolidated-Bathurst, supra* note 85.

[137]   [1992] 1 S.C.R. 952 [*Tremblay*].

[138]   2001 SCC 4, [2001] 1 S.C.R. 221 [*Ellis-Don*].

[139]   There were 48 members in 1982-83.

[140]   At the time, there were approximately 266 cases a year.

[141]   *Consolidated-Bathurst, supra* note 85, paras. 70-73.

majority also saw coherence as a goal to be fostered so that the outcome of disputes did not depend on the identity of the decision-maker. And last, in the majority's view, the fact that a privative clause protects the board's decisions made it even more incumbent on the board to take measures to avoid conflicting results.

At the same time, the Court recognized that fostering coherence should not compromise any panel member's capacity to decide in accordance with his conscience and opinions:

> It is obvious that no outside interference may be used to compel or pressure a decision maker to participate in discussions on policy issues raised by a case on which he must render a decision. It also goes without saying that a formalized consultation process could not be used to force or induce decision makers to adopt positions with which they do not agree. Nevertheless, discussions with colleagues do not constitute, in and of themselves, infringements on the panel members' capacity to decide the issues at stake independently. A discussion does not prevent a decision maker from adjudicating in accordance with his own conscience and opinions nor does it constitute an obstacle to this freedom. Whatever discussion may take place, the ultimate decision will be that of the decision maker for which he assumes full responsibility.[142]

The Court held that the relevant issue is whether there is *pressure* on the decision-maker to decide against his or her own conscience and opinions. It outlined the following conditions for the holding of such meetings so that natural justice would not be breached: that the discussions be limited to law or policy and not factual issues, and that the parties be given a reasonable opportunity to respond to any new ground arising from the meeting. In this regard, the Court approved of the checks and balances put in place by the Labour Relations Board—for example, not keeping minutes of the meeting, not keeping attendance, and not holding a vote at the end of the discussion.

Tremblay was decided a few years after *Consolidated-Bathurst*. In *Tremblay*, the Court clarified that the imposition of consultation meetings by a member of the board who was not on the panel could amount to inappropriate constraint. The Court also held that even in situations where the consultation process is said to be voluntary, it is important to see whether the operational practice of the tribunal shows evidence that the consultation, in fact, comprises systemic pressure.

In *Tremblay*, the decision issued after a consultation process was quite different from that in *Consolidated-Bathurst*. Although the consultations were optional, in theory (they were to be called by the decision-making member of the commission), the practice at the Commission des affaires sociales (CAS) made a consultation compulsory when a proposed decision was contrary to previous decisions.

Other factors that gave an appearance of constraint and an apparent lack of decisional independence at the CAS were that the president could refer a matter before another member for plenary discussion. The Supreme Court noted that, in such circumstances, a decision-maker may not feel free to refuse to submit a question to the consultation process. Because the statute expressly indicates that the individual decision-makers must decide matters, imposing group consultation on them amounts to an act of compulsion and goes against legislative intent. As well, the plenary meetings aimed to reach a consensus. Many of the

---

142   *Ibid.* at para. 80.

protective devices that the Court had approved in *Consolidated-Bathurst* did not exist at the CAS. In particular, unlike the practice of the Ontario Labour Relations Board, CAS took attendance, voted by a show of hands, and kept minutes of the meetings. These aspects created an appearance of "systemic pressure."

Finally, at issue in *Ellis-Don* was whether facts had been discussed at a full labour board meeting, contrary to the jurisprudential rules governing institutional decision making set out in *Consolidated-Bathurst* and *Tremblay*. Although *Ellis-Don* focused only on the issue of providing the parties with a full opportunity to respond to matters discussed at a plenary meeting and did not deal with the questions of pressure and independence, it is useful because it sets out concisely the jurisprudential rules governing intra-agency consultation.

c. Lead Cases

Since the time of the *Consolidated-Bathurst* trilogy, other tribunal practices for garnering consistency, developing policy, and addressing efficiency—another perennial concern in the face of the heavy workloads of tribunals—have come to the attention of the courts. One recent development is the use of lead cases. In the decision of *Geza v. Canada (Minister of Citizenship and Immigration)*,[143] the Immigration and Refugee Board instituted a procedure through which it attempted to select one of several similar refugee claims to create a full evidential record for all. The purpose of the lead case initiative was to enable the board to have one case in which there were informed findings of fact and a relatively thorough analysis of the relevant legal issues.[144] The board was attempting to deal efficiently with a large influx of refugee claims by the Hungarian Roma. Although chosen before many Roma had had their claims heard, the claim chosen was to be representative of the issues that recurred when the Hungarian Roma were seeking refugee status. The case used as the lead case was selected with the participation of the lawyer who had the largest inventory of pending Hungarian Roma claims. The minister of citizenship and immigration was invited to participate in the hearings. This claim was then heard by an experienced panel of the board chosen for its familiarity with the relevant country conditions, experience with case management of the Roma cases, and drawn from different regions of Canada. The appellants argued that the lead case initiative was designed to reduce the number of successful Roma refugee applications, and therefore showed bias. For the Court of Appeal, Evans J.A. held that, based on the entire factual matrix, a reasonable person would conclude that the lead case initiative was designed not only to generate consistency but also to reduce the number of positive decisions that might be rendered in favour of the 15,000 Roma claimants and to deter future claims. Justice Evans held that although there was no single fact that alone established a reasonable apprehension of bias, there were several facts that contributed collectively to a reasonable apprehension of bias. The decision in *Geza* is useful both for showing the bound-

---

143   [2005] 3 F.C.R. 3 (Fed. Ct.), rev'd [2006] 4 F.C.R. 377 (C.A.) [*Geza*].

144   In a similar vein, see also *Thamotharem, supra* note 117 (C.A.), and *Benitez v. Canada (Minister of Citizenship and Immigration)*, 2007 FCA 199, [2008] 1 F.C.R. 155, in which allegations of reasonable apprehension of bias were brought against the Immigration and Refugee Board for its creation of procedural guidelines that suggested the manner in which adjudicators should conduct their hearings.

aries between tribunal efficiency and bias, and for indicating that a reasonable apprehension of bias can arise from the totality of evidence, as opposed to a single, determinative fact.

d. Adjudicative Independence and the Legislative Process

In *Communications, Energy and Paperworkers Union of Canada, Local 707 v. The Alberta Labour Relations Board*,[145] the Alberta Labour Relations Board was consulted for its knowledge of the field by the executive branch of government in order to help the government implement a new legislative policy. As a result, the Board then faced both a legal battle in which it was said to lack independence and impartiality with respect to any matter it had to deal with touching on the labour law policy, and a grave loss of confidence by the unions affected by the policy. To many, this occurrence may ring contradictory in light of McLachlin C.J.'s now famous dicta in *Ocean Port Hotel* that all tribunals exist precisely to further the policy of the executive branch of government.[146] *Alberta Labour Relations Board* raises a fresh and interesting question of independence in administrative law—namely, how should feedback on the industry be transferred to the executive department that has responsibility for the tribunal? The question turns on how a tribunal can communicate such information while preserving its appearance of impartiality and independence from the executive branch of government. Central to this question of feedback is the protection of adjudicative independence, particularly on an institutional level.

e. Multifunctionality

Unlike courts, tribunals have been created to manage and oversee areas that are often polycentric in nature. This means that the expertise required of the tribunal members and staff is not only juristic expertise, which is needed to interpret the statute, but may also include expertise in the particular technical subject area.[147] The appointments process often reflects this diversity through requirements that a tribunal be composed of experts drawn not only from lawyers but also from other fields and sometimes even from the general public. For example, although classified as staff rather than members, the *Canadian International Trade Tribunal Act* has a provision for the appointment of technical experts.[148] These experts are mandated to assist the tribunal in an advisory manner.[149] The Alberta *Natural Resources Conservation Board Act* has a similar appointment provision.[150] However, it is not just the

---

[145] [2004] A.J. No. 83 (QL) [*Alberta Labour Relations Board*].

[146] *Ocean Port Hotel, supra* note 3 at para. 24. See also Lorne Sossin & Charles W. Smith, "The Politics of Transparency and Independence Before Administrative Boards" (2012) Sask. L. Rev. 13.

[147] France Houle provides a thoughtful definition of what it means to be an "expert" in the administrative law sense in France Houle, "Le fonctionnement du régime de preuve libre dans un système non-expert: Le traitement symptomatique des preuves par la Section de la protection des réfugiés" (2004) 38 R.J.T. 263. See also, generally, L. Jacobs & T. Kuttner, "The Expert Tribunal" in Jacobs & Mactavish *supra* note 2.

[148] *Canadian International Trade Tribunal Act*, R.S.C. 1985, c. 47 (4th Supp.), s. 15(2).

[149] *Ibid.*

[150] See *Natural Resources Conservation Board Act*, R.S.A. 2000, c. N-3, s. 23.

appointment of experts to a tribunal that serves to reflect a tribunal's polycentric nature. The structure of many enabling statutes themselves reflects the polycentric nature of the tribunal through the plurality of functions that the tribunal may be asked to perform.

For example, the Canadian International Trade Tribunal (CITT) is endowed with both broad powers of policy development and adjudicative powers. The CITT conducts inquiries and provides advice on economic, trade, and tariff matters as referred to it by the minister of finance or the governor in council. It also hears appeals of decisions made under various statutes by the Canada Revenue Agency.[151] This type of plurality of function has been called into question by litigants on judicial review in cases where staff research was not revealed to all the parties, raising issues of procedural fairness.[152] Many tribunals make available to the public their staff reports, research, and even training manuals and adjudicator decision-making guides, most often by posting them on their websites.[153] Some tribunals try to maintain a de facto separation of powers within their work, seemingly to avoid allegations that one aspect of the tribunal's work has had an inappropriate interference with another aspect of its work, causing a reasonable apprehension of bias.[154] One wonders, though, whether this may be an overly cautious internalization by tribunals of the judicial dictates on multifunctionality, especially if it hinders the expertise developed in one area of the tribunal's work from enriching the rest of the tribunal's work. This may occur, for example, by preventing the subject-matter knowledge collected through policy development from being available to adjudicators in their decision making.

The most common complaint in relation to a tribunal's multiplicity of functions stems from a perception by the user that a tribunal has the potential to act as both prosecutor and judge in the same matter. Generally, it has been held that overlapping functions are not a problem so long as sanctioned by statute enacted in conformity with the Constitution or applicable quasi-constitutional enactment.[155]

In some cases, tribunals may take their own proactive measures to reduce the appearance or reality that relations are too close between those acting in a prosecutorial fashion and

---

151 *Canadian International Trade Tribunal Act, supra* note 148, ss. 16, 18, 19. See also the mandate of the Canadian International Trade Tribunal, online: Canadian International Trade Tribunal <http://www.citt.gc.ca/mandate/index_e.asp>.

152 See, in particular, *Toshiba Corp v. Canada (Anti-Dumping Tribunal)* (1984), 8 Admin. L.R. 173 (F.C.A.).

153 See e.g. the publications of the Immigration and Refugee Board, which include policies, procedures, and research reports on various countries, online: Immigration and Refugee Board of Canada <http://www.irb-cisr.gc.ca/Eng/resrec/publications/Pages/index.aspx>.

154 Such allegations have been made in the literature: see e.g. Colin J. Bennett, "The Privacy Commissioner of Canada: Multiple Roles, Diverse Expectations and Structural Dilemmas" (2003) 46(2) Canadian Public Administration 218.

155 See the discussion of *Régie, supra* note 33 and accompanying text, and *Brosseau v. Alberta Securities Commission*, [1989] 1 S.C.R. 301 (holding that, if authorized by a constitutionally valid statute, the multiplicity of rules in one administrative body does not give rise to reasonable apprehension of bias). At issue in *Brosseau* was whether there was a reasonable apprehension of bias arising from the multiple roles, including investigation and adjudication, at the Alberta Securities Commission. The litigation was prompted by the fact that the Commission chair, in his investigative capacity, had received a report prior to the hearing from the deputy director of enforcement.

those performing adjudicative functions. Should such proactive measures be taken into account in determining whether a reasonable person could find a lack of impartiality vis-à-vis the tribunal? *Lippé* had indicated that the test for impartiality in a substantial number of cases is whether the system is structured in a way that creates a reasonable apprehension of bias on an institutional level. Several factors could be considered to decide whether such bias exists. Determining which factors to use was held to be a matter of looking at the tribunal in question, the way that it operates in practice, and any safeguards that may exist to prevent incidents of bias in practice. In the Federal Court decision of *Sam Lévy & Associés Inc. v. Mayrand*,[156] the Court held that although the superintendent of bankruptcy was statutorily endowed with powers of investigation and adjudication, the fact that he used his delegation powers to hive off adjudicative responsibilities was sufficient to avoid a reasonable apprehension of institutional bias and a violation of the right to a fair hearing under the federal *Bill of Rights*. The Alberta Queen's Bench decision of *Currie v. Edmonton Remand Centre*[157] illustrates how operational practice may have a negative effect on the outcome. In *Currie*, the court found institutional bias from the overlapping functions of the prison guards and the disciplinary board members. *Currie* dealt with the question of whether disciplinary hearings used in a provincial prison exhibited signs of institutional bias in a substantial number of cases. The disciplinary hearings were used to determine whether prisoners had committed breaches of acceptable standards of conduct within the prison and the appropriate punishment for contraventions of the rules and regulations of the correctional institution. However, those who were responsible for maintaining order in the institution were also placed on the disciplinary panels. This caused an appearance of conflict—in particular, an appearance that the institution's primary decision would be maintained at the expense of the prisoner having a fair opportunity to contest it.

The applicants argued that the provisions of the Alberta *Corrections Act*[158] and the Alberta *Correctional Institution Regulation*,[159] which allowed for this decision-making structure to exist, were contrary to ss. 7 and 11(d) of the Charter. The Alberta Queen's Bench found that, although s. 11(d) did not apply in this case, there was indeed a breach of s. 7 of the Charter. In addition to finding that none of the traditional guarantees of independence existed in this case, the Court's holding was also based, in part, on the fact that the culture of the institution and these types of hearings within them made it impossible for a prisoner to assert his side of the story.

In summary, multifunctionality is a current concern of many administrative bodies. Often, tribunals will use their own de facto methods of reducing the appearance of bias, which can be raised by the enabling statute. The degree to which these practices will or should be taken into account is a matter of debate and the effect that these practices have on the outcome can be quite significant.

---

[156] 2005 FC 702, [2006] 2 F.C.R. 543, Martineau J. [*Sam Lévy*].

[157] 2006 ABQB 858, 276 D.L.R. (4th) 143 [*Currie*].

[158] R.S.A. 2000, c. C-29, s. 15.

[159] Alta. Reg. 205/2001, ss. 43, 44(3), 44(5), and 45.

VI. Conclusion

This chapter has provided a historical overview of the law of tribunal independence in Canada, linking it to its jurisprudential roots in judicial independence and its stated goals of preserving impartiality and avoiding bias. It has also provided a critical look at current situations that have given rise to allegations of individual and institutional bias in the administrative state. The chapter has aimed to illustrate that, although security of tenure, financial security, and administrative control—the central tenets of judicial independence—may figure in the problems of independence, impartiality, and bias affecting administrative tribunals, they are by no means the main issues of independence, impartiality, and bias currently affecting tribunals in their everyday operational contexts. Portrayed in artistic terms, the administrative state is a pastiche: it is made up of a plurality of structures and decision-making methods, stemming from the legislature, the executive, and administrative bodies themselves. The context of any administrative body, therefore, needs to be taken into account in determining the standard to apply when bias is alleged. Ultimately, one wonders whether a fundamental reconceiving of the nature and purpose of administrative tribunals is a necessary precondition to guaranteeing impartiality in the administrative state, whether the concepts of independence and impartiality need a fresh look within the administrative context, or both. By calling attention to the issues of adjudicative independence that are intimately tied to the complex concept of "policy making" in the administrative state and to the issue of multifunctionality, this chapter serves both as a call for a greater empirical understanding of the true challenges to the work of administrative tribunals and a more genuine reflection of these challenges in legislative policy, measures of reform, and judicial review.

SUGGESTED ADDITIONAL READINGS

BOOKS AND ARTICLES

Bryden, Philip, "Structural Independence of Administrative Tribunals in the Wake of *Ocean Port*" (2003) 16 Can. J. Admin. L. & Prac. 125.

Carnwath, Lord Justice, "Tribunals and the Courts—the UK Model" (2011) 24 Can. J. Admin. L. & Prac. 5.

Comtois, Suzanne, "Le contrôle de la cohérence décisionnelle au sein des tribunaux administratifs" (1990) 21 R.D.U.S. 77.

Ellis, S. Ronald, "The Justicizing of Quasi-Judicial Tribunals (Part I)" (2006) 19 Can. J. Admin. L. & Prac. 303.

Heckman, Gerald, & Sossin, Lorne, "How Do Canadian Administrative Law Protections Live Up to International Human Rights Standards? The Case of Independence" (2005) 50 McGill L.J. 193.

Jacobs, Laverne, "A Wavering Commitment?: Administrative Independence and Collaborative Governance in Ontario's Adjudicative Tribunals Accountability—Legislation" (2010) 28(2) Windsor Y.B. Access to Just. 285.

Jacobs, Laverne, "Tribunal Independence and Impartiality: Rethinking the Theory after Bell and Ocean Port Hotel—A Call for Empirical Analysis" in Laverne A. Jacobs & Anne L. Mactavish, eds., *Dialogue Between Courts and Tribunals: Essays in Administrative Law and Justice (2001-2007)* (Montreal: Éditions Thémis, 2008) 45.

Kligman, Robert D., *Bias* (Toronto: Butterworths, 1998).

Macdonald, Roderick A., "The Accoustics of Accountability—Towards Well-Tempered Tribunals" in András Sajó, ed., *Judicial Integrity* (Leiden: M. Nijhoff Publishers, 2004) 141.

Mullan, David J., "Chapter 14: Bias and Lack of Independence" in *Administrative Law* (Toronto: Irwin Law, 2001).

Mullan, David J., "Common and Divergent Elements of Practices of the Various Tribunals: An Overview of Present and Possible Developments" in *Administrative Law: Principles, Practice and Pluralism* (Special Lectures of the Law Society of Upper Canada 1992) (Toronto: Carswell, 1993), 461.

Sossin, Lorne, "Administrative Law at Pleasure: *Keen v. Canada*," available online: <adminlawincontext.emp.ca>.

Sossin, Lorne, & Charles W. Smith, "The Politics of Transparency and Independence Before Administrative Boards" (2012) Sask. L. Rev. 13.

Whitaker, K., M. Gottheil, & M. Uhlmann, "Consistency in Tribunal Decision Making: What Really Goes on Behind Closed Doors …" in Laverne A. Jacobs & Anne L. Mactavish, eds., *Dialogue Between Courts and Tribunals: Essays in Administrative Law and Justice (2001-2007)* (Montreal: Les éditions Thémis, 2008).

Wyman, K.M., "The Independence of Administrative Tribunals in an Era of Ever Expansive Judicial Independence" (2001) 14 Can. J. Admin. L. & Prac. 61.

CASES

2747-3174 Québec Inc. v. Quebec (Régie des permis d'alcool), [1996] 3 S.C.R. 919.

Association des juges administratifs de la Commission des lésions professionnelles c. Québec (Procureur général), 2011 QCCS 1614 (decision on appeal).

Beauregard v. Canada, [1986] 2 S.C.R. 56.

Bell Canada v. Canadian Telephone Employees Association, [2003] 1 S.C.R. 884.

Brosseau v. Alberta Securities Commission, [1989] 1 S.C.R. 301.

Canadian Pacific Ltd. v. Matsqui Indian Band, [1995] 1 S.C.R. 3.

Chrétien v. Canada (Commission of Inquiry into the Sponsorship Program and Advertising Activities, Gomery Commission), 2008 FC 802; aff'd 2010 FCA 283.

Committee for Justice and Liberty v. National Energy Board, [1978] 1 S.C.R. 369.

Communications, Energy and Paperworkers Union of Canada, Local 707 v. the Alberta Labour Relations Board (2004), 351 A.R. 267 (Q.B.).

Ellis-Don Ltd. v. Ontario (Labour Relations Board), [2001] 1 S.C.R. 221.

Energy Probe v. Canada (Atomic Energy Control Board) (1984), 15 D.L.R. (4th) 48 (F.C.A.).

Geza v. Canada (Minister of Citizenship and Immigration), [2005] 3 F.C.R. 3 (Fed. Ct.); rev'd [2006] 4 F.C.R. 377 (C.A.).

International Woodworkers of America, Local 2-69 v. Consolidated-Bathurst Packaging Ltd., [1990] 1 S.C.R. 282.

Keen v. Canada (Attorney General), 2009 FC 353.

McKenzie v. Minister of Public Safety and Solicitor General et al. (2006), 61 B.C.L.R. (4th) 57 (Sup. Ct.); (2007), 71 B.C.L.R. (4th) 1 (C.A.); [2007] S.C.C.A. No. 601 (QL).

Newfoundland Telephone Co. v. Newfoundland (Board of Commissioners of Public Utilities), [1992] 1 S.C.R. 623.

Ocean Port Hotel Ltd. v. British Columbia (Gen. Manager Liquor Control), [2001] 2 S.C.R. 781.

Old St. Boniface Residents Assn. Inc. v. Winnipeg (City), [1990] 3 S.C.R. 1170.

R. v. Lippé, [1991] 2 S.C.R. 114.

R. v. S. (R.D.), [1997] 3 S.C.R. 484.

Reference Re Remuneration of Judges of the Provincial Court (P.E.I.), [1997] 3 S.C.R. 3.

Sam Lévy & Associés Inc. v. Mayrand, [2006] 2 F.C.R. 543 (Fed. Ct.).

Save Richmond Farmland Society v. Richmond (Township), [1990] 3 S.C.R. 1213.

Thamotharem v. Canada (Minister of Citizenship and Immigration), [2006] 3 F.C.R. 168 (C.A.).

Tremblay v. Quebec (Commission des affaires sociales), [1992] 1 S.C.R. 952.

Valente v. The Queen, [1985] 2 S.C.R. 673.

STATUTES

Alberta Bill of Rights, R.S.A. 2000, c. A-14, s. 1(a).

Canadian Bill of Rights, S.C. 1960, c. 44, ss. 2(e), (f), reprinted in R.S.C. 1985, App. III.

Canadian Charter of Rights and Freedoms, Part I of the *Constitution Act, 1982*, being Schedule B to the *Canada Act 1982* (U.K.), 1982, c. 11, ss. 7, 11(d).

Charter of Human Rights and Freedoms, R.S.Q., c. C-12, s. 23.

CHAPTER NINE

Standard of Review: Back to the Future?

AUDREY MACKLIN*
Faculty of Law, University of Toronto

* Thanks to Lorne Sossin for his editorial assistance and to the other contributors in the volume who kindly offered insights and corrections. I am also grateful to David Dyzenhaus for his constructive suggestions for the first edition, Jennifer Nedelsky for her helpful comments on the second edition, and Sheila Wildeman for her careful and incisive analysis and generous encouragement throughout.

I. Introduction

Judges who hear appeals from decisions made by other judges about the interpretation or application of a statutory provision have a straightforward task: to determine whether the lower court arrived at the "right" answer. If the appellate judges determine that the answer is "wrong," they will replace it with the "correct" answer. This description presupposes that there is always a single, correct answer, which consists of the one given by a majority of judges perched on the higher rung of the judicial ladder. The main exception arises where an appellate court is called on to review findings of fact. Here, higher courts may hesitate to intervene because they lack the trial judge's advantage of first-hand exposure to the evidence, especially viva voce testimony, and because revisiting factual determinations of little precedential value constitutes a poor allocation of scarce judicial resources.

Judicial review of administrative action elicits a different set of questions that do not generally arise in ordinary appellate jurisprudence: Is there always only a single correct answer?[1] Who is better situated to determine the answer, the first-level, specialist decision-maker or the generalist reviewing judge? What criteria can assist in assessing relative expertise?

At present, the short answer to these questions is that a court called on to review the interpretation or application of a statutory provision by an administrative decision-maker will usually determine that the decision made by the agency, board, or tribunal assigned primary responsibility under the statute merits deference. In *Baker*, the Supreme Court of Canada endorsed David Dyzenhaus's articulation of deference as respect: "Deference as respect requires not submission but a respectful attention to the reasons offered or which could be offered in support of a decision."[2]

Deference is then quantified through the standard of review applied by the court to the impugned decision. Less deference means stricter review. An issue warranting no deference from the reviewing court will be judged in terms of its "correctness." An issue attracting deference will only be set aside if it is "unreasonable." Under the contemporary doctrine of standard of review, courts never completely relinquish their entitlement to have the last word and, therefore, insist that no decision can be completely immunized from judicial scrutiny.[3]

The longer answer to these questions requires embarking on a journey through the history of judicial review, the rise of the administrative state, contested conceptions of the rule of law, and judicial oscillation between at least two methodologies: one, a default rule with exceptions; the second, a multi-factorial balancing test. As Bette Davis famously warned in *All About Eve*, "Fasten your seatbelts. It's going to be a bumpy night."

Don't forget Deference

---

[1] One might plausibly contend that this question is (or ought to be) equally apposite to appeal as to judicial review. See the discussion in David Dyzenhaus, "Constituting the Rule of Law: Fundamental Values in Administrative Law" (2002) 27 Queen's L.J. 445 at 469-70, n. 46. If there is not always a single correct answer on review, there is also not always a single correct answer on appeal.

[2] *Baker v. Canada (Minister of Citizenship & Immigration)*, [1999] 2 S.C.R. 817 at para. 65 [*Baker*]; for the facts of *Baker*, see Grant Huscroft's Chapter 5, From Natural Justice to Fairness: Thresholds, Content, and the Role of Judicial Review.

[3] See the discussion of *Crevier v. A.G. (Québec) et al.*, [1981] 2 S.C.R. 220, in part IV.A, Is Judicial Review Constitutionally Protected?

II. The Prequel

In Chapter 1, An Introduction to Administrative Law: Some History and a Few Signposts for a Twisted Path, Colleen Flood and Jennifer Dolling surveyed the diverse reasons for the creation of administrative agencies, tribunals, and commissions. Certain functions—for example, licensing, distribution of goods or resources, and the resolution of polycentric disputes—are ill-suited to resolution in a bipolar or adversarial judicial process. Some domains, such as engineering, the environment, securities, and telecommunications, require a level and type of technical or experiential expertise that judges lack. Other areas—for example, immigration, social assistance, and workers' compensation—generate such a high volume of cases (usually involving people of limited means) that the ordinary courts and judicial processes would be overwhelmed into paralysis. Concerns of efficiency, cost, and specialization militate in favour of an administrative regime. In the 20th century, ideological conflict between the expanding administrative state and the courts (incisively and passionately critiqued by the legal realists) led governments in the Anglo-American legal world to withdraw certain tasks from courts and allocate them to newly created, specialized agencies. The iconic case is labour law. Judicial deployment of traditional common-law doctrines of freedom of contract, protection of private property, privity of contract, and prohibition on contracts in restraint of trade consistently thwarted legislation designed to provide a measure of protection to workers, standardize minimum terms of employment, and enable the emergence of an industrial relations regime based on union representation.

Frustrated with judicial hostility toward the objectives of labour-relations legislation, the government not only established a parallel administrative regime of labour relations boards, but also enacted statutory provisions, known as privative or preclusive clauses, that purported to oust entirely judicial review of the legality of administrative action. Ordinarily, judicial review is available for breaches of procedural fairness, errors of law, abuse of discretion, or factual findings made in the absence of evidence.

So-called privative clauses were originally intended to prevent courts from interfering with substantive outcomes of administrative action through the doctrines of error of law or absence of evidence for findings of fact. A primary, but not exclusive, motive behind privative clauses was to direct the judiciary to respect the relative expertise of the administrative or regulatory body. Other reasons for privative clauses included the promotion of prompt and final resolution of disputes or the rationing of scarce judicial resources. Moreover, although the dominant narrative of the 20th century depicts a progressive administrative state using privative clauses to shield social welfare legislation from the conservative grasp of a retrograde judiciary, one should not assume that the politics of judicial review are uniform or static. In recent years, for example, the Australian government has perfected the use of the privative clause in the service of precluding judicial review of the interpretation and application of draconian legislation directed at asylum seekers.

Privative clauses vary in wording, but usually include a grant of exclusive jurisdiction over the subject matter, a declaration of finality with respect to the outcome, and a prohibition on any court proceedings to set the outcome aside. The following example from the Saskatchewan *Workers' Compensation Act, 1979* is typical:

> The board shall have exclusive jurisdiction to examine, hear and determine all matters and questions arising under this Act and any other matter in respect of which a power, authority or

discretion is conferred upon the board ... . The decision and finding of the board under this Act upon all questions of fact and law are final and conclusive and no proceedings by or before the board shall be restrained by injunction, prohibition or other proceeding or removable by *certiorari* or otherwise in any court.[4]

The privative clause poses a conundrum for the traditional conception of the rule of law. On the one hand, a legislative grant of authority is always circumscribed by the terms of the statute. The common law presumes that citizens retain access to the ordinary courts in order to ensure that creatures of statute do not exceed or abuse the power granted to them. Making government actors accountable to the ordinary (and independent) courts is a principle that Dicey espoused as essential to the rule of law. As the British jurist H.W.R. Wade wrote, the rule of law demands that "administrative agencies and tribunals must at all costs be prevented from being sole judges of the validity of their own acts."[5] As discussed below, the Supreme Court of Canada has even elevated judicial review to a constitutionally protected principle under s. 96 of the *Constitution Act, 1867*.

On the other hand, the doctrine of parliamentary supremacy dictates that the legislator enacts the law, and the court must interpret and apply the law in accordance with the legislator's intent. A privative clause pits the second principle against the first by stating rather clearly and unambiguously that the legislator intends to oust the courts from supervising the actions of the administrative decision-maker.

Not surprisingly, judges historically resisted the privative clause's "plain meaning" and circumvented it through the following chain of reasoning, most powerfully articulated in the House of Lords' *Anisminic*[6] case: decision-makers' jurisdiction is demarcated by statute; actions that exceed jurisdiction *purport* to be decisions or findings, but in actuality are nullities. Therefore, "decisions" or "findings" that are insulated by a privative clause do not include actions that exceed the jurisdiction granted to the decision-maker.

If a college of physicians and surgeons purported to suspend the licence of a dentist to practise dentistry, we might all agree that the putative suspension was beyond the jurisdiction of the college and not protected by a privative clause. However, few real cases present such starkly deviant administrative behaviour. Typically, the issue is the interpretation of a statutory provision, inferences from evidence whose relevance to the outcome depends on a particular statutory construction, or the exercise of discretion. Judges faced with a privative clause assigned themselves the task of determining whether the issue fell "within jurisdiction" and, therefore, within the ambit of the privative clause or was a "jurisdictional question" that determined the outer boundary of the decision-maker's authority. If the latter, a court was entitled to review the decision. At this juncture, and before the emergence of a variable standard of review, correctness was the implicit and exclusive standard of review. Rather like the early approach to natural justice, review in the face of a privative clause was an all-or-nothing affair. Either the issue was a jurisdictional question, and the courts treated it as they would an issue on appeal, or it was virtually inoculated from judicial oversight.

---

4 *Workers' Compensation Act, 1979*, S.S. 1979, c. W-17.1, s. 22, quoted in *Pasienchyk v. Saskatchewan (Workers' Compensation Board)*, [1997] 2 S.C.R. 890 at para. 5 [*Pasienchyk*].

5 H.W.R. Wade, *Administrative Law*, 4th ed. (Oxford: Clarendon Press, 1977).

6 *Anisminic Ltd. v. Foreign Compensation Commission*, [1969] 2 A.C. 147 (H.L.).

The effectiveness of privative clauses in deterring judicial intervention depended on the ease and frequency with which courts could designate an issue as determinative of jurisdiction, therefore warranting strict judicial scrutiny. Two techniques deployed by the courts were the "preliminary or collateral question" doctrine, and the "asking the wrong question" doctrine.

In the 1971 case of *Bell v. Ontario (Human Rights Commission)*,[7] the Supreme Court of Canada considered the interpretation of s. 3 of the Ontario *Human Rights Code*,[8] which, inter alia, proscribed discrimination on the basis of race in the provision of rental housing. The provision applied to rental of a "self-contained dwelling unit" and the landlord argued that the flat for rent in his house did not fall within the meaning of "self-contained dwelling unit." The landlord sought an order of prohibition to prevent the board of inquiry law professor Walter Tarnopolsky from investigating the complaint on the ground that it had no jurisdiction under the *Human Rights Code* over the rental of his unit. The Supreme Court of Canada held that ascertaining the meaning of "self-contained dwelling unit" was preliminary to the question whether the landlord had engaged in discrimination contrary to the *Human Rights Code*. According to Martland J., the definition of "self-contained dwelling unit" was "an issue of law respecting the scope of the operation of the Act, and on the answer to that question depends the authority of the board to inquire into the complaint of discrimination at all ... and a wrong decision on it would not enable the board to proceed further."[9] On the basis of the landlord's affidavit and photographs of his house, the majority of the Supreme Court determined that the rental unit was not "self-contained." The landlord "was not compelled to await the decision of the board on that issue before seeking to have it determined in a court of law."[10] In so stating, the majority tacitly communicated that it had nothing to learn or gain from permitting the board of inquiry to first offer its own interpretation of "self-contained dwelling unit."

In *Metropolitan Life Insurance Company v. International Union of Operating Engineers, Local 796*,[11] the Supreme Court of Canada addressed an Ontario Labour Relations Board certification of a union as the sole bargaining agent for a group of employees engaged in janitorial and building maintenance work. The provision that the union relied on for certification required evidence that at least 55 percent of the employees were members of the union. The union constitution provided for membership by "operating engineers" alone, but, in practice, that union had signed up workers of many occupational classifications. Almost two decades earlier, the Ontario Labour Relations Board had adopted a policy of imposing a uniform set of criteria for determining whether employees were members of a union applicant for certification. These consisted of an application for membership, followed by acceptance of membership, an assumption of the financial or other responsibilities of membership, and enjoyment of all the rights and privileges of union membership. Eligibility under the union constitution was only one factor and, even then, only an explicit

---

7   [1971] S.C.R. 756, rev'g *R. v. Tarnopolsky, Ex parte Bell*, [1970] 2 O.R. 672 [*Bell*].

8   R.S.O. 1990, c. H.19.

9   *Bell, supra* note 7 at 775.

10   *Ibid.* at 769.

11   [1970] S.C.R. 425 [*Metropolitan Life*].

constitutional exclusion from membership status (along with its rights and privileges) would be determinative. The board's reasons explained at length the rationale for its approach and specifically addressed why reliance on union constitutions as the determinant of union membership would produce incongruous outcomes and confer unfair advantages on some unions over others. In the particular case before it, the board considered that over 55 percent of the employees had become union members according to its criteria. The Ontario *Labour Relations Act*[12] contained a form of privative clause. The employer sought judicial review and ultimately appealed to the Supreme Court of Canada.

The Court ruled that the determination by the board was not protected by the privative clause. Although the question whether 55 percent of the employees were members of the union was undoubtedly an issue within the exclusive jurisdiction of the board, the board lost jurisdiction because it employed a faulty reasoning process. According to the Court, "the Board has failed to deal with the question remitted to it (i.e. whether the employees in question were members of the union at the relevant date) and instead has decided a question which was not remitted to it (i.e. whether in regard to those employees there has been fulfillment of the conditions [for membership devised by the Board])."[13] Implicit in the Court's reasoning was the assumption that the union constitution was determinative of membership; indeed, the Court did not engage at all with the rationale of the board in employing different criteria. The upshot of "asking the wrong question" was that even matters otherwise within the jurisdiction of a decision-maker (and thus protected by a privative clause) could become jurisdictional and subject to judicial scrutiny if the decision-maker engaged in a reasoning process that the Court deemed defective.

The doctrines of preliminary or collateral question and asking the wrong question were derided by academic commentators as formalistic, malleable, and instrumental devices manufactured by the courts to meddle in spheres where the legislature had deliberately and explicitly excluded them. Courts inclined to disagree with a decision could, with little effort, transform almost any issue into a preliminary or collateral question, or depict the tribunal as asking the wrong question, in order to impugn a decision as the product of a flawed chain of reasoning.

The doctrines described above have largely been discarded, but the language of jurisdiction lives on. Familiarity with the jurisprudential history of privative clauses and jurisdiction remains important for two reasons. First, the sources of judicial anxiety about jurisdiction, rooted in the rule of law, remain salient. Second, it is arguable that traces of the "preliminary or collateral question" and "asking the wrong question" doctrines are forgotten but not gone. For example, the assertion that a statutory provision is properly understood according to the principles of another area of law survives in the characterization of a legal question as one of "central importance to the legal system as a whole."[14] A reasoning process that inquires into the effect of a given interpretation on advancing the broader objectives of the statute may still be rejected as a flawed and self-aggrandizing attempt to expand the jurisdiction of the decision-maker.[15]

---

12   S.O. 1995, c. 1, Sch. A.

13   *Metropolitan Life, supra* note 11 at 435.

14   *Toronto (City) v. C.U.P.E., Local 79, infra* note 110 at para. 62, per LeBel J.; see also *U.E.S., Local 298 v. Bibeault*, [1988] 2 S.C.R. 1048 [*Bibeault*].

15   *Barrie Public Utilities v. Canadian Cable Television Association*, 2003 SCC 28, [2003] 1 S.C.R. 476 [*Barrie Utilities*].

III. The Blockbuster:
C.U.P.E. v. New Brunswick Liquor Corporation

C.U.P.E. v. N.B. Liquor Corporation[16] is to the standard of review what *Nicholson*[17] is to procedure and *Baker* is to discretion: a judgment that shifts the legal landscape onto new terrain.[18] The facts are straightforward. A public sector union, Canadian Union of Public Employees (CUPE), went on strike. Under the terms of the New Brunswick *Public Service Labour Relations Act*,[19] striking employees were prohibited from picketing and employers were prohibited from using replacement workers. Section 102(3) of the Act stated:

> 102(3) ... during the continuance of the strike
>
> (a) the employer shall not replace the striking employees or fill their position with any other employee, and
>
> (b) no employee shall picket, parade or in any manner demonstrate in or near any place of business of the employer.[20]

Section 101 of the Act contained a lengthy privative clause declaring, *inter alia*, that every "award, direction, decision, declaration, or ruling of the Board ... is final and shall not be questioned or reviewed in any court."[21]

The employer complained to the N.B. Public Service Labour Relations Board that the union was picketing, contrary to s. 102(3)(b), and the union complained that the employer was filling striking employees' positions with management personnel, contrary to s. 102(3)(a). The board upheld the employer's complaint and ordered the union to cease and desist picketing. It also upheld the complaint against the employer and ordered it to refrain from using management personnel to do work ordinarily performed by bargaining unit employees. The employer successfully sought judicial review of the board's order against it and, eventually, the union appealed to the Supreme Court of Canada.

The issue in the case was the interpretation of s. 102(3)(a). The employer argued that the provision should be interpreted to prohibit the temporary replacement of employees "with any other employee" or permanently filling their positions "with any other employee." Management personnel were not employees as defined in the Act, therefore s. 102(3)(a) was not breached by the use of management personnel to replace employees during the strike. The employer argued that the objective of the provision was to preserve the positions of the employees once the strike was over. The union argued that the phrase "with any other employee" only applied to permanently filling positions, and not to temporarily replacing employees during the strike.[22] Therefore, s. 102(3) also precluded the temporary replacement of employees by management personnel.

---

[16]   [1979] 2 S.C.R. 227 [*CUPE*].

[17]   *Nicholson v. Haldimand-Norfolk (Regional) Board of Commissioners of Police*, [1979] 1 S.C.R. 311.

[18]   See Grant Huscroft's Chapter 5, From Natural Justice to Fairness: Thresholds, Content, and the Role of Judicial Review; Sheila Wildeman's Chapter 10, Pas de Deux: Deference and Non-Deference in Action.

[19]   R.S.N.B. 1973, c. P-25 [PSLRA].

[20]   PSLRA, *supra* note 19, s. 102(3); *CUPE*, *supra* note 16 at para. 4.

[21]   PSLRA, *supra* note 19, s. 101(1); *CUPE*, *supra* note 16 at para. 14.

[22]   *CUPE*, *supra* note 16 at paras. 5-6.

Writing for the Supreme Court of Canada, Dickson J. (as he then was) paraphrased the board's approach to interpreting s. 102(3) as follows:

> It was the opinion of the board that when the Legislature saw fit to grant the right to strike to public employees, it intended through the enactment of s. 102(3) to restrict the possibility of picket-line violence by prohibiting strikebreaking, on the one hand, and picketing, on the other. This apparent intention, the board held, would be frustrated [by the employer's interpretation]. The result of such an interpretation would be that strikers would have been deprived of their right to picket, but the employer would not have been deprived of the right to employ strike-breakers.[23]

The Supreme Court allowed the union's appeal. However, it did not follow the extant analytical framework toward the conclusion that the interpretation of s. 102(3) was a question within the jurisdiction of the board and thus immunized from judicial review by the privative clause. Instead, Dickson J. canvassed the reasons for the existence of privative clauses, emphasizing the legislative choice to confer certain tasks on administrative actors, the specialized expertise and accumulated experience of administrative bodies, and the virtues of judicial restraint. In the case at bar, the interpretation of s. 102(3) "would seem to lie logically at the heart of the specialized jurisdiction confided to the Board."[24] As such, a court should only interfere (by labelling as jurisdictional error), an interpretation of the provision that is "so patently unreasonable that its construction cannot be rationally supported by the relevant legislation."[25]

The Supreme Court's judgment in *CUPE* did not break with earlier jurisprudence that invoked jurisdictional error to circumvent privative clauses. Rather, it reconfigured the analysis of when, why, and how the doctrine of jurisdictional error ought to be deployed. Most important, it conveyed a spirit of curial deference, a recognition that administrative decision-makers are not merely "inferior tribunals," but specialized bodies that possess a legislative mandate to apply their expertise and experience to matters that they may be better suited to address than an "ordinary court." This change of heart regarding the appropriate role of judicial review eventually transcended the confines of privative clauses to encompass substantive judicial review in general, including the exercise of discretion.

A reading of *CUPE* reveals three sources of the Supreme Court's doctrinal change. First, the Court situates the case in a broader reappraisal of the respective roles assigned by the legislature to the courts and to administrative bodies in the implementation of regulatory regimes.[26] According to Dickson J., courts should recognize and respect the fact that these specialized decision-makers bear primary responsibility for implementing their statutory mandate and may be better suited to the interpretive task than the generalist judge.

Second, the judgment candidly admits that, because the provision in dispute "bristles with ambiguities,"[27] no single interpretation could lay claim to being "correct." Instead, there

---

23   *Ibid.* at para. 7.

24   *Ibid.* at para. 15.

25   *Ibid.* at para. 16.

26   *Ibid.* at para. 15.

27   *Ibid.* at para. 4.

were several plausible interpretations, including that of the board, the majority of the New Brunswick Court of Appeal, and a minority opinion of the Court of Appeal. Dickson J. canvassed at length the basis for each possible interpretation, not in order to discern which one was correct, but to demonstrate why the board's interpretation "would seem at least as reasonable as the alternative interpretations suggested in the Court of Appeal" and, in any event, could not be described as patently unreasonable.[28] Although *CUPE* is concerned with a statutory provision whose ambiguity was attributable to poor drafting, it has been amplified in subsequent cases, such as *Corn Growers*[29] and *Domtar*,[30] into a more radical critique of the conceit that there is always only one correct interpretation of a statutory provision. Ambiguity, gaps, silences, and contradictions can rarely (if ever) be completely excised from text. This ineluctable interpretive choice makes it possible to ask who is better placed to make the choice—the tribunal or the court? In other words, indeterminacy of meaning also underwrites the plea for judicial humility that is at the heart of *CUPE*. Moreover, Dickson J.'s interpretive survey notably focused on the meaning of the provision in the context of the statute, its purpose, and the consequences of various interpretive options for the fulfillment of the legislative scheme's objectives. He did not resort to dictionary definitions of "fill" or "replace," invoke common-law presumptions about access to the courts, or employ mechanistic canons of statutory construction.

Finally, Dickson J. acknowledged the failure of prior judicial efforts to construct a coherent, principled means of distinguishing reviewable questions from those insulated by a privative clause. He noted that the "preliminary or collateral question" method is not helpful because one can, with little effort, characterize just about anything as preliminary or collateral. He admitted that identifying what is and is not jurisdictional can also be difficult, but counselled that "courts, in my view, should not be alert to brand as jurisdictional, and therefore subject to broader curial review, that which may be doubtfully so."[31] Unfortunately, the judgment does not set out an alternative, except to suggest that "jurisdiction is, typically, to be determined at the outset of the inquiry"[32] and, in the case at bar, the board's statutory authority over the parties (in this case, the union and the employer) and the subject matter (the conduct of a lawful strike), indisputably conferred jurisdiction "in the narrow sense of authority to enter upon an inquiry."[33] The issue then became whether the board did "something which takes the exercise of its powers outside the protection of the privative or preclusive clause."[34] According to Dickson J., short of a patently unreasonable interpretation of a statutory provision, courts should not interfere with the result reached by the administrative decision-maker. The shorthand description of *CUPE*'s outcome is that a

---

[28] *Ibid.* at para. 29.

[29] *National Corn Growers Assn. v. Canada (Import Tribunal)*, [1990] 2 S.C.R. 1324, Wilson J. [*Corn Growers*].

[30] *Domtar Inc. v. Quebec (Commission d'appel en matière de lesions professionnelles)*, [1993] 2 S.C.R. 756, L'Heureux-Dubé J. [*Domtar*].

[31] *CUPE, supra* note 16 at paras. 9-10.

[32] *Ibid.* at para. 9.

[33] *Ibid.* at para. 12.

[34] *Ibid.* at para. 16.

jurisdictional question is assessed according to a standard of correctness, while questions within jurisdiction are evaluated against a standard of "patent unreasonableness."

CUPE transformed the conceptual basis of substantive review through a reformulation of the institutional relationship between courts and the administrative state. As Dyzenhaus and Fox-Decent[35] observed, however, there is a certain irony in the fact that CUPE was decided only a year after Nicholson. The latter heralded a new era in procedural review by vastly expanding the range of administrative action subject to judicial scrutiny on grounds of procedural fairness. Meanwhile, CUPE signalled a radical break from the existing modes of substantive review by advocating judicial retreat from the interventionism of the past. Interestingly, both Nicholson and CUPE were and continue to be hailed by most commentators as progressive and forward-looking judgments.

IV. The Sequels

In the aftermath of CUPE, many provincial superior courts embraced the message of curial deference, although the Supreme Court of Canada itself displayed more diffidence. In particular, the majority of the Supreme Court seemed to disregard Dickson J.'s caution against labelling issues as jurisdictional in order to subject them to the more stringent correctness review.[36]

In Bibeault,[37] the Supreme Court of Canada demonstrated the gap between following the spirit of CUPE and abiding by its letter. The issue in the case was contentious in Quebec labour law. By a 7:4 majority, a specially convened full panel of the Quebec Labour Court upheld a labour commissioner's order. The Supreme Court of Canada disagreed.

Although the judgment by Beetz J. certainly cites CUPE, it is noteworthy that the word "deference" appears nowhere in the judgment. The task Beetz J. set for himself was the elaboration of a test for determining what constitutes a jurisdictional question (subject to correctness) and which questions are within a tribunal's jurisdiction (subject to patent unreasonableness). Beetz J.'s innovation was to propose a pragmatic and functional analysis for distinguishing between jurisdictional and non-jurisdiction-conferring provisions. The central question posed by the analysis is not whether a question is preliminary or collateral, but "did the legislator intend the question to be within the jurisdiction conferred on the tribunal?"[38]

---

35   David Dyzenhaus & Evan Fox-Decent, "Rethinking the Process/Substance Distinction: Baker v. Canada" (2001) 51 U.T.L.J. 193 [Dyzenhaus & Fox-Decent].

36   For example, in L'Acadie (Syndicat des employés de production du québec et de l'acadie v. Canada (Canadian human rights commission), [1989] 2 S.C.R. 879), decided a few years after CUPE, a unanimous Supreme Court of Canada resiled from the idea that jurisdiction ought to be determined at the outset and ruled that a jurisdictional question attracting a correctness standard could arise anytime and could apply not only to interpretation, but also to findings of fact, applications of law to facts, or in the fashioning of a remedy. Elsewhere in the jurisprudence, when addressing the capacity of tribunals to entertain Charter challenges to their constitutive statute, the Supreme Court described tribunal "jurisdiction over the whole of the matter" as jurisdiction over parties, subject matter, and remedy. Cuddy Chicks Ltd. v. Ontario (Labour Relations Board), [1991] 2 S.C.R. 5 at para. 12.

37   Supra note 14.

38   Ibid. at para. 120.

Responding to this question involves an examination not only of "the wording of the enactment conferring jurisdiction on the administrative tribunal, but the purpose of the statute creating the tribunal, the reasons for its existence, the area of expertise of its members and the nature of the problem before the tribunal."[39] By framing the question in terms of legislative intent, Beetz J. retains a formal commitment to parliamentary supremacy and a rejection of a contextual statutory interpretation. Similarly, he invokes the expertise of the tribunal as a relevant factor in the analysis, which hearkens back to *CUPE*'s plea for judicial humility. Nevertheless, in his application of the criteria, Beetz J. quickly concludes that the issue before the Court was indeed a jurisdictional question that the commissioner failed to answer correctly.[40] Rather than arrange the subsequent jurisprudence chronologically, we identify different jurisprudential instruments that play out the themes of *CUPE*—though not always harmoniously. The content given to each standard of review, as well as the actual application of the particular standard of review to the statutory provision at issue, is the topic of Sheila Wildeman's Chapter 10, Pas de Deux: Deference and Non-Deference in Action.

A. Is Judicial Review Constitutionally Protected?

A central common-law precept of statutory construction is that interpretation should express the will of the legislator. To the extent that the judiciary accepts the doctrine of parliamentary supremacy, a given interpretation is always defensible insofar as the legislator is free to amend the statutory provision if judicial interpretation does not properly capture the intended meaning. In theory, then, a legislator could revise and refine a privative clause in order to better effectuate the ouster of the courts. However, a few years after *CUPE*, the Supreme Court of Canada obviated the possibility of completely insulating provincial administrative bodies from judicial review. In *Crevier v. A.G. (Québec) et al.*,[41] the constitutionality of a privative clause in a Quebec statute was challenged on the basis that confiding final and unreviewable decision-making authority to a provincial administrative tribunal would violate s. 96 of the *Constitution Act, 1867*, by depriving federally appointed, s. 96 judges of a quintessential judicial function.[42] Writing for the Court, Laskin C.J.C. upheld the privative clause against s. 96 attack, but read it narrowly as permitting correctness review for challenges based on division of powers and, by implication, patent unreasonableness review for matters within jurisdiction. In other words, *Crevier* constitutionalized judicial review for jurisdictional questions, even in the face of a privative clause, thereby placing the matter beyond the reach of legislative amendment.[43]

---

[39]   *Ibid.* at para. 123.

[40]   But compare *Ivanhoe Inc. v. UFCW, Local 500*, 2001 SCC 47, [2001] 2 S.C.R. 565 [*Ivanhoe*], where the Court adopted a standard of patent unreasonableness for the interpretation of the same phrase in a slightly revised statute.

[41]   *Supra* note 3.

[42]   (U.K.), 30 & 31 Vict., c. 3. Section 96 grants jurisdiction over the appointment of superior court judges to the federal government, but has been interpreted to protect "essential" judicial functions associated with superior court judges.

[43]   See Mary Liston's Chapter 2, Governments in Miniature: The Rule of Law in the Administrative State.

In *Royal Oak*, the Supreme Court of Canada was confronted with a privative clause in s. 22 of the federal *Canada Labour Code*[44] that purported to thwart judicial review "on any ground ... including the ground that the ... decision ... is beyond the jurisdiction of the Board to make ... or that, in the course of any proceeding, the Board for any reason exceeded or lost its jurisdiction."[45] The Court did not pause to contemplate the legislator's intention in granting a tribunal exclusive jurisdiction to determine its own jurisdiction before proceeding to subject the decision to review, albeit on the more deferential standard of patent unreasonableness. As L'Heureux-Dubé J. stated in *Pasienchyk*, "[s]ince, as a matter of constitutional law, a legislature may not, *however clearly it expresses itself*, protect an administrative body from review on matters of jurisdiction, it also cannot be left to decide freely which matters are jurisdictional and which come within the Board's exclusive jurisdiction."[46] In terms of the rule-of-law tension between fidelity to parliamentary intent and the common-law presumption of access to the ordinary courts, the Supreme Court's expansive interpretation of s. 96 of the *Constitution Act, 1867*[47] ensures that the latter trumps the former.

The Supreme Court's devotion to the primacy of access to the ordinary courts remains to be tested where courts themselves (rather than the legislature) police access to first-level judicial review. As we have seen in *Baker* and will see in *Pushpanathan*, below, the *Immigration and Refugee Protection Act* imposes a written leave requirement on first-level judicial review.[48] Whereas legislatures purport to limit access to judicial review via a privative clause, a leave requirement endows Federal Court judges with authority to restrict access to judicial review by denying leave. The jurisprudence indicates that the threshold for leave is low and ought to be granted where the applicant makes "an arguable case,"[49] and denied only where it is "plain and obvious that the applicant would have no reasonable chance of succeeding."[50] Apart from descriptions of a quantitative threshold, there are no discernible qualitative criteria, no reasons requirement, and no appeal from a denial of leave. In practice, about 85 percent of applications for leave to seek judicial review of refugee decisions are denied, although there is radical variation in grant rates betweeen judges. One might contend that judicial consideration of a leave application constitutes a perfunctory form of access to the ordinary courts, but the fact that the leave process operates in an opaque and unaccountable manner makes this characterization difficult to sustain from a rule-of-law perspective.[51]

---

44   R.S.C. 1985, c. L-2.

45   *Royal Oak Mines Inc. v. Canada (Labour Relations Board)*, [1996] 1 S.C.R. 369 at para. 30 [*Royal Oak*].

46   *Pasienchyk, supra* note 4 at para. 55 (emphasis added).

47   *Supra* note 42.

48   *Immigration and Refugee Protection Act*, S.C. 2001, c. 27, s. 72.

49   *Bains v. Canada (Minister of Employment and Immigration)*, [1990] F.C.J. No. 457 (QL), 47 Admin. L.R. 317; 109 N.R. 239 (F.C.A.) [*Bains*].

50   *Saleh v. Canada (Minister of Citizenship and Immigration)*, 2010 FC 303, [1989] F.C.J. No. 825 (QL).

51   The Federal Court in *Bains, supra* note 49, described the leave requirement as "in reality the other side of the coin of the traditional jurisdiction to summarily terminate proceedings that dispose no reasonably arguable case." *Quaere* the analogy between judicial review of government action and private civil action. Note also that the applicant for judicial review bears the burden of satisfying a judge that leave ought to be granted, whereas the party opposing an action bears the burden of proof in a motion to strike.

B. Beyond Privative Clauses

The Supreme Court of Canada demonstrated its most enthusiastic embrace of *CUPE* by making "should the court defer?" a question asked not only where statutes contain privative clauses, but also where statutes contain finality clauses,[52] leave intact the option of judicial review, or even provide a full appeal to the courts on questions of law and fact.

Pezim v. British Columbia (Superintendent of Brokers)[53] is noteworthy because the issue concerned a question of law and the enabling statute provided for a right of appeal. Writing for the Court, Iacobucci J.'s judgment offers a time-lapse photograph of the rapid shift in the jurisprudence from the language of "jurisdiction" and "privative clause" to "expertise" and "deference."[54] The issue was whether newly acquired information about asset value constituted a "material change" requiring disclosure. At the outset of his review of principles of judicial review, Iacobucci J. hews closely to *Bibeault*, and states:

> The central question in ascertaining the standard of review is to determine the legislative intent in conferring jurisdiction on the administrative tribunal. ... Included in the analysis is an examination of the tribunal's role or function. Also crucial is whether or not the agency's decisions are protected by a privative clause. Finally, of fundamental importance, is whether or not the question goes to the jurisdiction of the tribunal involved.[55]

A few paragraphs later, Iacobucci J. declares that "even where there is no privative clause and where there is a statutory right of appeal, the concept of the specialization of duties requires that deference be shown to decisions of specialized tribunals on matters which fall squarely within the tribunal's expertise."[56]

The presence of a privative clause was apparently not so crucial after all, and the fundamentally important "jurisdictional question" was supplanted by "expertise" as the key determinant of standard of review.[57]

In the case at bar, there was no question but that the B.C. Securities Commission had jurisdiction over the parties (members of the board of directors of reporting issuers on the Vancouver Stock Exchange), the subject matter (disclosure of material change), and the remedy (suspension of trading). The Court identified several factors that contributed to the conclusion that the B.C. Securities Commission was a highly specialized tribunal and that an interpretation of material change in the B.C. *Securities Act*[58] "arguably goes to the core of its regulatory mandate and expertise" in regulating the securities market in the public interest.[59]

---

[52] A finality clause typically states that the decision of the agency is final and binding on the parties, but the clause says nothing about judicial review.

[53] [1994] 2 S.C.R. 557 [*Pezim*].

[54] See also *Canada (Director of Investigation and Research) v. Southam Inc.*, [1997] 1 S.C.R. 748 at para. 31 [*Southam*]: "There is no privative clause, and so jurisdiction is not at issue."

[55] *Pezim, supra* note 53 at 596.

[56] *Ibid.* at 593.

[57] See also *United Brotherhood of Carpenters and Joiners of America, Local 579 v. Bradco Construction Ltd.*, [1993] 2 S.C.R. 316.

[58] S.B.C. 1985, c. 83.

[59] *Pezim, supra* note 53.

Although the Court concluded that the interpretation of the statutory provision warranted curial deference, it conspicuously failed to describe the applicable standard of review as patently unreasonable. Instead, Iacobucci J. simply adverted to the need for considerable deference. Three years later, in *Canada (Director of Investigation and Research) v. Southam Inc.*,[60] Iacobucci J. made explicit what he had only hinted at in *Pezim*—namely, an intermediate standard of review between patent unreasonableness and correctness. He labelled the standard "reasonableness *simpliciter*" and declared it (retrospectively) as the standard of review applied in *Pezim*. To understand how the perceived need for a "middle ground" emerged, one should return to *Pezim*'s shift in emphasis from privative clauses to relative expertise. A binary focus on the presence or absence of a privative clause (and the attendant jurisdictional–non-jurisdictional question) aligns with two standards of review embodying the presence or absence of deference. Shifting to an emphasis on relative expertise does not map easily onto a dichotomy, which may help to explain the impetus driving the Court to insert reasonableness *simpliciter* into the spectrum.

Southam concerned a finding by the Competition Tribunal that Southam's acquisition of various newspapers within a given advertising market substantially lessened competition. By way of remedy, the tribunal gave Southam the option of divesting itself of one of two community papers. The statute provided for an appeal directly to the Federal Court of Appeal. Two aspects of the tribunal's decision were the subject of appeal to the Supreme Court: the dimensions of the relevant market within which to assess impact on competition and the remedy of divestment.

After reviewing various factors pertinent to the standard of review, Iacobucci J. concluded that some factors pointed toward deference and some away from it:

> Several considerations indicated deference: the fact that the dispute is over a question of mixed law and fact; the fact that the purpose of the *Competition Act*[61] is broadly economic, and so is better served by the exercise of economic judgment; and the fact that the application of principles of competition law falls squarely within the area of the Tribunal's expertise. Other considerations counsel a more exacting form of review: the existence of an unfettered statutory right of appeal from decisions of the Tribunal and the presence of judges on the Tribunal. Because there are indications both ways, the proper standard of review was found to fall somewhere between the ends of the spectrum. Because the expertise of the Tribunal, which is the most important consideration, suggests deference, Iacobucci J. concluded that a posture more deferential than exacting was warranted.[62]

The middle ground is, of course, reasonableness *simpliciter*: "An unreasonable decision is one that, in the main, is not supported by any reasons that can stand up to a somewhat probing examination." This examination entails an inquiry into the "evidentiary foundation or the logical process by which conclusions are sought to be drawn from it."[63] Although Iacobucci J. is not entirely clear on this point, he seems to regard the most deferential stan-

---

[60] *Southam, supra* note 54.

[61] R.S.C. 1985, c. C-34.

[62] *Southam, supra* note 54 at para. 54.

[63] *Ibid.* at para. 56.

dard of patent unreasonableness as appropriate only in the presence of a privative clause, where intervention must formally be justified by resort to the concept of jurisdiction.

The insertion of an intermediate standard of review did little to promote predictability or determinacy in this area of administrative law. Moreover, some contended that if three standards were better than two, four standards must be better than three, five better than four, and so on. Others suggested that the reasonableness standard ought to be applied flexibly—sometimes closer to correctness, sometimes closer to patent unreasonableness—depending on the balance of factors for and against deference in the particular case. The Supreme Court of Canada squelched both propositions in *Law Society of New Brunswick v. Ryan* and stood firm on three standards of review.[64]

V. Pragmatic and Functional Redux: Pushpanathan v. Canada

Shortly after *Southam*, the Supreme Court of Canada took the opportunity to consolidate and summarize the factors to be taken into account in determining the appropriate standard of review. *Pushpanathan v. Canada (Minister of Citizenship and Immigration)*[65] concerned the interpretation of a provision in the *Immigration Act*[66] (incorporating article 1F(c) of the *UN Convention Relating to the Status of Refugees*) that excludes from refugee status those persons "guilty of acts contrary to the purposes and principles of the United Nations." Pushpanathan had made a refugee claim in Canada. Before his claim was heard, he was convicted in Canada of the offence of conspiracy to traffic in a narcotic. He was subsequently excluded from refugee protection under article 1F(c) on the basis of his conviction. The issue in the case concerned whether "acts contrary to the purposes and principles of the United Nations" included a criminal conviction for drug trafficking in the country of asylum.[67] A distinctive feature of the *Immigration Act* (also applicable in *Baker*) was the mechanism for judicial review. The statute contained no privative clause or right of appeal. Instead, judicial review could only commence with leave of a judge of the Federal Court, and no reasons were required where leave was denied. If leave was granted and the case heard, the losing party could only appeal to the Federal Court of Appeal if the trial judge certified "a serious question of general importance."

Writing for the Court, Bastarache J. reformulated *Bibeault*'s pragmatic and functional question into "Did the legislator intend this question to attract judicial deference?" He organized the factors relevant to discerning this legislative intent into four categories: (1) privative clause, (2) expertise, (3) purpose of the act as a whole and of the provision in particular, and (4) nature of the problem (question of law, fact, or mixed law and fact). Jurisprudence after *Pushpanathan* routinely relied on these four categories. It remains unclear whether, where, and to what extent these factors exert influence after *Dunsmuir*. Therefore, acquaintance with the elements of the pragmatic and functional analysis remains important.

---

64 2003 SCC 20, [2003] 1 S.C.R. 247 [*Ryan*].

65 [1998] 1 S.C.R. 982 [*Pushpanathan*].

66 *Supra* note 48.

67 *Pushpanathan, supra* note 65 at para. 22.

Although the *Pushpanathan* Court identifies four separate factors, arguably there are only two ingredients in the deference calculus: the legislator's direct or indirect pronouncement about judicial supervision (privative clause, finality clause, common-law judicial review, statutory judicial review, appeal) and the reviewing court's assessment of the agency's relative expertise. The inquiry into statutory purpose and nature of the problem seem to address specific indicia of expertise. In *Pushpanathan* itself, the Court admits that "purpose and expertise often overlap,"[68] and that the basis for greater security of general questions of law than questions of fact relates to the relative expertise of courts versus agencies.[69] A year after Pushpanathan, *Baker* expanded the reach of the standard of review inquiry to encompass judicial review of discretion, as well as questions of fact, mixed fact and law, and law. The following survey summarizes the meaning ascribed to the four elements of the *Pushpanathan* test and provides examples of their application in various cases, bearing in mind the substantial overlap just described.

A. Privative Clause

Pushpanathan furthered the project of detaching the rationale of deference from privative clauses. By the time the Court reached *Pushpanathan*, the formal category of "jurisdiction" had been hollowed out: "a question which 'goes to jurisdiction' is simply descriptive of a provision for which the proper standard of review is correctness, based upon the outcome of the pragmatic and functional analysis."[70]

Privative clauses are not all identical, though the differences between them can be overstated by courts. In any event, as La Forest J. unhelpfully stated in *Ross v. New Brunswick Human Rights Commission*, "there are privative clauses and there are privative clauses."[71]

Under the pragmatic and functional test, the presence of a privative clause weighed in favour of curial deference. It never played a determinative role, however, because the designation of a matter as a jurisdictional question (correctness standard) or as a question within jurisdiction (patently unreasonable standard) had to await the outcome of the Court's assessment of expertise according to the remaining three factors. Put another way, the courts accepted that a privative clause amounts to a statutory direction from the legislator to defer to the administrative actor's expertise, but the courts also arrogated to themselves the authority to define and demarcate the scope of that actor's expertise. The Court often said that lack of expertise could outweigh a privative clause; the Court never said that a privative clause could outweigh the Court's estimation of the decision-maker's relative lack of expertise.

B. Expertise

The case law was clear that relative expertise was the most important factor in determining the standard of review. In *Pushpanathan*, the Court identified three steps in evaluating ex-

---

68   *Ibid.* at para. 36.

69   *Ibid.* at para. 37.

70   *Ibid.* at para. 28.

71   [1996] 1 S.C.R. 825 at para. 26.

pertise: "the court must characterize the expertise of the tribunal in question; it must consider its own expertise relative to that of the tribunal; and it must identify the nature of the specific issue before the administrative decision-maker relative to this expertise."[72] Where the tribunal possesses "broad relative expertise" that it brings to bear "in some degree" on the interpretation of highly general questions, the Court would show considerable deference, despite the generality of the issue.[73] Such was the case in *Southam* ("material change") and *Corn Growers* (interpretation of a treaty provision), where the Court applied the standard of patent unreasonableness in view of the tribunal's specialized expertise. In *Southam*, Iacobucci, J. describes the objectives of the *Competition Act* as more economic than "strictly legal." Business people and economists possess greater expertise than a "typical judge," who is more "likely to encounter difficulties in understanding the economic and commercial ramifications of the Tribunal's decisions and consequently ... less able to secure the fulfillment of the purpose of the *Competition Act* than is the Tribunal."[74] This judicial modesty in relation to certain regulatory domains was presaged in an earlier concurring judgment of L'Heureux-Dubé J. in *Corn Growers*, where she identifies "labour relations, telecommunications, financial markets and international economic relations" as examples where courts "may simply not be as well equipped as administrative tribunals or agencies to deal with issues which Parliament has chosen to regulate through bodies exercising delegated power."[75]

Unfortunately, the case law provided scant guidance on when the Court would valorize the agency's expertise as relevant to the interpretation of a question of law and when it would discount it. When describing the broad expertise of an agency, the Supreme Court attended to the agency's composition and specialized knowledge in comparison to a court. Evidence of distinctive expertise could come from statutory criteria for appointment (for example, non-legal qualifications, length of term, and security of tenure), a policy-making function, or a "non-judicial means of implementing the Act."[76]

In terms of broad expertise, bodies that dealt with economic, financial, or technical matters seem to sit at the apex. Members of, for example, securities commissions, international trade tribunals, and telecommunications bodies have all been recognized by the Court as possessing experience, expertise, and specialized knowledge that courts lack.

Labour boards, often protected by privative clauses, are in some ways the paradigmatic example of expert administrative tribunals. Indeed, the Supreme Court would typically acknowledge their specialized knowledge and expertise in relation to industrial relations.[77] Yet labour boards tend not to benefit as consistently from curial deference as some other bodies. Labour arbitrators are considered less expert than labour boards (even though the same people often engage in both decision-making activities), because arbitrators are usually

---

72   *Pushpanathan, supra* note 65 at para. 32.

73   *Ibid.* at para. 34.

74   *Southam, supra* note 54 at para. 49.

75   *Corn Growers, supra* note 29 at para. 80.

76   *Ibid.* at para. 32.

77   See e.g. *Canada (Attorney General) v. Public Service Alliance of Canada*, [1993] 1 S.C.R. 941; *Ivanhoe, supra* note 40; *Royal Oak, supra* note 45; *Toronto (City) Board of Education v. O.S.S.T.F., District 15*, [1997] 1 S.C.R. 487.

appointed by the parties on an ad hoc basis, and the arbitrator's task is confined to the interpretation and application of a particular collective agreement, rather than administration of the entire regime of industrial relations.[78] The ad hoc nature of the appointment usually counts against the expertise of certain human rights tribunals as well. More generally, the majority of the Supreme Court of Canada belittled the expertise of human rights tribunals and commissions, which they confined to fact-finding in the human rights context. The divergent judgments of La Forest J. (concurring) and L'Heureux-Dubé J. (dissenting) in *Canada (Attorney General) v. Mossop*[79] vividly illustrate the point.

To the extent that expertise was the animating principle of the pragmatic and functional test, it is perhaps unsurprising that the Court eschews deferring to human rights tribunals. Rights adjudication lies at the heart of the judicial function and institutional self-understanding. The Court found it difficult to concede anything but a narrow compass of relative expertise to another body charged with tasks that so closely resemble those performed by courts.

On the other hand, in both *Ryan*,[80] a case involving the sanction for misconduct imposed on a miscreant lawyer, and *Moreau-Bérubé v. New Brunswick (Judicial Council)*,[81] involving allegations of judicial misconduct, the Court went to some length to defend the superior expertise of professional discipline committees composed of lawyers and judges. Unlike a securities commission or a competition tribunal, the expertise of a law society or judicial council discipline committee could hardly be described as beyond the ken of most judges. Nevertheless, the *Ryan* majority explained that practising lawyers "may be more intimately acquainted with the ways that these [professional] standards play out in the everyday practice of law than judges who no longer take part in the solicitor–client relationship."[82] To the extent that at least one member of the committee is a layperson, the fact that the member is not a lawyer may place him or her "in a better position to understand how particular forms of conduct and choice of sanctions would affect the general public's perception of the profession and confidence in the administration of justice."[83] Ultimately, "owing to its composition and its familiarity with the particular issue of imposing a sanction for professional misconduct in a variety of settings, the Discipline Committee arguably has more expertise than courts on the sanction to apply to the misconduct."[84] As for the New Brunswick Judicial Council, Arbour J. concluded that a "council composed primarily of judges, alive to the delicate balance between judicial independence and judicial integrity, must in my view attract in general a high degree of deference."[85] The Court eventually decided on the intermediate standard of reasonableness in both cases.

---

[78] See e.g. *Dayco (Canada) Ltd. v. CAW Canada*, [1993] 2 S.C.R. 230.

[79] [1993] 1 S.C.R. 554 [*Mossop*].

[80] *Supra* note 64.

[81] 2002 SCC 11, [2002] 1 S.C.R. 249 [*Moreau-Bérubé*].

[82] *Ryan*, *supra* note 64 at para. 31.

[83] *Ibid.* at para. 32.

[84] *Ibid.* at para. 34.

[85] *Moreau-Bérubé, supra* note 81 at para. 60.

Decision-making bodies staffed by elected officials have proven problematic subjects for the evaluation of expertise (and for the application of the pragmatic and functional test as a whole). In *Baker*, the Court dealt with the humanitarian and compassionate discretion that was statutorily conferred on the minister of citizenship and immigration, but delegated to a civil servant. The Court found that the "fact that the formal decision-maker is the Minister is a factor militating in favour of deference. The Minister has some expertise relative to courts in immigration matters, particularly with respect to when exemptions should be given from the requirements that normally apply."[86] The basis of deference is unclear, given the acknowledgment that the minister is formally the decision-maker, but the actual decisions are made by a delegate. Is it because a minister is deemed expert in whatever portfolio he or she is assigned? Is it because the delegate is presumed to have expertise acquired through repeated processing of many humanitarian and compassionate applications? Is it because the minister is an elected official, and the grant of discretion to an elected official signals an entitlement to apply "political" factors, an activity in which politicians are more expert than judges?

In *Chamberlain v. Surrey School District No. 36*,[87] a local school board composed of elected trustees passed a resolution against authorizing three books depicting same-sex parented families to be used in the classroom. One challenge to the resolution was that the board acted outside its mandate under the *School Act*[88] in passing the resolution—that is, it exceeded its jurisdiction. The majority of the Court applied the pragmatic and functional test to arrive at a reasonableness standard of review, and found the resolution unreasonable. Writing for the majority, McLachlin C.J. described the board as expert in balancing "the interests of different groups, such as parents with widely differing moral outlooks, and children from many types of families," and acknowledged that, as locally elected representatives, the board is better placed to understand community concerns than the court."[89] However, McLachlin C.J. went on to find that, because the decision in question "has a human rights dimension" in which courts are more expert than administrative bodies, less deference is owed. Writing in dissent, Gonthier J. commented that, although the board's decision clearly had a human rights aspect, "courts should be reluctant to assume that they possess greater expertise than administrative decision makers with respect to all questions having a human rights component,"[90] especially in the context of local democracy. LeBel J.'s dissent challenges the premise that expertise ought to be the basis of curial deference toward elected officials in their legislative (as opposed to adjudicative) capacity. He notes that, in judicial review of municipal actors, "our Court has always focused on whether the action in question was authorized, not on whether it was reasonable."[91] In LeBel J.'s view, the animating principle is the separation of the judiciary and representative government and the need to

---

[86] *Baker, supra* note 2 at para. 59.

[87] 2002 SCC 86, [2002] 4 S.C.R. 710 [*Chamberlain*].

[88] R.S.B.C. 1996, c. 412.

[89] *Chamberlain supra* note 87 at para. 10.

[90] *Ibid.* at para. 143.

[91] *Ibid.* at para. 197.

protect each from illegitimate interference by the other. Application of the pragmatic and functional test, with the possible result of a reasonableness standard,

> fails to give due recognition to the board's role as a local government body accountable to the electorate. As long as it acts pursuant to its statutory powers, it is carrying out the will of the community it serves and in general is answerable to the community, not the courts. But if it purports to exercise powers it does not have, its actions are invalid.[92]

One way of understanding LeBel J.'s position is to posit that elected officials merit deference because they represent the will of the majority, not because of any expertise they may possess. The *ultra vires–intra vires* dichotomy is analogous to the inside–outside jurisdiction dichotomy, but is even more deferential to matters deemed *intra vires*. In certain respects, the disagreement between the majority and LeBel J. on this issue mirrors a similar debate about the application of the doctrine of reasonable apprehension of bias. Crudely put, it brings to the surface the question about the role of judicial review versus the ballot box in making elected officials accountable.

Although the Supreme Court prioritized expertise in formulating the standard of review, its inquiry is limited to the statutory role of the administrative actor, not to the particular individual occupying it. Courts will glean evidence of expertise from statute and surrounding context, but will not scrutinize the qualifications, competence, training, or experience of a specific decision-maker. Nor does administrative law provide a direct mechanism for imposing on the state an obligation to adopt a merit-based appointment process for non-elected decision-makers. Consider the *Back to School Act, 2001* (Toronto and Windsor),[93] wherein the statute empowered the minister of labour to appoint as arbitrator a person who "has no previous experience as an arbitrator" and who is not "mutually acceptable to both trade unions and employers."[94] Even the doctrine of independence of decision-makers adopts narrow and formal criteria for assessing independence from inappropriate government influence on decision-makers. In other words, independence identifies formal indicia of susceptibility to government influence, and standard of review examines formal indicia of expertise, but neither addresses actual competence. One might consider whether merit and competence ought to matter to the courts and, if so, how these concerns could be addressed in administrative law.[95] Is the standard of review a satisfactory proxy?

C. Purpose of the Statute as a Whole and the Provision in Particular

What aspect of statutory purpose is relevant to the standard of review? In *Pushpanathan*, the Court distilled prior jurisprudence into the following proposition: Where the statute or provision can be described as "polycentric"—that is, engages a balancing of multiple interests, constituencies, and factors or contains a significant policy element, or articulates the legal standards in vague or open-textured language, more judicial restraint is warranted.

---

92   *Ibid.* at para. 201.

93   S.O. 2001, c. 1, cited in *C.U.P.E. v. Ontario (Minister of Labour)*, 2003 SCC 29, [2003] 1 S.C.R. 539 at para. 81 [*Retired Judges*]. Note: This Act was repealed on December 15, 2009 (2009, c. 33, Sch. 20, ss. 5(1), 6).

94   *Back to School Act, supra* note 93, s. 11(4).

95   *Retired Judges, supra* note 93.

Disputes that more closely resemble the bipolar model of opposition between discrete parties and interests attract less curial deference. The rationale is that judges have less relative expertise in the former and more relative expertise in the latter. When discretion was added to the mix of provisions subject to review, courts tended to regard discretion-granting provisions as polycentric insofar as the exercise of discretion engaged consideration of multiple factors. Note, however, that discretionary decisions (such as the humanitarian and compassionate decision in *Baker*) may directly affect only a single individual or identifiable group of individuals, in contrast to the more diffuse benefits and burdens associated with conventional "polycentric" provisions. Courts have also identified provisions that confer positive discretion (a beneficial exemption from a rule) as attracting more deference.

D. The Nature of the Problem

Appellate and judicial review jurisprudence have long divided legal issues into questions of law, questions of mixed law and fact, and questions of fact. In administrative law, these conveniently map onto the spectrum of deference as less deference, neutral, and more deference, in accordance with courts' declining relative expertise: "Without an implied or express legislative intent to the contrary ... , legislatures should be assumed to have left highly generalized propositions of law to courts."[96]

The characterization of a matter as a question of law or as a question of mixed law and fact may not be straightforward,[97] and is complicated by the fact that characterizing an issue as a question of law does not necessarily preclude the possibility that the tribunal may possess greater expertise than a court in interpreting it, especially if the court otherwise regards the agency as highly expert, and the legal question relates to interpretation of a provision in the agency's enabling statute.[98]

One clue that judges looked for in distinguishing legal questions confided to the tribunal from those better resolved by the courts is the extent to which the determination will have precedential value in subsequent cases. The greater the precedential impact, the greater the assessment of expertise tilts toward the courts. The labelling of the issue as a "pure" question of law (*Barrie Utilities*);[99] a "concept derived from the common law or Civil Code" (*Bibeault*);[100] a general question of law (*Mossop*);[101] not scientific or technical (*Mattel*);[102] or a human rights issue (*Pushpanathan*,[103] *Chamberlain*[104]) was usually a reliable signal that the Court had concluded that the legal issue was one in which it believed itself to have superior expertise. In *Pushpanathan*, the Court relied on the unique provision in the

---

[96] *Ibid.* at para. 38.

[97] *Southam, supra* note 54 at paras. 34-35.

[98] See *Retired Judges, supra* note 93.

[99] *Supra* note 15.

[100] *Supra* note 14.

[101] *Supra* note 79.

[102] *Mattel, Inc. v. 3894207 Canada Inc.*, 2006 SCC 22, [2006] 1 S.C.R. 772 [*Mattel*].

[103] *Supra* note 65.

[104] *Supra* note 87.

Immigration Act (now the *Immigration and Refugee Protection Act*),[105] whereby a Federal Court judge must certify a "serious question of general importance"[106] in order for the litigants to proceed to the Federal Court of Appeal. The statutory requirement of generality and serious importance (as determined by the Federal Court judge) allowed the Court to declare that "s. 83(1) would be incoherent if the standard of review were anything other than correctness. The key to the legislative intention as to the standard of review is the use of the words 'a serious question of *general* importance.' "[107]

In *Baker*, decided a year later, the Court reiterated that s. 83(1) inclined away from deference, but quickly added that "this is only one of the factors involved in determining the standard of review."[108] Indeed, the Supreme Court of Canada in *Baker* also held that once leave to appeal was granted, appellate courts were not restricted to the certified question. In *Baker* itself, the Supreme Court addressed only obliquely the question identified by the Federal Court as a "serious question of general importance." Instead, the fact that the decision in *Baker* was discretionary seemed to exert the most significant influence in favour of deference. The Court ultimately arrived at the intermediate standard of reasonableness *simpliciter*.[109]

VI. Dunsmuir: And Then There Were Two

Ever since *Southam* ushered in the intermediate standard of review—reasonableness *simpliciter*—commentators, practitioners, and even some lower court judges have complained about the indeterminacy, impracticability, unpredictability, and sheer confusion generated by three standards of review. The balancing test for determining which of three standards of review should apply often produced indicators pointing toward and away from deference, thereby failing to provide predictable or reliable guidance to lawyers and litigants. Identifying criteria to distinguish the merely "unreasonable" from the "patently unreasonable" decision proved frustrating and elusive. In short, the "pragmatic and functional" test was neither.

In his concurring judgment in *Toronto (City) v. C.U.P.E., Local 79*,[110] LeBel J. canvassed the widespread discontent with the direction of Supreme Court jurisprudence. He provided a thorough and thoughtful analysis of the sordid history of the rise and application of three standards and issued a plea for the abandonment of three standards in favour of a return to "a two standard system of review, correctness and a revised unified standard of reasonableness."[111]

---

[105]   *Supra* note 48.

[106]   *Pushpanathan, supra* note 65 at para. 87 (*Immigration Act*, s. 83(1); *Immigration and Refugee Protection Act*, s. 82.3).

[107]   Pushpanathan, *ibid.* at para. 43 (emphasis added by the Court).

[108]   *Baker, supra* note 2 at para. 58.

[109]   The Supreme Court in *Baker* also undercut the logic of its own reasoning in *Pushpanathan* regarding s. 83(1). In *Baker, supra* note 2, the Supreme Court ruled that, once a question was "certified," the Federal Court of Appeal (and, a fortiori, the Supreme Court) was free to consider any other issue that was apposite to the disposition of the case, without filtering it through the s. 83(1) criterion of "serious question of general importance."

[110]   2003 SCC 63, [2003] 3 S.C.R. 77 [*CUPE, Local 79*].

[111]   *Ibid.* at para. 134.

Five years later, the *Dunsmuir* case gave the Court the occasion to heed LeBel J.'s *cri de coeur*.[112] Like *CUPE*, *Dunsmuir* arose out of New Brunswick, involved employment, and featured confounding statutory text.

Dunsmuir was dismissed from his civil service position in the Department of Justice. He received severance, but insisted that he was also owed a duty of fairness prior to termination. He grieved unsuccessfully, then appealed to an adjudicator. (The procedural fairness aspects of the case are discussed by Grant Huscroft in Chapter 5, From Natural Justice to Fairness: Thresholds, Content, and the Role of Judicial Review.) The adjudicator appointed to address Dunsmuir's grievance interpreted the relevant statutory provisions in a manner that allowed him to consider the reasons for discharge, even though the employer did not assert that Dunsmuir was dismissed for cause. The question of law was whether the adjudicator was entitled to inquire into whether the employer actually dismissed Dunsmuir for cause and, by extension, whether just cause existed. The adjudicator determined that the statute authorized him to inquire into the reasons for discharge as part of the grievance arbitration, but then went on to find that the dismissal was, on the facts, not for cause. One issue before the Supreme Court was the appropriate standard of review for the question of law concerning the adjudicator's authority to inquire into the reasons for dismissal.

The *Dunsmuir* majority acknowledged that its pragmatic and functional approach had attracted criticism for its "theoretical and practical difficulties" and that it had "proven difficult to implement." Binnie J, concurring, described it less charitably as "distracting" and "unproductive."

Despite the deficiencies of past jurisprudence, the Court did not resile from its post-*CUPE* endorsement of deference as an animating principle of substantive judicial review. En route to introducing the new standard-of-review analysis, the majority rehearsed the rationale for deference:

> Deference in the context of the reasonableness standard therefore implies that courts will give due consideration to the determinations of decision makers. As Mullan explains, a policy of deference "recognizes the reality that, in many instances, those working day to day in the implementation of frequently complex administrative schemes have or will develop a considerable degree of expertise or field sensitivity to the imperatives and nuances of the legislative regime."[113] In short, deference requires respect for the legislative choices to leave some matters in the hands of administrative decision makers, for the processes and determinations that draw on particular expertise and experiences, and for the different roles of the courts and administrative bodies within the Canadian constitutional system.[114]

For the Court, the problem lay not in the concept of deference or its virtues, but in the challenge of putting it into operation. After surveying the evolution of judicial review over the past 50 years, the majority offered the following diagnosis:

---

112 *Dunsmuir v. New Brunswick*, [2008] 1 S.C.R. 190 [*Dunsmuir*].

113 D.J. Mullan, "Establishing the Standard of Review: The Struggle for Complexity?" (2004) 17 Can. J. Admin. L. & Prac. 59 at 93.

114 *Dunsmuir, supra* note 112 at para. 49.

The Court has moved from a highly formalistic, artificial "jurisdiction" test that could easily be manipulated, to a highly contextual "functional" test that provides great flexibility but little real on-the-ground guidance, and offers too many standards of review. What is needed is a test that offers guidance, is not formalistic or artificial, and permits review where justice requires it, but not otherwise. A simpler test is needed.[115]

The Supreme Court of Canada followed the lead of LeBel J. and walked the legal test back from three to two standards of review—correctness and reasonableness. It rebranded the pragmatic and functional test as the standard-of-review analysis. It also adopted a different methodology for choosing between correctness and reasonableness.

The pragmatic and functional test, as synopsized in *Pushpanathan* and applied thereafter, laid out four factors to be evaluated and weighed. Although the judgment is not without ambiguity, the pattern of subsequent jurisprudence thus far suggests that the new standard of review methodology is no longer a balancing test, but appears to more closely resemble a defeasible rule: the default position is deference, unless one of the exceptions obtains.

The Court begins by casting the net of deference widely over a range of issues and situations: "Where the question is one of fact, discretion or policy, deference will usually apply automatically. We believe that the same standard must apply to the review of questions where the legal and factual issues are intertwined with and cannot be readily separated."[116] The Court ought to defer to the interpretation of a "discrete and special administrative regime in which the decision maker has special expertise."[117] On the basis of the pattern of past jurisprudence, the Court anticipates that "[d]eference will usually result where a tribunal is interpreting its own statute or statutes closely connected to its function, with which it will have particular familiarity."[118] Deference will even be warranted "where an administrative tribunal has developed particular expertise in the application of a general common law or civil law rule in relation to a specific statutory context."[119] The majority pauses to genuflect briefly before the privative clause, acknowledging it as "a statutory direction from Parliament or a legislature indicating the need for deference."[120]

Given all the situations that incline toward deference, when is deference not warranted? The majority identifies four circumstances where a standard of correctness should apply:

1. where the question of law is "of central importance to the legal system as a whole and outside the adjudicator's specialized area of expertise";[121]

2. in constitutional questions;

---

115   *Ibid.* at para. 43.

116   *Ibid.* at para. 53.

117   *Ibid.* at para. 54.

118   *Ibid.*

119   *Ibid.*

120   *Ibid.* at para. 55.

121   *Ibid.* at para. 60; see also para. 55.

3. in "true" questions of jurisdiction: "where the tribunal must explicitly determine whether its statutory grant of power gives it the authority to decide a particular matter";[122]

4. in "questions regarding the jurisdictional lines between two or more competing specialized tribunal."[123]

The majority says nothing about the standard of review for questions of procedural fairness, but Binnie J. plugs that hole by confirming that a standard of correctness will continue to apply: "On such matters ... , the courts have the final say. The need for such procedural safeguards is obvious. Nobody should have his or her rights, interests or privileges adversely dealt with by an unjust process."[124] Another way of stating this principle is to deny that standard of review is apposite to questions of procedural fairness. The only metric is whether the proceedings were conducted fairly.[125]

Although the majority judgment breaks with the past in some respects, it also maintains certain jurisprudential links. For instance, the majority counsels a two-step process for judicial review: first, courts "ascertain whether the jurisprudence has already determined in a satisfactory manner the degree of deference to be accorded with regard to a particular category of question."[126] If no precedent exists, then a court should proceed to applying the standard-of-review analysis. In so stating, the majority seems to assume that the new standard of review methodology will yield the same result as the old pragmatic and functional analysis. The Court also indicates that the application of the new standard of reasonableness will not undermine decisions that might have withstood the less exacting standard of patent unreasonableness. The Court addresses this concern directly when it reiterates that deference is "central to judicial review in administrative law," and affirms that "[t]he move towards a single reasonableness standard does not pave the way for a more intrusive review by courts."[127]

This deferential tenor of *Dunsmuir* would sit awkwardly alongside the belief that decisions previously sheltered under the standard of patent unreasonableness might henceforth be set aside as unreasonable. But does this mean that the new reasonableness is the same as the old "patent unreasonableness"? That also seems unlikely. Yet the Court seems to want to change the test without overruling any prior decisions. One way of finessing the dilemma is to imagine that the new technique for evaluating reasonableness will be neither the "somewhat probing" analysis proposed under reasonableness *simpliciter*, nor the "clearly irrational" benchmark of patent unreasonableness, but something qualitatively different. How reasonableness is measured is the subject of Chapter 10, Pas de Deux: Deference and Non-Deference in Action, by Sheila Wildeman.

---

122   *Ibid.* at para. 59.

123   *Ibid.* at para. 61.

124   *Ibid.* at para. 129.

125   See e.g. *Gismondi v. Ontario (Human Rights Commission)*, [2003] O.J. No. 419 (QL) (Ont. Div. Ct.).

126   *Dunsmuir, supra* note 112 at para. 62.

127   *Ibid.* at para. 48.

Another ambiguity in *Dunsmuir* emerges when the majority appears to revive *Pushpana-than*'s pragmatic and functional balancing approach only a few paragraphs after introducing the defeasible rule method of the standard-of-review analysis.[128] It is not clear how these two methodologies can be reconciled, or what advantage exists in maintaining both. The trend in the lower courts appears to be that if prior jurisprudence does not settle the standard of review, the defeasible rule approach is applied, and occasionally supplemented by a balancing of factors that conveniently arrives at the same conclusion as the defeasible rule.

When applying its new standard-of-review analysis to the legal issue raised in *Dunsmuir*, the majority proceeds swiftly to a deferential standard of review: the statute contains a full privative clause. The arbitrator was administering a discrete and specialized labour law regime that provided for prompt and final non-judicial remediation:

> Although the adjudicator was appointed on an ad hoc basis, he was selected by the mutual agreement of the parties and, at an institutional level, adjudicators acting under the *PSLRA* can be presumed to hold relative expertise in the interpretation of the legislation that gives them their mandate, as well as related legislation that they might often encounter in the course of their functions. ... The remedial nature of s. 100.1 and its provision for timely and binding settlements of disputes also imply that a reasonableness review is appropriate.[129]

While *Dunsmuir* engaged a question of law, it was not one of central importance to the legal system, and so the standard of reasonableness applied.

The Court's new standard-of-review test seems refreshingly simple and manageable. If the defect of the pragmatic and functional test was that it was conceptually coherent but practically indeterminate, the weakness of the majority's new standard of analysis approach is that it leaves various conceptual loose ends dangling. In other words, it may work fine in practice, but how well does it work in theory?

Chief among the outstanding concerns is the matter that preoccupies Justice Binnie in his concurring judgment: how can a single, invariant standard of deference (reasonableness) manage the diverse range of actors, issues, statutory review provisions, and expertise that the pragmatic and functional test previously identified and calibrated according to two standards of deference? Binnie J. asserts that the majority decision does not resolve this, but simply punts the task from the selection of the appropriate level of deference (reasonableness *simpliciter* or patent unreasonableness) to the application of the new reasonableness standard. He contends that the new reasonableness standard will inevitably devolve into a spectrum of deference that varies according to factors previously identified in the pragmatic and functional approach.[130] Rather like the *Dunsmuir* majority, this chapter (on the choice of standard of review) deflects this vexing issue to the next chapter (on the application of the chosen standard of review), and focuses here on matters more closely allied with the process of selecting between correctness and reasonableness.

---

[128] *Ibid.* at para. 64.

[129] *Ibid.* at paras. 68-69.

[130] This dilemma is heightened by the fact that no prior decision appears to be overruled. If patent unreasonableness meant something different than reasonableness *simpliciter*, it is difficult to see how a single standard of reasonableness could produce identical results to the pre-*Dunsmuir* results.

A. Whatever Happened to the Privative Clause?

Up to and including *CUPE*, the privative clause operated as the legislative signal for defer-ence. Under the pragmatic and functional test, the privative clause was demoted to one among many factors that a reviewing court would consider in determining the appropriate standard. In *Dunsmuir*, the privative clause is arguably rendered otiose. The default position is deference, there is only a single standard of reasonableness, and the privative clause does not trump the countervailing force of the exceptions to the presumption of deference. So what is the value added by the privative clause? In his concurring judgment, Binnie J. deliv-ers a tribute—or perhaps a requiem—for the unique heft of the privative clause:

> The existence of a privative clause is currently subsumed within the "pragmatic and functional" test as one factor amongst others to be considered in determining the appropriate standard of review, where it supports the choice of the patent unreasonableness standard … A system of judicial review based on the rule of law ought not to treat a privative clause as conclusive, but it is more than just another "factor" in the hopper of pragmatism and functionality. Its existence should presumptively foreclose judicial review on the basis of *outcome* on substantive grounds unless the applicant can show that the clause, properly interpreted, permits it or there is some legal reason why it cannot be given effect.[131]

Binnie J.'s insistence on the distinctiveness of privative clauses is linked to his prediction of the inevitable emergence of a spectrum of deference under the rubric of reasonableness. Thus he asserts that "a single standard of reasonableness cannot mean that the degree of deference is unaffected by the existence of a suitably worded privative clause. It is certainly a relevant contextual circumstance that helps to calibrate the intrusiveness of a court's re-view. It signals the level of respect that must be shown."[132]

Because the majority in *Dunsmuir* refuses to concede that the new standard of reason-ableness should, or will, evolve into a sliding scale of deference, it must reject the special role that Binnie J. assigns to privative clauses in calibrating the precise level of deference afforded under the rubric of reasonableness.

In *Canada (Citizenship and Immigration) v. Khosa*,[133] Rothstein J. mounts a spirited rear-guard action against the detachment of deference from privative clauses. He defends the primacy of legislative intent and the singularity of the privative clause by emphasizing the significance of its absence. Rather like Rip Van Winkle, Rothstein J. appears to have gone to sleep shortly after *CUPE* and woken up shortly after *Dunsmuir*. Dismayed by the evolution in the case law on standard of review, he is determined to "roll back the *Dunsmuir* clock" to an era where everyone agreed that "judge knows best" about questions of law and discre-tion, unless a suitably worded privative clause directed otherwise.[134]

Khosa concerned a discretionary decision by the Immigration Appeal Division of the Immigration and Refugee Board not to stay the deportation order of a non-citizen con-victed of dangerous driving causing death. The grounds for judicial review were enumerated

---

[131] *Dunsmuir, supra* note 112 at para. 143.

[132] *Ibid.*

[133] 2009 SCC 12, [2009] 1 S.C.R. 339 [*Khosa*].

[134] *Ibid.* at para. 25.

in s. 18.1(4) of the *Federal Courts Act*.[135] The statute was silent about the applicable standard of review, except to state that erroneous findings of fact warranted relief if made "in a perverse or capricious manner or without regard for the material before it."[136] Although Rothstein J. agreed with the majority that the appropriate standard of review was reasonableness, he insisted that the basis for deference lay exclusively in the language of the statutory provision dealing with errors of fact, not in any broader deferential stance derived from the common law.

According to Rothstein J., "where Parliament intended a deferential standard of review in s. 18.1(4), it used clear and unambiguous language. The necessary implication is that where Parliament did not provide for deferential review, it intended the reviewing court to apply a correctness standard as it does in the regular appellate context."[137] So, unless a statute contains a privative clause governing the entire statute or a provision stipulating deference in relation to a particular ground of judicial review (as in errors of fact under the *Federal Courts Act*), the default standard of review is correctness.

The majority of the Court did not share Rothstein J.'s nostalgia, but nor did it resolve the question of how to assign unique weight to the privative clause. Instead, the majority judgment in *Khosa* takes a perplexing detour through judicial discretion to deny prerogative relief en route to its conclusion. According to Binnie J., the standard of review structures residual judicial discretion to deny prerogative relief. Judicial deference to administrative decisions is thus recast as the method by which judges determine whether and why to withhold a remedy. The majority determined that deference was warranted in the case at bar and the appropriate standard of review is reasonableness, but not before reviving the *Pushpanathan* factors and offering the following gloss on the standard-of-review analysis: "A privative clause is an important indicator of legislative intent. While privative clauses deter judicial intervention, a statutory right of appeal may be at ease with it, depending on its terms."[138] Rather than clarify the weight that a privative clause exerts in favour of deference, *Khosa* adds uncertainty about the weight that a statutory appeal exerts against it. If nothing else, the application of the standard-of-review analysis in *Khosa* suggests equivocation on whether *Pushpanathan's* multifactor balancing approach can co-exist alongside *Dunsmuir's* defeasible rule methodology.[139] Nevertheless, they remain difficult to reconcile methodologically.

B. Whatever Happened to Jurisdiction?

Recall that the "jurisdictional question" arose as a judicial escape hatch from the strictures of privative clauses: a decision, determination, or order that exceeded the jurisdictional boundaries conferred by statute was a nullity and, therefore, not a genuine decision, determination,

---

[135]   R.S.C., 1985, c. F-7.

[136]   *Ibid.*, s. 18.1(4)(d).

[137]   *Khosa, supra* note 133 at para. 117.

[138]   *Ibid.* at para. 55.

[139]   For other examples of equivocation, see *Nolan v. Kerry (Canada) Inc.*, 2009 SCC 39, [2009] 2 S.C.R. 678; *Nor-Man Regional Health Authority Inc. v. Manitoba Association of Health Care Professionals*, 2011 SCC 59, [2011] 3 S.C.R. 616.

or order insulated from judicial review. But the demotion of privative clauses cast into question the raison d'être of its foil, the jurisdictional question. After *Southam*, a court could both justify deference in the absence of a privative clause and justify correctness scrutiny in the presence of a privative clause. Eventually, the jurisdictional question lost its formal, conceptual moorings and became merely a label affixed to the outcome reached by a judicial balancing of the four factors summarized in *Pushpanathan*. Serious attention to formal attributes of jurisdiction (authority over subject matter, parties, or remedy) virtually disappeared.

As applied by subsequent courts, *Dunsmuir* seemed to relinquish the *Pushpanathan* balancing test. But the judgment also revived the formal idea of jurisdiction as a boundary-drawing concept capable of rebutting a presumption of deference. The majority also invoked the dictum in *CUPE* that urged the courts to be sparing in their resort to the formal claim of jurisdiction. Thus far, the post-*Dunsmuir* Supreme Court seems committed to exercising restraint in labelling an issue as jurisdictional and thereby subject to the stricter standard of correctness. The best proof lies in *Dunsmuir* itself. Without expending much effort, the Court could have transformed the question "does the statute authorize the adjudicator to inquire into the existence of cause for dismissal?" into "does the adjudicator have jurisdiction to inquire into the existence of cause for dismissal?" Yet, the Court refrained from even posing the question in jurisdictional terms. The adjudicator had jurisdiction over the parties (the employer and employee) and over the subject matter (discharge, suspension, or other financial penalty), and that sufficed. In *Smith v. Alliance Pipeline*,[140] the Court swiftly disposed of an argument that the definition of "costs" under an expropriation statute is jurisdictional. Arbitration committees "doubtless have the authority to make the inquiry whether 'costs' under s. 99(1) refer solely to costs incurred in the proceedings before them, a determination that plainly falls within their statutory grant of power."[141]

The post-*Dunsmuir* Court has been so alert not to brand something as jurisdictional that the question before the courts is no longer "is this thing a jurisdictional question?," but "is there such thing as a jurisdictional question?" In *Northrop Grumman Overseas Services Corp. v. Canada (Attorney General)*,[142] the Court listed recent pre-*Dunsmuir* cases that treated as jurisdictional the question of whether a U.S. supplier had standing to make a complaint to the Canadian International Trade Tribunal (CITT). The Court noted that all parties accepted that the earlier case law remained authoritative in imposing a standard of correctness. Because the earlier jurisprudence determined the standard of review in "a satisfactory manner," the Court was relieved of the task of conducting a fresh standard-of-review analysis.[143] Later, in *Alberta (Information and Privacy Commissioner) v. Alberta Teachers'*

---

[140]   2011 SCC 7, [2011] 1 S.C.R. 160 [*Smith*].

[141]   *Dunsmuir*, supra note 112 at para. 36.

[142]   2009 SCC 50, [2009] 3 S.C.R. 309 [*Northrup Grumman*].

[143]   *Ibid.* at para. 10. For an interesting application of the correctness standard of review to the discharge of the Crown's duty to consult a First Nation before approving the grant of surrendered lands for agricultural purposes to a non-Aboriginal applicant, see *Beckman v. Little Salmon/Carmacks First Nation*, 2010 SCC 53, [2010] 3 SCR 103. While the adequacy of consultation was subject to correctness, the Court found no breach of the duty to consult, nor a breach of procedural fairness. The ultimate exercise of discretion regarding the grant application was reviewable on the basis of reasonableness.

Association,[144] a majority of the Court distanced itself from *Northrop Grumman*, claiming that it was based on "pre-*Dunsmuir* jurisprudence applying a correctness standard to this type of decision, not on the Court finding a true question of jurisdiction."[145] It seems troubling to rely on precedent to defend a standard of review based on a superceded legal test, while hinting that the current test would have yielded a different result. Precedent typically binds unless and until the legal test that produced it changes, and not thereafter. Indeed, only two years later, *Alberta (Information and Privacy Commissioner)* directly confronted the post-*Dunsmuir* endurance of jurisdictional questions in the context of the standard-of-review analysis.

Writing for six judges, Rothstein J. ventured that "the time has come to reconsider whether, for purposes of judicial review, the category of true questions of jurisdiction exists and is necessary to identifying the appropriate standard of review."[146] The core of Rothstein J.'s proposal resides in the admission that decades of administrative law jurisprudence have left him "unable to provide a definition of what might constitute a true question of jurisdiction."[147] Preserving a concept that is theoretically compelling, but practically unworkable and even superfluous seems only to invite the type of arcane and indeterminate legal wrangling that *Dunsmuir* sought to avoid. Because the Supreme Court already cast the cloak of constitutional protection over judicial review (thereby foreclosing any literal application of a privative clause), and *Dunsmuir* identified other criteria for applying the correctness standard, extinguishing the category of jurisdictional question jeopardizes neither the resilience of judicial review nor correctness scrutiny. In a technical sense, the majority leaves the issue unresolved, concluding instead that jurisdictional questions are exceptional and none have come before it since *Dunsmuir*.

A sympathetic reading of the majority judgment might proffer the hypothesis that the other post-*Dunsmuir* grounds for correctness review really amount to exemplars of situations typically regarded as "jurisdictional" in pre-*Dunsmuir* case law. In a jurisprudence chiefly notable for its lack of predictability, the correctness standard was most consistently applied to issues of procedural fairness, constitutionality, the "jurisdictional lines between competing specialized tribunals," and to questions of law elevated to "central importance to the legal system as a whole and ... outside the adjudicator's expertise."[148] One could argue that the work done by "jurisdiction" pre-*Dunsmuir* is performed post-*Dunsmuir* by these exceptions to the default presumption of *Dunsmuir* reasonableness, thereby rendering "jurisdiction" itself otiose.

Cromwell J. emphatically disagrees with the majority on the fate of jurisdiction, warning that the position espoused by Rothstein J. threatens to "undermine the foundation of judicial review of administrative action."[149] As Rothstein J. notes, however, Cromwell J.'s objec-

---

[144]   2011 SCC 61, [2011] 3 S.C.R. 654 [*Alberta (Information and Privacy Commissioner)*].

[145]   *Ibid.* at para. 10.

[146]   *Ibid.* at para. 34.

[147]   *Ibid.* at para. 42.

[148]   *Ibid.* at para. 30.

[149]   *Ibid.* at para. 92.

tion fails to take into account the bases for application of a correctness standard apart from the jurisdictional question.

Cromwell J.'s version of the standard-of-review analysis tempers the inclination toward reasonableness with "a more thorough examination of legislative intent when a plausible argument is advanced that a particular provision falls outside the 'presumption' of reasonableness review and into the 'exceptional' category of correctness review."[150] Cromwell J. does not actually conduct a thorough examination of legislative intent in the case at bar, or indicate what a plausible argument should contain, confining himself to the conclusory statement that the legislature did not intend a correctness standard to apply because "the power to extend time is granted in broad terms in the context of a detailed and highly specialized statutory scheme which it is the Commissioner's duty to administer and under which he is required to exercise many broadly granted discretions."[151] This quick concession seems curious, because Cromwell J. could have identified the fact that the interpretation of a statutory provision about timelines essentially concerns the process of investigation and adjudication, and the Court has consistently applied a correctness standard to matters of procedural fairness.

Binnie J. (Deschamps J. concurring) stakes out a conciliatory middle position between Rothstein J. and Cromwell J. He agrees with the latter that the concept of jurisdiction is "fundamental," but endorses Rothstein J.'s initiative "to euthanize the issue" on account of its practical disutility.[152] Binnie J.'s middle ground consists of two propositions. The first is a reiteration of his prediction that reasonableness will entail a spectrum of intensity of scrutiny, with the implication that the application of a reasonableness review may, in appropriate cases, look very similar to correctness review. The second is a revision of the "question of central importance to the legal system as a whole" exception to deference. Here, Binnie J. offers a broader and more generic exception for questions of law that "raise matters of legal importance beyond administrative aspects of the statutory scheme under review" and do not lie "within the core function and expertise of the decision maker."[153] If adopted, Binnie J.'s reformulation would appear to enlarge this exception.

It remains unclear whether the jurisdictional question will die a peaceful death or simply lay dormant until the Supreme Court decides to resurrect it. The boundary metaphor that underwrites jurisdiction is at once irresistible and impracticable. Perhaps it is no coincidence that the vocabulary of jurisdiction feels most natural when invoked in respect of entities that also happen to be geographically bounded, such as municipalities, provinces, and states. This makes all the more notable the 2012 judgment in *Catalyst Paper Corp. v. North Cowichan (District)*,[154] which concerned a municipal tax bylaw. The Supreme Court resolutely avoided the term "jurisdiction," or *vires*, and consistently spoke of deference and reasonableness.

---

150   *Ibid.* at para. 99.

151   *Ibid.* at para. 101.

152   *Ibid.* at para. 88.

153   *Ibid.* at para. 89.

154   2012 SCC 2 [*Catalyst*].

It is perhaps a fitting postscript to the narrative of jurisdiction in Canadian administrative law that even its contemporary defender, Cromwell J., took the opportunity to overrule *Bell v. Ontario Human Rights Commission*.[155] In *Halifax (Regional Municipality) v. Nova Scotia (Human Rights Commission)*,[156] the Court considered an appeal from an order of prohibition by a Nova Scotia chambers judge that had the effect of invalidating referral of a human rights complaint to a board of inquiry, thereby preventing the board of inquiry from considering whether the complaint fell within the purview of the Nova Scotia human rights statute. A unanimous Supreme Court rejected *Bell's* notion of "preliminary question" as both anachronistic and insufficiently respectful of "the considered opinion of the tribunal on legal questions, whether the tribunal's ruling is ultimately reviewable in the courts for correctness or reasonableness."[157] The Court also ruled that the appropriate standard of review in the case at bar was reasonableness.

C. Whatever Happened to Patent Unreasonableness?

Pity the legislators: long ago, they gave up trying to refine the privative clause in order to persuade judges that when they told the courts to "get out and stay out," they really meant it. If the privative clause was an exercise in communicating legislative intent about the role of the courts, suffice to say that the message was, if not lost, then reformulated in translation. The Court rationalized this through the constitutionalization of judicial review and a negotiation between the rule of law and an idea of parliamentary sovereignty envisioned as external to, or counterposed against, the rule of law.

Sometime after *Southam*, a few legislators switched tactics and decided instead to direct the courts on the legislature's intended standard of review by explicitly stating whether a reviewing court should apply correctness, unreasonableness *simpliciter*, or patent unreasonableness. For example, the B.C. *Administrative Tribunals Act*[158] (ATA) itemizes grounds of judicial review applicable to the tribunals subject to the ATA and matches each ground with a standard of review. In the case of judicial review of discretion, the ATA also lists factors relevant to determining whether discretion was exercised in a patently unreasonable way.[159] In Ontario, the *Human Rights Code* contains a privative clause stipulating that "a decision of the [Human Rights] Tribunal is final and not subject to appeal and shall not be altered or

---

155   *Supra* note 7.

156   2012 SCC 10.

157   *Ibid.* at para. 37.

158   S.B.C. 2004, c. 45.

159   If a tribunal's enabling statute has a privative clause, the standard of review is patent unreasonableness for questions of law and fact or the exercise of discretion for all matters over which "the tribunal has exclusive jurisdiction" (ATA, s. 58(1)). Common-law rules of natural justice and procedural fairness must be decided "having regard to whether, in all of the circumstances, the tribunal acted fairly" (ATA, s. 58(2)(b)), and a standard of correctness applies to "all other matters." Where the enabling statute has no privative clause, findings of fact are reviewable on the basis of no evidence or unreasonableness, questions of law are reviewable on correctness, the exercise of discretion is subject to a standard of patent unreasonableness, and procedural fairness is decided "having regard to whether, in all of the circumstances," the tribunal acted fairly (ATA, s. 59(5)).

set aside in an application for judicial review or in any other proceeding unless the decision is patently unreasonable."[160]

And then *Dunsmuir* came along, and out went patent unreasonableness.

The Supreme Court in *Khosa* acknowledges the predicament for parties dealing with statutes that incorporate the now obsolete common-law standard of "patent unreasonableness":

> Generally speaking, most if not all judicial review statutes are drafted against the background of the common law of judicial review. Even the more comprehensive among them, such as the British Columbia *Administrative Tribunals Act*,[161] can only sensibly be interpreted in the common law context because, for example, it provides in s. 58(2)(a) that "a finding of fact or law or an exercise of discretion by the tribunal in respect of a matter over which it has exclusive jurisdiction under a privative clause must not be interfered with *unless it is patently unreasonable*." The expression "patently unreasonable" did not spring unassisted from the mind of the legislator. It was obviously intended to be understood in the context of the common law jurisprudence, although a number of indicia of patent unreasonableness are given in s. 58(3). Despite *Dunsmuir*, "patent unreasonableness" will live on in British Columbia, but the *content* of the expression, and the precise degree of deference it commands in the diverse circumstances of a large provincial administration, will necessarily continue to be calibrated according to general principles of administrative law. That said, of course, the legislature in s. 58 was and is directing the B.C. courts to afford administrators a high degree of deference on issues of fact, and effect must be given to this clearly expressed legislative intention.[162]

How have courts interpreted statutory standards of "patent unreasonableness" post-*Dunsmuir*?

In *British Columbia (Workers Compensation Board) v. Figliola*,[163] the Supreme Court of Canada considered whether the B.C. Human Rights Tribunal exercised its discretion in a patently unreasonable fashion when it decided to adjudicate a Human Rights Code complaint that had already been rejected by a review officer of the B.C. Workers' Compensation Board. The Court was not required to interpret the term "patently unreasonable" post-*Dunsmuir*, because the ATA already defined it according to the traditional indicia of abuse of discretion.[164] In *Shaw v. Phipps*,[165] the Ontario Divisional Court held that "patently unreasonable" in the Ontario *Human Rights Code* should be interpreted against the legislative intent at the time of enactment. The Divisional Court reasoned that the Ontario Legislature's intent was to confer the highest level of deference available under general principles

---

160 *Human Rights Code, supra* note 8, s. 45.8.

161 *Supra* note 159.

162 *Khosa, supra* note 133 at para. 19.

163 2011 SCC 52, [2011] 3 S.C.R. 422 [*Figliola*].

164 ATA, *supra* note 158, s. 59(4) defines a patently unreasonable exercise of discretion as one where the discretion
    (a) is exercised arbitrarily or in bad faith,
    (b) is exercised for an improper purpose,
    (c) is based entirely or predominantly on irrelevant factors, or
    (d) fails to take statutory requirements into account.

165 2010 ONSC 3884.

of administrative law on the Human Rights Tribunal. In 2006, that standard was patent unreasonableness. The Supreme Court of Canada subsequently declared the highest level of deference available under general principles of administrative law to be reasonableness. Therefore, according the highest degree of deference to the tribunal's determination of liability and remedy post-*Dunsmuir* meant respecting those "questions within the specialized expertise of the Tribunal" unless "they are not rationally supported—in other words, they are unreasonable."[166]

D. What Is a Question of Central Importance to the Legal System as a Whole (and Outside the Decision-Maker's Area of Expertise)?

The standard of review approach articulated in *Dunsmuir* does not place expertise in the foreground as a discrete focus of the evaluation. Given the primacy of expertise in earlier jurisprudence, this seems odd. Perhaps the better reading of *Dunsmuir* is that the unmistakable tilt of the standard-of-review analysis toward deference presupposes the superior expertise of administrative decision-makers in interpreting and applying their home statutes, absent some indicator to the contrary.[167] In a sense, *Dunsmuir* deems administrative decision-makers as expert in applying their constitutive statutes, unless one of the exceptions applies. This posture contrasts with the view expressed by U.S. appellate judge (and scholar) Richard Posner, whose critique of poor-quality decision making by U.S. immigration adjudicators commenced with the declaration, "Deference is earned; it is not a birthright."[168] Questions of jurisdiction and constitutionality might be understood as illustrations of matters that lie outside the expertise of administrative decision-makers. Questions of "central importance to the legal system as a whole" are assigned to correctness review only if they are also "outside the specialized area of expertise of the administrative decision maker."[169] The *Dunsmuir* majority is also concerned about precedent: "Because of their impact on the administration of justice as a whole, such questions require uniform and consistent answers."[170] Issues concerning the jurisdictional boundaries between different administrative tribunals seem more ambiguously tied to expertise, but also link back to the allocation of questions of true jurisdiction to the correctness standard.

In *Celgene Corp. v. Canada (Attorney General)*,[171] and again in *Smith v. Alliance Pipeline*,[172] the majority affirmed that interpretation of the home statute "will usually attract a reasonableness standard of review."[173] One expects that most administrative decisions will

---

166   *Ibid.* at para. 42.

167   Rothstein J. strenuously objected to this presumption in *Khosa, supra* note 133, and reiterated precisely the opposite view: "If the legislature intended to protect expert decision-makers from review, it did so through a privative clause" (at para. 86).

168   *Kadia v. Gonzales*, 501 F.3d 817 at 821 (7th Cir. 2007).

169   *Dunsmuir, supra* note 112 at para. 60.

170   *Ibid.*

171   2011 SCC 1, [2011] 1 SCR 3 [*Celgene v. Canada*].

172   *Smith, supra* note 140.

173   *Ibid.* at para. 28.

satisfy this criterion most of the time, thereby assuring an expansive scope for the default position of deference.

In *Smith*, the majority went on to state that the nature of the task (discretionary award of costs), and the intertwining of fact and law, buttressed its conclusion that reasonableness is the operative standard, and no countervailing correctness factors were present.

In his *Dunsmuir* concurrence, Binnie J. expressed concern that the exceptional justification for intensified judicial scrutiny where an issue is of central importance and beyond the decision-maker's expertise would unleash needless and distracting debate in the lower courts. Thus far, few cases in which the parties have disputed whether a given legal question fits within the exemption have percolated upward. One might find clues as to its meaning in the pre-*Dunsmuir* case of *Toronto (City) v. C.U.P.E., Local 79*.[174] The Supreme Court considered the standard of review applicable to the relitigation of a criminal conviction in the course of a grievance arbitration. LeBel J. concurred with the majority's assessment that the question concerned common-law doctrines that went to the administration of justice. He agreed that the appropriate standard of review was correctness, because the issue concerned "a question of law that is both of central importance to the legal system as a whole and outside the adjudicator's specialized area of expertise."[175]

In *Mowat v. Canada*,[176] the Supreme Court considered the interpretation of s. 53(2)(c) of the *Canadian Human Rights Act*.[177] The provision authorizes a human rights tribunal to order the offending party to "compensate the victim for any or all of the wages that the victim was deprived of and for any expenses incurred by the victim as a result of the discriminatory practice." The question was whether "any expenses" included the complainant's legal fees.[178]

Although the *Dunsmuir* methodology presumes that the outcome of the pre-*Dunsmuir* pragmatic and functional analysis will align with the outcome of the post-*Dunsmuir* standard-of-review analysis, the situation of human rights tribunals gives the Supreme Court pause. As noted earlier, prior to *Dunsmuir*, human rights tribunals attracted little deference from the courts. The Supreme Court of Canada repeatedly insisted that the "superior expertise of human rights tribunals relates to fact-finding and adjudication in a human rights context and does not extend to general questions of law."[179] Interpretation of the home statute by human rights tribunals attracted no deference. So, if one relied on past jurisprudence about human rights tribunals' expertise, one would probably incline toward the standard of correctness. Indeed, if one focused more narrowly on the power of the tribunal to award costs, one might even characterize the issue as "jurisdictional" and thus subject to correctness. Yet, if one took seriously *Dunsmuir*'s recognition of the expertise of

---

174   *Supra* note 110.

175   *Ibid.* at para. 62.

176   *Canada (Canadian Human Rights Commission) v. Canada (Attorney General)*, 2011 SCC 53, [2011] 3 S.C.R. 471, *Canada (Attorney General) v. Mowat*, 2009 FCA 309, [2010] 4 F.C.R. 579 [*Mowat*].

177   R.S.C. 1985, c. H-6.

178   The legal issue in *Mowat* resembled the issue in *Smith v. Alliance Pipeline*, *supra* note 140—namely, the power to award costs. Although the Supreme Court adopted a standard of review of reasonableness in both cases, query whether the Court deferred equally to the respective administrative tribunals.

179   *Mowat*, *supra* note 176 at para. 29.

decision-makers in interpreting and applying their home statute, one would be pulled in the direction of reasonableness.

The Supreme Court acknowledges the dilemma, and resolves it by casting the issue of costs as neither jurisdictional nor a question of central importance to the legal system and outside the tribunal's expertise. The Court carefully steered a path that would enable it to arrive at a reasonableness standard of review with respect to costs without requiring it to disavow the pre-*Dunsmuir* jurisprudence that subjected human rights tribunals to correctness review on almost all other matters:

> There is no doubt that the human rights tribunals are often called upon to address issues of very broad import. But, the same questions may arise before other adjudicative bodies, particularly the courts. In respect of some of these questions, the application of the *Dunsmuir* standard of review analysis could well lead to the application of the standard of correctness. But, not all questions of general law entrusted to the Tribunal rise to the level of issues of central importance to the legal system or fall outside the adjudicator's specialized area of expertise. ... In this case, there is no doubt that the Tribunal has the power to award compensation for "any expenses incurred by the victim as a result of the discriminatory practice" ... . The issue is whether the Tribunal could order the payment of costs as a form of compensation. ... . Although the respondent submitted that a human rights tribunal has no particular expertise in costs, care should be taken not to return to the formalism of the earlier decisions that attributed "a jurisdiction-limiting label, such as 'statutory interpretation' or 'human rights,' to what is in reality a function assigned and properly exercised under the enabling legislation" by a tribunal. The inquiry of what costs were incurred by the complainant as a result of a discriminatory practice is inextricably intertwined with the Tribunal's mandate and expertise to make factual findings relating to discrimination. As an administrative body that makes such factual findings on a routine basis, the Tribunal is well positioned to consider questions relating to appropriate compensation under s. 53(2). In addition, a decision as to whether a particular tribunal will grant a particular type of compensation—in this case, legal costs—can hardly be said to be a question of central importance for the Canadian legal system and outside the specialized expertise of the adjudicator.[180]

The Court's standard-of-review analysis in *Mowat* remains silent on a problematic issue that preoccupied the Federal Court of Appeal when it decided the case.[181] In *Domtar*,[182] the Supreme Court ruled that inconsistent interpretations of a given statutory provision did not supply an independent ground for stricter judicial scrutiny where the appropriate stance was otherwise deferential. Although *Domtar* concerned the interpretation of a common phrase by two bodies constituted under different statutes, the reach of the Supreme Court's dictum was limited only by the possibility of direct operational conflict.[183] In *Mowat*, the

---

[180]   *Ibid.* at paras. 23-26.

[181]   *Mowat* (FCA), supra note 176.

[182]   *Supra* note 30.

[183]   In *Domtar, ibid.*, the Court had rejected the assertion that the precedential value of resolving inconsistency within or between tribunals constitutes an independent basis for adopting a correctness standard of review, unless the divergent decisions create an operational conflict, whereby compliance with one order would necessitate violation of the other. A significant concern for the Court in *Domtar* was the risk that real or appar-

Federal Court of Appeal was presented with conflicting interpretations of the same statutory provision by different panels of the same tribunal and, subsequently, by different Federal Court judges on judicial review. The Federal Court of Appeal described the problem as follows:

> The question has not been answered consistently by the Tribunal and is the subject of diverse opinions in the Federal Court. It comes before the Court for the first time. It is difficult, if not impossible, to conclude that the answer (either yes or no) can be said to fall within a range of possible acceptable outcomes. There is much to be said for the argument that where there are two conflicting lines of authority interpreting the same statutory provision, even if each on its own could be found to be reasonable, it would not be reasonable for a court to uphold both.[184]

The Federal Court of Appeal adopted the comments of Feldman J.A. in *Abdoulrab v. Ontario (Labour Relations Board)*,[185] and declared that "it accords with the rule of law that a public statute that applies equally to all affected citizens should have a universally accepted interpretation."[186] The values of certainty and consistency for the affected parties and the public at large led the Court of Appeal to characterize the question whether a human rights tribunal can order the losing party to pay the legal costs of the complainant as a "general question of law of central importance to the legal system as a whole and one that is outside the specialized area of the Tribunal's expertise."[187] It set aside the Human Rights Tribunal's affirmative response to the question as incorrect.

The Supreme Court of Canada in *Mowat* suppresses the issue of conflicting decisions and does not advert to it; one might interpret the silence as affirmation of *Domtar*. *Quaere* whether it should matter for purposes of designating a question as one of "central importance" that the legal question has already been the subject of conflicting decisions by the tribunal and by reviewing courts. If you were a member of that tribunal or representing a party before it, would you prefer that it be left to your peers to address divergent interpretations through institutional consistency mechanisms, or would you rather that the courts resolve the matter definitively by applying a correctness standard? Would it be legitimate to pre-empt future conflict by asserting a standard of correctness the first time the interpretation of a legal provision is contested? If not, when does it become appropriate to do so?

In the result, the Supreme Court in *Mowat* decided that the Human Rights Tribunal's inclusion of legal costs as "expenses" was unreasonable. Of course, the Supreme Court of Canada's decision had the convenient effect of ruling out one of only two possible interpretations of the statutory provision. The Supreme Court thus provided definitive guidance to subsequent decision-makers.

---

ent inconsistencies within or between tribunal decisions might become a pretext for undermining fidelity to the principles underlying curial deference. The Court also adverted to internal mechanisms available to tribunals to encourage consistency, and downplayed the virtues of consistency in relation to other important values served by deference.

[184]   *Mowat* (FCA), *supra* note 176 at para. 45.

[185]   2009 ONCA 491, 95 O.R. (3d) 641, 95 Admin. L.R. (4th) 121.

[186]   *Mowat* (FCA), *supra*, note 176 at para. 46.

[187]   *Ibid.* at para. 47.

VII. Spin-Offs

A. The Charter, Discretion, and the Standard of Review

Where a judicial review application raises several discrete issues, reviewing courts have sometimes calibrated the standard of review separately for each issue. Segmentation arises whenever one link in a decision chain attracts a different standard of review than other links in the chain. *Dunsmuir* offers relief from the complexity of this process by expanding the range of decisional steps to which deference will presumptively apply, but the problem remains where one or more elements of the decision attracts a standard of review of correctness.

In *Dunsmuir*, Binnie J. described segmentation in the following terms:

> Mention should be made of a further feature that also reflects the complexity of the subject matter of judicial review. An applicant may advance several grounds for quashing an administrative decision. He or she may contend that the decision maker has misinterpreted the general law. He or she may argue, in the alternative, that even if the decision maker got the general law straight (an issue on which the court's view of what is correct will prevail), the decision maker did not properly apply it to the facts (an issue on which the decision maker is entitled to deference). In a challenge under the *Canadian Charter of Rights and Freedoms* to a surrender for extradition, for example, the minister will have to comply with the Court's view of Charter principles (the "correctness" standard), but if he or she correctly appreciates the applicable law, the court will properly recognize a wide discretion in the application of those principles to the particular facts. The same approach is taken to less exalted decision makers. In the jargon of the judicial review bar, this is known as "segmentation."[188]

Unfortunately, neither Binnie J. nor his colleagues say anything further in *Dunsmuir* (or in subsequent cases) about the dilemmas posed by segmentation, or how to resolve them.

The intersection of discretion and the Charter provides an object lesson in some of the complexities of segmentation. Consider *Suresh*.[189] A provision of the *Immigration Act* (now IRPA) grants the minister discretion to deport a non-citizen who is deemed to be a threat to national security. The s. 7 constitutional issue was whether the minister could exercise his or her discretion to deport a non-citizen to a country where that person faced a substantial risk of torture. A deportation decision in this context consisted of various subquestions:

1. What is the meaning of national security?
2. Is the non-citizen a threat to national security?
3. What does torture mean?
4. Does the non-citizen face a substantial risk of torture?
5. Does deportation of a non-citizen to torture violate s. 7 of the Charter?

The Court does not articulate a standard of review for questions 1 and 3, but emphasizes that questions 2 and 4 attract deference, while question 5 is explicitly subject to correctness.

---

188   *Dunsmuir, supra* note 112 at para. 142.

189   *Suresh v. Canada (Minister of Citizenship and Immigration)*, 2002 SCC 1, [2002] 1 S.C.R. 3.

Had the Court said "yes" to question 5, then the determinations under questions 1 to 4 could have proceeded sequentially and discretely from one another. If questions 4 was reached and the answer was "yes," that would be the end of the story: no deportation. If the answer was "no," then the minister could deport to torture.

But the Court's answer to question 5 was neither "yes" nor "no." It was "no, unless there are exceptional circumstances." The Court effectively constrained but did not eliminate the discretion to deport to torture. The so-called *Suresh* exception directed the minister to consider the following additional question:

> 6. Do the benefits to Canada's national security of deporting the non-citizen outweigh the harm of deporting the non-citizen to torture?

What standard of review should apply at this stage? The Court is silent on this matter. On the one hand, the decision not to prohibit deportation to torture absolutely amounts to a decision that a decision-maker possesses discretion to deport to torture in some imaginable case. The exercise of balancing multiple factors usually attracts deference because of its indeterminacy, the interplay of factors, and the courts' stated reluctance to reweigh evidence on review. On the other hand, the Court itself invented the *Suresh* exception, and each balancing exercise under the rubric of exceptional circumstances risks the most extreme violation of a specific individual's Charter rights if the minister's calculus is mistaken. It seems inimical to the normative and institutional foundation of the Charter to defer to a minister's own determination of whether his or her discretionary decision violates an individual's Charter rights, but there is precedent indicating judicial willingness to do precisely that.[190]

In *Doré v. Barreau du Québec*,[191] the Supreme Court offered a path out of this methodological dilemma: "When Charter values are applied to an individual administrative decision, they are being applied in relation to a particular set of facts. *Dunsmuir* tells us this should attract deference."[192] The courts should recognize "the distinct advantage that administrative bodies have in applying the Charter to a specific set of facts and in the context of their enabling legislation."[193] Rather than attempt to retrofit the s. 1 *Oakes* test into the exercise of a

---

[190]   In practice, courts called on to review a ministerial decision to deport to torture have applied a standard of reasonableness but found the decision unreasonable. See e.g. *Jaballah (Re) v. Jaballah (Re)*, 2005 FC 399, [2005] 4 F.C.R. 359. See also *Lake v. Canada (Minister of Justice)*, 2008 SCC 23, [2008] 1 S.C.R. 761 [*Lake*], in which the Supreme Court deferred to the minister of justice's determination about whether surrender of a fugitive for extradition would violate the fugitive's ss. 6 and 7 rights under the Charter on the grounds that the decision in question was "largely a political decision, not a legal one" and "a fact driven inquiry" (paras. 37 and 38). This is a deeply problematic judgment that has the potential to insulate rights violating state conduct from the correctness standard, where the breach arises from the exercise of a broad statutory discretion that does not, on its face, violate the Charter. Many, if not most, individualized exercises of discretion can easily be characterized as "fact-driven." The claim that a decision is political rather than legal is conclusory and unhelpful, insofar as many "political" decisions have a legal dimension. Moreover, it is precisely because the violation of individual rights may be politically expedient that the Charter places legal limits on the exercise of political power.

[191]   2012 SCC 12.

[192]   *Ibid.* at para. 36.

[193]   *Ibid.* at para. 48.

case-specific discretion, the Court proposes a similar "proportionality" analysis that balances "the severity of the interference of the Charter protection with the statutory objectives."[194] If the outcome of that balancing "falls within a range of possible, acceptable outcomes," then it merits deference. The concluding declaration of the Court is that "[i]f, in exercising its statutory discretion, the decision-maker has properly balanced the relevant Charter values with the statutory objectives, the decision will be found to be reasonable."[195]

What this will mean in practice, of course, remains to be seen. How wide a margin of appreciation will the courts grant administrators in "properly" balancing the Charter against other objectives? Though the Court has repeatedly claimed to eschew re-weighing of factors in deferential review of discretion, it is difficult to conceive of a proportionality analysis that does not inquire into the appropriate weighting of the Charter right against other interests.

We live in an era where most governments take advice from government lawyers in drafting legislation in order to avoid flagrant unconstitutionality. It is also the case that many contemporary statutes look increasingly "skeletal." What goes on the bones of the statute is fleshed out through regulatory authority delegated to the governor in council or expansive and vague grants of statutory discretion to administrative decision-makers (including ministers). If Charter issues are increasingly likely to emerge in the exercise of broad discretion rather than in the text of a law, the scope and intensity of judicial oversight of Charter-impacting discretion will have profound implications for the level of rights protection within the Canadian legal order.

B. Reasoning About Reasons

Reasons straddle procedure and substance. As Grant Huscroft explains in Chapter 5, From Natural Justice to Fairness: Thresholds, Content, and the Role of Judicial Review, the duty to give reasons is a component of fairness. Reasons serve a number of purposes, not least of which is to communicate that the decision-maker has genuinely heard and considered the evidence and arguments presented. As the Supreme Court remarked in *Lake v. Canada (Minister of Justice)*, "The purpose of providing reasons is twofold: to allow the individual to understand why the decision was made; and to allow the reviewing court to assess the validity of the decision."[196] One might contend that reasons that do not adequately communicate the basis of the decision do not meet some minimal threshold that qualifies the text as "reasons." They fail as a matter of form.

Reasons also disclose the findings of fact, interpretations of law, applications of law to fact, and exercises of discretion that are the substance of the decision. Reasons contain the evidence of the reasonableness (or correctness, as the case may be) of those exercises of statutory authority. As you will see in Sheila Wildeman's Chapter 10, Pas de Deux: Deference and Non-Deference in Action, measuring the substantive reasonableness of a decision

---

194   *Ibid.* at para. 56.

195   *Ibid.* at para. 58.

196   *Lake, supra* note 190 at para. 46.

post-*Dunsmuir* includes assessing the justification, transparency, and intelligibility of the reasoning process.

There is obvious potential for overlap between assessing the formal adequacy of reasons as a matter of procedural fairness and evaluating the substantive content of reasons as a matter of merits review. Framing the ground-of-reasons review in terms of procedure rather than substance potentially invites a greater degree of judicial intervention via the correctness standard. This also depends on the ambit-of-adequacy review. The more a court demands of reasons in order to satisfy the procedural duty of fairness, the greater the potential for expansive and intrusive judicial review.

Finding a consistent "break point" between the form of reasons and the content of reasons proved challenging for lower courts, and different jurisprudential currents began to emerge.[197] Without adverting to this incipient debate, the Supreme Court of Canada abruptly terminated it.

In *Newfoundland and Labrador Nurses' Union v. Newfoundland and Labrador (Treasury Board)*,[198] Abella J., writing for the Court, stated: "I do not see *Dunsmuir* as standing for the proposition that the 'adequacy' of reasons is a stand-alone basis for quashing a decision, or as advocating that a reviewing court undertake two discrete analyses—one for the reasons and a separate one for the result."[199] Later, she explicitly minimized the scope of the duty to give reasons to bare form.

> It strikes me as an unhelpful elaboration on *Baker* to suggest that alleged deficiencies or flaws in the reasons fall under the category of a breach of the duty of procedural fairness and that they are subject to a correctness review. As Professor Philip Bryden has warned, "courts must be careful not to confuse a finding that a tribunal's reasoning process is inadequately revealed with disagreement over the conclusions reached by the tribunal on the evidence before it" .... .
> It is true that the breach of a duty of procedural fairness is an error in law. Where there are no reasons in circumstances where they are required, there is nothing to review. But where, as here, there *are* reasons, there is no such breach. Any challenge to the reasoning/result of the decision should therefore be made within the reasonableness analysis.[200]

VIII. Review of Standard of Review: I Laughed, I Cried, I Stood on My Chair and ...

The tensions lying at the heart of jurisprudence about the standard of review have not changed and will not go away. In its recent jurisprudence, the majority of the Supreme Court of Canada has staked out a position that, in principle, inclines toward deference. It has told and retold the story about why and when courts ought to defer to the decisions of

---

[197] See e.g. *Clifford v. Ontario Municipal Employees Retirement System*, 2009 ONCA 670 (2009), 93 Admin. L.R. (4th) 131; *Vancouver International Airport Authority v. Public Service Alliance of Canada*, 2010 FCA 158, [2011] 4 F.C.R. 425.

[198] 2011 SCC 62, [2011] 3 S.C.R. 708.

[199] *Ibid.* at para. 14.

[200] *Ibid.* at paras. 21-22.

administrative decision-makers. Each major iteration reveals shifts in emphasis; additional nuances; glosses on past recitations; and attempts to reconcile, distinguish, or conceal apparent anomalies. On rare occasions, we get a new plot twist: from two standards of review to three, then back to two (but not the same two); from the formalism of "preliminary or collateral question," to multifactor balancing, to a defeasible rule (or maybe not).

The job of discerning the appropriate standard of review became simpler after *Dunsmuir*, and for this students and practitioners of administrative law should feel relieved. But they should also attend to the prediction of Binnie J. in *Dunsmuir*. By streamlining the standard-of-review analysis and winnowing deference down to a single standard of reasonableness, the Court has not resolved the challenge of operationalizing deference in all its multifarious contexts. Rather, it has exported the task to the next stage of judicial review—namely, the application of correctness or reasonableness review to actual decisions. Thus, the conclusion of this chapter is really a prologue to Chapter 10 where, post-*Dunsmuir*, the action unfolds.

SUGGESTED ADDITIONAL READINGS

BOOKS AND ARTICLES

Canadian

Heckman, G., "Substantive Review in Appellate Courts Since Dunsmuir" (2009) 47 Osgoode Hall L.J. 751.

Jacobs, L., "Developments in Administrative Law: The 2007-2008 Term—The Impact of Dunsmuir" (2008) 43 Sup. Ct. L. Rev. (2d) 1-34.

Lahey, B., & D. Ginn, "After the Revolution: Being Pragmatic and Functional in Canada's Trial Courts and Courts of Appeal" (2002) 25 Dal. L.J. 259.

MacLauchlan, H.W., "Transforming Administrative Law: The Didactic Role of the Supreme Court of Canada" (2001) 80 Can. Bar Rev. 281.

McLachlin, The Honourable Justice B., "The Roles of Administrative Tribunals and Courts in Maintaining the Rule of Law" (1999) 12 Can. J. Admin. L. & Prac. 171.

Mullan, D., "Dunsmuir v. New Brunswick, Standard of Review and Procedural Fairness: Let's Try Again!" (2008) 21 Can. J. Admin. L. & Prac. 117.

Sossin, L., & C. Flood, "The Contextual Turn: Iacobucci's Legacy and the Standard of Review in Administrative Law" (2007) 57 U.T.L.J. 581.

International

Dyzenhaus, D., "The Politics of Deference: Judicial Review and Democracy" in M. Taggart, ed., *The Province of Administrative Law* (Oxford: Hart Publishing, 1997).

CASES

Alberta (Information and Privacy Commissioner) v. Alberta Teachers' Association, 2011 SCC 61, [2011] 3 S.C.R. 654.

Baker v. Canada (Minister of Citizenship and Immigration), [1999] 2 S.C.R. 817.

British Columbia (Workers' Compensation Board) v. Figliola, 2011 SCC 52, [2011] 3 S.C.R. 422.

Canada (Canadian Human Rights Commission) v. Canada (Attorney General), 2011 SCC 53, [2011] 3 S.C.R. 471.

Canada (Citizenship and Immigration) v. Khosa, 2009 SCC 12, [2009] 1 S.C.R. 339.

Canada (Director of Investigation and Research) v. Southam Inc., [1997] 1 S.C.R. 748.

Celgene Corp. v. Canada (Attorney General), 2011 SCC 1, [2011] 1 S.C.R. 3.

C.U.P.E. v. N.B. Liquor Corporation, [1979] 2 S.C.R. 227.

Dunsmuir v. New Brunswick, [2008] 1 SCR 190.

Newfoundland and Labrador Nurses' Union v. Newfoundland and Labrador (Treasury Board), 2011 SCC 62, [2011] 3 S.C.R. 708.

Nor-Man Regional Health Authority Inc. v. Manitoba Association of Health Care Professionals, 2011 SCC 59, [2011] 3 S.C.R. 616.

Pushpanathan v. Canada (Minister of Citizenship and Immigration), [1998] 1 S.C.R. 982.

Smith v. Alliance Pipeline Ltd., 2011 SCC 7, [2011] 1 S.C.R. 160.

Pas de Deux: Deference and Non-Deference in Action

SHEILA WILDEMAN*

Schulich School of Law, Dalhousie University

I. Introduction

In 2008, the Canadian case law on the standards of review structuring judicial oversight of substantive administrative decisions underwent a significant transformation. As Audrey Macklin explains in Chapter 9, Standard of Review: Back to the Future?, for roughly the previous 10 years, Canadian administrative law had featured three standards of review, representing, at least in theory, three distinct judicial postures toward disputed administrative decisions. These were correctness, wherein the decision under review was said to command low or no deference; reasonableness, wherein the decision commanded some, but not great, deference; and patent unreasonableness, wherein the decision commanded utmost

* This chapter includes revisions of my chapter from the first edition of this text, as well as reworked excerpts from my LL.M. thesis, "Romancing Reasonableness: An Aspirational Account of the Canadian Case Law on Judicial Review of Substantive Administrative Decisions Since *C.U.P.E. v. N.B. Liquor Corporation*" and new material. I wish to thank David Dyzenhaus and Audrey Macklin for their invaluable contributions to my understanding of administrative law. Thanks also to Lorne Sossin and Colleen Flood for their patient and helpful editorial assistance.

deference. With the issuing of the Supreme Court judgment in *Dunsmuir v. New Brunswick*,[1] the three standards were condensed into two: correctness and reasonableness, connoting, at least on a cursory view, a simpler binary opposition of non-deference versus deference.

This development was generally (if tentatively) welcomed as advancing the cause of simplifying substantive review. In particular, *Dunsmuir's* judicial downsizing of the standards of review and ostensible streamlining of the work of selecting a standard was regarded, not least by the judges issuing the decision, as enabling a freeing-up of judicial energies in order to engage more directly with the legal adequacy of administrative decisions. That is, the *Dunsmuir* court suggested (and, in this, all three judgments concurred) that it was high time to attenuate the long-standing preoccupation with "calibrating" or selecting the appropriate standard of review that had come to dominate this area of law.[2] Instead, judges and lawyers should now turn more promptly or directly to the core work of substantive review—that is, to answering the question: should the challenged decision stand or fall as a matter of law? Yet despite this urging to get down to the work at hand, the shift in orientation that is to be adopted in the wake of *Dunsmuir* forces renewed reflection on the sort of analysis that should drive substantive review, particularly where deference is warranted.

Chapter 9 introduced the complexities of the law on identifying the appropriate standard of review where an administrative decision is subject to judicial oversight. The present chapter revisits the law on the standards of review, shifting the focus from the application of the selected standard to the decision under review. It inquires, in particular, into the signposts that have been erected in and after *Dunsmuir* to direct the conduct of judicial review on a correctness or reasonableness standard, although it also asks what guidance may be drawn from the pre-*Dunsmuir* case law on these matters.

The question driving this chapter's inquiry into the meaning and application of the standards of review is, therefore, "What is required of administrative decision-makers in order to satisfy the expectations of substantive legality?" On taking up that question, we soon encounter deep tensions in this area of law. Indeed, as Audrey Macklin indicates in Chapter 9, the case law extending from *C.U.P.E. v. N.B. Liquor Corporation*[3] in 1979 to *Dunsmuir* in 2008 and beyond is animated by disputes wherein the legislatively conferred authority and sector-specific expertise of administrators may be said to have butted up against the constitutional responsibility of a judiciary charged with ensuring that administrative action remains within legal limits. The jurisprudence on the standards of review may be understood as a record of the shifting ways in which the long-standing tensions in the judicial–administrative (and moreover, judicial–legislative) relationship have been negotiated.

There is more than one approach to the study or interpretation of the underlying tensions to which I refer. The approach taken in this chapter foregrounds, even as it encourages you to question, what may be termed a romantic account of this area of law. The romantic

---

[1]   [2008] 1 S.C.R. 190 [*Dunsmuir*].

[2]   This shift in emphasis informs all three sets of reasons, although it is brought out most clearly in the concurring opinion of Binnie J. in *Dunsmuir, ibid.* at para. 145. See also *Alberta (Information and Privacy Commissioner) v. Alberta Teachers' Association*, 2011 SCC 61, [2011] 3 S.C.R. 654 at para. 38, Rothstein J. for the majority [*Alberta (Information and Privacy Commissioner)*].

[3]   [1979] 2 S.C.R. 227 [*CUPE*].

account has slowly risen to prominence over the past few decades of jurisprudence on substantive review. One can trace its (hesitant) evolution through the case law on deference, beginning with *CUPE* in 1979 and stretching through a line of cases wherein the work of substantive review has been progressively modelled not as a matter of judges patrolling the legal limits of administrative action, but rather as an expression of a wider constitutional project shared among the legislative, judicial, and executive/administrative branches.[4] This is the project of public justification—that is, of ensuring that state action is grounded in, and so may be publicly justified in light of, law.[5] The romantic account of substantive review thus expresses a model of constitutional ordering that we may refer to as "constitutional pluralism,"[6] wherein all three branches of government participate in working out the significance of the legal norms governing the exercise of state power. A plurality of sources of legal norms are understood to inform this (shared) project of public justification. These encompass not only statute law, but also—as we shall see is stated in *Baker*[7]—the Constitution (including the Charter), the common law and international law, instruments of "soft law" (for example, ministerial directives or departmental policies), and the "fundamental values of Canadian society."[8] Finally, the pluralist model of constitutional ordering that informs the romantic account of substantive review insists that the public justification of administrative action, in

---

[4] I traced this case law in the introduction to my chapter in the previous edition of this text: "A Fine Romance? The Modern Standards of Review in Theory and Practice" in *Administrative Law in Context*, C. Flood & L. Sossin, eds. (Toronto: Emond Montgomery, 2008) 221 at 231-32 ["A Fine Romance"]. Arguably, *Dunsmuir* and subsequent case law—in particular, *Doré v. Barreau du Québec*, 2012 SCC 12 [*Doré*] (discussed in section III.B)—represent new inroads for the romantic model, although, as related herein, such developments are not simple or uniform. The foundations for the model I am calling "romantic" are set out in D. Dyzenhaus, "The Politics of Deference: Judicial Review and Democracy" in M. Taggart, ed., *The Province of Administrative Law* (Oxford: Hart Publishing, 1997) 279.

[5] That contemporary approaches to administrative law are rooted in a commitment to a "culture of justification" is conveyed in a statement from McLachlin C.J. in 1999 (The Hon. Justice B. McLachlin, "The Roles of Administrative Tribunals and Courts in Maintaining the Rule of Law" (1999) 12 Can. J. Admin. L. & Prac. 171 at 174-75):

> [S]ocieties governed by the Rule of Law are marked by a certain ethos of justification. … Where a society is marked by a culture of justification, an exercise of public power is only appropriate where it can be justified to citizens in terms of rationality and fairness. … A culture of justification shifts the analysis from the institutions themselves to, more subtly, what those institutions are capable of doing for the rational advancement of civil society. The Rule of Law, in short, can speak in several voices so long as the resulting chorus echoes its underlying values of rationality and fairness.

See also D. Dyzenhaus, "Law as Justification: Etienne Mureinik's Conception of Legal Culture" (1998) 14 S.A.J.H.R. 11; D. Dyzenhaus & E. Fox-Decent, "Rethinking the Process/Substance Distinction: Baker v. Canada" (2001) 51 U.T.L.J. 193 ["Process/Substance"]; D. Dyzenhaus, "Constituting the Rule of Law: Fundamental Values in Administrative Law" (2002) 27 Queen's L.J. 445 ["Constituting the Rule of Law"].

[6] See "Constituting the Rule of Law," *ibid.* at 487-89. Dyzenhaus refers to this model of constitutional ordering as "democratic constitutionalism" and argues that it is implicit in the majority decision of L'Heureux-Dubé J. in *Baker v. Canada (Minister of Citizenship and Immigration)* [1999] 2 S.C.R. 817 [*Baker*].

[7] *Ibid.*

[8] *Ibid.* at paras. 56, 67.

order to count as public justification—that is, as legal reasons, not mere explanations—must take account of the important interests of, and so be undertaken in dialogue with, the individuals directly affected by state action.[9]

Despite the contemporary ascendance of the romantic account of substantive review and the model of constitutional ordering it implies, there remain in the case law vestiges of the major competing approach. This is the Diceyan model of administrative state ordering, discussed by Mary Liston in Chapter 2, Governments in Miniature: The Rule of Law in the Administrative State, and Geneviève Cartier in Chapter 11, Administrative Discretion: Between Exercising Power and Conducting Dialogue. That model asserts a strict separation of powers as among the legislative, executive/administrative, and judicial branches in constituting the administrative state.[10] That is, on the Diceyan model, the legislature is the proper source of the laws conferring authority on administrative decision-makers; administrative decision-makers execute or exercise the authority so conferred; and judges apply their law-interpretive capacities to ensure that administrative action remains within the limits of legislative intent.[11] But these strict Diceyan dividing lines are difficult to maintain—particularly (as Geneviève Cartier explains in Chapter 11) when it comes to administrative discretion. In effect, the Diceyan judge is caught between conflicting signals: to respect Parliamentary supremacy and legislative intent by ceding decision-making authority to administrative decision-makers, and to ensure that administrative decision-makers remain within the limits of law. The result, as Dyzenhaus and others have argued, is instability between two extremes of judicial conduct—abdication and supremacy—on review.[12] The first of these extremes seeks to express respect for parliamentary supremacy and legislative intent through non-interference with the "merits" of administrative decisions, while the second attempts to affirm the supervisory powers of the judiciary by closely hedging administrative authority within judicially ascertained legal or jurisdictional limits.

The instability between judicial abdication and judicial supremacy on review gives rise to what we may call the skeptical account of substantive review. The skeptic (the romantic's foil) regards the standards of review and, in particular, the idea of deferential review or re-

---

9   The approach to substantive review that I describe here is thus oriented by the overarching principles of the rule of law (requiring that state action be grounded in law) and democracy (not merely representative democracy, but an ideal of deliberative democracy aimed at facilitating active individual participation in the shaping of legal norms). See G. Cartier, "Administrative Discretion as Dialogue: A Response to John Willis (or: From Theology to Secularization)" (2005) 55(3) U.T.L.J. 623 at 644-56, and Chapter 11 herein. See also D. Dyzenhaus, "Constituting the Rule of Law," *supra* note 5 at 501:

     Legislatures and administrative tribunals have a role in the determination of the values considered fundamental to the Canadian social, political and legal order, as do the parties who challenge the state to show that its exercises of public power are accountable to those underlying values.

10   See "Constituting the Rule of Law," *supra* note 5 at 453-57.

11   *Ibid.* at 454-55, citing Dickson C.J. in *Fraser v. P.S.S.R.B.*, [1985] 2 S.C.R. 455 at 469-70 and *Cooper v. Canada (Human Rights Commission)*, [1996] 3 S.C.R. 854 at para. 10.

12   See D. Dyzenhaus, "Formalism's Hollow Victory" (2002) N.Z.L. Rev. 525 at 530-39; "The Politics of Deference," *supra* note 4 at 280-82; "Constituting the Rule of Law," *supra* note 5 at 448-51 and 454-58; D. Dyzenhaus and E. Fox-Decent, "Process/Substance," *supra* note 5 at 197-200 and 204-5. See also D. Mullan, "A Proportionate Response to an Emerging Crisis in Canadian Judicial Review Law?" (2010) N.Z.L. Rev. 233 at 251-53 ["A Proportionate Response?"].

view for reasonableness as a grand illusion distracting us from the underlying truth of this area of law. That truth is one of irreconcilable differences as between the legislative branch—and with it, administrative decision-makers democratically mandated to advance legislative policy—and the judicial branch, with its exclusive claim to determining the limits of law. Moreover, beneath the cloak of substantive review doctrine, the skeptic tends to discern a (judicial) discretion so wide that judges may, in many if not most cases, deploy their final say however they like—that is, to overturn those decisions that conflict with their particular values or policy preferences (including their sense of what is necessary to the coherence of the individualist common-law traditions in which they are steeped) and to uphold the decisions that do not so conflict. In short, the skeptic regards the romantic's promise of reconciliation under the shared banner of public justification as hollow.

Upon becoming better acquainted with the cases, students of this area of law may wish to resist the totalizing perspectives of either the romantic or the skeptic. Instead, they may opt to take a little from each. But one is a romantic at heart if, in the end, one is convinced that the point of the law on substantive review is to ground the decisions of both administrators and judges in a common commitment to public justification: a commitment that is reinforced, rather than undermined, by the different perspectives as well as capacities of the diverse institutional actors of the administrative state.

Our task is to keep in mind the above-noted concerns about the constitutional relationships proper to the administrative state while attending closely to what *Dunsmuir* reminds us is or should be the crowning moment of substantive review: that of applying the standard, and so bringing legal oversight directly to bear on a contested administrative decision. As noted, historically, the application of the standard has tended to play out as the weak final act of the substantive review judgment. For example, deferential review has often been conducted as if it amounted to no more than a sniff test[13] registering judicial intuitions that defy public articulation. Alternatively, where a correctness standard has been applied, the assessment of substantive legality has typically been conducted as if it were merely a matter of making the law (particularly the enabling statute) speak for itself—thus demanding uncritical assent to judicial assertions of a plain or otherwise unitary legislative intent. Both approaches may lead us to wonder whether other perspectives on the nature or import of the public values engaged (most notably, the perspective of the administrative decision-maker) are being suppressed. The attendant concern is that the substantive legality or illegality of the impugned decision has been asserted with insufficient justification. Such charges have lent increased potency to the skeptical thesis that, at the end of the day, substantive review is a judge's game.

By this chapter's end, we should be in a better position to evaluate whether the developments in and since *Dunsmuir* regarding application of the standards of review are likely to advance the reconciliation of the judiciary and administrative decision-makers under the rule of law that is the romantic's happy ending. Or, as the skeptic might suggest, are these latest twists in the law on the standards of review but a further installment in a long-running farce?

---

13 Or "puke test": see Dyzenhaus, "Constituting the Rule of Law," *supra* note 5 at 493 (n. 110), referring to the position of Wilson J. in *National Corn Growers Assn. v. Canada (Import Tribunal)*, [1990] 2 S.C.R. 1324.

The chapter proceeds as follows. Section II takes up the subject of statutory interpretation: specifically, competing approaches to statutory interpretation as they interact with the project of substantive review. This section lays some groundwork for what follows. Section III examines the standards of review as they have been described and, moreover, applied in the substantive review jurisprudence since *CUPE*, with a particular concern to alert the student to the state of the law post-*Dunsmuir*. Section III.A addresses the correctness standard, canvassing the rationales underlying this standard and then examining some examples from the case law in order to reflect further on those rationales. Section III.B turns to deferential review. It first examines aspects of the case law on the now-defunct standards of patent unreasonableness and reasonableness *simpliciter* that arguably remain essential to our understanding of the methods and substantive expectations of deferential review. It then takes up *Dunsmuir* and subsequent developments, asking how the refashioned reasonableness standard negotiates the tensions between deference to and supervision of administrative decisions. Again, the examination of judicial statements about reasonableness review is followed by an analysis of judgments applying the standard. Section IV offers some conclusions and raises some questions aimed particularly at the developing law on reasonableness review.

II. Statutory Interpretation and Substantive Review: Working Theories

Assessment of the substantive legality of an administrative decision is steeped in the work of statutory interpretation.[14] Therefore, before further broaching the subject of substantive review, it may help to briefly consider certain competing approaches to statutory interpretation. I suggest that these competing approaches imply competing models of the separation of powers—that is, conceptions of the proper work of, and so separation or interaction of, the legislative, executive or administrative, and judicial branches.[15] Thus adoption of one or another approach to statutory interpretation canvassed here may be significant to or determinative of the outcome of substantive review.

Let us start with the "modern principle" of statutory interpretation, articulated in the second edition of Driedger's *Construction of Statutes* and repeatedly endorsed by the Supreme Court:

---

14   "To a large extent judicial review of administrative action is a specialized branch of statutory interpretation": *U.E.S. Local 298 v. Bibeault*, [1988] 2 S.C.R. 1048 at 1087. Beetz J. (writing for the Court) is quoting S.A. de Smith, H. Street, & R. Brazier, *Constitutional and Administrative Law*, 4th ed. (Harmondsworth, UK: Penguin, 1981) at 588. Compare J.M. Keyes, "Judicial Review and the Interpretation of Legislation: Who Gets the Last Word?" (2006) 19 Can. J. Admin. L. & Prac. 119.

15   This section focuses on competing ways that judges understand (or appear to understand) the project of statutory interpretation—including competing perspectives on the role of administrative decision-makers in this project. Another question that we do not consider, although it is highly relevant to the project of substantive review, is whether administrators do or should approach statutory interpretation differently than judges. See S. Slinn, "Untamed Tribunal? Of Dynamic Interpretation and Purpose Clauses" (2009) 42 U.B.C.L. Rev. 125. Slinn builds on Edward Rubin's thesis that administrative tribunals tend to adopt dynamic interpretative practices in response to multiple sources of shifting and contending norms—not only the judiciary, but also the legislature, executive and the tribunal's constituency. See also E. Rubin, "Dynamic Statutory Interpretation in the Administrative State" (2002) Issues in Legal Scholarship, online: De Gruyter <http://www.bepress.com/ils/iss3/art2>.

Today there is only one principle or approach [to statutory interpretation], namely, the words of an Act are to be read in their entire context and in their grammatical and ordinary sense harmoniously with the scheme of the Act, the object of the Act, and the intention of Parliament.[16]

General judicial acceptance of this principle tends to obscure continuing conflicts among judges (and sometimes even among decisions of a single judge) as to the factors that should be deemed of primary relevance when interpreting contested statutory texts.[17] Here we may roughly distinguish what may be termed positivist approaches from pragmatic or normative approaches.[18]

In general terms, a positivist approach to statutory interpretation flows from the presumption that statutory language contains a singular and unified meaning that is stable over time.[19] Judges adhering to that presumption tend to accept that this stable meaning may be ascertained through interpretive techniques proper to and perfected by the judiciary. Those techniques may involve a strict focus on the statutory text or efforts to situate the text in its legislative context. On either variant of this approach, the objective is to "find" a determinate legislative intent.[20] A positivist approach to law or to law interpretation is often accompanied by a commitment to legal formalism. On this model, law is a self-contained system of formal concepts, and legal judgment consists in solving case-specific problems by making deductive and inductive links to that stable conceptual-legal system.[21] However, the interplay of legislative and common-law systems in administrative law tends to wreak havoc with formalism, strictly conceived.

A general criticism raised to the positivist approach to law interpretation is that it smuggles into legal judgment contestable value-driven choices, where those choices should

---

[16] E.A. Driedger, *Construction of Statutes*, 2d ed. (Toronto: Butterworths, 1983) at 87.

[17] See R. Sullivan, "Statutory Interpretation in the Supreme Court of Canada" (1998) 30 Ottawa L. Rev. 175 ["Statutory Interpretation"]; S. Beaulac & P. Côté, "Driedger's 'Modern Principle' at the Supreme Court of Canada: Interpretation, Justification, Legitimization" (2006) R.J.T. 131.

[18] Sullivan, "Statutory Interpretation," *ibid.*, distinguishes textualist and intentionalist (which I am loosely calling "positivist") from pragmatic (which I am calling "normative") approaches to statutory interpretation.

[19] See D. Dyzenhaus, "David Mullan's Theory of the Rule of (Common) Law" in G. Huscroft & M. Taggart, eds., *Inside and Outside Administrative Law: Essays in Honour of David Mullan* (Toronto: University of Toronto Press, 2006) 448 at 474 [*Inside and Outside*]: "[T]he point of the positivist conception of law is to insist that real law is the determinate content of valid law, where determinate means determinable in accordance with tests that do not rely on moral considerations and arguments, including arguments about the principles of an internal morality of law."

[20] Compare J. Gardner, "Legal Positivism: 5½ Myths" (2001) 46 Am. J. Juris. 199 at 218-22. Gardner argues that legal positivism is not committed to either textualism or originalism in statutory interpretation. Again, see "Statutory Interpretation," *supra* note 17.

[21] Katrina Wyman surveys the many deployments of the term formalism in legal academia in her article "Is Formalism Inevitable?" (2007) 57 U.T.L.J. 685. See, especially, 688 at note 7. Compare Dyzenhaus: "Formalism is formal in that it requires judges to operate with categories and distinctions that determine results without the judges having to deploy the substantive arguments that underpin the categories and distinctions." ("Constituting the Rule of Law," *supra* note 5 at 450.) The (a)political implications of formalism are elaborated by Sunstein: "[F]ormalism is an attempt to make the law both autonomous, in the particular sense that it does not depend on moral or political values of particular judges, and also deductive, in the sense that judges decide cases mechanically on the basis of preexisting law and do not exercise discretion in individual cases." (Cited in Wyman, *ibid.* at 688, note 7.)

be explicitly submitted for public justification.[22] In administrative law, a positivist approach may further be argued to work against deference, in that it restricts the potential for judges to acknowledge their own value-laden presumptions in the face of the potentially competing values or perspectives of administrative decision-makers. However, in the face of a privative clause, the positivist approach suffers ambivalence between acknowledgment of the legislature's explicitly granting administrative decision-makers exclusive interpretive authority over their enabling statutes and insistence that such authority is exclusive to the judiciary.[23]

In contrast, it is the explicit submission of the value-laden bases of legal judgment for public justification that marks a normative approach to statutory interpretation.[24] Such an approach proceeds on the assumption that contested matters of statutory interpretation cannot be resolved by exclusive reference to the text,[25] or even by situating the text in its social context,[26] but also require judgments about the competing values or social priorities informing alternative statutory constructions. This approach is reflected in the acknowledgment of Justice L'Heureux-Dubé in her judgment in the *Baker* case,[27] discussed elsewhere in this text, that all law interpretation involves the exercise of discretion—that is, discretion is not the exception in law, but the rule.[28] That is not to say that law is without any anchor beyond the whim of the judge. Rather, the normative model of law interpretation implies a conception of the rule of law in which the legitimacy of state action is contingent not on strict adherence to legislative or majority will, but on consistency with the important public values inscribed in our social and legal traditions.[29]

---

22   Sullivan, *supra* note 17 at 220-25.

23   For a compelling example of this tension, see Justice Rothstein's judgment in *Canada (Citizenship and Immigration) v. Khosa*, 2009 SCC 12, [2009] 1 S.C.R. 339 at para. 74 and, more generally, at paras. 76-98 [*Khosa*].

24   Sullivan, *supra* note 17 at 184-87 and 220-27 (on the "pragmatic" approach to interpretation).

25   Sullivan, *ibid.* at 185, makes this point, in part in light of a set of standard critiques of textualist and intentionalist approaches:

> [C]ommunication through natural language is never a sure thing; rules drafted by legislatures tend to be general and are often abstract; and legislatures cannot form intentions with respect to how these rules should apply to every possible set of facts.

26   The point is made by Hanoch Dagan, "The Realist Conception of Law" (2007) 57 U.T.L.J. 607 at 649:

> A prescription for sensitivity to situations and facts is vacuous without general normative commitments. These commitments are indispensible if we are to resolve—as law always needs to do—conflicts between the very demands and interests that case sensitivity exposes.

27   *Supra* note 6.

28   L'Heureux-Dubé writes (for the majority) in *Baker*, *supra* note 6 at para. 54:

> It is, however, inaccurate to speak of a rigid dichotomy of "discretionary" or "non-discretionary" decisions. Most administrative decisions involve the exercise of implicit discretion in relation to many aspects of decision making. To give just one example, decision-makers may have considerable discretion as to the remedies they order. In addition, there is no easy distinction to be made between interpretation and the exercise of discretion; interpreting legal rules involves considerable discretion to clarify, fill in legislative gaps, and make choices among various options.

29   As Sullivan, *supra* note 17 at 227, notes, this model is supported by the following statement of McLachlin C.J. for the Court in *Reference re Secession of Quebec*, [1998] 2 S.C.R. 217 at para. 67 [*Secession Reference*]:

> [A] system of government ... must be capable of reflecting the aspirations of the people. But there is more. Our law's claim to legitimacy also rests on an appeal to moral values, many of which are em-

In the administrative law context, it is possible to adopt the normative model of law interpretation while insisting on correctness review of administrative efforts at law interpretation. Such insistence may be made particularly where fundamental values are at stake in the interpretive exercise—for example, Charter rights, statutory human rights, or individual rights at common law.[30] This approach reflects a traditional understanding of judges as the exclusive arbiters of foundational legal values. However, over the past two decades, that traditional understanding of the role of the judge has been at least partially modified, in light of the commitment to constitutional pluralism described above. The now-ascendant approach in administrative law tends to recognize the normative contestability of (much) law interpretation and to regard (many if not most) law-interpretive problems as supportive of deference on review. As such, the modern (romantic or constitutional pluralist) model of substantive review reflects an understanding of administrative decision-makers—or, again, many of them—as aptly positioned to contribute to the shared work of determining how the basic commitments of the social, political, and legal order should inform or interact with the sector-specific values and policy objectives of administrative regimes.[31]

There are tensions in each of the approaches to statutory interpretation discussed so far, in terms of their implications for the relationship between courts and administrative decision-makers. A positivist insistence that there is one right answer in construing disputed statutory provisions seems inconsistent with one of the cornerstones of the law on deference that, as Audrey Macklin recounts in Chapter 9, was identified in *CUPE*—that is, the thesis that there may be more than one reasonable interpretation of disputed statutory language.[32] At the same time, a judge who adopts a positivist approach to statutory interpretation—and, moreover, a strict separation of powers approach to administrative state ordering—may resist the proposition that administrative decisions must accord with the "fundamental values" underlying statutory text (absent a formal constitutional challenge).[33] The constitutional pluralist, on the other hand, expresses deference by acknowledging a role for administrative decision-makers in the project of defending and elaborating the rule of

---

bedded in our constitutional structure. It would be a grave mistake to equate legitimacy with the "sovereign will" or majority rule alone, to the exclusion of other constitutional values.

See also Mary Liston's discussion of the *Secession Reference* in Chapter 2 of this text.

30 See "Constituting the Rule of Law," *supra* note 5 at 448-51, where Dyzenhaus points out that the Supreme Court's endorsement of "unwritten constitutional principles" in the *Secession Reference* is accompanied by other statements expressing a formalist vision of the separation of powers, whereby judges bear exclusive responsibility for working out those principles. For a recent articulation of a formalist vision of the separation of powers in the administrative law context, see the concurring judgment of Justice Cromwell in *Alberta (Information and Privacy Commissioner)*, *supra* note 2 at paras. 90-104, especially paras. 92-94 and 102-3.

31 The presumption of reasonableness review attaching to matters involving interpretation of the home statute, stated by the majority in *Dunsmuir* and confirmed by the majority in *Alberta (Information and Privacy Commissioner)*, *supra* note 2, may be understood as an endorsement, or partial endorsement, of constitutional pluralism. The *Doré* decision (*supra* note 4) further affirms the model's commitments.

32 Chapter 9, section III, The Blockbuster: *C.U.P.E. v. New Brunswick Liquor Corporation*.

33 The latter predisposition is now significantly blocked by the decision in *Doré* (*supra* note 4, discussed in section III.B, below, and by Evan Fox-Decent and Alexander Pless in Chapter 12). At least, this is the case where a disputed instance of law interpretation or application may be characterized as an exercise of administrative (and, moreover, adjudicative) discretion involving Charter values.

law. But he or she tends thereby to invest those decision-makers with a duty to consider and, perhaps, even to attribute determinative importance to the values the judge deems essential to the legitimate exercise of the relevant statutory powers.

Wade MacLauchlan has argued that the challenges facing substantive review on the way to a culture of justification lie precisely in devising better ways for tribunals to inform courts of the institutional and social policy considerations underlying their decisions. This includes instilling better practices of reason-giving among administrative decision-makers. Such institutional developments—accompanied by developments in the capacity or willingness of courts to exhibit appropriate sensitivity to administrative reasoning—are held out by MacLauchlan as potentially supplanting formalist and positivist tendencies to rely on manipulable notions of legislative intent and jurisdiction in this area of law.[34] As we explore in section III, recent developments in the law on substantive review have intensified the expectation that administrative decision-makers support, or justify, their decisions, including their interpretations of law—and that judges make special efforts to appreciate such justificatory efforts.

III. The Standards of Review in Theory and Practice

In what follows, we take up the standards of review as described and applied in the case law. The central question we seek to explore thereby is what, if any, contribution this evolving case law has made toward negotiating the tensions between the dual rule-of-law imperatives placed on judges engaged in substantive review—namely, to respect administrative decisions and to supervise the substantive legality of those decisions.

A. A Contested Correctness

1. Correctness Review in Theory

Let us begin with the standard of review most expressive of the institutional authority of the judiciary: review for correctness. As Audrey Macklin relates in Chapter 9, the majority in *Dunsmuir* indicates that a correctness standard will presumptively apply in certain types of cases, including those that raise constitutional questions,[35] "true questions of jurisdiction or *vires*,"[36] questions about the relative jurisdictional scope of different tribunals,[37] and questions of law that are "of central importance to the legal system as a whole and outside the adjudicator's specialized area of expertise."[38] Arguably, *Dunsmuir* has reduced the reach of correctness review by (1) lending increased specificity to the broad category of questions of

---

[34] H.W. MacLauchlan, "Transforming Administrative Law: The Didactic Role of the Supreme Court of Canada" (2001) 80 Can. Bar Rev. 281 at 293-94 and 297-98. Also see B. Lahey & D. Ginn, "After the Revolution: Being Pragmatic and Functional in Canada's Trial Courts and Courts of Appeal" (2002) 25 Dal. L.J. 259 at 325.

[35] *Dunsmuir, supra* note 1 at para. 58.

[36] *Ibid.* at para. 59.

[37] *Ibid.* at para. 61.

[38] *Ibid.* at para. 60.

"general" law previously attracting this standard and (2) indicating that a narrow approach should be taken to the category of jurisdictional questions.

At the same time, *Dunsmuir* indicates that there is no need to disturb existing doctrine on the conduct of correctness review—no need, that is, to modify our understanding of what it means to apply this standard from that which has held the field since *CUPE*. That may strike one as unsurprising. That is, "correctness" may at first appear so plain in meaning as to be beyond serious consideration for reform, or even comment. Asserting a requirement of correctness appears to amount merely to an insistence that the decision-maker get it right, full stop. On reflection, however, the meaning of "getting it right" and the method by which this is evaluated are less than transparent; indeed, in some cases, these matters have been hotly contested.

In *Law Society of New Brunswick v. Ryan*,[39] Iacobucci J. wrote that where a correctness standard is imposed, "the court may undertake its own reasoning process to arrive at the result it judges correct."[40] This may be contrasted to what we will see shortly has long been a key feature of deferential review—that is, the requirement that judges make an effort to consider the administrative decision-maker's reasoning on its own terms. Iacobucci J.'s description of correctness review in *Ryan* indicates, to the contrary, that the court need not put any effort into assessing the administrative decision-maker's reasons or casting those reasons in their best light.

The *Dunsmuir* majority confirms this point:

> When applying the correctness standard, a reviewing court will not show deference to the decision maker's reasoning process; it will rather undertake its own analysis of the question. The analysis will bring the court to decide whether it agrees with the determination of the decision maker; if not, the court will substitute its own view and provide the correct answer. From the outset, the court must ask whether the tribunal's decision was correct.[41]

The majority in *Dunsmuir* further states that the underlying rationale of the correctness standard is to "promot[e] just decisions and avoi[d] inconsistent and unauthorized application of law." [42] Arguably, one may distinguish in *Dunsmuir* and in the prior jurisprudence three related rationales. The first is rooted in the idea of jurisdiction—that is, the idea that certain matters fall within, and others outside, an administrative decision-maker's assigned area of authority. To defer to administrative decision-makers on the scope of their authority would invite the charge that the executive/administration has been permitted to usurp the role of the legislature. Moreover, judges of the superior courts, constitutionally vested with superintending and reforming powers as well as independence from the executive, may be understood as uniquely equipped to supervise tribunal jurisdiction. Closely aligned to this is a second rationale, based in expertise. Here the claim is that an administrative decision-maker should not command deference in matters over which it cannot claim expertise superior to that of the generalist judge. Traditionally, law interpretation was placed among

---

39   2003 SCC 20, [2003] 1 S.C.R. 247 [*Ryan*].

40   *Ibid.* at para. 50.

41   *Dunsmuir, supra* note 1 at para. 50.

42   *Ibid.*

these matters. However, as noted above, that Diceyan tenet has been progressively eroded by exceptions (even presumptions) acknowledging the law-interpretive capacities of administrative decision-makers. Finally, and typically raised in conjunction with the rationales relating to authority and expertise, is a third rationale based in the need for consistency and predictability in the legal system.[43] Here the argument is that judges, as legal generalists with the institutional capacity to produce binding precedents, are best placed to resolve contests about law interpretation where this is essential to the even-handed application of law. This rationale has purchase even (indeed particularly) where there may be a range of reasonable alternative interpretations that fit within the administrative scheme.

Together these rationales advance a set of practical and theoretical bases for maintaining correctness review as a fundamental feature of the law on substantive review. But if it is accepted that the modern case law on substantive review is increasingly shifting toward the model of administrative state ordering described above as constitutional pluralism, we must ask whether the perspectives or reasoning of administrative decision-makers are ever *not* of value in informing judicial oversight, even on such questions as the scope of their authority, or how fundamental legal (including constitutional) norms affect or interact with specific administrative regimes. Indeed, we might consider whether the correctness standard is now obsolete in the face of strengthened rationales for and guidance on the application of a context-sensitive standard of reasonableness. At the same time, we must consider whether or how the institutional values (for example, consistency) now promoted by the correctness standard might be secured in the absence of this standard.[44]

2. Correctness Review in Practice

We begin this section with two touchstone cases that serve to provoke reflection on the nature of correctness review before turning to more recent case law, including one post-*Dunsmuir* decision.

Two decisions of the Supreme Court that illustrate the tensions in correctness review are *U.E.S., Local 298 v. Bibeault*,[45] and *Canada (Attorney General) v. Mossop*.[46] *Bibeault*, decided in 1988, involved a school board's terminating janitorial service contracts with companies whose workers were on strike and then contracting with another company for such services. The question was, did this fit the criterion of "alienation or operation by another" of an "undertaking" under the successor employer provisions of Quebec's labour law? If so, the union representing the employees of the original companies would represent those of the new company, continuity of the collective agreement would be assured, and the strike would carry on. As Audrey Macklin explains in Chapter 9, one may detect a schism in the approach taken to this question in the judgment of Beetz J., which, on the one hand, consolidates a set of "prag-

---

43　Cf. D. Mullan, "Consistent Decision-Making—A Core Value for High Volume Jurisdiction Tribunals and Agencies?" (14 December 2010), online: Workplace Safety and Insurance Appeals Tribunal <http://www.wsiat.on.ca/english/documents/mullan25thSymposium.pdf>.

44　See David Dyzenhaus, "Constituting the Rule of Law," *supra* note 5 at 493-96, and Evan Fox-Decent and Alexander Pless in Chapter 12 of this text.

45　[1988] 2 S.C.R. 1048 [*Bibeault*].

46　[1993] 1 S.C.R. 554 [*Mossop*].

matic" and "functional" queries for discerning whether deference is due and, on the other, continues to convey a Diceyan concern to patrol the limits of administrative jurisdiction.[47]

It is the latter concern that animates the disposition of the case. Beetz J. concludes that the issue is jurisdictional, meaning that no deference is due. This conclusion turns on his determination that the statutory language includes terms of art at civil law, the interpretation of which demands general legal expertise. From there, the objective is to determine the right answer to the question: were the successor employer provisions engaged or not?

First, Beetz J. canvasses the purpose of the disputed provision (in light of the purpose of the statute as a whole); this is stated to be protection of "the benefits resulting from certification and the collective agreement."[48] He then situates that purpose in light of the principle, derived from attention to the four corners of the statute, that collective bargaining requires a single union, a single employer, and a single undertaking. That principle, in addition to analysis of the terms "alienation" and "undertaking" at civil law, leads Beetz J. to conclude that a legal relationship between employers (in transferring a single undertaking) is required to trigger the disputed provision. Against this background of analysis, Beetz J. concludes that the alternative construction accepted by the labour commissioner and upheld by a majority of the Labour Court gave the terms of art in question "a non-legal and even uncommon meaning"[49]—one that, moreover, was "inconsistent with the purpose of the *Labour Code*."[50] He suggests that the source of this inconsistency was a misguided "desire to protect the certification and collective agreement despite all the vicissitudes of the undertaking."[51]

The judgment of Beetz J. in *Bibeault* favours conceptual coherence as between the statute and the civil law over the context-inflected sympathies of the tribunal. Now, few will argue that coherence, in the law or in general, is inherently a bad thing. But on reading this case, we may ask ourselves whether we are convinced by the construction of the statute adopted by Beetz J. How important is it that terms of art at civil or common law are preserved from novel—or contextually informed—interpretations in administrative sectors? From Chapter 9 you have learned that, with *Dunsmuir*, not only is deference now arguably presumed on questions involving interpretation of the enabling statute, but that it "may also be warranted where an administrative tribunal has developed particular expertise in the application of a general common law or civil law rule in relation to a specific statutory context."[52] In light of this, how might a court approach the issues raised in *Bibeault* post-*Dunsmuir*?

Moving from the labour context to the human rights context, consider *Mossop*.[53] In this 1993 decision, a majority of the Supreme Court overturned a decision of the Canadian Human Rights Tribunal on the basis that the prohibited ground of "family status" (not

---

47   See Audrey Macklin's discussion in Chapter 9, section IV, The Sequels. Also see Dyzenhaus, "The Politics of Deference," *supra* note 4 at 291.

48   *Bibeault, supra* note 45 at para. 144.

49   *Ibid.* at para. 180.

50   *Ibid.* at para. 162.

51   *Ibid.*

52   *Dunsmuir, supra* note 1 at para. 54. And see *Nor-Man Regional Health Authority Inc. v. Manitoba Association of Health Care Professionals*, 2011 SCC 59.

53   *Supra* note 46.

otherwise defined in the *Canadian Human Rights Act*) could not be interpreted to extend protection to a same-sex couple. The majority, as well as two judges dissenting on the result, adopted a correctness standard of review.[54] (Here we encounter the not-uncommon phenomenon of judges agreeing on a correctness standard and then disagreeing on what the "right answer" is upon applying that standard.) L'Heureux-Dubé J. wrote a dissenting judgment adopting a patent unreasonableness standard.

The concurring majority judgments in *Mossop* express two variants of what I have described as a positivist approach to statutory interpretation. Lamer C.J. (Sopinka and Iacobucci JJ. concurring) grounds his analysis in legislative intent. This analysis is framed by a gesture toward the parallel universe of normative jurisprudence available only to claimants invoking the Charter.[55] That is, given that Mr. Mossop had opted to base his claim exclusively in arguments from statutory interpretation, Lamer C.J. suggests that the Court is bound by contextual indicia that "family status" was not intended to encompass same-sex relationships. Here he emphasizes the absence of "sexual orientation" from the statute's prohibited grounds of discrimination at the time the proceedings arose, even in the face of a recommendation by the Canadian Human Rights Commission that it be added. The failure of Parliament to act on the commission's recommendation, he reasons, amounted to its "refusal" to do so. Lamer C.J. states the principle driving his analysis as follows:

> Absent a *Charter* challenge of its constitutionality, when Parliamentary intent is clear, courts and administrative tribunals are not empowered to do anything else but to apply the law. If there is some ambiguity as to its meaning or scope, then the courts should, using the usual rules of interpretation, seek out the purpose of the legislation and if more than one reasonable interpretation consistent with that purpose is available, that which is more in conformity with the *Charter* should prevail.[56]

In this case, however, Lamer C.J. determined that the legislative intent was clear, so that no recourse to the Charter as an interpretive aid could be made.

In his concurring judgment, La Forest J. (writing for himself and Iacobucci J.)[57] also focuses on legislative intent. However, his judgment is more insistently fixed on the statutory text and, specifically, the word "family." He describes his approach as consistent with "the ordinary rules of statutory interpretation," which demand that one give "to the words used in a statute their usual and ordinary sense having regard to their context and to the purpose of the statute."[58] In applying this principle, however, La Forest J. emphasizes not the clear purpose of the *Canadian Human Rights Act*—that of eradicating discrimination—but the "usual and ordinary sense" of the word "family." His conclusion is that the "dominant" and thus

---

54   Audrey Macklin discusses the rationale behind selection of a correctness standard in *Mossop* in Chapter 9, section V, Pragmatic and Functional Redux: *Pushpanathan v. Canada* (under heading V.B, Expertise; see also heading V.D, The Nature of the Problem).

55   *Canadian Charter of Rights and Freedoms*, part I of the *Constitution Act, 1982*, being Schedule B to the *Canada Act 1982* (U.K.), 1982, c. 11 [the Charter].

56   *Mossop, supra* note 46 at 581-82.

57   The fact that Iacobucci J. concurs with the opinions of both Lamer J. and La Forest J. on the correct approach to statutory interpretation alerts us to the compatibility of these approaches.

58   *Supra* note 46 at 585.

ordinary sense of the word, or that which represents the consensus of the Canadian public, is the "traditional family." This is the meaning that therefore must be understood to have been Parliament's intent both when the statute was enacted and at the time the dispute arose.

L'Heureux-Dubé J. is alone in arguing that a patent unreasonableness standard (at the time, the only alternative to correctness review) should apply. However, her disposition of the matter is endorsed in the separate dissenting reasons of McLachlin and Cory JJ., who determine that a correctness standard is in order. This seems to indicate that for McLachlin and Cory JJ., the judgment of L'Heureux-Dubé J. represents the best account of the "right answer" to this interpretive dispute.[59] Thus, while our objective in this section is to consider correctness review, it is worth contrasting the approach taken by L'Heureux-Dubé J. to that of the majority.

The judgment of L'Heureux-Dubé J. is not the superficial gloss endorsed by some early on as the proper model of patent unreasonableness review.[60] And yet it distinguishes itself from the approach of the majority in two key ways. First, it takes an emphatically normative approach to statutory interpretation. L'Heureux-Dubé J. expresses the distance between her approach and that of the majority as follows:

> Even if Parliament had in mind a specific idea of the scope of "family status," in the absence of a definition in the Act which embodies this scope, concepts of equality and liberty which appear in human rights documents are not bounded by the precise understanding of those who drafted them. Human rights codes are documents that embody fundamental principles, but which permit the understanding and application of those principles to change over time. These codes leave ample scope for interpretation by those charged with that task.[61]

The point here is that, at least with human rights statutes, it is essential to orient interpretive judgment with reference to human rights principles (in this case, equality or non-discrimination). These are asserted in this passage not as statute-specific but as "fundamental." As such, they may be curtailed only by the most explicit expressions of legislative intent. Thus it seems that there is, if not a right answer in this case (and perhaps, for L'Heureux-Dubé J., there is), then at least a right and a wrong way of going about resolving the question. Both the reliance of La Forest J. on an "unexamined consensus" and the reliance of Lamer C.J. on legislative intent as inferred from legislative history come in for criticism as insupportably prioritizing the will of an ostensibly unitary majority over the human rights principles engaged by this instance of interpretation. In contrast, L'Heureux-Dubé J.'s judgment reflects a commitment to a model of the rule of law known as "common-law constitutionalism."[62]

---

[59] The implications of this are the subject of careful analysis in Dyzenhaus, "Constituting the Rule of Law," *supra* note 5 at 464-68.

[60] See the judgment of Wilson J in *National Corn Growers, supra* note 13.

[61] *Mossop, supra* note 46 at 621.

[62] See the discussion of normative approaches to statutory interpretation in section II, above. For an illuminating account of historical and contemporary features of common-law constitutionalism, see M.D. Walters, "'Common Public Law in the Age of Legislation': David Mullan and the Unwritten Constitution" in *Inside and Outside, supra* note 19 at 421, and "The Common Law Constitution in Canada: Return of *Lex Non Scripta* as Fundamental Law" (2001) 51 U.T.L.J. 91.

Under this model, statutes are understood not as closed systems but as requiring interpretation in light of the animating principles and values of the wider social and legal tradition.

The second major difference between L'Heureux-Dubé J.'s judgment and that of the majority (and here she also differs from her fellow dissenters) is, of course, her selection of a patent unreasonableness standard. Thus, while the tradition of common-law constitutionalism tends to place the burden of identifying and prioritizing fundamental values on the shoulders of judges alone, L'Heureux-Dubé J. indicates through her adoption of deference that the tribunal has a legitimate role in this enterprise. This is confirmed in her method of reasoning, which throughout draws on and amplifies the evidence and argument accepted by the tribunal. That is, the decision of the tribunal is drawn on not simply as a base of fact or policy separable from legal analysis, but as an exercise in statutory interpretation, which is itself a model of the interdependency of facts and values in legal judgment. As such, L'Heureux-Dubé J. demonstrates both a respect for Parliament's will to assign the tribunal the role of administering this statute, and a commitment to the idea (again, cast as a principle of law) that in administering the statute, the tribunal's task is to transcend narrow constructions of parliamentary will.

In agreeing with L'Heureux-Dubé J.'s disposition of the case, McLachlin and Cory JJ. indicate their support for the idea that the statutory text must be read in light of social context (and thus changing social conceptions of family), and with particular sensitivity to the ways that human rights principles inflect and are inflected by that text and context. Yet according to L'Heureux-Dubé J., this sensitivity is best served by careful attention to the reasons of the tribunal. In light of the fact that the other dissenters select a correctness standard, a question that arises is whether they are to be understood to say that the "right answer" would have been secured absent the tribunal's reasons or, alternatively, that in this case, correctness review is compatible with—even in some measure dependent on—attentiveness to tribunal reasoning.[63]

Since *Mossop* and, moreover, the introduction of review for reasonableness (as an alternative to deference attuned only to "patent" unreasonableness), the Court has indicated an increased willingness to accept that deference to human rights tribunals on matters involving interpretation of human rights statutes may, at least in some circumstances, be warranted—for instance, where the matter is "fact-intensive" or goes to tribunal processes.[64] At the same time, it has shown some willingness to defer to decisions affecting human rights even where the administrative decision-maker is not a human rights tribunal.[65] This trend receives further support with *Doré*,[66] which, as discussed in the next section, states that the

---

63   See Dyzenhaus, "Constituting the Rule of Law," *supra* note 5 at 467-68.

64   *Pushpanathan v. Canada (Minister of Citizenship and Immigration)*, [1998] 1 S.C.R. 982 at para. 45 [*Pushpanathan*]. More recent consideration of this question is found in *Canada (Canadian Human Rights Commission) v. Canada (Attorney General)*, 2011 SCC 53, [2011] 3 S.C.R. 471 [*Mowat*] at paras. 19-27. See Audrey Macklin's discussion of the issue in Chapter 9, section V, Pragmatic and Functional Redux: *Pushpanathan v. Canada* (under heading V.B, Expertise) and section VI, *Dunsmuir*: And Then There Were Two (under heading VI.D, What Is a Question of Central Importance to the Legal System as a Whole (and Outside the Decision-Maker's Area of Expertise)?).

65   For example, see *Council of Canadians with Disabilities v. VIA Rail Canada Inc.*, 2007 SCC 15, [2007] 1 S.C.R. 650. The decision is characterized not as law-interpretive but rather as a highly discretionary application of legal standards to the facts.

66   *Supra* note 4.

exercise of adjudicative discretion involving the balancing of Charter values with other legal values should generally attract deference.

It is not at all clear, however, that a decision like the one engaged in *Pushpanathan v. Canada (Minister of Citizenship and Immigration)*[67] would attract deference after *Doré*. In *Pushpanathan*, the Court applied a correctness standard of review to a decision of the Convention Refugee Determination Division of the Immigration and Refugee Board, involving interpretation of a provision of the *Immigration Act* excluding from refugee status persons who have "been guilty of acts contrary to the purposes and principles of the United Nations." The language had been incorporated from a UN convention. Here, the central matter in dispute was constructed not as an exercise of discretion (despite the necessary operation of discretion or of value-laden judgment in interpreting the provision), but rather as interpretation of a "general legal principle"—and the board was found not to have applicable experience or expertise. On applying a correctness standard, both the majority and dissenting judgments of the Supreme Court of Canada undertook an independent analysis of the interpretive problem. That is not to say that either took a positivistic, as opposed to normative, approach. Indeed, the selection and application of correctness review in this case is rooted less in the thesis that the question gives rise to one right answer than the thesis that judges hold a unique institutional capacity to adjudicate general legal principles of broad importance, in particular those affecting fundamental human rights.[68] Notably, the majority and dissent arrived at diverging interpretations based on diverging opinions about the proper balancing of competing values and objectives.

Correctness review has also continued to be applied in ways that suggest a more positivistic understanding of the enterprise of statutory interpretation. We may ask how the *Dunsmuir* majority's statement that a tribunal engaged in interpretation of its enabling statute will typically attract deference[69] would affect the analysis in the pre-*Dunsmuir* case, *Barrie Public Utilities v. Canadian Cable Television Assn.*[70] There, Gonthier J. for the majority characterized the phrase "the supporting structure of a transmission line" as a matter of "pure statutory interpretation"[71] attracting correctness review. He then proceeded to identify the plain meaning of this phrase. Yet the contrary interpretation (favoured by the Canadian Radio-television and Telecommunications Commission) arguably reflected cogent policy goals consistent with its mandate. Bastarache J., in dissent, criticized the majority's approach in comments that drew on the reasons of L'Heureux-Dubé J. for a unanimous Court in *Domtar Inc. v. Quebec (Commission d'appel en matière de lésions professionnelles)*:[72]

> Substituting one's opinion for that of an administrative tribunal in order to develop one's own interpretation of a legislative provision eliminates its decision-making autonomy and special expertise. Since such intervention occurs in circumstances where the legislature has determined

---

67 *Supra* note 64.

68 I discuss these judgments further in "A Fine Romance?," *supra* note 4 at 231-32.

69 "Deference will usually result where a tribunal is interpreting its own statute or statutes closely connected to its function, with which it will have particular familiarity" (*Dunsmuir, supra* note 1 at para. 54). See also the majority judgment in *Alberta (Information and Privacy Commissioner), supra* note 2.

70 2003 SCC 28, [2003] 1 S.C.R. 476 [*Barrie Utilities*].

71 *Ibid.* at para. 16.

72 [1993] 2 S.C.R. 756 [*Domtar*].

that the administrative tribunal is the one in the best position to rule on the disputed decision, it risks, at the same time, thwarting the original intention of the legislature. For the purposes of judicial review, statutory interpretation has ceased to be a necessarily "exact" science and this Court has, again recently, confirmed the rule of curial deference set forth for the first time in *Canadian Union of Public Employees, Local 963 v. New Brunswick Liquor Corp.*[73]

If statutory interpretation is not an "exact" science, then on what grounds can courts continue to apply correctness review to disputes of this sort, as such giving no credence or weight to tribunal interpretations? Again, as with *Bibeault*, we may ask whether or how *Barrie Utilities* might have been differently decided after *Dunsmuir*.

The post-*Dunsmuir* judgment of the Supreme Court in *Northrop Grumman Overseas Services Corp. v. Canada (Attorney General)*[74] offers a final example of a dispute about statutory interpretation that was resolved on a correctness standard. There the question was whether the Canadian International Trade Tribunal (CITT) had authority to hear a complaint brought by a non-Canadian corporation, Northrop Grumman Overseas. The corporation wished to argue that Public Works and Government Services Canada had not evaluated its bid for a procurement contract in accordance with the *Agreement on Internal Trade* (AIT). The statute governing the tribunal's authority, the *Canadian International Trade Tribunal Act*,[75] contemplated complaints from "potential suppliers" of procurement contracts under the AIT where certain threshold conditions were met. The question was: did those with standing before the CITT include non-Canadian corporations like Northrop Grumman? The CITT departed from its own precedents to decide that it could hear the complaint. On its analysis of the text and purposes of the CITT Act and Regulations in addition to the AIT, it determined that there was no basis on which to conclude that the "potential suppliers" who may make complaints under the AIT were restricted to Canadian suppliers.[76]

Both the Federal Court of Appeal[77] and the Supreme Court of Canada[78] applied a correctness standard to the CITT's decision, in light of past jurisprudence of the federal court and, more generally, a determination that the matter went to the tribunal's jurisdiction.[79]

---

[73] *Barrie Utilities, supra* note 70 at para. 128 (per Bastarache J.), quoting *Domtar, supra* note 72 at 775.

[74] 2009 SCC 50, [2009] 3 S.C.R. 309.

[75] R.S.C. 1985, c. 47 (4th Supp.).

[76] *Northrop Grumman Overseas Corp. v. Department of Public Works and Government Services* (12 September 2007), PR-2007-008, online: Canadian International Trade Tribunal <http://www.citt-tcce.gc.ca/procure/ Determin/archive_pr2h08r_e.asp>.

[77] *Canada (Attorney General) v. Northrop Grumman Overseas Services Corp.*, 2008 FCA 187, [2009] 1 F.C.R. 688.

[78] *Supra* note 74.

[79] *Ibid.* at para. 10. Rothstein J., writing for the Court, justifies selection of a correctness standard, first on the basis that recent case law from the Federal Court establishes that "a CITT decision on whether something falls within its jurisdiction" will attract correctness review. This is followed by the more categorical statement: "The issue on this appeal is jurisdictional in that it goes to whether the CITT can hear a complaint initiated by a non-Canadian supplier under the AIT. Accordingly, the standard of review is correctness." See David Mullan's critique of the courts' reliance on identification of a jurisdictional question to justify correctness review in this case, rather than identifying the concern for consistency as determinative (given that different panels of the tribunal had come to conflicting conclusions): D. Mullan, "Consistent Decision-Making," *supra* note 43 at 11.

Both courts concluded that the tribunal's decision should be quashed. They supported this result by way of close analysis of provisions of the AIT and the associated statutory instruments. In particular, the reviewing courts determined that article 502(1) of the AIT, which states that the AIT applies to procurement contracts "within Canada," specifically contemplates contracts between governmental parties and suppliers with a base of operations in Canada. This interpretation was attentive to an express purposes clause in which the section addressing procurements is described as seeking "to establish a framework that will ensure equal access to procurement for all Canadian suppliers."[80] Justice Rothstein, writing for the Supreme Court, additionally took account of the consequences for Canada's international trading relationships if foreign corporations were to gain rights under the AIT despite exclusion of those same rights from the international trade agreements negotiated with their home nations.[81]

One may be persuaded by the careful construction of the text of the CITT and AIT undertaken by the Federal Court of Appeal and Supreme Court of Canada, which is supported by analysis of the adverse consequences for Canada's international trading interests if the tribunal's interpretation were to be accepted. However, comparison of the way correctness review was conducted by the Court of Appeal and Supreme Court of Canada is arguably instructive. The Court of Appeal extensively details the tribunal's reasoning prior to launching into an examination of the AIT and relevant statutory instruments.[82] Subsequently, in disposing of the case, it specifically addresses the aspect of the tribunal's reasoning that, it holds, was in error—characterizing that error as a "failure to consider" a key element of the statutory scheme.[83] In this, the judgment of the Court of Appeal has some appearance of entering into a dialogue with the tribunal. In contrast, the Supreme Court references the arguments brought by the disappointed party without noting the reasoning of the tribunal in any detail. Moreover, neither court directly addresses the tribunal's purposive thesis that the economic objectives of the Act may be best satisfied by recognizing the standing of non-Canadian suppliers.[84] To simply enter into an independent analysis in the absence of direct engagement with the tribunal's reasoning is, of course, strictly in accord with the law on correctness review. Moreover, such an approach may be particularly appropriate to the Supreme Court's decision in this case, given that it adopts the reasoning of the Court of Appeal in significant part. However, the question to consider in comparing these judgments is whether the Court of Appeal takes the insights of the tribunal more seriously in its analysis—and, moreover, whether such an approach (which, again, is in tension with the basic tenets of correctness review) is to be preferred, precisely because it enables the parties, the wider public, and the tribunal itself to evaluate whether and how the decision to quash was justified.

Examination of how correctness review was applied in the above cases reveals tensions between a positivist approach to statutory interpretation, which looks to the text (or sometimes text and context) as a closed system indicative of a determinate legislative intent, and

---

80   *Northrop Grumman, supra* note 74 at paras. 22-24.

81   *Ibid.* at paras. 41-42.

82   *Supra* note 77 at paras. 13-24 (FCA).

83   *Ibid.* at paras. 79-81.

84   See the tribunal judgment, *supra* note 76 at para. 30.

a normative approach, which views problems of statutory interpretation in light of background assessments not only of social facts but also of competing value-laden purposes. Arguably the latter approach, taken seriously, begins to erode the idea that courts need not give any weight or respect to the justificatory efforts of tribunals, even on matters traditionally reserved for correctness review. This proposition is further supported by the observation that it may be difficult, if not impossible, ever to achieve a surgical separation of fact and law or policy and law.

The bedrock of correctness review is the concept of jurisdiction: the idea that administrative decision-makers do not enjoy unlimited authority and, moreover, do not enjoy authority (or final authority) on questions going to the scope of their mandate. Further, as we have seen, the correctness standard of review reflects the rule-of-law concern for stability in law, particularly in matters of general legal (including constitutional) significance. Yet for all that, the standard sits uneasily with the aspiration of integrating the work of administrative tribunals more fully into the constitutional order. For signals that this is indeed an aspiration that is proper to the modern jurisprudence on the standards of review, we must now turn to the alternative to correctness review: review for reasonableness.

B. Review for Reasonableness

Let us consider, then, what it means to express deference on review. More fully stated, the question pursued in the jurisprudence examined in this section is whether or how the imperatives of deference and supervision may be integrated where judges are tasked with reviewing the substantive legality of administrative decisions. This is the question at the heart of reasonableness review, one that has driven successive transformations in this area of law over the past three decades as courts have struggled to strike a principled balance between these imperatives. *The question is how do you balance the supervisory role of the judiciary with the deference given*

1. Enduring Questions from the Pre-Dunsmuir Case Law *to ADM's*

To begin with the pre-*Dunsmuir* deferential standards—patent unreasonableness and reasonableness *simpliciter*[85]—we know now that we must view with suspicion the case law that sought to distinguish between these standards by reference to the depth of probing or magnitude of error allowable under each. Such reasoning came in for authoritative criticism in *Dunsmuir*, as both conceptually empty and practically unhelpful. However, the pre-*Dunsmuir* jurisprudence may nonetheless assist in alerting us to two main areas of controversy about deference on substantive review that remain alive today: (1) controversies about the method or conduct of judicial reasoning on review that is most consistent with deference, and (2) controversies about the substantive indicia of reasonableness or unreasonableness.

What makes something reasonable or not

a. The Conduct of Deferential Review

The majority in *Dunsmuir* endorses (as fundamental to the law on deference) the statement from the 1979 decision in *CUPE* that statutory language may accommodate more than one

expanding on # 1 controversy

---

[85] For a more expansive examination of these standards, see "A Fine Romance?," *supra* note 4 at 233–47.

reasonable interpretation. That thesis is essential to a further proposition that has driven the last few decades of jurisprudence on the standards of review—namely, that there may be good reasons for courts to defer to tribunals' interpretations of law where those interpretations fall within the ambit of reasonableness. The question is: how are the limits of reasonableness to be discerned, consistent with deference?

Cases decided after *CUPE* at times manifested tensions in the impulse toward deference, as courts ostensibly deployed the standard of patent unreasonableness yet engaged in what appeared to be a search for the "right answer" to the matter in dispute.[86] Nonetheless, a basic principle of deference that prevailed both in the law on patent unreasonableness and reasonableness *simpliciter* was that the reviewing judge must not measure the decision against his or her sense of the "correct" decision.[87] That, however, raised the question of how to adjudge the legality of the decision under review, if not in light of the judge's opinion of the correct decision.

One response, which persisted until the shift to a single reasonableness standard in *Dunsmuir*, was to fix on the "depth of probing" allowable on patent unreasonableness as opposed to reasonableness review. This metaphor flourished despite the fact that, even before the rise of the reasonableness *simpliciter* standard in the mid-1990s, the case law had rejected the idea that deference meant refraining from careful engagement with administrative reasons.[88] That is, it was generally agreed that courts need not restrict their inquiries to, for example, the basic defensibility of the decision-maker's construction of the statute, absent consideration of how the law was applied in the case at hand. Still, the jurisprudence remained uncertain on how exactly to express deference, if not by "not looking" at the decision or aspects of it or by refusing to test it against the full set of statutory and evidentiary materials on the record.

A methodological alternative to independently seeking the "right answer" on reasonableness review—one that anticipates the developments we will see in *Dunsmuir*—is stated in *Ryan*, wherein Iacobucci J. urges judges to "stay close to the reasons" for an administrative decision, while searching for "a line of analysis within the given reasons that could reasonably lead the tribunal from the evidence before it to the conclusion at which it arrived."[89] Here Iacobucci J. revives the principle, reaching back to *CUPE*, that "a decision may satisfy the reasonableness standard if it is supported by a tenable explanation even if this explanation is not one that the reviewing court finds compelling."[90] This is bolstered by the further

---

[86] See the examples rehearsed in the judgment of LeBel J. in *Toronto (City) v. C.U.P.E., Local 79*, 2003 SCC 63, [2003] 3 S.C.R. 77 at paras. 96-99. The cases discussed include *Canada Safeway Ltd. v. RWDSU, Local 454*, [1998] 1 S.C.R. 1079 and *Lester (W.W.) (1978) Ltd. v. United Association of Journeymen and Apprentices of the Plumbing and Pipefitting Industry, Local 740*, [1990] 3 S.C.R. 644.

[87] *Ryan*, *supra* note 39 at para. 50. I discuss the case law supporting this point in more detail in "A Fine Romance?," *supra* note 4 at 233 and 236.

[88] See *National Corn Growers*, *supra* note 13, and the discussion of that case in "A Fine Romance?," *supra* note 4 at 236-38.

[89] *Supra* note 39 at paras. 49 and 55.

[90] *Ibid.* at para. 55.

statement that judges should assess the "basic adequacy of a reasoned decision," and so refrain from "seiz[ing] on one or more mistakes or elements of the decision which do not affect the decision as a whole."[91]

At the same time, Iacobucci J. in *Ryan* puts to rest the proposition that with the inception of the reasonableness standard, further and finer gradations of deference are implicitly registered on the spectrum of the standards of review—mirrored, perhaps, by distinctions in the allowable "depth of probing" or "magnitude of error." The persistence of the controversy was understandable. For if the reasonableness standard was forged in an attempt to better calibrate reviewing practices to the diversity of administrative contexts, then more standards would seem to mean even finer calibration. In *Ryan*, Iacobucci J. suggests that increasing efforts at fine-tuning when identifying the standard would only distract judges from the central work of "explaining why the decision was not supported by any reasons that can bear a somewhat probing examination."[92]

Two cases, both of which were decided under the patent unreasonableness standard, illustrate the challenge of adopting a mode of reasoning on review that avoids measuring the contested decision against the court's independent determination of the correct answer. The first (and arguably more successful) is Justice Dickson's judgment in *CUPE*.[93] The dispute about statutory interpretation at the heart of the case is discussed by Audrey Macklin in Chapter 9, and I will not take up the details here.[94] Instead I wish to briefly outline the reasons for claiming that Dickson J.'s judgment for the Court is exemplary of deference. What is exemplary about the judgment, I suggest, is its evaluation of the decision under review, not simply in light of the statutory purposes, but in light of the tribunal's own reasoning about those purposes.[95] That is, Dickson J. does not embark on a wholly independent assessment of the statutory scheme or the factors of mandatory relevance to the dispute. Rather, like L'Heureux-Dubé J. in *Mossop*, he repeatedly refers to, and may be said to amplify, the tribunal's purposive construction of the contested provision of the statute even as he inquires into the supportability of its interpretive conclusion. The importance of this approach becomes clear as Justice Dickson explains that a generalist judge (or one who "draws too heavily upon private sector experience") might find the tribunal's conclusions counterintuitive without the scaffolding of the tribunal's reasons, which canvass the historical trade-offs informing the regulation of public service labour relations.[96] In short, Justice Dickson grounds his analysis in a careful appraisal of the tribunal's reasons. And so this judgment remains a touchstone of what we have termed a constitutional pluralist orientation to the project of statutory interpretation on review.

---

91 *Ibid.* at para. 56. See also *Canadian Broadcasting Corp. v. Canada (Labour Relations Board)*, [1995] 1 S.C.R. 157 at paras. 48-49.

92 *Ryan, supra* note 39 at para. 46.

93 *Supra* note 3.

94 See Audrey Macklin, Chapter 9, section III, The Blockbuster: *C.U.P.E. v. New Brunswick Liquor Corporation*.

95 I discuss the judgment in more detail in "A Fine Romance?," *supra* note 4 at 235-36.

96 *CUPE, supra* note 3 at 242.

We may contrast this to another *CUPE* case, decided in 2003: *C.U.P.E. v. Ontario (Minister of Labour)*—often referred to as the *Retired Judges* case.[97] The decision of the majority in this case arguably stands as an example of the interpretive attitude of judicial supremacy, discussed in section II. According to the majority, the decision of the Ontario Minister of Labour to appoint only retired judges as the third members of tripartite hospital labour arbitration panels was patently unreasonable, because that decision failed to reflect consideration of labour relations experience and general acceptability within the labour relations community. On a purposive and historical analysis of the statutory scheme, these two factors were identified as having mandatory relevance to the exercise of the minister's broad statutory discretion. Yet the majority's extensive analysis of the statutory scheme, performed in an effort to discern the limits of the minister's discretionary powers, is conducted prior to, and wholly independent of, its formal adoption of a deferential standard or its application of that standard to the impugned decision. In other words, the majority independently ascertains, if not the "correct answer" to the matter in dispute, then the construction of the statute that is determinative of the result. Is this consistent with deference?[98]

Bastarache J.'s dissent in *Retired Judges* directs criticism at the excessive "probing" required to identify the majority's factors of mandatory relevance. Bastarache J. also argues that the majority's conclusion that the minister failed to consider certain factors is but a weak cover for its impermissible reassessment of the relative weight accorded by the minister to these and other factors.[99] We inquire further into this form of critique in a moment, in taking up the substantive indicia of unreasonableness. The main point for now is that the majority judgment in the *Retired Judges* case sits uneasily, not only with the traditional bar on revisiting administrative assessments of the weight accorded factors of relevance to their decisions, but with the methodological imperative of deference established above—that is, that judges "stay close" to the reasons of the decision-maker on review. We must acknowledge, however, that the latter imperative is far more likely to be satisfied where the decision under review is adjudicative or otherwise supported by formal reasons than in circumstances like those in *Retired Judges*, where the reasons were in effect judicially reconstructed in light of the legislative history and statements from members of the executive, along with responses given in the cross-examination of the minister's senior advisor.[100]

b. Substantive Indicia of (Un)reasonableness

We have seen that, from its inception in the mid-1990s, the law on reasonableness *simpliciter* review urged judges to attend closely to administrative decision-makers' reasons on review.

---

97   2003 SCC 29, [2003] 1 S.C.R. 539 [*Retired Judges*].

98   I discuss the case further in "A Fine Romance?," *supra* note 4 at 238-40. For a trenchant critique of the majority judgment, emphasizing the importance of the legislature's having left the disputed decision to the minister's "opinion," see G. Huscroft, "Judicial Review from CUPE to CUPE: Less Is Not Always More" in *Inside and Outside*, *supra* note 19 at 296. See also L. Sossin, "Empty Ritual, Mechanical Exercise or the Discipline of Deference? Revisiting the Standard of Review in Administrative Law" (2003) 27 Advocates' Q. 478, especially at 504-5.

99   *Retired Judges*, *supra* note 97, per Bastarache J. at paras. 35-36.

100   *Ibid.* at paras. 181-82.

Indeed, it may be said that what animates the subtle interposition of reasonableness *simpliciter* between correctness and patent unreasonableness review is a confidence in reason. This confidence is expressed, on the one hand, in the idea that judges are capable of appreciating the reasons of administrative decision-makers (though they must work to do so, by turning their mind to the statutory and wider institutional rationales for deference) and, on the other hand, in the idea that administrative decision-makers can communicate the reasonableness of their decisions to reviewing judges (though they too must work at this, by articulating their decisions in a manner that is sensitive to the demands of public justification).

This is confirmed in statements from Iacobucci J. in *Canada (Director of Investigation and Research) v. Southam*[101] on the links between deference, expertise, and reason-giving. He writes: "In the final result, the standard of reasonableness simply instructs reviewing courts to accord considerable weight to the views of tribunals about matters with respect to which they have significant expertise."[102] Yet to this Iacobucci J. appends an extended citation to the effect that unless experts are able to explain "to a fair-minded but less well-informed observer, the reasons for their conclusions," then "they are not very expert" and no deference is commanded.[103] That is, the expert status of a tribunal will not serve as a stand-alone justification for deeming a decision reasonable, absent reasons verifying the application of expertise to the matter at hand.

But apart from the imperative of "staying close" to administrative reasons on review, what guidance does the pre-*Dunsmuir* case law provide on the substantive indicia of reasonableness, or more pointedly, unreasonableness? Again we may draw on Iacobucci J.'s judgment in *Southam*, where he states:

> [A] court reviewing a conclusion on the reasonableness standard must look to see whether any reasons support it. The defect, if there is one, could presumably be in the evidentiary foundation itself or the logical process by which conclusions are sought to be drawn from it. An example of the former kind of defect would be an assumption that had no basis in the evidence .... An example of the latter kind would be a contradiction in the premises or an invalid inference.[104]

This description of reasonableness *simpliciter* review plays up a concern to identify decisions that have no basis in evidence or that fail to adhere to basic principles of practical reasoning or logic. Yet it arguably leaves out the sort of cases that have proven most challenging and controversial. That is, the case law on both patent unreasonableness and review for reasonableness *simpliciter* (and more recently, *Dunsmuir* reasonableness) has brought the challenges of deference into clearest focus where what is in issue is the decision-maker's construction of the values or ends to be advanced under the enabling statute. Just how the substantive limits of legality are to be identified in such cases is a central problem for reasonableness review.

---

[101]   [1997] 1 S.C.R. 748 [*Southam*].

[102]   *Ibid.* at para. 62.

[103]   *Ibid.*, citing R.P. Kerans, *Standards of Review Employed by Appellate Courts* (Edmonton: Juriliber, 1994) at 17.

[104]   *Southam, supra* note 101, at para. 56.

In *Ryan*, Iacobucci J. emphasizes (as Dickson J. had in *CUPE*) that, "[u]nlike a review for correctness, there will often be no single right answer to the questions"[105] attracting review for reasonableness. Here he directly engages problems of statutory construction hinging on the prioritization of competing statutory purposes:

> For example, when a decision must be taken according to a set of objectives that exist in tension with each other, there may be no particular trade-off that is superior to all others. Even if there could be, notionally, a single best answer, it is not the court's role to seek this out when deciding if the decision was unreasonable.[106]

This statement affirms the principle, long accepted in the case law (but, as we will see, increasingly subject to erosion or exceptions), that deferential review must avoid second-guessing administrators with respect to the weight or priority they assign to competing statutory purposes.[107] That is, traditionally, deference has been understood to mean that reviewing judges are prohibited from revisiting the relative weight placed by administrative decision-makers on the competing factors of relevance to their decisions—although they may insist, as a matter of law, that the decision-maker consider all factors of mandatory relevance (typically identified through a purposive construction of the statutory scheme). In this, "failing to consider a relevant factor" has taken on the character of an objective legal defect, while judgments about the weight to be accorded competing values, interests, or other considerations relevant to the statutory mandate have been deemed matters not of law but of discretion or policy, rightly falling to the administration. In *Southam*, Iacobucci J.'s refusal to revisit the weight placed by the tribunal on competing elements of a multi-factored economic analysis stands as a compelling illustration of how the prohibition may play out in practice.[108] But is the prohibition on revisiting the weight accorded by administrative decision-makers to the factors relevant to their decisions consistent with your intuitions about the substantive qualities of reasonableness in law or, for that matter, with the developing law on substantive reasonableness?

The prohibition was significantly called into question in *Baker*. There, the majority judgment of L'Heureux-Dubé J. exposed the potential for conflict between this imperative of deference as traditionally understood and the commitment to ensure that administrative decisions and decision-makers are fully integrated into the work of advancing the rule of law. You will recall that, on applying a reasonableness standard to the minister's (or rather, the minister's delegate's) exercise of discretion in that case, L'Heureux-Dubé J. determined that the notes of a junior officer, deemed to be the reasons for the decision, were inconsistent with "the values underlying the grant of discretion."[109] Moreover, L'Heureux-Dubé J. indicated that the values that underlie or set reasonable limits to discretionary powers issue

---

[105]   *Supra* note 39 at para. 51.

[106]   *Ibid.*

[107]   The most recent incursion on this principle, as discussed further below, is *Doré, supra* note 4.

[108]   See my discussion of *Southam* (*supra* note 101) in "A Fine Romance?," *supra* note 4 at 242-43.

[109]   *Baker, supra* note 6 at para. 65. The legal and factual background to the case, along with a more complete analysis, is provided by Geneviève Cartier in Chapter 11, Administrative Discretion: Between Exercising Power and Conducting Dialogue.

not only from a decision-maker's enabling legislation and associated regulations, but also from instruments of soft law (for example, departmental policies and guidelines), the common law ("the principles of administrative law"), the Constitution ("the principles of the rule of law" and "the principles of the *Charter*"), international law, and even what are tantalizingly (and, depending on one's perspective, perhaps worryingly) held out as the "fundamental values of Canadian society."[110] L'Heureux-Dubé J. concluded that the sources relevant to the case at hand (the statute, an international convention ratified but not incorporated into domestic legislation, and ministerial guidelines) established that "the rights, interests, and needs of children and special attention to childhood are important values that should be considered in reasonably interpreting the 'humanitarian' and 'compassionate' considerations that guide the exercise of the discretion."[111] Because the officer's notes failed to reflect that the decision-maker was "alive, alert, or sensitive to the interests of Ms. Baker's children,"[112] the decision failed to meet the standard of reasonableness *simpliciter*.

Following the ruling in *Baker*, commentators and courts alike were concerned to settle the matter of whether this decision was a straightforward example of the tradition of vitiating a discretionary decision for failure to consider a relevant factor at all (the children's interests). Or was it a departure from the traditional approach, amounting to a revisiting of the *weight* placed on a particular factor (those interests)? The comments of L'Heureux-Dubé J. left some uncertainty. At one point she wrote that the officer's notes were "completely dismissive of the interests of Ms. Baker's children." But in the next sentence, she wrote, "the failure to give serious weight and consideration to the interests of the children constitutes an unreasonable exercise of the discretion."[113] Further uncertainty arose from L'Heureux-Dubé J.'s suggestion that, depending on the circumstances, a discretionary decision-maker may be accorded deference in connection with the factors he or she deems relevant to a given decision, and not merely in connection with the weight he or she gives to mandatory relevant factors.[114] This represents an even more radical departure from the traditional approach to substantive review (even on a deferential standard)—antithetical to the constitutional traditionalist's view of the mandate of courts to patrol the limits of administrative jurisdiction.

In *Suresh v. Canada (Minister of Citizenship and Immigration)*,[115] the Court responded to some of these uncertainties. *Baker*, it stated, "does not authorize courts reviewing decisions on the discretionary end of the spectrum to engage in a new weighing process, but draws

---

[110] *Baker, supra* note 6 at paras. 56 and 67.

[111] *Ibid.* at para. 73.

[112] *Ibid.*

[113] *Ibid.* at para. 65. See the discussion of how these statements might be reconciled, in D. Mullan, "Deference from Baker to Suresh and Beyond—Interpreting the Conflicting Signals" in D. Dyzenhaus, ed., *The Unity of Public Law* (Portland, OR: Hart Publishing, 2004) 21 at 31-37 [*The Unity of Public Law*]. Among the more convincing interpretations is that the factor in question (the children's interests) read in light of the statute, the applicable ministerial guidelines, and international law, necessarily carries with it "elements of weight or degree."

[114] *Baker, supra* note 6 at para. 56: "In fact, deferential standards of review may give substantial leeway to the discretionary decision-maker in determining the 'proper purposes' or 'relevant considerations' involved in making a given determination."

[115] 2002 SCC 1, [2002] 1 S.C.R. 3 [*Suresh*].

on an established line of cases concerning the failure of ministerial delegates to consider and weigh implied limitations or patently relevant factors."[116] Here the possibility that certain factors may be deemed by courts to demand prioritization (or "*serious* weight and consideration") in light of statutory or other legal sources in particular cases is left open. The Court in *Suresh* does not address the proposition advanced by L'Heureux-Dubé J. in *Baker* that some discretionary decision-makers may receive deference in relation to the factors they deem to be relevant to their decisions.

The multiple, complex messages in *Baker*—endorsing, on the one hand, the idea that deference may even be directed at decision-makers' assessments of statutory purposes and so to their assessments of the considerations that are of mandatory relevance to their decisions, and on the other, the idea that those decision-makers must conform with the "values underlying the grant of discretion," even necessarily placing significant weight on one or another of these where the reviewing judge deems that to be required by the statutory text or context—express a tension that is basic to reasonableness review on the romantic account. That is, this tension is inherent in the idea of "deference as respect" advanced by David Dyzenhaus and explicitly endorsed by L'Heureux-Dubé J.[117] Such respect places confidence in the capacity of decision-makers to discern the limits of their legal mandates in a nuanced, context-sensitive fashion, while at the same time insisting that this capacity be demonstrated in their decisions. In other words, deference under this standard carries with it an expectation that decision-makers can and will identify, and evince appropriate sensitivity to, the values (including the significant individual interests) that should inform the exercise of their statutory powers. But, we may ask: is this really so different from correctness review? Is this just an old-time assertion of the courts' "jurisdiction"—and so of judges (historically prioritizing individual rights over the public purposes driving administrative mandates) having the last word on matters given to tribunals to decide? If not, how exactly is it different?

On the romantic account of substantive review, the decisions of judges on review must also be publicly justified. To that end, would it not be better that judges' background assessments of weight, where these assessments differ from those of administrative decision-makers, be explicitly stated and subjected to public scrutiny—thus alleviating the possibility of their covert operation? On turning to post-*Dunsmuir* developments, we will see that, with *Doré*,[118] the Supreme Court has unleashed a new set of possibilities for revisiting the weight accorded to competing legal values on reasonableness review—at least, where the decision is constructed as an exercise of adjudicative discretion and where Charter values are understood to be engaged.

In sum, although the logic of reasonableness *simpliciter* was drawn out of the law on patent unreasonableness—a line of case law ostensibly tolerant of administrative decisions that were unreasonable, though not "patently" so—the cases elaborating the new standard introduced new expectations of judicial attentiveness to administrative reasoning, along with

---

[116] *Ibid.* at para. 37.

[117] "Deference as respect requires not submission but a respectful attention to the reasons offered or which could be offered in support of a decision": *Baker, supra* note 6 at para. 65, citing "The Politics of Deference," *supra* note 4 at 286.

[118] *Supra* note 4.

new expectations that administrative decision-makers publicly justify their decisions. Arguably, these central features of reasonableness review begin to erode the logic underpinning the formal non-engagement with tribunal reasons that characterizes correctness review.[119]

2. Reasonableness Post-Dunsmuir

a. Dunsmuir Reasonableness in Theory

As Audrey Macklin has explained in Chapter 9, *Dunsmuir's* collapsing of patent unreasonableness and reasonableness *simpliciter* into a single standard of deferential review marks an effort to simplify this area of law and, at the same time, to set it on a more principled foundation. In place of the prior case law's shaky gestures to depth of probing and magnitude of error, the *Dunsmuir* majority makes tentative attempts to offer clearer guidance about what it means to express deference on review. Yet the majority does not pull the essential features of the revised reasonableness standard out of thin air, but rather builds on the foundations of the prior case law on deference, including Justice Iacobucci's descriptions of reasonableness review in *Southam*[120] and *Ryan*[121] and Justice Dickson's judgment in *CUPE*.[122] Those judgments centred on the idea that judges applying a reasonableness standard should closely attend to administrative reasoning, and that the decision should stand unless it "cannot be rationally supported by the relevant legislation"[123] or the evidence.

The question is whether *Dunsmuir* or the subsequent case law adds anything to the law on deferential review that might ease the historical tensions—at times wild mood swings—affecting this area of law. I refer to the aforementioned instability in the case law applying a deferential standard as between attitudes of judicial supremacy (setting strict limits of legality within which administrative reasoning is closely hedged) and attitudes of judicial abdication (for example, refusing to peer "too deeply" into the reasoning or evidentiary record, or to revisit administrative assessments of the relative weight of competing factors, including statutory objectives or legal values). Ultimately, we may be forced to conclude that the jury is still out on the success of *Dunsmuir* and the subsequent case law in negotiating these extremes. At the same time, read in light of the romantic's concern that the law on substantive review should help coordinate the work of judges and administrative decision-makers in a "culture of justification," the principles of reasonableness review asserted in and after *Dunsmuir* are arguably a step in the right direction.

---

119   See D. Dyzenhaus, "David Mullan's Rule of (Common) Law" in *Inside and Outside, supra* note 19 at 474-75. Dyzenhaus argues that reasonableness *simpliciter* "shears the correctness standard off the continuum of the standards of review." Also see "Constituting the Rule of Law," *supra* note 5 at 495.

120   *Supra* note 101.

121   *Supra* note 39.

122   *Supra* note 3.

123   *CUPE, ibid.* at 237, cited in *Dunsmuir, supra* note 1 at para. 35.

i. Deference as Respect

The passages in *Dunsmuir* offering guidance on the newly unified standard of reasonableness are explicitly grounded in the concept of deference "as respect"—or to quote the passage from Dyzenhaus's work on which the majority relies: deference as "not submission but a respectful attention to the reasons offered or which could be offered in support of a decision."[124] The longer passage in which the majority adopts this descriptor of deference is worth reproducing here:

> Deference is both an attitude of the court and a requirement of the law of judicial review. It does not mean that courts are subservient to the determinations of decision makers, or that courts must show blind reverence to their interpretations, or that they may be content to pay lip service to the concept of reasonableness review while in fact imposing their own view. Rather, deference imports respect for the decision-making process of adjudicative bodies with regard to both the facts and the law. The notion of deference "is rooted in part in a respect for governmental decisions to create administrative bodies with delegated powers" (*Canada (Attorney General) v. Mossop* ...). We agree with David Dyzenhaus where he states that the concept of "deference as respect" requires of the courts "not submission but a respectful attention to the reasons offered or which could be offered in support of a decision."[125]

In this statement, deference is said to be rooted "in part" in respect for legislative intent, as registered not merely in the existence of a privative clause but more generally in the legislature's conferring decision-making powers on administrative actors. In a further statement following close on the foregoing, the majority takes account of the pragmatic rationales for according deference to administrative decision-makers even on questions involving interpretation of law. Specifically, the majority cites David Mullan for the insight that according deference to tribunals

> recognizes the reality that, in many instances, those working day to day in the implementation of frequently complex administrative schemes have or will develop a considerable degree of expertise or field sensitivity to the imperatives and nuances of the legislative regime.[126]

The majority concludes with a statement of the diverse foundations for, and expressions of, "deference as respect" inscribed in the modern law on substantive review. These include

> respect for the legislative choices to leave some matters in the hands of administrative decision makers, for the processes and determinations that draw on particular expertise and experiences

---

[124] *Dunsmuir, ibid.* note 1 at para. 48, citing Dyzenhaus, "The Politics of Deference," *supra* note 4 at 286. As noted above, the passage is also cited with approval in *Baker, supra* note 6 at para. 65.

[125] *Dunsmuir, supra* note 1 at para. 48 (citing *Mossop, supra* note 46 at 596, L'Heureux-Dubé J. dissenting).

[126] *Ibid.* at para. 49. The quoted passage is from D. Mullan, "Establishing the Standard of Review: The Struggle for Complexity?" (2004) 17 Can. J. Admin. L. & Prac. 59 at 93. Recently, Abella J. in *Newfoundland and Labrador Nurses' Union v. Newfoundland and Labrador (Treasury Board)*, 2011 SCC 62 at para. 13 [*Newfoundland Nurses' Union*] has observed that *Dunsmuir's* statements on reasonableness review convey "a respectful appreciation that a wide range of specialized decision-makers routinely render decisions in their respective spheres of expertise, using concepts and language often unique to their areas and rendering decisions that are often counter-intuitive to a generalist."

[of administrative decision-makers], and for the different roles of the courts and administrative bodies within the Canadian constitutional system.[127]

These pronouncements on the purposes of substantive review and in particular on deference on review are made following an observation concerning statutory interpretation, wherein the majority endorses the key premise behind the attitude of deference taken to law interpretation—or at least, to *some* law interpretation—in *CUPE* and in the subsequent case law on deference. This is the premise that "certain questions that come before administrative tribunals do not lend themselves to one specific, particular result. Instead, they may give rise to a number of possible, reasonable conclusions."[128] That acknowledgment of the place of judgment, or discretion, in (at least *some* instances of) statutory interpretation is accompanied by the majority's recognizing the imperative that administrative decision-makers be accorded a "margin of appreciation within the range of acceptable and rational solutions" to interpretive problems.[129]

ii. Targets of Reasonableness Review: Reasons and Outcomes

The *Dunsmuir* majority's statement that administrative decision-makers attracting deference should be accorded a margin of appreciation prefaces a brief discussion of how a court is to conduct reasonableness review. First comes the statement: "A court conducting a review for reasonableness inquires into the qualities that make a decision reasonable, referring both to the process of articulating the reasons and to outcomes."[130] This is elaborated in the following manner:

> In judicial review, reasonableness is concerned mostly with the existence of justification, transparency and intelligibility within the decision-making process. But it is also concerned with whether the decision falls within a range of possible, acceptable outcomes which are defensible in respect of the facts and law.[131]

Some provincial courts of appeal subsequently interpreted this as mandating a two-stage inquiry, first into the reasoning process and then into whether the decision falls into the range of reasonable outcomes.[132] Courts must be mindful of the recent statement of Abella J., writing for a unanimous court in *Newfoundland and Labrador Nurses' Union v. Newfoundland and Labrador (Treasury Board)*, that *Dunsmuir* does not advocate "that a reviewing court undertake two discrete analyses—one for reasons and a separate one for the result."[133] Rather, the assessment of reasonableness "is a more organic exercise—the reasons

---

127   *Dunsmuir, supra* note 1 at para. 49.

128   *Ibid.* at para. 47.

129   *Ibid.*

130   *Ibid.*

131   *Ibid.*

132   See *Casino Nova Scotia v. Nova Scotia (Labour Relations Board)*, 2009 NSCA 4; *Communications, Energy and Paperworkers' Union, Local 1520 v. Maritime Paper Products Ltd.*, 278 N.S.R. (2d) 381 (C.A.); *Taub v. Investment Dealers Association of Canada*, 2009 ONCA 628.

133   *Supra* note 126 at para. 14.

must be read together with the outcome and serve the purpose of showing whether the result falls within a range of possible outcomes."[134] This is not to say that a reviewing court is in error if it begins with an examination of the decision-maker's reasoning process. Rather, it affirms the common-sense point that any inquiry into substantive reasonableness must evaluate whether the reasons support (justify) the outcome. At the same time, the statement that reasonableness review is an "organic exercise" reminds us that courts should not indulge in a reasons-independent assessment of the outcome in a manner that privileges the court's determination of the "right answer."

iii. The Criteria of Dunsmuir Reasonableness

We have seen that the *Dunsmuir* majority replaces the preoccupation with depth of probing and magnitude of error that once informed the law on deference with what are presented as three conceptual touchstones: "justification, transparency, and intelligibility."[135] These terms are stipulated, more than explained, in a manner that may be regarded as a gesture toward the horizon of future interpretations. Consider again the passage from the majority in *Dunsmuir*, quoted above:

> In judicial review, reasonableness is concerned mostly with the existence of justification, transparency and intelligibility within the decision-making process. But it is also concerned with whether the decision falls within a range of possible, acceptable outcomes which are defensible in respect of the facts and law.[136]

Here the three terms appear to be embedded in the "process of reasoning" aspect of reasonableness review. Yet the identification of "outcomes which are defensible in respect of the facts and the law" arguably requires application of at least the criterion of justification. Indeed, the application of all three criteria to both foci of reasonableness review (reasons and outcomes) is suggested in the majority judgment in *Khosa*,[137] in the statement that "as long as the process and the outcome fit comfortably with the principles of justification, transparency and intelligibility, it is not open to a reviewing court to substitute its own view of a preferable outcome."[138] In *Montréal (City) v. Montreal Port Authority*, LeBel J. (writing for the Court) averts to the criteria of reasonableness as follows:

> The concept of "reasonableness" relates primarily to the transparency and intelligibility of the reasons given for a decision. But it also encompasses a quality requirement that applies to those reasons and to the outcome of the decision-making process.[139]

All this talk about reasonableness may seem just that—all talk. But as we will see, these statements lead to some important developments regarding the conduct of reasonableness

---

[134] *Ibid.*

[135] *Dunsmuir, supra* note 1 at para. 47.

[136] *Ibid.*

[137] *Supra* note 23.

[138] *Ibid.* at para. 59.

[139] 2010 SCC 14 at para. 38.

review. In all these developments, the overarching question is how the concern for justification—which implicitly speaks to the normativity or value-ladenness of law, even reaching
to considerations of proportionality—is to be integrated with the other, more process-
oriented criteria.

iv. Post-Dunsmuir Developments

Here we take up three post-*Dunsmuir* developments concerning the significance or proper
application of the reasonableness standard. These developments speak to (1) the distinction
between review to determine whether the duty to give reasons has been met and review for
substantive reasonableness, (2) the effort to give content to the idea that reasonableness
"takes its colour from the context";[140] and (3) integration of proportionality analysis into
reasonableness review (specifically, review of adjudicative discretion implicating Charter
values). We also take note of some continuing controversies regarding (4) the interpretation
and application of statutory standards of patent unreasonableness.

1. "NO REASONS" VERSUS SUBSTANTIVE (UN)REASONABLENESS

The question at the heart of the *Newfoundland Nurses' Union* case[141] is how a court is to
proceed where it is alleged that there are gaps in administrative reasoning. The allegation
may be that the decision-maker has not addressed matters that would be determinative of
the outcome, or that the decision-maker has failed to lay down a clear reasoning path linking the evidence or law to the conclusions reached.

The first dimension of this problem is whether claims about the incompleteness or inadequacy of reasons should be decided through an inquiry into substantive reasonableness, or
alternatively, through an inquiry into whether the duty to provide reasons has been met as
a matter of procedural fairness. As Grant Huscroft and Audrey Macklin relate in Chapters 5
and 9, there was controversy among provincial courts of appeal on this point prior to the
Supreme Court's hearing the *Newfoundland Nurses' Union* case.[142] Without adverting to the
competing positions adopted in the appellate decisions, Abella J. indicates, first, that a low
threshold should apply in determining whether reasons have been provided as a matter of
procedural fairness and, second, that where questions arise concerning "the *quality*" of
reasons provided, this is a matter for substantive review. This leaves some uncertainty
around what it takes to qualify as even minimally adequate reasons for the purposes of procedural fairness. Yet the overall effect is to shift questions about whether reasons adequately
support or justify a decision to substantive review. This is not a mere formality. For it allevi-
ates both the prospect of inefficient doubling of advocates' and judges' efforts to address
sufficiency of reasons (on both procedural and substantive grounds) and the prospect that

---

140   *Khosa, supra* note 23 at para. 59.

141   *Supra* note 126.

142   Ontario's approach was to decide allegations of inadequacy or insufficiency of reasons as a matter of proced-
      ural fairness (i.e., as raising the question whether the reasons constituted reasons at all). See *Clifford v. On-
      tario Municipal Employees Retirement System*, 2009 ONCA 670. The Newfoundland Court of Appeal, in
      deciding the *Newfoundland Nurses' Union* case, took the position that such allegations fall under the head of
      substantive review: 2010 NLCA 13.

the imperatives of deference will be subverted by review of tribunal reasoning under the head of procedural fairness where the standard that traditionally applies is correctness.[143]

The second dimension of the problem addressed in the *Newfoundland Nurses' Union* case goes to how a court is to exhibit deference on reviewing a decision alleged to have fatal gaps in reasoning. Here some specifics may assist. The nurses' union was contesting a labour arbitrator's decision that the collective agreement did not permit the crediting of time spent as a casual employee when calculating an employee's vacation entitlement. Specifically, the union argued that the decision was inadequately supported by the arbitrator's reasons. In rejecting the union's position, Justice Abella rehearsed in brief the arbitrator's reasoning (the arbitrator "outlined the facts, the arguments of the parties, the relevant provisions of the collective agreement, a number of applicable interpretive principles," and then drew a conclusion).[144] In addition, Abella J. took note of the main inferences that the arbitrator had made from provisions of the collective agreement. According to Abella J., all this "provided a reasonable basis for the arbitrator's conclusion, based on a plain reading of the agreement itself."[145] Citing the Court of Appeal for the observation that "'a more comprehensive explanation' would have been preferable,"[146] Justice Abella nonetheless concurs with that court that the arbitrator's decision met the *Dunsmuir* criteria of "justification, transparency and intelligibility."[147]

Along the way, Abella J. makes some general statements on how judges are to express "deference as respect" when there are alleged gaps in administrative reasons. Most important is the statement that deference as respect—articulated in Dyzenhaus's now-authoritative phrasing as respect for "the reasons offered or which could be offered in support of a decision"[148]—may require looking beyond the reasons to the wider record of evidence and argument, "for the purpose of assessing the reasonableness of the outcome."[149] On this approach, it is recognized that "[a] decision-maker is not required to make an explicit finding on each constituent element, however subordinate, leading to its conclusion."[150]

In Chapter 5, Grant Huscroft raises concerns about the potential extension of the directive that courts consider the reasons that "could be offered" in support of a decision to cases in which no reasons have been given.[151] In such circumstances, we may question both the practical and constitutional capacity of a court to ascertain, independent of the administrative

---

143 See *Newfoundland Nurses' Union, supra* note 126 at para. 21. And see Alice Woolley, "The Continued Complexity of Administrative Law Post-Dunsmuir" (14 December 2010), online: The University of Calgary Faculty of Law Blog on Developments in Alberta Law <http://ablawg.ca/wp-content/uploads/2010/12/blog_aw_mitzel_dec2010.pdf> at 7.

144 *Newfoundland Nurses' Union, supra* note 126 at para. 5.

145 *Ibid.* at para. 7.

146 *Ibid.* at para. 9.

147 *Ibid.*

148 *Ibid.* at para. 12.

149 *Ibid.* at para. 15.

150 *Ibid.* at para. 16.

151 Grant Huscroft, Chapter 5, section V, The Content of the Duty of Fairness (under heading V.C, Specific Components of the Duty of Fairness, and heading V.C.7, The Duty to Give Reasons).

decision-maker, the bases on which the decision rests. But how, if not by evaluating the decision in light of what materials are available, is the reviewing court to assure itself of substantive legality? Huscroft suggests, drawing on further statements on this subject in *Alberta (Information and Privacy Commissioner)*,[152] that it would be preferable to remit the matter to the original decision-maker to give reasons after the fact. The awkwardness of such a call for reasons in retrospect illuminates the uneasy position, in a "culture of justification," of administrative decisions that are not supported by reasons in the first place.

As discussed in Chapter 5, Rothstein J.'s judgment for the majority in *Alberta (Information and Privacy Commissioner)* offers a more limited pronouncement on the sort of case in which judges may attend to the reasons that "could be offered" in support of a decision. Specifically, Rothstein J. addresses a situation in which a matter of determinative importance has implicitly been decided as part of a wider decision, but has not been discussed in the reasons. Moreover, the situation is one in which the party raising the issue in court failed to put the decision-maker on notice about the importance of giving reasons on the matter in the first place. In such cases, the reviewing judge has discretion to decide whether to hear the challenge.[153] The exercise of that discretion may be significantly informed by the prejudicial effect that this would have on the parties or tribunal, and by whether there are alternative means of ascertaining the reasons for the decision—for example, prior tribunal jurisprudence.[154] Justice Rothstein emphasizes, however, that adverting to the reasons that "could be offered" must not collapse into mere submission to tribunal decisions, no matter how thin their discernible basis in the evidence and law.[155] In the absence of alternative mechanisms for ascertaining the decision-maker's reasons, the court may decide not to hear the matter or, alternatively, may give the decision-maker the opportunity to give reasons after the fact.[156]

This discussion of the conduct of reasonableness review in the face of alleged gaps in reasons recalls a form of fatal error that we have already encountered in the law on deferential review (indeed, as Geneviève Cartier describes in Chapter 11, it is a traditional ground for the review of discretion): that of failing to consider a factor of mandatory relevance. Claims about fatal gaps in reasoning may attract similar questions about whether the gap reflects the decision-maker's failure to consider a relevant factor or, instead (and more controversially), the decision-maker's failure to attach to that factor the same relative priority as that favoured by the reviewing court.

2. CONTEXTUAL DIMENSIONS OF REASONABLENESS

Justice Binnie's concurring reasons in *Dunsmuir* included a suggestion that the simplicity introduced by the shift to a single reasonableness standard was likely to be accompanied, and perhaps undermined, by the emergence of distinct grades or shades of reasonableness review at the stage of applying the standard. Binnie J. observed that this fracturing of rea-

---

152   *Supra* note 2.

153   *Ibid.* at paras. 22-28.

154   *Ibid.* at paras. 26-28.

155   *Ibid.* at para. 54. Also see *Khosa, supra* note 23 at para. 63.

156   *Supra* note 2 at para. 55.

sonableness review was likely to occur by way of judicial consultation of contextual factors, including the factors traditionally canvassed at the stage of identifying the standard, to inform the expectations of reasonableness appropriate to the decision at hand.[157] This idea again surfaces in Justice Binnie's reasons for the majority in *Khosa*, where reasonableness is described as a standard that "takes its colour from the context."[158]

In his concurring opinion in *Dunsmuir*, Justice Binnie elaborated on this line of speculation by drawing on Rand J.'s observation in *Roncarelli v. Duplessis* that "there is always a perspective ... within which a statute is intended [by the legislature] to operate."[159] Binnie J. adds:

> How is that "perspective" to be ascertained? The reviewing judge will obviously want to consider the precise nature and function of the decision maker including its expertise, the terms and objectives of the governing statute (or common law) conferring the power of decision, including the existence of a privative clause and the nature of the issue being decided. Careful consideration of these matters will reveal the extent of the discretion conferred, for example, the extent to which the decision formulates or implements broad public policy. In such cases, the range of permissible considerations will obviously be much broader than where the decision to be made is more narrowly circumscribed, e.g., whether a particular claimant is entitled to a disability benefit under governmental social programs.[160]

Notably, one factor that is not mentioned in the above passage (a factor that has historically been absent from the standard of review analysis, though it is counted among the contextual factors relevant to calibrating the expectations of procedural fairness)[161] is the significance of the interests at stake. However, Binnie J. continues:

> In some cases, the court will have to recognize that the decision maker was required to strike a proper balance (or achieve proportionality) between the adverse impact of a decision on the rights and interests of the applicant or others directly affected weighed against the public purpose which is sought to be advanced. In each case, careful consideration will have to be given to the reasons given for the decision. To this list, of course, may be added as many "contextual" considerations as the court considers relevant and material.[162]

Again, the integration of proportionality analysis into reasonableness review is something that, as discussed further in a moment, has recently come to pass (or partially so) with *Doré*.[163]

---

[157]   *Dunsmuir, supra* note 1 at paras. 139 and 150-55, Binnie J.

[158]   *Khosa, supra* note 23 at para. 59. Also see *Mills v. Workplace Safety and Insurance Appeals Tribunal*, 2008 ONCA 436.

[159]   *Dunsmuir, supra* note 1 at para. 151, per Binnie J., citing the judgment of Rand J. in *Roncarelli v. Duplessis*, [1959] S.C.R. 121 at 140 [*Roncarelli*].

[160]   *Dunsmuir, supra* note 1 at para. 151.

[161]   *Baker, supra* note 6 at para. 25. And see L. Sossin & C.M. Flood, "The Contextual Turn: Iacobucci's Legacy and the Standard of Review in Administrative Law" (2007) 57 U.T.L.J. 581 at 596. (The calibration of deference, like the calibration of procedural fairness guarantees per *Baker*, should reflect, *inter alia*, the significance of any individual interests directly affected by the decision.)

[162]   *Dunsmuir, supra* note 1 at para. 151.

[163]   *Supra* note 4.

The post-*Dunsmuir* jurisprudence has sought to give more determinate content to the idea that reasonableness "takes its colour from the context." In *Alberta (Information and Privacy Commissioner)*, Justice Rothstein for the majority rejects those statements in Justice Binnie's concurring reasons, both in that case and in *Dunsmuir*, which raise the spectre of "variable degrees of deference."[164] Echoing the approach taken to reasonableness *simpliciter* review in *Ryan*, Rothstein J. states that "[o]nce it is determined that a review is to be conducted on a reasonableness standard, there is no second assessment of how intensely the review is to be conducted."[165] However, Rothstein J. continues, each instance of reasonableness review is nonetheless "governed by the context," in the sense that it must be informed by contextual factors such as the nature of question.

The idea that reasonableness review is governed by context—though it is not conducted on a spectrum involving shifting degrees of intensity or of deference—is further refined in *Catalyst Paper Corp. v. North Cowichan (District)*, a case that involved reasonableness review of a municipal bylaw.[166] There, McLachlin C.J. (writing for the Court) confirms that review for reasonableness "is an essentially contextual inquiry."[167] She continues, by way of orienting this inquiry: "[t]he fundamental question is the scope of decision-making power conferred on the decision-maker by the governing legislation."[168] This recalls the statements of Binnie J. in *Dunsmuir* on ascertaining the ambit of reasonableness by way of a contextual inquiry into the "perspective" properly imputed to statutory powers. Notably, McLachlin C.J.'s statements on the context-sensitivity of reasonableness review follow closely on her rejecting the principle from *Thorne's Hardware Ltd. v. The Queen*[169] that matters of municipal policy making are not subject to judicial review.[170] Rejection of that principle is consistent with the now-dominant logic of reasonableness review, which acknowledges the necessity of deference while maintaining that the exercise of statutorily delegated powers (including broad discretionary powers) is always bounded by limits of legality. We take up *Catalyst Paper* further, with attention to the way that McLachlin C.J. puts into action the idea that reasonableness review demands contextual analysis, in a moment, as part of our more general inquiry into how reasonableness review has been practised (as opposed to simply theorized) post-*Dunsmuir*.

3. DORÉ AND PROPORTIONALITY

We have seen that, traditionally, common-law substantive review featured a general prohibition against revisiting administrative judgments concerning the relative weight or importance to be assigned competing factors of relevance, from evidentiary considerations to policy goals or statutory purposes. We have also seen that, in *Baker*,[171] that prohibition came

---

164   *Supra* note 2 at para. 47, citing Binnie J. at paras. 85-87 and Binnie J.'s concurring reasons in *Dunsmuir*.

165   *Alberta (Information and Privacy Commissioner)*, *supra* note 2 at para. 47.

166   2012 SCC 2 [*Catalyst Paper*].

167   *Ibid.* at para. 18.

168   Ibid.

169   [1983] 1 S.C.R. 106 at 115.

170   *Catalyst Paper, supra* note 166 at paras. 14-15.

171   *Supra* note 6.

under some strain. Indeed, given that, as stated in *Baker*, discretion must be exercised in accordance with the values underlying the grant of discretion (values registered, *inter alia*, in the Constitution and Charter), it arguably makes no sense to attempt to divorce substantive legality from the weight accorded to such factors as "fundamental values."

Recent case law developments have further eroded the principle that the review of discretion should not revisit the weight assigned to competing factors—in particular, competing legal values—of relevance to the decision. The Supreme Court's unanimous judgment in *Doré*[172] states that where an exercise of discretion (or specifically "adjudicative discretion," applying discretionary powers to individual cases)[173] engages Charter values, judicial review should be conducted according to common-law principles of substantive review rather than under the s. 1 Charter framework for justifying a rights-infringement. Abella J.'s judgment in *Doré* further indicates that the appropriate standard of review (at least, where there are no other compelling factors in play) will be reasonableness—with "proportionality" serving, in such cases, as the central criterion of reasonableness. In Chapter 12, Evan Fox-Decent and Alexander Pless situate *Doré* within a wider set of jurisprudential developments involving the interaction of the Charter and administrative law. Here, we assess the implications of the decision for reasonableness review.

Proportionality analysis has in the past couple of decades made marked incursions into the common law on judicial review of substantive administrative decisions in the United Kingdom and in other common-law countries.[174] This has been the case not only with administrative decisions involving human rights, but also a wider class of discretionary decisions involving the balancing of competing values or interests understood not to implicate human rights.[175] The analysis has tended to be conducted in terms that parallel, even where they are not strictly equivalent to, the analysis proper to s. 1 of Canada's Charter (that is, the inquiry into whether an infringement of Charter-protected rights constitutes a "reasonable limit" that "can be demonstrably justified in a free and democratic society").[176]

---

[172]   *Supra* note 4.

[173]   This may be contrasted to, for example, regulation making (the form of executive discretion in issue in *Alberta v. Hutterian Brethren of Wilson Colony*, 2009 SCC 37, [2009] 2 S.C.R. 567).

[174]   See M. Taggart, "Proportionality, Deference, Wednesbury" (2008) N.Z.L. Rev. 423 ["Proportionality, Deference, Wednesbury"].

[175]   In "Correctness, Reasonableness and Proportionality: A New Standard of Judicial Review" (2005) 31 Man. L.J. 239 ["A New Standard"], Guy Régimbalt canvasses cases attracting proportionality review in other common-law jurisdictions and identifies, beyond cases clearly involving human rights, "those where the review is of a decision which imposes burdens (penalties and levies), and the review of policy laden discretionary decisions" (at para. 83). David Mullan ("A Proportionate Response?," *supra* note 12) takes note of certain "categories of unreasonableness" attracting proportionality review in the United Kingdom. He cites cases "held invalid because they manifestly failed to balance one or more (relevant) consideration, and those where the decision was held to be unreasonably onerous or oppressive." Mullan continues: "Under the first of these, the courts evaluate whether manifestly disproportionate weight has been attached to one or other considerations relevant to the decision. Under the second, the courts consider whether there has been a disproportionate interference with the claimant's rights or interests" (at 254).

[176]   Section 1 of the Charter has been the subject of extensive case law elaboration, beginning with Dickson J.'s 1986 judgment in *R. v. Oakes*, [1986] 1 S.C.R. 103 [*Oakes*]. The analysis requires an initial inquiry into whether the state action in issue was "prescribed by law," followed by an inquiry into whether the action was undertaken in pursuit of a pressing and substantial objective, and then an inquiry into proportionality. The

The view that some form of proportionality analysis should be integrated into the common law on reasonableness review has been propounded over the past decade by a number of Canadian commentators.[177] Evan Fox-Decent and Geneviève Cartier, for instance, argued that proportionality analysis was already implicit in the jurisprudence on reasonableness review, or at least in certain exemplary decisions (for example, *Baker*) in which reviewing judges insisted that administrative decisions must reflect the critical importance of the individual interests and legal values engaged.[178] In *Doré*, the Court accepts that, in some of its prior decisions, it had effectively endorsed oversight of the weight accorded by administrative decision-makers to Charter-protected interests within the common-law framework for substantive review.[179]

Doré builds on these precedents in an effort to resolve the ambivalence in the case law on whether administrative discretion affecting Charter-protected interests should be reviewed according to common-law administrative law principles of substantive review or under s. 1 of the Charter (and its judicial elaboration, the *Oakes* test[180]). The important background to this controversy is explained by Evan Fox-Decent and Alexander Pless in Chapter 12. The Court (Abella J. writing) determines that it is the common-law review of discretion, rather than the analysis under s. 1, that should apply—at least where what is in issue is the application of Charter values to an "individual administrative decision."[181] Among the central reasons for this are (1) that the *Oakes* analysis (and related jurisprudence, for instance on the s. 1 requirement that the state action be "prescribed by law")[182] was crafted specifically to guide judicial oversight of legislation and so lacks sensitivity to considerations proper to the oversight of executive or administrative decisions about individual cases and (2) that the common-law analysis of substantive legality now recognizes that administrative discretion

---

latter inquiry includes contemplation of (1) whether there was a "rational connection" between the rights-infringing action and the objective, (2) whether the means taken to pursue the objective were "minimally impairing," and (3) whether the benefits flowing from the targeted action outweigh the harms.

177   See D. Mullan, "A Proportionate Response?," *supra* note 12; G. Régimbalt, "A New Standard," *supra* note 175; E. Fox-Decent, "The Internal Morality of Administration" in *The Unity of Public Law*, *supra* note 113 at 143 ["The Internal Morality"]; G. Cartier, "The Baker Effect: A New Interface Between the Canadian Charter of Rights and Freedoms and Administrative Law—The Case of Discretion" in *The Unity of Public Law*, *ibid.* at 61 ["The Baker Effect"]. Also see D. Dyzenhaus, "The Politics of Deference," *supra* note 4 and "Constituting the Rule of Law," *supra* note 5.

178   E. Fox-Decent, "The Internal Morality," *supra* note 177; and G. Cartier, "The Baker Effect," *ibid.*

179   *Doré*, *supra* note 4 at paras. 30-34, 49, and 50.

180   *Supra* note 176. A few of the statements in this section are taken from my summary of *Doré* in the 2012 edition of the *Nova Scotia Barristers Society Bar Admission Course Materials (Administrative Law)* (Diana Ginn & Sheila Wildeman, 2012, on file with author).

181   *Oakes*, *supra* note 176 at para. 36.

182   In her reasons for judgment in *Doré*, *supra* note 4 at para. 38, Abella J. adds that "when exercising discretion under a provision or statutory scheme whose constitutionality is not impugned, it is conceptually difficult to see what the 'pressing and substantial' objective of a decision is, or who would have the burden of defining and defending it." Of course, in the first instance, the objective underlying the exercise of discretion would assumedly have to be identified and defended as part of the balancing of legal values that decision-makers are now expected to undertake. However, legitimate concerns about the shift in burden under s. 1 arise where there is no party defending the decision on review.

is internally structured by legal, including constitutional, limits: limits that the common-law analysis is uniquely equipped to assess in a context-sensitive manner. Abella J. therefore concludes that where the question on review is "whether an administrative decision-maker has taken sufficient account of *Charter* values in making a discretionary decision," the review will be conducted according to common-law administrative law principles.[183]

Abella J. further indicates that the exercise of adjudicative discretion affecting Charter values will generally attract deference and, thus, a reasonableness standard of review.[184] This represents a narrowing of *Dunsmuir's* presumption that decisions involving constitutional questions will attract a standard of correctness.[185] That is, the exercise of adjudicative discretion is carved off from situations in which "a tribunal is determining the constitutionality of a law, [in which case,] the standard of review is correctness."[186] We may ask here where cases in which Charter values may inform interpretation of a law (for example, as in *Mossop*) will fall.

The rationale for extending deference to adjudicative discretion is similar to the rationale for extending deference to administrative interpretations of law: "[a]n administrative decision-maker exercising a discretionary power under his or her home statute, has, by virtue of expertise and specialization, particular familiarity with the competing considerations at play in weighing *Charter* values."[187] It should be noted, however, that this understanding of administrative decision-makers as well-suited to integrating system-wide or fundamental values into their specialized areas of decision-making counters a long tradition of opinion that they are too embedded in sector-specific values or interests to warrant deference on such matters.[188] Whether there will be exceptions to the general principle of reasonableness review of adjudicative discretion affecting Charter values remains to be seen, and will depend on an analysis of the contextual factors noted in *Dunsmuir*.

Consistent with the ascendant logic of reasonableness review, the call for deference to discretionary decisions affecting Charter values in *Doré* is circumscribed by the imperative that the decisions reflect the "fundamental importance" of those values: "both decision-makers and reviewing courts must remain conscious of the fundamental importance of *Charter* values in the analysis."[189] This concern is more expansively conveyed by way of statements indicating that the central concern in reasonableness review of administrative

---

[183] *Doré, ibid.* at para. 43.

[184] *Ibid.* at paras. 3-7 and 52-54.

[185] The majority in *Dunsmuir, supra* note 1 at para. 58, states that questions involving the division of powers, "as well as other constitutional issues, are necessarily subject to correctness review because of the unique role of s. 96 courts as interpreters of the Constitution."

[186] *Doré, supra* note 4 at para. 43.

[187] *Ibid.* at para. 47.

[188] See, for example, the comments of Ruth Sullivan, *Sullivan on the Construction of Statutes*, 5th ed. (Markham, ON: LexisNexis, 2009) at 625: Most "non-judicial interpreters have little training in legal interpretation. Their focus tends to be narrow and coloured by the concerns and possibly by the biases of their own professional culture. They may have particular interests to promote on behalf of their department or agency of they may have strong views respecting the groups or problems regulated by their legislation. This may put them into an adversarial position with other interested parties." See also Margaret Allars, "On Deference to Tribunals, with Deference to Dworkin" (1994-95) 20 Queen's L.J. 163 at 204-6.

[189] *Doré, supra* note 4 at para. 54.

discretion affecting Charter values (like the central concern of the s. 1 analysis per *Oakes*) is proportionality. Abella J. writes:

> As this Court has noted, most recently in *Catalyst Paper Corp. v. North Cowichan (District)*, … the nature of the reasonableness analysis is always contingent on its context. In the *Charter* context, the reasonableness analysis is one that centres on proportionality, that is, on ensuring that the decision interferes with the relevant *Charter* guarantee no more than is necessary given the statutory objectives. If the decision is disproportionately impairing of the guarantee, it is unreasonable. If, on the other hand, it reflects a proper balance of the mandate with *Charter* protection, it is a reasonable one.[190]

Abella J. offers some further (if slim) guidance about the way in which administrative decision-makers are to "balanc[e] the *Charter* values with the statutory objectives." She writes, "In effecting this balancing, the decision-maker should first consider the statutory objectives."[191] Next, the decision-maker "should ask how the *Charter* value at issue will best be protected in view of the statutory objectives." Abella J. adds, "This is at the core of the proportionality exercise, and requires the decision-maker to balance the severity of the inter-ference of the *Charter* protection with the statutory objectives."[192] Here we may remark that the Charter values that administrative decision-makers are to identify and balance against other legal values are not intrinsically of a determinate or ranked weight. In the passage quoted, decision-makers are apparently to gauge the relative importance of (and possibilities for integration of) statutory objectives and Charter protections. But what tools are they to use in making this determination? Will it ever be necessary, for instance, to engage a formal analysis of rights-infringement on the model of the Charter jurisprudence? Will such ex-pectations vary depending on the nature of the interest engaged, the type of decision-maker, or other circumstances of the case?[193]

Where a court applies a reasonableness standard to such decisions, "the question be-comes whether, in assessing the impact of the relevant *Charter* protection and given the nature of the decision and the statutory and factual contexts, the decision reflects a propor-tionate balancing of the *Charter* protections at play."[194] As is the case at the minimal impair-ment stage of the *Oakes* analysis, "'courts must accord some leeway to the legislator' in the *Charter* balancing exercise, and the proportionality test will be satisfied if the measure 'falls within a range of reasonable alternatives' [or, per *Dunsmuir*,] 'falls within a range of pos-sible, acceptable outcomes.'"[195] To this we may add that it would be perfectly consistent with the existing law on reasonableness review for a court to quash an administrative decision for failure to take into account a Charter value that the court deems to be of mandatory rel-

---

190   *Ibid.* at para. 7 (citing *Catalyst Paper*, *supra* note 166).

191   *Doré*, *supra* note 4 at para. 55.

192   *Ibid.* at para. 56. Note the phrasing: the severity of the interference "of" (not "with") the Charter protection. This appears to connote interference of the Charter with the discretionary decision, rather than interference of the decision with the Charter (its impact on the protected interest). See note 194, *infra*.

193   I thank Audrey Macklin for urging me to raise these questions at this juncture.

194   *Doré*, *supra* note 4 at para. 57. Again notice the preposition: the impact "of" the Charter guarantee (on the decision), rather than the impact of the decision "on" the guarantee.

195   *Ibid.* at para. 56 (citing *Dunsmuir*, *supra* note 1 at para. 47).

evance to a particular exercise of discretion. Indeed this may mark an important emerging area of judicial intervention, whereby individuals who were once unable to amass the resources to force consideration of a Charter-protected interest may now find such considerations mandated or vindicated on review by way of the expectations placed on discretion at common law.

Doré may be understood as an expression of what we have been calling the romantic approach to substantive review, in its affirmation that Charter values must be fully integrated into administrative decision-making even as administrative decision-makers' efforts to balance Charter values with other legal values must attract deference on review. However, a number of questions now arise.

Abella J. states that *Doré*'s endorsement of common-law reasonableness review as the mechanism for overseeing administrative discretion affecting Charter values will not affect the potency of Charter guarantees in the affected administrative arenas.[196] For both the s. 1 analysis and, now, the reasonableness analysis centre on proportionality even as they admit of deference. Nonetheless, concerns may be raised about the implications of this shift. Abella J. draws on the precedent of *Hill v. Church of Scientology of Toronto*,[197] both for insights into the rationale for shifting to a values-balancing model and to illustrate how the values-balancing exercise may be conducted. Yet *Hill* endorses the balancing of Charter values against other legal values (instead of analysis of Charter rights infringement and s. 1 justification) in the context of a common-law action between private litigants. That is, in that case, there was understood to be no state action grounding or giving conceptual coherence to a Charter rights claim. On the side of the rationale for endorsing a values-balancing paradigm, *Doré* then suggests that the constitutional position of an administrative decision-maker exercising adjudicative discretion is less that of a government actor whose decisions

---

[196] *Ibid.* at para. 5.

[197] [1995] 2 S.C.R. 1130 [*Hill*]. This case involved a defamation suit brought by Hill (then a Crown attorney) against the Church of Scientology. The Church argued (*inter alia*) that the common law of defamation did not adequately reflect the Charter value of freedom of expression. Cory J. in *Hill* drew on *RWDSU v. Dolphin Delivery Ltd.*, [1986] 2 S.C.R. 573, for the principle that the common law is not subject to direct Charter challenge (as void because in violation of an individual's or group's Charter rights) absent government action relying on a common-law rule that allegedly breaches the Charter. Yet *Hill*, at paras. 83-91, confirms that judges must develop the common law in light of "Charter values." Cory J. indicates that this does not require application of the s. 1 framework for justifying a Charter breach; rather, what is required is a more flexible "balancing" of Charter and common-law values. In *Hill*, the common-law value of protection of reputation (which Cory J. links to the underlying value of dignity) is weighed against the Charter value of freedom of expression. In the result, the Court declines to make the primary change to the common law of defamation advanced by the Church (adoption of an "actual malice" standard), although Cory J. recognizes that s. 2(b) of the Charter may expand the defence of qualified privilege. See *Doré*, *supra* note 4 at para. 40:

> In *Hill v. Church of Scientology of Toronto* … this Court explicitly rejected the use of the s. 1 *Oakes* framework in developing the common law of defamation for two reasons. First, when interpreting a common law rule, there is no violation of a *Charter* right, but a conflict between principles, so "the balancing must be more flexible than the traditional s. 1 analysis," with *Charter* values providing the guidelines for any modification to the common law (para. 97). Second, the Court noted that "the division of onus which normally operates in a *Charter* challenge" was not appropriate for private litigation under the common law, as the party seeking to change the common law should not be allowed to benefit from a reverse onus (para. 98). As a result, the Court went on to "consider the common law of defamation in light of the values underlying the *Charter*" (para. 99).

themselves constitute potential rights-infringements than a neutral arbiter (like a judge) tasked with integrating Charter values into adjudicative judgment.[198] Oversight of such decisions will thereby not be conducted on the model of a direct Charter challenge, but rather with an eye to successful or unsuccessful integration of Charter values. Does one's comfort with this (romantic) shift in the constitutional character of administrative discretion itself shift depending on whether the decision-maker is, say, an adjudicative tribunal (like the disciplinary tribunal involved in *Doré*) or, for instance, a minister determining whether to deport a refugee to possible torture, as in *Suresh*?[199] Relatedly, are we convinced that the potency of Charter guarantees is unaffected by the shift to a model in which the breadth of administrative discretion is assessed (in the first and, in practice, typically the final instance, by the one exercising the discretion) through a relatively inchoate analysis of the relative weight of statutory purposes and competing Charter values?

A separate worry is that the values-balancing exercise endorsed in *Hill* is characterized as a less disruptive or abrupt intrusion on the integrity of the common law than a Charter rights-claim would be—that is, *Hill* stands for the incremental integration of Charter values into the common law.[200] Is incrementalism also to be the watchword in the exercise and review of administrative discretion? The propriety of incrementalism has been called into question in the s. 1 Charter context, where the importance of individual rights protections is to be privileged above administrative convenience or concerns about whether majority values have caught up with Charter guarantees.[201] Uncertainty about what if any carryover this principle has from *Hill* to *Doré* may cause one to question how much comfort the expansion of reasonableness review to encompass proportionality analysis should give those faced with executive or administrative action threatening their significant interests.

There is a further institutional dimension to the worry about whether *Doré* will promote or dilute Charter guarantees. That is, as we have seen, a traditional rationale for correctness review is to ensure consistency in the interpretation and application of system-wide or fundamental legal principles or values. The reasonableness standard, on the other hand, admits of variation among decision-makers as they select among "a range of possible, acceptable outcomes which are defensible in respect of the facts and law."[202] How much variation will be possible or acceptable where Charter values are in issue? Assuming that this itself depends on a contextual analysis, will such analysis be able to support the setting of strict limits to certain types of executive or administrative action?

---

198   The determination that judicial orders do not constitute government action for the purpose of application of the Charter is made in *Dolphin Delivery Ltd.*, *supra* note 197 at para. 36. Section 32 of the Charter states that the Charter applies to Parliament or provincial legislatures as well as the "government" of Canada and each province, thus vesting both the legislative and executive branches with a duty not to infringe Charter-protected rights.

199   *Supra* note 115. See Audrey Macklin's discussion of this point in Chapter 9, section VII, Spin-Offs, under heading VII.A, The Charter, Discretion, and the Standard of Review. Thanks to Audrey Macklin for raising this concern, which arises in part from the breadth of discretion traditionally accorded to ministers of the Crown.

200   *Hill*, *supra* note 197 at paras. 92-93 and 96.

201   See Iacobucci J.'s decision for the majority on the s. 1 issue in *Vriend v. Alberta*, [1998] 1 S.C.R. 493, at paras. 120-22.

202   *Dunsmuir*, *supra* note 1 at para. 47.

Beyond these questions relating to the potency of Charter guarantees upon their integration into administrative discretion are other significant questions about the reach of proportionality analysis into common law reasonableness review. For instance, will administrative decisions affecting important interests deemed not to engage Charter values (such as, potentially, decisions about professional licensing or entitlement to social assistance) remain subject to the traditional restriction against revisiting administrative assessments of weight? Or is there something to the criterion of "justification" imported into the law on reasonableness review since (at least) *Dunsmuir* that demands proportionality analysis in such cases as well?

In taking up selected applications of reasonableness review in the next section, we briefly examine the way that the reasonableness standard is applied in *Doré*, and so the judgment's (rather slight) illustration of how the common-law analysis of discretion in light of Charter values should proceed.

4. PATENT UNREASONABLENESS AS STATUTORY STANDARD

Controversy remains in the case law on the question of what, if any, significance should be attributed to patent unreasonableness review where that standard is statutorily mandated.[203] On one approach, following the common-law developments in *Dunsmuir*, review for patent unreasonableness admits of no distinction from reasonableness review. For to rely on the historical imperatives of restricted probing or tolerable grades of unreasonableness would invite the now-authoritative critique of inconsistency with the rule of law.[204] The contrary argument is that some significance must be given to the legislature's intention to preserve a distinct standard of patent unreasonableness. Just how the application of this standard, where statutorily mandated, may reflect both rule of law imperatives—that of public justification and that of respect for clear legislative language—remains unresolved.[205]

5. CONCLUSION: REASONABLENESS POST-DUNSMUIR

Having examined various judicial pronouncements on reasonableness review post-*Dunsmuir*, we may again ask: has the now-unified standard of reasonableness delivered workable conceptual or practical schema for guiding the efforts of judges to express deference—and, moreover, to supervise substantive legality—on review? In order to investigate our central question further, we must turn to how *Dunsmuir*'s refurbished reasonableness standard has been applied.

---

[203] See Audrey Macklin, Chapter 9, section VI, *Dunsmuir*: And Then There Were Two, under heading VI.C, Whatever Happened to Patent Unreasonableness?

[204] *Dunsmuir, supra* note 1 at para. 42.

[205] The Supreme Court of Canada did not take up the challenge of resolving or addressing these concerns in *British Columbia (Workers' Compensation Board) v. Figliola*, 2011 SCC 52, [2011] 3 S.C.R. 422. There, the Court adopted the statutory standard of patent unreasonableness from the *Administrative Tribunals Act*, S.B.C. 2004 c. 45, without comment on the complexities of applying that standard post-*Dunsmuir*. Moreover, both sets of concurring reasons applied the standard in a manner that, at least judged against the expectations of "tracking" the tribunal's reasoning, is arguably more consistent with correctness review than review for reasonableness. In this, *Figliola* arguably follows a line of examples of review of discretion that simultaneously endorse utmost deference while prioritizing independent judicial assessment of the statutory text and context.

b. Dunsmuir Reasonableness in Practice

In what follows, I suggest that review for *Dunsmuir* reasonableness has not as yet overcome the instability between the impulse toward judicial supremacy and the impulse toward judicial abdication that has historically marked the case law on deference. I begin with two judgments at opposite ends of the spectrum: *Dunsmuir* itself (offered as an example of judicial supremacy) and *Khosa*[206] (offered as an example of judicial abdication). I then turn to *Celgene Corp. v. Canada (Attorney General)*,[207] which I argue goes some distance toward exhibiting a more defensible variety of reasonableness review. The section ends with more recent case law illustrating the tensions arising as judges seek to operationalize the dictum that reasonableness take "its colour from context."

i. Dunsmuir: Judicial Supremacy in Practice?

In Chapter 9, Audrey Macklin discusses the facts of *Dunsmuir* along with the central question raised under the heading of substantive review in that case. This was whether an arbitrator's interpretation of certain statutory provisions governing the employment relationship between public servants and the government of New Brunswick—provisions located primarily in two provincial statutes, the *Civil Service Act* and the *Public Service Labour Relations Act*—was reasonable. Despite the *Dunsmuir* majority's stated commitment to deference to administrative decision-makers' field-sensitive interpretations of statutes they encounter on a frequent basis,[208] its application of a reasonableness standard to the arbitrator's decision proceeds fairly quickly to the conclusion that it was unreasonable and so an illegality. Most disturbing, as argued by David Mullan,[209] is that what appears to drive the majority's reasoning on this point is a prioritization of traditional common-law values to the exclusion of the competing values that the administrator arguably privileged in his construction of the statutory regime.

The arbitrator in *Dunsmuir* determined that the two statutes of relevance could be read so as to give a non-unionized public employee a right to inquire into whether ostensibly no-cause dismissal was in fact dismissal for cause, thereby potentially triggering a greater range of remedies than would be available under the common law of employment. According to the Supreme Court, this interpretation was insupportable. In coming to this conclusion, the majority enters briefly into an analysis of the statutory scheme, focused primarily on a term of the *Civil Service Act* preserving the common law of contract in the public employment relationship. The majority concludes that to allow a non-unionized employee to go behind no-cause dismissal would disrupt this statutory guarantee of an employment relationship structured in accordance with private law, in the absence of a clear statutory basis for such disruption.[210]

---

206   *Supra* note 23.

207   2011 SCC 1, [2011] 1 S.C.R. 3 [*Celgene*].

208   *Dunsmuir, supra* note 1 at para. 54.

209   "Dunsmuir v. New Brunswick, Standard of Review and Procedural Fairness for Public Servants: Let's Try Again!" (2008) 21 Can. J. Admin. L. & Prac. 117 at 137-40 ["Let's Try Again!"].

210   *Dunsmuir, supra* note 1 at paras. 72-76, especially para. 74.

In the face of this reasoning, Mullan asks: was the arbitrator's decision rightly construed as outside the range of reasonableness, gauged with reference to the reasoning process or the outcome?[211] Or did the decision instead fail to pass muster because of its starkly different weighting of the purposes reflected in the statutory scheme than that preferred by the Supreme Court? The arbitrator's ruling suggested a favouring of the statutorily protected employment interests of non-unionized public employees over the statutorily protected expectations (including common-law rights) of their employer.[212] To this end, the interpretation adopted arguably expanded the remedial purposes of the legislation to the furthest extent possible while, as Mullan points out, still giving effect to the terms of both statutes.[213] On this analysis, s. 20 of the *Civil Service Act*[214] (preserving the private law of employment) still had important effect—namely, the employer could continue to pursue no-cause dismissal in accordance with contract law rules of notice or pay in lieu. But where dismissal was in fact for cause, a grievance challenging the cause could be mounted despite the employer's attempt to convert for-cause into no-cause to avoid such a challenge.

Revisited in this manner, it is arguable that *Dunsmuir* might have been better decided if the normative dimensions of the reasoning—the prioritization of values or interests driving the case—had been made more explicit both at the administrative or arbitration level and at the level of judicial review. Instead, these are left as background assumptions to be dimly discerned behind the reasoning of a reviewing court apparently concerned with identifying a singular "right answer" to this interpretive problem.

ii. Khosa as Judicial Abdication: Still Battling the Weight Problem

If *Dunsmuir* stands at one extreme of review under the newly unified reasonableness standard (the extreme of judicial supremacy), the 2009 Supreme Court decision in *Khosa*[215] arguably stands at the other. In this, *Khosa*, too, forces us to reflect on the distance between aspiration and reality in the unfolding law on reasonableness review.

This case originated in an Immigration Appeal Division (IAD) decision denying Mr. Khosa humanitarian and compassionate relief from the legal consequence of removal from Canada following his conviction on charges of criminal negligence causing death. In upholding that decision on review, a majority of the Supreme Court made reference to the legal test setting out the mandatory considerations relevant to such decisions (known as the *Ribic* factors) and, in addition, closely tracked the decision of the tribunal in light of those considerations:

---

[211] "Let's Try Again!," *supra* note 209 at 139.

[212] Mullan asks whether the arbitrator's interpretation may have been one "that is more expansive in its protection of the rights of non-unionized employees, but one that is also consistent with a statutory objective of trying to achieve a satisfactory balance between the common law rights of employers and protecting the employment interests of non-unionized employees in a largely unionized workforce?" *Ibid.*

[213] *Ibid.*

[214] S.N.B. 1984, c. C-5.1.

[215] *Supra* note 23.

The majority [of the tribunal] considered that the last four *Ribic* factors were not particularly compelling for or against relief. As to the first two factors, the offence in question was "extremely serious" (para. 14) and the majority expressed particular concern over Khosa's refusal to accept without reservation the finding that he had been street racing. The IAD majority considered that this refusal "reflects a lack of insight into his conduct" (para. 15). As to Khosa's prospects for rehabilitation, the majority decided that there was insufficient evidence upon which to make a finding one way or the other (paras. 15 and 23). However, even if Khosa had good prospects for rehabilitation, "balancing all the relevant factors, ... the scale does not tip in [Khosa's] favour" (para. 23). Accordingly, "special relief" was denied.[216]

In this way, the majority of the Supreme Court adverted to the bases on which the IAD had grounded its decision to deny humanitarian and compassionate relief to Khosa. At the same time, it explicitly took account of *Dunsmuir's* exhortations to defer to administrative exercises of discretion and (in its brief reasons at the stage of applying the standard)[217] also the line of jurisprudence, which it roots in *Southam*,[218] prohibiting revisiting the weight assigned by an administrator to the factors relevant to the exercise of discretion. With these principles in the background to its analysis, the majority of the Court found no basis on which to disturb the decision of the IAD. Specifically, it stated: "[t]he weight to be given to the respondent's evidence of remorse and his prospects for rehabilitation [one of the *Ribic* factors] depended on an assessment of his evidence in light of all the circumstances of the case."[219]

Fish J.'s dissent in *Khosa* centred on his assertion that the principles of "justification, transparency and intelligibility"[220] inherent to reasonableness per *Dunsmuir* had not been adhered to by the tribunal. This assertion was grounded in what Fish J. took to be an inordinate focus in the tribunal's reasons on what it termed Khosa's "lack of insight": his non-admission of street racing in the wake of his conviction. That undue emphasis on one element of the evidence was argued by Fish J. to have effectively depleted all other evidence of its significance, in particular, evidence that was clearly in Khosa's favour. Fish J. writes:

---

216   *Ibid.* at para. 8. At para. 7, the *Khosa* majority writes:

> The majority of the IAD recognized (at para. 12) that its discretionary jurisdiction to grant "special relief" on humanitarian and compassionate grounds under s. 67(1)(c) of the *IRPA* should be exercised in light of the factors adopted in *Ribic v. Canada (Minister of Employment and Immigration)*, [1985] I.A.B.D. No. 4 (QL), and endorsed by this Court in *Chieu v. Canada (Minister of Citizenship and Immigration)*, 2002 SCC 3, [2002] 1 S.C.R. 84, at paras. 40, 41 and 90, namely:
>
> (1) the seriousness of the offence leading to the removal order;
>
> (2) the possibility of rehabilitation;
>
> (3) the length of time spent, and the degree to which the individual facing removal is established, in Canada;
>
> (4) the family and community support available to the individual facing removal;
>
> (5) the family in Canada and the dislocation to the family that removal would cause; and
>
> (6) the degree of hardship that would be caused to the individual facing removal to his country of nationality.

217   *Ibid.* at paras. 59-67.

218   *Supra* note 101.

219   *Khosa, supra* note 23 at para. 66.

220   *Ibid.* at para. 156 (per Fish J.).

While Mr. Khosa's denial of street racing may well evidence some "lack of insight" into his own conduct, it cannot reasonably be said to contradict—still less to outweigh, on a balance of probabilities—all of the evidence in his favour on the issues of remorse, rehabilitation and likelihood of reoffence.[221]

In support of this claim, Fish J. makes mention of evidence accepted by the sentencing judge following Khosa's criminal conviction, and argues that the IAD failed to justify its departure from those evidentiary findings:

The majority at the IAD made repeated reference to the denial. Toward the end of its decision, it stated that in light of Mr. Khosa's "failure ... to acknowledge his conduct and accept responsibility for ... street-racing ... , there is *insufficient evidence* upon which I can make a determination that [Mr. Khosa] does not represent a present risk to the public" (para. 23 (emphasis added)). I find that this conclusion is not only incorrect, but unreasonable. There was ample evidence suggesting that he posed no risk. The majority decision of the IAD simply disregarded virtually all of that evidence.[222]

Imputation of legal error to the tribunal based on its failure to consider—or to consider seriously—the evidence in tension with its conclusions is also reflected in the following passage from Fish J.'s judgment:

The IAD's cursory treatment of the sentencing judge's findings on remorse and the risk of recidivism are particularly troubling. While findings of the criminal courts are not necessarily binding upon an administrative tribunal with a distinct statutory purpose and a different evidentiary record, it was incumbent upon the IAD to consider those findings and to explain the basis of its disagreement with the decision of the sentencing judge. The majority decision at the IAD mentions only in passing the favourable findings of the criminal courts and does not explain *at all* its disagreement with them.[223]

In response, the *Khosa* majority charges that Fish J. has breached the prohibition on reweighing the evidence that it takes to be inherent to review on a deferential standard.[224] Here it is important to mention that the approach taken by Fish J. is described by him not as an exercise in reweighing, but rather as a determination that the tribunal's inordinate emphasis on one aspect of the evidence amounted to its ignoring the bulk of the evidence. That is, the error that Fish J. imputes to the tribunal has the character of a "failure to consider" relevant factors (or specifically, relevant evidence),[225] effected by way of an irrational preference for evidence that was not clearly probative of the central matters in issue.

---

221   *Ibid.* at para. 149.

222   *Ibid.* at para. 154.

223   *Ibid.* at para. 150 (emphasis in original).

224   *Ibid.* at para. 61 (per Binnie J. for the majority): "I do not believe that it is the function of the reviewing court to reweigh the evidence." And see para. 64: "It seems evident that this is the sort of factual dispute which should be resolved by the IAD in the application of immigration policy, and not reweighed in the courts."

225   *Ibid.* at para. 159 (per Fish J.): "To be sure, the majority at the IAD stated that even if it were to have found that Mr. Khosa did not present a risk to the public 'in balancing all the relevant factors, I determine the scale does not tip in [Mr. Khosa's] favour and decline to exercise favourable discretion' (para. 23). This sort of conclusory statement, however, cannot insulate the IAD's decision from review when the rest of its reasons demonstrate that its decision rests on an unreasonable determination of central importance, as in this case."

Khosa may be understood to confirm those statements in *Dunsmuir* indicating the importance of deference to expert tribunals in matters falling within their expertise. The majority's unwillingness to second-guess the tribunal's exercise of its broad discretion to exempt individuals from the ordinary operation of the statute (in a situation where the "margin of appreciation" may be said to be broad, in light of the traditional legislative signals supporting deference)[226] draws directly on Iacobucci J.'s strong warnings in *Southam*[227] against revisiting expert tribunals' weighing of relevant factors. However, one of the questions raised earlier, to which we now return, is whether the prohibition on revisiting weight may be adhered to—or if so, how—without coming into conflict with the rule of law concern for public justification. Fish J.'s reasons may be understood to draw on the idea, prominent in *Baker*, that decision-makers must demonstrate that they have been "alert" and "sensitive," not merely to the range of legal considerations in play but also to the weight of considerations that are of clear legal importance. *Baker* specifically requires that decision-makers be alert to the critical interests of those affected by their decisions. Might this imperative support oversight of the weight accorded to competing factors in a legal test where this is determinative of a decision affecting critical interests? This question has new traction following *Doré's* integration of proportionality analysis into reasonableness review of discretionary decisions affecting Charter values. Could the decision in *Khosa* be constructed as such a decision?

iii. Celgene: Respect for, not Submission to, Administrative Assessment of Statutory Purposes?

Let us turn to another case, this time arguably exemplary of the potential for reconciliation of concerns for deference and for supervision of legality in reasonableness review—despite the fact that the case arrived at the Supreme Court on the assumption that the proper standard of review was correctness. *Celgene*[228] involved judicial review of a decision of the Patented Medicine Prices Review Board centring on the board's interpretation of its home statute (the *Patent Act*). The disputed decision went to whether a pharmaceutical product distributed by Celgene Corp. from its base in the United States to Canadian purchasers in Canada could be construed as a drug "sold in any market in Canada." The board determined that the statutory condition was satisfied, with the consequence that the board had authority to demand pricing information to determine whether the prices were "excessive."

On the way to confirming the substantive legality of the board's decision, a unanimous Supreme Court (Abella J. writing) framed the question in issue as one of statutory interpretation.[229] While the proceedings in the lower courts had been conducted on a standard of correctness, the Supreme Court indicated that reasonableness was the appropriate standard for reviewing the board's interpretation of its home statute.[230] The ensuing judgment is arguably exemplary in its close and respectful attention to the reasoning of the Board—a matter

---

226   See the decision of the majority, *ibid.* at para. 62.

227   *Supra* note 101.

228   *Supra* note 207.

229   *Ibid.* at para. 1.

230   *Ibid.* at para. 34.

of particular importance, given that the board's interpretation had departed from ordinary principles of commercial law.[231]

Abella J.'s inquiry into the substantive legality of the decision is framed by the following remark in reference to the relevant provisions of the statutory scheme: "I acknowledge that these words may lend themselves to different interpretations. The question is whether the one selected by the Board is justified."[232] The attorney general, in defence of the board's interpretation, had argued that the words "sold in any market in Canada" were amenable to a broad, purposive interpretation, while Celgene argued that these words, and specifically the word "sold," yielded a "precise and unequivocal" meaning, indeed constituted "a legal term of art that should presumptively be given its private law, commercial meaning [that is,] a commercial contract of sale occurring in Canada."[233] In stating a preference for the attorney general's approach or, rather, in stating the opinion that inconsistency with the commercial construal of this term "does not mean that the Board misinterpreted the words 'sold' and 'selling,' "[234] Abella J. writes:

> In rejecting the technical commercial law definition, the Board was guided by the consumer protection goals of its mandate, concluding that Celgene's approach would undercut these objectives by preventing the Board from protecting Canadian purchasers of Thalomid and other foreign-sold SAP patented medicines.[235]

It is only after this reference to the board's purposive interpretation of the values animating its statutory mandate that Abella J. inquires into the legislative history and other bases of support for this construction. She prefaces this with the statement: "The Board's interpretive choice is supported by the legislative history."[236] The reasoning that follows is reminiscent of Justice Dickson's exploration of the statutory scheme in *CUPE*, in drawing on dimensions of the legislative history that illuminate the connection between the values prioritized in the board's reasoning and those identified at various moments in the enactment and reform of the statutory base of its authority.[237]

The final paragraphs of the judgment exhibit close attention to the interpretation of "sold" or "selling" relied on by the board. Here Abella J. cites the board's statements about its statutory mandate: statements identifying and assigning relative priority to the various interests or values engaged by that mandate. The passage cited starts with the board's observation that its mandate "includes balancing the monopoly power held by the patentee of a medicine, with the interests of purchasers of those medicines."[238] It concludes with an emphasis on the objective of ensuring "that the prices of patented medicines in Canada are not

---

[231]   *Ibid.* at para. 1.

[232]   *Ibid.* at para. 20.

[233]   *Ibid.* at para. 22.

[234]   *Ibid.* at para. 25.

[235]   *Ibid.*

[236]   *Ibid.* at para. 260

[237]   *Ibid.* at paras. 26-28.

[238]   *Ibid.* at para. 29.

excessive."[239] It is against this background that Abella J. affirms the reasonableness of the board's conclusion that

> in order to comply with that mandate, sales "in any market in Canada" for the purposes of the relevant provisions, should be interpreted to "include sales of medicines that are regulated by the public laws of Canada, that will be delivered in Canada, to be dispensed in Canada, and where, in particular, the cost of the medicine will be borne by Canadians—patients or taxpayers, as the case may be."[240]

Arguably, the conduct of substantive review in *Celgene* is expressive of "deference as respect for, not submission to" administrative reasoning. Like Justice Dickson's judgment in *CUPE* or Justice L'Heureux-Dubé's dissenting judgment in *Mossop*, the reasons of Abella J. draw on those of the tribunal (particularly where its reasoning departs from the ordinary presumptions of commercial law), closely considering and even amplifying the tribunal's reasoning while nonetheless checking it against the statutory scheme and circumstances of the case. In this, the reviewing court takes account of the value-laden purposive analysis explicitly driving the tribunal's decision, and concludes that this reasoning is rationally grounded in the statutory mandate.

Those keen to locate other examples of post-*Dunsmuir* deference conveying respectful attentiveness to tribunal perspectives on statutory purposes might examine the way that reasonableness review is conducted in a case discussed earlier, with reference to when and how a court might go about discerning the reasons that "could be offered" in support of a decision when those reasons are otherwise absent: *Alberta (Information and Privacy Commissioner)*.[241] Like *Celgene*, that case involved review of a decision that at first glance might strike the generalist as counterintuitive. This was the implicit determination of an adjudicator that notice of an extension of the statutorily mandated period in which to complete an inquiry could be given following the expiry of that period. In upholding the decision on review, the majority of the Court attended closely to the way that the tribunal (not the specific adjudicator, who had not been apprised of the issue as a matter of concern, but others within the administrative regime) had justified the decision. As in *Celgene*, the decision was justified at the tribunal level through interpretation of the disputed statutory provision in light of statutory purposes, as well as the practical exigencies of implementing the statutory mandate. The reviewing court exhibits deference by staying close to the tribunal's reasons while checking those reasons against the statutory framework and wider context—matters explicitly addressed in the tribunal's decision.

iv. Resurgent Tensions in (Context-Sensitive) Reasonableness Review: Catalyst Paper to Doré

I conclude this examination of how the reasonableness standard has been applied post-*Dunsmuir* with a brief discussion of some efforts to lend further specificity to the dictum that reasonableness "takes its colour from context." Earlier, we noted the statement from

---

239   *Ibid.*

240   *Ibid.* at para. 30.

241   *Supra* note 2.

Catalyst Paper that the concern for context in reasonableness review is directed in the main at determining "the scope of decision-making power conferred on the decision-maker by the governing legislation."[242] Arguably, this is precisely the sort of exercise that is undertaken (in a manner that I have suggested is consistent with "deference as respect") in the decisions discussed above (*Celgene* and *Alberta (Information and Privacy Commissioner)*). *Catalyst Paper* may, however, be said to evince new tensions between judicial supremacy and judicial abdication in the manner in which it seeks to ascertain the scope or limits of reasonableness.

Catalyst Paper involved a challenge to a municipal bylaw that imposed markedly higher property tax rates on industry compared with residents. Catalyst Paper Corp. argued that the considerations informing the difference in rates were not limited to objective criteria (such as consumption of municipal services), and that the bylaw was therefore unreasonable. A reasonableness standard was applied. In operationalizing the comments noted above on ascertaining the scope of legislatively conferred powers as an essential component of reasonableness review, McLachlin C.J. (writing for the Court) looked primarily to prior case law in which the scope and limits of municipal bylaw-making powers had been elucidated. This was necessarily supplemented by more direct attention to the statutory sources of the municipality's powers.[243]

It may be argued that reliance on case law along with independent analysis of the governing statute amounts to an overly judge-centric approach to the context-sensitive delimitation of reasonableness, reflecting an inadequate commitment to deference. And yet, as it turns out, the cases drawn on in *Catalyst Paper* reinforce the point that municipal politicians, in light of their democratic accountability as well as the broad terms in which their statutory powers tend to be conferred, enjoy significant discretion when it comes to bylaw making: a discretion legitimately informed by "an array of social, economic, political and other non-legal considerations."[244] The outcome of the case confirms the breadth of that discretion, in that the Court rejects the claim that the municipality exceeded its authority by not limiting the considerations informing the bylaw to those stipulated by the appellant.

On the way to this determination, however, the judgment takes some notable turns. For instance, among the cases on which McLachlin C.J. relies is the English judgment *Associated Provincial Picture Houses, Ltd. v. Wednesbury Corp.*[245] From *Wednesbury*, McLachlin C.J. extracts the principle that the decision of a public authority on a matter within its competence should be upheld unless so unreasonable that no reasonable authority could ever have come to it.[246] Following this approach, the chief justice states (hearkening back to the case

---

242 *Supra* note 166 at para. 18.

243 Curiously, the passages that McLachlin C.J. cites from *Dunsmuir* (paras. 55 and 57, as well as para. 64) as authority for consulting existing case law for guidance on the proper conduct of reasonableness review speak to consulting case law (or other elements of "context") for guidance on which standard to apply. See *Catalyst Paper, supra* note 166 at para. 18.

244 *Catalyst Paper, ibid.* at para. 19.

245 [1948] 1 K.B. 223 (C.A.) [*Wednesbury*].

246 This is one of three bases for review (the other two are failing to consider relevant factors and considering irrelevant factors) stated in the judgment of Lord Greene. More precisely, what has been termed *Wednesbury* unreasonableness is stated by Lord Greene, *ibid.* at 228-29, as follows: "It is true to say that, if a decision on a

law on "the wide variety of factors that elected municipal councillors may legitimately consider in enacting bylaws"):[247] "The applicable test is this: only if the bylaw is one no reasonable body informed by these factors could have taken will the bylaw be set aside."[248]

Wednesbury unreasonableness has inspired a long tradition of English case law seeking to lend specificity to its indeterminate (and tautological) content, along with an equally long tradition of criticism.[249] It is therefore perhaps surprising that this case would be unearthed in an attempt to demonstrate how a court should ascertain the limits of legality on a context-sensitive application of the reasonableness standard. Indeed, the gesture to *Wednesbury* unreasonableness in *Catalyst Paper* is arguably a chastening reminder of the morass of patent unreasonableness review, now recognized to have been an insufficiently sensitive instrument for identifying substantive unreasonableness in law.

However, McLachlin C.J. offsets the weakness of the central question from *Wednesbury* by excavating a more determinate pronouncement about the legal limits on municipal bylaws, now from an even older English decision, *Kruse v. Johnson*:

> *If, for instance, they were found to be partial and unequal in their operation as between different classes; if they were manifestly unjust; if they disclosed bad faith; if they involved such oppressive or gratuitous interference with the rights of those subject to them as could find no justification in the minds of reasonable men, the Court might well say, "Parliament never intended to give authority to make such rules; they are unreasonable and ultra vires."*[250]

McLachlin C.J. adds that a particular statutory regime may permit bylaws that contravene these common-law limits. But the primary point is that long-established case law adequately illuminates the starting assumptions in determining the scope of the relevant discretionary powers.

Catalyst Paper may be regarded as both a step back and a step forward for reasonableness review. It is a step back in pairing the flabby rhetoric of *Wednesbury* unreasonableness with

---

competent matter is so unreasonable that no reasonable authority could ever have come to it, then the courts can interfere. That, I think, is quite right; but to prove a case of that kind would require something overwhelming."

247   *Catalyst Paper, supra* note 166 at para. 24.

248   *Ibid.*

249   See Andrew Le Sueur, "The Rise and Ruin of Unreasonableness?" (2005) 10 Judicial Review 32 at 32–33. Le Sueur states the major criticisms of and proposals for common law reform of *Wednesbury* unreasonableness as follows:

> [I]t is a circular definition; it is an uncertain guide as to the extent of the "margin of discretion" to be permitted to a public authority in any given situation or (the flip side of the coin) the intensity of review to be conducted by the court; it is a cloak which may tempt lawyers and courts to deal with the merits of grievances rather than questions of legality. These conceptual weaknesses have led to proposals for the common law to recognise a number of *substantive* principles in place of unreasonableness (e.g., equality) or for the replacement of the reasonableness test with one of proportionality. [Emphasis in original.]

Dyzenhaus subjects the judgment of Lord Greene to critique of a form similar to that raised to patent unreasonableness review in *Dunsmuir* in "Formalism's Hollow Victory," *supra* note 12 at 542–48.

250   [1898] 2 Q.B. 91 at 99–100 (Div. Ct.), Lord Russell C.J., cited in *Catalyst Paper, supra* note 166 at para. 21 (emphasis in original).

what appears to be a rejuvenation of the judicial impulse to work out the limits of administrative legality in isolation from the reasoning of administrative decision-makers. On the side of the step forward, *Catalyst Paper* may be said to bring together a commitment to identifying contextual factors supportive of deference with a willingness to recognize indicia of illegality (the traditional grounds of review of municipal discretion from *Kruse v. Johnson*) that include unreasonable partiality to one or another class of interests and oppressive interference with individual rights. This may be viewed as a pre-*Doré* inroad toward incorporating proportionality analysis into reasonableness review.

If the emphasis placed on independent judicial ascertainment of the scope and limits of administrative powers in *Catalyst Paper* leaves us with a concern that review for substantive reasonableness may be tipping too far in the direction of judicial supremacy, the possibility of salvaging deference while remaining alert to the limits of substantive legality is suggested in another recent judgment, *Nor-Man*.[251] That decision involved a labour arbitrator's "creative" application of the equitable doctrine of estoppel at the remedial stage of a grievance. Again, the court prefaces its application of the reasonableness standard with a contextual analysis of the ambit of the arbitrator's discretionary powers. Its canvassing of the factors relevant to this determination is specifically attentive to the accumulated expertise of "arbitrators and academics"[252] regarding the legal principles and processes appropriate to the resolution of labour relations disputes. The factors identified include "the objectives and purposes of [the applicable labour relations statute], the principles of labour relations, the nature of the collective bargaining process, and the factual matrix of [the] grievance."[253] The question is whether the respect accorded in *Nor-Man* to context-saturated perspectives, and specifically to tribunal perspectives, on the values and the processes properly informing delegated decision making (that is, the factors of mandatory relevance to these decisions) may be extended to other administrative settings. If so, what responsibility—and moreover, what resources—do tribunals have to amass and effectively communicate those perspectives?[254]

---

[251]   *Supra* note 52. And see G. Heckman's commentary on the decisions below, "Nor-Man Regional Health Authority: Labour Arbitration, Questions of General Law and the Challenge of Legal Centrism" (2011) 35:1 Man. L.J. 63-83.

[252]   *Supra* note 52 at para. 50.

[253]   *Ibid.* at para. 60. Compare this list of factors with the forms of illegality stated in *Royal Oak Mines Inc. v. Canada (Labour Relations Board)*, [1996] 1 S.C.R. 369 at para. 68: "There are four situations in which a remedial order will be considered patently unreasonable: (1) where the remedy is punitive in nature; (2) where the remedy granted infringes the *Canadian Charter of Rights and Freedoms*; (3) where there is no rational connection between the breach, its consequences, and the remedy; and (4) where the remedy contradicts the objects and purposes of the Code."

[254]   Another case to consider for the manner in which it implements the dictum that reasonableness "takes its colour from context" is *Halifax (Regional Municipality) v. Nova Scotia (Human Rights Commission)*, 2012 SCC 10. There the Court draws on aspects of the statutory scheme (Nova Scotia's statutory human rights regime) to guide its review of the commission's decision to refer the complaint in issue to a board of inquiry. Cromwell J. (for the Court) stated, at para. 44, that "both the nature of the Commission's role in deciding to move to a board of inquiry and the place of that decision in the Commission's process are important aspects of that context and must be taken into account in applying the reasonableness standard." These contextual considerations underlie the Court's refusal to "assess the merits of the complaint," instead focusing on the reasonableness of the commission's decision to refer the complaint to the board of inquiry. See also *Mowat* (*supra* note 64), another case arising out of the statutory human rights setting and applying a reasonableness

A final example to consider, on context-sensitivity in the application of the reasonableness standard, is *Doré*.[255] We have already noted that the prospect of balancing Charter values against other legal values in the review of discretion introduces tensions between judicial supervision of those judgments (under the criterion of proportionality) and judicial abdication (arguably foregoing the prioritization of the individual right effected through the Charter analysis of rights infringement and justification).

In her judgment, Abella J. indicated that the determination that proportionality analysis is central to the review of discretionary decisions implicating Charter values is itself an illustration of how reasonableness takes its colour from context.[256] That is, the nature of the decision and importance of the affected interest inform the expectations of reasonableness (here, proportionality). On applying the standard to the impugned decision—a decision of the Disciplinary Council of the Barreau to reprimand a lawyer for statements he made in a letter to a judge—the Court determined that the decision was not proportionate in its weighing of the Charter-protected value of freedom of expression against the competing statutory value of professional civility. On the way to this determination, Abella J. considered the part of the lawyer's *Code of Ethics* that the council applied ("[t]he conduct of an advocate must bear the stamp of objectivity, moderation and dignity"), along with the public values advanced by that rule, as elaborated in academic and judicial commentary.[257] On the other side, the Court briefly took note of the fact that the Charter-protected interest in freedom of expression is engaged by the decision, while additionally citing sources of legal commentary concerning the public interest in ensuring that lawyers participate in critical discourse about the workings of justice system.[258] The implication is that these competing considerations should be reflected in the Disciplinary Council's decision. Abella J. stated: "Disciplinary bodies must therefore demonstrate that they have given due regard to the importance of the expressive rights at issue, both in light of an individual lawyer's right to expression and the public's interest in open discussion."[259]

In a single paragraph,[260] these expectations are applied to the council's reasoning. Among the key findings of the Court (made by way of citations to the council's decision) are that the council was "conscious" that application of the relevant term of the *Code of ethics* may constitute "a restriction on a lawyer's expressive rights," and that the council acknowledged that a lawyer "can suffer no restrictions when it is a question of defending clients' rights before the courts." Pitched against those considerations are a vivid set of insults drawn from the lawyer's letter (for example, the judge suffered from a "chronic inability to master any social skills" and was "pedantic, aggressive and petty in [his] daily life"), on which basis the council

---

standard to the tribunal's interpretation of (a process-oriented provision of) the home statute. But is the analysis in *Mowat*, which features a careful examination of the statutory text and context, eventuating in rejection of the apparently overly policy-infused reasoning of the tribunal, consistent with deference?

255   *Supra* note 4.

256   *Ibid.* at para. 7.

257   *Ibid.* at paras. 60-62.

258   *Ibid.* at paras. 63-65.

259   *Ibid.* at para. 66.

260   *Ibid.* at para. 70.

concluded that the "generally accepted norms of moderation and dignity" had been "overstepped." Following this brief rehearsal of the council's reasoning (and against the background of the preceding discussion of the competing legal values), the Court concluded that the decision to issue a reprimand satisfied the criterion of proportionality and, thus, the standard of reasonableness.

Judging from *Doré*, it appears that administrative decision-makers balancing Charter values will not (or not necessarily, depending on various factors) be expected to engage in formal rights analysis on the model of Charter jurisprudence, nor must they necessarily (but, again, perhaps in some cases they must) defend their decisions as, for instance, "minimally impairing."[261] What they must do is "demonstrate that they have given due regard" to the competing values engaged by their decisions.[262] Just what will be expected in the demonstration of "due regard" beyond the instance of *Doré*, and how competing considerations—such as the degree of impact on Charter-protected interests or the expertise (or parallel forms of accountability) attributed to the decision-maker—may be brought to bear in shaping those expectations, remains unclear. But, in general terms, the way that the reasonableness standard is applied in *Doré* brings together two important trends in reasonableness review:

1. supplementation of the insistence that courts "stay close to the reasons" of administrative decision-makers with an insistence that they first make efforts to ascertain the "perspective," or range of acceptable options, within which the decision is expected to stay; and

2. erosion of the once-dominant principle that courts may not revisit the weight accorded to competing factors (in particular, legal values) on review—although this erosion is, so far, restricted to adjudicative discretion implicating Charter values.

IV. Conclusion

Having inquired into the significance of the standards of review in theory and in practice, we should now understand that review of administrative decisions for substantive legality is not a simple matter of measuring those decisions against an objective standard of legal accuracy. Rather, it is about striking the proper relationships among legislatures, judges, administrators, and those affected by administrative decisions, in the common work of securing and advancing the rule of law. *Dunsmuir* marks an important development in the common law on substantive review, urging deeper reflection on the standards of review: both the rationales for and the practical implications of adopting one or the other of the now-dual standards. In particular, *Dunsmuir* has prompted renewed reflection on the meaning of reasonableness as a criterion of substantive legality and on the reviewing practices most consistent with deference. These developments may (and perhaps should) also inspire further critical inquiry into the significance and indeed the legitimacy of non-deference or correctness review.

---

261 *Ibid.* at para. 4.

262 *Ibid.* at para. 66.

Yet the path toward consensus on the purposes and proper conduct of substantive review is neither simple nor well-defined. *Dunsmuir* raises as many questions, particularly on the conduct of reasonableness review, as it resolves. That is not necessarily a criticism. As Michael Taggart has quipped, the common law "does not come with an owner's manual."[263] Perhaps, as the jurisprudence develops, the courts will identify further tools to assist in clarifying how the oversight of substantive legality may be reconciled with deference. The recent endorsement of proportionality review in overseeing discretionary decisions affecting Charter values is one example of judicial efforts in this regard.

The ongoing challenge posed by reasonableness review goes to how the commitment to deference—specifically, deference to the field-sensitivity of those with expertise or experience in areas of social practice remote from the experience of many judges—is to be reconciled with the judicial commitment to supervise administrative decisions, and more broadly, to uphold the rule of law. For many years, the jurisprudence on deference has focused on the process of review (for example, urging judges to "stay close to" tribunal reasons, rather than making an independent determination of the "right answer"). Although these principles remain vital to the project of substantive review, more recent developments in the jurisprudence have sought to clarify how judges may discern the limits of substantive reasonableness in specific decision-making contexts.

Here the romantic may welcome, in particular, the recent developments in *Doré*, whereby administrative discretion affecting Charter values is to be tested against the expectation of proportionality, even as the court's supervisory authority is to be exercised in a manner that is responsive (though not submissive) to the considerations driving administrative reasoning.[264] On the account developed herein, the romantic is concerned above all to defend the normative function of administration—that is, its co-participation in the work of lending specificity to the wider values of the constitutional order. On the other side, however, the emerging engagement of common-law substantive review with proportionality analysis may attract the skeptic's critique that this represents new inroads for the constitutionalization of administrative law: the creeping infusion of the work and oversight of administrative decision making with constitutional (in particular, Charter) norms, which, for the skeptic, amounts to an illegitimate colonization. This critique stems from long-standing concerns about the potential for individualist values to obstruct the important and, moreover, democratically underwritten public purposes animating the administrative state. Yet a further, diametrically opposed set of concerns also arise in response to *Doré*—from the side of the individual whose human rights are affected by executive or administrative action. For him or her, the concern is whether the rights guarantees of the Charter will be diluted in the course of administrative efforts to balance Charter and other legal values, and judicial deference thereto.

Will the integration of proportionality analysis into review for reasonableness, whether restricted to decisions in which Charter values are understood to be at stake, or extended to a wider class of discretionary decisions, properly be regarded as strengthening the position

---

263   M. Taggart, "Proportionality, Deference, Wednesbury," *supra* note 174 at 440.

264   Of course, it helps if (as in *CUPE*, *Mossop*, and *Celgene*) tribunals are explicit about the values and value-laden priorities driving their interpretations and resultant decisions.

of administrative decision-makers—and even more vitally, the individuals subject to administrative decisions—as co-participants in the work of public justification? In responding, one should carefully consider both the capacity (including resources) of administrative decision-makers to address proportionality in their reasoning, and the capacity of judges to express respect for administrative decision-makers' reasoning on questions of proportionality. I leave this final puzzle for the student to consider in light of the developing case law and his or her developing understanding of the proper mandates of, and relationships among, legislatures, administrative decision-makers, and courts.

SUGGESTED ADDITIONAL READINGS

ARTICLES

Canadian

Cartier, Geneviève, "The Baker Effect: A New Interface Between the Canadian Charter of Rights and Freedoms and Administrative Law—The Case of Discretion" in David Dyzenhaus, ed., *The Unity of Public Law* (Oxford: Hart Publishing, 2004) 61.

McLachlin, The Honourable Justice B., "The Roles of Administrative Tribunals and Courts in Maintaining the Rule of Law" (1999) 12 Can. J. Admin. L. & Prac. 171.

Mullan, David, "A Proportionate Response to an Emerging Crisis in Canadian Judicial Review Law?" (2010) N.Z.L. Rev. 233.

International

Dyzenhaus, David, "The Politics of Deference: Judicial Review and Democracy" in M. Taggart, ed., *The Province of Administrative Law* (Oxford: Hart Publishing, 1997) 279.

Fox-Decent, Evan, "The Internal Morality of Administration: The Form and Structure of Reasonableness" in David Dyzenhaus, ed., *The Unity of Public Law* (Oxford: Hart Publishing, 2004) 143.

CASES

Alberta (Information and Privacy Commissioner) v. Alberta Teachers' Association, 2011 SCC 61, [2011] 3 S.C.R. 654.

Barrie Public Utilities v. Canadian Cable Television Assn., 2003 SCC 28, [2003] 1 S.C.R. 476.

Canada (Attorney General) v. Mossop, [1993] 1 S.C.R. 554.

Canada (Citizenship and Immigration) v. Khosa, 2009 SCC 12, [2009] 1 S.C.R. 339.

Catalyst Paper Corp. v. North Cowichan (District), 2012 SCC 2.

Celgene Corp. v. Canada (Attorney General), 2011 SCC 1, [2011] 1 S.C.R. 3.

C.U.P.E. v. N.B. Liquor Corporation, [1979] 2 S.C.R. 227.

Doré v. Barreau du Québec, 2012 SCC 12.

Dunsmuir v. New Brunswick, 2008 SCC 9, [2008] 1 S.C.R. 190.

Newfoundland and Labrador Nurses' Union v. Newfoundland and Labrador (Treasury Board), 2011 SCC 62, [2011] 3 S.C.R. 708.

Nor-Man Regional Health Authority Inc. v. Manitoba Association of Health Care Professionals, 2011 SCC 59, [2011] 3 S.C.R. 616.

Northrop Grumman Overseas Services Corp. v. Canada (Attorney General), 2009 SCC 50, [2009] 3 S.C.R. 309.

CHAPTER ELEVEN

Administrative Discretion: Between Exercising Power and Conducting Dialogue

GENEVIÈVE CARTIER

Faculty of Law, University of Sherbrooke

I. Introduction

The Commission may cancel any permit at its discretion.

An Act Respecting Alcoholic Liquor, R.S.Q. 1941, c. 255, s. 35

The Minister is hereby authorized to exempt any person from any regulation made under sub-section 114(1) of the Act or otherwise facilitate the admission to Canada of any person where the Minister is satisfied that the person should be exempted from that regulation or that the person's admission should be facilitated owing to the existence of compassionate or humanitar-ian considerations.

Immigration Regulations, 1978, SOR/78-172, as amended by SOR/93-44

These provisions were at the heart of two of the most famous decisions ever handed down by the Supreme Court of Canada on the subject of administrative law: *Roncarelli v. Duplessis*[1] and *Baker v. Canada (Minister for Citizenship and Immigration)*.[2] They are but two examples of thousands of similar provisions in legislative as well as regulatory instruments[3] that confer "discretionary powers" (or, as they were sometimes called, "administrative powers") on executive decision-makers. The aim of this chapter is to present the state of the law relating to the exercise and review of discretion in Canada and to highlight the challenges that dis-cretion poses to the rule of law and to democracy.

Administrative discretion is not an easy concept to grasp. Generally speaking, it is associ-ated with the power of an administrative authority to make a choice between various op-tions: "The concept of discretion refers to decisions where the law does not dictate a specific outcome, or where the decision-maker is given a choice of options within a statutorily im-posed set of boundaries."[4] As such, discretion questions the view of the administrative state as a mere transmission belt between the legislature and the citizens, as the traditional articu-lation of the separation of powers used to depict it. According to this view, the executive simply "executes" the will of the legislature by putting into operation the projects developed by democratic representatives for their citizens. In practice, the margin of manoeuvre that is involved in making choices suggests that there is a space or distance between the expres-sion of the will of Parliament on the one hand, and acts of the executive on the other, so that running the government exceeds "mere execution." Discretion is exercised in that space.

If discretion gives the administrative state leeway to make decisions or adopt norms, is the administrative state governed by the rule of law?[5] In other words, is discretion a legal phenomenon, exercised in a space controlled by legal principles and subjected to judicial oversight, or is it a political phenomenon, exercised in a legal void and subjected to political

---

1   [1959] S.C.R. 121 [*Roncarelli*].

2   [1999] 2 S.C.R. 817 [*Baker*].

3   In 1975, Philip Anisman identified 14,885 powers of a discretionary nature in the Revised Statutes of Canada alone: see Philip Anisman, *A Catalogue of Discretionary Powers in the Revised Statutes of Canada* (Ottawa: Law Reform Commission of Canada, 1975).

4   *Baker*, *supra* note 2 at para. 52.

5   For the rule of law, see Mary Liston, Chapter 2, Governments in Miniature: The Rule of Law in the Admin-istrative State.

controls? Central issues on administrative discretion have precisely revolved around the question whether the space in which discretion is exercised is legally constrained or not. As we shall see, that question was first addressed through the perspective of a dichotomy between law and discretion: "quasi-judicial" decisions were based on law and therefore were legally constrained and controllable; "administrative" (or discretionary) decisions were based on policy and could not be so controlled. Over time, however, the influence of the law–discretion dichotomy was increasingly undermined, to a point where the distinction between decisions based on discretion and those based on law came to be seen as residing in the degree, not in the nature, of the constraints within which they are made.[6]

Section II of this chapter offers an overview of the role of discretion in the administrative state. It also briefly presents the positions of a number of influential academics on the question of discretion. Section III exposes the structure of the law relating to the exercise and review of discretion as it stood from *Roncarelli* to *Baker*. Section IV explores *Baker* and its implications for that part of administrative law and it also analyzes the impact of *Dunsmuir v. New Brunswick*[7] and the challenges that both decisions raise for administrative lawyers. In the conclusion, I raise the question of the relationship between discretion and democracy. I also suggest that a conception of discretion as "dialogue" might be a promising way to take up both the rule of law and the democratic challenges, although, as we shall see, it is a conception that remains vulnerable to judicial retreats.

II. The Role of Discretion and How It Was Viewed by Academics

A. The Role of Discretion in the Administrative State

Because discretion is part of the daily routine of many administrative decision-makers, understanding the role of that kind of power is a sensible starting point to any substantial analysis of the concept of discretion.

Discretion is essential to contemporary government: bringing the various legislative schemes that are put in place by Parliament down to the individual requires some measure of flexibility on the executive's part, either because Parliament cannot foresee every individual case that is likely to arise (and therefore chooses to let the executive decide in each case according to its own appreciation of the situation) or because it does not have the necessary expertise or knowledge to craft the norms that should apply in any given area of activity (and therefore chooses to let the executive adopt the norms).

1. Discretion to Decide Individual Cases

A great many statutory and regulatory provisions confer discretionary powers on administrative decision-makers, to be exercised in individual cases. The adoption of that kind of

---

[6] G. Van Harten, D. Mullan & G. Heckman, *Administrative Law: Cases, Text, and Materials*, 6th ed. (Toronto: Emond Montgomery, 2010) at 954.

[7] [2008] 1 S.C.R. 190 [*Dunsmuir*].

provision is justified by the fact that the legislator or regulating authority cannot imagine all the particular situations that are likely to arise under any given scheme, so it is impossible for them to formally conceive a comprehensive set of binding rules. Delegating discretion to decide in each case gives the decision-maker presented with concrete facts the ability to make a decision that is both adapted to that set of facts and also compatible with the legislative or regulatory scheme within which the decision-maker operates.

Baker is a good example of that kind of discretionary power.[8] In that case, the *Immigration Act*[9] required that applications for permanent residence be made outside Canada, before the arrival in Canada of the applicant. However, a regulatory provision adopted pursuant to the Act provided that the minister could exempt someone from the application of any statutory or regulatory provision, or otherwise facilitate his or her admission to Canada, if the minister was satisfied that compassionate and humanitarian reasons justified such an exemption or facilitation. When called on to decide under that provision, the minister was given the ability to take into account a variety of factual situations that, although not specifically mentioned in the statute, led to "exemption" or "facilitation." The *Roncarelli* case is another example: the Liquor Commission, the administrative authority responsible for the application of the *Alcoholic Liquor Act*,[10] was delegated the power to "cancel any [liquor] permit at its discretion." Here, the statute did not even provide any formal restriction on the discretionary power, an aspect that would be central to that case.[11]

2. Discretion to Adopt General Norms

An impressive number of statutory provisions expressly confer discretionary powers on administrative decision-makers to adopt binding rules of general application. These rules are often referred to as "regulations," but they may also be termed "bylaws," "orders," "tariffs," etc. The justification for delegating the discretionary power to adopt general norms is explored elsewhere in this book (see Andrew Green, Chapter 4, Regulations and Rule Making: The Dilemma of Delegation). Generally speaking, such a justification is twofold. First, it resides in the need for expertise, which members of Parliament do not always have, given the immense variety of fields that are subjected to state intervention. Specific ministries or administrative bodies are often better equipped for such a task. Second, it responds to the problem of time (which legislators do not have when it comes to articulating specific provisions in a number of contexts) and information (which is always incomplete and which results in the need for rule modification, which is most efficiently carried out through regulation rather than legislation): delegation of rule-making powers to the executive increases the efficiency and flexibility of legislative schemes.

The executive endowed with discretion also has implicit power to adopt non-binding rules, such as "directives," "guidelines," and "manuals." These non-binding instruments are

---

8   For the facts of *Baker*, see Grant Huscroft, Chapter 5, From Natural Justice to Fairness: Thresholds, Content, and the Role of Judicial Review.

9   R.S.C. 1985, c. I-2.

10   *An Act Respecting Alcoholic Liquor*, R.S.Q. 1941, c. 255.

11   A detailed analysis of this case will be found in section III, below.

increasingly referred to as "soft law."[12] Soft law may play various roles. For instance, when discretion to decide individual cases is delegated to an administrative authority that, in practice, confers its actual exercise on many front-line officers who act simultaneously,[13] directives or guidelines may establish non-binding rules intended for decision-makers, with a view to enhancing coherence and fairness in administrative decision making. In other instances, soft law is used to set policy orientations that are likely to determine the way in which a particular legislative or regulatory scheme will be applied (see Andrew Green, Chapter 4).

While it could be said that administrative discretion was a relatively minor phenomenon at the turn of the 20th century, the emergence and growth of the welfare state caused a dramatic expansion of that kind of power. As life became more complex and as citizens' demands for state intervention intensified, the government needed a variety of flexible tools and considerable leeway for action in order to give concrete expression to its projects. This translated into more parliamentary delegations of discretion to decide individual cases or to adopt general norms. Recent calls for a reduced role for the government did not significantly alter that trend. So to say that discretion is not only here, but that it is here to stay is pretty much uncontroversial.

What is controversial, however, is the nature of the legal regime that applies to that kind of power. To understand the evolution of that legal regime, presented in sections III and IV, it is useful to refer to the perspective and vision of academic commentators because they provide an analytical tool that helps us better understand and contrast the various trends in legal thinking about discretion.

B. Discretion and Academics

Academic debates on discretion are roughly divided between authors who associate discretion with arbitrariness and those who view discretion as an instrument that allows the welfare state to reach its legitimate objectives.

In 1885, A.V. Dicey published *An Introduction to the Study of the Law of the Constitution*,[14] in which he set out his conception of the rule of law (on the rule of law, see Mary Liston, Chapter 2, Governments in Miniature: The Rule of Law in the Administrative State). In what he describes as the first "meaning" of this concept, he affirms that citizens living in a state governed by the rule of law can be subjected to state punishment only if they have breached *the law*. Dicey contrasts *law* with *discretion*, which he associates with arbitrary power:

> [The rule of law means] the absolute supremacy or predominance of regular law as opposed to the influence of arbitrary power, and *excludes the existence* of arbitrariness, or prerogative, or even *of wide discretionary authority on the part of the government*. Englishmen are ruled by the

---

12   See Andrew Green, Chapter 4, Regulations and Rule Making: The Dilemma of Delegation.

13   For instance, in *Baker*, the discretion delegated to the minister was actually exercised by many immigration officers (by virtue of a specific provision in the statute conferring powers on the minister).

14   A.V. Dicey, *An Introduction to the Study of the Law of the Constitution*, 10th ed. by E.C.S. Wade (London: Macmillan, 1959) (first edition published in 1885).

law, and by the law alone; a man may with us be punished for a breach of law, but he can be punished for nothing else.[15]

In his view, "wherever there is discretion there is room for arbitrariness, and ... in a republic no less than under a monarchy discretionary authority on the part of the government must mean insecurity for legal freedom on the part of its subjects."[16]

Dicey agreed that the executive might need discretionary powers in exceptional circumstances—times of trouble, war, invasion, and the like. In such cases, executive discretion was acceptable because Parliament needed to adopt a statute to authorize the delegation and also because citizens could ultimately resort to the courts, which would ensure that statutory language was construed in light of common-law principles developed over time that protected the liberty of the subject. However, Dicey fiercely condemned the kind of legislative delegations of discretion that became commonplace in the welfare state. In his opinion, those delegations were problematic for two reasons. On the one hand, statutes delegating discretion were systematically framed to deprive courts of their supervisory power.[17] On the other hand, the discretionary matters that the executive was called on to decide were substantively extralegal: they dealt with "public business," which, in Dicey's view, courts were unsuited to decide. In other words, although judges were trained to answer questions of law (for example, "Was the right to freedom of expression violated by the executive?"), they were unable to settle "public business" (for example, "Does the public interest require the delivery of a permit in that part of the city?").

Dicey thus sharply contrasted law with discretion. In his view, decisions of the executive based on law (that is, quasi-judicial decisions) could be properly controlled by courts, but decisions based on discretion could not, because they dealt with public business and were therefore made in a "lawless void."

In the late 1920s, in *The New Despotism*,[18] Lord Hewart followed Dicey in condemning what he perceived as the propensity of the executive to manipulate Parliament in order to be freed from judicial control. He too denounced the legislative techniques that placed "a large and increasing field of departmental authority and activity *beyond the reach of the ordinary law*"[19] and made those decision-makers a law unto themselves.[20] Some time after Lord Hewart's outburst, F.A. Von Hayek added his voice to those who expressed the view that discretion was contrary to the rule of law. In his *Road to Serfdom*,[21] he described the rule of law as a set of principles whose ideal is the prevention of arbitrary government. He formed the view that discretion, with its absence of rules announced beforehand, prevented

---

[15]   *Ibid.* at 202 (emphasis added).

[16]   *Ibid.* at 188.

[17]   A technique that was often used to attain that objective consisted in articulating parliamentary delegations of discretion in language that sought to give discretionary decisions the force of statutes.

[18]   Lord Hewart, *The New Despotism* (London: Ernest Benn, 1929).

[19]   *Ibid.* at 11 (emphasis added).

[20]   *Ibid.* at 14.

[21]   F.A. Von Hayek, *The Road to Serfdom* (Chicago: University of Chicago Press, 1944) at 80ff.

citizens from knowing how the state will use its coercive powers and was therefore contrary to the rule of law.[22]

As a reply to those who conceived and denounced discretion as arbitrariness, supporters of the welfare state perceived discretion as an instrument of welfare. W.A. Robson, in contrast to Dicey, strongly supported state intervention and the setting up of administrative authorities. He did not view discretion as intrinsically arbitrary. For him, the legitimacy of the administrative state depended on administrative tribunals "exhibiting a ... judicial frame of mind,"[23] or a "spirit of justice":[24] when endowed with discretion, they would hear the controversies with an open mind, further only authorized purposes, and avoid being influenced by extraneous considerations.[25]

Robson agreed, however, that while the creation of administrative tribunals proved necessary in order to escape from the rigidities of the processes and methods of the law (either through the possibility to consider imponderables or through the exercise of discretion), these tribunals had to remain under appropriate legal control.[26] In Robson's opinion, ordinary courts had failed to demonstrate their ability to appropriately control administrative tribunals and authorities. On the one hand, they had developed a dual approach to judicial control that was based on what he viewed as a disputable distinction between "law" and "discretion" (courts claimed they could control the former, not the latter). On the other hand, he thought courts were unfit to deal with the realities of administrative authorities. As a substitute, he favoured the creation of a specialized court of law that, freed from the framework of an unworkable distinction between law and discretion and attentive to the particularities of the administrative state, could exercise control over all the activities of the executive.

Following Robson, W.I. Jennings expressed the view that Dicey's constitutional theory was ill-founded, so that contending that discretion was contrary to the rule of law was pointless. Jennings did not, however, argue that discretionary powers should go uncontrolled. Like Robson, he supported the creation of an administrative court, which he thought could be a specialized division of the High Court. He thought that this would circumvent the prejudices that ordinary courts had traditionally expressed against the government of the welfare state.[27] In a similar vein, J. Willis was highly critical of the judicial approach to administrative law, which he thought expressed clear hostility toward the administrative state. He was equally unsupportive of a conceptual approach, which in his view involved either a categorization of functions to be shared between the judiciary and the executive, or the adoption of Dicey's theory of the rule of law. Rather, Willis favoured what he termed a "functional" approach to administrative law,[28] one that focuses on the questions of "who is best fitted to

---

[22] *Ibid.* at 80.

[23] W.A. Robson, *Justice and Administrative Law: A Study of the British Constitution*, 3d ed. (London: Stevens & Sons, 1951) at 38.

[24] *Ibid.* at 418.

[25] *Ibid.* at 408-9, 610.

[26] *Ibid.* at 408.

[27] W.I. Jennings, *The Law and the Constitution*, 5th ed. (London: University of London, 1959) at 55.

[28] J. Willis, "Three Approaches to Administrative Law: The Judicial, the Conceptual, and the Functional" (1935) 1 U.T.L.J. 53.

exercise discretion" and "who is best fitted to control that exercise." Overall, however, and notwithstanding harsh criticism, Dicey's thinking exercised a profound and enduring influence on the way in which courts conceived of their supervisory role in the administrative state. Indeed, the law–discretion dichotomy structured the law of judicial review in various ways until *Baker*, and recent judicial decisions suggest that, even as of today, it has not entirely disappeared from the legal landscape. It is to the description of this complex evolution that we now turn.

III. Discretion from Roncarelli to Baker

Until the decision of the Supreme Court in *Baker*, the traditional approach to judicial supervision of administrative exercises of discretion operated under specific heads or grounds of review, usually grouped under the expression "abuse of discretion." This framework thus differed from that used for the review of administrative interpretations of the law, which proceeded as described by Audrey Macklin and Sheila Wildeman in Chapters 9, Standard of Review: Back to the Future?, and 10, Pas de Deux: Deference and Non-Deference in Action, respectively. This section presents the various grounds of review under the traditional approach to the judicial control of discretion, but it also analyzes the importance of *Roncarelli* on this part of administrative law and it sketches the elements that led to the fundamental change of approach elaborated in section IV.

Roncarelli is usually viewed as the pivotal chapter of the story of judicial review of discretion in Canada.[29] This decision is remarkable in many aspects, but for our purposes, it is instructive for two reasons. On the one hand, it clearly affirms that, even at the highest levels of executive action, discretion is limited by legal principles, although, as we shall see, the nature of those principles was debated. On the other hand, the set of majority and minority opinions respectively articulate two visions of discretion between which courts have been oscillating for decades. A close analysis of *Roncarelli* is therefore inescapable.

Frank Roncarelli owned a high-class, prosperous restaurant in Montreal. He sued the premier of Quebec, Maurice Duplessis, for damage caused by the cancellation of his liquor licence. A majority of judges gave judgment for Roncarelli, in light of two fundamental factual findings. First, even though the licence had been formally cancelled by the Quebec Liquor Commission, the latter had acted on Duplessis's orders. Second, the authorities had been motivated by a desire to curb what they perceived to be seditious activities of the Jehovah's Witnesses and to punish Roncarelli. A member of that sect, Roncarelli acted as a bailsman for close to 400 of his fellow members, who were arrested for illegally distributing pamphlets. Duplessis considered that in so using the money he earned with his liquor licence, Roncarelli was making an illegitimate use of a privilege that was granted to him by the province.

For Rand J., not only did Duplessis lack any legal basis for acting in the circumstances of the case, but so did the commission, notwithstanding the wording of the relevant statutory

---

29 See also the discussion of *Roncarelli* in Mary Liston, Chapter 2, Governments in Miniature: The Rule of Law in the Administrative State, and the special issue of the *McGill Law Journal*, dedicated to the 50th anniversary of the decision: (2010) 55 McGill L.J. 375-741.

provision, which stipulated that the commission could "cancel any permit at its discretion."[30] In his view, even in the case of formal delegations of apparently unfettered discretion, there were always implied limits to its exercise.

Rand J. emphasized that Roncarelli had not done anything wrong and was merely acting as a private, honourable citizen: having a religion, earning his living, and exercising his right to act as bailsman. In addition, the authorities had cancelled the licence in order to "halt the activities of the Witnesses, to punish the appellant ... and to warn others."[31] Hence, "the de facto power of the Executive over its appointees at will to such a statutory public function [had been] exercised deliberately and intentionally to destroy the vital business interests of a citizen."[32] In Rand J.'s view, however, the commission was a "public service"[33] that had to "serve"[34] the purpose of the statute and that owed a "public statutory duty" toward Roncarelli.[35] This was particularly important because the occupations and businesses that were regulated (the administration and sale of alcohol) "would be free and legitimate"[36] absent restriction in legislation. This was "steadily becoming of concern to citizens generally"[37] because an increasing number of activities became subject to statutory limitations, such as requirements of permits. For Rand J., "[i]n public regulation of this sort there is no such thing as absolute and untrammelled 'discretion,'"[38] even when the formal statutory language indicates otherwise.

Rand J. also insisted that the regulatory framework and, more specifically, the requirement of a permit had important consequences for permit holders: "[a]s its exercise continues, the economic life of the holder becomes progressively more deeply implicated with the privilege while at the same time his vocation becomes correspondingly dependent on it."[39] This necessarily influenced the way in which the cancellation of a permit could be carried out. When action was "dictated by and according to the arbitrary likes, dislikes and irrelevant purposes of public officers acting beyond their duty,"[40] administration was not made "according to law,"[41] and this was susceptible to result in the disintegration of the rule of law.[42] The following excerpt clearly encapsulates Rand J.'s approach to discretion:

---

[30] *Alcoholic Liquor Act, supra* note 10, s. 35, quoted in *Roncarelli, supra* note 1 at 139.

[31] *Roncarelli, ibid.* at 133.

[32] *Ibid.* at 137.

[33] *Ibid.* at 139.

[34] *Ibid.* at 140.

[35] *Ibid.* at 141.

[36] *Ibid.* at 140.

[37] *Ibid.*

[38] *Ibid.*

[39] *Ibid.*

[40] *Ibid.* at 142.

[41] *Ibid.*

[42] *Ibid.*

Here, the act done was in relation to a public administration affecting the *rights of a citizen to enjoy a public privilege*, and a *duty implied by the statute toward the victim was violated*. The existing permit was an interest for which the appellant was entitled to *protection against any unauthorized interference*, and the illegal destruction of which gave rise to a remedy for the damages suffered.[43]

In sum, for Rand J., discretion could not be viewed as a pure exercise of power, as an instrument in the hands of a decision-maker enabling him or her to make any decision he or she sees fit. For discretion to be legally exercised, it had to pursue legitimate purposes and take into account the situation of the individual affected by the decision.

By contrast, in his dissenting opinion, Cartwright J. took the perspective of the decision-maker as the starting point of his analysis. He formed the view that no actionable wrong had been committed through the cancellation of Roncarelli's licence. The authorities had honestly entertained the opinion that Roncarelli did not deserve to enjoy this privilege because he supported members of a group who attempted to disrupt public order, and courts could not "inquire as to whether there was sufficient evidence to warrant its formation or as to whether it constituted a reasonable ground for cancellation of the permit."[44] The specific language of the statute did not contain any guidance as to the "circumstances under which [the commission could] cancel a permit":[45] the commission, therefore, had unfettered discretion to so determine. Cartwright J. insisted that the decision to cancel the licence was an administrative, as opposed to a quasi-judicial decision, which prevented courts from intervening in the decision of the commission:

> A tribunal that dispenses justice, i.e. every judicial tribunal, is concerned with legal rights and liabilities, which means rights and liabilities conferred or imposed by "law"; .... .
>
> In contrast, non-judicial tribunals of the type called "administrative" have invariably based their decisions and orders, not on legal rights and liabilities, but on policy and expediency. ...
>
> A judicial tribunal looks for some law to guide it; an "administrative" tribunal, within its province, is a law unto itself.[46]

For Cartwright J., then, the decision-maker endowed with a broadly worded delegation of discretionary power could not be the subject of control by the courts as long as he or she acted within the limits explicitly set forth in the statute. Where no formal limits were prescribed and the delegating statute conferred entire discretion on the decision-maker, the latter was "a law unto itself."

Two observations must be made at this point. On the one hand, Rand J.'s opinion in *Roncarelli* generally stands for the proposition that discretion is limited or constrained by legal principles. However, as we alluded to at the beginning of this section, different interpretations of the nature of those principles have been suggested. One interpretation of Rand J.'s opinion is that the legal regime applicable to executive exercises of discretion lies in the

---

43   *Ibid.* at 143 (emphasis added).

44   *Ibid.* at 164.

45   *Ibid.* at 167.

46   *Ibid.* (emphasis added), quoting *Ashby et al.*, [1934] O.R. 421 at 428, 3 D.L.R. 565, 62 C.C.C. 132 (C.A.).

text of the delegating statute, read in the light of a number of principles "underlying" that text. Those principles are usually associated with interpretive presumptions aimed at identifying the intention of Parliament. A second interpretation suggests that those principles are "unwritten" principles that are a constitutive part of the legal regime of discretion and that their identification does not depend on the written text of the delegating statute but rather lies in the fundamental values of our legal order.[47] The first interpretation largely dominated administrative law in the years that followed *Roncarelli*. Two reasons might explain why. First, it was more easily reconcilable with the orthodox conception of law, positivism, which postulates that only valid positive rules, as opposed to "unwritten" principles reflective of values, are binding on judges.[48] Second, the interpretation was also compatible with the *ultra vires* rule that generally governed the law of judicial review of executive action, according to which courts would strike down excesses of jurisdiction or abuses of power, where jurisdiction or power were understood as those delegated by statute.

On the other hand, Rand J.'s and Cartwright J.'s respective opinions reveal diametrically opposed views of discretion. Rand J. focused on the perspective of the individual, suggesting a bottom-up approach to that kind of power: he insisted on the necessity to take into account the purpose of the statutory framework involved, but also to keep in mind that the exercise of public power requires being attentive to the individual affected by a decision, even when (and perhaps, especially when) wide discretion is conferred on public decision-makers. By contrast, Cartwright J. emphasized the need for public authorities to be free from legal control absent statutory indications suggesting otherwise, revealing a top-down approach to discretion. The first perspective points to the need to respect individual freedom; the second seeks to protect the public decision-maker's margin of manoeuvre. For decades, courts have been oscillating between these two different conceptions of discretion.

With *Roncarelli* as a background, we can now expose more specifically the heads or grounds of review in the traditional approach to the judicial control of discretion. Those grounds express the idea that courts will only police the legality of discretionary decisions and that, absent "abuse of discretion," they will not intrude into their merits.

A. Unauthorized Object or Purpose, Irrelevant Considerations

A number of judicial pronouncements have established that decision-makers must exercise discretion in conformity with the purposes authorized by the delegating statute. Likewise, they have held that discretion cannot be exercised on the basis, or in the light of, "irrelevant" considerations, or in failing to take into account relevant considerations. The two situations often overlap. In the first case, courts must identify the object authorized by the statute and then determine whether that object or purpose has been followed or not. Similarly, in the second case, the question whether a consideration is relevant or not is usually answered with reference to the object of the statute. These grounds of review are by far the most frequently invoked. A few examples illustrate that kind of case.

---

[47] For a discussion of the distinction between "underlying" and "unwritten," see D. Dyzenhaus, "The Deep Structure of Roncarelli v. Duplessis" (2004) 53 U.N.B.L.J. 111.

[48] *Ibid.*

In *Roncarelli*, the majority decided that the cancellation of Roncarelli's permit had been made with a view to punishing him for his religious affiliation and his action as bailsman and that this justified invalidating the decision to cancel. In *Smith & Rhuland Ltd. v. The Queen*,[49] the Supreme Court held that an administrative authority (in that case a labour board) entrusted with the discretionary power to certify a union as a bargaining unit could not exercise its power to refuse certification on the basis that the secretary-treasurer of the union had communist allegiance. More recently, in *Shell Canada Products Ltd. v. Vancouver (City)*,[50] the city of Vancouver had voted a resolution expressing its intention not to do business with Shell until that company withdrew from South Africa, then under the apartheid regime. A narrow majority formed the view that the object of the resolution was to join an international movement of boycott in order to exert pressure on the company to retreat from South Africa. As such, it did not pursue "municipal purposes," which limited the powers of the city to its territory.

B. Bad Faith

As we saw above in *Roncarelli*, Duplessis was found to have used his discretion to cancel a liquor licence with a view to punishing the licence holder for supporting the cause of members of a religious movement that was overtly hostile to the Catholic Church. This prompted Rand J. to say that "'[d]iscretion' necessarily implies good faith in discharging public duty; there is always a perspective within which a statute is intended to operate; and any clear departure from its lines or objects is just as objectionable as fraud or corruption."[51] Although Rand J. referred to bad faith, Duplessis's behaviour was also said to be incompatible with the object of the statute and also based on improper considerations.

In *Landreville v. Town of Boucherville*,[52] the city was found to have used its power to expropriate, not for a legitimate purpose, but with a view to prevent a resident from operating his quarry. While Beetz J. admitted that "the burden of proof is a heavy one when it involves establishing the commission of an 'abuse of power equivalent to fraud' and 'resulting in a flagrant injustice,'"[53] he formed the view that both the official documents of the city and the circumstances of the case established bad faith.

C. Acting Under Dictation or Influence

Courts presume that when Parliament chooses to delegate discretion to a particular decision-maker, only the latter can actually exercise it. Therefore, any indication that one acted under the dictation or influence of another person suggests that the exercise of authority was not empowered by Parliament. In *Roncarelli*, the decision-maker was found to

---

49   [1953] 2 S.C.R. 95.

50   [1994] 1 S.C.R. 231.

51   *Roncarelli, supra* note 1 at 140.

52   [1978] 2 S.C.R. 801.

53   *Ibid.* at 809.

have exercised his power under the dictation of Duplessis, which was not permitted by the delegating statute that conferred the power to decide on the Liquor Commission.

D. Wrongful Delegation of Powers

The preceding reasoning is also invoked in a slightly different way. Courts assume that discretion is bestowed on executive decision-makers on the basis of their expertise or particular situation in the administrative machinery, so that an administrative authority must exercise discretion itself without delegating that responsibility to another (except when simple matters of execution are involved, in which case delegation is possible because then the exercise of the power does not require any particular ability or expertise). Hence, in *Vic Restaurant Inc. v. Montreal (City)*,[54] the city of Montreal had adopted a bylaw that made the delivery of permits conditional on the authorization of a number of directors of service, including the chief of police. This was found to be an illegal subdelegation of the power to make a decision, because the bylaw did not provide precise norms on which the chief of police could rely, de facto conferring on him the power to make those norms.

E. Fettering of Discretion

Decision-makers cannot decide in advance how they will exercise their discretion. They must consider the particulars of each situation and make a decision on the merits of each case. Otherwise, they transform the nature of the power that was delegated to them. This kind of situation is most likely to arise in contexts where directives or guidelines are used to structure the exercise of discretion, as we alluded to in section II. If directives or guidelines are applied in a way that prevents the decision-maker from using his or her margin of manoeuvre in each case, he or she then transforms the discretionary power into a non-discretionary one. The legality of using those directives thus requires decision-makers to actually exercise discretion and to depart from the guidelines when cases demand it.

Likewise, the no-fettering rule justifies important aspects of the doctrine of legitimate expectations (see Grant Huscroft, Chapter 5, From Natural Justice to Fairness: Thresholds, Content, and the Role of Judicial Review). Under this doctrine, a decision-maker who makes declarations, promises, or engagements may create a legitimate expectation that they will be respected or honoured. Yet, Canadian courts have refused to hold decision-makers to their promises or conducts, partly on the basis that this would fetter their discretion. Only procedural rights can be obtained when a decision-maker purports to go back on a promise.

F. Unreasonableness

On some occasions, courts invoked the notion of "unreasonableness" to reinforce an argument already made on the basis of one of the specific grounds of review just mentioned. But as a separate ground of review, unreasonableness was rarely invoked because, in contrast to the notion of reasonableness associated with the control of decisions based on law (see

---

[54] [1959] S.C.R. 58.

Audrey Macklin, Chapter 9, and Sheila Wildeman, Chapter 10), the notion of unreasonableness expressed in the context of discretion was usually understood in the *Wednesbury*[55] sense of "something so absurd that no sensible person could ever dream that it lay within the powers of the authority."[56] That definition was later reformulated by the House of Lords as "a decision which is so outrageous in its defiance of logic or of accepted moral standards that no sensible person who had applied his mind to the question to be decided could have arrived at it."[57] The conditions required to make a case of unreasonable exercise of discretion were therefore very demanding and rarely established before the courts.

Among those grounds, by far the most frequently invoked was the first, which also presented important difficulties in its application. Indeed, identifying the purpose that a given power must pursue, or the considerations that are relevant to its exercise, involved interpreting the delegating statute. Given the controversies surrounding the very conception of discretion and the nature of the principles limiting its exercise, as highlighted in *Roncarelli*, judicial decisions were not always easy to reconcile in a coherent whole. This was illustrated by the periodic resurfacing of the "law unto itself" approach to discretion in the years that followed *Roncarelli* and by the tendency of courts to oscillate between the majority and minority approaches expressed in that decision.[58] For example, in *Thorne's Hardware Ltd. v. The Queen*,[59] the Supreme Court expressed the view that "the possibility of striking down an order in council on jurisdictional or other compelling grounds remains open, [but] it would take an egregious case to warrant such action"[60] and that "[d]ecisions made by the Governor in Council in matters of public convenience and [necessity] are final and not reviewable in legal proceedings."[61]

By and large, the approach to judicial control of discretion just described maintained the law–discretion dichotomy in that it expressed a form of control that differed from that which applied to decisions based on law. Recall that at the time, the latter were approached along the lines of the doctrines of "preliminary or collateral questions" and "asking the wrong question" (see Audrey Macklin, Chapter 9) thereby authorizing intrusive judicial control on the substance. By contrast, the various grounds of review (enumerated above) illustrate that discretionary decisions were approached from a perspective that sought to preserve the freedom of the decision-makers to decide on the substance and to limit judicial intervention to policing the surrounding legal limits within which such freedom was exercised.

The law–discretion dichotomy persisted even with the emergence of the politics of deference inaugurated in *C.U.P.E. v. N.B. Liquor Corporation*.[62] As we saw from preceding chapters,

---

55 Named after the famous dictum by Lord Greene in *Associated Provincial Picture Houses Ltd. v. Wednesbury Corporation*, [1948] 1 K.B. 223.

56 *Ibid.* at 229.

57 *Council of Civil Service Unions v. Minister for the Civil Service*, [1985] A.C. 374 at 410 (H.L.).

58 See D.J. Mullan, "Judicial Deference to Executive Decision-Making: Evolving Concepts of Responsibility" (1993) 13 Queen's L.J. 137.

59 [1983] 1 S.C.R. 106 [*Thorne's*]. See Andrew Green's discussion of *Thorne's* in Chapter 4, Regulations and Rule Making: The Dilemma of Delegation.

60 *Ibid.* at 111.

61 *Ibid.*

62 [1979] 2 S.C.R. 227 [*CUPE*].

the Supreme Court mandated courts to adopt an attitude of deference toward administrative determinations of law, suggesting that the latter had to be protected from systematic judicial control (see Audrey Macklin, Chapter 9, and Sheila Wildeman, Chapter 10). What came to be termed a "pragmatic and functional approach"—now the "standard of review analysis"—was used to determine the degree of deference applicable in each case. At first glance, this seemed to narrow the gap between the judicial approach to discretion and its approach to law, because courts were invited to restrain their interventions in both cases. But different reasons justified these apparently similar results.

The hands-off approach to administrative interpretations of non-jurisdictional questions of law was justified by the idea that law interpretation was not the monopoly of the courts and that, in many cases, expert, administrative agencies were just as qualified as courts, and sometimes better qualified, to interpret a statutory provision. This stance moved away from the general understanding of the separation of powers, because it implied that it was legitimate for the executive to exercise powers of a judicial nature. By contrast, the hands-off approach to discretion was precisely dictated by the necessity to maintain the judiciary in a position that was compatible with a formal view of the separation of powers. Because discretion required choices that could be based on political or policy considerations, subjecting discretion to substantive legal scrutiny was viewed as putting courts on the slippery slope of politics. Therefore, the heads of review limited the potential for intrusion into the substance of those decisions and maintained the judiciary in a position that was compatible with a formal view of the separation of powers.

Thus, in the field of discretion, the justification for restraint was not based on judicial "deference," the recognition of a legitimate role for the executive in law interpretation, but on judicial "abstinence,"[63] the necessity to keep the judiciary away from decisions that were viewed as being outside the realm of the law. Although both review approaches recognized that "unreasonable" decisions mandated intervention, the nature of the latter differed. In cases of discretion, unreasonableness was understood in the *Wednesbury* sense and did not seem to require any serious involvement with the merits of the decision because the defect it punished was to clearly appear on its face. By contrast, in the context of the review of executive interpretations of the law, *CUPE* defined a patently unreasonable decision as one that could not be "rationally supported by the relevant legislation."[64]

The law–discretion dichotomy therefore seemed firmly entrenched in judicial review of administrative action. However, another decision of the Supreme Court handed down the same year as *CUPE* paved the way for the profound restructuring of the law of judicial review that would occur 20 years later.

As explained by Grant Huscroft in Chapter 5, in *Nicholson v. Haldimand-Norfolk Regional Police Commissioners*,[65] the Supreme Court expressly stated that the distinction between law and discretion was not a reliable criterion for determining the domain of application of procedure in administrative matters. On the one hand, it was very difficult to make formal

---

63 The expression is from R.A. Macdonald, "Judicial Review and Procedural Fairness in Administrative Law: I" (1980) 25 McGill L.J. 520 at 534.

64 *CUPE, supra* note 62 at 237.

65 [1979] 1 S.C.R. 311 [*Nicholson*].

distinctions between legal (or "quasi-judicial") decisions and discretionary (or "administrative") ones; on the other hand, the focus on formal categories masked a fundamental aspect to be considered in the discussion, that of the consequences of a decision for the individual concerned. In so saying, the Court questioned the justification for using precisely this distinction for the purpose of judicial control of administrative decisions. In other words, if the difficulty (if not the impossibility) to neatly differentiate law and discretion, together with the necessity to shift the focus of the analysis toward the individual concerned, justified changing the conditions of application of procedural rights, it became increasingly difficult to maintain that distinction as a justification for exercising different forms of control for law and discretion. The tensions thus created eventually resulted in the Supreme Court's decision in *Baker*, which marked a turning point in the law of discretion in Canada.

IV. Discretion from Baker to Dunsmuir and Beyond

A. The Contemporary Framework of Analysis

The facts of *Baker* are described more fully by Grant Huscroft in Chapter 5. The *Baker* case was concerned with the legality of the minister's refusal to exempt Ms. Baker from the application of the *Immigration Act*. Such exemptions could be accorded if the minister was satisfied that compassionate and humanitarian considerations existed. One of the arguments that were made on behalf of Ms. Baker was that the minister's decision was unreasonable because insufficient attention had been given to the interests of her children.

L'Heureux-Dubé J., speaking for the Court on this particular question, elucidated the proper approach for the review of administrative discretion. She recalled that traditionally, the control of that kind of decision was limited to the specific grounds of abuse of discretion, as opposed to the review of decisions interpreting rules of law, which proceeded under the "pragmatic and functional approach," as it was then termed (see Audrey Macklin, Chapter 9). In her opinion, the traditional approach to the review of discretion, with its limited grounds of review, incorporated two central ideas. One is that the decision-maker must be given an important margin of manoeuvre when exercising discretion.[66] The other idea is that the decision-maker must nonetheless act within certain limits:

> [D]iscretionary decisions, like all other administrative decisions, must be made within the bounds of the jurisdiction conferred by the statute. … [It] must be exercised in a manner that is within a reasonable interpretation of the margin of manoeuvre contemplated by the legislature, in accordance with the principles of the rule of law (*Roncarelli v. Duplessis* …), in line with general principles of administrative law governing the exercise of discretion, and consistent with the *Canadian Charter of Rights and Freedoms* (*Slaight Communications v. Davidson* …).[67]

In her opinion, no strict dichotomy could be made between discretionary and non-discretionary decisions: decisions made by the executive could never be neatly associated with either category, because they were usually composed of a mixture of characteristics

---

66   *Baker, supra* note 2 at para. 53.

67   *Ibid.*

that prevented such a classification. Moreover, the exercise of discretion and the interpretation of rules of law could not be easily differentiated, notably because both involved making choices between two courses (action or inaction), or between various options opening up in cases of legal silence or ambiguity.[68]

The review of discretion could follow the pragmatic and functional approach, L'Heureux-Dubé J. said, because the factors it put forward to determine the applicable standard of review in any given case could accommodate the specificity of discretionary powers. This would not lead to more intervention into that kind of decision, because the pragmatic and functional approach would take into account that discretion inherently requires leeway, while recognizing that "discretion must be exercised in accordance with the boundaries imposed in the statute, the principles of the rule of law, the principles of administrative law, the fundamental values of Canadian society, and the principles of the *Charter*."[69] In the circumstances, she concluded that the minister's decision had to be reviewed on the standard of reasonableness *simpliciter* (as it then existed: see Sheila Wildeman, Chapter 10) and that, on the facts of the case, the decision failed to meet the required standard. The reasons that supported the decision showed that the officer failed to give "serious weight and consideration to the interests of the children."[70] As such, this demonstrated that it was "inconsistent with the *values* underlying the grant of discretion"[71] and therefore unreasonable.

L'Heureux-Dubé J. argued that the reasonableness of the exercise of a discretionary power conferred by Parliament depended on the words "compassionate and humanitarian considerations" and their meaning.[72] The relevant provisions showed that Parliament's intention was that decision-makers exercise discretion "in a humanitarian and compassionate manner."[73] Now, to be able to determine the meaning of those crucial words (stated differently, to determine "whether the approach taken by the immigration officer was within the boundaries set out by the words of the statute and the values of administrative law"),[74] the Court had to engage in a process of statutory interpretation, through a contextual approach. Such a contextual interpretation required taking into account the objectives of the *Immigration Act*, international instruments, and ministerial guidelines. These indications revealed that "[c]hildren's rights, and attention to their interests, are central humanitarian and compassionate values in Canadian society."[75] Therefore, a reasonable exercise of the power required close attention to the interests and needs of the children.

By applying the pragmatic and functional approach to the control of discretion, *Baker* marked the end of the law–discretion dichotomy in the domain of substantive judicial review. The Supreme Court recognized that the substance of discretionary decisions could be

---

[68] *Ibid.* at para. 54.

[69] *Ibid.* at para. 56.

[70] *Ibid.* at para. 65.

[71] *Ibid.* (emphasis added).

[72] *Ibid.* at para. 66.

[73] *Ibid.*

[74] *Ibid.* at para. 67.

[75] *Ibid.*

made subject to a control based on reasonableness. As a result, the Court moved away from Dicey's conception of discretion, because he conceived discretion as exercised on the basis of considerations that were not part of the law, and therefore impossible to control judicially. The approach put forward by the Court in *Baker* is much closer to the perspective endorsed by Robson, Jennings, and Willis, who had emphasized the difficulty of differentiating decisions on the basis of their discretionary or non-discretionary content and the need to confer the control of administrative decisions to institutions attentive to the distinctive features of public administration.[76] The pragmatic and functional approach aimed at the same objective. In other words, if it was not possible to clearly differentiate in any given case discretion from law, the differentiation could not be the basis for the determination of the approach to judicial review.

In addition, the *Baker* case softened the dichotomy between procedure and substance. The Court not only required that reasons be given for decisions having important consequences for the individuals concerned, but also required that those reasons demonstrate that the decision made was sensitive and attentive to the situation of those individuals. *Baker* thus recognized that procedure may affect the substance of the decision.[77] More generally, *Baker* is in line with the decision of the Supreme Court in *Nicholson*,[78] which shifted the starting point for determining the legality of executive action, from the nature of the power to the consequences of the exercise of that power on the individual. This is clear from the rationale put forward by the Court for imposing a duty to give reasons on decision-makers endowed with extensive discretionary powers:

> The profound importance of [a humanitarian and compassionate] decision to those affected ... militates in favour of a requirement that reasons be provided. It would be unfair for a person subject to a decision such as this one, which is so critical to their future not to be told why the result was reached.[79]

Therefore, the duty to give reasons does not depend on the kind of power that is exercised by the executive, but rather on the consideration that the dignity of the individual requires that he or she be told why a decision that is critical to his or her future was made.

Baker thus moves closer to a conception of discretion as exercised in a "space controlled by law,"[80] as opposed to a conception of discretion as inherently political or giving the executive "free reign within legal limits."[81]

As explained by Audrey Macklin and Sheila Wildeman (see Chapters 9 and 10), the Supreme Court's decision in *Dunsmuir* reassessed the approach to be taken to judicial review of decisions of administrative decision-makers generally. On the one hand, *Dunsmuir* said

---

76   For further details, see text under section II.B, "Discretion and Academics," above.

77   Further discussion of this argument will be found in D. Dyzenhaus & E. Fox-Decent, "Rethinking the Process/Substance Distinction: Baker v. Canada" (2001) 51 U.T.L.J. 193.

78   *Supra* note 65.

79   *Baker, supra* note 2 at para. 43.

80   Dyzenhaus & Fox-Decent, *supra* note 77 at 218.

81   *Ibid.* at 204.

that there ought to be only two standards of review: correctness and reasonableness. On the other hand, to identify the applicable standard, one must first determine whether it has already been established in a satisfactory manner in the jurisprudence. Only if no standard of review has been so established will one need to use the "standard of review analysis," a substitute for the "pragmatic and functional approach," to identify the proper level of deference in a given case. In regard to the review of discretion more specifically, *Dunsmuir* does not depart from *Baker's* general orientation: both questions of law and of discretion are to be reviewed under the same approach. *Dunsmuir* does, however, clearly indicate that questions of discretion "generally attract a standard of reasonableness"[82] and that "deference will usually apply automatically"[83] to that kind of decision.

As the following section illustrates, while *Baker* and *Dunsmuir* set aside the distinction between law and discretion for the purpose of determining the approach to judicial review, they do not completely eliminate the challenges involved in that part of administrative law.

B. The Challenges

1. What Is Left of the Previous Approach?

Baker left us with the difficult question of the remaining role of the categories or heads of review that characterized the traditional "abuse of discretion" approach. This question emerges because *Baker* suggests that those heads of review still have a role to play: recall that "discretion must still be exercised ... in line with general principles of administrative law governing the exercise of discretion."[84] Those principles very probably refer to the grounds for review described in the preceding section. How, then, can we reconcile the standard of review analysis with the necessity to ensure the conformity of executive exercises of discretion with those distinct grounds?

As suggested by David Mullan,[85] one might think that those among the previous grounds of review that rely in large part on questions of fact (bad faith, wrongful delegation of power, acting under dictation, or fettering of discretion), are unaffected by that approach. However, the grounds more closely related to an exercise of statutory interpretation (such as unauthorized object or purpose, irrelevant considerations, or reasonableness) might need to be approached in conformity with the appropriate standard of review. In more concrete terms, this could mean that reviewing courts will be called on to intervene only if it was unreasonable (because *Dunsmuir* suggests that this would very probably be the applicable standard in the case of discretion) for a decision-maker to have considered X or Y as a relevant or irrelevant factor, or to have considered X or Y to be the object or purpose of the statute. This is suggested by the following passage of L'Heureux-Dubé J.: "deferential standards of review

---

82 *Dunsmuir, supra* note 7 at para. 51.

83 *Ibid.* at para. 53.

84 *Baker, supra* note 2 at para. 53.

85 D.J. Mullan, "Deference from Baker to Suresh—Interpreting Conflicting Signals" in D. Dyzenhaus, ed., *The Unity of Public Law* (Oxford: Hart Publishing, 2004) 21 at 24ff.

may give substantial leeway to the discretionary decision-maker in determining the 'proper purpose' or 'relevant considerations' involved in making a given determination."[86]

This aspect of *Baker* has not been clearly settled by the Supreme Court, but there are indications courts will not easily give up on determining those elements based on what seems to be a correctness standard. Three examples will illustrate that point. In *Lake v. Canada (Minister of Justice)*,[87] LeBel J., speaking for the Court, seems to be saying that the question whether a particular consideration is a relevant factor to the decision to extradite or not is for the Court to decide on a correctness standard (in this case, the consideration that the appellant had already been convicted), while it was for the minister of justice to determine, on a standard of reasonableness, if the factor was met in that particular case.[88] In *Montréal (City) v. Montreal Port Authority*,[89] LeBel J., again speaking for the Court, said that the exercise of discretion by the authority was based on an interpretation of the relevant statute and regulations that was fundamentally flawed[90] and "contrary to the[ir] objective,"[91] suggesting that the determination of the object or purpose of the statute was for the Court to make on a correctness standard. In *Kane v. Canada (Attorney General)*,[92] Evans J. found that a decision of the Public Service Staffing Tribunal was unreasonable because it failed to consider a relevant, although not mandatory, consideration. Stratas J., dissenting, expressed the view that Evans J.'s approach had been set aside in *Baker* and *Dunsmuir*, and that the question whether a consideration was relevant or not was for the tribunal to decide on a standard of reasonableness, not for the Court. The Supreme Court granted leave to appeal,[93] and it is to be hoped that it will shed light on the precise impact of *Baker* on that account.

2. The Level of Deference

Dunsmuir raises questions more directly related to the relevance and impact of the standard of correctness in judicial review of discretionary decisions. Recall that in *Baker*, L'Heureux-Dubé J. said that discretion "must still be exercised in a manner that is within *a reasonable interpretation of the margin of manoeuvre contemplated by the legislature*."[94] *Dunsmuir*'s clear indication that questions of discretion will generally be reviewed on a standard of reasonableness is compatible with that aspect of *Baker*. Hence, in *Montreal Port Authority*, LeBel J., after highlighting the discretionary nature of the decision-making power of the authority, said that this "resolves the question of the appropriate standard of review"[95] as being reasonableness. However, Supreme Court pronouncements indicate that the discretionary nature

---

86   *Baker, supra* note 2 at para. 56.

87   [2008] 1 S.C.R. 761 [*Lake*].

88   *Ibid.* at paras. 43 and 45.

89   [2010] 1 S.C.R. 427 [*Montreal Port Authority*].

90   *Ibid.* at para. 40.

91   *Ibid.* at 42.

92   2011 FCA 19.

93   December 1, 2011: (2 December 2011) *S.C.C. Bulletin* 1775, LeBel, Fish, and Cromwell JJ.

94   *Baker, supra* note 2 at para. 53 (emphasis added).

95   *Montreal Port Authority, supra* note 89 at para. 36.

of the decision is not necessarily the determining factor for the identification of the standard of review. In fact, the "interpretation of the margin of manoeuvre" inherent in exercises of discretion may also be viewed either as implying the interpretation of the home statute—which *Dunsmuir* says is to be reviewed on a standard of reasonableness[96]—or as involving a "true question of jurisdiction"—to be reviewed on a standard of correctness.[97] For example, in *Smith v. Alliance Pipeline Ltd.*,[98] the majority of the Court affirmed that the question whether the Arbitration Committee had the authority to determine the nature and amount of the costs that could be awarded in the context of the disputes it was called to settle was a question involving the interpretation of its home statute, hence calling for the standard of reasonableness.[99] By contrast, in *ATCO Gas & Pipeline Ltd. v. Alberta (Energy & Utilities Board)*,[100] the statute allowed the board to impose "any additional conditions that [it] considers necessary in the public interest."[101] For Binnie J., the question what is necessary in the public interest is "for the Board to decide."[102] On the contrary, Bastarache J., writing for the majority, was of the view that this was a question going to jurisdiction, which was for the court to decide on a standard of correctness.

Because these situations are not easily differentiated, there may be reasons for concern as to the level of deference that is likely to be applied by the courts on judicial review of discretion under the contemporary approach. The recent decision of the Supreme Court in *Alberta (Information and Privacy Commissioner) v. Alberta Teachers' Association*,[103] which questions the relevance of the category of "true questions of jurisdiction" in the standard of review analysis, points to future developments that might simplify the issue, at least in cases like *ATCO*.

As this chapter was going to press, the Supreme Court handed down *Doré v. Barreau du Québec*,[104] a judgment that raises the question of the applicable standard of review of discretionary decisions challenged on the basis of Charter arguments (on this question, see, generally, Evan Fox-Decent and Alexander Pless, Chapter 12, The Charter and Administrative Law: Cross-Fertilization or Inconstancy?). Speaking for a unanimous Court, Abella J. writes that the Charter framework—the *Oakes* test developed under s. 1—is inappropriate in the case of judicial challenges to administrative decisions as applied to individual cases, as opposed to "a law or other rule of general application."[105] For those individual cases, the Court points to a proportionality inquiry that would "integrat[e] the spirit of s. 1 into judicial review."[106] Moreover, while there were clear indications in the case law that administrative

---

[96] *Dunsmuir, supra* note 7 at para. 54.

[97] *Ibid.* at para. 59.

[98] [2011] 1 S.C.R. 160 [*Smith*].

[99] *Ibid.* at paras. 28-29.

[100] [2006] 1 S.C.R. 140 [*ATCO*].

[101] *Ibid.* at para. 89.

[102] *Ibid.*

[103] 2011 SCC 61.

[104] 2012 SCC 12.

[105] *Ibid.* at para. 39.

[106] *Ibid.* at para. 57.

decisions dealing with Charter arguments were to be reviewed on a standard of correctness, in *Doré* the Court indicates that the standard of reasonableness is more appropriate in such a context, because "[e]ven where Charter values are involved, the administrative decision-maker will generally be in the best position to consider the impact of the relevant Charter values *on the specific facts of the case*."[107] The full impact of the decision still needs to be assessed.[108]

3. To "Reweigh" or Not to "Reweigh"

Recall that, in *Baker*, the Court formed the view that a number of elements (the purposes of the legislation, administrative guidelines, and the international *Convention on the Rights of the Child*[109]) pointed to the interests of Baker's children as an important element to be taken into account in the decision to deport her or not. On the facts of the case, the Court found that the decision-maker had failed to give "serious weight and consideration to the interests of the children."[110] In so concluding, the Court clearly suggested that the evaluation of the reasonableness of the decision to deport Baker included the evaluation of the "weight" that had been given to a consideration that was viewed particularly relevant to the decision: the interests of Baker's children. During the months that followed *Baker*, that aspect of the decision became the focus of judicial debate and academic discussion: when called on to review the validity of any given exercise of discretion, can the reviewing court "reweigh" the considerations that were taken into account by the decision-maker? In *Suresh v. Canada (Minister of Citizenship and Immigration)*,[111] the Supreme Court clearly said no: the authority required to "weigh" the relevant considerations in *Baker* was the minister, not the reviewing court:

> *Baker* does not authorize courts reviewing decisions on the discretionary end of the spectrum to engage in a new weighing process, but draws on an established line of cases concerning the failure of ministerial delegates to consider and weigh implied limitations and/or patently relevant factors.[112]

Reviewing courts must therefore limit themselves to ensuring that only relevant considerations have been taken into account; weighing is for the decision-maker alone.

The Supreme Court has reaffirmed this position on a number of occasions. For example, in *Lake*, the Court said that the minister "is in the best position to determine whether the factors weigh in favour or against extradition"[113] and that the "reviewing court's role is not

---

107   *Ibid.* at para. 54 (emphasis in the original).

108   See Sheila Wildeman, Chapter 10, Pas de Deux: Deference and Non-Deference in Action, for an overview of some of the most difficult issues raised by *Doré* in relation to the general question of deference.

109   Can. T.S. 1992, No. 3.

110   *Baker, supra* note 2 at para. 65.

111   [2002] 1 S.C.R. 3 [*Suresh*].

112   *Ibid.* at para. 37.

113   *Lake, supra* note 87 at para. 41.

to re-asses the relevant factors."[114] In *Canada (Citizenship and Immigration) v. Khosa*,[115] Fish J., dissenting, would have invalidated the decision of the Immigration Appeal Division denying special, discretionary relief from a removal order, because it was based on a factor that could not reasonably be said to "outweigh, on a balance of probabilities—all of the evidence"[116] in the applicant's favour. However, the majority disagreed: reweighing was not the function of the reviewing court.[117]

One can of course wonder how this is any different from the pre-*Baker* era: as we saw from the various heads of review that were used to control discretion, courts were limited to just that same role. Moreover, if we accept that discretion is not intrinsically different from law, as *Baker* indicates, then discretion should be subjected to a form of control that permits an evaluation of the reasonableness of the decision. Now, since the difference between a reasonable and an unreasonable decision sometimes depends on the relative importance, or weight, given to the relevant considerations at play, it is difficult to reconcile the principles established in *Baker* with the position in *Suresh*, *Lake*, and *Khosa*, according to which reviewing courts must not "reweigh" the considerations at play.

It is interesting to compare these decisions with *Németh v. Canada (Justice)*,[118] which adopts a different perspective, closer to *Baker*'s teachings. In that decision, the Court criticized the minister's decision in a case related to the surrender for extradition of a refugee. The Court agreed that the relevant statute set out mandatory grounds for refusing surrender for extradition and that those grounds had to "be considered as a whole."[119] However, in the Court's view, the minister "*failed to give sufficient weight* or scope to Canada's *non-refoulement* obligations."[120] Such a conclusion is clearly at odds with *Suresh*, *Lake*, and *Khosa*, but it will take some time to assess the extent to which it signals a real shift toward the *Baker* view.

V. Conclusion

No one today denies the central, indeed, the necessary role played by discretion in the day-to-day functioning of the administrative state. Discretion allows the administrative state the flexibility that is required in order either to make individual decisions adapted to particular situations, or to conceive general, regulatory norms that will structure the way in which a particular legislative scheme is to be concretized. As we saw, however, the proper place of discretion within a state governed by the rule of law is not easy to find. From *Roncarelli* to *Baker*, courts oscillated between a view of discretion as governed by politics and one governed by legal principles. The latter now seems formally recognized by the judiciary, but as

---

[114]   *Ibid.*

[115]   [2009] 1 S.C.R. 339 [*Khosa*].

[116]   *Ibid.* at para. 149.

[117]   *Ibid.* at paras. 61, 64, and 66.

[118]   [2010] 3 S.C.R. 281 [*Németh*].

[119]   *Ibid.* at para. 58.

[120]   *Ibid.* (emphasis added).

we saw from the preceding analysis of recent case law, the concrete application of such a view of discretion presents important challenges that the courts have not entirely overcome.

In addition to its complex relationship with the rule of law, discretion questions democracy. Simply put, if executive decision-makers define the norms according to which individual cases are to be decided, or simply make individual decisions in the absence of formal legislative norms, can we say that discretion is compatible with democratic values? It is my contention that a particular conception of discretion, termed "discretion as dialogue," as opposed to a conception of "discretion as power," is likely to take up both the challenge of the rule of law and the challenge of democracy. In what follows, and by way of conclusion, I briefly advance this conception for further thought.

As I suggested at the beginning of section III, courts have been oscillating between two different conceptions of discretion at least since *Roncarelli*. I term these contrasting conceptions as "dialogue" and "power." When conceived as the former, administrative discretion must be approached from a bottom-up perspective and thought of as a dialogue[121] between the individual affected by the decision and the public authority making that decision. The exercise of discretion is here viewed as triggering a process of communication between the decision-maker and the individual concerned, in a way that prevents the former from unilaterally imposing its decision on the latter. Dialogue builds primarily on a bottom-up approach to discretionary power and seeks to foster a reciprocal relationship between the decision-maker and the individual. The distinctive features of a conception of discretion as dialogue relate to the content of the communication that it involves and to the effect that the dialogue produces on the outcome of the decision-making process. As to the content, it first allows the individual to expose the particularities of his or her situation and requires the decision-maker to demonstrate openness and listening. Second, it requires the parties to transcend their particular position in order to deliberate on the norms and values that should govern the exercise of discretion. The effect of the dialogue is essentially to narrow the range of outcomes that a decision-maker is legally entitled to reach, because the decision must be responsive to the dialogue that preceded it.

This notion of "discretion as dialogue" is different from what I term "discretion as power" — that is, discretion exercised from a top-down perspective or as a "one-way projection of authority,"[122] where discretionary powers are seen as "direct descendants of what were once considered to be unreviewable or unjusticiable executive prerogatives."[123]

In *Roncarelli*, Rand J. set the stage for a conception of discretion as dialogue that sharply contrasted to Cartwright J.'s view of discretion as an exercise of power, unchallengeable in courts, except when the statute explicitly indicates that such a challenge is authorized. In my view, discretion should be conceived as a dialogue for two reasons.

---

121 This expression has been used by J. Handler and L. Sossin. See J. Handler, "Dependent People, the State, and the Modern/Postmodern Search for the Dialogic Community" (1988) 35 U.C.L.A. L. Rev. 999; and L. Sossin, "The Politics of Discretion: Towards a Critical Theory of Public Administration" (1993) 36 Can. Pub. Adm. 364. But Handler and Sossin focus on cases involving vulnerable people, while I contend that dialogue applies to every exercise of discretion.

122 L.L. Fuller, *The Morality of Law*, rev. ed. (New Haven, CT: Yale University Press, 1969) at 191-95, 204, 209.

123 D. Dyzenhaus, "Introduction" in D. Dyzenhaus, ed., *The Unity of Public Law*, *supra* note 85 at 2.

First, dialogue best explains the development that has occurred in administrative law over the past 30 years. More specifically, it explains why courts have been willing to impose procedural obligations on decision-makers exercising discretion (for example, *Nicholson*) and also an obligation to justify their decisions through a duty to give reasons when the decision has important effects on an individual (for example, *Baker*). Such findings can hardly be reconciled with a view of discretion as power, because such a view posits that the decision-maker is free to impose the decision as he or she sees fit from his or her point of view.

Second, discretion as dialogue not only explains but also justifies the evolution of the law of discretion, because it suggests how discretion is compatible with both the rule of law and democracy. On the one hand, discretion as dialogue, through its requirement of justification, places executive action within the realm of the rule of law through participation and accountability. On the other hand, by creating venues for communication and deliberation, discretion as dialogue allows the individual to participate in the articulation of the norms that will be applied to him or her and substantiates the democratic value of public action. In concrete terms, this could translate in the following way. Suppose that the associate dean of the Faculty of Law has discretion to make changes to the course schedule, but those changes are only made on request and for good reasons. Discretion as dialogue requires the associate dean to listen to the student asking for a change, and also allows the student to express what he or she sees as good reasons in general for agreeing to those requests. As a result, not only does the student expose his or her particular case, but also participates in the articulation of the norms that might guide the decision-maker in treating the request.

The question whether dialogue is likely to impose itself as the background metaphor in the years to come is not an easy one to answer. Three considerations may give reasons for concern. First, while *Baker* clearly put aside the view of discretion as exercised in a legal void, there is still considerable judicial resistance to assessing the substance of discretionary decisions on a standard of reasonableness that goes beyond absurdity or arbitrariness. The refusal (*Németh* excepted) to "reweigh" the factors supporting an administrative decision is one indication of that judicial attitude. Second, a recent decision of the Supreme Court clearly points to a reintroduction of the process/substance distinction in administrative law.[124] That distinction, which *Baker* had considerably weakened, threatens the justification for dialogue, because it does not recognize that processes may affect substance, making individual participation considerably less valuable. Third, when governments are overly sensitive to questions of national security and emergency, as they are now, temptations are great to fall back on a view of discretion that moves away from considerations of participation and accountability.[125] We are never far away from reverting to discretion as a "law unto itself." It is my contention, however, that to have at least a clear view of the competing articulations of discretion at play in these troubled times is the best weapon to protect individual liberty, democracy, and the rule of law.

---

[124]   *Newfoundland and Labrador Nurses' Union v. Newfoundland and Labrador (Treasury Board)*, 2011 SCC 62.

[125]   On the challenges that those preoccupations present for administrative law, see Craig Forcese, Administering Security: The Limits of Administrative Law in the National Security State, available online at <adminlawincontext.emp.ca.>.

SUGGESTED ADDITIONAL READINGS

BOOKS AND ARTICLES

Cartier, G., "Administrative Discretion and the Spirit of Legality: From Theory to Practice," (2009) 24 C.J.L.S. 313.

Cartier, G., "Administrative Discretion as Dialogue: A Response to John Willis (or: From Theology to Secularization)" (2005) 55 U.T.L.J. 629.

Dyzenhaus, D., "The Deep Structure of Roncarelli v. Duplessis" (2004) 53 U.N.B.L.J. 111.

Mullan, D.J., "Deference from Baker to Suresh and Beyond—Interpreting Conflicting Signals" in D. Dyzenhaus, ed., *The Unity of Public Law* (Oxford: Hart Publishing, 2004) 21.

CASES

Baker v. Canada (Minister for Citizenship and Immigration), [1999] 2 S.C.R. 817.

Lake v. Canada (Minister of Justice), [2008] 1 S.C.R. 761.

Montréal (City) v. Montreal Port Authority, [2010] 1 S.C.R. 427.

Németh v. Canada (Justice), [2010] 3 S.C.R. 281.

Roncarelli v. Duplessis, [1959] S.C.R. 121.

Smith v. Alliance Pipeline Ltd., [2011] 1 S.C.R. 160.

Suresh v. Canada (Minister for Citizenship and Immigration), [2002] 1 S.C.R. 3.

The Charter and Administrative Law: Cross-Fertilization or Inconstancy?

EVAN FOX-DECENT*
Faculty of Law, McGill University

ALEXANDER PLESS**
Department of Justice, Government of Canada

*   We are indebted to Colleen Flood, Robert Leckey, Mary Liston, Sara Gauthier, and Lorne Sossin for valuable comments and suggestions.

** The views expressed in this chapter are my own and do not necessarily reflect those of my employer the Department of Justice or the Attorney General of Canada. I am indebted to Evan Fox-Decent for the invitation to contribute to this chapter and to Elisabeth, Oscar, Emma, Ollie and my parents, for their patience and inspiration.

I. Introduction

Armed with an understanding of how courts treat both substantive and procedural review of administrative decisions from Chapters 5, 9, 10, and 11, it is now necessary to examine how the court's approach changes when an administrative decision appears to engage a Charter protected right. The relationship between administrative law and the Charter is complex and still unfolding. If a decision touches a Charter right, front-line decision-makers and reviewing courts alike determine the requirements of legality using the Charter, administrative law principles, or some combination of the two. There is an emerging consensus that the Charter does not replace the common law, but rather embodies and supplements fundamental legal principles contained within it.

This chapter sets out various ways in which judicial review at common law has influenced understandings of the Charter, as well as the manner in which the Charter has influenced review of administrative decisions when a Charter right is clearly at stake. As we shall see, the influence runs in both directions and has significant implications for judicial review of both the procedure and substance of administrative action. In the realm of procedure, the courts rely on the common-law doctrine of procedural fairness to interpret the principles of fundamental justice set out in s. 7 of the Charter.[1] Until recently, when courts reviewed the substance, rather than the procedural aspects, of a decision that engages a Charter right, they tended to review the decision using the analytical framework developed in *R. v. Oakes*[2] to test the validity of the legislation. Now they suggest an administrative law approach adapted to consider Charter values. Taken together, the general features of the relationship between Charter jurisprudence and administrative law suggest that each is porous and open-textured to the other. Put generously, the relationship between the Charter and administrative law exhibits a cross-fertilization of principles and approaches that inform judicial review of administrative action. Put somewhat less generously, in the relevant cases, the courts have yet to develop a consistent framework for determining when they will decide the merits with resort to the Charter rather than administrative principles (or administrative principles plus the Charter), leaving litigants no practical option but to argue both.

This chapter has three main sections: sections II, III, and IV. Section II explores the relationship between the common-law duty of procedural fairness and the principles of fundamental justice found in s. 7 of the Charter. In section III we examine the different approaches courts have used to review decisions when a Charter right is at issue. Section III refers to ideas and concepts developed at common law, so it is best to read Audrey Macklin, Chapter 9, Standard of Review: Back to the Future?, and Sheila Wildeman, Chapter 10, Pas de Deux: Deference and Non-Deference in Action, on common-law substantive review prior to reading section III.

A further and separate issue raised by the advent of the Charter is whether administrative tribunals and agencies have jurisdiction to apply the Charter to their enabling statutes. The issue is controversial because administrative bodies, as creatures of statute belonging to

---

1   *Canadian Charter of Rights and Freedoms*, part I of the *Constitution Act, 1982*, being Schedule B to the *Canada Act 1982* (U.K.), 1982, c. 11 [the Charter].

2   [1986] 1 S.C.R. 103 [*Oakes*].

the executive, are not normally viewed as having authority to refuse to apply the very legislation the legislature has entrusted them to implement. Nonetheless, the Supreme Court has affirmed that the Charter is "not some holy grail which only judicial initiates of the superior courts may touch,"[3] and has found that agencies may have jurisdiction to apply the Charter if they have authority to decide questions of law. Section IV discusses the legal basis and practical effects of agency jurisdiction over the Charter.

II. Procedural Fairness and the Principles of Fundamental Justice

As discussed by Grant Huscroft in Chapter 5, From Natural Justice to Fairness: Thresholds, Content, and the Role of Judicial Review, the duty of procedural fairness in administrative law requires decision-makers to provide a fair hearing to individuals subject to their authority. And, as Laverne Jacobs discusses in Chapter 8, Caught Between Judicial Paradigms and the Administrative State's Pastiche: "Tribunal" Independence, Impartiality, and Bias, at a minimum, this usually means that front-line decision-makers must hear the other side and decide the matter before them impartially and independently. The duty does not mean that the individual must receive an oral hearing (very often written submissions are enough), but the individual must receive notice of the proceedings and have a full and fair opportunity to respond to the facts and contentions on which the decision-maker may ultimately rely. Implicit in the duty to hear the other side is a duty to disclose all facts and contentions, barring considerations such as privacy and national security, which may justify non-disclosure. In some cases the individual may have a right to legal counsel. These safeguards are frequently referred to as participatory rights, and they apply prior to the decision. If the decision affects an important interest, such as continued residency in Canada, the decision-maker owes the individual reasons for the decision. The duty to give reasons applies after the decision has been made.

In addition to the duty of fairness that applies at common law to a vast array of public entities—probably any entity that exercises or purports to exercise statutory powers[4]—a duty of fairness may also be owed under the Charter. The class of entities to which the Charter applies may be narrower than those captured by the common-law duty of fairness. Where the Charter does apply, the duties are considerable.[5] What does the Charter require in terms of procedural fairness or a fair hearing? The Charter stipulates that "[e]veryone has the right to life, liberty and security of the person and the right not to be deprived thereof

---

[3] *Nova Scotia (Workers' Compensation Board) v. Martin; Nova Scotia (Workers' Compensation Board) v. Laseur,* [2003] 2 S.C.R. 504 at para. 29 [*Martin*], per Gonthier J., citing with approval McLachlin J.'s (as she then was) dissenting dictum in *Cooper v. Canada (Human Rights Commission)*, [1996] 3 S.C.R. 854 at para. 70 [*Cooper*].

[4] See e.g. the definition of "federal board, commission or other tribunal" at s. 2 of the *Federal Courts Act*, R.S.C. 1985, c. F-7 and the discussion in *Federal Courts Practice 2012*, B.J. Saunders, D.J. Rennie, & G. Garton (Toronto: Carswell, 2011).

[5] Compare, for example, *McKinney v. University of Guelph*, [1990] 3 S.C.R. 229, where the court concludes that the Charter does not apply to a university, with *Kane v. Bd. of Governors of U.B.C.*, [1980] 1 S.C.R. 1105, where a university is found to owe a duty of fairness.

except in accordance with the principles of fundamental justice."[6] Section 7 is the only rights-conferring provision in the Charter that refers to the principles of fundamental justice and, within the Charter's substantive rights-conferring provisions, only these principles have been found to include procedural fairness.[7] The presence of the principles of fundamental justice within s. 7 has led to that section's emergence as the primary source of procedural safeguards within the Charter.[8]

To access procedural safeguards in the context of s. 7, complainants must first cross the "threshold" of establishing that their "life, liberty or security" interests are impaired by the relevant decision. Section 7 only applies to legislation or decisions that impair a person's interests in their life, liberty, or security of the person. The right to life has been interpreted to mean one's right to live and be free of state conduct that increases the risk of dying. The right to liberty implies at least two elements: freedom from physical restraint and freedom to make fundamental life choices. The right to security of the person has both a physical and a psychological component. The physical component is engaged where there is a threat of physical harm. The psychological component is engaged only where the state imposes severe psychological harm. If the affected individual cannot establish that an impugned decision touches a s. 7 interest, procedural fairness may still be due, but as a matter of common law, or the *Bill of Rights*, rather than as a consequence of s. 7 and the principles of fundamental justice.

A further important threshold issue in this context concerns the relationship of procedural fairness to legislation. Legislation can (and often does) determine the content of available procedures.

The common law does not empower judges to impose procedures in the face of clear statutory language that dictates less stringent (or even no) procedural safeguards.[9] Under s. 7, however, the procedural requirements of the principles of fundamental justice are constitutional requirements. In other words, if a s. 7 interest is engaged, procedural fairness comes into play by means of the principles of fundamental justice, and legislation must conform to them in order to be lawful.[10] Other non-Charter sources of procedural safe-

---

6   The Charter, *supra* note 1, s. 7 (emphasis added).

7   Arguably s. 1 implicitly contains procedural fairness (or something much like it) within the idea that infringements of rights must be limited to those that can be "demonstrably justified in a free and democratic society." Similarly, the preamble refers to the rule of law, and procedural fairness might also be inferred. See Mary Liston, Chapter 2, Governments in Miniature: The Rule of Law in the Administrative State, for discussion of the sense in which procedural fairness informs the rule of law and the idea of a common-law constitution.

8   Sections 8 though 14 are sometimes regarded as elaborations of the principles of fundamental justice in the detention context. Naturally, the courts look to the common law to guide their interpretation of these procedural rights. But these rights are parasitical on invasive state action, and so in this sense they are not substantively "right-conferring" in the sense in which s. 7 guarantees to everyone the right to life, liberty, and security of the person independently of anything the state does.

9   *Ocean Port Hotel Ltd. v. British Columbia (General Manager, Liquor Control and Licensing Branch)*, 2001 SCC 52, [2001] 2 S.C.R. 781 [*Ocean Port*].

10 The Supreme Court's decision in *Doré v. Barreau du Québec*, 2012 SCC 12, discussed in detail below adds a wrinkle to the application of s. 7 procedural rights. The requirements of procedural fairness are typically reviewed on the standard of correctness. *Doré* establishes that administrative decisions raising Charter concerns are evaluated on the standard of reasonableness. If a decision involves establishing procedures in a case

guards that ordinary legislation cannot oust would be the *Bill of Rights*,[11] the doctrine of the honour of the Crown under s. 35 of the *Constitution Act, 1982*,[12] and fiduciary obligations owed by the Crown to Aboriginal peoples under that same section of the *Constitution Act, 1982* (see Janna Promislow and Lorne Sossin's discussion in Chapter 13, In Search of Aboriginal Administrative Law). The *Bill of Rights* is rarely argued. Presumably because its early jurisprudence created a number of unusual and complex restrictions to its application, it is perceived as ineffective. But litigants ignore it at their peril. Where it applies, the *Bill of Rights* provides procedural safeguards that cannot be overridden "unless it is expressly declared by an Act of the Parliament of Canada that it shall operate notwithstanding the *Canadian Bill of Rights*."[13] It is worth remembering that half the Court in *Singh* found the very same procedural guarantees for the applicant in the *Bill of Rights* that the other half found in s. 7.[14] The important difference is that under the *Bill of Rights* it is not necessary to show that life, liberty, or security of the person is at stake in order to obtain the relevant procedural protection.

Although *Ocean Port* is often cited for the proposition that clear statutory requirements can oust common-law guarantees, this is only true in jurisdictions that do not have quasi-constitutional guarantees like the *Bill of Rights*.[15] Any decision taken under statutory authority conferred by Parliament may potentially give rise to procedural rights under the *Bill of Rights*.[16]

The remainder of this section now examines the content of the principles of fundamental justice in various statutory contexts. As we shall see, the common law of procedural fairness informs both the specific content of the principles (for example, oral hearings, disclosure, the duty to give reasons, and timely decision-making) and the reasons for interpreting them

---

that engages s. 7 rights, it might be argued that it should be reviewed on the standard of reasonableness. Indeed, one of the first cases to cite *Doré* raised precisely this query. See *Alberta Health Services v. Alberta Union of Provincial Employees*, 2012 ABQB 243.

[11] *Canadian Bill of Rights*, S.C. 1960, c. 44, reprinted in R.S.C. 1985, app. III [*Bill of Rights*].

[12] Being Schedule B to the *Canada Act 1982* (U.K.), 1982, c. 11.

[13] *Bill of Rights, supra* note 11, s. 2.

[14] In *Singh, infra* note 18, only six judges participated in the decision.

[15] At the federal level, the *Bill of Rights* functions like the Quebec Charter functioned in *2747-3174 Québec Inc. v. Quebec (Régie des permis d'alcool)*, [1996] 3 S.C.R. 919 [*Régie*], to fix quasi-constitutional guarantees of procedural fairness that cannot be varied except where the statute is expressly declared to operate notwithstanding the *Bill of Rights*. Notice that in a jurisdiction with no such quasi-constitutional guarantee, the common law yields to a clear statutory requirement. See the discussion in *Ocean Port, supra* note 9, at para. 28 explaining why *Régie* does not apply in British Columbia.

[16] Unwritten constitutional principles may also complicate the usual story of the supremacy of clear legislation over the common law. Judges have imposed a duty to give reasons where an unwritten constitutional principle was at stake (protection of minorities) and the relevant legislation was silent on the issue: *Lalonde v. Ontario (Commission de restructuration des services de santé)* (2001), 56 O.R. (3d) 577 (C.A.). It remains to be seen whether they would do the same in similar circumstances if confronted with express legislation that barred the imposition of such a duty. In two cases in which the rule of law was alleged to operate as an unwritten constitutional principle, the Supreme Court declined to invalidate the impugned legislation: *British Columbia v. Imperial Tobacco Canada Ltd.*, 2005 SCC 49, [2005] 2 S.C.R. 473; *British Columbia (Attorney General) v. Christie*, 2007 SCC 21 [*Christie*]. For discussion of the rule of law cases, see Mary Liston, Chapter 2.

to have particular contents in some decision-making contexts but not in others.[17] And as in the common-law context, the specific procedural requirements of the principles of fundamental justice are determined flexibly but on a standard of correctness. For further discussion on determining and applying the standards of review see also Audrey Macklin, Chapter 9 and Sheila Wildeman, Chapter 10.

A. Oral Hearings and the Scope of Section 7

In 1985, *Singh v. Minister of Employment and Immigration*[18] established that the principles of fundamental justice include procedural fairness. *Singh* involved seven refugee claimants who had no opportunity to present their cases in oral hearings before either the decision-maker at first instance (formally the minister, acting on the recommendation of the precursor to today's Immigration and Refugee Board, the Refugee Status Advisory Committee) or the Immigration Appeal Board (IAB) on appeal. The statutory scheme at the time provided for the possibility of an oral hearing, but only before the IAB on appeal, and *only* if the IAB concluded on the basis of the asylum seeker's written submissions that there were reasonable grounds to believe that the claimant could make a successful claim at an oral hearing. Thus, the statutory scheme precluded the IAB from granting an oral hearing to claimants who failed to set out "reasonable grounds." Because the statutory scheme excluded the possibility of an oral hearing in these cases, the common law of procedural fairness could not "supply the omission of the legislature";[19] there was no omission but rather a clear exclusion.

Six judges took part in the judgment: three found an infringement of s. 7 of the Charter and three found an infringement of s. 2(e) of the *Canadian Bill of Rights*. Wilson J. wrote the Charter portion of the judgment, finding that "everyone" in s. 7 includes "every human being who is physically present in Canada,"[20] and that the security interest "must encompass freedom from the threat of physical punishment or suffering as well as freedom from such punishment itself."[21] As a consequence, Wilson J. held that s. 7 applied to Singh (the threshold was crossed) and, although he did not have a constitutional right to remain in Canada per se, he did have a constitutional right to have his claim determined in accordance with the principles of fundamental justice. She concluded that the interests protected under s. 7 are of such importance that generally an oral hearing will be required when those interests are engaged. Where credibility is at stake, as it almost always is in refugee cases, she found it "difficult to conceive of a situation"[22] in which the claimant would not be entitled to prior discovery of the minister's case and an oral hearing. She affirmed the conventional wisdom that resort to the Charter should be reserved for cases in which ordinary statutory interpret-

---

17   For an earlier, but still exemplary, discussion of the relationship between the common law and the principles of fundamental justice, see J.M. Evans, "The Principles of Fundamental Justice: The Constitution and the Common Law" (1991) 29 Osgoode Hall L.J. 51.

18   [1985] 1 S.C.R. 177 [*Singh*].

19   *Cooper v. Wandsworth Board of Works* (1863), 14 C.B. (N.S.) 180, 143 E.R. 414 (C.P.) at 420.

20   *Singh, supra* note 18 at para. 35.

21   *Ibid.* at para. 47.

22   *Ibid.* at para. 59.

ation cannot provide a remedy. She held that this was one such case because the principles of fundamental justice in the refugee claimant context require an oral hearing, and the statute itself expressly barred some refugee claimants from receiving such a hearing. *Singh* remains a vivid example of how review under the Charter can overcome clear legislation, usually an insurmountable obstacle to relief at common law.

Singh is also a foundational case in Canadian immigration law for both its recognition that s. 7 applies to non-citizens and its impact on Canada's statutory and institutional framework regarding refugee claimants. At no small cost, the government overhauled the statutory scheme and established the Immigration and Refugee Board to ensure that all refugee claimants will receive a fair hearing in accordance with the principles of fundamental justice.

Notice, however, that although the constitutional status of the Charter is required to overcome the language of the statutory scheme then in place, Wilson J. relies on the common-law idea from civil and criminal procedure that credibility is best assessed through an evaluation of oral testimony. In other words, the Charter can take a complainant across the normally insuperable threshold of a clear statutory bar to certain procedures; however, once the threshold is crossed it is still the common law that determines the content that the procedure must have to pass constitutional muster.

B. Incorporation of the Common-Law Framework Under Section 7

Chapter 1, An Introduction to Administrative Law: Some History and a Few Signposts for a Twisted Path, by Colleen Flood and Jennifer Dolling, and Chapter 5 by Grant Huscroft have already described the landmark case of *Baker v. Canada (Minister of Citizenship and Immigration)*[23] in which the Supreme Court drew together a wide body of jurisprudence to establish a framework for determining the content of procedural fairness in a particular case. Recall that the framework the Court established in *Baker* for determining the content of procedural fairness ("the *Baker* framework") is composed of five non-exhaustive contextual factors, none of which is necessarily determinative. The first concerns the nature of the decision: the more the decision can be said to be judicial or quasi-judicial in nature, adjudicative rather than administrative, the weightier the procedural safeguards must be. The second factor is the role and place of the decision within the statutory scheme. For example, if the decision constitutes an exception to the general principles of the scheme, fewer protections are due. On the other hand, if procedural safeguards are present elsewhere in the Act, and if the decision is final, these considerations would militate in favour of more stringent procedures. The third factor is the importance, in practical terms, of the decision to the individual affected. The fourth is legitimate expectations. Legitimate expectations can arise as a result of past practices or representations of public officials that, if present, may provide a basis for procedural safeguards that would not otherwise be available. The fifth factor calls for a measure of deference to the minister's or agency's choice of procedure.

The Court in *Baker* applied this framework to determine only the content of Ms. Baker's participatory rights; she had a right to make written submissions and to have those submissions fully considered, but she was not entitled to an oral hearing. As well, her children were

---

23   [1999] 2 S.C.R. 817 [*Baker*].

denied independent standing on the grounds that their interest in the proceedings could be communicated to the minister and defended by Baker's legal counsel. The Court considered the issues of bias and the duty to give reasons independently of the *Baker* framework. However, as we shall now see in *Suresh v. Canada (Minister of Citizenship and Immigration)*,[24] arguably, where the *Baker* framework is applied in the context of a s. 7 claim, it may generate a substantive duty to give reasons as a principle of fundamental justice. *Suresh* involved a convention refugee detained on a security certificate for alleged links with the Liberation Tigers of Tamil Eelam (LTTE). The Federal Court upheld the certificate and, in the subsequent deportation hearing, the adjudicator found Suresh to be inadmissible as a refugee on grounds of membership in a terrorist organization. Pursuant to s. 53(1)(b) of the *Immigration Act* in force at the time,[25] the minister proceeded to issue an opinion that Suresh constituted a danger to the security of Canada and should be deported, notwithstanding an acknowledgment that Suresh would face a risk of torture upon his return to Sri Lanka. Suresh challenged the minister's decision on constitutional and administrative law grounds. The Court held that "barring extraordinary circumstances, deportation to torture will generally violate the principles of fundamental justice protected by s. 7 of the *Charter*,"[26] but ultimately the case was decided in Suresh's favour because the minister had breached the s. 7 principles of fundamental justice by failing to provide Suresh with adequate procedural safeguards and reasons for the decision.

Unlike the statutory provisions under scrutiny in *Singh*, s. 53(1)(b) of the *Immigration Act* did not require the minister to adopt or follow any particular procedure. The minister notified Suresh that she intended to consider issuing a "danger opinion" against him and gave him the opportunity to make submissions to her. Those submissions were considered by an immigration officer who weighed the importance of Canada's commitment to fight terrorism against the risk of torture to Suresh. The officer recommended in a memorandum to the minister that she issue an opinion under s. 53(1)(b) that Suresh constitutes a danger to Canada. Suresh did not have an opportunity to see or respond to the officer's memorandum, which the Court described as "more like a prosecutor's brief than a statement of reasons for a decision."[27]

Without the guidance of statute, the Court turned to the *Baker* framework to assess the adequacy of the procedure afforded Suresh: "Insofar as procedural rights are concerned, the common law doctrine summarized in *Baker, supra*, properly recognizes the ingredients of fundamental justice."[28] It is worth noting that despite its reliance on *Baker* to determine the

---

[24]   [2002] 1 S.C.R. 3 [*Suresh*].

[25]   R.S.C. 1985, c. I-2 (superseded by the *Immigration and Refugee Protection Act*, S.C. 2001, c. 27).

[26]   *Supra* note 23 at para. 76. This is a notable instance in which the principles of fundamental justice are deemed to contain substantive as well as procedural guarantees. It is also an instance in which international law guides the Court's interpretation of the Charter. The international/domestic law nexus is explored by Gerald Heckman in Chapter 14, The Role of International Human Rights Norms in Administrative Law. Examination of the substantive guarantees implicit in the principles of fundamental justice is more a matter of constitutional than administrative law and, generally, beyond the scope of this book.

[27]   *Suresh, supra* note 24 at para. 126.

[28]   *Ibid.* at para. 113.

content of the s. 7 guarantee, the Court emphasizes that "the common law is not constitutionalized."[29] It would seem that the Court perceives the possibility of cases where the procedural requirements of fundamental justice would be different under s. 7 and the common law. It is difficult to imagine circumstances where this would be the case. If s. 7 is engaged, procedural requirements are likely to be very significant, but it does not follow that the common-law analysis would not produce the same result.

C. The Duty to Disclose and the Right to Reply

Weighing together the five factors referred to above, the Court concluded that Suresh did not have a right to an oral hearing, but he did have the right to disclosure of the materials on which the minister would base her decision, including the memorandum from the immigration officer who initially reviewed Suresh's case under s. 53(1)(b) of the *Immigration Act*. Suresh also had the right to reply to the claims set out in the memorandum, including claims relevant to the threat he posed to Canada and the risk of torture he would face if deported. The minister then had an obligation to consider Suresh's submissions as well as those of her staff.

Let us now explore further the interaction between the Charter, statutes, and the common law by considering what would have happened if the immigration officer who prepared the memorandum was a lawyer whose legal advice the minister explicitly sought and whether his report to the minister could be fairly characterized as a legal opinion. The Court said that Suresh was entitled to disclosure "[s]ubject to privilege or similar valid reasons for reduced disclosure, such as safeguarding confidential public security documents."[30] In *Pritchard v. Ontario (Human Rights Commission)*[31] (a case of judicial review at common law rather than review under the Charter), the Court held that the common-law doctrine of solicitor–client privilege barred a complainant before the Ontario Human Rights Commission from obtaining disclosure of a legal opinion drafted by the commission's in-house counsel.[32]

In principle, an ordinary statute can oust privilege because privilege is a doctrine of the common law (the Court in *Pritchard* said that any such legislation would be interpreted restrictively). It seems to follow that a duty to disclose found to inhere in the principles of fundamental justice could also reduce the effect of privilege. However, the Court in *Pritchard* found that meeting the requirements of procedural fairness does not require the disclosure of a privileged legal opinion. Thus, if the reason disclosure is required in *Suresh* is that procedural fairness is a feature of the principles of fundamental justice, and procedural fairness does not require disclosure of a legal opinion, then the immigration officer's

---

[29]   *Ibid.* at para. 114.

[30]   *Ibid.* at para. 122.

[31]   [2004] 1 S.C.R. 809 [*Pritchard*].

[32]   The issue whether the minister could use solicitor–client privilege to block disclosure of the immigration officer's memorandum did not arise in *Suresh* because the minister simply did not disclose the report prior to making her decision. Although the report was drafted prior to the decision, it was provided to Suresh only after the decision was made, apparently as reasons for the decision.

memorandum may not be discoverable if the minister can convince a court that the memorandum is, in substance, a legal opinion. To pierce privilege, a complainant would have to distinguish procedural fairness at common law (the context in *Pritchard*) from procedural fairness under s. 7.

D. The Duty to Give Reasons

Another area of procedural fairness influenced by *Suresh* is the duty to give reasons. *Baker* established that decision-makers have a duty to give reasons whenever important interests are at stake. In *Baker*, the notes of a junior officer were deemed to satisfy the reasons requirement even though this officer did not make the final decision, and even though the notes were so riddled with stereotypes and prejudice that the Court found that they gave rise to a reasonable apprehension of bias. After *Baker*, some courts interpreted the duty to require no more than a symbolic or even box-ticking exercise,[33] while others interpreted the obligation to require a substantive justification of the impugned decision.[34] In *Suresh*, the Court held that the minister herself (not a delegated officer) must provide "responsive" reasons that demonstrate both that the individual is a danger to Canada and that there are no substantial grounds to believe he or she would be subject to torture. Unlike *Baker*, the Court did not separate its discussion of participatory rights from its treatment of the duty to give reasons; both were informed by contextual analysis conducted under the *Baker* framework. Specifically, the Court made much of the importance of the security interest arising from torture to justify its expansive reading of the duty to give reasons. The Court's attentiveness to the sheer brutality of torture suggests that the justificatory burden under the duty to give reasons is likely to become heavier in rough proportion to the significance of the interest, even in non-Charter contexts.

Because the duty to give reasons is part of the duty of procedural fairness, courts have traditionally reviewed it on a standard of correctness. A decision will be quashed on this standard if it does not prescribe the same outcome as the reviewing court would have prescribed. Moreover, the correctness standard is brought to bear on procedural questions without application of the context-sensitive approach the courts have developed to determine the standard of review applicable to particular substantive decisions. In the wake of *Dunsmuir v. New Brunswick*,[35] two standards of review are now available, correctness and reasonableness. For discussion of these standards, see Audrey Macklin, Chapter 9, and Sheila Wildeman, Chapter 10. It seems that the line between procedure and substance vanished in *Suresh*, and, at the time, it was far from clear which standard of review would be used to assess "responsive" reasons given in a similar future case.

---

33   *Liang v. Canada (Minister of Citizenship and Immigration)*, [1999] 4 F.C. D-54, [1999] F.C.J. No. 1301 (T.D.) (QL).

34   See e.g. *VIA Rail Canada Inc. v. National Transportation Agency*, [2001] 2 F.C. 25 (C.A.); and *Gray v. Director of the Ontario Disability Support Program* (2002), 59 O.R. (3d) 364, 212 D.L.R. (4th) 353, [2002] O.J. No. 1531 (C.A.) (QL).

35   2008 SCC 9, [2008] 1 S.C.R. 190 [*Dunsmuir*].

The Court's recent decision *Newfoundland and Labrador Nurses' Union v. Newfoundland and Labrador (Treasury Board)*,[36] discussed in more detail by Grant Huscroft in Chapter 5, raises serious doubt that inadequate reasons will give rise to a violation of procedural fairness. Although the decision arises in a non-constitutional context, the Court's reasons are likely to be applicable if the issue were to arise under s. 7. In this case, Abella J., writing for a unanimous court, rejects the proposition that the adequacy of reasons is a stand-alone basis for quashing a decision.[37] The assessment of the reasonableness of an outcome, she explains, is not to be undertaken in two steps, one for the reasons and one for the outcome; rather, it is a "more organic exercise."[38] She goes on to say that "it strikes me as an unhelpful elaboration on *Baker* to suggest that alleged deficiencies or flaws in the reasons fall under the category of a breach of the duty of procedural fairness and that they are subject to a correctness review."[39] The net result of this is that if reasons are provided at all, it seems that the duty has been complied with, and that the adequacy of those reasons will be assessed together with the outcome in the substantive review, perhaps on a reasonableness rather than correctness standard of review.

E. The Right to State-Funded Legal Counsel

In the administrative realm, the presence of lawyers is sometimes viewed as a hindrance to speedy, inexpensive, and conciliatory dispute resolution, and procedural fairness does not necessarily entail a right to legal counsel even at one's own expense.[40] The Supreme Court has held that neither procedural fairness nor the rule of law in the administrative setting requires the state to fund legal representation.[41]

In certain circumstances, however, where a decision impairs a s. 7 interest, the state must provide the individual with legal counsel in order to satisfy the requirements of the principles of fundamental justice. In *New Brunswick (Minister of Health and Community Services) v. G.(J.)*,[42] the New Brunswick minister of health and community services sought to extend for six months a previous custody order over an indigent complainant's three young children. Lamer C.J. for the majority and L'Heureux-Dubé J. for the concurring minority held that a forced separation would have "a serious and profound effect"[43] on the parent's psychological

---

[36]   2011 SCC 62 [*Newfoundland Nurses' Union*].

[37]   *Ibid.* at para. 14.

[38]   *Ibid.*

[39]   *Ibid.* at para. 21.

[40]   *Re Men's Clothing Manufacturer's Association of the Ontario and Toronto Joint Board, Amalgamated Clothing and Textile Worker's Union* (1979), 222 L.A.C. (2d) 328 (H.W. Arthurs), quashed (1979), 104 D.L.R. (3d) 441 (Ont. Div. Ct.).

[41]   *Christie, supra* note 16. At a more general level, *Christie* may also be read to suggest that the Supreme Court will not use unwritten constitutional principles (in this case the rule of law) to invalidate legislation. In *Christie*, a provincial tax scheme was alleged to impair the ability of the underprivileged to obtain legal representation and access to the courts.

[42]   [1999] 3 S.C.R. 46 [*G.(J.)*].

[43]   *Ibid.* at para. 60.

integrity and stigmatize her, thereby engaging her right to security of the person.[44] Furthermore, the custody hearing in such cases is adversarial and held in a court of law. Given the seriousness of the interest, the complexity of the proceedings, and the limited capacities of the individual, Lamer C.J. found that the principles of fundamental justice required a fair hearing and that in these circumstances a fair hearing required the Crown to provide legal aid to the parent.

   G.(J.) also offers insight into why a majority of the Supreme Court has never found an infringement of s. 7 to be justified under s. 1. Lamer C.J. notes that s. 7 infringements are not easily saved under s. 1 because the rights protected under s. 7 are very significant, and because "rarely will a violation of the principles of fundamental justice, specifically the right to a fair hearing, be upheld as a reasonable limit demonstrably justified in a free and democratic society."[45] Although the Court in *Suresh* insisted that "the common law [of procedural fairness] is not constitutionalized" but rather "is used to inform the constitutional principles that apply,"[46] there is no question that enfolding procedural fairness into the s. 7 principles of fundamental justice has elevated the duty of fairness to new heights. The consistent refusal of a majority of the Supreme Court to find a s. 7 infringement justified under s. 1 signals the remarkable extent to which the right to a fair hearing has been constitutionalized.

F. Undue Delay

A further element of procedural fairness concerns the timeliness with which administrative proceedings are conducted. The Constitution does not refer explicitly to unreasonable delays before administrative agencies, but in *Blencoe v. British Columbia (Human Rights Commission)*,[47] Bastarache J. speaking for the majority, acknowledged the possibility that an undue delay in the resolution of a human rights complaint could infringe the security interest protected under s. 7. Specifically, it is possible that an inordinate and undue delay could result in stigmatization and an impairment of the psychological integrity of the alleged wrongdoer, but, as we shall see, the threshold to cross is set very high, to the point of it being difficult to imagine a delay that could actually constitute an infringement of s. 7.

   Blencoe had been a minister in the government of British Columbia in March 1995 when one of his assistants accused him of sexual harassment. A month later the premier removed him from Cabinet and the New Democratic Party caucus. In July and August 1995, two women filed sexual harassment complaints against Blencoe with the B.C. Council of Human Rights (later the B.C. Human Rights Commission). Hearings were eventually scheduled before the B.C. Human Rights Tribunal in March 1998, after the commission had completed its preliminary investigation and some 30 months after the initial complaints were filed. Media

---

44   *Ibid.* at paras. 60-61 and 116.

45   *Ibid.* at para. 99. It is also noteworthy that Lamer C.J. finds the infringement unjustifiable solely on the basis of the legal aid policy's deleterious effects; in other cases in which the Court refers to deleterious effects, the reference comes only after the Court has already determined that the Crown failed to satisfy some other aspect of the test from *Oakes* (for example, lack of minimal impairment).

46   *Suresh, supra* note 24 at para. 114.

47   [2000] 2 S.C.R. 307 [*Blencoe*].

attention was intense. The Court recognized that Blencoe's career as a politician was finished, that he suffered clinical depression, that his financial resources were depleted, and that he and his family had moved twice to flee the stigmatizing effects of the outstanding complaints. Nonetheless, Bastarache J. found that even on the assumption that the delay was a cause of Blencoe's grief, "[t]he state has not interfered with the respondent and his family's ability to make essential life choices,"[48] and so the state did not infringe Blencoe's s. 7 security interest.

Wareham v. Ontario (Ministry of Community and Social Services)[49] reveals a potentially more liberal approach to issues of delay and abuse of process. Janice Wareham brought a class action on behalf of persons with disabilities. She claimed that she and the class she represented suffered maladministration under the Ontario Disability Support Program (ODSP). At the time of writing, the case was still before the courts, but the province brought a motion to strike the statement of claim as disclosing no cause of action. The province brought a motion to strike the statement of claim as disclosing no cause of action. The Ontario Court of Appeal allowed the plaintiffs to amend the s. 7 aspect of their claim to include an attack on the process used to determine eligibility for ODSP benefits. The plaintiffs had alleged that, in practice, the ODSP eligibility determination process was Kafkaesque. The court referred to Lorne Sossin's finding that the process was a case study of "bureaucratic disentitlement," which is "a series of structural and situational features of the welfare eligibility process which together have the effect of discouraging applicants and demoralizing recipients."[50] In other words, the cumulative effect of the various steps in the ODSP eligibility procedure was to cause such delay and hardship for applicants that conceivably the overall procedure itself constitutes an infringement of the principles of fundamental justice.

G. Ex Parte, in Camera Hearings

In the wake of the events of September 11, 2001, many liberal democracies, including Canada, enacted legislation to give police and security services added powers to investigate and prosecute terrorism. Canada, however, already had comprehensive legislation in place within its *Immigration and Refugee Protection Act* (IRPA)[51] that permitted the detention of foreign nationals and permanent residents (not citizens) suspected of terrorism or of having an association with terrorist organizations. Detainees under the IRPA are not charged criminally and do not benefit from a presumption of innocence and other due process guarantees that permeate the criminal justice system. This scheme eventually gave rise to *Charkaoui v. Canada (Citizenship and Immigration).*[52]

Canadian security agencies alleged that Adil Charkaoui, Hassan Almrei, Mohamed Harkat, Mohamed Zeki Mahjoub, and Mahmoud Jaballah were involved with terrorist organizations. Charkaoui is a permanent resident. The others are foreign nationals who had

---

48 *Ibid.* at para. 86.

49 2008 ONCA 771 [*Wareham*].

50 *Ibid.* at para. 30, citing Lorne Sossin, "Boldly Going Where No Law Has Gone Before: Call Centers, Intake Scripts, Database Fields, and Discretionary Justice in Social Assistance" (2004) 42 Osgoode Hall L.J. 363 at 399.

51 *Supra* note 25.

52 2007 SCC 9 [*Charkaoui*].

been recognized as convention refugees. The minister of citizenship and immigration and the minister of public safety and emergency preparedness issued security certificates against them pursuant to s. 77 of the IRPA, leading to their detention pending deportation.

Under ss. 78-84 of the IRPA, the detention and the reasonableness of security certificates are subject to review by the Federal Court. During the review process, prior to amendments to the IRPA enacted in 2008, *ex parte* and *in camera* hearings (closed-door hearings in which neither the person named on the certificate nor his or her lawyer is present) were held at the request of the Crown if the judge believed that disclosure of some or all of the evidence on which the certificate was based could undermine national security. The judge then provided to the named person a summary of the evidence, but not its sources or any other details that might compromise national security. The judge could receive and rely on evidence withheld from the named person that would be inadmissible in a court of law, such as uncorroborated hearsay evidence provided by foreign security agencies known to use torture. If the judge determined that the certificate was reasonable, there was no appeal or opportunity for further judicial review.

McLachlin C.J., for a unanimous Supreme Court, found that these proceedings doubly engaged s. 7 because persons subject to security certificates face detention pending deportation (the liberty interest), and because the person's removal may be to a place where his or her life or freedom would be threatened (the security interest). The Court held that the review procedure violated the principles of fundamental justice because it denied the named person a fair hearing. A fair hearing, the Court said, requires a judge to decide the case on the basis of all the relevant facts and law. Unlike an inquisitorial system in which judges play an investigative role, in an adversarial system such as ours, judges do not have the power to investigate and gather evidence. As a consequence, the Court found, Federal Court judges may have to decide on the reasonableness of the Crown's case without the benefit of having the evidence adequately tested. A similar problem affects the law the reviewing judge must consider to meet the requirements of a fair hearing. The named person is precluded from raising legal objections to the evidence, or from basing legal arguments on it. As a result, the judge may have to decide the matter without a full and fair appraisal of all the facts and law at issue.

A further implication of the secrecy required by the statutory scheme is that the named person may never know the case that he or she has to meet, because it may be based, in whole or in part, on undisclosed material. In perhaps the sharpest language in her judgment, the chief justice said that the "principle [of knowing the case to meet when liberty is in jeopardy] has not merely been limited; it has been effectively gutted."[53]

An important aspect of the Court's ruling on the principles of fundamental justice concerns the issue whether reviewing judges may balance the interests of the individual against those of society at the s. 7 stage of determining the content of the principles of fundamental justice. In *Thomson Newspapers Ltd. v. Canada (Director of Investigation and Research, Restrictive Trade Practices Commission)*,[54] La Forest J. wrote as part of the majority and found that determining their content requires a "just accommodation between the interests of the

---

53 *Ibid.* at para. 64.

54 [1990] 1 S.C.R. 425 [*Thomson*].

individual and those of the state."[55] Similarly, in *Ruby v. Canada (Solicitor General)*, Arbour J., writing for the Court, held that "[i]n assessing whether a procedure accords with the principles of fundamental justice, it may be necessary to balance the competing interests of the state and the individual."[56] In *Charkaoui*, however, the Court affirmed its more recent holding in *R. v. Malmo-Levine* that s. 7 does not permit "a free-standing inquiry ... into whether a particular legislative measure 'strikes the right balance' between individual and societal interests in general."[57] Such balancing, the Court said, should be conducted under s. 1. Nonetheless, in *Khawaja v. Canada (Attorney General)*,[58] Richard C.J. of the Federal Court of Appeal relied heavily on *Ruby* and *Thomson* when he balanced the interests of the state and the individual within s. 7 in favour of the state. *Khawaja* came down just months after *Charkaoui* and upheld the constitutionality of *ex parte* sessions mandated under s. 38 of the *Canada Evidence Act*[59] for the purpose of reviewing sensitive information that the government wishes to keep secret.

To remedy the procedural shortcomings of the statutory scheme in *Charkaoui*, the Court suggested that a special advocate (an independent, security-cleared lawyer) could be appointed to represent the named person during *in camera* proceedings. The Crown's failure to incorporate such a measure, or to otherwise correct the procedural defects referred to above, led the Court to conclude that the violation of s. 7 could not be saved under s. 1 because the infringement did not minimally impair the right at stake. Canada has since amended the IRPA to provide for a special advocate.[60] The advocate, however, once he or she goes behind closed doors, is not permitted to communicate with the named person except with the judge's authorization. As a result, the advocate may not be able to ask the named person for an explanation of facts or events presented as grounds for detention, such as trips to the Middle East or Central Asia, visits to certain websites, or apparent associations with terror suspects. Exculpatory explanations may exist and be forthcoming but for the shroud of secrecy that still envelops security certificate proceedings.

Interestingly, the Court's endorsement of the use of a special advocate system takes place in its s. 1 analysis and not in the analysis of the requirement of natural justice under s. 7.[61] As a result, it is unclear whether the Court is of the view that using special advocates is consistent with the principles of fundamental justice, or whether the special advocate system is inconsistent with s. 7 but justified under s. 1. This marks the first time the Court has seriously entertained an infringement of s. 7 being saved by s. 1. Moreover, this may mean that a special advocate program in a non-constitutional context would not be consistent with the common-law duty of fairness, because the content of the common-law duty informs and so is similar to the procedural content of s. 7. If this is so, such a program could be upheld only

---

55   *Ibid.* at para. 176.

56   [2002] 4 S.C.R. 3 at para. 39 [*Ruby*].

57   *R. v. Malmo-Levine*, [2003] 3 S.C.R. 571 at para. 96, cited in *Charkaoui*, *supra* note 52 at para. 21.

58   2007 FCA 388.

59   R.S.C. 1985, c. C-5.

60   *An Act to amend the Immigration and Refugee Protection Act (certificate and special advocate) and to make a consequential amendment to another Act*, S.C. 2008, c. 3.

61   *Charkaoui*, *supra* note 52 at paras. 70-87.

if supported by clear statutory language that explicitly limited the reach of the common law of procedural fairness.

In the 2008 case *Charkaoui v. Canada (Citizenship and Immigration)* (*Charkaoui II*),[62] the Supreme Court reviewed the policy of the Canadian Security Intelligence Service (CSIS) of destroying operational notes, including notes relied on to issue a security certificate against Charkaoui. The Court held that the Crown has an obligation to retain (not destroy) such documents, because they must be available for assessment by the reviewing judge. Speaking more generally to the duty to disclose, the Court said that the security certificate procedure brings s. 7 interests into play, and as a result a "form of disclosure of all the information that goes beyond the mere summaries which are currently provided by CSIS to the ministers and the designated judge is required to protect the fundamental rights affected by the security certificate procedure."[63]

Charkaoui and *Charkaoui II* figure in a line of cases stretching back to *Singh* in which s. 7 has provided procedural safeguards to non-citizens who historically were vulnerable to unstructured discretionary authority subject only to limited review. Nonetheless, the bigger question that is easily lost in the minutiae of Charter review of specific statutory provisions, and which was never asked by the Court, is whether it is at all just to incarcerate foreign nationals and permanent residents without the protection of fundamental criminal law principles, such as the rules of evidence, the idea that the Crown must prove its case beyond a reasonable doubt, the proscription against double jeopardy, and the presumption of innocence. These principles lie at the heart of our justice system because they are constitutive of the rule of law, and because deprivations of liberty arising from detention are so serious. Sections 7 through 14 of the Charter reflect and embody these principles, and those sections are supposed to apply to "everyone," regardless of civil and political status. They remain in place for citizens. But for others who have yet to attain citizenship, and who are subject to security certificates rather than criminal law, the Charter's safeguards against arbitrary prosecution are silenced because, in the case of security certificates, there is no prosecution at all.

III. Review of Administrative Decisions Under the Charter

We turn now to examine how the Court deals with administrative decisions that appear to engage rights protected by the Charter. Such cases are common. Indeed, the Supreme Court has had occasion to study dozens of such cases since the coming into force of the Charter. Regrettably, for students and litigants, the Court's approach has been less than constant. As this second edition was on its way to the printer, the Supreme Court released its decision in *Doré v. Barreau du Québec*.[64] Abella J., writing for a unanimous Court, squarely addresses the inconstancy discussed in this chapter and lays the foundation for a new approach. As we will see, *Doré* resolves a significant debate as to the appropriate approach to take where ad-

---

62 2008 SCC 38, [2008] 2 S.C.R. 326 [*Charkaoui II*].

63 *Ibid.* at para. 50.

64 2012 SCC 12 [*Doré*].

ministrative decisions engage the Charter. Some questions remain unaddressed and some new ones arise.

The inconstancy we observe resides in differing views and approaches as to whether, when, and how to conduct a s. 1 analysis of an administrative decision that infringes a protected right. Should only the legislation that authorizes the decision be subject to s. 1, and the decision be subject to just administrative law analysis if the law is justifiable under s. 1? Should both the decision and the law be subject to s. 1, or merely the decision itself? Or should courts and litigants employ an administrative law analysis of the decision that takes into consideration Charter values and requirements? It is this last approach that won favour with the unanimous court in *Doré*. But all these approaches have been endorsed by the Supreme Court or members of the Court in different cases in recent years. The table at the end of this chapter sets out the diversity of views in the cases discussed. This section aims to sort through the different approaches, to describe them, and to assess them critically. While *Doré* goes a long way to addressing some of the uncertainty residing in the previous case law, it would be imprudent to ignore the tensions that *Doré* aims to resolve. Many lie just below the surface and are likely to require attention as the Court applies the new approach.

The facts in *Doré* are straightforward. The appellant, Mr. Doré, was a lawyer practising in Quebec. After a particularly difficult day in court in front of Justice Boilard, Mr. Doré returned to his office and wrote Boilard J. a letter "man to man." With what might be described charitably as colourful prose, Mr. Doré expressed reservations as to Boilard J.'s suitability for the office of a judge. The Supreme Court generously reproduced the entire letter.[65] Boilard J. did not receive the letter "man to man," but rather "lawyer to judge," and forwarded a copy of the letter to the Chief Justice of the Quebec Superior Court who in turn forwarded a copy to the Barreau du Québec, the professional order responsible for the discipline of lawyers in Quebec. Notwithstanding the fact that Boilard J.'s conduct that provoked the letter in the first place would ultimately be sanctioned by the Canadian Judicial Council, Mr. Doré was found to have run afoul of Quebec's *Code of ethics of advocates*—in particular s. 2.03, which requires that "[t]he conduct of an advocate must bear the stamp of objectivity, moderation and dignity." The Barreau suspended Mr. Doré from the practice of law for three weeks. In doing so, they rejected his argument that s. 2.03 violated the Charter. They accepted that the section infringed s. 2(b) of the Charter but found that the violation was justified under s. 1. Mr. Doré appealed the decision to Quebec's Tribunal des professions. He abandoned his argument that s. 2.03 of the Code itself violated s. 2(b) of the Charter, pursuing instead a complaint that the decision taken under s. 2.03 violated the Charter. The Tribunal des professions applied a standard of correctness to the decision. Relying on LeBel J.'s separate concurring reasons in *Multani*[66]—an approach rejected by the majority in *Multani* and discussed in detail below—the Tribunal des professions upheld the decision. That approach rejects a formal application of the *Oakes* test in favour of an inquiry focused on whether the decision-maker has achieved "proportionality or, more specifically, minimal limitation of the guaranteed right."[67] The decision of the Tribunal des professions was upheld

---

[65] *Ibid.* at para. 10.

[66] *Multani v. Commission scolaire Marguerite-Bourgeoys*, 2006 SCC 6, [2006] 1 S.C.R. 256 [*Multani*].

[67] *Doré, supra* note 64 at para. 19. See also *Multani, supra* note 66 at para. 155.

on judicial review. The Quebec Court of Appeal also upheld the decision, but only after having applied the *Oakes* test (the Supreme Court describes this as a "full s. 1 analysis").[68] Finally, a unanimous Supreme Court upheld the decision, but established a new approach that explicitly rejects relying on the *Oakes* test. The *Oakes* test, Abella J. explained, is appropriate for dealing with a "law" or rules of general application, but not for an administrative decision that is said to violate the rights of a particular individual.[69] In these cases, the decision will be reviewed on the reasonableness standard, adjusted for its context, such that the decision will be affirmed as reasonable only if it reflects a "proper balance" of the implementation of statutory purposes with Charter protection.[70] The challenges of applying this approach to different cases will be discussed below.

It is important to note that in many respects the new approach is not revolutionary. First, as the Court points out, it builds on approaches that have been adopted from time to time throughout the entire history of the Charter. Second, the critical core of the *Oakes* analysis has always required deference to legislative choice. Although the *Oakes* test contains four distinct steps, almost every piece of legislation that fails the test stumbles at the minimal impairment stage where deference to legislative choice has been consistently recognized. Indeed, the manner that deference to legislative choice is applied in the *Oakes* test is expressed with exactly the same language as we find under reasonableness review in administrative law: in both cases the government's action must fall within a range of reasonable alternatives.[71]

The rest of this section on the review of administrative decisions under the Charter is divided into three parts organized loosely around the framework established by the Supreme Court in *Slaight Communications Inc. v. Davidson*.[72] Much of the reasoning of *Slaight* has been abandoned by the Court in *Doré*, but, as we shall see, the distinction it sets out may take on new importance. Prior to *Doré* we were of the view that the *Slaight* framework offered little analytic value. Now it appears that it houses a significant distinction that the Court will have to grapple with in the future. As a result, in the first part below, the *Slaight* framework is described. This framework sets out a distinction between actions that are based on express statutory authority to infringe a protected right and those that are based on imprecise or discretionary authority. The discussion includes a critical evaluation of the purpose of this dichotomy. The second and third parts deal respectively with each branch of the framework (that is, express and imprecise authority to infringe a protected right).

A. The Slaight Framework and Doré

The Supreme Court first considered the application of the Charter to an administrative decision in *Slaight*.[73] Mr. Davidson worked for Slaight Communications as a salesperson for

---

68   *Doré, supra* note 64 at para. 21.

69   *Ibid.* at para. 36.

70   *Ibid.* at para. 7.

71   *RJR-MacDonald Inc. v. Canada (Attorney General)*, [1995] 3 S.C.R. 199 at para. 160.

72   [1989] 1 S.C.R. 1038 [*Slaight*].

73   *Ibid.*

almost four years prior to his termination. A labour adjudicator found that he had been dismissed unjustly. The adjudicator enjoyed broad discretionary authority under the *Canada Labour Code* to impose a remedy. Part of the remedy consisted of a "positive order" that required the employer to write an unembellished, factual letter of reference setting out Mr. Davidson's success relative to annual sales targets, as well as the fact that the adjudicator had found Mr. Davidson's dismissal to be unjust. The adjudicator also made a "negative order" requiring Slaight to provide the letter, and only the letter, to prospective employers making inquiries about Mr. Davidson's employment at Slaight. In other words, to protect the integrity of the positive order, Slaight was forbidden from making any negative comments about Mr. Davidson's work performance to possible future employers. Slaight sought judicial review, arguing that both the positive and the negative order infringed its freedom of expression guaranteed under s. 2(b) of the Charter, and that the infringement could not be justified under s. 1.

Dickson C.J. wrote for the majority and held that although the positive and negative orders infringed s. 2(b), in both cases the infringement could be saved under s. 1. The chief justice found that the orders were both rationally connected to the laudable purpose of the enabling legislation as well as proportionate to its ultimate end—that is, remedying inequality of bargaining power between employers and employees, especially when employees are seeking employment and are at their most vulnerable. He also held that the orders were reasonable in the administrative law sense, though he declined to offer any analysis to substantiate this claim apart from the idea that "[a]dministrative law unreasonableness, as a preliminary standard of review, should not impose a more onerous standard upon government than would Charter review."[74] He said that administrative law review remained important, but for "questions untouched by the Charter," such as questions of fact, because "[i]n contrast to s. 1, patent unreasonableness rests to a large extent on unarticulated and undeveloped values and lacks the same degree of structure and sophistication of analysis."[75] In *Doré*, Abella J. explains away these concerns by reminding us of the context in which *Slaight* was written—one where the Charter's relationship to administrative law was in its infancy. She further explains that in the 30 years since the *Slaight* decision, administrative law has developed and come to embrace an approach that reviews discretion "in light of constitutional guarantees and the values they reflect."[76]

Although the majority reasons are written by Dickson C.J., he expressly adopts Lamer J.'s (dissenting in part) analytic framework.[77] The first step in Lamer J.'s framework is to determine whether the disputed order was made pursuant to legislation that confers "either expressly or by necessary implication, the power to infringe a protected right."[78] If that is the case, then the legislation itself must satisfy the requirements of s. 1 of the Charter. If, however, as was the case in *Slaight*, the legislation provides broad or imprecise discretion and the authority to infringe a protected right is not express, then the order itself must be justified

---

74 *Ibid.* at 1040.

75 *Ibid.* at 1049.

76 *Doré*, *supra* note 64 at para. 35.

77 *Slaight*, *supra* note 72 at 1048.

78 *Ibid.* at 1079.

in accordance with s. 1. If the order cannot be justified under s. 1, the administrative tribunal has necessarily exceeded its jurisdiction; if, on the other hand, it is justified, then the administrative tribunal has acted within its jurisdiction.

As we will see in the next section dealing with cases where express authority infringed a Charter right, the fact that the legislation was justified under s. 1 did not guarantee that the Supreme Court would not also subject the decision itself to the requirements of s. 1. Sometimes it did, sometimes it did not. To make matters worse, the same inconstancy existed in cases where there was imprecise authority to infringe the Charter. Sometimes judges in those cases opted for an administrative law rather than a s. 1 analysis of the decision. Most of the time the Court required s. 1, but not always, and there were no definitive criteria for knowing in advance which way the Court would go. *Doré* now tells us explicitly that a decision itself will *not* invite application of the *Oakes* test. As a result, the dichotomy in *Slaight* takes on a new meaning. A person who has his or her rights infringed as the result of an express authority to do so appears to be in a different position than a person who sees his or her rights infringed by a decision based on an imprecise authority. As will be discussed below, there are at least two significant differences. First, the constitutionality of the rule itself will be reviewed on the correctness standard, whereas an individual decision based on imprecise authority will be reviewed on a standard of reasonableness. Second, the evidentiary burden of satisfying the *Oakes* test will fall on the person seeking to defend the rule, not the person attacking it. In the case of an individual decision based on imprecise authority, the burden of demonstrating that the decision is unreasonable falls on the party seeking to have the decision reviewed.[79]

B. Express Authority to Infringe a Protected Right

As we have seen, the *Slaight* framework makes clear that when legislation expressly authorizes the infringement of a Charter right, the legislation itself must satisfy the requirements of s. 1. This approach is affirmed in *Doré*.[80] *Slaight* was silent, however, on what to do with orders resulting from such legislation. Did Lamer J. intend for there to be a s. 1 analysis of orders made pursuant to legislation that expressly authorizes an infringement of a Charter right? Or, did he intend that only the legislation be subject to s. 1 and that the order must satisfy only the requirements of administrative law? Following *Doré*, it is now clear that the order will not be subject to the *Oakes* analysis even if the law or rule that authorizes it could be. In *Doré*, s. 2.03 of the Code could have been contested (indeed, before the disciplinary committee it was), but its constitutionality was not at issue before the Supreme Court. Had it been, one assumes that the section would have been subjected to *Oakes*, while the decision would have been assessed for reasonableness.

The *Extradition Act*[81] is a paradigmatic example of legislation that expressly authorizes the infringement of a Charter right. In its usual application, the decision-maker is authorized to infringe a citizen's s. 6 Charter right to remain in Canada. Courts have consistently

---

79   It is well established that a person seeking judicial review bears the burden of establishing that the decision attacked is unreasonable (or incorrect). See e.g. *Khosa, infra* note 84 at para. 146.

80   *Doré, supra* note 64 at para. 36.

81   S.C. 1999, c. 18.

found that ordinary exercises of this right-infringing authority are justified under s. 1. It does not follow, of course, that any and every case of extradition is immunized from Charter review. On the contrary, every extradition order is a prima facie infringement of a protected right. So the Crown must show that each particular case is a justified limitation on the individual's s. 6 right, even if after *Doré* the Crown need not satisfy each formal requirement of the *Oakes* test.[82]

In *Doré*, the Supreme Court relied on LeBel J.'s reasons in *Lake*, an extradition case, as an example of how the reasonableness standard can embrace constitutional values. In *Lake*, a unanimous Supreme Court refused to apply an explicit s. 1 analysis to the minister's decision.[83] Writing for the Court, LeBel J. does not cite *Oakes* or rely on the proportionality test established in that case. Instead, he conducts a reasonableness analysis that sounds in administrative law and follows the approach set out in *Dunsmuir*.

Before *Doré*, with *Slaight* and *Lake* in mind, it was already tempting to conclude that where a law expressly confers authority to infringe a protected right and this general authority can be justified under s. 1, then it is only necessary to determine whether a particular exercise of that authority is reasonable in the administrative law sense. On this approach, it could be argued, the "reasonableness" analysis captures the s. 1 considerations as part of a wider inquiry within which, following *Dunsmuir*, the range of reasonable outcomes is determined.[84] *Doré* makes clear that this is precisely the approach to be followed.

However, it is difficult to see why the reasonableness analysis, which is primarily concerned with "justification, transparency and intelligibility within the decision-making process,"[85] would *necessarily* screen out decisions that fail to satisfy the requirements of s. 1.[86] In *Lake*, for example, the Court does not engage in the minimal impairment inquiry that lies at the core of the *Oakes* analysis. *Doré* relies on *Lake*, but insists that there is, nonetheless, conceptual harmony between a reasonableness review and the *Oakes* framework. If it is true that the reasonableness analysis engages the same considerations as *Oakes*, what is gained by not following the framework of *Oakes* explicitly? For Abella J. in *Doré*, the choice between the two approaches is not about choosing between levels of protection. It is about different analytic approaches that she appears to believe would produce the *same* results. Introducing the new approach, she explains, makes it "possible to reconcile the two regimes [the *Oakes* test and administrative law review] in a way that protects the integrity of each."[87]

Moreover, as Abella J. points out in *Doré*, the decision in *Lake* does not entirely resist a s. 1 analysis. *Lake* expressly follows *Controni*, which stands for the proposition that "while extradition constitutes a *prima facie* infringement of a Canadian citizen's mobility rights

---

82 *United States of America v. Cotroni; United States of America v. El Zein*, [1989] 1 S.C.R. 1469. Consider also *Little Sisters Book and Art Emporium v. Canada (Minister of Justice)*, 2000 SCC 69, [2000] 2 S.C.R. 1120 [*Little Sisters*].

83 *Lake v. Canada (Minister of Justice)*, 2008 SCC 23, [2008] 1 S.C.R. 761 at para. 34 [*Lake*].

84 *Dunsmuir, supra* note 35 at para. 47, and see application in *Canada v. Khosa (Citizenship and Immigration)*, 2009 SCC 12, [2009] 1 S.C.R. 339 at para. 59 [*Khosa*].

85 *Dunsmuir, supra* note 35 at para. 47.

86 This seems to be the basis of the majority's complaint in *Multani* about Deschamps and Abella JJ.'s approach. See *Multani, supra* note 66 at para. 16.

87 *Doré, supra* note 64 at para. 4.

under s. 6(1) of the *Charter*, that infringement can be justified under s. 1."[88] The form of that s. 1 analysis is unprecedented in *Lake*. According to LeBel J., the Court owes deference to the minister's evaluation of whether the infringement of s. 6 is justified in accordance with s. 1.[89] Although it would not be unusual for the Court to show deference to the minister's evaluation of relevant factors as to whether Canada should defer to the interests of a requesting state to prosecute a Canadian citizen, it is the first time that the Court finds that deference is owed to the s. 1 justification itself. Recall that in *Dunsmuir* the majority avers that a constitutional issue will be decided on the standard of correctness.[90] Deference to the minister's purported s. 1 analysis is particularly puzzling in *Lake* because the minister's decision, as it is described by the Ontario Court of Appeal, shows no sign of having actually conducted a s. 1 analysis.[91] This means that not only does the attorney general not bear the burden of demonstrating that the decision is justified in the manner that would be required under s. 1, but that the minister is owed deference on whether the infringement is justified or not. If *Lake* is indeed the model that *Doré* adopts for all administrative decisions that engage Charter rights, it appears that the burden on the party called to defend the infringement—the government—has become dramatically lighter.

As noted above, the decision in *Doré* affirms the distinction from *Slaight* between cases where there is an explicit authority to infringe the Charter and where there is not, but now with the crucial consequence that resolving this matter will determine whether review is conducted on a standard of correctness (if the authority is explicit) or reasonableness (if the authority is imprecise or discretionary). This distinction is likely to create significant litigation over what kind of authority is being exercised. Presumably the aggrieved party will seek to locate the source of the infringement in the statute itself while the defendant will try to say that the authority is imprecise and that only the reasonableness standard should apply. *Little Sisters* is a good example of a case where establishing the source of the infringement can be complex.[92]

Little Sisters was a bookstore catering to gay and lesbian communities. The store imported 80 to 90 percent of its erotica from the United States. The *Customs Tariff* prohibited the importation of obscene materials. The trial judge found "not only that Customs officials had wrongly delayed, confiscated, destroyed, damaged, prohibited or misclassified materials imported by the appellant bookstore on numerous occasions, but that these errors were caused by the 'systemic targeting ... [of the store's importations].' "[93] The case was one of express legislative authority to infringe a protected right but both the rule and its application were subjected to a s. 1 analysis.[94] The Court does this in one, single pass—all the while

---

[88] *Lake, supra* note 83 at para. 28.

[89] *Ibid.* at para. 37.

[90] *Dunsmuir, supra* note 35 at para. 58. See also Chapters 9 and 10 on the standards of review.

[91] *United States of America v. Lake* (2006), 212 C.C.C. (3d) 51 at para. 16 (Ont. C.A.).

[92] *Little Sisters, supra* note 82 at para. 71.

[93] *Ibid.* at para. 1.

[94] *Ibid.* at para. 134. Binnie relies on *Slaight, supra* note 72, for the proposition that the order itself must also be subject to a s. 1 analysis, but, as we have discussed, *Slaight* does not say this for orders based on express authority. The order at issue in *Slaight* was based on imprecise authority, so the Court did not address the validity of the law itself.

examining whether the legislation or its particular application could be justified. Notice how this approach would be inconstant with *Doré*. Now only the law would be subject to *Oakes*, whereas its application would be assessed for reasonableness. The majority concludes that the authority to infringe was justified, while the particular exercises of discretion were not.[95] Admittedly, there was little doubt that the particular application of the statute was unconstitutional; the real issue was whether the infringement lay in the statute or merely its application. Dissenting, Iacobbucci J. made a compelling case that legislation authorizing the infringement of protected rights must also contain safeguards to ensure that its administration will permit infringement only where infringement is justifiable.

More recently, in *PHS Community Services*, McLachlin C.J., for a unanimous Court, reiterated that "as with all exercises of discretion, the Minister's decisions must conform to the *Charter*."[96] The Court conducted a full *Charter* analysis of the statute and the particular decision, as it did in *Little Sisters*. At issue in *PHS* was the constitutionality of the minister of health's refusal to grant an exemption to the application of the *Controlled Drugs and Substances Act*[97] [CDSA] to allow for the operation of a safe injection site for heroin addicts. The Court first considered the constitutionality of s. 4 of the CDSA, which criminalizes the possession of controlled substances like heroin. It found that the provision engaged s. 7 of the Charter, but, because there was a safety valve—the possibility to grant an exemption—it did so in a manner that respected the principles of fundamental justice.[98] Thus, it became necessary to determine whether the particular exercise of discretion under s. 56, in this case the minister's refusal to grant an exemption, was legal. The Court could have conducted an administrative law analysis of the particular decision. Instead, the unanimous Court conducted a s. 7 and a s. 1 analysis, concluding that the decision violated the Charter on grounds that it could not be justified under s. 1.

Notice the role of the s. 1 analysis in *PHS*. Since *Doré*, in cases where there is no need to test the legislation and therefore no *Oakes* analysis, it is unclear whether the reasonableness analysis in its present form would provide a basis for intervention in a case like *PHS*.

C. Imprecise Authority to Infringe Charter Rights

Prior to *Doré*, the law was no more predictable with respect to imprecise grants of discretion than it was with express grants of authority to infringe Charter rights. We now know that generally a formal *Oakes* test is not required where imprecise grants of discretion are in play, but that a proportionality inquiry of some form must take place. As the Court points out in *Doré*, a major recent case that applied the *Oakes* test to an administrative decision was *Multani v. Commission scolaire Marguerite-Bourgeoys*.[99] The Court's approach in *Doré* cannot be appreciated without understanding the vigorous debate in *Multani* on how best to treat such

---

95   See *Little Sisters*, *supra* note 82 at paras. 150 and 154.

96   *Canada (Attorney General) v. PHS Community Services Society*, 2011 SCC 44, [2011] 3 S.C.R. 134 at para. 117 [*PHS*].

97   S.C. 1996, c. 19.

98   *PHS*, *supra* note 96 at paras. 113 and 114.

99   *Multani*, *supra* note 66.

orders. *Multani* dealt with a decision by a school board to prohibit an orthodox Sikh student from wearing a kirpan, a religious object that resembles a dagger. The school board considered the object a weapon notwithstanding the student's undertaking to wear it sewn within his clothing. The carrying of weapons at school was prohibited by the school's *Code de vie*.

Charon J., for a majority of the Court, followed the *Slaight* framework and applied a s. 1 analysis to the decision. In powerful concurring reasons, Deschamps and Abella JJ. rejected the *Oakes* analysis altogether and insisted that the matter be analyzed through the lens of administrative law. LeBel J., in separate concurring reasons, offered a further variation on the theme. Despite the debate, Charron J.'s was the position adopted by a clear majority of the Court. For the majority in *Multani*, when faced with the argument that administrative action based on imprecise authority infringes the Charter, one only conducts a traditional Charter analysis without evaluating the decision through the traditional administrative law framework. This approach is now explicitly rejected by *Doré*.

The majority's approach in *Multani* was problematic. It is worth recalling some of the reasons why and assessing the extent to which *Doré* resolves them. First, there was an unavoidable practical problem for litigants. When you go to court in first instance to complain about an administrative decision based on a general or imprecise authority, you cannot know that the court will agree with you that it limits a right protected by the Charter and that the limit will not be saved by s. 1. Indeed, as we will see below, there are also plenty of cases where the court decides that it can resolve your case without resorting to a Charter analysis or even deciding whether Charter rights are engaged. *Baker* is an example of this.[100] *Doré* has not entirely resolved this. First, it is not clear, based on *Doré*, whether deference is owed to an administrative decision-maker's assessment of whether there has been an infringement of a Charter right at all. In *Doré* it was clear that the disciplinary action infringed Mr. Doré's freedom of speech protected by s. 2(b) of the Charter. Of course, there are lots of cases, such as *Baker*, where the infringement will not be obvious at all. Ordinarily we would think that this question will be evaluated on the correctness standard, but this is not certain in light of *Doré*.

Another problem with the majority's approach in *Multani* was that it failed to consider the administrative law implications of cases where a Charter right was infringed, but the infringement could be justified under s. 1. Thus, in addition to his or her constitutional arguments, an applicant may want to raise arguments that attack the reasonableness or correctness of the decision from the point of view of administrative law. For example, in a case where the court may find a limit on a Charter right, but not a violation because the infringement is justified, you may want to argue that the infringement is relevant to the administrative law analysis. You would certainly argue that a decision that limited a Charter right invited a higher standard of procedural fairness. A decision to stop you from carrying an

---

100   The Supreme Court's decision in *G.(J.)*, *supra* note 42 was rendered two months after *Baker* (and was heard only five days after). In *G.(J.)* the Court recognized that a parent's forced separation from her children can infringe s. 7. Also, Mavis Baker suffered a psychiatric illness that evidence suggested might not have been treated adequately were she returned to her native Jamaica. We know from *Chaoulli v. Quebec (Attorney General)*, 2005 SCC 35, [2005] 1 S.C.R. 791, and *Blencoe*, *supra* note 47, that this too may have given rise to a claim under s. 7. Nevertheless, the Court essentially ignores Charter issues and decides the case on wholly administrative law principles with the result that the case had a far greater precedential impact than it would have had if it had been decided on Charter grounds.

ordinary knife at school would probably invite little or no procedural protection, whereas a decision to stop you from carrying a knife that also happened to be of religious significance would, presumably, invite a much higher level of procedural protection. You would also be well-advised to argue that the fact that a Charter right was infringed was one of the contextual factors that should be considered in assessing the reasonableness of the decision.[101] So, even if prior to *Doré* you were satisfied that the settled view in Canadian law is that an administrative decision that purportedly infringes a Charter right must be analyzed through the lens of the ordinary Charter analysis, you would still have wanted to advance your case within the traditional administrative framework unless you are prepared to concede that, except for your constitutional challenge, there was no other problem with the legality of the decision. *Doré* goes a long way to resolving this problem. Interestingly, however, because the Court will not conduct an explicit and distinct *Oakes* analysis, the constitutional dimension of the issue will not be explicit or distinct. It will be rolled into the overall reasonableness analysis. A reviewing court may not be forced to explicitly adjudicate whether a right is infringed and whether the infringement is justified, especially if the issue is cast as one that touches Charter values that in the case do not necessarily crystallize in a Charter right (for example, see the discussion of *Chamberlain* below).

Recall that in *Multani* the majority suggested one approach—to conduct a purely constitutional analysis—whereas two different concurring opinions, one from Abella and Deschamps JJ., and another from LeBel J., suggested different approaches. Abella and Deschamps JJ. preferred an analytic framework that mirrors the traditional administrative law approach now set out in *Dunsmuir*. LeBel J. suggested a hybrid approach that combined factors of both approaches. In the cases that followed *Multani* and preceded *Doré*, the Court had not expressly returned to the debate. Litigants (and students!) could not be certain whether the majority's view had really won the day. Recall that LeBel J. wrote for a unanimous Court in *Lake* just a year after *Multani*. We now know that *Lake* planted the seed for a solution to resolving the diverse views expressed in *Multani*.

The solution, however, raises some of its own problems. If the correct reading of *Doré* is that express authority to infringe a Charter right requires the *Oakes* analysis, but imprecise authority does not, one can legitimately question why, when the Constitution is the supreme law of Canada, there would be two different approaches to determining the constitutionality of government action depending on whether it is expressly authorized by legislation or not. One can easily imagine imprecise discretion being codified in such a way as to contain in the statute an express power to do the very same thing that an administrator had done under an imprecise or general grant. Indeed, if it had not been for the "decision" in *Multani* to not accept the proposed accommodation, the constitutional attack would have been directed to the rule and not the individual decision. Why should these two situations of a limit on a prescribed right be treated differently? In *Doré*, Abella J. does not squarely address whether the new approach will yield a more relaxed standard of scrutiny, though the introduction of the reasonableness standard points in this direction. Recall that she says that the integrity of both can be respected with the approach she adopts.[102] Much of her explanation would lead one to think that she perceives the new approach as merely adapting the same

---

101   *Khosa, supra* note 84 at para. 59.

102   *Doré, supra* note 64 at para. 3.

requirements (those of s. 1) to different types of problems—but in no way diminishing the scrutiny. For Abella J. (relying on her joint reasons with Deschamps J. in *Multani* and LeBel J.'s approach in *Lake*) the *Oakes* test is suitable for assessing "principles of general application" not "individual administrative decision[s]" that are "in relation to particular set of facts."[103] This is a puzzling distinction because, ever since the early days of the Charter, the Court has consistently resisted analyzing Charter questions in the abstract, and has insisted that a law be tested in its actual application. So, arguably, every s. 1 analysis we have ever seen has dealt with individual cases "in relation to a particular set of facts."[104] It is true that in many cases a rule of general application is at issue, but it is tested in respect of how it is applied to a particular case and, typically, its constitutionality is determined only insofar as necessary with respect to the facts proved before the court.

We might wonder whether the different approaches matter. In *Multani*, there are three different approaches, but they all reach the same conclusion—that the school board's decision is illegal. One can legitimately ask whether it makes any difference to the outcome which approach you take. This question takes on a new importance with the Court's decision in *Doré*. Now that we know that a formal *Oakes* analysis is usually unnecessary for administrative decisions, we want to know whether it matters. Put another way, faced with the same decision, is it possible that a traditional s. 1 analysis would lead a court to intervene when a reasonableness/administrative law analysis would not? The answer to this question is that these different approaches might well produce different results even though they did not in *Multani*. The majority view in *Multani* adopted a traditional Charter analysis that is, for all intents and purposes, identical to the approach the Court would have taken if it had been asked to evaluate a law that purportedly infringed a Charter right. First, the Court would have inquired as to whether the applicant had demonstrated that the law, either in purpose or effect, infringed a right protected by the Charter. In the event that the answer was yes, the burden would shift to the government (or the party defending the action) to demonstrate that the action could be justified in accordance with s. 1 of the Charter.

Deschamps and Abella JJ. suggest that the correct approach would follow the traditional administrative law framework, but in a manner that is consistent with the applicant's Charter rights. Following this approach, the evaluation as to whether the decision was reasonable would be informed by the extent to which the decision interfered with Charter rights. What this means in the abstract is difficult to grasp. Their reasons, however, make their approach clear: they conclude that the decision is unreasonable because, among other things, the school board failed to take into consideration Multani's Charter rights. Suppose the school board *had* seriously considered the applicant's Charter rights and *had* wrestled with the practical considerations and dangers of allowing him to wear the kirpan, and yet *still* concluded that the kirpan should be prohibited? This would have all the trappings of a reasonable decision. Judges will strike down a decision where the decision-maker fails to take account of relevant considerations (for example, Charter rights), but they are reluctant to "reweigh" the

---

103   *Ibid.* at para. 36.

104   See e.g. *Reference re Same-Sex Marriage*, 2004 SCC 79, [2004] 3 S.C.R. 698 at para. 51; *Danson v. Ontario (Attorney General)*, [1990] 2 S.C.R. 1086 at 1093; *MacKay v. Manitoba*, [1989] 2 S.C.R. 357 at 361–62; *Hy and Zel's Inc. v. Ontario (Attorney General); Paul Magder Furs Ltd. v. Ontario (Attorney General)*, [1993] 3 S.C.R. 675.

weight the decision-maker gives to those considerations.[105] It seems possible, then, that the decision would have been upheld under the approach of the concurrency, whereas the majority, reviewing the issue on a standard of correctness, would strike down the decision as an unjustifiable infringement of freedom of religion. One can imagine that applying the reasonableness approach puts pressure on the court to revisit the rule against reweighing. Indeed, it appears that according to *Doré* a decision is reasonable *only* when the decision-maker has struck the "appropriate balance" between its mandate and the Charter rights at issue.[106] Testing whether an appropriate balance has been struck necessarily involves an inquiry into the weight accorded the countervailing considerations.

Moreover, Deschamps and Abella JJ. in *Multani* were not just suggesting a different analytic framework. They explicitly reasoned that an administrative decision is not susceptible to justification under s. 1 of the Charter.[107] On one reading this would mean that any decision that infringed a Charter-protected right would automatically be invalid because it could not be saved by s. 1. Although this is one interpretation of their reasons, *Doré* makes it clear that that is not what they intended. The better view is that justification is included in assessing the reasonableness of the decision.

It is important to note that their difference with the majority in *Multani* is not the absence of express *statutory* authority, but rather that s. 1 ought only to be applied to a "norm or rule of general application"[108] and not to a particular decision. They clearly managed to win over the rest of the Court in *Doré* because this is precisely the basis for the new approach. Notice that in *Greater Vancouver Transportation Authority*, where Deschamps and Abella JJ. join the majority, there is no *statutory* authority: the issue dealt with a *rule* rather than a particular decision.[109] In that case, the Court found that the Greater Vancouver Transportation Authority policy prohibiting non-commercial advertising was in fact a "limit prescribed by law" and subjected the non-statutory policy to the s. 1 analysis having found that it infringed s. 2(b) of the Charter. If Deschamps and Abella JJ. believed that authority to infringe a Charter right must flow expressly from statutory authority, then (considerations of deference to prior majority rulings aside) they would not have accepted that s. 1 could be applied to the non-statutory policy at issue in *GVTA*. It would seem to follow that if the issues had been framed differently to attack only the *Code de vie* in *Multani*, they would presumably have accepted the traditional s. 1 analysis. The view that individual decisions are not necessarily amenable to the same analysis as rules or norms had received some endorsement from the Court before *Doré* and since *Multani*. Consider *Alberta v. Hutterian Brethren of Wilson Colony*.[110] The case involved the constitutionality of the requirement that all drivers' licences bear a photo of the licence holder. The Hutterian Brethern respondents

---

[105]   *Khosa, supra* note 84 at paras. 60-64.

[106]   *Doré, supra* note 64 at paras. 7, 57, and 58. Note also that in *Lake, supra* note 83, the Court says the minister must apply the "correct test" but is owed deference in the application of the test.

[107]   *Multani, supra* note 66 at para. 100 et seq.

[107]   *Ibid.* at para. 113.

[109]   *Greater Vancouver Transportation Authority v. Canadian Federation of Students—British Columbia Component*, 2009 SCC 31, [2009] 2 S.C.R. 295 at para. 58 et seq. [*GVTA*].

[110]   2009 SCC 37, [2009] 2 S.C.R. 567 [*Hutterian Brethren*].

sincerely believed that the second commandment prohibits them from having their photos taken and that, as a result, the licensing requirement violated their freedom of religion. McLachlin C.J. penned the majority reasons. Although an administrative decision was not at issue, there was a debate before the Court arising from the lower court decisions as to whether the analytic framework of s. 1 or the test for reasonable accommodation applicable under human rights legislation should be employed. The majority, of which Deschamps J. was a member, held that s. 1 should be applied where legislation is at issue, but that if government *action* or *practice* is at issue, another analytic approach, like reasonable accommodation, may be appropriate. McLachlin C.J. cited both Charron J.'s majority reasons and Deschamps and Abella JJ.'s concurring reasons in *Multani* in support of this proposition.[111] Finally, although in no way departing from the majority's view in *Multani*, McLachlin C.J. adopted a stance reminiscent of Deschamps and Abella JJ.'s argument that s. 1 is ill-suited to particular decisions. McLachlin C.J. emphasized that laws are different from particular decisions when it comes to a s. 1 analysis.[112]

All this, it turns out, would be relied on in *Doré*. As a result, *Doré* might be read to blur the line between the *Oakes* analysis as an analytic tool on the one hand and compliance with s. 1 of the Charter on the other. It is one thing to say that individual discretionary decisions are "ill-suited" to the *Oakes* test, it is quite another to say that they are a type of government action that can legally infringe a Charter right without needing to satisfy s. 1 of the Charter. Notice that the requirements of *Oakes* and s. 1 are not identical. Section 1 provides that "[t]he *Canadian Charter of Rights and Freedoms* guarantees the rights and freedoms set out in it *subject only to such reasonable limits prescribed by law as can be demonstrably justified in a free and democratic society*."[113] *Oakes* provides an analytic framework to assess whether a given rule satisfies these requirements. Its components—a pressing and substantial objective, rationally connected to a minimally impairing infringement whose benefits are not outweighed by its interference with a protected right—are not provided for in s. 1. However, s. 1 *does* require that the limit be reasonable, that it be prescribed by law, and importantly, that its reasonableness be *demonstrably justified*. Abella J.'s reasons in *Doré*, however, do not expressly distinguish between the requirements of s. 1 and the requirements of *Oakes*. For example, to demonstrate that a s. 1 analysis of an individual decision is "awkward," Abella J. asks rhetorically: "On whom does the onus lie, for example, to formulate and assert the pressing and substantial objective of an adjudicated decision, let alone justify it as rationally connected to, minimally impairing of and proportional to that objective?"[114] Prior to *Doré* the answer to that question was clear: it was based on the language of s. 1. The party that sought to uphold the infringement of a right protected by the Charter (the government) had the burden of *demonstrating* that it was a reasonable limit.[115] There is no analogue in administrative law that imposes a similar burden on the government when a Charter right is infringed. Indeed, under the Charter framework alone rights are absolutely guaranteed *except*

---

111   *Ibid.* at paras. 66-68.

112   *Ibid.* at para. 69.

113   The Charter, *supra* note 1 (emphasis added).

114   *Doré, supra* note 64 at para. 4.

115   See e.g. *Irwin Toy Ltd. v. Quebec (Attorney General)*, [1989] 1 S.C.R. 927 at 986.

where the infringement can be demonstrably justified to be a reasonable limit prescribed by law in a free and democratic society.

Notice that LeBel J.'s approach in *Multani* does not expressly reject a s. 1 analysis but merely denies that all the steps may be necessary in the case of an individualized decision. He still recognizes that the justificatory burden rests on the party defending the infringement. He dispenses with the entire s. 1 (or s. 1-like) analysis in a single paragraph that deals with the test holistically and concludes that the school board failed to show that its prohibition was justified. And yet in *Lake*, he found that the justification of the infringement is wholly subsumed under an administrative law reasonableness analysis.

With *Doré*, and following Deschamps and Abella JJ.'s approach in *Multani* and LeBel J.'s in *Lake*, where the Court is not applying the traditional s. 1 analysis, the government actor appears to be relieved of its considerable burden of explicitly justifying the decision in accordance with s. 1. Moreover, Charter remedies are not obviously available to an applicant who succeeds on administrative law grounds alone. A determination that a decision is unreasonable because it fails to consider protected rights as part of an administrative law inquiry, as Deschamps and Abella JJ. conclude in *Multani*, may not give rise to a remedy under s. 24.

A further set of cases—cases where Charter rights were implicated yet the Court preferred to resolve them on administrative law grounds—will be of concern to litigants who worry that the salience of Charter issues could be lost under the new approach. In a previous version of this chapter, pre-dating *Doré*, we identified these cases under the heading "Avoiding Charter Issues," in part because the Court seemed to avoid, rather than engage, Charter issues when disposing of these cases. In *Doré*, almost all these cases are cited as having inspired the new approach. Abella J. refers to those cases saying that they "applied an administrative law/judicial review analysis in assessing whether the decision-maker took sufficient account of Charter values."[116] That characterization is puzzling because, in many of the cases that she mentions, the Court expressly resists addressing Charter arguments. In *Baker*, for example, the first case on Abella J.'s list, Heureux-Dubé J. expressly states that "[b]ecause, in my view, the issues raised can be resolved under the principles of administrative law and statutory interpretation, I find it unnecessary to consider the various Charter issues raised by the appellant."[117] It is true that while Heureux-Dubé J. states on several occasions that any exercise of discretion must be consistent with Charter values, she never evaluates whether a Charter right is engaged by the decision, nor whether the decision-maker "took sufficient account of Charter values."[118] It is important to note, however, that she certainly could have done so. *Baker* was decided in the same year as *G.(J.)*, and in *G.(J.)* the Court found that a forced separation of a mother from her children would trigger s. 7. Ms. Baker's deportation could have forced her to leave her children behind to further their best interests, arguably engaging the same s. 7 security interest that was impaired in *G.(J.)*. The Court did not address the Charter, electing instead to resolve the dispute on administrative law grounds.

---

[116] *Doré, supra* note 64 at para. 32.

[117] *Baker, supra* note 23 at para. 11.

[118] *Doré, supra* note 64 at para. 32.

Abella J. also refers to *Chamberlain* as an example of the approach advanced in *Doré*. As in *Baker*, however, McLachlin C.J., writing for the majority, expressly concludes that the "appeal does not fall to be determined on the basis of the *Charter*."[119] *Chamberlain* was a case involving an allegation of discrimination based on sexual orientation in the public school system.[120] In this case, a kindergarten–grade 1 (K–1) teacher asked the Surrey School Board to approve as supplementary learning resources three books that depicted same-sex parented families. The board refused. McLachlin C.J. found that the decision should have been reviewed as a matter of administrative law on the then-available middle standard of reasonableness *simpliciter*. She held that the board's decision was unreasonable because it failed to respect the principles of tolerance and secularism set out in its enabling legislation and regulations. It is this aspect of the decision that Abella J. cites in *Doré*.[121] In dissent, Gonthier and Bastarache JJ. agreed that the case should be reviewed on administrative law principles. They did, however, conclude that discrimination was not made out on the facts because same-sex parenting could still be discussed at the K–1 level, and because human sexuality—including homosexuality—was addressed in later grades. In coming to that conclusion, it is interesting to note that they too refuse to engage in a Charter analysis. However, in stark contrast to McLachlin C.J. who does not mention Charter rights at all, they see a role in the reasonableness analysis for Charter considerations, concluding that "this case engages the s. 15, s. 2(a) and s. 2(b) rights of *both* the appellants and the parents who expressed their views to the School Board—and all must be considered as imported into the review of the School Board's decision."[122]

To the same end, Abella J. cites *Trinity Western* in support of the idea that courts can use administrative law to examine whether "the decision-maker took sufficient account of Charter values."[123] In that case, the B.C. College of Teachers refused to grant the Evangelical Trinity Western University (TWU) permission to assume full responsibility for its educational program. TWU required faculty and students to sign its TWU Community Standards code, which described same-sex relations as a "sexual sin."[124] The B.C. College of Teachers worried that TWU was promoting a culture of discrimination that could be passed from TWU teacher-graduates to children attending public school. Iacobucci and Bastarache JJ., writing for the majority, (L'Heureux-Dubé J. dissenting) found that analysis under the Charter was inappropriate because there was no evidence that s. 15 equality interests of school children were affected. The decision of the B.C. College of Teachers, they held, punished TWU for its religious beliefs alone, and not for any wrong it had committed. The proper subject of censure, the majority said, is conduct rather than belief, such as discriminatory conduct in the classroom. Because there was no evidence that TWU graduates had engaged in discriminatory conduct, the majority could not conclude that TWU graduates would adversely affect the s. 15 interests of B.C. school children.

---

119   *Chamberlain v. Surrey School District No. 36*, 2002 SCC 86, [2002] 4 S.C.R. 710 at para. 73 [*Chamberlain*].

120   *Ibid.*

121   *Doré, supra* note 64 at para. 49.

122   *Chamberlain, supra* note 119 at para. 126 (emphasis in original).

123   *Doré, supra* note 64 at para. 32.

124   *Trinity Western University v. College of Teachers*, 2001 SCC 31, [2001] 1 S.C.R. 772 [*Trinity Western*].

However, the majority clearly thought that the impugned decision infringed TWU's freedom of religion by declining TWU's request to assume full responsibility for its program on the basis of its beliefs. Contending values—freedom of religion versus equality—were undeniably at stake. Nonetheless, Iacobucci and Bastarache JJ., for the majority, declined to apply the Charter despite a powerful dissent by L'Hereux-Dubé J. to that effect; they did not review the decision under ss. 2(a) and 1 of the Charter. They preferred an approach that might be compared with Abella and Deschamps JJ.'s approach in *Multani*, but they never recognized that a Charter right was clearly infringed (either s. 2 or s. 15).

Notice that Iacobucci and Basterache JJ. did not resist the Charter analysis because they preferred a different analytic approach, but because they were not convinced that there was evidence that a Charter right was infringed.[125] And, interestingly, they certainly did not perceive the decision-maker as especially well-placed to evaluate the Charter claims. In determining the standard of review, Iacobucci and Basterache JJ. for the majority concluded that "the Council is not particularly well equipped to determine the scope of freedom of religion and conscience and to weigh these rights against the right to equality in the context of a pluralistic society. … All this to say that even if it was open to the BCCT to base its decision on perception rather than evidence of actual discrimination or of a real risk of discrimination, there is no reason to give any deference to that decision."[126] Despite the conclusion that deference was not owed, a majority of the Court in *Trinity Western* examined the decision with an eye to determining whether sufficient consideration was given to the Charter rights at issue. So, in this sense the decision is likely indicative of the approach favoured by the Court in *Doré*.

D. Conclusion

With *Doré*, the Supreme Court provided much needed clarity to the debate over whether to apply the *Oakes* analysis to administrative decisions that infringe Charter rights. *Doré* is clear that the administrative law approach and the standard of reasonableness will apply. The Court emphasized that this approach will nonetheless work "the same justificatory muscles: balance and proportionality."[127] Whether this approach will provide the same protection for parties as they would have received with the *Oakes* test remains to be resolved in future cases. Abella J. suggests that it should, but a number of aspects of the decision are problematic from the point of view of the strong protection previously afforded under the *Slaight/Multani* framework. At very least, the party defending decisions alleged to infringe Charter rights seems to be relieved of the obligation of demonstrably justifying the infringement. This alone may produce challenges for the Court. As awkward as the *Oakes* test may have been to apply to individual adjudicative decisions, it had the merit of plainly reflecting the burden-of-proof requirements of s. 1 of the Charter.

---

125   *Ibid.* at para. 36

126   *Ibid.* at para. 19.

127   *Doré, supra* note 64 at para. 5.

Some questions to watch for:

- What is the burden on a party defending a decision that infringes a Charter right? What does the party need to demonstrate?
- What is the standard of review on the issue of whether a Charter right is engaged by an administrative action? For example, is deference owed to an administrative decision-maker who decides that a Charter right is not engaged (or what if they don't consider the issue at all)?
- Are constitutional remedies available in a case where an administrative decision is found to be unreasonable because it fails to properly consider Charter values?
- Are Charter values the same as Charter rights within the new approach?
- Will deference apply when a decision-maker's Charter analysis does not fall within the expertise of its "home statute"?

IV. Agency Jurisdiction Over the Charter

It is a commonplace principle of statutory interpretation that administrative tribunals and courts alike should endeavour to interpret legislation in light of the Charter and the values contained therein. Sometimes, however, unambiguous statutory provisions may appear to infringe Charter rights under any reasonable interpretation, and thus a tribunal's application of the interpretive principle referred to above would be tantamount to a refusal to obey the law the legislature has entrusted it to implement. The first subject of this section is whether administrative agencies, as creatures of statute, have authority to interpret and apply the Charter to their enabling legislation for the purpose of refusing to give effect to provisions found to violate the Charter. The second subject is the authority of administrative bodies to grant remedies under s. 24(1) of the Charter.

A. The Old Trilogy and "Jurisdiction Over the Whole Matter"

The Supreme Court initially considered the first issue in a trilogy of cases: *Douglas/Kwantlen Faculty Assn. v. Douglas College*,[128] *Cuddy Chicks Ltd. v. Ontario (Labour Relations Board)*,[129] and *Tétreault-Gadoury v. Canada (Employment and Immigration Commission)*.[130] La Forest J. wrote the majority reasons in each of these decisions. He held that because s. 52(1) of the *Constitution Act, 1982* declares the Constitution to be the supreme law of the land and inconsistent law of no force and effect, administrative decision-makers with the power to interpret law must also interpret and respect this supreme law. Therefore, although administrative agencies cannot declare infringing statutory provisions to be invalid (a power reserved to the courts), s. 52(1) authorizes them to both apply the Charter to their enabling legislation and refuse to give effect to provisions they determine to be inconsistent with it.

---

[128]   [1990] 3 S.C.R. 570 [*Douglas College*].

[129]   [1991] 2 S.C.R. 5 [*Cuddy Chicks*].

[130]   [1991] 2 S.C.R. 22.

The Supreme Court pointed out that it retained authority to review agency determinations of Charter issues on a standard of correctness. Perhaps more significant, however, the Court deployed a restrictive understanding of what it would mean for an agency to have authority to interpret law, and thus authority to apply the Charter. In *Cooper*, the Court later characterized this authority as one that must evince a "general power to consider questions of law."[131] This power had to be conferred by the enabling legislation because agencies have no inherent authority to decide questions of law, but it could be granted explicitly or implicitly. In *Cuddy Chicks*, the Court described this authority as "jurisdiction over the whole of the matter before it, namely, the parties, subject matter and remedy sought."[132] Specifically, the authority to interpret law had to be more than the authority required to implement the legislation's basic policies and programs, because all public officials had to be capable of this much interpretation, and the Court was not prepared to say that all public officials had jurisdiction to apply the Charter.

Although the majority in *Douglas College* were careful to insist that their recognition of agency jurisdiction over the Charter did not offend the separation of powers, their restrictive understanding of authority to consider questions of law shares the separation-of-powers concerns raised by Lamer C.J. in his concurring judgment in *Cooper*. Lamer C.J. thought that recognizing agency jurisdiction over the Charter undermined the separation of powers according to which the legislature makes law and the executive applies it: permitting agencies to apply the Charter to their enabling legislation appeared, he said, to let the executive decide the limits of its own jurisdiction. Conventional wisdom has the legislature determining those limits at first instance through legislation, and the judiciary policing them once they are established through judicial review. Lamer C.J. held that allowing tribunals to hear Charter challenges to their enabling legislation means that "the executive can defeat the laws of the legislature,"[133] thus inverting the relationship between the legislature and the executive.

The Court's restrictive view of authority to consider questions of law led to the much-criticized *Cooper* decision. The case turned on whether the Canadian Human Rights Commission or a tribunal struck under it had jurisdiction to apply s. 15 of the Charter to s. 15(c) of the *Canadian Human Rights Act*.[134] Section 15(c) of the Act stipulated that it was not a discriminatory practice for an employer to terminate an individual if the individual reached the normal age of retirement for employees occupying a similar position. La Forest J., for the majority, held that the legislation did not confer on the commission an explicit power to consider questions of law, and that no such power was implicit to the statutory scheme because the commission's role within it was to screen complaints rather than adjudicate them. Thus, the commission had to apply s. 15(c) of the Act to the appellants in *Cooper*, disqualifying their case as one that could be sent to a tribunal for adjudication. As a consequence, neither the commission nor a tribunal could review the constitutional validity of the impugned provision. McLachlin J. (as she then was, and with L'Heureux-Dubé J.) dissented,

---

[131]   *Cooper, supra* note 3 at para. 46.

[132]   *Cuddy Chicks, supra* note 129 at 14.

[133]   *Cooper, supra* note 3 at para. 25.

[134]   R.S.C. 1985, c. H-6.

insisting that "[a]ll law and law-makers that touch the people must conform to [the Charter]"[135] and that the commission had the power to consider questions of law.

B. Vindication of the Dissent in Cooper?

Seven years later, a series of unanimous decisions emerged that confirmed the dissenters' more generous understanding of what it means for a tribunal to have authority to consider questions of law. As we shall see, however, the vindication of the dissent in *Cooper* may not be complete. Two judgments were released together, *Nova Scotia (Workers' Compensation Board) v. Martin; Nova Scotia (Workers' Compensation Board) v. Laseur*;[136] the third is *Paul v. British Columbia (Forest Appeals Commission)*.[137] The leading case is *Martin*.

In *Martin*, the Nova Scotia *Workers' Compensation Act* and its regulations excluded chronic pain sufferers from receiving benefits under the regular workers' compensation system and provided, in lieu of benefits usually available to injured workers, a four-week functional restoration program beyond which no further benefits were available. As a result of the statutory exclusion, the Workers' Compensation Board denied benefits to two workers suffering chronic pain. The workers appealed the board's decision to the Workers' Compensation Appeals Tribunal. They alleged that the legislation infringed s. 15(1) of the Charter by denying them equality under the law and discriminating against them on the basis of their disabilities. The Appeals Tribunal held that it had jurisdiction to hear the Charter argument, and concluded that the statutory exclusion violated the Charter as the complainants alleged. The Appeals Tribunal then went on to adjudicate the claims without giving effect to the infringing legislation. The board challenged the Appeals Tribunal's jurisdiction to hear the Charter argument.

Gonthier J. wrote for the Court and rejected the board's challenge, finding that "[a]dministrative tribunals which have jurisdiction—whether explicit or implied—to decide questions of law arising under a legislative provision are presumed to have concomitant jurisdiction to decide the constitutional validity of that provision,"[138] and that the Appeals Tribunal had such jurisdiction. He relied on the old trilogy and overruled *Cooper* to the extent that it went the other way.

Martin's most important novelty is that it eschewed the prior restrictive understanding of what it means for an agency or tribunal to have authority to consider questions of law. The inquiry into legislative intent on this matter does not rely on whether the legislature intended the tribunal to apply the Charter. The question is "whether the empowering legislation implicitly or explicitly grants to the tribunal the jurisdiction to interpret or decide *any* question of law."[139] Gonthier J. rejected the distinction made in *Cooper* between "general" and "limited" questions of law. However, he restricted the inquiry to one that must focus on

---

135   *Cooper, supra* note 3 at para. 70.

136   *Supra* note 3.

137   2003 SCC 55, [2003] 2 S.C.R. 585 (agency jurisdiction extends to determinations of Aboriginal rights enshrined in s. 35 of the *Constitution Act, 1982*).

138   *Martin, supra* note 3 at para. 3.

139   *Ibid.* at para. 36 (emphasis in original).

whether the tribunal has the power "to decide questions of law arising under the challenged provision."[140] These powers typically reside in tribunals with adjudicative functions, but Gonthier J. made it clear that the presence or absence of adjudicative authority is not necessarily determinative.

If the legislation does not expressly grant jurisdiction to consider questions of law, the jurisdiction may still be present implicitly and inferred from a series of factors: "the statutory mandate of the tribunal in issue and whether deciding questions of law is necessary to fulfilling this mandate effectively; the interaction of the tribunal in question with other elements of the administrative system; whether the tribunal is adjudicative in nature; and practical considerations, including the tribunal's capacity to consider questions of law."[141] The guiding principle that informs the application of these factors (save perhaps practical considerations) is whether the legislature intended the tribunal to have jurisdiction to decide questions of law.

The presence of such an intent does not, however, end the inquiry; it merely establishes a rebuttable presumption that the agency has jurisdiction to apply the Charter. The presumption can be rebutted, Gonthier J. said, by pointing to an explicit or implied statutory withdrawal of authority to determine constitutional questions.

Despite the Court's unequivocal recognition of agency jurisdiction to hear Charter challenges, some tension remains. The tension arises from the requirement of legislative intent and one of its immediate consequences: legislatures can amend and enact law to withdraw tribunal jurisdiction over the Charter. Various provincial legislatures have omnibus legislation that insulates their statutes from agency scrutiny of constitutional matters. For example, in 2004 British Columbia passed the *Administrative Tribunals Act*,[142] a comprehensive justice reform measure that expressly denies most provincial administrative tribunals jurisdiction over Charter issues. The attorney general of British Columbia justified the jurisdiction-depriving sections of the Act on several grounds.[143] In his second-reading speech to the legislative assembly, he claimed that courts are more expert than most tribunals with respect to complex and far-reaching Charter questions. He also worried that permitting agencies to resolve these questions would require laypersons to hire (costly) legal counsel where they would not otherwise have to do so. He expressed concern over the drain on resources and

---

140   *Ibid.* at para. 37.

141   *Ibid.* at para. 41. For an insightful discussion of the explicit/implicit distinction in *Martin*, and possible uncertainties regarding its application, see J.M. Evans, "Principle and Pragmatism: Administrative Agencies' Jurisdiction Over Constitutional Issues" in G. Huscroft & M. Taggart, eds., *Inside and Outside Canadian Administrative Law: Essays in Honour of David Mullan* (Toronto: University of Toronto Press, 2006) at 377-420.

142   S.B.C. 2004, c. 45, ss. 43-45. The Labour Relations Board and the Securities Commission are exceptions to the rule and can decide Charter questions. Other B.C. tribunals can determine constitutional issues related to federalism, but cannot apply the Charter. Yet others cannot determine any constitutional issues. Alberta has passed similar legislation: *Administrative Procedures Amendment Act, 2005*, S.A. 2005, c. 4. In *Tranchemontagne v. Ontario (Director, Disability Support Program)*, [2006] 1 S.C.R. 513, the Supreme Court reaffirmed that legislatures can preclude tribunals from considering Charter questions through clear legislation, though the bar in that case was specific to the relevant statute.

143   British Columbia, Legislative Assembly, *Official Report of Debates*, vol. 25, no. 15 (18 May 2004) at 11193 et seq., as cited in Deborah K. Lovett, "Administrative Tribunal Jurisdiction Over Constitutional Issues and the New Administrative Tribunals Act" (2005) 63 Advocate 177 at 191-92.

the additional time required to settle Charter challenges at the agency level. These resource and access to justice problems, he said, would be exacerbated by the non-binding nature of tribunal decisions over Charter issues, because similar questions would have to be decided anew in subsequent proceedings.

Both proponents and critics of agency jurisdiction over the Charter claim that their policy is the one that, overall, minimizes the expense and time required to settle an administrative dispute involving a Charter challenge. No one denies that if the tribunal does not have jurisdiction to hear a Charter challenge, separate judicial review proceedings must be launched. Critics of agency jurisdiction reply that these constitutional issues are likely to come before the courts in any event, and thus addressing them in the tribunal adds considerable cost and time to the final resolution of the matter. As yet, no comparative empirical studies examine similar cases before similar tribunals in which one jurisdiction's tribunals have competence to consider Charter issues while the other's do not. Studies of this nature are needed to advance this aspect of the debate past the current speculation.

The unchallenged doctrinal assumption that merits further reflection is that agency jurisdiction to apply the Charter depends on legislative intent. Recall that the idea underlying this assumption is that tribunals have no inherent jurisdiction to decide questions of law (including constitutional questions), and so all such jurisdiction must issue from the legislature. However, the mere fact that tribunals rely on the legislature for jurisdiction to decide questions of law does not imply that the legislature has authority to deprive them of jurisdiction to apply the Charter to their enabling legislation.

Arguably, respect for the supremacy of the Constitution requires agencies to have due regard for the Charter—independently of legislative intent—whenever they interpret ordinary legislation to decide questions of law. Otherwise, tribunals are not treating the Constitution as the supreme law with which all other law must conform. Put another way, a plausible interpretation of the principle of constitutional supremacy is that the legislature cannot confer on agencies the authority to decide questions of law without necessarily conferring on them the authority to apply the Charter. This is entirely consistent with the idea that tribunals have no inherent jurisdiction and so must receive all their legal powers from statute. The issue is whether those legal powers can be exercised without regard for the Charter. At the level of decision-making where Charter rights are at stake, we have seen in section III that the *Slaight* framework to review directs tribunals to evaluate their prospective decisions in light of both the Charter and its analytical framework. To require tribunals to assess provisions of their enabling statutes in the same light is simply asking them to do at the general level that which they are already doing in particular cases, regardless of legislative intent. Yet, as we shall now see, the legislative-intent basis of agency jurisdiction over the Charter became more deeply entrenched in the Supreme Court's most recent ruling on agency jurisdiction to grant remedies under s. 24(1), *R. v. Conway*.[144]

C. Remedies Under Section 24(1)

Section 24(1) provides that anyone whose Charter rights have been infringed may apply to a "court of competent jurisdiction" to obtain a remedy that is appropriate and just in the

---

[144]   2010 SCC 22, [2010] 1 S.C.R. 765 [*Conway*].

circumstances." In *Conway*, Abella J., writing for the Court, built on the rationale in *Martin* to develop a "new approach" for determining when a board or tribunal can grant a specific remedy under s. 24(1).[145] There is a sense in which *Conway* is to s. 24(1) what *Martin* is to s. 52(1): in both cases, the Court relaxes the prior test for determining whether a board or tribunal has jurisdiction to grant the relevant remedy.

Conway has spent most of his adult life in mental health institutions. In 1984 he was found not guilty by reason of insanity of sexual assault with a weapon. In 2006 he complained of various abuses and Charter rights violations. He sought an absolute discharge under s. 24(1) before the Ontario Review Board. After an eight-day hearing, the board rejected Conway's request for discharge, finding that he was "an egocentric, impulsive bully" with "continued paranoid and delusional ideation," and that he would pose a risk to public safety if released.[146]

On review, Abella J. held that the board had jurisdiction to grant Charter remedies generally, but not the remedy of an absolute discharge. The first stage of the analysis, she said, is to determine whether the board is a "court of competent jurisdiction" within the meaning of s. 24(1). Whereas the prior case law, originating with *Mills v. The Queen*,[147] called for an inquiry into whether the agency had jurisdiction over the particular s. 24(1) remedy sought, Abella J. held that the time had come to ground the initial inquiry on a more general and institutional question: "Does this particular tribunal have the jurisdiction to grant *Charter* remedies generally?"[148] She held that the test for resolving this question is precisely the test from *Martin*, which asks whether the tribunal has jurisdiction to decide questions of law, and if so, whether that jurisdiction has been removed by the legislature. The advantage of this approach, Abella J. said, is that it attributes Charter jurisdiction "to the tribunal as an institution, rather than requiring litigants to test, remedy by remedy, whether it is a court of competent jurisdiction."[149] If the board is found to be a court of competent jurisdiction, then the inquiry moves to whether the board has jurisdiction to grant the remedy sought. This issue is to be determined by legislative intent, as discerned from the board's statutory mandate, structure, and function.[150]

In *Conway*, the Court found that the board was a quasi-judicial body authorized to decide questions of law in relation to persons detained for wrongful acts for which they were not criminally responsible (NCR patients). The board is established by, and operates under, part XX.1 of the *Criminal Code*.[151] Section 672(1) of the *Criminal Code* provides for appeals from the board's decisions on questions of law. So, as a general matter, Abella J. found the board to be a court of competent jurisdiction for purposes of s. 24(1). She then had to determine whether the remedy of an absolute discharge was available to Conway in light of the

---

[145]   *Ibid.* at para. 18.

[146]   *Ibid.* at para. 13.

[147]   [1986] 1 S.C.R. 863.

[148]   *Conway, supra* note 144 at para. 22.

[149]   *Ibid.* at para. 23.

[150]   Sometimes the legislature makes this task easy by expressly *excluding* authority to consider Charter questions. See, for example, s. 45 of the B.C. *Administrative Tribunals Act, supra* note 142.

[151]   R.S.C. 1985, c. C-46.

board's mandate and function. At its annual review hearings of NCR patients, the board is required under part XX.1 to weigh and consider the public's interest in protection from dangerous persons, the patient's mental condition, and the patient's liberty interest and other needs. If the NCR patient poses a significant risk to the public, the board is barred by statute from granting the individual an absolute discharge. Because the board found that Conway continued to pose a risk to public safety, it could not grant him an absolute discharge under s. 24(1) of the Charter. Nor could the board grant Conway specific treatment orders and ameliorative detention conditions, as he had requested in the alternative, because these too lay beyond the board's statutory authority. In the result, the Court denied Conway's application for s. 24(1) remedies.

While the "new approach" from *Conway* is intended to avoid forcing litigants to "test, remedy by remedy, whether [the board] is a court of competent jurisdiction,"[152] its method still forces litigants to "test, remedy by remedy," whether the board has jurisdiction with respect to the remedy sought. Because this has always been the critical question at issue in s. 24(1) cases, in practice the "new approach" may turn out to be old wine in new bottles.[153] It is also unclear whether the new approach will result, as it is intended to do, in a lessening of the bifurcation of proceedings. Boards and tribunals after *Conway*, when petitioned for a s. 24(1) remedy, are not to begin with an assessment of the Charter claim that there has been a rights violation. At no point in *Conway* does the Court consider this matter. The inquiry is directed solely to the availability of the remedy. Presumably, if the remedy were available in *Conway*, a consideration of the merits would have been necessary. But because the remedy is unavailable, the board would never get to the merits of the case, and so Conway would have to go to court if he wished to have a public institution determine whether his Charter rights had been violated.

Less clear still is the content of s. 24(1), as a constitutional remedial provision, given that provision's strict dependence on the board's statutory scheme. The Court could have read s. 24(1) as conferring on all "courts of competent jurisdiction" a statute-independent jurisdiction to do whatever is "appropriate and just in the circumstances" to remedy a Charter violation. As with all administrative action, exercise of this jurisdiction would be subject to judicial review. But by grounding jurisdiction over s. 24(1) on the statutory scheme alone, rather than on the statutory scheme *and* the Charter considered as a power-conferring enactment, it appears that applicants are entitled to petition boards for only those remedies and orders that are already available under the statute. Additional cases will be needed to determine whether agency jurisdiction to grant remedies under s. 24(1) has any independent substance.

---

152 *Conway*, *supra* note 144 at para. 23.

153 Lorne Sossin & Andrea Hill, "Social Rights and Administrative Justice" in *Reconceiving Human Rights Practice for the New Social Rights Paradigm*, research project, online: Social Rights in Canada <http://socialrightscura .ca>; see also: Steve Coughlan, "Tribunal Jurisdiction Over Charter Remedies: Now You See It, Now You Don't" (2010) 75 C.R. (6th) 238.

V. Conclusion

The relationship between administrative law and the Charter is sometimes uncertain, but important. As we have seen, there are significant areas of overlap—notably s. 7 of the Charter and the requirements of procedural fairness—but also generally with respect to the constitutional role of the judiciary reviewing executive action. As a result, there is significant cross-pollination such that developments in one area will often, and even necessarily, give rise to changes in the other.

Cases involving judicial review of administrative action that may affect Charter rights are common. The courts have had numerous occasions to address such issues in a diversity of circumstances. Their approach, however, has been less than constant, in particular with respect to whether, when, and how to evaluate administrative decisions under s. 1 of the Charter. The court's recent decision in *Doré* is a strong indication that the future will be more stable than the past. While there was considerable uncertainty as to when a traditional s. 1 analysis would be engaged, the court has now identified a vast area of decision making that engages Charter rights where the *Oakes* analysis will not be relied on. The Court has prudently reserved the challenges of determining precisely how this will play out for later cases.

Finally, the scope of authority of administrative tribunals to apply the Charter is increasingly clear and arguably more generous. The authority of administrative tribunals to grant remedies under s. 24 of the Charter is also better defined and possibly more extensive than it ever has been. Although it is too early to say, this may give rise to an increase in applications for such relief before administrative tribunals, which in turn will give the Court occasion to determine whether s. 24 can ground remedies not already available under the tribunal's enabling statute.

Different Approaches to Reviewing Administrative Decisions That Engage Charter Rights

Case	Administrative analysis, Charter, both, or hybrid?	If administrative analysis, was the decision reasonable?	Was a Charter right infringed by the legislation or the decision?	Justified under s. 1?
Doré	hybrid administrative and Charter	reasonable	decision	yes, reasonable decision
Slaight (Dickson C.J. +3)	Charter	n/a	decision	yes, both
Slaight (Lamer J.)	both	unreasonable	decision	one yes, one no
Slaight (Beetz J.)	Charter	n/a	decision	no, both
Baker (L'Heureux-Dubé J. +4)	administrative	unreasonable	n/a	n/a
Little Sisters (Binnie J. +5)	Charter	n/a	decision	no
Little Sisters (Iacobucci J. +2))	Charter	n/a	both	no
Trinity Western (Iacobucci, Bastarache JJ.)	administrative	unreasonable	n/a	n/a
Trinity Western (L'Heureux-Dubé J.)	both	reasonable	decision	no
Chamberlain (McLachlin C.J. +5)	administrative	unreasonable	n/a	n/a
Chamberlain (Gonthier, Bastarache JJ.)	hybrid administrative and Charter	reasonable	n/a	n/a
Chamberlain (LeBel J.)	administrative with reserve	unreasonable	n/a	n/a
Multani (Charron J. +4)	Charter	n/a	yes	no

Different Approaches to Reviewing Administrative Decisions That Engage Charter Rights

Case	Administrative analysis, Charter, both, or hybrid?	If administrative analysis, was the decision reasonable?	Was a Charter right infringed by the legislation or the decision?	Justified under s. 1?
Multani (Abella, Deschamps JJ.))	hybrid administrative and Charter	unreasonable	n/a	n/a
Multani (LeBel J.)	Charter, not all factors of s. 1	n/a	decision	no
Lake (LeBel J. +8)	Charter, but with deference s. 1	unclear	both	yes
PHS (McLachlin C.J. +8)	Charter	n/a	both	legislation yes, decision no

SUGGESTED ADDITIONAL READINGS

BOOKS AND ARTICLES

Choudhry, S., & K. Roach, "Racial and Ethnic Profiling: Statutory Discretion, Constitutional Remedies, and Democratic Accountability" (2003) 41 Osgoode Hall L.J. 1.

Evans, J.M., "Principle and Pragmatism: Administrative Agencies' Jurisdiction Over Constitutional Issues" in G. Huscroft & M. Taggart, eds., *Inside and Outside Canadian Administrative Law: Essays in Honour of David Mullan* (Toronto: University of Toronto Press, 2006) 377-420.

Evans, J.M., "The Principles of Fundamental Justice: The Constitution and the Common Law" (1991) 29 Osgoode Hall L.J. 51.

Leckey, Robert, "Prescribed by Law/Une règle de droit" (2007) 45 Osgoode Hall L.J. 3 at 571-620.

Lovett, D.K., "Administrative Tribunal Jurisdiction Over Constitutional Issues and the New Administrative Tribunals Act" (2005) 63 Advocate 177.

Van Harten, G., G. Heckman & D. Mullan, *Administrative Law: Cases, Text, and Materials*, 6th ed. (Toronto: Emond Montgomery, 2010) 276-80.

Sossin, Lorne, "Discretion Unbound: Reconciling the Charter and Soft Law" (2002) 45 Can. Public Admin. 465.

CASES

Canada (Attorney General) v. PHS Community Services Society, 2011 SCC 44, [2011] 3 S.C.R. 134.

Canada (Prime Minister) v. Khadr, 2010 SCC 3, [2010] 1 S.C.R. 44.

Charkaoui v. Canada (Citizenship and Immigration), 2007 SCC 9, [2007] 1 S.C.R. 350.

Conway, R. v., 2010 SCC 22, [2010] 1 S.C.R. 765.

Doré v. Barreau du Québec, 2012 SCC 12.

Lake v. Canada (Minister of Justice), 2008 SCC 23, [2008] 1 S.C.R. 761.

Mills v. The Queen, [1986] 1 S.C.R. 863.

Multani v. Commission scolaire Marguerite-Bourgeoys, 2006 SCC 6, [2006] 1 S.C.R. 256.

Newfoundland and Labrador Nurses' Union v. Newfoundland and Labrador (Treasury Board), 2011 SCC 62.

Nova Scotia (Workers' Compensation Board) v. Martin; Nova Scotia (Workers' Compensation Board) v. Laseur, 2003 SCC 54, [2003] 2 S.C.R. 504.

Singh v. Canada (Minister of Employment and Immigration), [1985] 1 S.C.R. 177.

Slaight Communications Inc. v. Davidson, [1989] 1 S.C.R. 1038.

Suresh v. Canada (Minister of Citizenship and Immigration), 2002 SCC 1, [2002] 1 S.C.R. 3.

Wareham v. Ontario (Ministry of Community and Social Services), 2008 ONCA 771.

CHAPTER THIRTEEN

In Search of Aboriginal Administrative Law

JANNA PROMISLOW*
Faculty of Law, Thompson Rivers University

LORNE SOSSIN**
Osgoode Hall Law School

* Thanks are due to Colleen Flood and Arthur Wilson for their helpful comments and to the other authors for their enthusiastic support of this chapter. I am also grateful to Albert Peeling for our many conversations on the subject.

** Some of the ideas in this chapter are adapted from L. Sossin, "Aboriginal Administrative Law" (2011) U.B.C. L. Rev. (forthcoming). I am grateful to Andrea Hall for her excellent research assistance.

I. What Is Aboriginal Administrative Law?

Aboriginal administrative law is about the intersection of three bodies of law: administrative law (referring to Canadian administrative law, as discussed in the rest of this text), indigenous law (referring to the internal law of indigenous peoples),[1] and Aboriginal law (referring to Canadian law about the state's relationships with Aboriginal peoples and Aboriginal peoples' rights). Described as an intersection, we start from the assumption that none of these bodies of law exists in isolation from the others and understand that these bodies of law have a mutual influence upon each other. Thus the name "Aboriginal administrative law" is meant to capture the interaction of the legal principles from each of administrative, indigenous, and Aboriginal law.

In addressing the interaction of these bodies of law as part of administrative law,[2] this chapter builds upon the work of the Royal Commission on Aboriginal Peoples (RCAP) in recognizing Aboriginal governments as one of three orders of government, and the work of scholars who claim that indigenous law, along with the common law and civil law, are the founding legal traditions of Canada.[3] Each has an autonomous existence in Canada, but it is fair to say that what makes Canadian public law a distinct, if not unique project, is the meaningful relationships between legal traditions as well as different spheres of law. Interactions between different spheres and systems of law have many parallels in Canadian public law. For example, the founding of Canada required interaction between principles of statutory and constitutional interpretation, and later, the adoption of the "living tree" approach to Canadian federalism. The introduction of the *Canadian Charter of Rights and Freedoms*[4] similarly led to intermingling between common law and fundamental rights, such as grafting common-law procedural fairness as one of the "principles of fundamental justice" under s. 7 of the Charter. Indigenous laws and perspectives have been acknowl-

---

[1] Although in many contexts, the international language of "indigenous peoples" may be preferable, we will refer to indigenous peoples as Aboriginal peoples, following the language of s. 35 of the *Constitution Act, 1982*, being Schedule B to the *Canada Act 1982* (U.K.), 1982, c. 11, thus signalling that First Nations, Inuit, and Metis peoples are included in this term.

[2] It is worth noting that the intersection of legal spheres and traditions that we address might also be addressed as part of the discussion of indigenous legal traditions and Aboriginal law.

[3] John Borrows, *Canada's Indigenous Constitution* (Toronto: University of Toronto Press, 2010) at 113-18 [John Borrows, *Indigenous Constitution*]; Report of the Royal Commission on Aboriginal Peoples (Ottawa: The Commission, 1996) [RCAP], "Governance," vol. 2, c. 1, online: Indian and Northern Affairs Canada <http://www.collectionscanada.gc.ca/webarchives/20071211052559/http://www.ainc-inac.gc.ca/ch/rcap/sg/sh2_e.html#2.%20Governance>; James [sákéj] Youngblood Henderson, "Empowering Treaty Federalism" (1994) 58 Sask. L. Rev. 241; and, related, Brian Slattery, "The Organic Constitution: Aboriginal Peoples and the Evolution of Canada" (1996) 34 Osgoode Hall L.J. 101.

[4] Part 1 of the *Constitution Act, 1982*, being Schedule B to the *Canada Act 1982* (U.K.), 1982, c. 11.

edged and incorporated into the rights recognized under s. 35 of the *Constitution Act, 1982*, although this interaction has been fraught with debate and criticism.[5]

The idea of Aboriginal administrative law also emerges from the ongoing evolution of Aboriginal self-government in Canada. A great deal of advocacy, adjudication, and analysis has focused on the Aboriginal right to self-government under the Canadian Constitution. In contrast, very little attention has been devoted to what happens the day after self-government agreements are achieved, when the focus shifts to implementing, rather than seeking, recognition of self-government rights. Administrative law is an important component of implementation, as well as part of the design and structure of Aboriginal governments.[6] It is also an important mechanism through which the decisions of Aboriginal governments will be recognized and integrated into Canadian public law. Self-government negotiations in comprehensive land claim processes have begun to answer questions regarding the institutions and mechanisms of Aboriginal government outside of statutory frameworks (for example, the *Indian Act*),[7] such as how indigenous governance traditions are or are not reflected in the elected and executive arms of governments, and the jurisdictions they will exercise. Even these answers lead to more questions: How will courts and governments treat the laws and decisions made by Aboriginal governments? How will Aboriginal governments deal with questions of procedural justice in their decision-making processes? Will people who are adversely affected by administrative and regulatory decisions of Aboriginal governments have the same recourses to the same kinds of bodies as the rest of the country such that Aboriginal agencies, boards, and commissions will emerge as parallel structures to the federal and provincial agencies, boards, and commissions? Or might Aboriginal governments find alternative institutional forms to express and protect administrative justice?[8]

Against this backdrop, in this chapter we present Aboriginal administrative law as an emerging, distinctive, and perhaps unique, branch of administrative law that is capable of responding to and incorporating concepts of fairness, independence, and accountability in Aboriginal contexts. We discuss it as a pan-Aboriginal concept, encompassing sufficient flexibility and generality to respond to differences in Aboriginal governance traditions and institutions, much as administrative law already encompasses a diverse range of governance contexts. Within this concept, we include at least three separate but related contexts.[9]

---

[5] See e.g. Kent McNeil, Aboriginal Title and the Supreme Court of Canada: What is Happening? (2006) 69 Sask. L. Rev. 281-308; Gordon Christie "A Colonial Reading of Recent Jurisprudence: Sparrow, Delgamuukw and Haida Nation" (2005) 23:1 Windsor Y.B. Access Just. 17-53; and Minnawaanagogiizhigook (Dawnis Kennedy), "Reconciliation Without Respect? Section 35 and Indigenous Legal Orders" in Law Commission of Canada, ed., *Indigenous Legal Traditions* (Vancouver: UBC Press, 2007) 77-113.

[6] For a discussion of other aspects of implementation, see Stephanie Irlbacher-Fox, "Justice Authorities in Self-Government Agreements: The Importance of Conditions and Mechanisms of Implementation" in John D. Whyte, ed., *Moving Toward Justice* (Purich Publishing & Saskatchewan Institute for Public Policy, 2008) 130-41.

[7] R.S.C. 1985, c. I-5.

[8] For an example of a governance approach from an Aboriginal point of view, see John Borrows, "Constitutional Law From a First Nation Perspective: Self-Government and the Royal Proclamation" (1994) 28 U.B.C. L. Rev. 1 [Borrows, "Constitutional Law"].

[9] Another context in which to contemplate Aboriginal administrative law is in relation to how institutions and processes intended to further reconciliation and settle past grievances with Aboriginal peoples should be designed—for example, the Specific Claims Tribunal (online: the Specific Claims Tribunal <http://www.sct-

what is meant by Public Institution

A. Developing Administrative Justice for Aboriginal Self-Government

The first context involves the development of administrative justice by Aboriginal communities as they assume control over their own public institutions through mechanisms of self-government. To begin this discussion, we first need to clarify what is encompassed within our discussion of Aboriginal self-government.

Aboriginal self-government is evolving through a number of different approaches, processes and instruments. Importantly, this field is not characterized by a linear move from statutorily defined governmental powers under the *Indian Act* to negotiated self-government achieved through land claims or self-government negotiations. Instead, evolutions toward greater self-government are occurring through changing legislative frameworks as well as negotiations to define government-to-government relationships on specific issues and to redefine Aboriginal governments outside the confines of the *Indian Act*. To facilitate our discussion, we refer to Shin Imai's helpful delineation of four non-exclusive types of Aboriginal self-government:

1. sovereignty and self-government, which involve recognition of the inherent authority of an indigenous government to govern over a defined territory, as illustrated by comprehensive self-government agreements like the Nisga'a agreement;

2. self-management and self-administration, under which Aboriginal communities exercise powers that derive from the state, such as *Indian Act* band councils or Metis settlement councils under Alberta's *Metis Settlements Act*;

3. co-management and joint management, which describe Aboriginal participation in land and resource management through Aboriginal representation in decision-making institutions, as illustrated by the Mackenzie Valley Environmental Impact Review Board in the Northwest Territories; and

4. participation in public government, as illustrated by the government of Nunavut over which Inuit control is, at least for now, secured by the demographics of the territory.[10]

The discussion below encompasses all four of these types of self-governance, recognizing that elements of more than one type may be present in a given context.

Regardless of the approach to self-government, administrative justice is significant to achieving self-government structures that meet the self-determining aims and needs of Aboriginal communities. Addressing both the structures of accountability and decision making within Aboriginal governments as well as the principles of administrative justice that may guide the work of those institutions and their partnerships with state institutions, administrative justice is an expression of societal values. As we explore in this chapter, administrative justice in Aboriginal governance contexts may be informed by both indigenous law

---

trp.ca/hom/index_e.htm>) and the Truth and Reconciliation Commission (online: Aboriginal Affairs and Northern Development Canada <http://www.ainc-inac.gc.ca/ai/rqpi/trc/index-eng.asp>). This exploration, however, is beyond the scope of this chapter.

10   Shin Imai, "Indigenous Self-Determination and the State" in Benjamin J. Richardson, Shin Imai, & Kent McNeil, eds., *Indigenous Peoples and the Law: Comparative and Critical Perspectives* (Oxford and Portland: Hart Publishing, 2009) 285.

as well as Canadian law, but arriving at an appropriate mix of indigenous and Canadian traditions in the administration of self-government demands attention.

B. Applying Administrative Law to Aboriginal Decision-Makers

The second context in which Aboriginal administrative law plays out is in relation to how existing administrative law principles and doctrines are applied to Aboriginal decision-makers. The starting point for this discussion is that decision making by *Indian Act* band governments (or Metis settlement councils under the Alberta *Metis Settlements Act*) is typically reviewable by Canadian courts on administrative law grounds.[11] Applying administrative law to Aboriginal decision making is thus a long-standing feature of the governance of at least First Nations peoples. Should new forms of Aboriginal self-government alter this relationship?

This question points to the need to examine what may be different about Aboriginal governments, and whether administrative law principles with respect to concepts such as independence and deference may be inadequate to accommodate judicial review of Aboriginal decision-makers. As discussed above, there are many different forms of self-government that differ in their sources of authority, governance structures, and incorporation of indigenous law and governance traditions. A key issue then, is how the particular type of decision-maker and the nature and context of the decision should be taken into consideration in applying administrative law to Aboriginal decision-makers. By the same token, we need to question what approaches and concepts developed by Aboriginal decision-makers (for example, related to concepts of fairness, impartiality, and independence) will have implications in other administrative law settings.

Following the available jurisprudence to date, our attention in this section of the chapter is focused on the move from judicial review of *Indian Act* bands to the accountability of decision-makers under the authority of governments formed through modern treaty processes.

C. Respecting Aboriginal Rights and Jurisdictions: The Duty to Consult and Accommodate

The third and most-developed context in which to consider Aboriginal administrative law centres on Canadian governments. Against a history of governments not implementing commitments made to Aboriginal peoples and delayed settlement of their claims, the Supreme Court has insisted that Aboriginal peoples be consulted and accommodated, as appropriate, regarding both proven and unproven Aboriginal rights.[12] In developing the scope and content of these constitutional duties, the courts have borrowed heavily on administrative law principles, processes, and remedies. This convergence between procedural justice and Aboriginal law is enough to bring it within the scope of a distinctive Aboriginal administrative

---

11   *Gabriel v. Canatonquin*, [1978] 1 F.C. 124 (T.D.), aff'd [1980] 2 F.C. 792 (C.A.); *Sparvier v. Cowessess Indian Band No. 73*, [1993] 3 F.C. 142, 13 Admin. L.R. (2d) 266 (T.D.) [*Sparvier*].

12   *Haida Nation v. British Columbia (Minister of Forests)*, 2004 SCC 73, [2004] 3 S.C.R. 511 [*Haida Nation*].

law, but the duty to consult is also importantly linked to self-government, the focus in the other two contexts of Aboriginal administrative law identified above.

The duty to consult and accommodate arises most commonly in relation to decisions about the management of land and resources, picking up where self-government and the mechanisms of negotiated forms of government-to-government interaction have not been defined (or where there are gaps in a negotiated agreement and its implementation, as was the case in *Little Salmon/Carmacks*).[13] Aboriginal communities may claim full or shared jurisdiction over the land and resources in issue, and thus consultation and accommodation can be understood as a decision-by-decision bridge to more stable forms of interaction between Aboriginal communities and governments. In the context of unsettled land claims, negotiated consultation protocols and shared decision making on resource management have been employed as a step toward modern treaties or as a way to arrive at government-to-government relationships without resolving the underlying land and rights claims.[14] In the context of historical treaties, joint decision-making models and land-use planning efforts are also beginning to be developed, which may assist in implementing consultation obligations in a predictable framework that is respectful of Aboriginal rights and jurisdictions.[15] Nevertheless, the case-by-case consideration of a duty to consult and accommodate does not address governance relationships directly, and the administrative law approach to consultation often falls short of respecting Aboriginal rights and jurisdictions. Is this *administrative* law borrowing up to the Aboriginal law task of reconciliation? How are administrative law principles being adapted in the context of Aboriginal law obligations? And how will this borrowing impact administrative law outside of Aboriginal law obligations? Can, and how can, administrative law tools be adapted to serve the aims of broadening of Canadian public law to encompass indigenous legal traditions and governments?

---

13   *Beckman v. Little Salmon/Carmacks First Nation*, 2010 SCC 53, [2010] 3 S.C.R. 103 [*Little Salmon/ Carmacks*].

14   One example is the Consultation Interim Measures Agreement from July 27, 2009 between Ontario, Canada, and the Algonquins of Ontario (online: Ontario Ministry of Aboriginal Affairs <http://www.aboriginalaffairs .gov.on.ca/english/negotiate/algonquin/algonquin.asp>) regarding a claim that dates back to 1983, and the parties are nearing an agreement in principle (see Mohammed Adam, "Algonquin Land Claim Deal Near, Lawyer Says," *Ottawa Citizen*, 14 February 2012). A second example is found in the reconciliation agreements between British Columbia and the Haida Nation, the Coastal First Nations, and the Haisla Nation, respectively. They are committed to establishing shared decision-making structures in relation to land and resources within particular geographic boundaries without resolving the land and rights claims of these nations (online: British Columbia <http://www.newrelationship.gov.bc.ca/agreements_and_leg/reconciliation.html>).

15   For example, Ontario's *Far North Act, 2010*, S.O. 2010, c. 18, establishes a framework under which joint bodies may be established. The statement of purpose in this Act (s. 1) uses the terminology "community based land use planning," shying away from recognizing Aboriginal jurisdictions but still indicating its purposes as conducting land-use planning in a manner that is consistent with the recognition and affirmation of s. 35 Aboriginal and treaty rights, including the duty to consult. The *Far North Act* has been much criticized by Ontario First Nations, particularly the Nishnawbe Aski Nation, as well as other commentators. See Penelope Simons & Lynda Collins, "Participatory Rights in the Ontario Mining Sector: An International Human Rights Perspective" (2010) 6 McGill J.S.D.L.P. 177 at 202-4 (First Nations powers limited and inconsistent with international commitments); contrast Bruce Pardy & Annette Stoehr, "The Failed Reform of Ontario's Mining Laws" (2011) 23 J. Envtl. L. & Prac. 1 at 8, 9 (process as cumbersome, unpredictable/too discretionary, and giving too much power to First Nations with regard to land use).

We pursue these questions by considering the duty to consult and accommodate alongside the duty of fairness, identifying and questioning the appropriateness of both commonalities and differences between the two in light of the underlying purposes of both administrative and Aboriginal law.

The remainder of this chapter addresses each of these three contexts in turn, providing an introduction and overview of the concepts in an emerging and complex area of administrative law. More time is devoted to the duty to consult and accommodate, in part because this context is the most developed, and in part because this aspect of Aboriginal administrative law has already had far-reaching impacts on government decision making, particularly in the lands and resource sectors, affecting the practice of administrative law far beyond Aboriginal law specialities.

An overarching theme in this chapter is the expectation that developments in Aboriginal administrative law will reverberate in administrative law more generally. Particularly apparent in relation to duty to consult and accommodate, we view the adaptation of principles and institutions from one area of public law to another, and between indigenous and Canadian legal traditions, as part of the dynamic of administrative law more generally. Introducing Aboriginal administrative law demonstrates this dynamic and encourages both students and practitioners to think creatively and flexibly about administrative law. Equally important, the concerns underlying Aboriginal law—respecting Aboriginal peoples and reconciliation—suggest some limitations and cautions with respect to the extension of administrative law into the three contexts identified above. Thus, this chapter is intended to contribute to a thoughtful and principled approach to the development of Aboriginal administrative law.

II. Developing Administrative Justice for Aboriginal Self-Government

As in other parts of this chapter, our presumption is that the boundaries of legal systems are porous; that both Canadian and indigenous law have been and will continue to be affected by the other. This characteristic of law is emphasized by John Borrows in relation to indigenous law, which he describes as living, adaptable, and imperfect traditions that have "ancient roots [but] can also speak to the present and future needs of all Canadians."[16] Canadian law (and western systems of law more generally) can be similarly characterized as open and affected by diverse influences and processes of diffusion.[17] As Val Napoleon suggests, it may be that "the most crucial process that a people must consider in seeking to understand their own legal order and the legal orders of others is how laws change over time."[18] Understanding indigenous legal systems, and indeed all legal systems, as adaptable,

---

16 Borrows, "Constitutional Law," *supra* note 8 at 10.

17 See e.g. William Twining, "Social Sciences and the Diffusion of Law" (2005) 32 J.L. & Soc'y 203.

18 Val Napoleon, Ayook: Gitksan Legal Order, Law, and Legal Theory (PhD thesis, University of Victoria, Faculty of Law, 2009) [unpublished] at 290.

creates the space necessary to understand indigenous law as a political as well as a cultural phenomenon.[19]

From such starting points, we move away from the concern for the "aboriginality" of the practices and principles of administrative justice in Aboriginal governments, as directed by the Aboriginal rights jurisprudence,[20] to consider how the systems of administrative justice that are adopted or continue to be in place within Aboriginal governance meet the needs and aspirations of Aboriginal communities and facilitate relationships with the Canadian state.

The incorporation of indigenous law and values in the approach to administrative justice within Aboriginal self-governance remains critically important to the self-governance aims of Aboriginal communities but difficult to achieve. One difficulty is identified by Paul Nadasdy, who points out that participating in land claims and self-government processes involves discourses of governance that are foreign to indigenous practices and lifestyles and, consequently, can transform indigenous governance.[21] Although transformation and change should not be presumed to produce negative outcomes,[22] Aboriginal communities and critical scholars have earned their skepticism regarding the assimilative nature of the interaction and the potential to reinscribe the harms of colonial impositions. A second challenge is drawing on legal traditions that support decentralized, non-state governance to inform governance institutions that parallel or share jurisdiction with the institutions of the Canadian state. Val Napoleon's work on Gitksan law and legal theory, for example, illustrates the decentralized nature of Gitksan government and the lack of specialized decision-makers but also a tradition rich in mechanisms of transparency, accountability, and accessibility. Such values are demonstrated in the requirement that most community business—whether decisions about access or ownership of resources, changes in leadership, or resolving disputes within a house (the main governance institution)—be conducted openly in the feast house. Moreover, such decision making is supported by extensive consultation with those affected by the issue beforehand, as well as the formal appointment of individuals to witness the proceedings, thereby creating a public record and ensuring that the decisions reached are accessible to all.[23] Witnesses are selected from guests at the feast whose lineages are un-

---

19   For discussion, see *ibid.* at 289-90.

20   See e.g. Lamer C.J.C.'s statement in *R. v. Van der Peet*, [1996] 2 S.C.R. 507 at para. 20, that "[t]he task of this Court is to define aboriginal rights in a manner which recognizes that aboriginal rights are *rights* but which does so without losing sight of the fact that they are rights held by aboriginal people because they are *aboriginal* … . The Court must define the scope of s. 35(1) in a way which capture *both* the aboriginal and the rights in aboriginal rights" (emphasis in original). For comment and criticism, see John Borrows, *Recovering Canada: The Resurgence of Indigenous Law* (Toronto: University of Toronto Press, 2002) at 60, and Mark D. Walters, "Promise and Paradox: The Emergence of Indigenous Rights Law in Canada" in *Indigenous Peoples and the Law, supra* note 10 at 47.

21   Paul Nadasdy, *Hunters and Bureaucrats: Power, Knowledge and Aboriginal-State Relations in the Southwest Yukon* (Vancouver: UBC Press, 2003). For related concerns, see Christie, *supra* note 5.

22   For discussion, see Twining, *supra* note 17 at 232 and 237 and Nicole Roughan, "The Association of State and Indigenous Law: A Case Study in 'Legal Association' " (2009) 59 U.T.L.J. 135.

23   Napoleon, *supra* note 18, especially the cases outlined in chapter 3 and at 309, where she defines "public witnessing and accountability" as a general working principle of Gitksan legal theory and the steps involved in managing disputes among the Gitksan.

related to the hosts and are given roles and degrees of responsibilities that depend on their relationship to the host group.[24]

As the Gitksan example demonstrates, some indigenous approaches to the administration of government that could, with due care and attention, inform the conduct of business in more centralized government structures arrived at through negotiations. However, as the brief overview of administrative justice within the different types of Aboriginal self-government that follows illustrates, the challenges of implementing such approaches through governance institutions are formidable.

A. Participation in Public Government, Co-Management, and Shared Management

Public government models rely on demographics and Aboriginal participation to achieve Aboriginal self-government aspirations. Co-management and shared management boards involve Aboriginal participation on administrative bodies outside Aboriginal communities, whose decisions affect those communities. Reservations concerning both of these approaches to self-government reflect the critique from critical legal scholarship noted above that transplanted legal instruments have a limited capacity for transformative political change. Can such regulatory and administrative settings provide the space necessary for adaptation that can transform regulation to reflect local values? What other measures and concerns should inform our assessment of the success of such approaches?

Canada's most ambitious instance of indigenous self-government to date—the Nunavut Land Claims Agreement (NLCA)—established the Territory of Nunavut in 1999. The NLCA specifies that the number of Inuit employed in the public service be representative of Inuit in Nunavut society.[25] This figure was set at 50 percent for April 1, 1999, and was intended to slowly increase to 85 percent to reflect the fact that Inuit comprise the overwhelming majority of Nunavut residents. The structures of the Nunavut government, on the other hand, are familiar Canadian governance institutions. Apart from the consensus nature of the Nunavut legislature, government is organized into line departments and central agencies (such as the Department of Finance), with hierarchical leadership and specialized bureaucracies.[26] Inuit values and political aspirations were thus intended to be achieved through their strong demographic majority and participation in the territorial government.[27] While the success of Nunavut as an expression of a distinctly Inuit form of self-governance is hotly

---

[24] *Ibid.* at xv, citing Richard Overstall, "Encountering the Spirit in the Land: 'Property' in a Kinship-Based Legal Order" in John McLaren, Andrew R. Buck, & Nancy E. Wright, eds., *Despotic Dominion: Property Rights in British Settler Societies* (Vancouver: UBC Press, 2004) 22 at 28.

[25] *Nunavut Land Claims Agreement Act,* S.C. 1993, c. 29, s. 23.2.1.

[26] See, generally, Graham White, "Governance in Nunavut: Capacity vs. Culture?" (2009) 43 J. Can. Stud. 57.

[27] The establishment of a separate land claims organization, Nunavut Tunngavik Incorporated (NTI), representing the Inuit beneficiaries of the claim, also has an important role and influence on governance in Nunavut (*ibid.* at 60-61). Natalia Loukacheva explains that the public governance model does not preclude the Inuit from pursuing separate, self-government institutions within Nunavut in the future (*The Arctic Promise: Legal and Political Autonomy of Greenland and Nunavut* (Toronto: University of Toronto Press, 2007) 49.

debated and continually evaluated,[28] Paul Okalik, the first premier of Nunavut, offers his perspective as follows: "What we sought and attained in our land claims negotiation was a legislated guarantee that Inuit would participate in a meaningful way in the decision-making process in our territory. In Nunavut, we were able to guarantee the rights of self-government within a public governance structure."[29]

The emphasis in Paul Okalik's comments is on meaningful participation in decision making, an aim that is behind the establishment of co-management boards that are part of the NCLA as well as other claims. Sari Graben has explored how such participatory processes have led to the adaptation of regulatory instruments that are, for all intents and purposes, a transplanted form of Aboriginal self-governance.[30] Using the Mackenzie Valley Environmental Impact Review Board (MVEIRB) case study, a co-management board in the Northwest Territories that was mandated by land claim agreements in the Gwich'in and Sahtu territories,[31] she describes how Aboriginal communities provided input into the guidelines used by the board and the impact of this participation. Furthermore, Graben finds those guidelines, in part because of the incorporation of Aboriginal governance principles, have proved instrumental in fostering private negotiation between indigenous communities and industry as a central feature of environmental assessment.

One further context in which co-management processes are becoming more common is in British Columbia, through "reconciliation agreements."[32] Called "shared" and "joint" decision making in this context, the structures established in these reconciliation agreements are notable for several reasons. The Haida Gwaii Management Council (HGMC), for example, was established by the joint operation of the *Haida Gwaii Reconciliation Act*[33] and a resolution of the Haida Nation, pursuant to the Kunst'aa Guu-Kunst'aayah Reconciliation Protocol, signed by the Haida Nation and British Columbia in 2009. Similar to the land claims boards established through the land claims and subsequent legislation, the HGMC consists of two members of the Haida Nation appointed by resolution after consultation with British Columbia, two members appointed by the lieutenant governor in council after consultation with the Haida Nation, and a chair appointed by resolutions of each party.[34]

---

28   For two perspectives, see Loukacheva, *ibid.*, and White, *supra* note 26.

29   Paul Okalik, "Nunavut: The Road to Indigenous Sovereignty" (2007) 2 Intercultural Human Rights Law Review 11 at 14.

30   Sari Graben, "Writing the Rules of Socio-Economic Assessment: Adaptation Through Participation" (paper presented at the annual meeting of the Law and Society Association, Renaissance Chicago Hotel, Chicago, IL, May 27, 2010, Osgoode CLPE Research Paper 23/2010).

31   See "Preamble," *Mackenzie Valley Resource Management Act*, S.C. 1998, c. 25.

32   For reconciliation agreements reached to date, see online: British Columbia <http://www.newrelationship .gov.bc.ca/agreements_and_leg/reconciliation.html>, and *supra* note 14.

33   S.B.C. 2010, c. 17, s. 3 [HGRA].

34   British Columbia Board Resourcing and Development Office, Directory of Agencies, Haida Gwaii Management Council, online: British Columbia <http://www.fin.gov.bc.ca/BRDO/boardView.asp?boardNum =215137> [BRDO document]. In contrast, the members of the MVEIRB are all appointed by the federal minister of Aboriginal Affairs and Northern Development. There is an equal number of nominations from the federal and territorial governments on the one hand, and from Aboriginal land claimant organizations on the other hand. Nominations for the chair generally come from other Review Board members (online: Mackenzie Valley Review Board <http://www.reviewboard.ca/about>).

HGMC members are required to adhere to natural justice, impartiality, and procedural fairness in their work, but also function on consensus decision-making model, where the consensus of four of the five members demonstrates a sufficient degree of consensus.[35] A key difference from the northern land claim context is the functions of these bodies. MVEIRB is an environmental assessment board; other northern co-management boards have responsibilities such as permitting decisions with respect to land and water use. By contrast, the HGMC's mandate is to make strategic policy decisions dealing specifically with forest resources and heritage sites.[36] Significantly, the HGMC has been created outside the strictures of the B.C. treaty process, which has proven unacceptable to several B.C. First Nations. The joint Haida Nation and B.C. authorities relied on to establish the HGMC demonstrate the possibility of a different, non-hierarchical relationship between the First Nation and the province.[37] Although it is too early to evaluate the HGMC or other shared management structures created through recognition agreements, there will be much to learn from the experience, including the application of administrative law principles in structuring the work of such joint bodies bridging indigenous and Canadian governments.

B. Self-Management and Self-Administration

The nature of the powers of *Indian Act* band councils has long been a point of confusion. Specifically, courts have not always recognized that these councils may exercise powers derived from inherent rights of self-governance in addition to, or as "interfered with," by the powers delegated through the *Indian Act*.[38] To understand the nature of *Indian Act* band councils and their powers, one must be aware of the colonial history and policies that have intruded upon and reshaped First Nations governments.[39]

Two areas in which amendments to the *Indian Act* have permitted First Nations to develop laws based on band "custom" are in relation to band elections and band membership. The control over membership was introduced in 1985 when Bill C-31 was introduced as part of a package to correct the legacy of Indian status rules that discriminated against women.[40]

---

[35] BRDO document, *ibid.* The MVEIRB has well-developed rules of procedure, as mandated by statute, in which the application of the common-law duty of procedural fairness is confirmed, online: Mackenzie Valley Review Board <http://www.reviewboard.ca/upload/ref_library/MVEIRB_RulesofProcedure_0505.pdf>).

[36] HGRA ss. 1, 4, 5, and 7.

[37] For a discussion of the significance of non-hierarchical structures in the association of indigenous and state law, see Roughan, *supra* note 22.

[38] See Walters, *supra* note 20 at 31, where he favours the approach taken in *Bone v. Sioux Valley Indian Band No. 290*, [1996] 3 C.N.L.R. 54 (F.C.T.D.) (authority from inherent governance powers; context of a dispute regarding custom election code) over the approach in *Heron Seismic Services Ltd. v. Muscowpetung Indian Band*, [1991] 2 C.N.L.R. 52 (Sask. Q.B.) (authority from statute; context of a dispute over an account for work done drilling wells on reserve).

[39] See Walters, *supra* note 20, and Hamar Foster, "Canada: 'Indian Administration' from the Royal Proclamation of 1763 to Constitutionally Entrenched Aboriginal Rights" in Paul Havemann, ed., *Indigenous Peoples' Rights in Australia, Canada and New Zealand* (Auckland and New York: Oxford University Press, 1999) 351.

[40] The rules implemented through Bill C-31 in 1985 (*An Act to Amend the Indian Act*, S.C. 1985, c. 27) have since also been found to be discriminatory against women: *McIvor v. Canada (Registrar of Indian and Northern Affairs)*, 2009 BCCA 153.

The default position with respect to both electoral and membership codes is that the rules set out in the *Indian Act* apply until a First Nation initiates a process to adopt its own codes. Aboriginal Affairs and Northern Development Canada reports that of the 617 recognized First Nations in Canada, 341 have implemented community or custom election codes[41] while Kirsty Gover reports that 243 First Nations have adopted membership codes.[42]

Although administrative law should foster respect for band customs, those customs must also be approached with caution, particularly for *Indian Act* band "custom rules," which claim to be representative of Aboriginal communities but can involve substantial subjective discretion. Through seeking this balance, Aboriginal administrative law can seek to develop a more nuanced approach in dealing with the complexities of Aboriginal governance and "intra-band" disputes.[43]

C. Self-Government and Sovereignty

The RCAP suggested three models of Aboriginal government: the nation government model, the public government model, and the community of interest model. In each of these models, an Aboriginal government, "would have powers and authorities in respect of law making (legislative); administration and policy making (executive); and interpretation, application and enforcement of law (judicial)."[44] The legislative component, "may resemble historical structures, existing structures (a council) or government structures common to other Canadian governments (such as a legislative assembly)."[45] Likewise, the executive may be composed of individuals, such as chiefs, bodies, or councils. Finally, judicial powers will most likely rest with those Aboriginals seen as providing good "counsel and wisdom," such as elders and women.[46] In the end, the RCAP provides a useful point of departure but surprisingly little in the way of specific models that might inform Aboriginal administrative law. As with so much in the field of Aboriginal and constitutional law, the focus has been on achieving recognition of Aboriginal self-government, rather than on what happens the day after.

It should not be surprising that Aboriginal approaches to justice under self-government show similarities to the Canadian model given the nexus of history and culture. One example of this can be seen in the Nisga'a Administrative Decisions Review Board. The Nisga'a Lisims Government is defined in Chapter 1 of the Nisga'a Final Agreement to mean, "the government of the Nisga'a Nation described in the Nisga'a Constitution." Chapter 11 of the Nisga'a Final Agreement describes in some detail the powers of the Nisga'a Lisims Government, and the relationship of those powers to those of the federal and provincial governments. Section 16 of Chapter 11 provides that the Nisga'a Lisims Government will create

---

41   Online: Aboriginal Affairs and Northern Development Canada <http://www.aadnc-aandc.gc.ca/eng/1323193986817>.

42   Kirsty Gover, *Tribal Constitutionalism* (Oxford: Oxford University Press, 2011) 74.

43   For a discussion regarding custom elections, see Val Napoleon, "Aboriginal Discourse: Gender, Identity, and Community" in *Indigenous Peoples and the Law, supra* note 10, 233 especially at 248-52.

44   RCAP, "Models of Aboriginal Government: An Overview," *supra* note 3, vol. 2, c. 3.

45   *Ibid.*

46   *Ibid.*

appropriate procedures for the review of administrative decisions of Nisga'a Institutions. That power has been exercised in the establishment of the Nisga'a Administrative Decisions Review Board, pursuant to the Nisga'a *Administrative Decisions Review Act, 2000*.[47]

The *Nisga'a Administrative Decisions Review Act* sets out the authority and process of the board. Apart from a provision authorizing translation of a hearing into the Nisga'a language (though stipulating that the language of hearings, unless ordered otherwise, is English),[48] there appears to be little in the legislation denoting that this tribunal is different than other Canadian tribunals created to review executive decision making across the country.[49] The board has the power to set aside a government decision complained against if it is found to have been made beyond the jurisdiction of the decision-maker, reached unfairly, or based on an incorrect finding in law. In other words, the Act creates a board very much within the Canadian administrative law tradition. Thus far, the board has received very few complaints and has been concerned primarily with disputes relating to elections.[50] In *Azak v. Nisga'a Nation*,[51] the B.C. Human Rights Tribunal found that the Nisga'a Lisims government and the board fall under federal jurisdiction with respect to human rights. As such, the B.C. Human Rights Code had no application to decisions of the board. This case demonstrates the complexity of not just bijuralism, but also federalism, which is knit into the fabric of Canadian and Aboriginal administrative law.

One of the important functions of Canadian administrative law is its role in ensuring the accountability of government decision-makers. When considered in the context of Aboriginal self-government, vital questions arise as to who has the authority to monitor the accountability of Aboriginal decision-makers, and the standards against which accountability should be judged in those circumstances. One concern is that when Aboriginal institutions are subject to Canadian administrative review, traditional principles of administrative law will not adequately account for these alternative structures of accountability. It is therefore relevant to look at examples of how Canadian courts have assessed the accountability of Aboriginal decision-makers and the structures within which they operate, considered here in relation to Aboriginal decision-makers.

As Rothstein J. (as he then was) stated in *Sparvier v. Cowessess Indian Band*, in which the election of a Band Chief under a custom election code was challenged by one of the unsuccessful candidates:

---

[47] See *Nisga'a Administrative Decisions Review Act, NLGSR 2000/04* (2008), online: Nisga'a Lisims Government Wilp Si'Ayuukhl Nisga'a <http://nisgaalisims.ca/files/nlg/Nisga_a_Administrative_Decisions_Review_Act_-_Unofficial_Consolidation__January_4_2008_.pdf>.

[48] *Ibid.*, s. 14(2).

[49] Although it is common to have tribunal members recite an oath of impartiality upon appointment, the Act provides that in the case of the Nisga'a Administrative Decisions Review Board, that oath is taken before the Council of Elders. The oath reads: "Do you solemnly swear or affirm that you will faithfully, truly and impartially, without fear or favour and to the best of your judgment, skill and ability, perform the office of member of the Nisga'a Administrative Decisions Review Board and that you will not, except in the discharge of your duties, disclose to any person any of the evidence or other matter brought before the Board." *Ibid.* at 19.

[50] This assessment is based on a conversation with Angela D'Elia and Jim Aldridge, counsel to the Nisga'a Lisims Government, in the fall of 2009. The decisions of the board do not appear to be published.

[51] [2003] B.C.H.R.T.D. No. 75 (QL).

While I accept the importance of an autonomous process for electing band governments, in my opinion, minimum standards of natural justice or procedural fairness must be met. I fully recognize that the political movement of Aboriginal People taking more control over their lives should not be quickly interfered with by the courts. However, members of bands are individuals who, in my opinion, are entitled to due process and procedural fairness in procedures of tribunals that affect them. To the extent that this Court has jurisdiction, the principles of natural justice and procedural fairness are to be applied.[52]

A more recent illustration of the intersection of administrative law approaches to accountability and Aboriginal self-government occurred in *Lafferty v. Tlicho Government*.[53] This case, occurring in the context of government structures recognized through a comprehensive claims process, involved three dissident chiefs who challenged a law enacted by the Tlicho government. Under s. 13 of the Tlicho Constitution, the validity of laws enacted by the Tlicho Assembly may be challenged by way of an appeal to that Assembly (at least until the Assembly enacts laws creating a different appeal body). The dissident chiefs who used this process, and participated both as appellants and members of the Tlicho Assembly, did not obtain a favourable result, and so chose to dispute the law in the Canadian courts. Justice Richard of the Supreme Court of the Northwest Territories struck out the chiefs' claim as an abuse of process because the claim had, "already been adjudicated upon by the process chosen by the Tlicho in developing their *Constitution*."[54] Justice Richard further affirmed Tlicho self-government by holding that, "[t]he most that could be said for the Applicants' position … is that there is concurrent jurisdiction,"[55] but the "[c]ourt cannot simply ignore the fact that the Tlicho Assembly has, under the Constitution, already ruled on the validity of the impugned law."[56] Overall, Justice Richard saw the applicants' claim as disrespectful of the newly established Tlicho self-government,[57] even going so far as to override criticisms of the Tlicho government's accountability. For instance, he observed that, "[w]hile it may appear an anomaly to have a legislative body … re-constitute itself into an adjudicative body (the Tlicho assembly under section 13.3) to hear a challenge to the validity of one of its own laws, that is the process that the Tlicho people decided upon in adopting the Tlicho *Constitution*."[58]

The *Tlicho* case seems to confirm the autonomy of decisions made by Aboriginal governments, so long as adequate internal accountability exists. In the Tlicho example, it did not matter that the accountability mechanism in question was unique to the Aboriginal context.

---

52 *Sparvier, supra* note 11 at para. 47.

53 *Lafferty v. Tlicho Government*, [2009] 3 C.N.L.R. 151 (N.W.T.S.C.), appeal dismissed on grounds of mootness, 2010 NWTCA 4 [*Tlicho*].

54 *Ibid.* at para. 42.

55 *Ibid.* at para. 41.

56 *Ibid.* at para. 42.

57 *Ibid.* at para. 38.

58 *Ibid.* at para. 23.

III. Applying Administrative Law to Aboriginal Decision-Makers

In this section, we explore the importance of Aboriginal decision-making contexts in the development of administrative law in Canada.

A. How Do We Assess Independence?

It is perhaps a coincidence that the leading precedent from the Supreme Court of Canada on the meaning of independence in administrative decision making arose in the context of an Aboriginal tribunal: *Canadian Pacific Ltd. v. Matsqui Indian Band.*[59] As discussed by Laverne Jacobs in Chapter 8, Caught Between Judicial Paradigms and the Administrative State's Pastiche: "Tribunal" Independence, Impartiality, and Bias, *Matsqui* involved appeals from tax assessments of real estate within reserves. The particular issue was whether lands granted to Canadian Pacific by the Crown were, by definition, excluded from lands "within a reserve." Canadian Pacific lost at the tribunal level, so it applied to the Federal Court, Trial Division for judicial review. Canadian Pacific argued that the provisions permitting band members to sit on the assessment appeal tribunal raised a reasonable apprehension of bias. Joyal J. struck out the application on the ground that the issues raised could be litigated within the assessment appeal structure itself.[60] Joyal J. did not deal with reasonable apprehension of bias. An appeal to the Federal Court of Appeal was allowed.[61] The band appealed to the Supreme Court of Canada, where Canadian Pacific argued that the assessment appeal procedures were not an adequate alternative to judicial review because the appeal tribunals themselves gave rise to a reasonable apprehension of bias, in part based on the tribunals' lack of independence. Lamer C.J. concluded that the judicial independence principles first developed in *Valente*[62] apply to administrative tribunals on the basis of natural justice principles, but that the test for institutional independence may be less strict than for courts:

> Therefore, while administrative tribunals are subject to the Valente principles, the test for institutional independence must be applied in light of the functions being performed by the particular tribunal at issue. The requisite level of institutional independence (i.e., security of tenure, financial security and administrative control) will depend on the nature of the tribunal, the interests at stake, and other indices of independence such as oaths of office.
>
> In some cases, a high level of independence will be required. For example, where the decisions of a tribunal affect the security of the person of a party (such as the immigration adjudicators ...), a more strict application of the Valente principles may be warranted. In this case, we are dealing with an administrative tribunal adjudicating disputes relating to the assessment of property taxes. In my view, this is a case where a more flexible approach is clearly warranted.[63]

---

59   [1995] 1 S.C.R. 3 [*Matsqui*].

60   [1993] 1 F.C. 74 (T.D.).

61   [1993] 2 F.C. 641 (C.A.).

62   *Valente v. The Queen*, [1985] 2 S.C.R. 673 [*Valente*]. This principle focused on three objective guarantees of adjudicative independence: security of tenure, financial independence, and administrative independence.

63   *Matsqui, supra* note 59 at paras. 83-84.

Although Lamer C.J. carried fewer judges on this point than Sopinka J. (who would have preferred to see how the tribunal functioned in practice before resolving the independence question),[64] his view was nonetheless adopted by the Court in subsequent cases.

In considering the validity of the Aboriginal Band's Tax Assessment Review Committee, the majority reasons of Sopinka J. made numerous references to Aboriginal self-government. Justice Sopinka prefaced his analysis with the caveat that, "[c]onditions of institutional independence must take into account their operational context,"[65] and then stressed that the most significant contextual factor in this case was that the purpose of the tax assessment scheme was to foster Aboriginal self-government.[66] This led him to resolve that, "before concluding that the by-laws in question do not establish band taxation tribunals with sufficient institutional independence, they should be interpreted in the context of the fullest knowledge of how they are applied in practice."[67]

The Court was split on whether the challenge should have been raised before the committee itself before being brought to Court, but the majority held that the committee lacked sufficient administrative independence from the Band chiefs and councils. For example, the committee members could be fired at any time and their compensation was left to the discretion of the Band. In his reasons, Chief Justice Lamer observed:

> [W]hile I agree that the larger context of Aboriginal self-government informs the determination of whether the statutory appeal procedures established by the appellants constitute an adequate alternative remedy for the respondents, I cannot agree with Sopinka J.'s conclusion that this context is relevant to the question of whether the bands' tribunals give rise to a reasonable apprehension of bias at an institutional level. In my view, principles of natural justice apply to the bands' tribunals as they would apply to any tribunal performing similar functions.[68]

After determining that "members of the appeal tribunals perform adjudicative functions not unlike those of courts,"[69] Lamer C.J. found that, "under the By-laws, there is nothing to prevent the Band Chiefs and Councils from paying tribunal members only *after* they have reached a decision in a particular case, or not paying the members at all."[70] In addition, he found that tribunal members could be removed from their positions at any time by the Band, which left open the possibility of "considerable abuse."[71]

As already quoted above, in coming to this conclusion, Chief Justice Lamer did admit that, "the larger context of Aboriginal self-government informs the determination of whether the statutory appeal procedures established by the appellants constitute an adequate alternative remedy for the respondents."[72] Yet, he did not see how this was relevant

---

64 *Ibid.* at paras. 117-23.

65 *Ibid.* at para. 113.

66 *Ibid.* at para. 114.

67 *Ibid.* at para. 115.

68 *Ibid.* at para. 74.

69 *Ibid.* at para. 92.

70 *Ibid.* at para. 94 (emphasis in original).

71 *Ibid.*

72 *Ibid.* at para. 74.

to the question of whether the bands' tribunals give rise to a reasonable apprehension of bias at an institutional level. In other words, the Supreme Court simply grafted the test for judicial independence onto the context of administrative tribunals generally and an Aboriginal dispute resolution tribunal specifically. Is Aboriginal decision making simply an additional example of delegated statutory authority within the framework of Canadian administrative law, and/or a parallel but distinct decision-making context with inherent sources of constitutional authority and an administrative law of its own?

B. Is the Canadian Ideal of Independence Applicable in Aboriginal Contexts?

As stated in the introduction to this chapter, a tension exists between those features of administrative law with a valid claim to universality and those that are culturally, and perhaps temporally, specific.

The desire that administrative decision-makers should be subject to statutory mandates but insulated from political manipulation has become a central motif in Canadian administrative law. As examined by Laverne Jacobs in Chapter 8, from labour boards to liquor control boards, or human rights tribunals to international trade tribunals, independence has become one of the most common grounds on which to challenge administrative decisions. While the Supreme Court remains divided on the extent to which Aboriginal tribunals require modified administrative law principles in the context of independence, the question remains whether such an ideal of independence resonates with Aboriginal traditions. According to John Borrows:

> Aboriginal peoples need recognition of their own independent norms, and dispute resolution mechanisms to ensure that accomplishments are consistent with stewardships. These mechanisms need not be courts, but they should possess an independence from band councils that would enable them to act as a countervailing source of authority within the community.
>
> • • •
>
> Ironically, well-intentioned attempts to "fix" First Nations political structures by making them more accountable may end up doing just the opposite: further entrenching top-down, elected, hierarchical politics that has little respect for First Nations traditions of polyfunctional decision-making and dispute resolution structures. If the proposals are implemented, they may make it even more difficult to diffuse power throughout Indian communities in the future. What is needed, before the creation of administrative law codes, are First Nations-designed adjudicative or dispute resolution bodies that can independently review decisions of the executive and legislative bodies in the band. There must be bodies that can independently articulate legal principles of stewardship and responsibility whenever a dispute arises.[73]

While Borrows was not referring specifically to *Matsqui*, the Supreme Court's approach seems to fit with the hierarchical politics that Borrows discourages those in positions of political and legal authority outside the Aboriginal context from doing. More broadly, the

---

73   John Borrows, "Stewardship and the First Nations Governance Act" (2003) 29 Queen's L.J. 103 at 121 and 123 [Borrows, "Stewardship"].

debate in *Matsqui* raises the question of which administrative law principles are culturally specific and which are universally applicable. Arguably, rules against self-dealing and bias arise in any public decision-making process conducted under the rule of law. Is the concern for institutional independence similarly universal?

A hallmark of Canadian administrative law is arguably its ability to develop varying approaches to questions of fairness, independence and accountability to apply within disparate settings within the administrative state (government departments, hospitals, prisons, universities, regulatory agencies, adjudicative tribunals, etc.). Impartiality, as discussed by Laverne Jacobs in Chapter 8, is a good example. An understanding of what constitutes a reasonable apprehension of bias developed in the context of a utility board (where, for example, a member makes public statements relating to the issue during hearings and may be perceived to have decided the issue before hearing all of the evidence[74]) may not be applied in the same way in the context of immigration decision making (where, for example, an immigration officer must consider the best interests of children in making a deportation decision and may be considered biased when expressing views contrary to a child's best interests).[75] Yet the same principles are held to govern each body under Canadian administrative law. Do Aboriginal communities present a particularly distinct administrative setting in which to apply conventional administrative law doctrines, or do such communities require different doctrines altogether?

Justice Louis LeBel once wrote:

> [N]ot all administrative bodies are the same. Indeed, this is an understatement. At first glance, labour boards, police commissions, and milk control boards may seem to have about as much in common as assembly lines, cops, and cows! Administrative bodies do, of course, have some common features, but the diversity of their powers, mandate and structure is such that to apply particular standards from one context to another might well be entirely inappropriate.[76]

The question is, can we construct a standard of review with respect to governing institutions of First Nations drawn from standards applied to Canadian administrative bodies, or must a unique framework be developed that is consistent with the customs, traditions, spiritual beliefs and historical realities of Aboriginal peoples? In other words, a discussion of Aboriginal administrative law necessarily engages the limits of pluralism in public law. It reveals the tension between those features of administrative law with a claim to universality, and those which may be reduced, ultimately, to a particular culture's view of justice at a particular time in its history.

C. Appropriate Level of Deference

To take a familiar concept from administrative law, what level of deference should apply when Aboriginal decision making is impugned in applications for judicial review in Canad-

---

74   See *Newfoundland Telephone Co. v. Newfoundland (Board of Commissioners of Public Utilities)*, [1992] 1 S.C.R. 623 [*Newfoundland*].

75   See *Baker v. Canada (Minister of Citizenship and Immigration)*, [1999] 2 S.C.R. 817 [*Baker*].

76   *Blencoe v. British Columbia (Human Rights Commission)*, 2000 SCC 44, [2000] 2 S.C.R. 307 at para. 158.

ian courts? In what circumstances should those courts overturn Aboriginal government or agency decision making? Where Aboriginal and Canadian regulatory jurisdictions apply to a given matter or individual, which should take precedence and why? These areas of the convergence of Aboriginal and Canadian administrative law principles remain largely unsettled. However, recent jurisprudence such as the *Tlicho* case[77] (discussed above) suggests that, for at least the foreseeable future, Canadian courts and doctrines of deference will determine the scope left to develop administrative decision making consistent with Aboriginal values.

IV. Respecting Aboriginal Rights and Jurisdictions: The Duty to Consult and Accommodate

Nowhere is the convergence of Aboriginal and administrative law more apparent than in the duty to consult and accommodate. In this section, we provide an overview of the duty as well as a comparison with the duty of fairness before exploring a few specific issues in greater depth. This section also highlights the potential for growth and learning between Aboriginal law and administrative law: the influence of administrative law on the duty to consult is obvious, but influence goes both ways and the language of Aboriginal consultation obligations is already identifiable in other areas of public law.[78]

A. Overview of the Duty to Consult and Accommodate

In 2004, *Haida Nation*[79] ushered new life into the procedural obligations relating to constitutionally protected Aboriginal rights. Aboriginal and treaty rights under s. 35 of the *Constitution Act, 1982*[80] protect the collective rights of Aboriginal peoples and the special relationship between the Crown and Aboriginal peoples, stemming in part from the colonial history of Canada.[81] Although an obligation to consult Aboriginal peoples in order to justify regulatory infringements of their constitutional rights was already part of the s. 35 jurisprudence,[82]

---

[77] *Tlicho, supra* note 53.

[78] For discussion, see Lorne Sossin, "The Duty to Consult and Accommodate: Procedural Justice as Aboriginal Rights" (2010) 23 Cdn. J. Admin. L. & Prac. 93-113 [Sossin (2010)] and David Mullan, "The Duty to Consult Aboriginal Peoples—The Canadian Example" (2009) 22 Can. J. Admin. L. & Prac. 107 [Mullan].

[79] *Haida Nation, supra* note 12.

[80] *Constitution Act, 1982, supra* note 1.

[81] On the sources of the Aboriginal rights protected by s. 35, see e.g. John Borrows, *Indigenous Constitution, supra* note 3; Brian Slattery, "The Generative Structure of Aboriginal Rights" (2007) 38 Sup. Ct. L. Rev. (2d) 595 [Slattery]; Mark D. Walters, "The 'Golden Thread' of Continuity: Aboriginal Customs at Common Law and Under the Constitution Act, 1982" (1999) 44 McGill L.J. 711; Kent McNeil & David Yarrow, "Has Constitutional Recognition of Aboriginal Rights Adversely Affected their Definition?" (2007) 37 Sup. Ct. L. Rev. (2d) 177.

[82] *R. v. Sparrow*, [1990] 1 S.C.R. 1075 [*Sparrow*]; *Delgamuukw v. British Columbia*, [1997] 3 S.C.R. 1010 [*Delgamuukw*]; *Halfway River First Nation v. British Columbia (Ministry of Forests)*, 1999 BCCA 470, 178 D.L.R. (4th) 666 [*Halfway River*]. See also Patrick Macklem & Sonia Lawrence, "From Consultation to Reconciliation: Aboriginal Rights and the Crown's Duty to Consult" (2000) 79 Can. Bar Rev. 252.

Haida Nation, along with *Taku River Tlingit*[83] and *Mikisew Cree*[84] ("the *Haida Nation* trilogy"), which followed shortly after, gave this obligation wider scope and force. The *Haida Nation* trilogy's key renovation of previous iterations of the Crown's obligation to consult Aboriginal peoples was the requirement that the Crown consult with Aboriginal communities both before and after the proof or settlement of the Aboriginal or treaty rights at stake.[85] In light of the pre-proof nature of the *Haida Nation* duty, consultation obligations derive from the honour of the Crown rather than the rights themselves.[86]

The honour of the Crown is damaged when the Crown undertakes or sanctions activities with the potential to derogate from Aboriginal rights before those rights have been properly recognized and accommodated through negotiations or otherwise. As the Court said in *Haida Nation*:

> The Crown, acting honourably, cannot cavalierly run roughshod over Aboriginal interests where claims affecting these interests are being seriously pursued in the process of treaty negotiation and proof. It must respect these potential, but yet unproven, interests .... To unilaterally exploit a claimed resource during the process of proving and resolving the Aboriginal claim to that resource, may be to deprive the Aboriginal claimants of some or all of the benefit of the resource. That is not honourable.[87]

To preserve the Aboriginal rights and interests pending recognition and settlement, the duty to consult and, if appropriate, accommodate thus arises where the claimed Aboriginal right would potentially be negatively affected by proposed government conduct. Further explored below, government conduct includes decisions such as permits and licences to allow resource use or changes to decision-making structures that regulate the use of land and water. Given the wide variety of government departments and agencies in which such decisions are made, the evolving duty to consult and accommodate has had a significant impact on government decision-making processes, at least with respect to lands and resource management.[88]

The *Haida Nation* trilogy made it clear that the renewed duty to consult and accommodate shares many concepts and techniques with the administrative law duty of fairness. In *Haida Nation*, the Supreme Court stated that "regard may be had to the procedural safe-

---

83 *Taku River Tlingit First Nation v. British Columbia (Project Assessment Director)*, 2004 SCC 74, [2004] 3 S.C.R. 550 [*Taku River Tlingit*].

84 *Mikisew Cree First Nation v. Canada (Minister of Canadian Heritage)*, 2005 SCC 69, [2005] 3 S.C.R. 388 [*Mikisew Cree*].

85 In *Little Salmon/Carmacks*, *supra* note 13, the Court clarified that the honour of the Crown also applies to modern treaty settlements, allowing courts to supplement negotiated consultation requirements if the honour of the Crown so demands.

86 See, generally, Dwight G. Newman, *The Duty to Consult: New Relationships with Aboriginal Peoples* (Saskatoon: Purich Publishing, 2009) [*Newman*].

87 *Haida Nation*, *supra* note 12 at para. 25.

88 The emphasis on lands and resources in the duty to consult jurisprudence follows the lands and resources focus of Aboriginal rights jurisprudence to date. This focus should not, however, be seen to preclude the duty's potential application to other types of government decisions in areas such as education, health policy, intellectual property, or other areas in relation to which treaty or Aboriginal rights may be credibly asserted.

guards of natural justice *mandated by administrative law*" in discharging the duty,[89] while *Taku River Tlingit* demonstrated that the duty could be carried out within regular administrative processes, such as environmental assessment. In *Little Salmon/Carmacks*, the Supreme Court again highlighted this relationship. In that case, the Court considered the argument that administrative law principles, "for all their tremendous value, are not tools toward reconciliation of Aboriginal people and other Canadians."[90] Writing for the majority, Binnie J. rejected this argument, stating that "[a]dministrative law is flexible enough to give full weight to the constitutional interests of the First Nation."[91]

The close relationship between the duty to consult and accommodate and the duty of fairness is evident in the analytic structure of the two duties. Both involve two steps: threshold and content. Within these steps, the duty to consult has its own, distinct tests. At the threshold step, the duty to consult is triggered when government contemplates conduct that might affect the exercise of an Aboriginal right. In *Rio Tinto*, the Supreme Court delineated three elements within this trigger: Crown knowledge of an Aboriginal right; Crown contemplation of an action (or decision); and the possibility that the contemplated action may adversely affect the exercise of the right.[92] With respect to the first element, the nature of the Crown knowledge required depends on the type of right in issue. Where treaty rights are in issue, the Court has held that the Crown will always have notice of the rights contained in the treaty.[93] In other contexts, the knowledge element is satisfied by credible assertions of rights and Crown knowledge of "the potential existence" of an Aboriginal right, a standard that ensures that the duty arises before proof or recognition of such rights.[94] Further, knowledge may be attributed to the Crown ("constructive knowledge") when, for example, the government is aware of an Aboriginal group's traditional occupation of an area.[95]

A preliminary question that has begun to receive some attention in the courts is identifying the appropriate Aboriginal consultation partners,[96] a trigger issue relating to credible claims that may also raise questions of standing. *Little Salmon/Carmacks* confirmed that consultation proceeds with the Aboriginal community rather than a particular member of the community, even when an individual's interest is particularly affected, as was the case

---

[89] *Haida Nation, supra* note 12 at para. 41 (emphasis added).

[90] *Little Salmon/Carmacks, supra* note 13 at para. 45.

[91] *Ibid.* at para. 47.

[92] *Rio Tinto Alcan Inc. v. Carrier Sekani Tribal Council*, 2010 SCC 43, [2010] 2 S.C.R. 650 at para. 31 [*Rio Tinto Alcan*].

[93] *Mikisew Cree, supra* note 84 at para. 34. Given that treaty rights are not entirely determined by the text of the historic treaties (*R. v. Marshall*, [1999] 3 S.C.R. 456), it is worth considering whether this presumption ought to be limited to notice of "at least" the rights outlined in the text of the treaty.

[94] *Haida Nation, supra* note 12 at para. 35.

[95] *Rio Tinto Alcan, supra* note 92 at para. 40.

[96] See the discussion in Newman, *supra* note 86 at 38-40, 70-72; Janna Promislow, Book Review of Newman, *ibid.* (2010) 48 Osgoode Hall L.J. 183 at 187-88; and more generally, Brent Olthuis, "The Constitution's Peoples: Approaching Community in the Context of Section 35 of the Constitution Act, 1982" (2009) 54 McGill L.J. 1.

for the affected trapline owner in *Little Salmon/Carmacks*.[97] Beyond this point, however, the issue quickly becomes complex and must be understood in relation to a history that involves (among other features) *Indian Act* band membership rules that excluded many individuals on the basis of gender and marriage or other criteria; high migration rates of First Nations individuals from reserves to urban centres as a result of on-reserve conditions; the absence of a legislative framework for the recognition of Metis communities or individuals outside of Alberta's *Metis Settlements Act*; imperfect recognition of First Nations under federal policies leading to unrecognized bands and the splintering of larger "national" groupings into band-level First Nations; and poor recognition and knowledge of Aboriginal communities' traditional territories. Against this history, identifying the appropriate consultation partners may involve rights claims by more than one Aboriginal community or organization in respect of the same geography and activities;[98] rights claims by unrecognized or non-status Aboriginal communities;[99] and issues regarding who may represent communities in consultation.[100]

The other two elements of the duty's trigger—Crown conduct and the potential for adverse effects on the rights—are also defined broadly. While the common law duty of fairness excludes preliminary decisions, meaningful consultation of a standard capable of upholding the honour of the Crown may require that consultation occur early and throughout multi-step government decision-making processes such as environmental assessments.[101] The duty also applies to decisions that may not have an immediate impact on Aboriginal rights; for example, the development of strategic plans and decision-making frameworks such as the water management plan in issue in *Tsuu T'ina Nation*.[102] The application of the duty to consult to strategic and planning decisions—decisions of a distinctly policy nature—means

---

[97] *Little Salmon/Carmacks, supra* note 13 at para. 35. Further comment on this issue may be forthcoming from the Supreme Court in *Moulton Contracting Ltd. v. Behn*, 2011 BCCA 311, leave to appeal to the Supreme Court of Canada granted, 2012 CanLII 17819 (S.C.C.). In that case, the Behn family is attempting to assert a breach of the duty to consult as a defence in a civil claim for damages. The B.C. Court of Appeal denied the family, as individual members of a First Nation, the standing to challenge the validity of government permits based on a breach of the government's duty to consult in issuing those permits.

[98] See e.g. *Nlaka'pamux Nation Tribal Council v. Griffin*, 2009 BCSC 1275, [2009] 4 C.N.L.R. 213 [*Nlaka'pamux Nation*], varied on appeal on a different issue, *Nlaka'pamux Nation Tribal Council v. British Columbia (Environmental Assessment Office)*, 2011 BCCA 78.

[99] See e.g. *Campbell v. British Columbia (Forest and Range)*, 2011 BCSC 448.

[100] See e.g. *Newfoundland and Labrador v. Labrador Métis Nation*, 2007 NLCA 75, 288 D.L.R. (4th) 641, leave to appeal to the Supreme Court of Canada refused (2008 CanLII 32711 (S.C.C.)). The Court of Appeal, at para. 46, found that Aboriginal communities with credible rights claims may choose their agents for consultation, including non-rights holding corporate bodies. The Court of Appeal, at para. 36, also found that it was unnecessary for the claimant group to finally decide whether they were ethnically Metis or Inuit for the purposes of establishing a credible claim that triggers the duty to consult. For related concerns regarding the definition of the class that may be certified to represent Aboriginal rights holders in a class action, see *Kwicksutaineuk/Ah-Kwa-Mish First Nation v. Canada (Attorney General)*, 2012 BCCA 193.

[101] See e.g. *Dene Tha' First Nation v. Canada (Minister of Environment)*, 2006 FC 1354, [2006] F.C.J. No. 1677 (QL) [*Dene Tha'*], aff'd in *Canada (Minister of Environment) v. Imperial Oil Resources Ventures Ltd.*, 2008 FCA 20. See also, Newman, *supra* note 86 at 54-55.

[102] *Tsuu T'ina Nation v. Alberta (Environment)*, 2010 ABCA 137, [2010] A.J. No. 479 (QL) [*Tsuu T'ina Nation*]. See also *Rio Tinto Alcan, supra* note 92 at para. 44.

that the duty to consult applies to decisions that may be excluded by the legislative exemption under a duty of fairness, an issue that will be pursued in greater detail further below.[103]

Past Crown conduct and past impacts or infringements of Aboriginal rights will not, on their own, trigger the duty to consult. This issue was recently clarified in *Rio Tinto Alcan*, in which the Carrier Sekani Tribal Council First Nations argued that the continued negative impact on their Aboriginal fishing rights caused by a dam built on the Nechako River, British Columbia, in the 1960s gave rise to a duty to consult. The dam supported a power plant for an aluminum smelter and B.C. Hydro purchased the extra power produced by the power plant. When the energy purchase agreement between B.C. Hydro and Rio Tinto Alcan came up for renegotiation and approval, the Carrier Sekani argued that the B.C. Utilities Commission had an obligation to ensure that there was adequate consultation before approving the renegotiated agreement. The Supreme Court disagreed, holding that because the renegotiation of the energy purchase agreement created no new impact on the fishing rights in issue—that is, it did not further alter the water levels in the river—the duty to consult was not triggered in this case. The limit on the threshold of the duty drawn in *Rio Tinto Alcan* does not preclude the consideration of cumulative impacts of development where, unlike in *Rio Tinto Alcan*, the current Crown conduct can be less clearly detached from the adverse effects of past Crown conduct. However, it is unclear and contested how to define the scope of the duty to consult in such cases, particularly when past impacts must be addressed in the consultation process and accommodated, or whether the consultation process should only seek to address the impact of the most recent Crown conduct.[104]

Rio Tinto Alcan clarifies the forward-looking nature of the duty, with the Court addressing historical grievances by allowing that past breaches of the duty to consult may give rise to a damages remedy.[105] This forward-looking direction is a key indication of how the Supreme Court envisions the role of the duty to consult and accommodate in supporting reconciliation.[106] It is also a key issue for the development of Aboriginal administrative law, which requires robust procedural safeguards capable of ensuring that Aboriginal perspectives are respected within Crown decision-making processes: perspectives that may not accept the separation of past or future from current resource management decisions as a matter of law, justice, or reconciliation.

---

[103]   See, generally, Mullan, *supra* note 78 at 128-29.

[104]   For example, contrast *Upper Nicola Indian Band v. British Columbia (Minister of Environment)*, 2011 BCSC 388, [2011] B.C.J. No. 559 (QL) (*Rio Tinto Alcan, supra* note 92, was relied on to exclude consideration of the original impacts of a 1960s transmission line right-of-way in the consultation process around a proposed new high voltage line to run parallel to the old one) and *West Moberly First Nations v. British Columbia (Chief Inspector of Mines)*, 2011 BCCA 247, 18 B.C.L.R. (5th) 234 [*West Moberly First Nations*], leave to appeal to the S.C.C. refused, 2012 CanLII 8361 (S.C.C.) (*Rio Tinto Alcan* distinguished to permit consideration of historical impacts of exploration on the Burnt Pine caribou herd in consultations about licensing decisions that would allow the expansion of coal exploration activities. The consideration of historical impacts is seen as essential to a proper understanding of the potential impacts of the present licensing decision).

[105]   *Rio Tinto Alcan, supra* note 92 at para. 49.

[106]   For a discussion of the reconciliation under s. 35, see Mark D. Walters, "The Morality of Aboriginal Law" (2006) 31 Queen's L.J. 470; Borrows, *Indigenous Constitution, supra* note 3; Slattery, *supra* note 81; and Kent McNeil, "Reconciliation and Third-Party Interests: Tsilhqot'in Nation v. British Columbia" (2010) 8 Indigenous L.J. 7.

Parallel to the duty of fairness, the duty to consult is easily triggered. And again, parallel to the duty of fairness, the broad application of the duty is balanced by the variable content of the duty that is managed through a contextual spectrum analysis. The content of the duty to consult is determined in relation to the preliminary assessment of the strength of the rights claim (where unproven) and the seriousness of the potential adverse impacts of the Crown action on the exercise of those rights.[107] Rights claims that appear tenuous to the Crown or less intrusive impacts such as a short disruption of harvesting practices will still trigger the duty but will attract only light consultation obligations, such as mere notice. Strong rights claims and/or serious impacts on the exercise of those rights attract "deep" consultation obligations, including accommodation. The overall aim of this spectrum analysis is to en-sure that the content of the duty accords with the honour of the Crown in the particular setting in which the duty has been triggered.

With the exception of accommodation, the content of the duty to consult is very similar to the procedural requirements required to satisfy a right to be heard. The content of the duty to consult is thus most like the duty of fairness at the lighter end of the spectrum, as illustrated in *Little Salmon/Carmacks*. The duty in *Little Salmon/Carmacks* was triggered by an application for an agricultural land grant that affected one third of 1 percent of a Little Salmon/Carmacks First Nation member's trapline.[108] In the Court's assessment, this was a small impact meriting consultation obligations at the lower end of the spectrum. Although the First Nation argued that its interests had not been taken seriously and required accom-modation, the Court found that the duty to consult was satisfied by notice of the decision and opportunities to state its concerns to the Yukon government decision-makers involved in the decision. As Nigel Bankes observed, the content of consultation in *Little Salmon* was "no greater than that which would be provided by the application of standard principles of administrative law."[109]

The potential requirement of accommodation is where the content of the duty to consult parts company with the content of the duty of fairness most significantly. Characterized as a substantive rather than a procedural requirement, *Haida Nation* was clear that accommoda-tion is only required where "appropriate," as determined through the spectrum analysis.[110] The parameters of accommodation—when it is required and what constitutes adequate ac-commodation—comprise one of the least-developed and most controversial areas in the duty to consult jurisprudence. As described in *Haida Nation*, accommodation with respect to at least unproven Aboriginal rights is about "seeking compromise" through "good faith efforts to understand each other's concerns and move to address them."[111] As a result, con-sultation and accommodation does not have to result in agreement. Instead, Aboriginal

---

107   *Haida Nation*, *supra* note 12 at para. 39.

108   *Little Salmon/Carmacks*, *supra* note 13 at para. 21.

109   He also comments that "[t]his impoverished view of the duty to consult is hardly likely to contribute to the constitutional goal of inter-societal reconciliation" (Nigel Bankes, "Little Salmon and the Juridical Nature of the Duty to Consult and Accommodate," online: ABlawg.ca archives <http://ablawg.ca/2010/12/10/little-salmon-and-the-juridical-nature-of-the-duty-to-consult-and-accommodate> [Bankes, *Little Salmon*]).

110   See e.g. *Haida Nation*, *supra* note 12, at paras. 10, 20, 37 and others.

111   *Ibid.* at para. 49.

parties' consent to the contemplated conduct will be required only in rare cases in relation to established rights.[112] In *Delgamuukw*, for example, the possibility of a consent require- ment was contemplated in relation to the regulation of harvesting activities on recognized Aboriginal title land.[113]

The lack of a consent requirement has been criticized as illustrative of the assimilative tendencies of the duty and how the structure of the duty is not capable of respecting Aborig- inal perspectives and aspirations.[114] For many Aboriginal parties, the lack of a consent re- quirement is seen as inconsistent with their laws and jurisdiction over their lands, which require them to be the stewards of their lands.[115] In addition, Aboriginal communities point out that the United Nations Declaration on the Rights of Indigenous Peoples (UNDRIP), which Parliament formally endorsed in 2010,[116] sets the consultation standard as the "free, prior and informed consent" (FPIC) of indigenous peoples to activities affecting their lands or territories (article 32). The scope and meaning of FPIC is being developed in inter- national law in a manner that might usefully be brought to bear on the Canadian approach to consultation and consent, but these international commitments and developments have yet to be referred to by Canadian courts.[117]

Consent and accommodation are not contentious in every consultation process: Aborig- inal parties may support the contemplated activities; accommodation of their concerns may be possible through changes to the planned activities; or compensation may be available for the anticipated infringements or impacts on rights.[118] Some cases are "hard cases" in which the balancing and compromise envisioned by the Court in *Haida Nation* are simply not available. In *West Moberly First Nations*, for example, the expansion of the coal exploration activities in issue would negatively impact the core habitat of the already threatened Burnt Pine Caribou Herd.[119] The majority of the B.C. Court of Appeal accepted that the devasta- tion of the Herd and its habitat also seriously impacted the First Nations' Treaty 8 hunting rights, but found less common ground on whether accommodation should address the past

---

[112] *Ibid.* at para. 48.

[113] *Delgamuukw, supra* note 82 at para. 168.

[114] Gordon Christie "Developing Case Law: The Future of Consultation and Accommodation" (2006) 39 U.B.C. L. Rev. 139 [Christie (2006)].

[115] See e.g. Treaty 3's Manito Aki Inakonigaawin or Great Earth Law, online: The Official Website of the Grand Council of Treaty #3 <http://www.gct3.net/grand-chiefs-office/laws-and-policies>.

[116] For Canada's position, see "Frequently Asked Questions" (on Canada's endorsement of the UNDRIP), on- line: Aboriginal Affairs and Northern Development Canada <http://www.aadnc-aandc.gc.ca/eng/ 1309374807748>.

[117] See e.g. *Saramaka People v. Suriname (Preliminary Objections, Merits, Reparations, and Costs)*, November 28, 2007, Series C No. 172 IACHR 5, esp. paras. 133-34. For a helpful discussion of FPIC, see Simons & Collins, *supra* note 15. For the treatment of international human rights law in Canadian administrative law, see Ger- ald Heckman, Chapter 14, The Role of International Human Rights Norms in Administrative Law.

[118] The law, of course, does not always dictate the approach taken by the parties. In many cases, the Crown and/ or developer are willing to consider some forms of accommodation, or may be willing to satisfy Aboriginal legal requirements, where the duty to consult law may not require it. For a discussion of related consultation practices, see Newman, *supra* note 86, Chapter 4.

[119] *West Moberly First Nations, supra* note 104.

impacts or just the present exacerbation. The trial judge's order had included a specific accommodation measure—a rehabilitation plan for the caribou herd—that took past harms into account. In the trial judge's view, the rehabilitation plan was the only accommodation measure that would be reasonable in light of the past harms and the state of the Burnt Pine Herd, and so ordered it specifically. The majority at the Court of Appeal reversed this order, agreeing that consultation had been inadequate and remitting the matter for further consultation, but without agreeing on whether an accommodation measure addressing past harms would ever be appropriate.[120]

Judicial reluctance to order specific accommodation measures, illustrated in *West Moberly First Nations*, is due in part to the reasonableness standard of review and the deference this standard demands. *Little Salmon/Carmacks* clarified that no deference is owed to decision-makers in determining the legal and constitutional limits of their discretion, and thus: "[a] decision maker who proceeds on the basis of inadequate consultation errs in law. Within the limits established by the law and the Constitution, however, the [decision-maker's] decision should be reviewed on a standard of reasonableness"[121] in accordance with *Dunsmuir v. New Brunswick*.[122] This restatement is potentially discordant with the direction from *Haida Nation*, where McLachlin C.J.C. stated that "The process itself would likely fall to be examined on a standard of reasonableness. Perfect satisfaction is not required; … government is required to make reasonable efforts to inform and consult. This suffices to discharge the duty."[123] The potential discordance lies in whether the "process of consultation" is part of the adequacy of consultation or part of the decision, as delineated in *Little Salmon/Carmacks*. In *Haida Nation*, McLachlin C.J.C. also discussed the possibility of deference at other stages of the review as a result of the factual nature of the initial assessments involved in the determinations of existence and scope of the duty and that therefore "a degree of deference to the findings of fact of the initial adjudicator may be appropriate."[124]

McLachlin C.J.C.'s comments in *Haida Nation* suggest that there may be more opportunities for deference in review of consultations than is apparent from the statement in *Little Salmon/Carmacks*. Moreover, interpretation of the standards of review applicable since *Little Salmon/Carmacks* confirm that lower courts still see room for deference to the Crown in the "process" of consultation and not just with respect to the outcomes.[125] This issue warrants further attention, which we pursue below through a comparison to the standards of

---

120   Chief Justice Finch refrained from deciding whether the rehabilitation plan was an appropriate accommodation measure but left it open as a possibility pending further consultation. Justice Hinkson, concurring in the result, found the rehabilitation plan to be inappropriate because accommodation should not be concerned with "remedying harm caused by past events" (*ibid.* at para. 180). Justice Garson wrote in dissent but agreed with Justice Hinkson that accommodation should be causally connected to the present contemplated conduct.

121   *Little Salmon/Carmacks, supra* note 13 at para. 48.

122   2008 SCC 9, [2008] 1 S.C.R. 190 [*Dunsmuir*].

123   *Haida Nation, supra* note 12 at para. 62.

124   *Ibid.* at para. 61.

125   *West Moberly First Nations, supra* note 104 at paras. 141 (Finch C.J., concurring), 174 (Hinkson J. concurring), and 189-198 (Garson J., dissenting, but not on this point); *Adams Lake Indian Band v. British Columbia*, 2011 BCSC 266 at para. 52 [*Adams Lake*], appeal in process, BCCA 38926.

review applied to matters of procedural fairness, followed by discussion of two other areas of convergence (and divergence) between the duty to consult and administrative law.

B. Standard of Review: Procedure, Substance, and Specialized Decision-Makers

As discussed by Audrey Macklin in Chapter 9, Standard of Review: Back to the Future?, the standard of review applied by a court in its review of an administrative decision-maker depends on the nature of the first decision-maker, his or her expertise on the issue in question, and contextual factors that suggest that more or less deference is owed in order to ensure the proper roles of legislatures, executives, and courts are respected. The courts retain the expertise on questions of (common-law) procedural fairness, and so the standard of correctness applies. On questions of law, however, the majority in *Dunsmuir* indicates that deference may be owed where the question of law, or mixed fact and law, falls within the decision-makers particular expertise and the necessary legislative signals, especially a privative clause, are present.[126] One further feature of standard of review analysis worth bearing in mind originates in the parameters of appellate review: the reluctance of appellate courts to interfere with the findings of fact of the initial trier of fact, in light of their position of relative disadvantage in assessing the credibility of witnesses giving oral testimony.

How do these concerns behind the standards of review play out in relation to the duty to consult? Beginning with what is clear, the application of the deferential standard to the outcome of consultation is consistent with judicial review in other contexts. The final result of the consultation process—the Crown's decision regarding how to proceed, including choices around appropriate accommodation—are understood in the duty to consult jurisprudence as "substantive" outcomes. With respect to the outcomes, the standard of reasonableness as described in *Dunsmuir* applies: "reasonableness is concerned mostly with the existence of justification, transparency and intelligibility within the decision-making process. But it is also concerned with whether the decision falls within a range of possible, acceptable outcomes which are defensible in respect of the facts and law."[127] Interestingly, in *West Moberly First Nations*, Chief Justice Finch elaborated on the idea of "meaningfulness" that attaches to the reasonableness standard in this context: "A reasonable process is one that recognizes and gives full consideration to the rights of Aboriginal peoples, and also recognizes and respects the rights and interests of the broader community."[128]

Echoing debates surrounding reasonableness review of discretionary decisions infringing Charter rights, several commentators have critiqued the application of the reasonableness standard in light of the constitutional nature of the interests at stake. They argue that

---

[126] *Dunsmuir, supra* note 122 at paras. 53-55.

[127] *Ibid.* at para. 47.

[128] *Supra* note 104 at para. 141. See also para. 154: "the consultation was not meaningful and was therefore not reasonable." Nigel Bankes suggests that consultation outcomes should be assessed against those described in *Halfway River, supra* note 82 at para. 160: that the representations of Aboriginal communities in consultation be "seriously considered and, wherever possible, demonstrably integrated into the proposed plan of action" (Bankes, *Little Salmon, supra* note 109).

greater judicial scrutiny of the resulting accommodation of Aboriginal parties would better implement protection for Aboriginal rights and better serve the reconciliation purposes of Aboriginal law.[129] However, the courts have been consistent in their application of the reasonableness standard to the outcomes of consultation. This approach follows from *Haida Nation*, which treats reconciliation as better served by fostering an improved dialogue while retaining the Crown's responsibility to make land-use decisions and balance competing interests in the process. This approach is also consistent with *Doré v. Barreau du Québec*,[130] discussed elsewhere in this text, which confirms the appropriateness of reasonableness review of discretionary decisions where constitutional rights are at stake.

Where there is less certainty, however, is with respect to whether deference also creeps into the review of the "process" of consultation. Binnie J. in the *Little Salmon/Carmacks* decision, describes the issue to be reviewed on a correctness standard as one of *adequate* consultation. By contrast, consultation cases both before and after *Little Salmon/Carmacks*, have applied the reasonableness standard to the "process of consultation and [whether] accommodation is unreasonable."[131] In review of procedural fairness, however, the process or actions of the decision-maker are included within the concept of "adequate" procedures. Under the *Baker* framework, consideration of and respect for the procedural choices of decision-makers is part of the determination of the content required by the duty of fairness.[132] As Grant Huscroft points out in Chapter 5, From Natural Justice to Fairness: Thresholds, Content, and the Role of Judicial Review, the choice of procedures is only one of five factors that must be taken into account in determining the content of the duty, a determination that is distinct from whether the duty has been met. Once content is determined, decision-makers cannot be wrong in whether they satisfied their duty or not. Is there a basis for treating the question whether the duty to consult has been met differently from the question whether the duty of fairness has been met? Is there a basis for treating the adequacy of the process of consultation (a procedural question) as part of the outcome of consultation (a substantive one)?

A grounded consideration of how the duty to consult plays out suggests there are differences between the two duties that might be relevant to where the line between process and substance should be drawn. The brief discussion earlier in this chapter regarding the importance of negotiated consultation protocols and joint decision-making models in implementing the duty to consult suggest the question of how to consult, and consideration of Aboriginal communities' view on the consultation process itself can be important. Where negotiated consultation processes are present, the duty to consult reaches into the realm of self-government and facilitating respect for Aboriginal jurisdictions. In such cases, it would

---

129   Sossin (2010), *supra* note 78 at 103, where he also reviews the arguments of other commentators. See also Mullan, *supra* note 78 at 130; but also note the inconsistency of the Supreme Court in its approach to the review of decisions where constitutional rights are at stake. See Evan Fox-Decent & Alexander Pless, Chapter 12, The Charter and Administrative Law: Cross-Fertilization or Inconstancy?, for discussion.

130   2012 SCC 12.

131   *Ahousaht First Nation v. Canada (Fisheries and Oceans)*, 2008 FCA 212 at para. 34, 37 C.E.L.R. (3d) 89. See also *West Moberly First Nations*, *supra* note 104; *Adams Lake*, *supra* note 125; and *Ke-Kin-Is-Uqs v. British Columbia (Minister of Forests)*, 2008 BCSC 1020, [2009] 1 C.N.L.R. 30 at para. 252.

132   *Baker*, *supra* note 75.

be fair to consider the process of consultation to be a distinct outcome of consultation. Another factor in favour of flexible assessment of the consultation process is that the process and depth of consultation required might change along the way, in light of information exchanged at the initial or later stages. At its best, consultation is a responsive learning process. In many cases, however, the choice of procedures by the Crown in carrying out the duty to consult will not reflect such lofty aspirations, and may instead reflect the limitations of the Crown's resources, the limitations of the Aboriginal communities' resources to participate, and might be complicated by the presence of consultation obligations to different Aboriginal communities who may not agree on consultation processes or the desired outcomes.[133]

These considerations point to the need for courts to provide space for the Crown to develop processes to implement the duty to consult in a manner that will be acceptable to Aboriginal communities as well as within the limitations of Crown resources and the need to balance polycentric interests. However, these considerations point equally to the need for courts to scrutinize the nature of the consultation process as part of their assessment of adequacy. In *West Moberly First Nations*, Garson J. (in dissent, but not on this point) distinguished *Little Salmon/Carmacks* and applied the reasonableness standard to the review of the consultation processes arising in relation to a Treaty 8 right: "In my view, [*Little Salmon/Carmacks's*] adoption of a higher standard [of review] was attributable to the fact that the case concerned the construction of a modern, comprehensive treaty; a precise document negotiated by sophisticated and well resourced parties. In that case, the Crown argued that the treaty was a complete code and there was no obligation to consult beyond the treaty itself."[134] Keeping in mind that this argument was rejected by the majority in *Little Salmon/Carmacks*, Garson J. further relied on a statement in *Rio Tinto Alcan* "'[c]onsultation itself is not a question of law, but a distinct constitutional process requiring powers to effect compromise and do whatever is necessary to achieve reconciliation of divergent Crown and Aboriginal interests.' Compromise is a difficult, if not impossible, thing to assess on a correctness standard."[135] This observation is undoubtedly true; compromise does not produce the "right" decision, which is, in theory, the aim of a review for correctness. Nor does the complex balancing of interests in the reconciliation process reflect the standard account of judicial expertise. However, it is incongruent that public authorities are required to justify their procedural choices to a higher standard under the common-law duty of fairness than under the constitutional duty to consult and accommodate Aboriginal rights. *Baker* demonstrates that it is possible for courts to defer to decision-makers in their procedural choices while still requiring them to get the content right. Moreover, Garson J.'s reasoning suggests that more deference is owed to the Crown when the implementation of its constitutional obligations is dependent on discretion than when it has reached a negotiated agreement with a First Nation, which results in a clearer statement of the constitutional obligations and requires legislative action to be implemented. This result does not accord with rationales behind deferential standards of review described above and elsewhere in this text. Legislative

---

133   See e.g. *Nlaka'pamux Nation, supra* note 98.

134   *West Moberly First Nations, supra* note 104 at para. 195.

135   *Ibid.* at para. 197, quoting from *Rio Tinto Alcan, supra* note 92 at para. 74.

action to circumscribe administrative decision making generally signals the need for greater deference not less. This result also does not accord with the guidance from *Haida Nation*.

One of the biggest differences between review of the duty to consult and review of the duty of fairness and the decisions of administrative decision-makers more generally, is the state of implementation of the duty to consult. In administrative law contexts, legislative signals and tribunal expertise ground the application of the reasonableness standard. According to *Dunsmuir*, deference is also owed to administrative decision-makers on questions of mixed fact and law. Such deference is owed in relation to the nature of the initial finder of facts and his or her expertise and experience in making such a finding. In *Haida Nation*, McLachlin C.J.C. anticipated the extension of these applications of deference to the duty to consult context through the development of legislated consultation processes and tribunals to administer the duty to consult that did not yet exist.[136] If such infrastructure existed, it would give rise to the usual bases for deference such as expertise.[137] Thus, decisions on questions of mixed fact and law, such as the assessment of strength of rights claims and adverse impacts of Crown actions, would be owed deference by a reviewing court because of legislative choices to delegate such decisions to expert, neutral bodies. Unless such processes are in place, the Crown, which is one of the parties in the consultation and the consultation dispute, retains the decision-making authority with respect to such questions of mixed fact and law as well the resulting choice of procedures.

In general, such legislation still does not exist and governments' implementation of the duty to consult relies heavily on policy.[138] Provincial legislation has been passed recognizing the s. 35 duty to consult, but has generally not defined the content of the duty nor established specialized tribunals to resolve disputes regarding consultation processes or outcomes. The recent amendments to the Ontario *Mining Act*[139] provide an example of a step toward this direction, with provisions (not yet in force) empowering the minister to designate individuals or a body to hear and consider consultation disputes and make recommendations, and giving the minister a broad remedial discretion to address the dispute after considering those recommendations.[140] However, the Court's anticipation of such develop-

---

136 See related discussion in *Halalt First Nation v. British Columbia (Environment)*, 2011 BCSC 945 at paras. 78-84, appeal in process 2011 BCCA 39264.

137 *Haida Nation*, *supra* note 12 at para. 60. *Rio Tinto Alcan*, *supra* note 92 provides an example of a standard of review analysis where a tribunal was the first adjudicator of the adequacy of the duty to consult and the way in which a statutory regime governing the applicable standards of review may alter the analysis. However, the B.C. Court of Appeal noted that the Supreme Court erred in their interpretation of the proper standard of review under the B.C. *Administrative Tribunals Act*, S.B.C. 2004, c. 45: *Lavender Co-Operative Housing Association v. Ford*, 2011 BCCA 114 at paras. 37-58. Thanks to M. Cheryl Crane for pointing out this error and discussion to us.

138 For discussion, see Newman, *supra* note 86, Chapter 4. For an argument that development of regulatory regime to oversee and fully implement the duty to consult and accommodate is key to ensuring judicial deference to government decision making, and therefore greater certainty in regulation of natural resource development, see Anthony Knox & Thomas Isaac, "Judicial Deference and the Significance of the Supreme Court of Canada's Decisions in Haida and Taku River" (2006) 64 Advocate 487 [Knox & Isaac].

139 R.S.O. 1990, c. M.14.

140 Section 170.1. For discussion of the Ontario *Mining Act* generally, see Simons & Collins, *supra* note 15 and Pardy & Stoehr, *supra* note 15.

ments in *Haida Nation* has generally gone unfulfilled. In the meantime, *Rio Tinto Alcan* confirms that like other constitutional issues, tribunals must consider the adequacy of consultation processes where the mandate has been conferred by the tribunal's constituent legislation.[141]

In light of this state of implementation, and in light of the complexities of multi-staged and negotiated consultation processes, it may be necessary to consider whether the standards of review and bases for deference play out so differently in judicial review of consultation decisions that these administrative law concepts require reconfiguration. However, an overly deferential treatment of Crown consultation decisions may discourage further Crown action to implement the duty, and thus hinder the protection of the unproven Aboriginal rights the duty was intended to protect. The absence of legislative action to implement the duty to consult (as anticipated in *Haida Nation*) thus suggests that a correctness standard should apply to the review of the adequacy of consultation processes.

C. The Constitutional Nature of the Obligation

The duty to consult and accommodate is owed only to Aboriginal collectivities, as a matter of constitutional law. The restricted application of this set of procedural obligations is unique, flowing from the constitutional recognition of Aboriginal and treaty rights. The constitutional nature of the duty is also unique. Fundamental justice under s. 7 of the Charter gives rise to procedural safeguards that are capable of being articulated as "constitutional rights" in relation to specific decisions, such as a right to reasons in relation to the deportation decision at issue in *Suresh*, discussed elsewhere in this text. A finding of inadequate due process under s. 7 is also capable of invalidating clearly legislated decision-making processes.[142] By contrast, the duty to consult and accommodate is a constitutional "obligation" that rests with the Crown as opposed to a constitutional "right" that belongs to Aboriginal communities. The Court has described the duty as a "valuable adjunct" to the unwritten constitutional principle of the honour of the Crown,[143] and an "essential corollary to the honourable process of reconciliation that s. 35 demands ... [that] preserves the Aboriginal interest pending claims resolution."[144] But consultation is not an Aboriginal right in and of itself. Instead, the constitutional rights in issue remain s. 35 rights, and the duty to consult and accommodate is a constitutional duty that arises in relation to those rights, by means of the honour of the Crown.

If the Aboriginal law context were parallel to s. 7 of the Charter, the honour of the Crown would be parallel to the principle of fundamental justice, protecting important constitutional rights by constitutionalizing procedural safeguards on the basis of a highly contextualized analysis of the procedural safeguards required in relation to a particular decision. Presumably,

[141]   *Rio Tinto Alcan, supra* note 92 at para. 55. For discussion of the role of tribunals, see Zena Charowsky, "The Aboriginal Law Duty to Consult: An Introduction for Administrative Tribunals" (2011) 74 Sask. L. Rev. 213.

[142]   See e.g. Justice Wilson's decision in *Singh v. Minister of Employment and Immigration*, [1985] 1 S.C.R. 177 and the discussion in Evan Fox-Decent and Alexander Pless's Chapter 12.

[143]   *Little Salmon/Carmacks, supra* note 13 at paras. 42 and 44.

[144]   *Haida Nation, supra* note 12 at para. 38.

the unwritten nature of the honour of the Crown should not render it less potent as a constitutional principle than fundamental justice. However, in *Little Salmon/Carmacks*, the Court avoided this parallel structure. As Justice Binnie explained, a constitutional "right" to be consulted would mean that "more or less every case dealing with consultation in the interpretation and implementation of treaties becomes a constitutional case. The trouble with this argument is that the content of the duty to consult varies with the circumstances."[145] This concern, however, is apparently unproblematic in the s. 7 context. For example, while concerned not to constitutionalize the common law in *Suresh*, the Court was nevertheless content to employ the common law framework for dealing with the variability of the content of fundamental justice in relation to s. 7 rights.[146] Given that the Court has crafted a similar and familiar framework around the variability of the duty to consult, the Court's explanation for avoiding a rights-based approach to Aboriginal consultation obligations leaves something to be desired. A more robust basis than variability of content might be found in the nature of the rights at stake. Section 7 interests in "life, liberty, and security of person" are proven before constitutional relief can be accessed while Aboriginal rights do not have to be proven before the consultation obligations arise. Nevertheless, the unusual status of Aboriginal consultation obligations poses a challenge for ensuring that the constitutional nature of the interests at stake are properly respected. Moreover, where consultation obligations arise in relation to proven or settled Aboriginal rights, the comparison to s. 7 procedural rights cannot be so easily dismissed.

These initial differences point to the different sources and objectives of procedural fairness, fundamental justice, and administrative law on the one hand, and of the duty to consult and Aboriginal law on the other. As discussed above and in other chapters, administrative law, procedural fairness, and fundamental justice address the legitimacy of state decision making through rules, process, and principles that maintain accountability and allow for participation. The duty to consult and accommodate, on the other hand, is about maintaining the honour of the Crown in ongoing processes "of fair dealing and reconciliation," obligations that flow "from the Crown's assertion of sovereignty over an Aboriginal people and de facto control of land and resources that were formerly in the control of that people."[147] Because state sovereignty gives rise to this need for processes of reconciliation, the duty to consult is also, unquestionably, about the legitimacy of state decision making and exercises of power. Where procedural fairness is about developing procedural safeguards within *existing* state structures, the duty to consult and accommodate is arguably about developing procedural safeguards that can support *changing* state structures, given its role in preserving Aboriginal interests in advance of or parallel to ongoing negotiations aimed at more complete resolutions of Aboriginal claims.[148]

145　*Little Salmon/Carmacks, supra* 13 at para. 44.

146　*Suresh v. Canada (Minister of Citizenship and Immigration)*, 2002 SCC 1, [2002] 1 S.C.R. 3 at para. 114 [*Suresh*]. For discussion, see Evan Fox-Decent and Alexander Pless, Chapter 12.

147　*Haida Nation, supra* note 12 at para. 32.

148　*Ibid.* at para. 38. See also Brian Slattery, "Aboriginal Rights and the Honour of the Crown" (2005) 29 Sup. Ct. L. Rev. (2d) 433. Many commentators are skeptical that the duty to consult and accommodate as currently constituted is capable of this kind of "two-way" reconciliation and accommodation, and some note the development bias and assimilative tendency of the duty to consult jurisprudence; see e.g. Christie (2006), *supra*

A more conservative view of the duty to consult is also possible, emphasizing instead the role of the duty to consult as a mechanism to integrate Aboriginal rights within existing administrative structures. In *Little Salmon/Carmacks*, for example, the Court emphasized that Aboriginal rights exist within the Canadian legal system and are closely aligned with the fulfillment of the duty to consult with procedural fairness and administrative law more generally.[149] Under this view, reconciliation is achieved by ensuring that Aboriginal interests are considered within existing decision-making structures and that attention is paid to working out the balance between Aboriginal concerns, third-party interests, and the broader public interests within those decision processes.[150]

Under either view of the duty's contribution, the duty to consult is similar to the duty of fairness or fundamental justice in that both support the legitimacy of state decision making and shape the exercise of state power. The difference is that they do so in relation to different challenges to state legitimacy: the duty of fairness supports the maintenance and evolution of the administrative state, the duty to consult supports processes that aim at a larger integration and/or restructuring.

D. The Legislative Exemption

In light of the different sources and challenges addressed by the duty of fairness and the duty to consult, it is not surprising that there are differences in the scope of decisions to which they apply. One such difference is found in the treatment of policy and legislative decisions. Under a duty of fairness, legislative decisions are exempt from common-law procedural obligations. By contrast, and as noted above, the duty to consult applies to strategic and planning decisions that would likely fall under the legislative exemption in relation to a duty of fairness (and are otherwise unlikely to attract much procedural content, given the factors considered under the *Baker* spectrum analysis). Further, the question of whether the duty to consult applies to the decisions of legislative bodies has been raised in the jurisprudence and remains open and undecided. Are there principled reasons to restrict this approach to the duty to consult or to expand it to administrative law contexts?

As discussed by Grant Huscroft in Chapter 5, the old legislative limitation on the duty to fairness is muddled by the lack of a clear definition of what constitutes a "legislative decision." In the dated and much criticized lead case, *Inuit Tapirisat*,[151] the Cabinet decision in issue was held to be legislative because of the nature of the decision-making body (ministers of the Crown who can be held politically accountable in Parliament) as well as the policy or general nature of the decision. In *Reference re Canada Assistance Plan*[152] and *Wells v. Newfoundland*,[153]

---

note 114 and Veronica Potes, "The Duty to Accommodate Aboriginal Peoples Rights: Substantive Consultation?" (2006) 17 J. Envtl. L. & Prac. 27.

[149] *Little Salmon/Carmacks, supra* note 13 at paras. 45-47. Similarly, strands of the s. 35 jurisprudence have emphasized that Aboriginal rights cannot "strain" the Canadian legal framework—*Mitchell v. M.N.R.*, 2001 SCC 33, [2001] 1 S.C.R. 911; *R. v. Marshall; R. v. Bernard*, 2005 SCC 43, [2005] 2 S.C.R. 220.

[150] See e.g. Knox & Isaac, *supra* note 138.

[151] *Att. Gen. of Can. v. Inuit Tapirisat et al.*, [1980] 2 S.C.R. 735. See Grant Huscroft, Chapter 5 for more discussion.

[152] *Reference Re Canada Assistance Plan (B.C.)*, [1991] 2 S.C.R. 525 at 558.

[153] *Wells v. Newfoundland*, [1999] 3 S.C.R. 199 at paras. 59-61 [*Wells*].

the Court affirmed that in pursuing policy agendas through legislation, Cabinet will not be subject to a duty of fairness. In *Authorson*[154] the Court confirmed that once a policy proposal reaches Parliament, the three readings in the Senate and House of Commons are all the process required for legislative decisions, even in light of quasi-constitutional due process obligations under the *Canadian Bill of Rights* and fiduciary obligations owed by the Crown to the affected individuals—in this case, disabled war veterans.

The legislative exemption from the duty of fairness has two inter-related but separable components: the nature of the decision, particularly whether it is general or policy in nature; and the nature of the decision-maker, and particularly whether the open, political processes of legislative assemblies apply. Both components engage the separation of powers and how courts respect and, hopefully, reinforce democratic accountability. With respect to the first component, David Mullan proposes that the duty to consult opens the door for acknowledging the participatory rights for citizen groups "seeking input into policy oriented or 'legislative' decisions."[155] The basis for this proposition is clear. Under the duty to consult threshold analysis, government conduct clearly includes general, polycentric decisions by the executive that might be called "legislative" under a duty of fairness analysis.[156] Moreover, the duty to consult and accommodate encompasses participation in the design of the decision processes: the rule making around large projects with significant impacts on the Aboriginal interests at stake.[157] So the key question in pursuing Mullan's proposition is whether there are principled reasons for the differences in threshold when it comes to policy decisions.

There are principled reasons for the application of the duty to consult to policy decisions. The requirement that consultation occur early and throughout government decision-making processes implies that consultation will be more effective if Aboriginal peoples are involved in the design of those decision-making processes. Aboriginal participation in policy processes that affect Aboriginal rights is clearly required by both the constitutional nature of their interests (and constitutional priority in relation to proven or recognized rights) and the imperatives of reconciliation that Aboriginal interests are taken into account in decision making and preserved pending a more final resolution. (Indeed, involving Aboriginal communities in policy formation links us back to the self-government processes that underpin the development of a distinctive Aboriginal administrative law.) The question is whether the purposes of the duty to consult that require its application to policy decisions also justify maintaining a different scope of participatory rights in relation to policy-making for other citizens or citizen groups.

It might be argued that the constitutional nature of the interests is sufficient to differentiate the scope of Aboriginal participatory rights from the scope of the participatory rights of other citizens in relation to policy decisions.[158] Alternatively, it might be argued, as Mullan

---

154   *Authorson v. Canada (Attorney General)*, [2003] 2 S.C.R. 40 at para. 37 [*Authorson*].

155   Mullan, *supra* note 78 at 128.

156   *Rio Tinto Alcan, supra* note 92 at para. 44; *Tsuu T'ina Nation, supra* note 102.

157   *Dene Tha', supra* note 101.

158   In *Adams Lake, supra* note 125 at para. 128, Justice Bruce relies on the constitutional character of the duty to consult to find that there is "no justification for insulating [the impugned order in council] from the duty to consult simply because it has a legislative character."

does, that broad participatory rights are, practically speaking, essential to the aims of the duty to consult: "Reconciliation will not come from keeping the competing interests apart, but rather from bringing them together in processes that will provide effective engagement on the part of all substantially affected interests."[159] These arguments engage the competing approaches to reconciliation, canvassed above. It is not necessary to choose between the competing views of reconciliation to address whether the constitutional purposes and interests behind the duty to consult justify restricting the inclusion of policy decisions to the duty to consult. The constitutional priority of Aboriginal interests is a limit on government conduct and not on the procedural rights of other citizens. The expansion of the duty of fairness to encompass policy decisions made by the executive has been argued to be justifiable on its own merits, whether because the theoretical line between administrative and policy decisions is unsustainable or because the formal theory of the separation of powers upon which this line was drawn has been discredited.[160] The broader scope of the duty to consult does not change or restrict this argument. If anything, it opens the door to procedural fairness in decisions that are legislative in nature by demonstrating that procedural rights with respect to policy decisions do not threaten the separation of powers and further refine what separates legislative and executive decision making, as we will see below.

The second component of the legislative exemption—the nature of the decision-maker and the application of procedural rights to open, political processes of legislative assemblies—is more complex and engages the constitutional basis of the duty to consult more directly. Whether under a duty of fairness or a duty to consult, the legislative limitation on procedural rights is presumably justified with respect to the decisions taken by and within legislative assemblies.[161] Procedural rights give rise to obligations that are owed by and in relation to the acts of the *executive* branch of government. This apparently clear line is, however, complicated by the role of Cabinet as the primary proposer and drafter of legislation as well as its primary role, at least in majority governments, in advancing legislation within legislative assemblies. And as Major J. commented in *Wells v. Newfoundland*, "The separation of powers is not a rigid and absolute structure. The Court should not be blind to the reality of Canadian governance that, except in certain rare cases, the executive frequently and de facto controls the legislature."[162] The question, then, becomes at what point and how far into the process of proposing and advancing legislation should procedural obligations (whether under a duty to consult or a duty of fairness) apply? And what remedies would procedural safeguards provide with respect to procedurally deficient legislative acts of the executive?

The duty to consult cases has begun to address these questions. While in *Rio Tinto Alcan*, the Supreme Court left "the question of whether government conduct includes legislative action" for another day,[163] the Alberta Court of Appeal has come up against this issue in a

---

[159] Mullan, *supra* note 78 at 129.

[160] See the discussion in Grant Huscroft, Chapter 5, and Genevieve Cartier, "Procedural Fairness in Legislative Functions: The End of Judicial Abstinence?" (2003) 53 U.T.L.J. 217 [Cartier].

[161] Cartier, *ibid.*

[162] *Wells, supra* note 153 at para. 54. In *Wells*, this reality meant that the Crown was liable in contract and not under a duty of fairness.

[163] *Supra* note 92 at para. 44. *Rio Tinto Alcan* was decided several months after *Tsuu T'ina Nation*.

couple of cases. In *Lefthand*, Justice Slatter was content to rely on *Authorson* to pronounce that "[t]here can ... be no duty to consult prior to the passage of legislation" including the passage of regulations and orders in council.[164] However, in *Tsuu T'ina Nation* the Alberta Court of Appeal accepted that the Crown's consultation obligations applied to the development of a water management plan, a plan that was adopted by an order in council. The more difficult issue defined by the Court in this case was whether quashing the order in council would be an appropriate remedy. The difficulty this issue raises is whether the constitutional procedural obligation of a duty to consult will give rise to a substantive limit on the legislative authority of Cabinet. The First Nations in *Tsuu T'ina Nation* withdrew their request for the order in council preferring to seek a declarative remedy, thereby allowing the court to leave the "interesting question as to whether a free-standing duty to consult is a constitutional imperative under section 35" for another day.[165]

As noted earlier in this section, the parallels between fundamental justice under s. 7 and under the duty to consult would appear to provide a basis for parallel substantive relief under the duty to consult. If this parallel is accepted, the answer to Alberta Court of Appeal's interesting question should be yes.[166] However, the Supreme Court's reluctance to attribute the same constitutional status to the duty to consult as given to procedural safeguards under s. 7 suggests that the answer might be no. In any event, the possibility of a substantive constitutional remedy based on procedural obligations is premised specifically on the constitutional nature of the duty to consult and thus not relevant in the context of common-law procedural fairness. Apart from this specific remedy, however, the application of the duty to consult to traditionally legislative decisions such as orders in council holds significant potential to transfer into the duty of fairness.

Tsuu T'ina Nation illustrates that legislative decisions made by the executive council fall within the scope of the duty to consult. The Cabinet decision in issue in *Tsuu T'ina Nation* was made pursuant to a delegated legislative authority, and the Court of Appeal confirmed that the mode by which the government policy was adopted—the order in council—did not immunize the executive actors from the duty to consult. Echoing the Supreme Court's comments in *Wells*, the Court of Appeal commented that "even if the Legislature itself does not have a duty to consult prior to passing legislation, the duty may still fall upon those assigned the task of developing the policy behind the legislation, or upon those who are charged with

---

164　*R. v. Lefthand*, 2007 ABCA 206 at para. 38, 77 Alta. L.R. (4th) 203, leave to appeal to the Supreme Court of Canada refused, 2008 CanLII 6384.

165　*Tsuu T'ina Nation, supra* note 102 at para. 51. The courts in British Columbia have also encountered this issue and have also avoided quashing a legislative act by Cabinet as a result of inadequate consultation. In *Adams Lake, supra* note 125, the B.C. Supreme Court considered the Adams Lake Indian Band's application to quash an order in council establishing the former recreation area of Sun Peaks as an incorporated municipality in light of inadequate consultation and accommodation prior to the passage of the order in council. Justice Bruce discussed this remedy as possible, but held that it was an inappropriate and unnecessary remedy in the circumstances.

166　This answer might be encouraged by considering the comments of the Supreme Court in *Authorson, supra* note 154 at para. 50, where the Court reviewed *Re B.C. Motor Vehicle Act*, [1985] 2 S.C.R. 486, and stated, "Although this Court has not yet recognized substantive rights stemming from due process, *Re B.C. Motor Vehicle Act* indicates its willingness to recognize that, in the proper circumstances, guarantees of process or justice may confer substantive protections."

making recommendations concerning future policies and actions."[167] The manner and extent to which the duty to consult applies to the development of legislative proposals to be tabled in a legislative assembly, remains undeveloped. But as noted above in relation to the first component of the legislative exemption, there is no principled reason to restrict any such developments to the Aboriginal administrative law context. Instead, Aboriginal administrative law is challenging this traditional limitation on procedural rights by forcing a consideration of the role of the executive in relation to the development of policy, including primary and secondary legislation. Outside of judicial review, it is worth noting that government actors have been working to align the legislative process and their consultative obligations in a manner that extends consultation quite a long way into the legislative drafting process. For example, the Kunst'aa Guu-Kunst'aayah Reconciliation Protocol between British Columbia and the Haida Nation, discussed above, included an explicit mutual commitment to review each other's draft legislation to implement the protocol.[168] Such developments as well as future judicial consideration of the issue will undoubtedly be relevant in considering the future of the legislative exception to the duty of fairness.

E. Other Possibilities and Points of Cross-Fertilization

In this brief review of the many parallels and the points of difference between the duty to consult and accommodate and the duty of fairness, we do not have the space to address numerous other issues that deserve further attention. For example, the unique allowance for the Crown to delegate "procedural aspects" of the duty to consult to third parties may hold useful further reflections on the procedural/substantive divide in administrative law. Concerns about the role of tribunals in reviewing the adequacy of Crown consultation efforts as part of their decision making are deeply related to the role of tribunals in considering constitutional questions and the tensions around this role in other parts of administrative law. A comparative consideration of remedies under the duty to consult relative to other areas of administrative law might produce interesting reflections. The list goes on.

The comparisons pursued have served to highlight that although administrative law and Aboriginal law are about different things, similar problems arise in each—namely, ensuring adequate transparency and participation in decision making for those affected by particular decisions. The most substantial differences exist where the constitutional nature of the duty, and its particular role in preserving Aboriginal interests pending claims resolution and promoting reconciliation, mandates a broader application of the duty to consult and more substantive remedies. Nevertheless, the constitutional distinctiveness of the duty to consult has not stopped it from moving into administrative law in a variety of contexts. From the emphasis on consultation in determinations of whether collective bargaining rights have been violated in *Health Services and Support*,[169] to the reliance on the duty to consult cases

---

[167] *Tsuu T'ina Nation, supra* note 102 at para. 55. See also *Canadian Society of Immigration Consultants v. Canada (Citizenship and Immigration)*, 2011 FC 1435, discussing the relationship in administrative law between executive and legislative action.

[168] Article 6.6, *supra* note 32.

[169] *Health Services and Support—Facilities Subsector Bargaining Assn. v. British Columbia*, 2007 SCC 27, [2007] 2 S.C.R. 391.

to interpret statutory consultation obligations regarding children's educational programs and plans under the *School Act* as encompassing reasonable accommodation in *Hewko*,[170] there is great potential for cross-fertilization between the duty to consult and accommodate, fundamental justice, and the duty of fairness. It is clear that the Court's adoption of a process-oriented, dialogic approach to Aboriginal law in the duty to consult is part of a broader direction toward procedural approaches to managing substantive problems and has much to offer the development of procedural thinking in other areas of public law.[171]

V. Conclusion

This chapter has attempted to explore different perspectives on the emerging field of Aboriginal administrative law. We examined the application of administrative law principles in Aboriginal contexts, the forms and types of administrative justice that may be developed by Aboriginal communities in the context of self-government, and the relationship between Aboriginal and Canadian systems of administrative justice in the context of the duty to consult and accommodate. This chapter is intended as a point of departure, rather than a synthesis of existing bodies of law. We hope this chapter contributes to a broader and deeper dialogue about the future of Aboriginal administrative law.

SUGGESTED ADDITIONAL READINGS

BOOKS AND ARTICLES

Canadian

Christie, Gordon, "Developing Case Law: The Future of Consultation and Accommodation" (2006) 39 U.B.C. L. Rev. 139.

Knox, Anthony & Thomas Isaac, "Judicial Deference and the Significance of the Supreme Court of Canada's Decisions in Haida and Taku River" (2006) 64 Advocate 487.

Mullan, David, "The Duty to Consult Aboriginal Peoples—The Canadian Example" (2009) 22 Can. J. Admin. L. & Prac. 107.

Newman, Dwight G., *The Duty to Consult: New Relationships with Aboriginal Peoples* (Saskatoon: Purich Publishing, 2009).

Slattery, Brian, "Aboriginal Rights and the Honour of the Crown" (2005) 29 Sup. Ct. L. Rev. (2d) 433.

---

170   *Hewko v. B.C.*, 2006 BCSC 1638 (CanLII). Thanks to Freya Kodar for drawing this case to our attention. Regarding the potential cross-fertilization of concepts of reasonable accommodation, see David Robitaille & Sébastien Grammond, "Le processus d'accommodement religieux et autochtone dans les institutions publiques canadiennes: Quelques comparaisons" (2009) 50 C. de D. 75.

171   See e.g. Lorne Sossin, "The Promise of Procedural Justice" in A. Dodek & D. Wright, eds., *Public Law at the McLachlin Court: The First Decade* (Toronto: Irwin, 2011).

Sossin, Lorne, "The Duty to Consult and Accommodate: Procedural Justice as Aboriginal Rights" (2010) 23 Can. J. Admin. L. & Prac. 93-113.

International

Imai, Shin, "Indigenous Self-Determination and the State" in Benjamin J. Richardson, Shin Imai & Kent McNeil, eds., *Indigenous Peoples and the Law: Comparative and Critical Perspectives* (Oxford and Portland: Hart Publishing, 2009) 285.

Potes, Veronica, "The Duty to Accommodate Aboriginal Peoples Rights: Substantive Consultation?" (2006) 17 J. Envtl. L. & Prac. 27.

CASES

Beckman v. Little Salmon/Carmacks First Nation, 2010 SCC 53, [2010] 3 S.C.R. 103.

Canadian Pacific Ltd. v. Matsqui Indian Band, [1995] 1 S.C.R. 3.

Haida Nation v. British Columbia (Minister of Forests), 2004 SCC 73, [2004] 3 S.C.R. 511.

Lafferty v. Tlicho Government, [2009] 3 C.N.L.R. 151.

Rio Tinto Alcan Inc. v. Carrier Sekani Tribal Council, 2010 SCC 43, [2010] 2 S.C.R. 650.

Sparvier v. Cowessess Indian Band No 73, [1993] 3 F.C. 175, 13 Admin. L.R. (2d) 266 (TD).

West Moberly First Nations v. British Columbia (Chief Inspector of Mines), 2011 BCCA 247, 18 B.C.L.R. (5th) 234, leave to appeal to the Supreme Court of Canada refused, 2012 CanLII 8361 (SCC).

CHAPTER FOURTEEN

The Role of International Human Rights Norms in Administrative Law

GERALD HECKMAN
Faculty of Law, University of Manitoba

I. Introduction

If we define administrative law as the set of principles and rules that places limits on the exercise by administrative decision-makers of their statutory power or authority, then international human rights law is, and has long been, relevant to administrative lawyers. However, it only garnered significant attention as a source of administrative law after the controversial judgment of the Supreme Court of Canada in *Baker v. Canada (Minister of Citizenship and Immigration)*.[1] More recently, the Court has focused on the role of international human

---

[1] [1999] 2 S.C.R. 817 [*Baker*]. For the facts of *Baker*, see Grant Huscroft, Chapter 5, From Natural Justice to Fairness: Thresholds, Content, and the Role of Judicial Review.

rights norms in defining *constitutional* limits to governmental power and, in particular, to state encroachments on freedom of association in the collective bargaining context.[2]

International human rights norms may influence the substantive review of administrative decisions in several ways. Canadian decision-makers must exercise discretionary powers and interpret their enabling statute "in accordance with the boundaries imposed in the statute, the principles of the rule of law, the principles of administrative law, the fundamental values of Canadian society, and the principles of the *Charter*."[3] This chapter will show that international human rights norms are relevant to defining several of these boundaries. First, the interpretation of a statutory provision may be influenced by a relevant international right or obligation, especially when the statute was expressly enacted to implement this right or obligation in Canada. Second, the fundamental values of Canadian society may be reflected in the international rights and obligations that bind Canada's governments through custom or convention. The meaning of rights and freedoms under the *Canadian Charter of Rights and Freedoms*[4] may also be influenced by the scope and content of Canada's international human rights obligations, many of which the Charter was intended to implement. Finally, where an official's discretionary decision could frustrate proceedings initiated by an individual before an international treaty body to clarify his or her rights under the treaty, this may be a mandatory relevant consideration to the official's exercise of the discretionary power. In sum, public officials and administrative agencies may be required, in a variety of circumstances, to exercise their statutory discretions or interpret their enabling legislation in a manner that conforms with or sufficiently accounts for international human rights norms or the values underlying these norms.

The provisions of international human rights treaties may also have an impact on the review of administrative decisions for procedural defects. In *Baker*, the Supreme Court recognized that the legitimate expectations of the person challenging a decision could be a factor in determining what procedures are required by the common-law duty of procedural fairness. Moreover, the Court left open the possibility that the terms of an international instrument ratified by Canada could give rise to a legitimate expectation,[5] an approach it later adopted in *Suresh*,[6] to define the content of fundamental justice under s. 7 of the Charter. In that case, the Court confirmed that it would look to international law as evidence of the principles of fundamental justice. Thus, international human rights norms may be relevant to defining the content of procedural fairness and fundamental justice and, in the latter case, may factor into a challenge of the constitutional sufficiency of statutory procedures.

It is no accident that many of the materials referred to in this chapter to describe the influence of international law on administrative law in Canada—including judicial decisions, statutes, regulations, and guidelines—are from the immigration and refugee law con-

---

2 See *Health Services and Support—Facilities Subsector Bargaining Assn. v. British Columbia*, 2007 SCC 27, [2007] 2 S.C.R. 391 [*Health Services*] discussed in section IV.D, *infra*.

3 *Baker, supra* note 1 at para. 56. The Supreme Court used these words to describe the boundaries applicable to the exercise of discretionary power, but in doing so, rejected any rigid dichotomy of "discretionary" or "non-discretionary" decisions.

4 Part I of the *Constitution Act, 1982*, being Schedule B to the *Canada Act 1982* (U.K.), 1982, c. 11 [*Charter*].

5 *Baker, supra* note 1 at para. 29.

6 *Suresh v. Canada (Minister of Citizenship and Immigration)*, 2002 SCC 1, [2002] 1 S.C.R. 3 at para. 60 [*Suresh*].

text. This does not mean that international human rights law is not relevant in other spheres of administrative decision making. This reflects only that it is an important source of state obligations toward non-citizens and that, absent sufficient express legal protections for their clients, immigration and refugee lawyers have more frequently and consistently raised international human rights norms in argument before administrative decision-makers and reviewing courts.[7] As these norms continue to proliferate and more attention is paid to them by advocates,[8] judges, and administrative decision-makers,[9] the opportunities to apply them in other administrative contexts will only multiply.[10]

Because many readers may not be familiar with public international law and, in particular, international human rights law, section II of this chapter sets out a brief synopsis of the sources of international law. Section III describes the rules that govern the reception of international law into Canada's domestic legal order. Section IV of this chapter examines how international human-rights norms affect the review by courts of the interpretation by officials and agencies of their enabling legislation, including discretionary powers, and whether this legislation complies with the Charter. Section V describes the role of international human rights law in administrative procedure and, in particular, the duty of decision-makers to act in accordance with the rules of procedural fairness and the principles of fundamental justice.

II. A Short Introduction to International Human Rights Law

International law is derived from several sources.[11] The most important of these are international custom (customary international law) and international treaties (conventional international law).

Rules of customary international law are "reflected in the practice or conduct of states" and "accepted by them, expressly or tacitly, as being binding on the international plane."[12] A

---

7   Audrey Macklin, "The State of Law's Borders and the Law of States' Borders" in David Dyzenhaus, ed., *The Unity of Public Law* (Oxford: Hart Publishing, 2004) 173 at 174.

8   See e.g. *Re Regina Qu'Appelle Health Region*, [2010] S.L.R.B.D. No. 4 (QL) at para. 3, where a union unsuccessfully sought from the Saskatchewan Labour Relations Board a declaration that Saskatchewan's *Public Service Essential Services Act*, S.S. 2008, c. P-42.2 violated both workers' right to freedom of association under s. 2(d) of the Charter and provisions of the *Freedom of Association and Protection of the Right to Organise Convention, 1948*, an international treaty defining workers' freedom to associate in the workplace.

9   See e.g. *Erickson v. Ontario (Ministry of the Environment)*, [2011] O.E.R.T.D. No. 29 at para. 520 (QL), where the Ontario Environmental Review Tribunal accepted that the precautionary principle, as developed at international law, was relevant to the interpretation and application of Ontario's *Environmental Protection Act*, R.S.O. 1990, c. E.19.

10 See e.g. Russell J. Juriansz, "International Law and Canadian Courts: A Work in Progress" (2009) 25 N.J.C.L. 171 at 179. And see Gerald Heckman & Lorne Sossin, "How Do Canadian Administrative Law Protections Measure Up to International Human Rights Standards?" (2005) 50 McGill L.J. 193.

11 Statute of the International Court of Justice, as found in the *Charter of the United Nations*, 26 June 1945, Can. T.S. 1945 No. 7, c. 14 [UN Charter].

12 Thomas Buergenthal & Harold Maier, *Public International Law in a Nutshell*, 2d ed. (St. Paul, MN: West Publishing, 1990) 22.

practice that meets these two requirements and qualifies as customary law is obligatory for all states that have not objected to it.[13] To establish that a legal norm is a rule of customary international law, there must be evidence that states have consistently and generally (universality is not required) followed the rule[14] and that they have acted in this manner because they were of the view they were obliged to do so under international law rather than for reasons of political expediency.[15] Some norms expressed in international instruments of "universal" character may eventually give rise to customary rules of international law. Whether a rule of customary law has crystallized from a treaty norm depends on whether ratification of the treaty is widespread among interested states and whether these states extensively and uniformly accept that the treaty provision sets out a rule of law that is binding as custom.[16]

Customary law is not static, and groups of states may create a new customary regime by introducing a new rule backed up with consistent and general practice. Moreover, an international treaty may displace otherwise applicable customary rules as between the parties to that treaty.[17] This is not true of *jus cogens*, or peremptory norms of customary international law, which are recognized by the international community of states as norms "from which no derogation is permitted and which can be modified only by a subsequent norm of general international law having the same character."[18] States cannot contract out of peremptory norms by acquiescing to their breach or by ratifying inconsistent treaties. Accordingly, the burden of proof to establish their existence is high. The International Court of Justice has held that peremptory norms derive "from the outlawing of acts of aggression, and of genocide, as also from the principles and rules concerning the basic rights of the human person including protection from slavery and racial discrimination."[19] The prohibition against torture may also have reached the status of a peremptory norm.

Most international human rights norms find their source in conventional, rather than customary, international law. Following the Second World War, to further their pledge under the United Nations (UN) Charter to promote "universal respect for, and observance

---

13   As Brownlie notes, a state may "contract out of a custom in the process of formation" by persistently objecting to it: Ian Brownlie, *Principles of Public International Law*, 6th ed. (Oxford: Oxford University Press, 2003) 11 [Brownlie (6th ed.)].

14   Ian Brownlie, *Principles of Public International Law*, 5th ed. (Oxford: Oxford University Press, 1998) 5-6 [Brownlie (5th ed.)]. Evidence of official state conduct could include diplomatic correspondence, state policies and legislation, executive decisions, treaties, and UN General Assembly resolutions.

15   *Opinio juris* (opinion of justice), the sense among states that they are obligated under international law to follow a certain practice, is sometimes implied on the basis of the evidence of a consistent and general practice: *Asylum Case* (1950), 17 I.L.R. 280 at 285.

16   Alan Brudner, "The Domestic Enforcement of International Covenants on Human Rights: A Theoretical Framework" (1985) 35 U.T.L.J. 219 at 248. See also Brownlie (5th ed.), *supra* note 14 at 12, who notes that non-parties may, by their conduct, accept that the provisions of an international convention represents general international law.

17   Buergenthal & Maier, *supra* note 12 at 25. In this sense, conventions play a role analogous to that of statutory law in common-law domestic legal systems.

18   Vienna Convention on the Law of Treaties, 23 May 1969, Can. T.S. 1980 No. 37, UN Doc. A/Conf. 39/26, art. 53 [Vienna Convention].

19   *Barcelona Traction*, [1970] I.C.J. Rep. 33 at para. 34.

of, human rights and fundamental freedoms for all,"[20] states engaged in an intense international effort, coordinated by the UN, to codify human rights and fundamental freedoms in declarations and treaties. Regional international organizations—the Organization of American States (OAS), the Council of Europe, and the Organization of African Unity—also developed treaty-based systems for the protection of human rights. These instruments form "a vast body of legal norms, a veritable human rights code, that gives meaning to the phrase 'human rights and fundamental freedoms.'"[21] Canada is a party to many important multilateral and regional international treaties that bind Canada at international law, some of which are discussed below.[22] Canada has also adopted important declarations, including the Universal Declaration of Human Rights (UDHR),[23] which, while not formally binding at international law, may "have solemn effects as the formal act of a deliberative body of global importance."[24] International treaties to which Canada is not a party are also important sources of human rights norms that could eventually bind Canada if they become customary international law.[25]

---

[20] UN Charter, *supra* note 11, arts. 55(c), 56.

[21] Thomas Buergenthal, Dinah Shelton, & David Stewart, *International Human Rights*, 3d ed. (St. Paul, MN: West Publishing, 2002) 33.

[22] These include the UN Charter, *supra* note 11; the International Covenant on Civil and Political Rights, 16 December 1966, [1976] Can. T.S. No. 47 [ICCPR]; the International Covenant on Economic, Social and Cultural Rights, 16 December 1966, [1976] Can. T.S. No. 46 [ICESCR]; the Convention Against Torture and Other Cruel, Inhuman or Degrading Treatment or Punishment, 25 May 2000, [2002] Can. T.S. No. 5 [CAT]; the 1951 Convention Relating to the Status of Refugees, 28 July 1951, [1969] Can. T.S. No. 6 [1951 Convention]; the International Convention on the Elimination of All Forms of Racial Discrimination, 21 December 1965, [1970] Can. T.S. No. 28; the Convention on the Rights of the Child, 20 November 1989, [1992] Can. T.S. No. 3 [CRC]; the Convention on the Elimination of All Forms of Discrimination Against Women, 18 December 1989, [1982] Can. T. S. No. 31 [CEAFDAW]; and the Charter of the Organization of American States, 30 April 1948, [1990] Can. T.S. No. 23 [OAS Charter].

[23] GA Res. 217(III), UN GAOR, 3d Sess., Supp. No. 13, UN Doc. A/810 (1948) [UDHR]. The UDHR has acquired a moral and normative status unlike that of any other declaration. The repeated reliance of state governments and international organizations on the UDHR as an authoritative expression of human rights has likely given to some of its provisions the status of customary international law: Buergenthal, Shelton, & Stewart, *supra* note 21 at 41-43. See also the American Declaration of the Rights and Duties of Man, 2 May 1948, 43 A.J.I.L. 133, art. 2 [ADRDM]. The ADRDM contains and defines the fundamental rights proclaimed by OAS member states in art. 3(l) of the OAS Charter: *Interpretation of the American Declaration of the Rights and Duties of Man Within the Framework of Article 64 of the American Convention on Human Rights* (1989), Advisory Opinion OC-10/89, Inter-Am. Ct. H.R. (Ser. A), No. 10 at paras. 45-46.

[24] H.J. Steiner & P. Alston, *International Human Rights in Context: Law, Politics, Morals*, 2d ed. (Oxford: Oxford University Press, 2000) 142, describing the impact of UN General Assembly declarations.

[25] These include the American Convention on Human Rights, 22 November 1969, 65 A.J.I.L. 679 [American Convention]; the European Convention for the Protection of Human Rights and Fundamental Freedoms, 4 November 1950, 213 U.N.T.S. 221 [ECHR]; and the African Charter of Human and Peoples' Rights, 27 June 1981, 1520 U.N.T.S. 217 [African Charter]. In interpreting a state's human rights obligations under the ADRDM, the Inter-American Commission on Human Rights takes the American convention into account even if the state has not ratified it because the convention represents, in many cases, "an authoritative expression of the fundamental principles set forth in the American Declaration": OAS, Inter-American Commission on Human Rights, *Report on the Situation of Human Rights of Asylum Seekers Within the Canadian Refugee Determination System*, OEA/Ser.L/V/II.106/Doc. 40, rev. 28 February 2000 at para. 38 [IACHR Report]. The ECHR is a particularly important source of international norms for Canada because it is historically

Broadly speaking, international human rights treaties contain several kinds of provisions that may be relevant to Canadian administrative decision-makers, reviewing courts, and public lawyers. Some guarantee substantive rights at international law to individuals. These range from the right to freedom from torture or cruel, inhumane, or degrading treatment, conferred by the International Covenant on Civil and Political Rights (ICCPR) and the Convention against Torture,[26] to the right to the opportunity to gain one's living by work that one freely chooses or accepts, granted by the International Covenant on Economic, Social and Cultural Rights (ICESCR).[27] Others impose substantive obligations on states' parties at international law, like the Convention on the Rights of the Child's (CRC's) duty on states' social welfare institutions, courts of law, administrative authorities, or legislative bodies to take into account the best interests of the child as a primary consideration in all actions concerning children.[28] Many treaties require states to provide an "effective remedy" to persons whose substantive treaty rights are violated.[29] In conjunction with the right to an effective remedy, substantive rights may imply institutional or procedural safeguards without which the substantive rights cannot be effectively implemented. Other treaty provisions expressly guarantee institutional and procedural rights at international law, such as the ICCPR right to a fair and public hearing by a competent, independent, and impartial tribunal established by law in the determination of one's rights and obligations in a suit at law,[30] or the CRC right of children, in expressing their own views on matters affecting them, to be heard in any judicial and administrative proceedings affecting them, either directly, or through a representative or an appropriate body.[31] The rights and obligations set out in the international treaties to which Canada is a party are clearly binding on Canada at international law. The extent to which they are sources of domestic law that bind Canadian courts and constrain the powers of administrative decision-makers is the more difficult question addressed in the following sections of this chapter.

Although many international human rights treaties comprise enforcement mechanisms, they rely primarily on the institutions of the signatory states to enforce their guarantees in domestic law. For example, most of the major UN treaties establish treaty bodies charged

---

and conceptually related to the ICCPR, a treaty ratified by Canada. The drafting of these treaties was conducted, in part, contemporaneously, and important linkages can be drawn between their respective provisions: see P. van Dijk, "'The Interpretation of Civil Rights and Obligations' by the European Court of Human Rights—One More Step to Take" in F. Matscher & H. Petzold, eds., *Protecting Human Rights: The European Dimension—Studies in Honour of Gérard Wiarda*, 2d ed. (Berlin: Carl Heymans Verlag KG, 1990) 137.

[26]   CAT, *supra* note 22; ICCPR, *supra* note 22, art. 7. These provisions were considered by the Supreme Court of Canada in *Suresh*, *supra* note 6. Compare ECHR, *supra* note 25, art. 3; American Convention, *supra* note 25, art. 5.

[27]   ICESCR, *supra* note 22, art. 6(1). This provision was considered by the Supreme Court of Canada in *Slaight Communications*, *infra* note 129.

[28]   CRC, *supra* note 22, art. 3.

[29]   ICCPR, *supra* note 22, art. 2(3). Compare ECHR, *supra* note 25, art. 13; American Convention, *supra* note 25, art. 25; ADRDM, *supra* note 23, art. XVIII.

[30]   ICCPR, *supra* note 22, art. 14.

[31]   CRC, *supra* note 22, art. 12.

with the task of supervising states' parties' implementation of the rights set out in their constituent treaties. Treaty bodies carry out several supervisory functions, including reviewing periodic reports submitted by states' parties regarding their implementation efforts,[32] issuing interpretive guidelines (general comments) that give meaning to specific treaty provisions, investigating systemic violations of treaty rights,[33] and reviewing petitions alleging treaty violations by a state party filed by other states[34] or by individuals.[35] However, consistent with the primacy of state laws and institutions in protecting human rights, individual petitions are admissible before UN treaty bodies only if the petitioners have exhausted all domestic remedies available to vindicate the rights in question.[36] Canadian institutions may enforce the rights and obligations expressed in international human rights treaties or in customary international law in one of several ways.[37] For example, Parliament or the provincial legislatures may draft laws to achieve compliance with international human rights norms. In turn, administrative decision-makers may interpret their statutory powers in a manner consistent with international human rights norms. Canadian courts may also give effect to such norms in individual cases, including those that involve procedural or substantive challenges to the decisions of administrative decision-makers. The principles governing whether courts may give effect to a norm of international law—the rules of reception—are discussed in the next section of this chapter.

III. Rules of Reception of International Law

What rules govern whether and in what circumstances Canadian courts may take international norms into account and how these norms can shape the interpretation of statutes and constitutional provisions? Despite efforts by Canada's Supreme Court to clarify the rules of reception of international law into domestic law,[38] they are not as clear as they should be. The Court has been criticized for, among other things, failing to rigorously analyze and apply conventional international law in cases where it was arguably binding, or at least persuasive, in Canada's legal system.[39] In this section, I examine the reception of both customary and conventional international human rights law.

---

32   ICCPR, *supra* note 22, art. 40.

33   CAT, *supra* note 22, art. 20.

34   ICCPR, *supra* note 22, art. 41.

35   Optional Protocol to the International Covenant on Civil and Political Rights, 16 December 1966, [1976] Can. T.S. No. 47, art. 1 [Optional Protocol].

36   *Ibid.*, art. 5(2)(b).

37   For a full listing, see Armand de Mestral & Evan Fox-Decent, "Implementation and Reception: The Congeniality of Canada's Legal Order to International Law" in Oonagh E. Fitzgerald, ed., *The Globalized Rule of Law* (Toronto: Irwin Law: 2006) 31 at 42-56 [de Mestral & Fox-Decent, "Implementation and Reception"].

38   See, notably, *R. v. Hape*, 2007 SCC 26.

39   Stephen J. Toope, "The Uses of Metaphor: International Law and the Supreme Court of Canada" (2001) 80 Can. Bar Rev. 534 at 536-38.

A. Reception of Customary International Human Rights Law

After a lengthy period of relative uncertainty, the Supreme Court confirmed, in its 2007 decision in *R. v. Hape*, that the reception of customary international law into Canadian law is governed by the doctrine of adoption, whereby customary rules of international law are incorporated automatically, as they evolve, into domestic law:

> [F]ollowing the common law tradition, it appears that the doctrine of adoption operates in Canada such that prohibitive rules of customary international law should be incorporated into domestic law in the absence of conflicting legislation. The automatic incorporation of such rules is justified on the basis that international custom, as the law of nations, is also the law of Canada unless, in a valid exercise of its sovereignty, Canada declares that its law is to the contrary. Parliamentary sovereignty dictates that a legislature may violate international law, but that it must do so expressly. Absent an express derogation, the courts may look to prohibitive rules of customary international law to aid in the interpretation of Canadian law and the development of the common law.[40]

There is a sharp contrast between the Court's tentative conclusion that, absent an express derogation, courts "may" look to customary international law to "aid" in the interpretation of Canadian law and the development of the common law and its stronger restatement of the doctrine of adoption in the preceding lines of its judgment. Under that doctrine, absent an express statutory derogation, customary international law *is* Canadian law and thus directly binding on Canadian courts.[41] This contrast may be evidence of the Court's unease with strong presumptions requiring the invocation of international law.

B. Reception of Conventional International Human Rights Law

As a matter of international law, an international treaty is binding on Canada if it is signed and ratified by Canada and has entered into force.[42] The effect of a ratified treaty on Canada's domestic law is another question entirely. Traditionally, conventional international law and Canadian domestic law have been conceived of as two separate regimes residing on entirely distinct planes. This "dualist" relationship is founded on the doctrine of separation of powers between the executive and legislature, which underpins the legal sovereignty of Parliament. Under this traditionalist account, the federal executive may exercise its prerogative power to sign and ratify international treaties that bind Canada on the international

---

40 *Hape, supra* note 38 at para. 39.

41 See Armand de Mestral & Evan Fox-Decent, "Rethinking the Relationship Between International and Domestic Law" (2008) 53 McGill L.J. 573 at 583 et seq. [de Mestral & Fox-Decent, "Rethinking the Relationship"].

42 By signing a treaty, the state expresses its intent to be bound by the treaty obligations in the future. The state formally expresses its final consent to be bound by a treaty by ratifying the treaty, usually by depositing a declaration to this effect with other states' parties or an agreed-upon depository like the UN Secretariat. Typically, a treaty provides that it comes into force once a specified number of states have ratified it: see e.g. ICCPR, *supra* note 22, arts. 48 and 49. See, generally, Mark Freeman & Gibran van Ert, *International Human Rights Law* (Toronto: Irwin Law, 2004) 57-58.

plane, but only Parliament or the provincial legislatures can enact laws that affect legal rights and obligations within Canada.[43] If treaties created legally enforceable rights and obligations without the need to enact enabling legislation, the federal executive could legislate without the consent of Parliament or the provincial legislatures.[44] Thus, international treaty provisions must be "implemented" or "transformed" into domestic law to impose obligations or confer rights legally enforceable in domestic courts. From the traditionalist perspective, an "automatic" domestic application of treaty norms by courts leads to a "democratic deficit," which must be cured by legislative or constitutional reforms to enhance legislatures' involvement in the decision to ratify international treaties.[45] A distinct but related objection to the domestic application of international treaty norms without specific legislative implementation is that federal treaty-making may affect areas of provincial legislative jurisdiction and lead to violations of Canada's constitutional division of powers.[46]

The claim that a treaty obligation binding on Canada at international law is "irrelevant" unless implemented by a specific statute following the treaty's ratification is hotly contested for a number of reasons. First, "not all implementing legislation is obviously so."[47] For example, Parliament may enact statutes for the purpose of implementing a treaty obligation without referring to the treaty. Moreover, "legislation that was not originally intended to implement a treaty may later be relied upon by the federal government as its means of doing so."[48] Canada ratifies most international human rights treaties without adopting implementing legislation, on the assumption that Canadian constitutional, statutory, and common-law regimes already conform to the treaty norms.[49] Controversially, despite this claim of conformity, the Canadian government resists attempts to enforce human rights treaty norms in Canadian courts on the ground that, absent implementing legislation, they are not binding

---

43 *Baker, supra* note 1 at paras. 80-83, per Iacobucci J., dissenting. See also *Baker v. Canada (Minister of Citizenship and Immigration)* (1996), 142 D.L.R. (4th) 554 at 563-64 (F.C.A.) [*Baker* (FCA)].

44 *Attorney General for Canada v. Attorney General for Ontario (Labour Conventions)*, [1937] A.C. 326 (P.C.) [*Labour Conventions*]; Hugh M. Kindred, *International Law: Chiefly as Interpreted and Applied in Canada*, 7th ed. (Toronto: Emond Montgomery, 2006) 206 [Kindred, *International Law*]. The jurisdiction to enact laws to implement a treaty resides with Parliament or the provincial legislatures, depending on the particular legislative subject matter dealt with by the treaty.

45 Joanna Harrington, "Redressing the Democratic Deficit in Treaty Law Making: (Re-)Establishing a Role for Parliament" (2005) McGill L.J. 465 at 468. For a detailed description of Canadian practice regarding the negotiation and implementation of treaties and a proposal for a federal *Canada Treaties Act* to bring greater unity to the relationship between international and domestic law, see de Mestral & Fox-Decent, "Rethinking the Relationship," *supra* note 41 at 538 et seq.

46 See *Labour Conventions, supra* note 44.

47 Freeman & van Ert, *supra* note 42 at 166.

48 *Ibid.* at 167. Canada's government claims that "many laws and policies, adopted by the federal, provincial and territorial governments, assist in the implementation of Canada's international human rights obligations": *ibid.*, n. 94. For an enumeration of the different modes of treaty implementation used in Canada, see de Mestral & Fox-Decent, "Rethinking the Relationship," *supra* note 41 at 617 et seq.

49 Irit Weiser, "Effect of International Human Rights Treaties Ratified Without Implementing Legislation" in *The Impact of International Law in the Practice of Law in Canada* (The Hague: Kluwer Law, 1999) 132 at 132. Toope, *supra* note 39 at 538.

in Canadian law.[50] Many now convincingly argue that express statutory implementation of a treaty is required only if the treaty purports to alter existing domestic law,[51] and that implementation should be inferred where Canada premises its ratification on the prior conformity of Canadian legislation, common law, and administrative policy.[52] Indeed, Canada's Department of Foreign Affairs now states that "the government can accept the obligations within many treaties without new legislation."[53]

Others challenge the traditionalist view by questioning the very basis of the formal separation of powers doctrine—the legislature's monopoly over the production of domestic legal norms. They point out that courts have long constrained the administrative state's exercise of statutory powers by insisting that it conform with "fundamental" or "constitutional" common-law values,[54] including the duty of procedural fairness in administrative law.[55] In their view, courts' increasing reliance on norms expressed in international human rights treaties (whether implemented by statute or not) is best understood as "the judicial updating of the catalogue of values to which the common law subjects the administrative state" from "pre-democratic, property-based values, to a more modern set of democratic values, including fundamental human rights."[56]

The Supreme Court appeared to endorse the traditionalist approach when it stated, in *Baker*,[57] that "[i]nternational treaties and conventions are not part of Canadian law unless they have been implemented by statute."[58] Despite this pronouncement, it is clear that "unimplemented" treaties may still influence statutory interpretation through a well-established

---

50   See *Baker* (FCA), *supra* note 43; *Ahani v. Canada (M.C.I.)* (2002), 58 O.R. (3d) 107 (C.A.), leave to appeal denied, [2002] S.C.C.A. No. 62 (QL) [*Ahani*]. See also K. Norman, "Taking Human Rights Lightly: The Canadian Approach" (2001) 12 N.J.C.L. 2 at 291.

51   S. Toope & J. Brunnée, "A Hesitant Embrace: The Application of International Law by Canadian Courts" (2002) 40 Can. Y.B. Int'l Law 3 at 26-27 [Toope & Brunnée, "Hesitant"]. See *Labour Conventions*, *supra* note 44 at 347 per Lord Atkin: the performance of treaty obligations requires legislative action "if they entail alterations of existing domestic law." See also *Francis v. The Queen*, [1956] S.C.R. 618 at 626, Rand J.: statutory action is needed if treaties "purport to change existing law" or restrict future legislative action.

52   Toope & Brunnée, "Hesitant," *supra* note 51 at 26; J. Brunnée & S. Toope, "A Hesitant Embrace: Baker and the Application of International Law by Canadian Courts" in Dyzenhaus, *supra* note 7, 357 at 363 [Brunnée & Toope, "Embrace"]. See also Hugh M. Kindred, "The Use and Abuse of International Legal Sources by Canadian Courts: Searching for a Principled Approach" in Fitzgerald, *supra* note 37, 5 at 15-17; de Mestral & Fox-Decent "Implementation and Reception," *supra* note 37 at 54-55.

53   (2008), online: Canada Treaty Information <http://www.treaty-accord.gc.ca/procedures.aspx> at para. 6.2. For a contrary view reflecting the traditionalist approach to implementation, see William A. Schabas & Stéphane Beaulac, *International Human Rights and Canadian Law—Legal Commitment, Implementation and the Charter*, 3d ed. (Toronto: Thomson Carswell, 2007) at 60.

54   David Dyzenhaus, Murray Hunt, & Michael Taggart, "The Principle of Legality in Administrative Law: Internationalisation as Constitutionalisation" (2001) 1 O.U.C.L.J. 5 at 7, 34 ["Principle of Legality"]. See also John Mark Keyes & Ruth Sullivan, "A Legislative Perspective on the Interaction of International and Domestic Law" in Fitzgerald, *supra* note 37, 277 at 292 et seq.

55   de Mestral & Fox-Decent "Implementation and Reception," *supra* note 37 at 57-58; *Knight v. Indian Head School Division No. 19*, [1990] 1 S.C.R. 653 at paras. 22 and 24.

56   "Principle of Legality," *supra* note 54 at 7, 34.

57   *Supra* note 1.

58   *Ibid.* at para. 69.

principle of statutory interpretation that legislation will be presumed to conform to international law, including customary international law and treaty obligations:

> The presumption of conformity is based on the rule of judicial policy that, as a matter of law, courts will strive to avoid constructions of domestic law pursuant to which the state would be in violation of its international obligations, unless the wording of the statute clearly compels that result. ... [T]he presumption has two aspects. First, the legislature is presumed to act in compliance with Canada's obligations as a signatory of international treaties and as a member of the international community. In deciding between possible interpretations, courts will avoid a construction that would place Canada in breach of those obligations. The second aspect is that the legislature is presumed to comply with the values and principles of customary and conventional international law. Those values form part of the context in which statutes are enacted, and courts will therefore prefer a construction that reflects them. The presumption is rebuttable, however. Parliamentary sovereignty requires courts to give effect to a statute that demonstrates an unequivocal legislative intent to default on an international obligation.[59]

Several academics claim that courts should and do apply the presumption of conformity with international law to interpret legislation that does not implement a treaty ratified by Canada, because the underlying rationale of the presumption—to avoid an unintended breach of Canada's international obligations through judicial misconstruction of a statute—applies as much to ordinary laws as it does to implementing legislation.[60] Notwithstanding the Supreme Court's assertion in *Hape* that the presumption of conformity is a "general principle" of statutory interpretation, it is too early to conclude that the Court has embraced a general duty on courts to interpret domestic legislation in conformity with unimplemented treaties. For example, the Court followed a more restrained approach to the reception of international norms in *Baker* when it applied "a *permissive* rule *allowing* courts to have regard to Canada's treaty obligations as an *aid* to statutory interpretation."[61] We begin our review of the impact of international human rights norms on the substantive review of administrative decisions with a closer examination of the *Baker* decision.

IV. International Human Rights Norms and the Substantive Review of Administrative Decision Making

A. The Role of Unimplemented Treaties

Baker, an illegal overstayer facing removal to Jamaica by Canadian immigration authorities, asked the minister of citizenship and immigration to exercise her discretion under the *Immigration Act*[62] to allow her, on humanitarian and compassionate grounds, to remain in

---

59   *Hape, supra* note 38 at para. 53.

60   Freeman & van Ert, *supra* note 42 at 156. Toope & Brunnée, "Hesitant," *supra* note 51 at 32. See also *Canadian Foundation for Children, Youth and the Law v. Canada (Attorney General)*, 2004 SCC 4, where the Supreme Court interpreted in conformity with the CRC and the ICCPR a provision of the *Criminal Code* that predated these treaties and was thus not enacted to implement them.

61   John Currie, *Public International Law* (Toronto: Irwin Law, 2001) 222-23, 226 (emphasis added).

62   R.S.C. 1985, c. I-2 (repealed).

Canada where she could care for her Canadian-born children and continue treatment for paranoid schizophrenia. The minister denied her application. Although the Supreme Court decided *Baker* on the procedural issue of bias, it also held that this was an unreasonable exercise of discretion because a review of the notes of the immigration officer who examined Baker's case revealed that his decision was not made in a manner that showed attentiveness and sensitivity to the best interests of Baker's children. The Court's assessment of the reasonableness of the decision was informed by the objectives of the *Immigration Act*, in particular family reunification, ministerial guidelines that emphasized preserving family connections, and the values underlying the CRC. The Act, the guidelines, and the CRC indicated that emphasis on the rights, interests, and needs of children, and special attention to childhood were "important values that should be considered in reasonably interpreting 'humanitarian' and 'compassionate' considerations that guide the exercise of the discretion."[63] The Court rejected Baker's claim that in assessing her application, the minister of citizenship and immigration should have given primacy to the best interests of her children as required by article 3(1) of the CRC[64] because, in its view, the CRC was not implemented by statute and article 3(1) was thus not part of Canadian law and could not apply directly to structure the minister's discretion under the Act.[65] However, L'Heureux-Dubé J., for the majority, ruled that the CRC still played an important role:

> [T]he values reflected in international human rights law may help inform the contextual approach to statutory interpretation and judicial review. As stated in R. Sullivan, Driedger on the Construction of Statutes (3rd ed. 1994) at p. 330:
>
> > [T]he legislature is presumed to respect the values and principles enshrined in international law, both customary and conventional. These constitute a part of the legal context in which legislation is enacted and read. *In so far as possible, therefore, interpretations that reflect these values and principles are preferred.*[66]

The decision that values reflected in an unimplemented international treaty may help inform the interpretation, exercise, and judicial review of statutory discretion sparked an animated debate. Iacobucci and Cory JJ. dissented on this point, arguing that allowing reference to an unincorporated treaty during the process of statutory interpretation allowed Baker to "achieve indirectly what cannot be achieved directly, namely, to give force and effect within the domestic legal system to international obligations undertaken by the executive alone that have yet to be subject to the democratic will of Parliament."[67] Arguably, however, the majority did not go far enough in giving effect to the CRC, which is ratified, in

---

63   *Baker, supra* note 1 at para. 73.

64   *Supra* note 22, art. 3(1) reads: "In all actions concerning children ... the best interests of the child shall be a primary consideration."

65   But see de Mestral & Fox-Decent, "Implementation and Reception," *supra* note 37 at 54-55 for the argument that the CRC had in fact been implemented into Canadian law.

66   *Baker, supra* note 1 at para. 70 (emphasis in original).

67   *Ibid.* at para. 80.

force, and thus binding on Canada. Unlike other international norms, the CRC is not "potentially persuasive," but obligatory: the Court should have applied the presumption of conformity of domestic law with Canada's international obligations, requiring it to strive, as far as possible, to interpret the *Immigration Act* in conformity with Canada's obligations under article 3 of the CRC. Instead, *Baker* prescribes only that the values underlying the CRC "may help inform" courts' "interpretive effort,"[68] a less demanding interpretive onus, appropriate in relation to international norms not binding on Canada. Curiously, when the Supreme Court reaffirmed the presumption of conformity and its application to treaty norms in *Hape*, it did not mention *Baker* or acknowledge this inconsistency.

Craig Scott argues that *Baker* changed courts' focus from the "bindingness" to the "persuasiveness" of international norms:

> [I]t is not simply a rule-of-law concern with the formal legal status of Canada's international legal commitments that determines the depth of interpretive influence of international norms on statutory interpretation but also (and more so) those commitments' resonance with Canadian law and society's fundamental constitutive values and principles. ...
>
> While the [interpretive presumption of legislative conformity with international law] ... is generally applicable to Canada's international commitments, the normative force of any given commitment being called in aid must vary with the subject matter of the international norms and with some appreciation of how the context in which it has been produced relates to our "free and democratic" ideals. In other words, *Baker* helps us understand how international human rights law has a special interpretive force within Canada's legal order.[69]

This characterization of *Baker* may answer the dissenting judges' challenge to the legitimacy of the majority's decision to take into account a value expressed in an unimplemented treaty in assessing the reasonableness of the minister's decision. The value of attentiveness to the best interests of children was reflected not only in the CRC, but also in the objectives of the *Immigration Act* and in the guidelines drafted by the minister's department to structure immigration officers' exercise of humanitarian and compassionate discretion. It already resonated with values that had significance in Canadian law. Arguably, then, requiring immigration officers' attentiveness or sensitivity to the best interests of children as a precondition to their reasonable exercise of humanitarian and compassionate discretion was neither illegitimate nor revolutionary.

What is the implication of the idea that the impact on statutory interpretation of an international human rights norm from an unimplemented treaty depends on its resonance with Canadian legal values? Most of the civil and political rights in international human rights treaties, including the right to be free from arbitrary arrest or detention, the right to be heard by an impartial and independent decision-maker, and the right to be free from discrimination, have great resonance in Canada's legal system. What about social and economic rights?

---

[68]   Brunnée & Toope, "Embrace," *supra* note 52 at 372.

[69]   Craig Scott, "Canada's International Human Rights Obligations and Disadvantaged Members of Society: Finally into the Spotlight?" (1999) 10 Const. Forum Const. 97 at 100, 101. See also "Principle of Legality," *supra* note 54 at 33.

They have a high potential impact on administrative decision making, which is largely concerned with individuals' entitlement to public goods and services provided or regulated by the modern state.[70]

Under the ICESCR, individuals are entitled to "the enjoyment of the highest attainable standard of physical and mental health," and states' parties must create conditions to "assure to all medical service and medical attention in the event of sickness."[71] The Committee on Economic, Social and Cultural Rights has noted that health facilities, goods, and services must be affordable for all, and that all are entitled to equal and timely access to appropriate treatment of prevalent diseases, illnesses, injuries, and disabilities, including the provision of essential drugs.[72] There is a strong presumption that retrogressive measures in relation to the right to health are not permissible, and that the state party has the burden of proving that such measures "have been introduced after the most careful consideration of all alternatives and that they are duly justified by reference to the totality of the rights provided for in the Covenant in the context of the full use of the State party's maximum available resources."[73] The committee also defines as a core obligation of state parties to "provide essential drugs as from time to time defined under the WHO Action Programme on Essential Drugs."[74] ICESCR norms, as developed by the committee in its general comment, could be argued to be relevant considerations for the exercise by provincial officials of the discretion to list or delist, in the public interest, certain drugs from provincial drug formularies or treatments from provincial Medicare schedules of benefits.[75] Could it be argued that the ICESCR's "right to health" resonates with Canadian legal values? Although the Supreme Court has not recognized a free-standing constitutional right to health care,[76] it has determined that state interference with Canadians' ability to access vital health care by purchasing private health insurance where the government is failing to deliver care in a reasonable manner engages constitutionally protected life and security of the person interests.[77]

---

[70]   My consideration of provisions of the ICCPR and ICESCR in this section to illustrate the potential influence of international human rights norms on substantive review does not indicate that I consider these treaties to be unimplemented in Canadian law. Indeed, strong arguments can be made that many of Canada's obligations under these instruments were implemented, notably through enactment of the *Charter of Rights and Freedoms*: see section IV.D, below.

[71]   ICESCR, *supra* note 22, art. 12.

[72]   Committee on Economic, Social and Cultural Rights, *General Comment 14—The Right to the Highest Attainable Standard of Health (Art. 12)*, UN Doc. E/C.12/2000/4 at paras. 12(b)(iii), 17.

[73]   *Ibid.* at para. 32.

[74]   *Ibid.* at para. 43(d).

[75]   See e.g. *Ontario Drug Benefit Act*, R.S.O. 1990, c. O.10, ss. 16-20; *Ontario Drug Benefit Regulations*, O. Reg. 201/96, as am. by O. Reg. 559/06, s. 11 et seq. The Ontario Drug Benefit Program covers most of the cost of prescription drug products listed on the Ontario Drug Benefit Formulary for over 2 million Ontarians who are seniors or who receive social assistance or provincial disability support.

[76]   *Chaoulli v. Quebec (Attorney General)*, 2005 SCC 35, [2005] 1 S.C.R. 791 at para. 104. For a critical assessment of the *Chaoulli* decision, see Colleen M. Flood, Kent Roach, & Lorne Sossin, eds., *Access to Care, Access to Justice: The Legal Debate Over Private Health Insurance in Canada* (Toronto: University of Toronto Press, 2005).

[77]   *Chaoulli, supra* note 76 at para. 124. International norms could be relevant factors in assessing the reasonableness of the decisions of provincial authorities to refuse to reimburse patients for out-of-province care that is not available to them in a timely manner in their home province. These reimbursement schemes were de-

Another area of administrative decision making that could be influenced by international norms is the state regulation of residential tenancies. Article 11(1) of the ICESCR guarantees to all the right to adequate housing. The committee has interpreted this right to include the right to security of tenure guaranteeing legal protection against forced eviction: "Evictions should not result in rendering individuals homeless or vulnerable to the violation of other human rights."[78] Before it was repealed and replaced by the Ontario legislature in 2006, the Ontario *Tenant Protection Act* allowed for expedited evictions without a hearing and did not require adjudicators with the Ontario Rental Housing Tribunal to consider the risk that evicted households could become homeless. In its review of Canada's fifth periodic report, the committee noted that "many evictions occurred on account of minimal arrears of rent without due consideration of [Canada's] obligations under the Covenant."[79] It could be argued, on the basis of article 11 of the ICESCR as interpreted by the committee, that the risk of homelessness should be a mandatory relevant consideration in the Landlord and Tenant Board's decision whether or not to grant an application for eviction.[80] Indeed, these and other sources of international norms were considered in the successful challenge of the constitutionality of a municipal bylaw's prohibition against erecting temporary shelter on public property, used to evict homeless persons from a public park.[81] It is noteworthy that both the provision of health care and the regulation of residential tenancies are largely, if not entirely, matters within provincial legislative jurisdiction. As mentioned previously, courts or administrative decision-makers who adopt a traditionalist view of the role of international norms in domestic law may be reluctant, on division of powers grounds, to give "automatic" domestic effect in areas of provincial jurisdiction to treaties ratified by the federal executive.

Following *Baker* and notwithstanding *Hape*, it remains unclear to what extent Canadian courts will apply the common law's interpretive presumption of conformity to interpret statutes in a manner consistent with international obligations that flow from treaties not implemented by statute. Canadian legislatures could clarify the role of specific international norms as Parliament did in the immigration and refugee protection context after *Baker*. It directed courts, tribunals, and administrators to interpret and apply the provisions of the *Immigration and Refugee Protection Act* consistently with international norms.[82] It expressly

---

scribed by the dissenting judges, at para. 264, as an important "safety valve," the administration of which could be supervised under s. 7 of the Charter. See e.g. *Flora v. Ontario (Health Insurance Plan, General Manager)*, 2008 ONCA 538. Additional evidence of resonance with Canadian legal values can be found in Arbour J.'s dissenting judgment in *Gosselin v. Québec (Attorney General)*, 2002 SCC 84, [2002] 4 S.C.R. 429, recognizing that s. 7 protects the positive right to life and security of person. The majority of the Supreme Court in *Gosselin* did not expressly reject this interpretation of s. 7. However, when the Court has subsequently applied s. 7, albeit in cases asserting state deprivations of life, liberty, and security of the person (the negative s. 7 right), it has been silent on the existence of a positive s. 7 right.

78   Committee on Economic, Social and Cultural Rights, *General Comment 7—The Right to Adequate Housing (Art. 11(1) of the Covenant): Forced Evictions*, UN Doc. E/1998/22, annex IV at para. 17.

79   Concluding Observations on Canada's 4th and 5th Periodic Reports, E/C.12/CAN/CO/5, 22 May 2006, 36th Sess.

80   *Residential Tenancies Act, 2006*, S.O. 2006, c. 17, s. 83.

81   *Victoria (City) v. Adams*, 2008 BCSC 1363 [*Adams*]; aff'd 2009 BCCA 563.

82   S.C. 2001, c. 27, s. 3(3)(f) [IRPA].

implemented article 3 of the CRC by requiring immigration officials deciding humanitarian and compassionate applications to take into account the best interests of a child directly affected by their decisions.[83] The following section examines the impact of international human rights norms that are implemented in this manner on substantive review.

B. Implemented International Human Rights Norms and the Substantive Review of Discretion

In interpreting a statute that expressly implements an international treaty, courts must rely on the provisions of that treaty.[84] In *Pushpanathan v. Canada (Minister of Citizenship and Immigration)*,[85] the Supreme Court reviewed the Immigration and Refugee Board's (IRB's) interpretation of a provision in the *Immigration Act* that implemented a clause in the 1951 Convention Relating to the Status of Refugees excluding from refugee protection individuals "guilty of acts contrary to the purposes and principles of the United Nations."[86] Since the statutory provision sought to implement the 1951 Convention, the Court was bound to "adopt an interpretation consistent with Canada's obligations under the Convention,"[87] which it determined by analyzing the convention's text and applying the rules of treaty interpretation articulated in the Vienna Convention.[88] The Court reviewed the IRB's determination on a correctness basis, largely because the interpretation of an international human rights convention was a pure question of law of precedential value over which it could claim more expertise than the IRB.[89]

---

83   *Ibid.*, s. 25.

84   Traditionally, courts would not resort to the text of an underlying treaty as an aid to interpreting the provisions of implementing legislation unless they were satisfied that the text was patently ambiguous: Kindred, *International Law*, *supra* note 44 at 202-3. In *National Corn Growers Assn. v. Canada (Import Tribunal)*, [1990] 2 S.C.R. 1324 at 1371, the Supreme Court jettisoned this requirement and held that it was proper to refer to the treaty at the outset of the interpretive inquiry, because implementing statutes can reveal latent ambiguities. But see Stéphane Beaulac, "International Law and Statutory Interpretation: Up with Context, Down with Presumption" in Fitzgerald, *supra* note 37, 331 at 349-51.

85   [1998] 1 S.C.R. 982 [*Pushpanathan*].

86   Adopted 28 July 1951, entry into force 22 April 1954, art. 1(6)(c), online: Office of the United Nations High Commissioner for Human Rights <http://www2.ohchr.org/english/law/refugees.htm>.

87   *Pushpanathan, supra* note 85 at para. 51.

88   Article 31 of the Vienna Convention, *supra* note 18 requires that a treaty be "interpreted in good faith in accordance with the ordinary meaning to be given to the terms of the treaty in their context and in light of its object and purpose." Article 32 recognizes that if this approach to interpretation leaves the meaning of a treaty provision ambiguous or obscure or leads to manifestly absurd or unreasonable results, recourse may be had to supplementary means of interpretation, including the preparatory work of the treaty and the circumstances of its conclusion. In *Pushpanathan*, on the basis of the convention's aim of protecting the human rights of refugees and on the travaux préparatoires, the Court held, at paras. 73-75, that only persons responsible for serious and sustained violations of fundamental human rights amounting to persecution should be excluded from refugee protection.

89   *Pushpanathan, supra* note 85 at para. 45 et seq. But see *National Corn Growers, supra* note 84, where the Court applied a deferential standard in its review of the Canadian Import Tribunal's interpretation of the *Special Import Measures Act*, R.S.C. 1985, c. S-15, including the tribunal's decision to refer to the General Agreement on Tariffs and Trade (GATT), which the Act was intended to implement. Such a standard was appropriate in light of the presence, in the specialized tribunal's enabling statute, of a privative clause.

In *Németh v. Canada (Justice)*,[90] the Supreme Court of Canada's interpretation of several provisions of the IRPA and *Extradition Act*[91] defining the scope of the minister's authority to extradite a refugee was heavily influenced by its very careful analysis of how Parliament had chosen to implement the prohibition at international law against the refoulement of Convention refugees in both statutes. The Némeths, Hungarian Roma, had been recognized by the IRB as refugees. A few years later, Hungary sought their extradition to face fraud charges. Canada's minister of justice ordered their surrender despite claims that they feared persecution in Hungary. He determined that to successfully resist their extradition, they had to establish that they would face persecution on their return to Hungary. The Némeths claimed that s. 115 of the IRPA implemented the principle of non-refoulement from the 1951 Convention by providing that a person recognized as a Convention refugee shall not be removed from Canada to a country where he or she would be at risk of persecution. In particular, they argued that an interpretation of s. 115 that precluded removal by extradition until their refugee status had ceased or been revoked through the processes set out under the IRPA was necessary to implement Canada's obligations under the Convention. Cromwell J., writing for a unanimous court, agreed that "where possible, statutes should be interpreted in a way which makes their provisions consistent with Canada's international treaty obligations and principles of international law."[92] However, he determined that, properly construed, "removal" in s. 115 was used solely in connection with "removal orders" under IRPA and did not extend to removal by extradition.[93] Accordingly, the presumption that s. 115 implemented Canada's international obligations in the context of extradition was rebutted by the unambiguous and clear meaning of that statutory provision.[94] Justice Cromwell determined that "the *IRPA* does not and was not intended to implement Canada's international obligations against *refoulement* in the context of expulsion by extradition,"[95] a role assigned in his view to s. 44 of the *Extradition Act*, which required the minister to refuse to make a surrender order in certain circumstances. Similarities in language and the legislative history leading to its enactment showed that s. 44(1)(b) was inspired by the provisions of the European Convention on Extradition and the UN Model Treaty on Extradition. It was thus reasonable to infer that s. 44(1)(b) was adopted to serve the purpose identified for these provisions—"protection against prejudice in the requesting state, particularly when extradition would constitute a violation of the requested state's obligations in relation to *non-refoulement*"[96]—and was Canada's "primary legislative vehicle to give effect to Canada's *non-refoulement* obligations when a refugee is sought for extradition."[97] Accordingly, the

---

[90] 2010 SCC 56 [*Németh*].

[91] S.C. 1999, c. 18.

[92] *Németh, supra* note 90 at para. 34.

[93] *Ibid.* at paras. 26-31.

[94] Moreover, Justice Cromwell held that the Némeths' claim that extradition could be ordered only if a previous finding that a person was a refugee had been formally set aside was inconsistent with the temporal nature of refugee status under the Convention and was not supported by more specific international norms: *ibid.* at paras. 50-52.

[95] *Ibid.* at para. 41.

[96] *Ibid.* at para. 81.

[97] *Ibid.* at para. 77.

international norms governing refugee protection played an important role in the interpretation of the provision:

> This clear link between s. 44(1)(b) and Canada's international obligations under the Refugee Convention has important implications for its interpretation and application in the refugee context. The Refugee Convention has an "overarching and clear human rights object and purpose," and domestic law aimed at implementing the Refugee Convention, such as s. 44(1)(b), must be interpreted in light of that human rights object and purpose: *Pushpanathan* ... . Section 44(1)(b), when applied to the situation of a refugee whose extradition is sought, must be understood in the full context of refugee protection.[98]

The Court decided that the closing words of s. 44(1)(b), which provides that the minister shall refuse surrender if satisfied that "the request for extradition is made for the purpose of prosecuting or punishing the person by reason of their race [or other Convention grounds] ... or [if] the person's position may be prejudiced for any of those reasons,"[99] should be interpreted broadly as "protecting a refugee against *refoulement* which risks prejudice to him or her on the listed grounds in the requesting state whether or not the prejudice is strictly linked to prosecution or punishment."[100] Moreover, imposing on a refugee the burden of proving that persecution would in fact occur and that the conditions which led to the conferral of refugee protection had not changed was "not compatible with Canada's international undertakings with respect to *non-refoulement* or with the requirements of fundamental fairness to the refugee."[101] In the opinion of the Court, by imposing such a burden on the Némeths and by failing to address s. 44(1)(b) in his decision to surrender them, the minister had made an unreasonable decision.

The *Németh* decision illustrates that before a court relies on the terms of an international treaty to interpret a statutory provision, it will first ascertain whether the legislature in fact intended the specific provision to implement the treaty. In some cases, this intention will be clear. For example, following the Supreme Court's decision in *Baker*, Parliament amended the *Immigration Act* to expressly require officials to take into account the best interests of children directly affected by their decisions, consistent with Canada's obligations under the CRC.[102] It also enacted s. 3(3)(f) of the IRPA, which provides that the Act "is to be construed and applied in a manner that ... complies with international human rights instruments to which Canada is signatory." The wording of s. 3(3)(f) is not limited to specific international instruments or to treaties addressed to refugees, nor does it require that these instruments be ratified. On its face, it extends to all human rights instruments to which Canada was already, and would become, a signatory. Interpreting s. 3(3)(f) for the first time in *De Guzman v. Canada (Minister of Citizenship and Immigration)*, the Federal Court of Appeal was troubled by the provision's broad scope, which made the meaning of IRPA "subject to ... an amorphous and open-ended body of international instruments," and trans-

---

98   *Ibid.* at para. 86.

99   *Ibid.* at para. 56.

100   *Ibid.* at para. 96.

101   *Ibid.* at para. 105.

102   IRPA, *supra* note 82, ss. 28(2)(c), 60, 67(1)(c), 68(1), 69(2).

ferred considerable power from Parliament to the executive.[103] It decided that s. 3(3)(f) meant that international human rights instruments that were binding at international law (signed and, if necessary, ratified by Canada) were "determinative of how IRPA must be interpreted and applied, in the absence of a contrary legislative intention."[104] It suggested in *obiter* that Parliament intended that non-binding international human rights instruments be used, as in the *Baker* approach, only as persuasive and contextual factors in the interpretation and application of IRPA.[105] In sum, in the immigration and refugee protection context, s. 3(3)(f) clarifies the role of international instruments that bind Canada at international law. Whether expressly implemented by statute or not, such instruments are determinative of the meaning of IRPA's provisions and the validity of decisions made pursuant to these provisions unless they reveal a contrary legislative intention.[106]

Thiara v. Canada (Citizenship and Immigration)[107] illustrates how s. 3(3)(f) of the IRPA has been used to challenge the substance of an immigration officer's discretionary decision. The applicant, who was to be removed from Canada, applied to remain on humanitarian and compassionate grounds, arguing that she was needed to raise her Canadian-born daughters in Canada. She claimed that forcing her to return with her daughters to India would not be in their best interests because of the poverty, poor educational opportunities, and other problems faced by young girls there and would be inconsistent with the UDHR guarantee of parental choice in children's education[108] and the CEAFDAW obligation on states' parties to eliminate discrimination against women in education.[109] Forcing her to leave her children in Canada would also violate the ICESCR and CRC, which required states' parties to support family unity and parents' child-rearing responsibilities.[110] The immigration officer dismissed her application. Thiara sought judicial review, arguing that the

---

[103]   2005 FCA 436 at para. 86 [*De Guzman*].

[104]   *Ibid.* at para. 87.

[105]   *Ibid.* at para. 89.

[106]   De Guzman had received permanent resident status on the basis of a misrepresentation: she had not told immigration officials that she had two sons in the Philippines. Because of her misrepresentation, she was barred by s. 117(9)(d) of the *Immigration and Refugee Protection Regulations* from later sponsoring her two sons' admission to Canada. She challenged this lifetime ban on sponsorship, claiming that IRPA did not authorize the enactment of regulations that made it non-compliant with international human rights instruments to which Canada was a signatory. In her view, the regulation subjected her family to arbitrary or unlawful interference contrary to art. 17 of the ICCPR and did not treat the best interests of her children as a primary consideration, in violation of art. 3 of the CRC. The Federal Court of Appeal found that, on the whole, IRPA did comply with these international instruments, because De Guzman's sons could apply for admission on humanitarian and compassionate grounds under s. 25 of IRPA, which directed immigration officers to consider their best interests. *Kim v. Canada (Citizenship and Immigration)*, 2010 FC 149, also well illustrates the impact of s. 3(3)(f) on the IRPA's interpretation. There, the Federal Court required at para. 74, that in determining whether a child had a well-founded fear of persecution, defined by the Supreme Court as the "sustained or systematic violation of basic human rights" and was a Convention refugee under s. 96 of IRPA, the Refugee Protection Division inform itself of the distinctive human rights of children recognized in the CRC.

[107]   2007 FC 387 [*Thiara*], upheld on appeal, 2008 FCA 151.

[108]   UDHR, *supra* note 23, art. 26.

[109]   CEAFDAW, *supra* note 22, art. 10.

[110]   ICESCR, *supra* note 22, art. 10; CRC, *supra* note 22, art. 18.

officer's failure to mention any international instruments in her decision meant that she had ignored them. The court rejected her claim, finding that the officer had in fact determined that it would be in the children's best interest to remain in Canada, but that this factor was outweighed by Thiara's past misrepresentations to Citizenship and Immigration Canada. The officer's failure to specifically cite the international instruments in her decision did not indicate that her decision was unreasonable, because her analysis of the best interests of the children was "cogent, considered and thoughtful, signifying that she was sensitive to the issues raised in the CRC, UDHR and so on."[111]

Significantly, s. 3(3)(f) does not require that each provision of IRPA in isolation assure Canada's compliance with international human rights instruments. In *Idahosa v. Canada (Public Safety and Emergency Preparedness)*,[112] a failed refugee claimant from Nigeria sought to prevent her impending removal from Canada by obtaining an order from the Ontario Court of Justice granting her temporary custody of her Canadian-born children and prohibiting their removal from Canada without further order from that court. She then asked a federal immigration enforcement officer to stay her removal on the grounds that removal would preclude her from exercising the right and responsibility to care for her children conferred by the Ontario custody order. She claimed the benefit of s. 50 of the IRPA, which stayed a removal order "if a decision that was made in a judicial proceeding ... would be directly contravened by the enforcement of the removal order." Idahosa argued that s. 50 should be interpreted and applied consistently with provisions of the UDHR, the ICCPR, and the CRC, which protect the best interests of children and the parent-child relationship. The enforcement officer refused to stay her removal, a decision upheld on judicial review by the Federal Court and Federal Court of Appeal. The Court of Appeal decided that a contextual interpretation of s. 50 did not support an interpretation that would enable non-nationals to defer their removal by obtaining custody orders when there was no genuine dispute about custody.[113] It found that these international human rights instruments did not prohibit the deportation of foreign nationals simply because removal would result in separation from their children. Moreover, compliance with international human rights instruments could not be assessed with regard to s. 50 in isolation:

> [A]ny assessment of whether a statutory provision violates Canada's international legal obligations must be made on the basis of the statute as a whole. IRPA provides opportunities for the consideration of the best interests of the children of those subject to deportation. The interests of Ms. Idahosa's children have been considered by the officer who determined her H & C [humanitairan and compassionate] application and in the PRRA [pre-removal risk assessment].

---

111 *Thiara, supra* note 107 at para. 41. See also *Canada (Citizenship and Immigration) v. Okoloubu*, 2008 FCA 326, where the Federal Court of Appeal upheld an immigration officer's dismissal of a humanitarian and compassionate application rejecting a non-citizen's claim that deportation would separate him from his spouse and child and interfere with his private family life contrary to art. 17 of the ICCPR and breach Canada's obligations under arts. 23 and 24 to protect the family unit and the interests of children. The Court upheld the officer's decision despite her finding that she did not have jurisdiction to deal with international law because she had "addressed in substance the different and important interests at stake, giving careful weight to the interests of the child and the importance of the family unit": *ibid.* at para. 60 (*Okoloubu*).

112 2008 FCA 418 [*Idahosa*].

113 *Ibid.* at para. 39.

While great weight must be given to the best interests of children in administrative decision-making, they do not necessarily outweigh all other considerations.[114]

This section has shown that conventional international human rights norms may play a significant role in the substantive review of discretionary decisions. For example, courts interpret the scope of statutory powers consistently with the human rights obligations that they are intended to implement. In the immigration context, officials are subject to a statutory obligation to interpret and apply the provisions of the IRPA in a manner that complies with the international human rights instruments to which Canada is signatory.

C. Norms of Customary International Law and Substantive Review

Norms of customary international law, particularly in the area of environmental protection, have also influenced the substantive review of the decisions of public bodies, including municipal councils. In *114957 Canada Ltée (Spraytech, Société d'arrosage) v. Hudson (Town)*,[115] the Supreme Court sought to determine whether a bylaw enacted by the town of Hudson restricting the use of pesticides was authorized by a general power under the Quebec *Cities and Towns Act*[116] to enact bylaws to "secure peace, order, good government, health and general welfare" in the municipality. A majority of the Court found, on the basis of ordinary principles of statutory interpretation that the purpose of the town's bylaw fell squarely within its power to secure citizens' health. Relying on the *Baker* approach, the majority added that its interpretation of the *Cities and Towns Act* was consistent with the precautionary principle, which had arguably crystallized into a norm of customary international law. The majority's reference to the *Baker* approach in discussing the application of customary law to statutory interpretation is problematic.[117] Under the common-law rules of reception, customary norms are binding on Canada at international law and directly applicable in Canadian law. They should not be treated, following *Baker*, as only potentially relevant to statutory interpretation.[118] Norms of customary international law may also constrain the discretionary powers of governments to decline to conduct environmental assessments of activities with serious transborder environmental impacts.[119]

---

[114] *Ibid.* at para. 54.

[115] [2001] 2 S.C.R. 241 [*Spraytech*].

[116] R.S.Q., c. C-19.

[117] Brunnée & Toope, "Embrace," *supra* note 52 at 378-79.

[118] Brunnée & Toope suggest that because the Court did not formally determine that the precautionary principle was custom, it may have intended only to recognize that as a non-binding international norm, the principle could inform statutory interpretation and judicial review: *ibid.* at 379. For discussion of the continuing evolution of the precautionary principle at international law and its relevance to the exercise of discretionary power by administrative decision-makers, see Chris Tollefson & Jamie Thornback, "Litigating the Precautionary Principle in Domestic Courts" (2008) 19 J. Envtl. L. & Prac. 33.

[119] Neil Craik argues that the federal minister of the environment's discretionary power under the *Canadian Environmental Assessment Act*, S.C. 1992, c. 37, to initiate an environmental assessment must be exercised consistently with an emergent international customary obligation to undertake such an assessment where proposed industrial activity may have a significant adverse impact in a transboundary (international) context, in particular, on a shared resource: Neil Craik, "Transboundary Environmental Assessment in Canada: International and Constitutional Dimensions" (2010) 21 J. Envtl. L. & Prac. 107 at 134.

Administrative decisions must also comply with Charter principles. Here again, the Supreme Court appears to have adopted the *Baker* approach, referring to international instruments as part of the context of Charter interpretation.[120] As shown below, Canadian courts' approach to the use of international human rights law in Charter interpretation suffers from the same uncertainties and inconsistencies as does their approach to the interpretation of statutes.

D. The Use of International Law in Charter Interpretation

The Charter is an important locus of reception of international law norms in Canada's legal system. Fulfilling Canada's obligations under the UDHR and ICCPR was a major impetus to drafting and adopting the Charter: the language of the general limitation clause in s. 1, the legal rights in ss. 7-14, and the right to equality in s. 15 were derived from analogous provisions in the ICCPR.[121] Moreover, Canada represents to domestic audiences and international treaty bodies that the Charter gives effect to provisions of these treaties.[122] Accordingly, it would be open to courts or administrative decision-makers to recognize the Charter as legislation intended to implement these and other important international human rights instruments. Some academics argue that the Supreme Court should treat binding international human rights laws, whether customary or conventional, as "presumptively protected" by the Charter, while non-binding international instruments, such as General Assembly declarations, and the views of UN treaty bodies should be treated as "relevant and persuasive sources for *Charter* interpretation."[123] Others object to applying the presumption of conformity to Charter interpretation because it would allow the federal executive to "unilaterally amend" Canada's constitution.[124]

---

[120]   The role of the Charter in administrative law is discussed by Evan Fox-Decent and Alexander Pless in Chapter 12, The Charter and Administrative Law: Cross-Fertilization or Inconstancy?

[121]   Anne Bayefsky, *International Human Rights Law—Use in Canadian Charter of Rights and Freedoms Litigation* (Toronto: Butterworths, 1992) 49. See also G.V. La Forest, "The Expanding Role of the Supreme Court of Canada in International Law Issues" (1996) 34 Can. Y.B. Int'l Law 89 at 97.

[122]   Presenting Canada's fourth periodic report regarding the ICCPR's implementation to the UN Committee on Human Rights, Canada's representative stated that the Charter "was the primary mechanism" for implementing the ICCPR and that the Charter's provisions "were based on the Covenant": UN Human Rights Committee, Summary Record of the 1738th Meeting: Canada (17 March 1999), UN Doc. CCPR/C/SR.1738, online: United Nations <http://www.unhchr.ch/tbs/doc.nsf/0/ec6cd11696c500a8c1256bb90034dd47?Opendocument>. Similarly, the Canadian government informed the Inter-American Commission on Human Rights that it implemented the ADHR through refugee protection laws and its general legal system and that the Charter shared many of the ADHR's principles: IACHR Report, *supra* note 25 at para. 36. Finally, as noted by Ross J. in *Adams*, *supra* note 81 at para. 98, Canada informed the Committee on Economic, Social and Cultural Rights that s. 7 of the Charter must be interpreted consistently with Canada's obligations under the ICESCR not to deprive persons of the basic necessities of life: Summary Record of the 5th Meeting, ESC, 8th Sess., 5th Mtg, U.N. Doc. E/C.12/1993/SR.5 (25 May 1993).

[123]   Freeman & van Ert, *supra* note 42 at 194-95.

[124]   Irit Weiser, "Undressing the Window: Treating International Human Rights Law Meaningfully in the Canadian Commonwealth System" (2004) 37 U.B.C. L. Rev. 113 at 148. But see Toope & Brunnée, "Hesitant," *supra* note 51 at 45, n. 140 and 49, n. 200.

In *Reference Re Public Service Employee Relations Act (Alta.)*, Dickson C.J. recognized that, as a party to international human rights treaties with provisions similar or identical to those in the Charter, Canada had "obliged itself internationally to ensure within its borders the protection of certain fundamental rights and freedoms which are also contained in the *Charter*."[125] Consequently, "[t]he general principles of constitutional interpretation require that these international obligations be a relevant and persuasive factor in *Charter* interpretation":[126]

> The content of Canada's international human rights obligations is, in my view, an important indicia of the meaning of "the full benefit of the *Charter*'s protection." I believe that the *Charter* should generally be presumed to provide protection at least as great as that afforded by similar provisions in international human rights documents which Canada has ratified.
>
> In short, though I do not believe the judiciary is bound by the norms of international law in interpreting the *Charter*, these norms provide a relevant and persuasive source for interpretation of the provisions of the *Charter*, especially when they arise out of Canada's international obligations under human rights conventions.[127]

Freeman and van Ert claim that this passage reveals two approaches to the use of international law in Charter interpretation.[128] The first paragraph speaks of a presumption that the Charter should be interpreted in conformity with Canada's international obligations. The second holds that international norms should be viewed by courts as relevant and persuasive, but not binding. In contrast, Currie argues that these statements set out a single "hierarchical interpretive approach":

> [T]he minimum content prescription, applicable to international human rights treaties which Canada has ratified, is simply a particularization—rather than a contradiction—of the relevant and persuasive influence that all international human rights law (whether internationally binding on Canada or not) should have in Charter interpretation.[129]

In subsequent decisions,[130] the Supreme Court appeared to emphasize that international norms provide a broader context within which to determine the scope and content of Charter

---

[125]   [1987] 1 S.C.R. 313 at para. 59 [*Alberta Reference*].

[126]   *Ibid.*

[127]   *Ibid.* at paras. 59-60, dissenting on another point.

[128]   Freeman & van Ert, *supra* note 42 at 193.

[129]   John H. Currie, "International Human Rights Law in the Supreme Court's Charter Jurisprudence: Commitment, Retrenchment and Retreat—In No Particular Order" (2010), 50 S.C.L.R. (2d) 423 at 429 [Currie, Commitment]. In *Slaight Communications Inc. v. Davidson*, [1989] 1 S.C.R. 1038 at 1056-57 [*Slaight Communications*], speaking for a majority of the Court, Dickson C.J. reiterated the minimum content prescription and the principle that Canada's international human rights obligations (whether arising from custom or treaty) should "inform" not only the interpretation of Charter rights but what can constitute reasonable limits to these rights under s. 1 of the Charter.

[130]   *Slaight Communications, ibid.*: Canada's international human rights obligations should "inform" the interpretation of Charter rights. See also *Kindler v. Canada (Minister of Justice)*, [1991] 2 S.C.R. 779; and *United States v. Burns*, 2001 SCC 7, [2001] 1 S.C.R. 283 [*Burns*].

rights, a "weaker version" of the presumption of conformity that does not require the court to "strive for an interpretation that is consistent with international norms."[131]

In *Suresh*, the Court extended this less constraining approach to norms of customary international law. The *Immigration Act* gave the minister of citizenship and immigration the discretion to decide that a refugee found to be inadmissible on the ground of membership in a terrorist organization was a danger to the security of Canada and could be removed to a country where his or her life or freedom would be threatened. The Court held that its inquiry into whether Suresh's deportation to a country where he faced a substantial risk of torture violated the principles of fundamental justice under s. 7 would be "informed not only by Canadian experience and jurisprudence, but also by international law, including *jus cogens*":[132]

> [T]he principles of fundamental justice expressed in s. 7 … and the limits on rights that may be justified under s. 1 … cannot be considered in isolation from the international norms which they reflect. A complete understanding of the [*Immigration Act*] and the *Charter* requires consideration of the international perspective.[133]

However, international norms were not binding or even determinative:

> International treaty norms are not, strictly speaking, binding … unless they have been incorporated into Canadian law by enactment. However, in seeking the meaning of the Canadian Constitution, courts may be informed by international law. Our concern is not with Canada's international obligations *qua* obligations; rather our concern is with the principles of fundamental justice. We look to international law as evidence of these principles and not as controlling in itself.[134]

Despite international law's "virtually categoric" rejection of deportation to torture, the Court concluded that under Canadian law, the minister retained an exceptional discretion to deport to torture after balancing the probability of prejudice to national security and the importance of the security interest at stake with the serious consequences of deportation to the deportee.[135] As long as the minister considered the correct factors in the balancing exercise, courts could not question the weight she accorded to them.[136]

---

131   Toope & Brunnée, "Hesitant," *supra* note 51 at 33.

132   *Suresh, supra* note 6 at para. 46.

133   *Ibid.* at para. 59. To properly review the international perspective, courts should consider "the various sources of international human rights law—declarations, covenants, conventions, judicial and quasi-judicial decisions of international tribunals, [and] customary norms": *ibid.* at para. 46. In deciding whether the *Criminal Code* prohibition on polygamous relationships was constitutionally valid and, in particular, whether it was justified under s. 1 of the Charter, the B.C. Supreme Court considered extensive arguments on conventional and customary international norms relating to polygamy: see *In Reference re: Criminal Code of Canada (B.C.),* 2011 BCSC 1588 at para. 794 et seq., 1279-81 and 1351.

134   *Ibid.* at para. 60.

135   *Ibid.* at paras. 76-78.

136   *Ibid.* at para. 41. The Court could intervene only if the decision was "unreasonable on its face, unsupported by evidence, or vitiated by failure to consider the proper factors or apply the appropriate procedures" (*ibid.*). For more discussion of judicial review of discretionary decisions in the national security context, see Craig Forcese, "Administering Security: The Limits of Administrative Law in the National Security State" in Colleen

Suresh sent a mixed message regarding the potential of international human rights norms to shape the interpretation of Charter rights.[137] The Court did hold that decision-makers must consider the influence of international norms in determining the procedural and substantive content of fundamental justice under s. 7, a more onerous duty than its direction in *Slaight Communications* that Canada's international human rights obligations "should" inform Charter interpretation.[138] On the other hand, its "international norms as evidence" approach to the role of international law in Charter interpretation allowed the Court to sidestep the question whether the prohibition on torture is a peremptory norm of customary international law.[139] Peremptory norms of international customary law are more than "evidence" of fundamental justice; they are automatically incorporated and directly enforceable in Canadian law to the extent that they are not incompatible with a contrary statute or established principle of common law. Applying the presumption of conformity, the Court could have read down the minister's statutory discretion consistently with the international customary prohibition on torture.[140] Alternatively, it could have decided that the prohibition, incorporated into Canada's common law, was a fundamental tenet of Canada's legal system, and hence a substantive principle of fundamental justice under s. 7 of the Charter. The prohibition on torture would have constitutional force; the *Immigration Act* would be inoperative to the extent that it conflicted with the prohibition.[141] Instead, looking at international law merely as "evidence" of the content of fundamental justice, the Court came to a conclusion that seems extraordinary: although "international law rejects deportation to torture, even where national security interests are at stake,"[142] fundamental justice nevertheless permits the minister to exercise an extraordinary discretion to deport refugees to torture.

More recently, the Supreme Court re-emphasized the role of the presumption of conformity with international law in Charter interpretation. In *Hape*, a majority of the Court held that s. 8 of the Charter, which protects individuals from unreasonable search and seizure, could not be enforced in criminal investigations carried out in another state's territory unless that state consented to the Charter's application.[143] The Court found support for this narrow construction of the Charter's application in the jurisdictional principles of customary

---

M. Flood & Lorne Sossin, eds., *Administrative Law in Context* (Toronto: Emond Montgomery, 2008) 289-307, available online at <adminlawincontext.emp.ca>.

[137]   For a full discussion, see Gerald Heckman, "International Human Rights Law Norms and Discretionary Powers: Recent Developments" (2003) Can. J. Admin. L. & Prac. 16 [Heckman, "Recent Developments"].

[138]   *Supra* note 129.

[139]   *Suresh, supra* note 6 at para. 65. There was no lack of evidence, including legal, academic, and judicial authority, to support the recognition of the absolute prohibition on torture as a peremptory norm: see Heckman, "Recent Developments," *supra* note 137 at 52.

[140]   Evan Fox-Decent, "Suresh and Canada's Obligations Regarding Torture" (2001) 12 N.C.L.J. 425 at 446.

[141]   Neither s. 7 nor s. 1 balancing was appropriate in *Suresh* because the *jus cogens* norm prohibiting torture "should have been directly controlling within Canadian law to preclude deportation": Toope & Brunnée, "Hesitant," *supra* note 51 at 49.

[142]   *Suresh, supra* note 6 at para. 75.

[143]   *Hape, supra* note 38 at para. 69.

international law.[144] It declared that "[i]n interpreting the scope of application of the *Charter*, the courts should seek to ensure compliance with Canada's binding obligations under international law where the express words are capable of supporting such a construction."[145] *Hape* illustrates that the application of the presumption of conformity may sometimes justify a less generous interpretation of Charter protection. For this reason, Currie views its application with trepidation and prefers the minimum content presumption developed in *Alberta Reference* and endorsed in *Slaight*.[146] Under the minimum content presumption, international norms, including international human rights norms of a relatively rudimentary or retrograde nature, establish a floor—not a ceiling—for the content of Charter protections.

In *Health Services*,[147] released a day after *Hape*, the Court found support for its conclusion that access to collective bargaining fell within the Charter's guarantee of freedom of association[148] in Canada's international obligations under the ICESCR, ICCPR, and UN International Labor Organization (ILO) Convention No. 87.[149] Significantly, the Court did not articulate the presumption of conformity using the strong language it used in *Hape*. Reiterating the traditionalist view that "the incorporation of international agreements into domestic law is properly the role of the federal Parliament or the provincial legislatures,"[150] it cited *Suresh* for the proposition that "Canada's international obligations can *assist* courts charged with interpreting the *Charter*'s guarantees."[151] Relying on *Alberta Reference*, it concluded that it was "reasonable to infer" that s. 2(d) of the Charter should be interpreted "as recognizing at least the same level of protection"[152] as the international conventions to which Canada is a party that protect union members' right to collective bargaining as part of their freedom of association. In *Ontario (Attorney General) v. Fraser*,[153] a majority of the Court, applying the principles in *Health Services*, found that an Ontario law that extended to agricultural workers the right to form an employees' association to make representations to their employers and have these views considered in good faith complied with s. 2(d) of the Charter, despite its failure to impose a statutory duty to bargain in good faith, recognition of the principles of exclusivity and majoritarianism, and a statutory mechanism to resolve bargaining impasses or disputes relating to the interpretation and administration of collective agreements. Justices Rothstein and Charron, while concurring in the result, would have overturned *Health Services* on the basis that it had improperly "constitutionalized"

---

144   *Ibid.* at para. 56.

145   *Ibid.*

146   Currie, Commitment, *supra* note 129 at 441 and 459.

147   *Supra* note 2.

148   *Ibid.* at para. 79.

149   Convention (No. 87) Concerning Freedom of Association and Protection of the Right to Organize, 68 U.N.T.S. 17, [1973] Can. T.S. No. 14, adopted 9 July 1948, ratified 23 March 1972, entered into force 23 March 1973.

150   *Health Services, supra* note 2 at para. 69.

151   *Ibid.* (emphasis added). See also para. 78: "Canada's *current* international law commitments … provide a *persuasive* source for interpreting the scope of the *Charter*" (emphasis added).

152   *Ibid.* at para. 79.

153   2011 SCC 20 [*Fraser*].

collective bargaining.[154] In particular, they argued that the majority had inappropriately interpreted the scope of Canada's international obligations based on an ILO Convention[155] that Canada had not ratified.[156] Justices Rothstein and Charron also held that ILO Convention No. 98 did not support a model of compulsory collective bargaining which, in their view, *Health Services* had read into s. 2(d) of the Charter. The majority reiterated that "*Charter* rights *must* be interpreted in light of Canadian values and Canada's international and human rights commitments."[157]

Responding to Justice Rothstein's criticism, the majority held that "the fundamental question ... is whether Canada's international obligations support the view that collective bargaining is constitutionally protected in the minimal sense discussed in *Health Services*."[158] It observed that the majority in *Health Services* had relied on three international conventions that Canada had endorsed and, moreover, that the ILO Committee on Freedom of Association, relying on Convention 87, had found a violation of freedom of association in the *Health Services* dispute. This most recent formulation of the role of international law in Charter interpretation suggests that an analysis of Canada's international obligations is an obligatory, not an optional, part of Charter interpretation. However, the majority's insistence, in response to Justice Rothstein's challenge, that its Charter analysis was influenced only by Canada's international obligations, obscures the fact that international human rights obligations set out in treaties not ratified by Canada may still be relevant and persuasive guides to the Charter's interpretation, even though they do not presumptively define the minimum content of Charter guarantees.

In sum, the Supreme Court's jurisprudence on the role of international rights norms in Charter interpretation leaves many significant questions unanswered.[159] First, the Court alternated between mandatory and permissive approaches to the consideration of international human rights norms in Charter interpretation, holding in *Slaight* that Canada's international obligations *should* inform Charter interpretation and in *Fraser* that Charter rights *must* be interpreted in light of Canada's human rights commitments. Second, the Court adopted many different standards describing the influence of international human rights norms on Charter interpretation. These range from the minimalist approach that international human rights norms are "evidence" of or "inform" the content of Charter rights (*Suresh*) to a rule that, in interpreting the Charter's scope and application, courts should seek to ensure compliance with Canada's binding obligations under international law where express words are capable of supporting such a construction (*Hape*) to the view that "similar provisions in international human rights documents which Canada has ratified"[160]

---

154   *Ibid.* at para. 231 et seq.

155   Convention (No. 98) concerning the application of the principles of the right to organize and bargain collectively, 96 U.N.T.S. 257.

156   *Fraser, supra* note 153 at para. 248.

157   *Ibid.* at para. 92 (emphasis in original).

158   *Ibid.* at para. 93.

159   See Currie, commitment, *supra* note 129 at 451 et seq.

160   *Alberta Reference, supra* note 125 at para. 59.

presumptively define the minimum content of Charter guarantees (*Alberta Reference*). Third, the Court has not clearly expressed the difference between the roles played in Charter interpretation by non-binding and binding international human rights norms—though its decision in *Fraser* clearly recognizes that such a difference exists. Finally, the Court has frequently not distinguished between the role played in Charter interpretation of international norms related to human rights and that played by norms unrelated to human rights.[161] Currie has remarked that the Court's approach to the role of international human rights norms in Charter interpretation is in a "continual state of upheaval," appears "confused" or "arbitrary," silences informed discussion of the principles governing this area "as there are no such clearly governing principles,"[162] and may dissuade litigants and their counsel from appealing to international human rights norms and trial courts from relying on them.[163] Currie suggests that the Court should always presume that Canada's international human rights obligations define the minimum content of the Charter's guarantees and that it should afford non-binding international rights norms relevant and persuasive interpretive status. His suggestion would both foster coherence in Canadian courts' approach to international human-rights norms and tend to maximize the domestic protection of human rights.[164]

---

[161]   See *Hape*, *supra* note 38 at para. 55: "the Court ... has sought to ensure consistency between its interpretation of the *Charter* ... and Canada's international obligations and the relevant principles of international law." However, Currie observes that the Court's recognition in *Hape*, at para. 101, reiterated in *Canada (Justice) v. Khadr*, 2008 SCC 28, [2008] 2 S.C.R. 125 at para. 2, that "the principles of international law and comity of nations, which normally require that Canadian officials operating abroad comply with local law, do not extend to participation in processes that violate Canada's international human rights obligations" might reflect the Court's view that norms of a human rights character rank higher than other international law norms on a spectrum measuring their normative influence on Charter interpretation: Currie, Commitment, *supra* note 129 at 448-49. Such an approach would be consistent with Scott's reading of *Baker* (*supra* note 69)—that the normative force of an international commitment varies with its subject matter.

[162]   Currie, Commitment, *supra* note 129 at 453-54.

[163]   *Ibid.* at 457. This may be illustrated in *Adams*, *supra* note 81, where the B.C. Supreme Court determined that a municipal bylaw prohibiting the erection of temporary shelter on public property infringed the s. 7 Charter rights of homeless persons evicted from a tent city set up in a Victoria city park. The trial judge accepted, over the objections of British Columbia's attorney general, that international instruments relating to the right to adequate housing and to an adequate standard of living should "inform" the court's interpretation of the scope and content of s. 7. However, she made no distinction between the degree of influence attributable to international instruments binding on Canada (e.g., the ICESCR) and those that are not (e.g. the Istanbul Declaration on Human Settlements and Habitat Agenda adopted by the UN Conference on Human Settlements (Habitat II) in Istanbul (Turkey) in 1996 (UN Doc. A/CONF. 165/14) later endorsed by the UN General Assembly (U.N. Doc. A/RES/51/177 (11 Feb. 1997)). Moreover, the trial judge made no further mention of these norms in her legal analysis finding a breach of s. 7.

[164]   Currie, Commitment, *supra* note 129 at 460-65. But see Graham Hudson, who argues, on the basis of a review of South African jurisprudence, that the presence of clear and robust rules in South Africa's Constitution governing the applicability of international law has not resulted in courts' more principled use of international norms. Hudson concludes that "formal rules, procedures and principles cannot alone engender living respect for international legal authority and ... there are good grounds for believing that formally non-legal factors such as political economy, ideology and judicial personality obstruct the full realization of international law": Graham Hudson, "Neither Here Nor There: The (Non-)Impact of International Law on Judicial Reasoning in Canada and South Africa" (2008) 21 Can J. L. & Juris. 321 at 352.

E. Discretion and Rights of Access to International Human Rights Bodies

Should administrative decision-makers, in exercising discretionary powers, take into account proceedings pending before an international human rights body that may bear on the validity of their decision at international law?[165] This question was raised before the Ontario Court of Appeal in *Ahani*.[166] The Canadian government considered that Ahani, like Suresh, was a danger to the public and wished to deport him. Unlike Suresh, Ahani had not made out a *prima facie* case that there may be a substantial risk of torture upon his removal to Iran. Having exhausted all domestic remedies in resisting deportation, Ahani petitioned the UN Human Rights Committee, claiming that his removal by Canada violated several provisions of the ICCPR, including his right not to be returned to a state where he could be tortured, his right to a fair hearing, and his right to a review of the legality of his detention without delay. The committee made an official request to the government of Canada to stay the deportation until it could consider Ahani's petition. Ahani contended that by adhering to the ICCPR and Optional Protocol, Canada had granted individuals like him the limited right to obtain the committee's views on whether their ICCPR rights had been breached. Ahani further argued that it was a principle of fundamental justice that Canada also provide him with a fair process and effective means to ensure that he could exercise this limited right. In particular, Ahani claimed the right to an injunction prohibiting his removal to Iran until the committee considered his communication and expressed its views thereon. He argued that while not binding on Canada, the committee's views had moral suasion, and the petition process should be allowed to run its course.

A majority of the Ontario Court of Appeal rejected Ahani's argument because, in its view, the ICCPR and the petition procedure under the Protocol were not legislatively incorporated into Canadian law. Neither had any legal effect beyond "informing" the content of the principles of fundamental justice under s. 7.[167] Ahani could thus not "enforce" Canada's international obligations in a domestic court. Further, these obligations were limited; Canada had not committed to be bound by the final views of the committee or to stay its domestic proceedings until the committee delivered its views. Acceding to Ahani's request for a stay would "convert a non-binding request in a Protocol, which has never been part of Canadian law, into a binding obligation enforceable in Canada by a Canadian court, and more, into a constitutional principle of fundamental justice."[168] By signing the Protocol, Canada had provided Ahani and others a right to seek the committee's views qualified by Canada's right to reject these views and to enforce its own laws before they were delivered.[169]

---

[165] For an extensive discussion of the role of discretion in administrative law, see Geneviève Cartier, Chapter 11, Administrative Discretion: Between Exercising Power and Conducting Dialogue.

[166] *Supra* note 50. For a complete discussion of this question, see Heckman, "Recent Developments," supra note 137.

[167] Arguably, the ICCPR and the Protocol were implemented in Canadian law: de Mestral & Fox-Decent "Implementation and Reception," *supra* note 37 at 54-55.

[168] *Ahani* (C.A.), *supra* note 50 at para. 33.

[169] *Ibid.* at para. 42.

Dissenting, Rosenberg J. would have recognized Ahani's right to seek an injunction preventing his removal until the committee had presented its views on his communication. Rosenberg J. held that if Parliament created a statutory right to review a decision that could affect an individual's security of the person, it was a principle of fundamental justice that the state could not unreasonably frustrate that right or render it practically illusory, a principle he was prepared to extend to the petition process under the Protocol.[170] In his view, the principle that international conventions could not bind Canada unless they were incorporated into Canadian law was intended to protect Parliament and the people of Canada from executive law making; the executive could not rely on that principle to shield it from the consequences of its voluntary ratification of the ICCPR and the Protocol,[171] including Canada's conferral on the committee of jurisdiction to receive and consider communications from individuals claiming to be victims of violations by Canada of their rights under the ICCPR:

> [Ahani] does not claim that the views of the Committee about our process for removing him would create legal rights that could be enforced in a domestic court. He claims only the limited procedural right to reasonable access to the Committee upon which the federal government has conferred jurisdiction. He submits that the government having held out this right of review, however limited and non-binding, should not be entitled to render it practically illusory by returning him to Iran before he has a reasonable opportunity to access it. I agree with that submission and that it is a principle of fundamental justice that individuals in Canada have fair access to the process in the Protocol. By deporting ... [Ahani] to Iran, the government will deprive [him] of this opportunity.[172]

Canada is clearly not bound to comply with the committee's views,[173] but on a fair reading, the Protocol contemplates that individuals be afforded an opportunity to submit communications to the committee and, if these are deemed admissible, to have the committee review the communications and deliver its views to the petitioners and to Canada for consideration. This interpretation is consistent with the principle of effectiveness in international law that human rights instruments like the ICCPR and the Protocol should be interpreted to

---

[170] *Ibid.* at paras. 86-89.

[171] *Ibid.* at para. 92.

[172] *Ibid.* at para. 93. Ahani was owed only a right of "reasonable" access to the committee, because fundamental justice, according to the *Suresh* decision, required that the protection of society be balanced against the individual's interest to security of the person. Such balancing could be performed by a court as part of the test for granting an interlocutory injunction: *ibid.* at para. 107.

[173] See *Dadar v. Canada (Minister of Citizenship and Immigration)*, 2006 FC 382. Canadian authorities had determined that Dadar, a permanent resident and refugee, was a danger to the public in view of his criminal convictions and issued an order for his removal. Dadar petitioned the United Nations Committee Against Torture, which concluded that there were "substantial grounds ... for believing that [Dadar] may risk being subjected to torture if returned to Iran" (*Dadar* at para. 10). Nevertheless, the Federal Court refused Dadar's application for a stay of deportation. After carefully examining the committee's decision, the Court held, at para. 27, that it contained no evidence that suggested that a ministerial delegate's conclusion that the Iranian regime posed no risk to Dadar (a decision upheld on judicial review) was "anything other than accurate." Noting that the committee's decision was not binding on Canada, the Court held, at para. 23, that: "it is not for the judiciary to second guess Canada's decision not to adopt the UNCAT decision. Rather, it is a matter for a 'court of public or international opinion, not for a court of law.' "

make their safeguards "practical and effective."[174] A corollary to this principle is that states may not, and should not, be presumed to intend to take steps that would render the rights recognized in a treaty that they have ratified nugatory or ineffective. If a petitioner establishes that his or her deportation would prevent him or her from submitting a communication or prevent the committee from considering it and delivering its views to the petitioner and Canada, deportation would not be consistent with the purpose of the Protocol. Without "reasonable" or "fair" access to the process in the Protocol, it would be nothing more than a "hollow sham … or cruel charade."[175] In its views on Ahani's communication, the committee determined that Canada had breached its obligations under the Protocol by deporting Ahani in the face of its request that he not be removed until it had dealt with his petition. It held that "flouting" the committee's authority to request interim measures, especially by irreversible measures such as deportation to face torture or death in another country, "undermined" the protection of Covenant rights through the Optional Protocol.[176]

The *Immigration Act* conferred on the minister a broad discretion to deport individuals determined to be a danger to the security of Canada, but was silent as to the timing of the deportation. Under the *Baker* approach, which recognized that discretionary powers are constrained by the values and principles contained in international law, the adverse impacts of deportation on the effectiveness of Ahani's limited right to communicate with the committee should have been a mandatory relevant consideration in the exercise of the minister's discretion. Failure to consider this factor should have rendered her decision to deport Ahani without delay unreasonable. Moreover, the minister was bound to exercise her discretion to deport Ahani consistently with the principles of fundamental justice under s. 7 of the Charter, whose content, according to *Suresh*, is informed by Canada's international obligations. Rosenberg J.'s recognition that fundamental justice does not countenance executive acts that frustrate even a limited right to review the legality of a decision that affects an individual's security of the person is entirely consistent with the principle of effectiveness in international human rights law. Here, fundamental justice arguably required that the merits of Ahani's communication (whether it raised a serious question) and the magnitude of the harm to Ahani caused by his deportation (whether the harm was irreparable) be balanced against the government's interest in deporting him before the committee released its views on the merits of his communication.

International human rights norms clearly have a role to play in the substantive review of administrative decision making. Administrative decisions based on the interpretation of statutory powers or discretions intended to implement an international human rights treaty obligation may be reviewed on the basis that the decision-maker incorrectly or unreasonably interpreted the statute by giving it a meaning inconsistent with the international treaty

---

174 M.N. Shaw, *International Law*, 4th ed. (Cambridge: Cambridge University Press, 1997) 660.

175 *Ahani, supra* note 50 at para. 98, citing *Briggs v. Baptiste*, [2000] 2 A.C. 40 at para. 47 (P.C.). See also *Barbados (A.G.) v. Boyce* (2006), CCJ (8 November 2006), where the court gave effect to convicted murderers' legitimate expectation that Barbados would not execute them before considering the views of a treaty body regarding their complaint that mandatory capital punishment infringed their rights under an international treaty.

176 *Ahani v. Canada*, Communication No. 1051/2002, UN Doc. CCPR/C/80/D/1051/2002 (2004) at paras. 8.1-8.2. For a full discussion of the committee's views, see Gerald Heckman, "International Law and Procedural Safeguards in Deportation Proceedings: Ahani v. Canada" (2004) 17 R.Q.D.I. 81.

norm. Canadian courts would be justified to intervene on judicial review where an administrative decision-maker fails to apply the presumption of conformity and interpret statutory powers in a manner consistent with international human rights obligations set out in a binding but unimplemented treaty. Instead, Canadian courts have followed the *Baker* approach: international human rights norms from ratified but unimplemented treaties, though binding on Canada at international law, *may* be considered as persuasive and contextual factors in interpreting and applying statutory provisions. Accordingly, administrative decisions, including discretionary decisions, may be challenged on the ground that they are inconsistent with the values behind such international human rights norms. Whether such a challenge will succeed may depend on how deeply these international norms resonate with fundamental values of the Canadian legal system. Courts have also applied the *Baker* approach to norms of customary international law,[177] even though they are, as confirmed in *Hape*, directly applicable in Canadian law. Discretionary decisions may be challenged if they are inconsistent with Charter rights. Canada's international human rights obligations are relevant to such challenges because they, arguably, presumptively define the minimum content of Charter protections or, at the very least, serve as evidence of their meaning. Finally, although it may be possible to challenge a decision-maker's exercise of discretionary power on the basis that he or she failed to consider the impact of the decision on an affected individual's access to an international human rights remedy, such challenges have so far not succeeded.[178]

The following section shows that many international human rights norms guarantee basic procedural safeguards in the context of state decision making affecting fundamental interests, including the rights to life, liberty, and security of the person. As explained in the following section, they may also serve to challenge administrative decision making—but on procedural rather than substantive grounds.

V. The Role of International Human Rights Norms in the Procedural Review of Administrative Decisions

The procedural fairness norms set out in international human rights treaties resonate deeply with Canadian legal values. As Grant Huscroft discusses in Chapter 5, From Natural Justice to Fairness: Thresholds, Content, and the Role of Judicial Review, procedural fairness is a basic tenet of Canada's legal system and a principle of fundamental justice under s. 7 of the Charter. Consistent with the previous discussion in the context of substantive review, international norms could also be called upon to influence the development of procedural safe-

---

177   See *Spraytech*, *supra* note 115.

178   For a recent example, see *Mugesera c. Kenney*, 2012 QCCS 116 (CanLII). Mugesera, a Rwandan national, was found to be inadmissible to Canada because he had, on the balance of probabilities, given a speech that constituted an incitement to murder, genocide, or hatred and which (there were reasonable grounds to believe) constituted a crime against humanity. He filed a petition with the United Nation's Committee Against Torture claiming that he would be tortured upon his return to Rwanda. The committee issued a request for interim measures asking Canada to stay removal until it could consider Mugesera's petition. Relying on the reasoning set out by the Ontario Court of Appeal in *Ahani*, the Quebec Superior Court denied Mugesera's application for a stay of his removal.

guards in Canada. In *Baker*, the applicant had invited the Federal Court of Appeal and the Supreme Court to find that she had a legitimate expectation, based on the terms of the CRC, that her children would be afforded a hearing by the immigration officer considering her humanitarian and compassionate application. In particular, article 12 of the CRC provides that children have the right "to be heard in any judicial or administrative proceedings affecting the child, either directly or through a representative or an appropriate body." This provision appeared to entitle Baker's children to participate directly in the humanitarian and compassionate application process. In fact, the interests of Baker's children had only been considered through the written submissions of Baker's own counsel. The Supreme Court decided that the CRC's terms did not give rise to a legitimate expectation on Baker's part that specific procedural rights above what would normally be required under the duty of fairness would be accorded.[179] The CRC was not "the equivalent of a government representation about how [humanitarian and compassionate] applications will be decided, nor does it suggest that any rights beyond the participatory rights [afforded by common-law procedural fairness] will be accorded."[180] The Federal Court of Appeal more clearly explained its concerns at the prospect of giving effect to the right of Baker's children to direct representation in the humanitarian and compassionate application. It warned that giving judicial force to the procedural provisions of the CRC, a treaty ratified by the federal executive but not formally implemented by the legislative branches, would have a significant impact on decision making by provincial authorities involving children, notably the administration of family law and the provision of legal aid for family law and child custody proceedings— matters of provincial jurisdiction.[181]

Curiously, in rejecting Baker's legitimate expectations argument, the Supreme Court made no mention of the High Court of Australia's judgment in *Minister for Immigration and Ethnic Affairs v. Teoh*,[182] which was raised by the applicant and discussed at length by the Federal Court of Appeal. In *Teoh*, the High Court had recognized that ratified but unimplemented international treaties could influence administrative decision making through the doctrine of legitimate expectations. The minister's delegate had decided that there were insufficient compassionate grounds to allow Teoh's application for a permanent entry permit, despite the fact that his deportation jeopardized the livelihood of his Australian children. A majority of the High Court decided that Australia's ratification of the CRC gave rise to a legitimate expectation that the minister's delegate would, in conformity with the CRC, treat the best interests of Teoh's children as a primary consideration in his decision. His failure to do this, or to allow Teoh to argue against a decision inconsistent with his legitimate expectation, breached procedural fairness. The majority held that Australia's ratification of the CRC was

> not to be dismissed as a merely platitudinous or ineffectual act, particularly when the [CRC] evidences internationally accepted standards to be applied by courts and administrative authorities

---

179 The doctrine of legitimate expectations is discussed further by Grant Huscroft in Chapter 5.

180 *Baker, supra* note 1 at para. 29.

181 *Baker* (FCA), *supra* note 43 at para. 30.

182 (1995), 183 C.L.R. 273 [*Teoh*].

in dealing with basic human rights affecting the family and children. Rather, [it] is a positive statement by the executive government of this country to the world and to the Australian people that the executive government and its agencies will act in accordance with the Convention. That positive statement is an adequate foundation for a legitimate expectation, absent statutory or executive indications to the contrary, that administrative decision-makers will act in conformity with the Convention and treat the best interests of the children as "a primary consideration."[183]

Dissenting, McHugh J. complained that the majority's ruling effectively allowed the executive to amend Australian law by ratifying an international convention without involving the political branches of government, a view accepted by the Federal Court of Appeal in *Baker*.[184] For this reason, successive Australian governments rejected *Teoh*'s holding,[185] and publicly declared that the act of entering into a treaty did not give rise to legitimate expectations that could form the basis for challenging administrative decisions.[186] Several High Court judges have since hinted that *Teoh* should be revisited.[187]

Although the Supreme Court dismissed Baker's legitimate expectations argument, it left open the possibility that an international instrument ratified by Canada could, in other circumstances, give rise to a legitimate expectation.[188] In *Suresh*, the Court took into account the legitimate expectation raised by the terms of the Convention Against Torture in determining that Suresh was owed more procedures under the principles of fundamental justice in s. 7. To determine the procedural requirements of fundamental justice, it applied the common-law approach to determining the content of the duty of procedural fairness.[189] Several factors weighed in favour of substantial procedural safeguards, including the absence of any appeal procedure, the determinative nature of the minister's decision, and the serious personal, financial, and emotional consequences for Suresh of deportation from Canada. The Court also considered whether Suresh had a legitimate expectation of additional procedure. It noted that the CAT prohibits the deportation of persons to states where there are "substantial grounds" for believing they would be "in danger of being subjected to

---

183 *Ibid.* at 291.

184 *Ibid.* at 316. See *Baker* (FCA), *supra* note 43 at para. 39.

185 H. Charlesworth et al., "Deep Anxieties: Australia and the International Legal Order" (2003) 25 Sydney L. Rev. 423 at 437 ["Anxieties"].

186 Attempts to enact legislation to counteract *Teoh* have been unsuccessful: "Anxieties," *ibid.* at 449. However, controversy over the decision led to important reforms to enhance parliamentary participation in the treaty-making process: Harrington, *supra* note 45 at 491-97.

187 *Re Minister for Immigration and Multicultural Affairs; ex parte Lam*, [2003] H.C.A. 6 at para. 102, per McHugh and Gummow JJ., and para. 145 per Callinan J. Academics have also criticized *Teoh* as a disingenuous application of the legitimate expectations doctrine: Michael Taggart, "Legitimate Expectation and Treaties in the High Court of Australia" (1996) 112 L.Q.R. 50; Murray Hunt, *Using Human Rights Law in English Courts* (Oxford: Hart Publishing, 1997) at 251-59.

188 *Baker, supra* note 1 at para. 29.

189 *Suresh, supra* note 6 at paras. 113-15. For a description of the common-law approach, see Grant Huscroft, Chapter 5, and for a detailed discussion of the interface between s. 7 and administrative law, see Evan Fox-Decent and Alexander Pless, Chapter 12.

torture." In the Court's view, it was "only reasonable that the same executive that bound itself to the CAT intends to act in accordance with the CAT's plain meaning."[190] Given "Canada's commitment to the CAT," and the requirement of "substantial grounds" to trigger the obligation of non-refoulement, the Court found that Suresh was entitled to an opportunity to demonstrate and defend those "grounds."[191] Suresh was not owed a full hearing or complete judicial process, but was entitled to examine the material upon which the minister based her decision to deport (subject to claims of privilege); respond to the minister's case and challenge her information regarding the threat he posed to national security, the risk of torture, and the value of assurances from foreign governments that he would not be tortured; and obtain written reasons from the minister justifying her final decision.[192]

Although *Suresh* indicates that it is possible to seek procedural review of administrative decisions on the grounds that the procedures provided by the decision-maker did not live up to the legitimate expectations of the applicant based on the terms of a ratified international treaty, it is unclear when such an argument will be successful given its dramatically different treatment by the Court in *Baker* and *Suresh*. More guidance is needed from the courts as to when state obligations in ratified conventions can or cannot raise legitimate expectations.

VI. Conclusion

There is no doubt that international human rights norms from binding international treaties, customary international law, or non-binding international instruments can play an important role in the substantive and procedural review of administrative decisions. It is also obvious that much work remains to be done to precisely delineate what that role is and, one hopes, to strengthen it. Much of the theoretical groundwork has already been laid in the burgeoning academic commentary on this subject. It is now incumbent on public lawyers to familiarize themselves with the international human rights norms that are relevant to their area of practice and raise them in individual cases. Administrative decision-makers, reviewing courts, and, ultimately, the Supreme Court of Canada must seize the opportunities so created to bring clarity and certainty to the relationship between international law and Canadian administrative and constitutional law: no less than the effective domestic enforcement of significant international human rights depends on it.

---

[190]   *Ibid.* at para. 119.

[191]   *Ibid.*

[192]   *Ibid.* at paras. 121-27.

SUGGESTED ADDITIONAL READINGS

BOOKS AND ARTICLES

Brunnée, Jutta, & Stephen Toope, "A Hesitant Embrace: Baker and the Application of International Law by Canadian Courts" in David Dyzenhaus, ed., *The Unity of Public Law* (Oxford: Hart Publishing, 2004).

Currie, John H., "International Human Rights Law in the Supreme Court's Charter Jurisprudence: Commitment, Retrenchment and Retreat—In No Particular Order" (2010), 50 S.C.L.R. (2d) 423.

de Mestral, Armand & Evan Fox-Decent, "Rethinking the Relationship Between International and Domestic Law" (2008) 53 McGill L.J. 573.

Fitzgerald, Oonagh E., ed., *The Globalized Rule of Law* (Toronto: Irwin Law, 2006).

Freeman, Mark, & Gibran van Ert, *International Human Rights Law* (Toronto: Irwin Law, 2004).

Heckman, Gerald, "International Human Rights Law Norms and Discretionary Powers: Recent Developments" (2003) 16 Can. J. Admin. L. & Prac. 31.

Schabas, William A., & Stéphane Beaulac, *International Human Rights and Canadian Law—Legal Commitment, Implementation and the Charter*, 3d ed. (Thomson Carswell, Toronto: 2007).

van Ert, Gibran, *Using International Law in Canadian Courts*, 2d ed. (Toronto: Irwin Law, 2008).

CASES

Ahani v. Canada (Minister of Citizenship and Immigration) (2002), 58 O.R. (3d) 107 (C.A.).

Baker v. Canada (Minister of Citizenship and Immigration), [1999] 2 S.C.R. 817.

De Guzman v. Canada (Minister of Citizenship and Immigration), 2005 FCA 436.

Health Services and Support—Facilities Subsector Bargaining Assn. v. British Columbia, 2007 SCC 27, [2007] 2 S.C.R. 391.

Minister for Immigration and Ethnic Affairs v. Teoh (1995), 183 C.L.R. 273.

R. v. Hape, 2007 SCC 26, [2007] 2 S.C.R. 292.

Suresh v. Canada (Minister of Citizenship and Immigration), 2002 SCC 1, [2002] 1 S.C.R. 3.

CHAPTER FIFTEEN

Making a Federal Case Out of It: The Federal Court and Administrative Law

CRAIG FORCESE

Faculty of Law, University of Ottawa

I. Introduction

Earlier chapters in this book have focused on the broad sweep of administrative law. This chapter shifts focus and concentrates instead on one particular venue of administrative law practice: the Federal Courts of Canada. It is, of course, true that the Federal Courts of Canada are not the only superior courts in which administrative law issues arise. The provincial superior courts and the Supreme Court of Canada are generalist courts and have jurisdiction to deal with administrative law matters.

The Federal Courts, however, are distinguished by two qualities. First, they exercise a virtual monopoly on the administrative judicial review function in relation to the federal executive. Second, because of the narrowness of their jurisdiction, that monopoly makes Federal Courts mostly administrative law courts. Federal Court judges are, in other words, the closest things to administrative law specialists in the Canadian judicial system. For both these reasons, Federal Courts deserve special attention in a volume on administrative law.

The chapter begins with a review of the structure and jurisdiction of the Federal Courts. It then canvasses a series of fundamental issues related to federal judicial review, including basic judicial-review procedure and issues surrounding the grounds of review and remedies at the federal level.

II. Structure and Jurisdiction of the Federal Courts

A. Federal Courts as Statutory Courts

The Federal Courts are "statutory courts"—that is, they are created by federal statute and have only the jurisdiction conferred on them by that statute. Constitutionally, the authority to create the Federal Courts lies in Parliament by virtue of s. 101 of the *Constitution Act, 1867*.[1] In addition to authorizing a national supreme appeal court, that provision empowers Parliament to "provide for the Constitution, Maintenance, and Organization ... any additional Courts for the better Administration of the Laws of Canada."[2]

As s. 101 "statutory courts," the Federal Courts differ from the provincial superior courts. The latter—also known as "s. 96" courts, in reference to s. 96 of the *Constitution Act, 1867*—are courts of inherent jurisdiction. "Jurisdiction" "is shorthand for the collection of attributes that enables a court or tribunal to issue an enforceable order or judgment."[3] "Inherent," in this context, means automatic or default jurisdiction. Although provincial statutes may prescribe their structural attributes, the ultimate origin of s. 96 courts lies in the *Constitution Act, 1867* and their jurisdiction is inherited from courts in the United Kingdom. In an ancient maxim recently cited with approval by the Supreme Court of Canada, "nothing shall

---

1   30 & 31 Vict., c. 3. (U.K.).

2   *Ibid.*, s. 101. Other s. 101 courts include the Tax Court of Canada and the Court Martial Appeal Court of Canada. The first court deals with tax matters and is, essentially, a special, tax-specific, administrative court. The second hears appeals from court martials applying the Code of Service Discipline to members of the Canadian Forces. As such, it is principally a criminal law court, albeit one that applies rules more extensive than those applicable to civilians. This chapter does not deal with either of these specific bodies.

3   *Canada (Attorney General) v. TeleZone Inc.*, 2010 SCC 62, [2010] 3 S.C.R. 585 at para. 44 [*TeleZone*].

be intended to be out of the jurisdiction of a Superior Court, but that which specially appears to be so; and, on the contrary, nothing shall be intended to be within the jurisdiction of an Inferior Court [in this context, courts other than the Royal Courts and their successors] but that which is so expressly alleged."[4]

Thus, while the Federal Courts have only those powers given to them by their constituting (or other) federal statute, the provincial superior courts have all judicial powers not expressly removed from them. Moreover, it is no small thing to strip judicial powers from provincial superior courts. Parliament does have the power to give exclusive federal administrative judicial review jurisdiction to the Federal Courts.[5] However, in the Supreme Court's words, the "ouster of jurisdiction from the provincial superior courts in favour of vesting exclusive jurisdiction in a statutory court … requires clear and explicit statutory wording to this effect."[6]

In the result, the actual jurisdiction of the Federal Courts is anemic relative to that of the provincial superior courts, and the Federal Courts must have particular regard to statutory authorization in the exercise of their judicial powers. As the Federal Court has itself warned repeatedly: "The Federal Court is a statutory court whose jurisdiction cannot be presumed, unlike provincial superior courts, whose jurisdiction is both general and inherent. There must be a statutory basis for the Federal Court to have jurisdiction in a given case."[7] As discussed below, the key statutory basis for Federal Court jurisdiction is the *Federal Courts Act*.[8]

B. Administrative Law Jurisdiction of the Federal Courts

1. The Federal Court of Canada and the Federal Court of Appeal

The *Federal Courts Act*[9] constitutes the Federal Courts. Specifically, it creates both a Federal Court of Canada (FCC), once known as the Federal Court—Trial Division, and a Federal Court of Appeal (FCA). The FCC is principally a court of first instance—that is, it is the first court that hears a particular dispute. The FCA is an appellate court, hearing appeals from the FCC and other federal judicial bodies, such as the Tax Court of Canada.

In some areas of Federal Courts jurisdiction, this pattern of trial court and court of appeal operates much as it would in any superior court. Thus, the FCC has concurrent jurisdiction with the provincial superior courts to hear civil claims brought against the federal government. This means that plaintiffs may choose to bring their action before either the

---

[4] *Peacock v. Bell* (1667), 1 Wms. Saund. 73, 85 E.R. 84 at 87-88, cited with approval in *TeleZone, supra* note 3 at para. 43.

[5] *TeleZone, supra* note 3 at para. 45, citing *Canada Labour Relations Board v. Paul L'Anglais Inc.*, [1983] 1 S.C.R. 147 at 154.

[6] *Ordon Estate v. Grail*, [1998] 3 S.C.R. 437 at para. 46, cited with approval in *TeleZone, supra* note 3 at para. 42.

[7] *Pontbriand v. Federal Public Service Health Care Plan Administration Authority*, 2011 FC 1029, [2011] 4 F.C.R. D-11 at para. 2. See also *DRL Vacations Ltd. v. Halifax Port Authority*, 2005 FC 860, [2006] 3 F.C.R. 516 at para 6.

[8] R.S.C. 1985, c. F-7.

[9] *Ibid.*

FCC or a s. 96 court. If they opt for the FCC as the court with original jurisdiction, any appeal from the trial of that action is to the FCA and, from there, with leave, to the Supreme Court of Canada.

This simple description does not, however, adequately capture the jurisdictional division of labour between the FCC and the FCA. In the administrative law area, it is not always the case that the FCC is inevitably the court of first instance. Most notably, there are a number of administrative tribunals enumerated in s. 28 of the *Federal Courts Act* for whom the FCA is the court of first instance on judicial review. These special tribunals include, among others, the Canadian International Trade Tribunal, the Public Service Labour Relations Board, the Copyright Board, and the Competition Tribunal.

Any applicant must be attentive to s. 28, or risk filing their application for judicial review in the wrong court. That said, the vast majority of applications for judicial review are not against decisions by administrative bodies listed in s. 28, and thus the FCC has the original jurisdiction. The balance of this chapter focuses on this more commonplace route.

2. The Federal Court's Exclusive Jurisdiction

Section 18 of the *Federal Courts Act* specifies that, subject to the above-discussed s. 28, the FCC has "exclusive original jurisdiction":

> (a) to issue an injunction, writ of *certiorari*, writ of prohibition, writ of *mandamus* or writ of *quo warranto*, or grant declaratory relief, against any federal board, commission or other tribunal; and
>
> (b) to hear and determine any application or other proceeding for relief in the nature of relief contemplated by paragraph (a), including any proceeding brought against the Attorney General of Canada, to obtain relief against a federal board, commission or other tribunal.

Section 18 is the source of the FCC's vast role in Canadian administrative law. It purports to give the FCC "exclusive" powers to issue classic administrative law remedies (and hear any application in relation to these) for any "federal board, commission or other tribunal." "Exclusive" means, in essence, a monopoly, subject to considerations discussed below.

For its part, "federal board, commission or other tribunal" is expansively defined in s. 2 of the Act as:

> any body, person or persons having, exercising or purporting to exercise jurisdiction or powers conferred by or under an Act of Parliament or by or under an order made pursuant to a prerogative of the Crown, other than the Tax Court of Canada or any of its judges, any such body constituted or established by or under a law of a province or any such person or persons appointed under or in accordance with a law of a province or under s. 96 of the *Constitution Act, 1867*.

Note the sweep of this paragraph. Somewhat counterintuitively, "board, commission or other tribunal" need only be a single "person." So long as that person is deploying powers conferred by a federal statute *or* under the royal prerogative, administrative judicial review jurisdiction lies with the FCC.

Because, as a practical matter, all the powers that matter in federal administrative action are conferred by statute or under royal prerogative, the FCC has administrative judicial review authority over all federal administrative action. As the Supreme Court noted recently, "[t]he federal decision makers that are included [by s. 2] run the gamut from the Prime Minister and major boards and agencies to the local border guard and customs official and everybody in between."[10]

The question has occasionally arisen as to how exclusive the FCC exclusive jurisdiction really is. As already noted, s. 96 courts guard their jurisdictional prerogatives closely. It is clear that Parliament can assign federal courts powers to conduct administrative judicial review authority. It is also clear that Parliament cannot assign federal courts exclusive federal *constitutional* judicial review authority: as the Supreme Court noted recently, Parliament "cannot operate to prevent provincial superior court scrutiny of the constitutionality of the conduct of federal officials."[11] At best, constitutional review jurisdiction is concurrent, shared by both provincial superior and federal courts. Accordingly, an attack on administrative action that is, in turn, grounded in an attack on an allegedly unconstitutional statute can be brought in either s. 96 or federal courts.

Further, the Federal Courts' s. 18 jurisdiction does not include issuance of the remedy of *habeas corpus*, except in narrow circumstances.[12] For this reason, the provincial superior courts retain *habeas corpus* jurisdiction in relation to federal administrative action in circumstances where that remedy's own requirements are met.[13]

III. Judicial Review Before the Federal Courts

In addition to defining the Federal Courts' jurisdiction, the *Federal Courts Act* creates a relatively comprehensive guide to the manner of, and basis for, judicial review of federal administrative action. This includes special rules relating to certain types of statutory appeals, standing, limitation periods, grounds of review, and remedies.

A. Statutory Appeals

As discussed earlier by Cristie Ford in Chapter 3, Dogs and Tails: Remedies in Administrative Law, applicants must exhaust all other remedies—such as statutory appeals—before applying for judicial review. Failure to exhaust this administrative appeal option may be a basis for the denial of a remedy on judicial review, a concept as true at the federal level as it is at the provincial.[14]

---

10 *TeleZone, supra* note 3 at para. 3. Section 2 does exempt other judges from FCC supervision and those provincial agencies constituted by a provincial law who might have occasion to apply federal law. But these are limited exceptions.

11 *Canada (Attorney General) v. McArthur*, 2010 SCC 63, [2010] 3 S.C.R. 626 at para. 14.

12 Section 18 also gives the FCC "exclusive original jurisdiction to hear and determine every application for a writ of *habeas corpus ad subjiciendum*, writ of *certiorari*, writ of prohibition or writ of *mandamus* in relation to any member of the Canadian Forces serving outside Canada." This power is obviously less sweeping than that found in other parts of s. 18, being limited to members of the Canadian Forces overseas.

13 *May v. Ferndale Institution*, 2005 SCC 82, [2005] 3 S.C.R. 809 at para. 32.

14 See e.g. *Fast v. Canada (Minister of Citizenship and Immigration)*, 2001 FCA 368.

1. Section 18.5

The *Federal Courts Act* adds a more robust bar to judicial review in the face of at least some forms of statutory appeal:

> if an Act of Parliament expressly provides for an appeal to the Federal Court, the FCA, the Supreme Court of Canada, the Court Martial Appeal Court, the Tax Court of Canada, the Governor in Council or the Treasury Board from a decision or an order of a federal board, commission or other tribunal made by or in the course of proceedings before that board, commission or tribunal, that decision or order is not, to the extent that it may be so appealed, subject to review or to be restrained, prohibited, removed, set aside or otherwise dealt with, except in accordance with that Act.[15]

Put simply, where a statutory appeal from an administrative decision-maker lies in one of the bodies listed in the section, there can be no judicial review of the same subject matter covered by that appeal.

A point to be carefully underscored: s. 18.5 is a rigid bar on judicial review. Where it applies, there is no further analysis required. As the Federal Court has noted, "Parliament's clear intention ousts judicial review by the Federal Court under s. 18.1 of the *Federal Courts Act* and this intention also removes the necessity for this Court to test whether the prescribed review route provides for an adequate alternative remedy."[16]

This is a sensible and unsurprising limitation for those statutory appeals that go from an administrative body to a court itself. It would make little sense, for example, for judicial review to be available before the Federal Court when the same issue may be statutorily appealed to the FCA. Section 18.5 also reaches more than courts, however, and includes circumstances where an appeal lies to the governor in council (GIC) or the Treasury Board. The result may create some confusing patterns.

2. The Sometimes Tricky Operation of Section 18.5

There are circumstances where statutory appeals may be available to *both* the FCA *and* the GIC. The *Telecommunications Act* authorizes the GIC to "vary or rescind" a decision of the Canadian Radio and Telecommunications Commission (CRTC) made under that statute.[17] That same Act creates an appeal from the CRTC to the FCA "on any question of law or of jurisdiction."[18]

Both the common-law doctrine of exhaustion and s. 18.5 demand that any challenge to a decision of the CRTC under the *Telecommunications Act* must come in the form of an

---

15 *Federal Courts Act, supra* note 8, s. 18.5.

16 *Abbott Laboratories, Ltd. v. M.N.R.*, 2004 FC 140, [2005] 1 F.C.R. D-40 at para. 40.

17 S.C. 1993, c. 38, s. 12.

18 *Ibid.*, s. 64.

appeal to the FCA or to the GIC.[19] Presumably, an applicant would select the FCA where questions of "law or jurisdiction" are at issue. In other instances, where the challenge is to the policy wisdom of the CRTC decision, recourse to the GIC would likely be preferred. What happens next varies between these two sorts of appeals.

In instances where an appeal is brought to the FCA, there will *never* be judicial review. Section 18.5 of the *Federal Courts Act* bars judicial review of the CRTC matter that is on appeal. Once the FCA issues its appeal decision, that decision is not amenable to judicial review—the FCA is not a federal "board, commission or other tribunal" under the *Federal Courts Act*. Instead, it is a court, and any further challenge to any of its determinations are simply taken up the regular court appeal chain to the Supreme Court of Canada, with leave.

If the CRTC decision were instead appealed to the GIC under s. 12 of the *Telecommunications Act*, the pattern would be slightly different. Again, s. 18.5 would preclude judicial review of a CRTC matter that is subject to appeal to the GIC—that appeal must be exhausted. Once it is exhausted, and the GIC issues its determination, judicial review does become a possibility: the GIC decision is not subject to any additional statutory appeal. Because the GIC is a "federal board, commission or other tribunal," it is itself subject to judicial review before the Federal Court. Thus the FCC could judicially review the GIC appeal decision. A litigant unhappy with the outcome of that FCC judicial review could then appeal that decision up the regular court appeal chain to the FCA and from there to the Supreme Court of Canada, with leave.

Note the differential impact of s. 18.5 in these two scenarios. In the first, where the statutory appeal is to the FCA, s. 18.5 has the end-effect of creating an appeal-*only* route. In the second, where the statutory appeal is to the GIC, s. 18.5 prioritizes that appeal over judicial review. Then, once the GIC completes its task, judicial review re-emerges as a sort of "one step removed from the CRTC decision" possibility.

3. Leave Requirements and Judicial Review

Generally speaking, there is no requirement that leave be obtained before an applicant brings an application for judicial review before the Federal Court. One significant, subject-matter specific exception to this observation relates to immigration matters. Under the *Immigration and Refugee Protection Act*,[20] judicial review must be commenced via an application for leave brought before the Federal Court.[21] These may or may not be granted and constitute an extra hurdle for judicial review applications in the immigration context.

---

[19] Note that the CRTC has roles under other statutes as well; readers should thus be attentive to the appeal rules that may exist under these other instruments. The pattern may not be the same as described for the *Telecommunications Act*. To add an extra layer of complexity, in those statutes where the CRTC is amenable to judicial review (that is, where there is no statutory appeal triggering s. 18.5), judicial review would go first to the FCA because the CRTC is one of the bodies listed in s. 28 of the *Federal Courts Act*.

[20] S.C. 2001, c. 27.

[21] *Ibid.*, s. 72.

B. Standing

The *Federal Courts Act* provides that "[a]n application for judicial review may be made by the Attorney General of Canada or by anyone directly affected by the matter in respect of which relief is sought."[22] This provision provides standing as of right to the government of Canada and standing to persons "directly affected" by federal, administrative decision making.

For a person to be directly affected, "the decision at issue must be one which directly affects the party's rights, imposes legal obligations on it, or prejudicially affects it directly."[23] There are, however, some decisions so general that it is difficult to envisage them being of sufficient direct affect vis-à-vis any single person. If standing rules were not relaxed in these circumstances, they would immunize the government from challenge. Accordingly, the Federal Courts do recognize "public-interest standing," something that exists where the three-part test established by the Supreme Court in *Canadian Council of Churches v. Canada (Minister of Employment and Immigration)*[24] is met. The applicant must show that a serious issue has been raised; it must have a genuine or direct interest in the outcome of the litigation; and there must be no other reasonable and effective way to bring the matter to court.

Seriousness of the issue "encompasses both the importance of the issues and the likelihood of their being resolved in favour of the applicant," with the latter measured by considering whether the applicant has a "fairly arguable case."[25] The requirement of genuine or direct interest sufficient to satisfy the test for public-interest standing relates, at least in part, to the experience and expertise of the applicant in relation to the subject matter of the litigation.[26] Last, the "reasonable and effective means" threshold amounts to asking whether there is a more appropriate applicant: "public interest standing may still be denied if there are other individuals who are more directly affected than the applicant, and are reasonably likely to institute proceedings to challenge the administrative action in question."[27]

As this book goes to press, a case is before the Supreme Court that may invite the court to reconsider and possibly broaden its public interest standing test.[28] The case involves a constitutional challenge, but as in the past, a change in public-interest standing in constitutional matters will likely spill over to administrative law.

---

22   *Federal Courts Act, supra* note 8, s. 18.1(1).

23   *League for Human Rights of B'Nai Brith Canada v. Odynsky*, 2008 FC 732 at para. 24, cited with approval in *Friends of the Canadian Wheat Board v. Canada (Attorney General)*, 2011 FCA 101, [2011] 2 F.C.R. D-1 at para. 21.

24   [1992] 1 S.C.R. 236.

25   *Sierra Club of Canada v. Canada (Minister of Finance)*, [1999] 2 F.C. 211 at paras. 38 and 39 (T.D.).

26   *Ibid.* at para. 53.

27   *Ibid.* at para. 69.

28   *Downtown Eastside Sex Workers United Against Violence Society v. Canada (Attorney General)*, 2010 BCCA 439, application for leave granted 2011 CanLII 19610 (S.C.C.) (S.C.C. Case Information Docket 33981).

C. Limitation Periods

The *Federal Courts Act* also establishes an unusually demanding limitation period on applications for judicial review: "An application for judicial review in respect of a decision or an order of a federal board, commission or other tribunal shall be made within 30 days after the time the decision or order was first communicated by the federal board, commission or other tribunal to the office of the Deputy Attorney General of Canada or to the party directly affected by it."[29] A judge may extend this time either before or after its expiry, but, to receive such an extension, the applicant must "show a continuing intention to pursue the application, that the application has some merit, that no prejudice to the respondent arises from the delay, and that a reasonable explanation for the delay exists."[30]

Note that even if a court accepts an extension on the statutory limitation period, it retains a discretion to deny a remedy on the basis of unreasonable delay.[31]

We should also note that the limitation period applies only to circumstances where there has been an actual administrative decision, as opposed to a challenge to a persisting situation. The limitations clock does not, for example, attach to a circumstance in which "an application for judicial review is sought for an order in the nature of mandamus, prohibition or declaratory relief for redress against a state of affairs that is by its very nature continuing and on-going and is alleged to be invalid or unlawful."[32]

D. Grounds of Review

Among the most difficult issues raised by the Federal Court's administrative law role are the grounds of review available to applicants challenging federal executive decisions. The *Federal Courts Act* specifies that "[t]he Federal Court may grant relief ... if it is satisfied that the federal board, commission or other tribunal

(a) acted without jurisdiction, acted beyond its jurisdiction or refused to exercise its jurisdiction;

(b) failed to observe a principle of natural justice, procedural fairness or other procedure that it was required by law to observe;

(c) erred in law in making a decision or an order, whether or not the error appears on the face of the record;

(d) based its decision or order on an erroneous finding of fact that it made in a perverse or capricious manner or without regard for the material before it;

(e) acted, or failed to act, by reason of fraud or perjured evidence; or

(f) acted in any other way that was contrary to law.[33]

---

[29] *Federal Courts Act*, *supra* note 8, s. 18.1(2).

[30] *Stanfield v. Canada*, 2005 FCA 107 at para. 3, applied to s. 18.1 by, *inter alia*, *Sander Holdings Ltd. v. Canada (Minister of Agriculture)*, 2006 FC 327, 289 F.T.R. 221 at para. 29 (aff'd 2007 FCA 322, 370 N.R. 274).

[31] *Ibid.* at para. 34.

[32] *Maple Leaf Foods Inc. v. Consorzio Del Prosciutto Di Parma*, 2009 FC 1035 at para. 19.

[33] *Federal Courts Act*, *supra* note 8, s. 18.1(4).

Great care is required in reading this language. In the past, some courts have interpreted the grounds of review listed in s. 18.1(4) as also prescribing the standard of review,[34] although that reasoning has not survived the Supreme Court's decision of *Canada (Citizenship and Immigration) v. Khosa*.[35] The exact matter before the Court in the latter case was "the extent to which, if at all, the exercise by judges of statutory powers of judicial review (such as those established by ss. 18 and 18.1 of the *Federal Courts Act* …) is governed by the common law principles lately analysed by our Court in *Dunsmuir v. New Brunswick*."[36] A majority of the Court concluded that s. 18.1(4), although clearly prescribing grounds of review, was largely silent on the standard of review to be applied. Accordingly, it was entirely proper for the Court to turn to the common law (as recently revised by *Dunsmuir*) in determining what standard of review it would apply to the ground of review in question.

Extrapolating from *Khosa*, we might make the following observations about the key grounds enumerated in s. 18.1(4).

1. *Acting Without Jurisdiction*

As the Supreme Court noted in *Khosa*, "jurisdictional issues command a correctness standard."[37] Once again, however, special caution is warranted because jurisdictional issues are virtually non-existent in the common-law administrative law jurisprudence and their invocation in the *Federal Courts Act* has, so far, not resuscitated them. Although, in *Dunsmuir*, the Supreme Court appeared to open the door a crack to a new creature known as a "true question of jurisdiction," it has held its shoulder against that door to prevent any further embellishment of the concept. As the Court observed in 2011, "our Court has held since *Dunsmuir* that issues which in other days might have been considered by some to be jurisdictional, should now be dealt with under the standard of review analysis in order to determine whether a standard of correctness or of reasonableness should apply."[38]

2. *Procedural Fairness*

In *Khosa*, the Supreme Court observed "procedural issues (subject to competent legislative override) are to be determined by a court on the basis of a correctness standard of review."[39] More generally, there is nothing unusual or unique in the Federal Court approach to common law procedural fairness. The procedural fairness described elsewhere in this book is that applied at the Federal Court. Indeed, Federal Court jurisprudence is the source of much of that general law on procedural fairness. This reflects, in part, the fact that, at the federal

---

[34] See *Mugesera v. Canada (Minister of Citizenship and Immigration)*, 2005 SCC 40, [2005] 2 S.C.R. 100 at paras. 37 and 38 [*Mugesera*].

[35] 2009 SCC 12, [2009] 1 S.C.R. 339 [*Khosa*].

[36] *Ibid.* at para. 1.

[37] *Ibid.* at para. 42.

[38] *Canada v. Canada*, 2011 SCC 53, [2011] 3 S.C.R. 471 at para. 24 [*Canada v. Canada*].

[39] *Khosa, supra* note 35 at para. 43.

level, there is no codified procedural statute intended to apply to all or some significant part of federal administrative action. This places federal administrative decision making on a very different procedural footing than, for instance, Ontario provincial equivalents governed by the *Statutory Powers Procedures Act*.[40] (Note that it is an error to assert that the Federal Court may or can apply these provincial laws—they *do not apply* to federal administrative decision making.)

That said, one area that is distinctly federal is the *Canadian Bill of Rights*.[41] The procedural guarantees found in ss. 1(a) and 2(e) of that instrument apply exclusively to the federal level. Thus, to the extent there is a jurisprudence interpreting these provisions (and it is a slender jurisprudence), it originates in the Federal Courts.

Sections 1(a) and 2(e) of the *Bill of Rights* read:

> 1. It is hereby recognized and declared that in Canada there have existed and shall continue to exist without discrimination by reason of race, national origin, colour, religion or sex, the following human rights and fundamental freedoms, namely,
>
> (a) the right of the individual to life, liberty, security of the person and enjoyment of property, and the right not to be deprived thereof except by due process of law. ...
>
> 2. Every law of Canada shall, unless it is expressly declared by an Act of the Parliament of Canada that it shall operate notwithstanding the *Canadian Bill of Rights*, be so construed and applied as not to abrogate, abridge or infringe or to authorize the abrogation, abridgment or infringement of any of the rights or freedoms herein recognized and declared, and in particular, no law of Canada shall be construed or applied so as to ...
>
> (e) deprive a person of the right to a fair hearing in accordance with the principles of fundamental justice for the determination of his rights and obligations.[42]

One reason that these provisions have received relatively little treatment by the courts is because of their overlap with both common-law procedural fairness and s. 7 of the Charter. For the most part, the jurisprudence seems to treat the *Bill of Rights* provisions as alternative sources of the same sorts of procedural protections offered by the common law and the Charter—that is, procedural rights under the Bill are different in source but not in kind from those found at common law or in s. 7 of the Charter. There are, however, a number of caveats to this point.

First, unlike the common law (but like the Charter), a statute does not displace *Bill of Rights* procedural entitlements (unless the *Bill of Rights* is expressly excluded by that statute). Like the Charter, therefore, the *Bill of Rights* is available to challenge *statutory* provisions that curtail procedural rights.

However, unlike the Charter, the trigger for the application of s. 1(a) of the *Bill of Rights* includes more than simply life, liberty, and security of the person. It also includes property. This gives it a much more expansive reach than s. 7 of the Charter.

---

40   R.S.O. 1990, c. S.22.

41   S.C. 1960, c. 44.

42   *Ibid.*, ss. 1(a) and 2(e).

For both these reasons, the *Bill of Rights* may be the sole source of procedural rights available to litigants presented with a statutory annulment of procedural rights in circumstances where property interests (but not life, liberty, or security of the person) are engaged.

A second caveat to the observation that the *Bill of Rights* procedural rights dovetail with those provided by common law and the Charter flows from some slender jurisprudence on the concept of "due process" in s. 1(a). There is a hint in the jurisprudence that "due process" in this context may reach "substantive due process," a concept that is not truly explored to date.[43] In a somewhat antiquated case, one Federal Court judge concluded that "due process requires, in addition to a fair hearing, a total process which provides for the making of a decision authorized by law, a means for rationally relating the facts in the case to criteria legally prescribed, as in this case, by Parliament."[44] This definition has never caught on, but it is notable that, were it to do so, it would give s. 1(a) a coverage more closely associated with substantive grounds for administrative judicial review. Specifically, rationally relating fact to applicable legal standards is the sort of decision-making process one would associate with reasonable exercises of discretion.

3. Error of Law

Again, there is nothing unique about Federal Court application of this ground. Despite quite different language in a predecessor case,[45] *Khosa* establishes that an error of law may be reviewable on correctness *or* reasonableness grounds. Which standard applies depends on consideration of the sorts of issues raised by *Dunsmuir* and its successors—for example, in a recent case, the Supreme Court has emphasized as a justification for reasonableness review the fact that the statute in question involved "the home statute or a closely related statute" applied "by an expert decision-maker."[46] The other variables that point toward correctness versus reasonableness review of errors of law are discussed elsewhere in this book.

4. Erroneous Finding of Fact

As with errors of law, there is an earlier jurisprudence assigning standard of review significance to the phrase "perverse and capricious manner or without regard for the material before it."[47] Some courts envisaged this language as connoting "patent unreasonableness" under the pre-*Dunsmuir* tripartite standard-of-review approach, while others applied a reasonableness *simpliciter* concept. This debate fell away after *Dunsmuir* and, for its part, *Khosa* holds that "it is clear from s. 18.1(4)(d) that Parliament intended administrative fact finding to command a high degree of deference. This is quite consistent with *Dunsmuir*. It

---

43　*Authorson v. Canada (Attorney General)*, 2003 SCC 39, [2003] 2 S.C.R. 40 at para. 51.

44　*Smith, Kline & French Laboratories v. Attorney General*, [1986] 1 F.C. 274 (T.D.); aff'd [1987] 2 F.C. 359 (C.A.).

45　See *Mugesera*, *supra* note 34 at para. 37, asserting that errors of law under s. 18.1(4) are reviewable on a standard of correctness.

46　*Canada v. Canada*, *supra* note 38 at para 44.

47　See again *Mugesera*, *supra* note 34 at para. 38.

provides legislative precision to the reasonableness standard of review of factual issues in cases falling under the *Federal Courts Act.*"[48]

5. Other Way Contrary to Law

This provision serves as a basket clause allowing the evolution of new grounds of review. Error of discretion is an obvious ground of review not expressly mentioned elsewhere in s. 18.1(4) that reasonably falls within this category.[49] As Audrey Macklin observes in Chapter 9, Standard of Review: Back to the Future?, *Dunsmuir* establishes that courts will generally review errors of discretion using the reasonableness standard.

One final note on grounds of review relates to the nature of proceedings before the Federal Court. Judicial review applications are heard on the record—that is, they do not involve the presentation of viva voce evidence by, for example, witnesses testifying in court. Instead, at issue before the court is the record of decision made by the decision-maker in question, as demonstrated either by the documents produced by that decision-maker in rendering its decision or, for more informal decisions, by affidavits describing the decision. As a consequence, judicial review applications bear more resemblance to appellate court proceedings than to trial-like proceedings.

E. Remedies

A last issue relating to administrative judicial review before the Federal Courts is remedies. As already noted, the Federal Court has exclusive, original jurisdiction under s. 18 "to issue an injunction, writ of *certiorari*, writ of prohibition, writ of *mandamus* or writ of *quo warranto*, or grant declaratory relief, against any federal board, commission or other tribunal."[50] A more formal remedies section is found at s. 18.1:

> (3) On an application for judicial review, the Federal Court may:
>
> (a) order a federal board, commission or other tribunal to do any act or thing it has unlawfully failed or refused to do or has unreasonably delayed in doing; or
>
> (b) declare invalid or unlawful, or quash, set aside or set aside and refer back for determination in accordance with such directions as it considers to be appropriate, prohibit or restrain, a decision, order, act or proceeding of a federal board, commission or other tribunal.[51]

In essence, this language simply encapsulates in textual form the meaning of the prerogative writs of *certiorari*, *mandamus*, and prohibition and the ordinary remedies of declaration and injunction discussed by Cristie Ford in Chapter 3, Dogs and Tails: Remedies in Administrative Law. In this respect, it equips the Federal Courts with the same remedies as the provincial superior courts, operating under an unmodified common-law administrative

---

48   *Khosa, supra* note 35 at para. 46.

49   *Telfer v. Canada (Revenue Agency)*, 2009 FCA 23, [2009] 2 F.C.R. D-15 at para. 23.

50   *Federal Courts Act, supra* note 8, s. 18(1)(a).

51   *Ibid.*, ss. 18.1(3)(a) and (b).

remedy regime. Further, like these common-law remedies, the Federal Courts' power to award remedies is purely discretionary: s. 18.1(3) uses the word "may." As a consequence, the Act "preserves the traditionally discretionary nature of judicial review."[52]

In practice, therefore, the circumstances in which the Federal Courts will award relief are not greatly different from those in which provincial superior courts will now act. For instance, in deciding whether to "order a federal board, commission or other tribunal to do any act or thing it has unlawfully failed or refused to do or has unreasonably delayed in doing,"[53] the Federal Court has employed the common-law tests for the writ of *mandamus*. Likewise, in deciding whether to exercise its discretion to deny a remedy, the Federal Court has looked to considerations similar to those contemplated by provincial superior courts, including "prematurity, mootness, waiver, impermissible collateral attack, conduct, the existence of an alternate remedy, or on the basis of a broader assessment of the balance of convenience between the parties."[54]

That said, there are a few potential differences between the federal and provincial remedies systems. First, relief under s. 18.1(3) "while doubtless modelled on the forms of relief available under the prerogative orders and the declaration and injunction, are not necessarily encrusted with the same technicalities that at one time hampered the development of the common law remedies of judicial review."[55] This is particularly true in the area of standing and procedure. To the extent that different common-law remedy rules had embedded in them distinct rules of procedure and standing, the Federal Court regime abolishes those in favour of the system established in the *Federal Courts Act*. Put another way, one follows the same process regardless of the administrative law remedy one is seeking. That hasn't always been the case at the provincial level, although modern provincial judicial review statutes echo the *Federal Courts Act* in consolidating judicial review procedure into a single process, irrespective of the remedy sought.

Second, there is a modest statutory embellishment on the common law remedies standard found in s. 18.1:

> (5) If the sole ground for relief established on an application for judicial review is a defect in form or a technical irregularity, the Federal Court may:
>
> (a) refuse the relief if it finds that no substantial wrong or miscarriage of justice has occurred; and
>
> (b) in the case of a defect in form or a technical irregularity in a decision or an order, make an order validating the decision or order, to have effect from any time and on any terms that it considers appropriate.[56]

---

52   *Canadian Pacific Ltd v. Matsqui Indian Band*, [1995] 1 SCR 3 para 31.

53   See e.g. *Vaziri v. Canada (Minister of Citizenship and Immigration)*, 2006 FC 1159, [2007] 2 F.C.R. D-2 at para. 38.

54   *Mwesigwa v. Canada (Minister of Citizenship and Immigration)*, 2011 FC 1367 at para. 15.

55   *Sierra Club of Canada v. Canada (Minister of Finance)*, [1999] 2 F.C. 211 (T.D.) at para. 47.

56   *Federal Courts Act, supra* note 8, ss. 18.1(5)(a) and (b).

IV. Conclusion

In summary, the federal system of administrative law is a variant to that applied provincially. The Federal Court issues a vast number of administrative law cases every year, and as a close perusal of the cases cited elsewhere in this book suggests, federal cases have been the source of many important developments in the administrative law. This is particularly the case in the area of common-law procedural fairness.

However, both students and practitioners of administrative law must be wary of a number of important considerations in approaching administrative practice in front of Federal Courts. First, because the Federal Courts are statutory bodies, they are unusually attentive to a statutory basis for their authority. Second, that statutory basis simplifies matters to an important extent by prescribing in detail guidance on issues such as standing, limitation periods, grounds of review, and remedies.

Nevertheless, we should exercise caution in relation to these statutory prescriptions. For one thing, the *Federal Courts Act*'s limitation period is unusually brief, and inattentive applicants may quickly find their applications dismissed as untimely. For another, the statutory codification of grounds of review does not in any real way answer the question of standard of review. Accordingly, Federal Court practitioners, like other administrative lawyers, must pay close attention to Supreme Court jurisprudence on standard of review machinations. Likewise, the codification of remedies in the statute is incomplete, in the sense that much of the common law on remedies remains relevant, as do the discretionary bases for declining to issue a remedy.

Put another way, the *Federal Courts Act* is the place to start in understanding administrative judicial review at the federal level. It is not, however, the final answer in any judicial review analysis.

CHAPTER SIXTEEN

Getting the Story Out: Accountability and the Law of Public Inquiries

PETER J. CARVER
Faculty of Law, University of Alberta

I. Accountability and the Public Inquiry

On December 9, 2007, a jury in New Westminster, B.C. convicted Robert William Pickton of six counts of murder with respect to women who had gone missing from Vancouver's notorious downtown eastside area over the previous several years. During the trial, the jury heard a recording in which Pickton boasted to a jailhouse informant that he had actually killed 49 women. Investigators who pored over Pickton's farm property identified the DNA of 32 missing women in all. It is widely believed that Pickton is the most prolific serial killer in Canadian history. The criminal conviction of Robert Pickton, and the appeals that upheld the conviction over the subsequent four years, closed one chapter in this tragic story.[1]

The disappearance of dozens of women from the Vancouver area between 1995 and 2002 had not gone unnoticed during that time. Family members and friends of the women, many of them of aboriginal descent, pressed the Vancouver police department throughout this period to step up its efforts to find out what was happening and to treat the unprecedented phenomenon as a serious criminal matter. The police repeatedly responded that because most of the women were known to be drug addicts and sex trade workers, their disappearances represented nothing more than the comings and goings of a transient population. This continued even after an internationally known profiler on the Vancouver police force concluded that the number of women involved suggested that a serial killer was at work, and after Pickton had been charged with attempted murder of a woman in the late 1990s in circumstances similar to many of the disappearances.[2] As time passed, the friends and family members of the missing women became a unified and vocal advocacy group. However, it was only when the search of Pickton's farm following his arrest in 2002 on weapons charges turned up effects and remains of some of the women that it dawned on everyone, including police, that family members' worst fears had been well founded.

The criminal trial brought a degree of accountability to Robert Pickton for his acts. It was not, however, directed at making accountable the public officials and systems that appeared to have failed so badly in protecting women in Vancouver's downtown eastside. Accountability means many different things. One meaning is that persons who have harmed others by their actions will be found responsible and made to "pay for" the harm they caused, through punishment or paying compensation. The justice system is the social institution designed to achieve accountability in this sense. Legal accountability through the justice system is directed at wrongdoing defined in advance by established norms of behaviour. It involves a retrospective inquiry into past events. To the degree that legal accountability is concerned with the future, it is limited to remediating the harm caused by and between the individuals involved. The model is adversarial in that it assumes a contest between two or more parties seeking to prove different versions of facts and law. Coercive in nature, the model builds in many protections for the individual. These include strict rules for ensuring that only evidence relevant to the question of liability is received, and that the onus of proving liability is placed on the alleging party.

---

[1] Stevie Cameron, *On the Farm: Robert William Pickton and the Tragic Story of Vancouver's Missing Women* (Toronto: Vintage Canada, 2010).

[2] The charges were stayed by the Crown purportedly because of the victim's failure to appear in court (*ibid.* at 158). This matter forms part of the missing women inquiry's mandate.

What the family members of the missing women, and indeed much of the public, wanted following the Pickton trial was a different kind of accountability. They wanted answers to questions about what police, prosecution, and other officials had done before and during the missing women investigation. Had sufficient resources been devoted to the investigation in a timely way? Did the Vancouver police and the Royal Canadian Mounted Police (RCMP) communicate with each other in an effective manner and share leads? How had police responded to tips they received about Mr. Pickton well before his arrest? Did bureaucratic infighting interfere with investigative work? Were women living in the downtown eastside, especially aboriginal women, systemically devalued? And most important, what steps could be taken to reduce or eliminate the chances that something so awful could ever happen again? These questions called for accountability in the sense of "getting the story out," of finding out who did what and when and why, and how similar events should be handled in the future. Historically, in Canada, an important mechanism for achieving accountability in this sense has been the public inquiry. Justice Cory of the Supreme Court of Canada described the difference between an inquiry and liability-based proceedings in these terms:

> A commission of inquiry is neither a criminal trial nor a civil action for the determination of liability. It cannot establish either criminal culpability or civil responsibility for damages. Rather, an inquiry is an investigation into an issue, event or series of events. The findings of a commissioner relating to that investigation are simply findings of fact and statements of opinion reached by the commissioner at the end of the inquiry. They are unconnected to normal legal criteria. They are based upon and flow from a procedure which is not bound by the evidentiary or procedural rules of a courtroom. There are no legal consequences attached to the determinations of a commissioner. They are not enforceable and do not bind courts considering the same subject matter.[3]

In September 2010, the government of British Columbia issued an order in council creating the Commission of Inquiry into the Missing Women, to be headed by retired Justice and former Attorney General Wally Oppal. The inquiry's public hearings commenced in late 2011. Its report is scheduled to be released at the end of October 2012, just before the publication of this volume. Throughout this chapter, reference will be made to the missing women inquiry to illustrate various points.[4]

There are two principal reasons for including a discussion of public inquiries in an introductory text on administrative law. First, both administrative law and public inquiries serve the important function of making government operations transparent and responsible to the public. As a mode of accountability, however, judicial review suffers from some of the limitations of most formal legal processes. Its focus is generally directed at specific acts of governmental decision making. Remedies in judicial review are rarely systemic, and frequently go only so far as to require that decision-makers start their process over again. On the policy level, judicial review is generally silent. It is therefore worth considering public

---

[3] *Canada (Attorney General) v. Canada (Commission of Inquiry on the Blood System)*, [1997] 3 S.C.R. 440 at para. 34 [*Krever Commission*].

[4] As you make your way through the chapter, you may find it helpful to refer to the commission's website: Missing Women Commission of Inquiry <http://www.missingwomeninquiry.ca>.

inquiries as an alternative recourse to judicial review for those aggrieved by alleged government misconduct. This is explored in a general way in section I.A of this chapter, which deals with the different kinds of public inquiries known in the Canadian tradition and the problems of balancing the public interest with individual rights in the holding of an inquiry.

Second, public inquiries operate within the context of administrative law principles. Inquiries are exercises in delegated executive power and are subject to most rules of administrative law. However, because inquiries engage largely in investigative fact-finding and recommending functions, and much less in adjudicative and order-making functions, they provide a different context in which to see administrative law in operation.

A. Types of Public Inquiries

The terms "royal commission," "judicial inquiry," and "public inquiry" are used almost interchangeably in media accounts.[5] Nevertheless, these terms have different shades of meaning that are worth noting. The term "royal commission" refers to the fact that inquiries used to be established by executive government pursuant to royal prerogative powers. Most inquiries are now appointed pursuant to the federal and provincial inquiry statutes that exist in each Canadian jurisdiction. The term "judicial inquiry" is a colloquial term that reflects the fact that governments frequently name current or former judges to be inquiry commissioners. This is especially true of inquiries whose main purpose is the investigation of and reporting on a series of factual events, such as the missing women inquiry. However, there is no requirement that an inquiry be headed by a judicial official. In the Canadian experience, many inquiries are led by non-judges.

This chapter uses the term "public inquiry." It does so because of the connotations of the word "public" that assist in understanding how inquiries in this country generally work. For one thing, inquiries are largely directed at the actions of public authorities and public officials. While nothing prevents lawmakers from establishing inquiries to look into the actions of private persons, it would be questionable to spend public resources where the findings had no implications for past or future government regulation. The decision to appoint an inquiry should meet a public-interest test. The term "public inquiry" implies another important feature of inquiries in Canada: they are usually carried out in public view. It is through the public nature of inquiry proceedings that the inquiry achieves one of its most important purposes: to assure members of the public that the "full story" is finally coming out, that actions and decisions that were taken behind closed doors will be exposed to the light of day.

Two kinds of public inquiries are familiar in Canadian experience: the policy inquiry and the investigative inquiry. The policy inquiry is directed at the study of broad issues of social or regulatory concern, with the purpose of changing law and policy. The Royal Commission

---

5   For a discussion of the historical use and meaning of these terms, see Chapter 2, "Nature and Purposes of Commissions of Inquiry" in Ed Ratushny, *The Conduct of Public Inquiries: Law, Policy and Practice* (Toronto: Irwin Law, 2009) 11-20. See also the Introduction by Ruel in Simon Ruel, *The Law of Public Inquiries in Canada* (Toronto: Carswell, 2010). Both books are excellent resources on all facets of the law governing public inquiries in Canada.

on Aboriginal Peoples (RCAP)[6] in the early 1990s, and the Commission on the Future of Health Care in Canada ("the Romanow Commission"),[7] which reported in 2002, are examples of policy inquiries.

An investigative inquiry is directed at uncovering and reporting on the facts of an event or series of events in which one or more persons were seriously harmed, or which comprised an instance of alleged public misconduct (that is, a political scandal). The Oliphant inquiry into the business relationship between former Prime Minister Brian Mulroney and Canadian-German businessman Karlheinz Schreiber is an example of an investigatory inquiry.[8]

Purely investigatory inquiries are, however, relatively infrequent in Canadian experience. Many more inquiries are combined with investigative and policy functions. The missing women inquiry is such a combined inquiry. The inquiry's terms of reference set out both functions:

> 4. The terms of reference of the inquiry to be conducted by the commission are as follows:
> (a) to conduct hearings, in or near the City of Vancouver, to inquire into and make findings of fact respecting the conduct of the missing women investigations;
> (b) consistent with the *British Columbia (Attorney General) v. Davies*,[9] to inquire into and make findings of fact respecting the decision of the Criminal Justice Branch on January 27, 1998, to enter a stay of proceedings on charges against Robert William Pickton of attempted murder, assault with a weapon, forcible confinement and aggravated assault;
> (c) to recommend changes considered necessary respecting the initiation and conduct of investigations in British Columbia of missing women and suspected multiple homicides;
> (d) to recommend changes considered necessary respecting homicide investigations in British Columbia by more than one investigating organization, including the co-ordination of those investigations; ...

Under British Columbia's *Public Inquiry Act*,[10] investigative and policy review functions are separately referred to as "hearing commissions" and "study commissions."[11] In other jurisdictions, the functions have often been termed phase 1 and phase 2 processes, which reflects the common practice of commissions of inquiry with combined functions to divide their proceedings into two distinct phases, with different parties, hearing procedures, and reports. The following discussion examines how investigative or phase 1 inquiries and policy or phase 2 inquiries pursue accountability at both the individual and organizational

---

6   See *Report of the Royal Commission on Aboriginal Peoples* (Ottawa: Queen's Printer, 1996), online: Aboriginal Affairs and Northern Development Canada <http://www.aadnc-aandc.gc.ca/eng/1100100014597>.

7   Health Canada, *Commission on the Future of Health Care in Canada*, online: Health Canada <http://www.hc-sc.gc.ca/hcs-sss/com/fed/romanow/index-eng.php>.

8   See the Canada Archives website for the Oliphant inquiry at <http://epe.lac-bac.gc.ca/100/206/301/pco-bcp/commissions/oliphant/2010-07-20/english/index.php.htm>.

9   2009 BCCA 337, B.C.L.R. (4th) 26.

10   S.B.C. 2007, c. 9.

11   The missing women inquiry was designated to encompass both functions by the order in council of September 2010: "2(1) A hearing and study commission, called the Missing Women Commission of Inquiry, is established under section 2 of the Public Inquiry Act."

levels. Section II of this chapter looks at several of the more important principles of administrative law that are applicable to public inquiries. The chapter concludes in section III by raising questions about the overall benefit of public inquiries.

B. The Policy Inquiry

Policy inquiries raise relatively few legal issues. Governments establish policy inquiries to develop new approaches to complex social policy issues. Not infrequently, governments are accused of establishing policy inquiries in order to forestall having to make decisions on complex or controversial social issues. The activity of policy inquiries is legislative in nature in the sense that it is prospective (not historical), broad-based or general in impact (not specific or individualized), and open to political/policy input (not restricted by stringent rules of relevance), the features that distinguish legislative from adjudicative decision making.

The Supreme Court has ruled that legislative decision making and "quasi-legislative" decision making do not attract fair process protections at common law,[12] even where government officials have created legitimate expectations of fair process.[13] These principles create a lacuna in administrative law, leaving decision-makers unbounded by anything other than statutory requirements to hear the affected public when it comes to the most important of all governmental functions: law-making. The appropriate procedural right with respect to law making seems likely to be a "right to consult"—that is, a right to give one's input to a legislative decision-maker. The public inquiry is one means of addressing this gap. Inquiries act in a consultative fashion with governments and, in turn, engage the public in this consultative activity.

The nature of a true consultative process is that the advice given in consultation should be received with respect and serious attention, even if the decision-maker decides not to accept it. Policy inquiries generally operate like formalized consultative processes. Most of them adopt public hearing processes similar to those adopted in the investigative inquiries. As a consequence, policy inquiries present an intriguing combination of formal hearing-like processes with a form of legislative function. Commissions of inquiry have also adopted a number of creative methods for obtaining public input, including public opinion surveys, online consultations, and holding public meetings at different geographic locations. An interesting question is whether a government might in certain circumstances, which include raising expectations from past practice, create a legal duty on itself to hold a policy inquiry as a form of consultation.[14]

---

12   *Att. Gen. of Can. v. Inuit Tapirisat et al.*, [1980] 2 S.C.R. 735.

13   See *Reference re Canada Assistance Plan (B.C.)*, [1991] 2 S.C.R. 525 and *Mount Sinai Hospital Center v. Quebec (Minister of Health and Social Services)*, 2001 SCC 41, [2001] 2 S.C.R. 281, per Binnie J., concurring.

14   In Ontario, a series of judicial review challenges were brought with respect to the hearings and findings of the Ontario Hospital Restructuring Commission in the mid-1990s, including its alleged failure to adequately consult with interested members of the community. See e.g. *Pembroke Civic Hospital v. Ontario (Health Services Restructuring Commission)* (1997), 36 O.R. (3d) 41 (Div. Ct.). However, the commission was a delegated decision-maker, having the power to order hospital restructuring, and so these cases are not directly applicable to the public inquiry situation.

The success of policy inquiries is often measured by whether the recommendations made by inquiry commissioners are adopted in whole or in part by governments. In this sense, the quality of an inquiry's hearings and final report will undoubtedly contribute to its success. In general, however, the degree to which recommendations are accepted turns on many other factors of a political nature—timing, context, and the inclinations of the government of the day in making the recommended changes. Reports that issue from the Phase Two process of a combined investigative and policy inquiry have an advantage in this respect. The immediacy and specificity of the issues that led to their creation can create momentum for acceptance of their recommendations.

Policy inquiries can have a significant impact on public discourse even without having their recommendations implemented. One way in which they contribute in this manner is through the generation of research. Policy commissions present an occasion for gathering the best available data and thinking on the subject at hand.[15] More important, policy inquiries may serve to mobilize public participation or, more accurately, cause groups to mobilize in order to take advantage of the opportunity presented by an inquiry. The best example of this phenomenon is the Royal Commission on the Status of Women in the early 1970s, around which the coalition of women's groups formed and became the National Action Committee on the Status of Women (NAC).[16]

C. The Investigative Inquiry

The investigative inquiry serves to uncover the truth about events that have already happened. Cory J. commented on the value of the fact-finding function of the inquiry in *Phillips v. Nova Scotia*:

> One of the primary functions of public inquiries is fact-finding. They are often convened, in the wake of public shock, horror, disillusionment, or scepticism, in order to uncover "the truth." Inquiries are, like the judiciary, independent; unlike the judiciary, they are often endowed with wide-ranging investigative powers. In following their mandates, commissions of inquiry are, ideally, free from partisan loyalties and better able than Parliament or the legislatures to take a long-term view of the problem presented. Cynics decry public inquiries as a means used by the government to postpone acting in circumstances which often call for speedy action. Yet, these inquiries can and do fulfill an important function in Canadian society. In times of public questioning, stress and concern they provide the means for Canadians to be apprised of the conditions pertaining to a worrisome community problem and to be a part of the recommendations that are aimed at resolving the problem. Both the status and high public respect for the commissioner and the open and public nature of the hearing help to restore public confidence not only in the institution or situation investigated but also in the process of government as a whole.[17]

---

15 See e.g. the "Resources/Research" link for the Romanow commission on the Health Canada website at <http://www.collectionscanada.gc.ca/webarchives/20071115024341/www.hc-sc.gc.ca/english/care/romanow/index1.html>.

16 See Jill Vickers, Pauline Rankin, & Christine Appelle, *Politics as if Women Mattered: A Political Analysis of the National Action Committee on the Status of Women* (Toronto: University of Toronto Press, 1993).

17 *Phillips v. Nova Scotia (Commission of Inquiry into the Westray Mine Tragedy)*, [1995] 2 S.C.R. 97 at para. 62 [*Phillips*].

In this regard, public inquiries share some qualities of other formal processes that have the investigation of historical incidents as their raison d'être. Such processes include coroner's inquests, fatality inquiries,[18] and ombudsperson investigations.[19] Unlike some investigative processes, however, the public inquiry is not solely concerned with ascertaining historical facts. It is also intended to bring transparency to the investigation itself by carrying the investigation out in public. Justice Samuel Grange, who headed the Ontario commission of inquiry into the unexplained deaths of children at Toronto's Hospital for Sick Children in the 1980s, experienced surprise on discovering the significance of this dual nature of the inquiry:

> I remember once thinking egotistically that all the evidence, all the antics, had only one aim: to convince the commissioner who, after all, eventually wrote the report. But I soon discovered my error. They are not just inquiries; they are public inquiries. … I realized that there was another purpose to the inquiry just as important as one man's solution to the mystery and that was to inform the public. Merely presenting the evidence in public, evidence which had hitherto been given only in private, served that purpose. The public has a special interest, a right to know and a right to form its opinion as it goes along.[20]

A dramatic example of this phenomenon occurred with the sponsorship (or Gomery) inquiry. The inquiry's exposure of financial improprieties in the distribution and management of federal government funds in Quebec in the post-1995 referendum period dominated headlines for weeks at a time in 2003-4. The televised hearings of the inquiry attracted massive audiences in Quebec and had a profound effect on public opinion in the province.[21] The power of the inquiry as an instrument for accountability must be balanced against what is at stake for the individuals whose decisions, actions, and lives are at the heart of any particular investigation, which includes those, often described as "victims," who suffered harm as a consequence of government action or inaction. Take Maher Arar as an example. Mr. Arar, a Syrian-born Canadian citizen living in Ottawa with his wife and two children, was rendered to Syria by American authorities after landing in New York on a return flight to Canada from a visit to his parents in Tunisia. This occurred in October 2002, just over a year following the terrorist attack on the World Trade Center. Based in part on information received from the RCMP and Canadian Security Intelligence Service (CSIS), American of-

---

18 See e.g. *Fatality Inquiries Act*, R.S.A. 2000, c. F-9.

19 See e.g. *Ombudsman Act*, R.S.B.C. 1996, c. 340. See discussion of the ombudsperson complaint and investigation process as an alternative to judicial review in Cristie Ford, Chapter 3, Dogs and Tails: Remedies in Administrative Law. Note that ombudsperson investigations generally take place in confidence, which encourages candour in government responses to ombudsperson queries, but arguably limits the social accountability benefits of the process.

20 S.G.M. Grange, "How Should Lawyers and the Legal Profession Adapt?" in A. Paul Pross, Innis Christie, & John A. Yogis, eds., *Commissions of Inquiry* (Toronto: Carswell, 1990) 154-55, and quoted by Cory J. in *Phillips, supra* note 17 at para. 63.

21 The sponsorship, or Gomery, inquiry produced two reports: *Who Is Responsible? Fact Finding Report* (Ottawa: Queen's Printer, 2005) [*Who Is Responsible?*] and *Restoring Accountability* (Ottawa: Queen's Printer, 2006). Documents prepared for website access by the sponsorship inquiry are now available online: Library and Archives Canada <http://epe.lac-bac.gc.ca/100/206/301/pco-bcp/commissions/sponsorship-ef/06-03-06/www.gomery.ca/en/default.htm>.

ficials apparently decided Mr. Arar represented a security threat. Mr. Arar was held in a Syrian prison for over a year, during which time he was repeatedly beaten and tortured during questioning about his alleged involvement with radical Islamic organizations. Following his release and return to Canada in 2003, Mr. Arar and many other Canadians demanded that an inquiry be held into the actions of Canadian government authorities leading to and during his imprisonment in Syria. The result was the Arar inquiry, conducted by Mr. Justice Dennis O'Connor over a two-year period.[22] Mr. Arar knew that his own actions would come under intense scrutiny in the course of the inquiry in addition to his physical and emotional injuries.

The second group of individuals directly affected by a public inquiry are those persons whose decisions and actions are the subject of the investigation. In the mid- to late 1990s, perceived conflict between the public interest in investigative inquiries and the interests of persons investigated caused a near-crisis in the world of Canadian public inquiries. Three inquiries into high-profile tragedies—the Krever commission into the Canadian blood system's use of tainted blood products, the Somalia inquiry into mistreatment of Somali prisoners by Canadian peacekeeping forces, and the Westray inquiry into a deadly coal mine explosion in Nova Scotia—became embroiled in lengthy litigation brought by both the subjects of investigation and witnesses. Delays caused by the many applications for judicial review in the course of the Somalia inquiry ultimately contributed to the controversial decision made by the government of Canada to terminate the inquiry before it could complete its evidence-gathering process. It seemed to many observers that public inquiries had become too expensive, time-consuming, and litigation-prone to be effective.[23]

The principal opinions in *Krever Commission* and *Phillips*, both written by Justice Peter Cory, sent the message that the public interest value of investigative inquiries outweighs concerns about their potential harm to the individual interests of witnesses and subjects of investigation. Both cases addressed one of the two main interests that have been viewed as most threatened by public inquiries: (1) rights of persons who may face criminal charges for matters being inquired into, and (2) reputational interests of those whose conduct may be called into question.

1. Balancing the Rights of Individuals Facing Criminal Charges

In *Starr v. Houlden*,[24] the Supreme Court of Canada quashed an Ontario public inquiry called to inquire into the actions of an individual and a private corporation involved in political fund-raising activities. The Court confirmed that public inquiries are not permitted to make findings of civil or criminal liability against individuals. In the *Starr* case, the inquiry's

---

[22] Commission of Inquiry into the Actions of Canadian Officials in Relation to Maher Arar, *Report of the Events Relating to Maher Arar: Factual Background*, vols. I and II (Ottawa: Queen's Printer, 2006); *Report of the Events Relating to Maher Arar: Analysis and Recommendations* (Ottawa: Queen's Printer, September 2006); and *A New Review Mechanism for the RCMP's National Security Activities* (Ottawa: Queen's Printer, December 2006).

[23] This "crisis" of the 1990s was partly responsible for the 1999 Conference on Commissions of Inquiry at Queen's University, which produced the valuable collection of essays in Allan Manson & David Mullan, eds., *Commissions of Inquiry: Praise or Reappraise* (Toronto: Irwin Law, 2003) [*Commissions of Inquiry*].

[24] [1990] 1 S.C.R. 1366 [*Starr*].

terms of reference prohibited the commissioner from making a finding of criminal liability but authorized him to state whether the individual had acted in ways that were described as a breach of an offence set out in the *Criminal Code*. The majority of the Court ruled that this effectively turned the inquiry into a substitute police investigation and prosecution without the protections of those procedures, and that this was *ultra vires* the provincial government.

Compelled testimony and document production are significant investigative tools of inquiries, giving inquiries a distinct investigative advantage in this respect over criminal trials. In the criminal setting, accused persons have the right under s. 11(c) of the Charter[25] not to testify. The danger from a civil liberties perspective is that governments may use inquiries and the power to compel witnesses to testify as a means to get around the right against self-incrimination. Indeed, the power of public inquiries to compel testimony from persons suspected of being responsible for an act or acts of wrongdoing has led to pointed questions about whether inquiries pose an improper threat to the rights of individuals.

The *Phillips* litigation addressed this issue in circumstances in which two mine managers summoned to testify before the provincial inquiry into the Westray mine disaster were also facing criminal prosecution with respect to the same events. The managers applied to quash the subpoenas issued by the inquiry and for an order quashing, or at least staying, the inquiry proceedings until after the criminal charges had been resolved. They argued that it would breach their Charter rights against self-incrimination to be compelled to testify at the inquiry in advance of any criminal trial and, further, that the publicity attending the hearings and findings of the inquiry would deny them a fair trial pursuant to s. 11(d) of the Charter.

By the time the matter was argued before the Supreme Court, the managers had opted to be tried by judge alone, without a jury. The criminal trial was in fact under way. In these circumstances, the majority of the Court lifted a stay of the inquiry imposed by the Nova Scotia Court of Appeal, but declined to rule on the issues of compellability or publicity, finding them to be moot. However, Justices Cory, Iacobucci, and Major gave lengthy concurring reasons addressing the compellability and fair trial questions for the sake of future cases. Cory J. concluded that witnesses should be compellable at a public inquiry, irrespective of whether they may be subject to prosecution for the same acts being investigated by the inquiry, so long as the inquiry serves a legitimate public purpose (that is, it is not intended as a substitute form of criminal investigation). Justice Cory found sufficient protection for witnesses in Charter sections 13 and 7. Section 13 prohibits the use of a person's testimony in subsequent criminal proceedings against him. Section 7 provides "derivative use immunity" as a matter of fundamental justice, barring the Crown from introducing evidence into a criminal trial that would not have been obtained "but for" the compelled testimony.

With respect to the risk that publicity attending inquiry proceedings might make a fair trial impossible, Cory J. said that governments must be allowed to take the risk of losing the power to prosecute an accused person, rather than have the judiciary adopt a blanket rule that would prevent public inquiries from going ahead where this risk exists. In short, the important role played by public inquiries justifies maintaining the general Canadian position of making witnesses compellable in all proceedings other than their own criminal

---

25   *Canadian Charter of Rights and Freedoms*, part I of the *Constitution Act, 1982*, being Schedule B to the *Canada Act 1982* (U.K.), 1982, c. 11 [Charter].

trials, so long as their right to fair process can otherwise be preserved. Although Cory J.'s opinion represented a minority position, it remains the clearest statement of the situation in Canadian law.

2. Balancing Reputational Interests

Wayne MacKay and Moira McQueen note that assigning blame for things that go wrong is often what members of the public mean by accountability:

> An integral part of this growing demand for accountability is the concept of blaming. When things go wrong, people want to know whom to blame for the state of affairs. ... The focus on blame is often justified by the argument that no remedial action can be effectively taken until the causes of a disaster or problem have been completely unearthed. However, this explanation is contradicted by the fact that public and media attention seems to die down fairly quickly once names have been named. ... This may suggest that what the public wants, and what public inquiries aim to achieve, is the public shaming of those found to have acted inappropriately, rather than tangible punishment.[26]

Although public inquiries cannot directly result in penal sanctions, damage to a person's reputation may result merely from having one's name mentioned at, or being called to testify before, a public inquiry, let alone being found in an inquiry report to be responsible for misconduct. For politicians, the damage done to reputation by a public inquiry may result in a lost election, as was the case for the Liberal government of Prime Minister Paul Martin in 2006 following the sponsorship inquiry.

In the *Krever Commission* case, Commissioner Krever served notices at the conclusion of the formal hearing process on approximately 90 individuals and organizations pursuant to s. 13 of the federal *Inquiries Act*,[27] which reads:

> No report shall be made against any person until reasonable notice has been given to the person of the charge of misconduct alleged against him and the person has been allowed full opportunity to be heard in person or by counsel.

The notices set out the possible findings of misconduct that might be made in the final report and invited the recipients of the notices to make a response to the commission before it reached its conclusions. Dozens of the recipients of notices sought judicial review, objecting to matters such as the timing and detail of the notices. The Supreme Court confirmed in its *Krever Commission* ruling that the potential harm to reputation justified procedural protections at common law including adequate notice. This right could enhance or "fill out" rights set out in the statute. The Court concluded that Commissioner Krever had provided reasonable notice and opportunity to respond.

---

26 A. Wayne MacKay & Moira G. McQueen, "Public Inquiries and the Legality of Blaming: Truth, Justice and the Canadian Way" in *Commissions of Inquiry, supra* note 23, 249-92 at 250-51. On the subject of inquiries and reputation also see Peter Doody, "Commissions of Inquiry, Fairness and Reasonable Apprehension of Bias: Protecting Unnecessary and Inappropriate Damage to Reputation" (2009) 23 Can. J. Admin. L. & Prac. 19.

27 R.S.C. 1985, c. I-11.

Citing *Starr v. Houlden*, several of the recipients of notices argued that inquiries lack the constitutional authority to make individual findings of misconduct or, in other words, that Commissioner Krever could not "name names." The Court distinguished its ruling in *Starr* by saying that it applied in the particular circumstances of an inquiry that was established solely to investigate acts of specific individuals. The Court also distinguished between an inquiry's making findings of "misconduct," which are permissible, and making findings of civil or criminal liability, which are not. The blood system inquiry was both a policy and an investigative inquiry and could only fulfill its broader policy purpose if it was allowed to make findings about individual responsibility for past decisions and actions. Justice Cory cautioned inquiry commissioners to avoid stating findings in terms that might convey the incorrect impression that they had found an individual to be civilly or criminally liable, but added that a commissioner "should not be expected to perform linguistic contortions to avoid language that might conceivably be interpreted as importing a legal finding."[28] Reputations might be harmed in the process. Although this possibility justified extending procedural fairness to the affected individuals, it should not stand, however, in the way of the inquiry's work:

> These findings of fact may well indicate those individuals and organizations which were at fault. Obviously, reputations will be affected. But damaged reputations may be the price which must be paid to ensure that if a tragedy such as that presented to the Commission in this case can be prevented, it will be.[29]

Peter Doody has argued that some of the fears concerning the Krever commission's fault-finding activity did indeed come true.[30] The commission report contributed to an RCMP investigation that resulted in charges of criminal negligence causing bodily harm against several blood system officials, all to great attendant publicity. Ten long years after the inquiry completed its work, the trial judge in the criminal matter acquitted the accused, and concluded, contrary to the inquiry's findings, that they had acted in an exemplary fashion. Benotto J. commented: "The events here were tragic. However, to assign blame where none exists is to compound the tragedy."[31]

II. Public Inquiries and Administrative Law Principles

Public inquiries are exercises in delegated government authority. For this reason, inquiries operate within the context of administrative law. The practice of lawyers before commissions of inquiry is an administrative law practice. The same skills that serve counsel who appear before labour boards, broadcast regulators, environmental review boards, and other tribunals also serve those who represent parties and witnesses at inquiry hearings. The same understanding of the principles governing the exercise of delegated public power will in-

---

28   *Krever Commission, supra* note 3 at para. 52.

29   *Ibid.* at para. 39.

30   *Supra* note 26 at 24–25.

31   *R. v. Armour Pharmaceutical Company*, 2007 CanLII 40864, 226 CCC (3d) 448 at para. 307 (Ont. S.C.), Benotto J.

form that practice. The major principles of administrative law concern the lawful delegation of authority, issues of procedural fairness, and the substantive review of governmental decision making. The discussion in this section of the chapter tracks these principles by looking at the following three subjects:

1. Establishing public inquiries, including terms of reference, constitutional limits on the scope of an inquiry, and the role and independence of commissioners of inquiry.

2. Procedural fairness issues—that is, the rules governing the conduct of the investigative and hearing process.

3. Substantive review of the rulings and findings of a commission of inquiry.

A. Establishing an Inquiry

1. Delegation of Authority

The power to call a public inquiry into a matter of governance was long understood to be a prerogative power of the Crown. In Canada, Parliament and nine provinces have adopted inquiry statutes that formalize certain aspects of inquiry activity.[32] Royal commissions and public inquiries are now appointed pursuant to the statutory provisions and clothed with the powers expressly set out by statute. In addition to general inquiry statutes, most jurisdictions make provision for inquiries to be conducted in specified areas of activity.[33] It is also not uncommon for regulatory statutes to authorize ministers of the Crown to appoint someone to investigate and report on a matter or an event, and to grant them the powers of a commissioner under the general inquiry statute.[34]

Inquiry statutes take the following general form. First, they set out the nature of matters that may be the subject of an inquiry. The federal *Inquiries Act* authorizes two kinds of inquiries, a Part I inquiry into "any matter connected with the good government of Canada or the conduct of any part of the public business thereof,"[35] and a Part II departmental inquiry into "the state and management of the business, or any part of the business, of [a] department."[36] The Nova Scotia statute provides for a broader mandate covering "any public matter in relation to which the Legislature may make laws,"[37] under which the provincial government

---

[32] *Public Inquiries Act*, R.S.A. 2000, c. P-39; *Public Inquiry Act, supra* note 10; *Inquiries Act*, R.S.N.B. 1973, c. I.11 (repealed); *Public Inquiries Act, 2006*, S.N.L. 2006, c. P-38.1; *Public Inquiries Act*, R.S.N.S. 1989, c. 372; *Public Inquiries Act, 2009*, S.O. 2009, c. 33, sched. 6; *Public Inquiries Act*, R.S.P.E.I. 1988, c. P-31; *An Act respecting public inquiry commissions*, R.S.Q., c. C-37; *Public Inquiries Act*, R.S.S. 1978, c. P.38. Manitoba does not have a public inquiries statute, but authorizes inquiries under other statutory instruments, including stand-alone statutes establishing individual inquiries and their terms of reference.

[33] See e.g. in Ontario the *Hospitals and Charitable Institutions Inquiries Act*, R.S.O. 1990, c. H.15.

[34] See e.g. the federal *Railway Safety Act*, R.S.C. 1985, c. 32 (4th Supp.), s. 40(2), with respect to investigations into railway accidents.

[35] *Supra* note 27, s. 2.

[36] *Ibid.*, s. 6.

[37] *Public Inquiries Act, supra* note 32, s. 2.

authorized the Westray inquiry into the operations of a private company (in addition to the regulation of mining activities).

Second, the statutes grant powers of compulsion to commissioners authorizing them to summon witnesses, place witnesses under oath, and cite for contempt, as well as to order production of documentary evidence. These are important investigatory powers that can only be granted by statute. Third, the statutes extend procedural protections to persons being investigated or persons who may be subject to adverse findings of fact in an inquiry report. These statutory procedural rights should be viewed as minimum protections that do not exclude additional protections provided by the common law of administrative law.

Governments in Canada usually initiate public inquiries by an order in council issued under the authority of an inquiry statute. This is not necessarily the case. However, a government that establishes an inquiry outside the authority of its inquiry statute may encounter questions about why it is doing so. This happened in Quebec in the fall of 2011. For two years media stories about corruption in the construction industry and its influence on local politics had swirled about. In October 2011 Premier Charest announced that his government would appoint Quebec Superior Court Justice France Charbonneau to head an inquiry into corruption in the construction industry. Premier Charest said that the government did not believe it necessary to establish the inquiry under Quebec's *Act Respecting Public Inquiry Commissions*[38] and clothe it with all the powers granted by that statute. Critics quickly raised doubts about the government's good faith. When Justice Charbonneau herself said that she needed the powers of the statute to adequately perform the task assigned to her, the government changed course. Premier Charest designated the inquiry by order under the statute, expanded its resources, and appointed two new commissioners to form an inquiry panel with Justice Charbonneau.

2. Appointing an Inquiry Commissioner

Governments can appoint whomever they wish to conduct public inquiries, subject to objections going to an alleged apprehension of bias (see below under the heading II.A.5, "Reasonable Apprehension of Bias"). With respect to investigative and combined inquiries, it is a common practice to appoint sitting or retired justices of a superior court. Nevertheless, inquiries are executive government functions. Justice David McDonald, who chaired the commission of inquiry into RCMP activities in the late 1970s, described the status of a sitting justice acting as an inquiry commissioner in these terms:

> The Commission is not a Court. It is not a branch of the judiciary. It fulfils Executive or administrative functions. … Very often a Judge is the sole commissioner or chairman of a group of commissioners. One reason a Judge is chosen is that his livelihood is secure in that he can be removed from office only by joint address of the Houses of Parliament. This fact, which lies at the root of the cherished independence of the judiciary, increases the likelihood that the inquiry will not be influenced by considerations to which ordinary segments of the Executive are

---

[38]   R.S.Q., c. C-37.

susceptible. Putting it another way, it ensures that the inquiry will be conducted at arm's length from the Executive.[39]

Dickson C.J. pointed out in *Re Residential Tenancies Act, 1979*[40] that because Canada does not operate on a strict separation of powers basis, members of the judiciary can carry out executive functions. This does not happen in the United States, for instance, where it would be unconstitutional for a federal judge to conduct an inquiry into governmental affairs.

In response to the common practice of sitting justices being named to conduct public inquiries, the Canadian Judicial Council (CJC) has developed a Protocol on the Appointment of Judges to Commissions of Inquiry.[41] The protocol seeks to assist judges who may be approached about taking on a commissioner's role and their chief justices with respect to the appropriate considerations for making the decision to accept. According to the CJC, such requests should always be made by a government first to the chief justice, not the individual judge. Relevant considerations are said to include the time the judge would be taken away from judicial duties and the terms of reference being proposed for the inquiry. This raises an interesting question: To what extent should a prospective commissioner of inquiry engage in discussions or negotiations with the government over the inquiry's mandate or terms of reference? Justice O'Connor, who conducted the Walkerton and Arar inquiries, agrees with the CJC that the discussions should be detailed and that the commissioner be satisfied that the mandate is one of public importance and is capable of being fulfilled on the terms proposed.[42] Nevertheless, as both the CJC and Justice O'Connor note, many inquiries deal with controversial matters. A commissioner may well be called on during the course of an inquiry to interpret the terms of reference under which he or she is operating. For this reason, it may make sense for a prospective appointee to leave the drafting of the substantive terms largely to government, while ensuring that matters dealing with inquiry resources and logistics are appropriately addressed.

3. Terms of Reference or Inquiry Mandate

Setting the mandate or terms of reference for an inquiry is a crucial step in determining what the inquiry is intended and able to achieve. By setting the terms of reference, governments exercise significant control over how far-reaching an inquiry will be. Of course, the more politically sensitive the subject matter is, the more likely opposition politicians, the media, and members of the public will take an active role in monitoring and shaping the government's decision making in this regard. In the case of alleged improper cash payments made

---

[39] *Re Commission of Inquiry Concerning Certain Activities of the Royal Canadian Mounted Police* (1978), 94 D.L.R. (3d) 365 at 370.

[40] [1981] 1 S.C.R. 714 at 728.

[41] See <http://www.cjc-ccm.gc.ca/cmslib/general/JIC-CIsc-protocol-finalE-August-2010.pdf>. The CJC has also developed a Reference Guide for Judges Appointed to Commissions of Inquiry: <http://www.cjc.gc.ca/cmslib/general/cjc_guide_judges_commissions_inquiry_en.pdf>.

[42] Dennis R. O'Connor & Freya Kristjanson, "Why Do Public Inquiries Work?" in Ronalda Murphy & Patrick Molinari, eds., *Doing Justice: Dispute Resolution in the Courts and Beyond* (Toronto: Canadian Institute for the Administration of Justice, 2007).

by German businessman Karlheinz Schreiber to former Prime Minister Brian Mulroney, Stephen Harper's Conservative government asked an outside individual, David Johnston, since appointed governor general of Canada, to give advice on whether an inquiry should be held and what its terms of reference should be. This move followed the previous government's decision to conduct a "pre-inquiry inquiry" into the Air India disaster before establishing the full public inquiry into that matter.[43] These actions represent attempts by governments to give the appearance of an independent, arm's-length process for deciding on the structuring of an inquiry. Nevertheless, the ultimate decision rests with executive government.

The terms of reference set out in an order represent the "law of the inquiry" and have binding force on the inquiry commissioner. Nevertheless, it is useful to remember that terms of reference are a form of delegated legislation, or regulatory law. In the case of the Somalia inquiry in the mid-1990s, the Federal Court of Appeal took the position that, as with other regulatory law, an inquiry's terms of reference can be modified by the executive at its discretion (see the discussion of independence under the heading II.A.4, "Independence of Inquiries," below).

The latter point was picked up in an interesting way by the British Columbia Court of Appeal in *British Columbia v. Commission of Inquiry into the Death of Frank Paul (the Davies Commission)*.[44] The commission was created to inquire into the circumstances surrounding the death of Frank Paul, an aboriginal man who died on a Vancouver street after being released from custody by police officers despite his being in a severely intoxicated and vulnerable state. The terms of reference included the phrase "to make findings of fact regarding circumstances relating to Mr. Paul's death, including findings of fact respecting the response of ... the Criminal Justice Branch of the Ministry of Attorney General to the death of Mr. Paul."[45] Commissioner Davies ruled that his mandate included investigating how and why the Crown had exercised its prosecutorial discretion not to lay charges against any of the police officers involved, and acceded to a request to subpoena former prosecutors (now judges) to testify. The Ministry of the Attorney General sought judicial review to quash this decision, arguing that the principle of prosecutorial independence made such questioning improper. The Court of Appeal dismissed the application. It said that the principle of prosecutorial independence had a basis in the separation of powers, but that as public inquiries are part of executive government, not the judiciary, the principle did not apply. Further, the court noted, citing the Federal Court of Appeal's decision in *Dixon*, the government could always change the inquiry's terms of reference if it wished to do so and was prepared to explain its actions to the public. In *Davies*, the B.C. Court of Appeal implicitly criticized the attorney general for having advised the provincial Cabinet on the inquiry's terms of refer-

---

43   See *Lessons to Be Learned: The Report of the Honourable Bob Rae, Independent Advisor to the Minister of Public Safety and Emergency Preparedness, on Outstanding Questions with Respect to the Bombing of Air India Flight 182* (Ottawa: Queen's Printer: November 2005), online: <http://www.publicsafety.gc.ca/prg/ns/ai182/repl-eng.aspx>.

44   *Supra* note 9.

45   *Ibid.* at para. 9.

ence, presumably including their constitutionality, and then turning around and applying for judicial review to obtain a narrow reading of those terms on constitutional grounds.[46]

The commissioner of an inquiry plays an important role in interpreting the terms of reference. The more brief or general the wording of the terms, the more interpretive work is necessary. Depending on how broadly the commissioner understands the scope of his or her inquiry, the more evidence will be relevant, the more questions will be probed, and the more witnesses will be called. This has significant implications for the cost and time needed for an inquiry, as well as for the nature of its findings. A commission's interpretation of its terms of reference is subject to judicial review. This is a form of "substantive review" (see discussion under section II.C, Substantive Review, below).

4. Independence of Inquiries

To what degree are public inquiries independent? The credibility and effectiveness of an inquiry depends very much on the degree to which it is and appears to be independent of executive government. It may be true to say, however, that the independence of public inquiries is more a matter of personal integrity, enforced at the level of politics, than a matter of law. As noted, inquiries are created by executive government, and the executive sets the terms of reference, time frames for reporting, and budgets, and appoints commissioners for an inquiry. While the constitutional principle of judicial independence protects the judicial careers of judges serving as commissioners of inquiry, it does not likely extend to an inquiry itself. In Chapter 8, Caught Between Judicial Paradigms and the Administrative State's Pastiche: "Tribunal" Independence, Impartiality, and Bias, Laverne Jacobs discusses the state of the law going to whether administrative tribunals of an adjudicative nature attract the constitutional principle of independence. Inquiries, of course, are not adjudicative bodies.

The clearest challenge to date to the independence of a public inquiry occurred with the Somalia inquiry. The evidence given at the public hearings of this inquiry into the abuse of Somalis in Canadian military custody caused considerable embarrassment to military and civilian officials and led to the resignation of the chief of defence forces. When the commissioners asked for a third extension of the deadline for the hearings and final report, the government of Prime Minister Chrétien refused. This decision effectively terminated the inquiry. A legal challenge alleging that the decision exceeded Cabinet's authority and violated the rule of law succeeded at first instance, but was rejected by the Federal Court of Appeal. Marceau J. stated:

> It has often been suggested, expressly or impliedly, especially in the media but also elsewhere, that commissions of inquiry were meant to operate and act as fully independent adjudicative bodies, akin to the Judiciary and completely separate and apart from the Executive by whom they were created. This is a completely misleading suggestion, in my view. The idea of an investigative body, entirely autonomous, armed with all of the powers and authority necessary to uncover the truth and answerable to no one, may well be contemplated, if one is prepared to disregard the risks to individuals and the particularities of the Canadian context. But a commission under Part I of the *Inquiries Act* is simply not such a body. ... All this, however, does

---

[46]   *Ibid.* at paras. 70-77.

not alter, in any way, the basic truth that commissions of inquiry owe their existence to the Executive. As agencies of the Executive, I do not see how they can operate otherwise than within the parameters established by the Governor in Council.[47]

The Federal Court of Appeal's decision in *Dixon* raises important questions concerning inquiry independence. It implies that an inquiry's terms of reference, which can be changed at will by Cabinet, do not provide a firm foundation for independence. However, fears that the experience with the Somalia inquiry will make it easier for governments to interfere in the operations of public inquiries have not borne fruit. Governments know that interfering with the mandate or the proceedings of a public inquiry in mid-course may not only undermine the inquiry's credibility, but also create a political firestorm. In this way, commissioners of inquiry are not powerless in their relationship with the executive that created an inquiry.[48]

Recent statutory reforms raise new questions concerning the independence of public inquiries. As noted, public inquiry statutes have replaced prerogative power as the source of government authority to initiate inquiries in all Canadian jurisdictions. This development occurred roughly between 1960 and 1980. Even so, most inquiry statutes remained brief, general statements of the authority that could be delegated to commissioners of inquiry. In the last four years, Ontario and British Columbia have rewritten their inquiry statutes, making them significantly more detailed and directive with respect to the conduct of public inquiries. The reform of Ontario's legislation is particularly noteworthy in this regard.[49] The Glaude inquiry raised concerns in that province about the risks of inquiries running "out of control." That inquiry is estimated to have cost $53 million and gone well past its intended completion date by the time it concluded in 2009. Almost immediately on its completion, the government of Ontario introduced new legislation that includes several provisions that set out limits and accountability measures on inquiry operations. Among other things, the *Public Inquiries Act, 2009* makes it a duty of an inquiry to be "financially responsible and [operate] within its budget";[50] allows inquiries to rely on forms of written and documentary evidence that would not generally be admissible in court proceedings;[51] bars inquiries from holding public hearings unless expressly so authorized in the order establishing the inquiry;[52]

---

47   *Dixon c. Canada (Gouverneur en conseil)*, [1997] 3 F.C. 169 at para. 13 (C.A.); leave to appeal to the Supreme Court of Canada dismissed, January 8, 1998. See critical comment on the Federal Court of Appeal decision by Inquiry Commissioner Peter Desbarats, "The Independence of Public Inquiries: Dixon v. Canada" (1997) 36 Alta. L. Rev. 252. It might be noted that concerns in the United States over the role of independent prosecutors not subject to executive or congressional supervision became a major issue in the year following the Somalia inquiry as a result of prosecutor Kenneth Starr's investigation into the private life of President Bill Clinton. See Cass Sunstein, "Unchecked and Unbalanced: Why the Independent Counsel Act Must Go" (2002) 38 American Prospect, online: The American Prospect <http://prospect.org/article/unchecked-and-unbalanced>.

48   It is worth noting that in the missing women inquiry, Justice Oppal requested a one-year extension of his mandate from the original date for reporting of December 31, 2011 to the end of 2012, but was given only six months to June 30, 2012, possibly putting significant time pressure on the Inquiry.

49   *Ontario Public Inquiries Act, 2009*, *supra* note 32. The legislation was brought into force on June 1, 2011.

50   *Ibid.*, s. 5(c).

51   *Ibid.*, s. 9(1).

52   *Ibid.*, s. 14.

and obliges a commission to deliver its final report on the date set out in the order.[53] A provision permitting the attorney general to release any unfinished work of an inquiry where it fails to provide its final report on time had not been proclaimed as of the time of writing.[54] While these legislative parameters have benefits in terms of clarifying responsibilities, they also have the potential for making inquiries more like ordinary government activities, subject to statutory mandates and ministerial oversight, and less like the independent operators they have often been viewed to be.

5. Reasonable Apprehension of Bias

The appointment of a particular individual as a commissioner of inquiry might be challenged on grounds of bias should that person have prior involvement with interested parties or a conflict of interest. Concerns of this nature were raised in public on the appointment of Wally Oppal as commissioner in the missing women inquiry. Mr. Oppal had served as attorney general of British Columbia from 2005 to 2009, and so had ministerial responsibility for the Crown's conduct of the Pickton trial, including decisions made by the Crown about how many murder charges to lay, and whether untried charges should be pursued after the initial convictions. No applications for Mr. Oppal's disqualification on this basis were brought to court prior to the inquiry's commencement.

Claims of bias on the part of commissioners have tended to arise more in connection with their conduct during an inquiry. The most striking finding of bias against an inquiry commissioner arose in the context of the sponsorship inquiry. Following the issuance of the phase 1 report that found Prime Minister Chretien responsible for maladministration of the sponsorship program, Chretien launched a challenge to Commissioner Gomery's impartiality. He cited a number of statements Justice Gomery made to the media during the course of the inquiry, including a description of Chrétien's ordering of autographed golf balls to give to other world leaders as "small town cheap." Justice Teitelbaum of the Federal Court of Canada agreed that the statements created a reasonable apprehension of bias on Justice Gomery's part, both with respect to a prejudgment of the issues before hearing all the evidence, and with respect to a predisposition against Chretien personally. In a tart judgment, Justice Teitelbaum expressed disapproval of a commissioner's commenting to the media during the conduct of the inquiry:

> The media is not an appropriate forum in which a decision maker is to become engaged while presiding over a commission of inquiry, a trial, or any other type of hearing or proceeding. Indeed, the only appropriate forum in which a decision maker is to become engaged is within the hearing room of the very proceeding over which he or she is presiding. Comments revealing impressions and conclusions related to the proceedings should not be made extraneous to the proceedings either prior, con- currently or even after the proceedings have concluded.

---

[53] *Ibid.*, s. 20(1).

[54] *Ibid.*, s. 20(4), which reads, "If a commission does not for any reason deliver its report, the Minister may publish any unfinished work of the commission, and that work shall be treated as if it had been published by the commission."

I stress that even in public inquiries where the purpose of the proceedings is to educate and inform the public, it is not the role of decision makers to become active participants in the media. First and foremost, a decision maker's primary duty is to remain impartial, with an open mind that is amenable to persuasion. It is only when all the evidence is heard and after deliberating on that evidence that a decision maker is to form conclusions and, finally, to issue a judgment or report on the basis of these conclusions.[55]

During the Somalia inquiry, Commissioner Mr. Justice Gilles Letourneau was reported to have made private comments about a witness before the inquiry to the effect that "Brigadier General Beno had not given straight answers and perhaps Beno had been trying to deceive." On learning of these remarks, Beno sought to have Justice Letourneau disqualified for having created a reasonable apprehension of bias. The Federal Court of Appeal (from which bench Justice Letourneau had been appointed to the inquiry) rejected Beno's application.[56] The Court distinguished between a public inquiry and a trial process for purposes of the bias test. Because an inquiry is not an adjudicative process, a more relaxed bias standard is appropriate. At the same time, the Court rejected the idea of going so far as to apply the "closed mind" test to inquiries:

> Depending on its nature, mandate and function, the Somalia Inquiry must be situated along the *Newfoundland Telephone* spectrum somewhere between its legislative and adjudicative extremes. Because of the significant differences between this Inquiry and a civil or criminal proceeding, the adjudicative extreme would be inappropriate in this case. On the other hand, in view of the serious consequences that the report of a commission may have for those who have been served with a section 13 notice, the permissive "closed mind" standard at the legislative extreme would also be inappropriate. We are of the opinion that the Commissioners of the Somalia Inquiry must perform their duties in a way which, having regard to the special nature of their functions, does not give rise to a reasonable apprehension of bias.[57]

6. *Constitutional Issues*

Delegated authority in Canada is subject to the constraints and obligations imposed by the Constitution. A government's decision to appoint an inquiry and its drafting of the inquiry's terms of reference may thus be open to constitutional challenge. Provincially appointed inquiries have been particularly subject to challenge on federalism grounds, especially with respect to whether they invade the federal jurisdiction over criminal law.

---

55   *Chrétien v. Canada (Ex-Commissioner, Commission of Inquiry into the Sponsorship Program and Advertising Activities)*, 2008 FC 802, [2009] 2 F.C.R. 417 at paras. 104-5; aff'd [2010] F.C.J. No. 1274 (C.A.) (QL) (oral reasons 26 October 2010, amended reasons 5 November 2010). For further discussion of the *Chrétien* case, see Chapter 8, Laverne Jacobs, Caught Between Judicial Paradigms and the Administrative State's Pastiche: "Tribunal" Independence, Impartiality, and Bias.

56   *Beno v. Canada (Commissioner and Chairperson, Commission of Inquiry into the Deployment of Canadian Forces to Somalia)*, [1997] 2 F.C. 527 (C.A.).

57   *Ibid.* at para. 26.

In the 1970s, a series of cases went to the Supreme Court of Canada addressing the jurisdiction of provinces to inquire into criminal activities, and into activities of the RCMP as a federally regulated institution. In *Di Iorio v. Warden of Montreal Jail*,[58] the Court permitted a Quebec inquiry into organized crime to proceed as falling within provincial jurisdiction over "the administration of justice" in s. 92(14) of the *Constitution Act, 1867*. A year later, in *A.G. of Que. and Keable v. A.G. of Can. et al.*,[59] the Court ruled that while a provincial inquiry may investigate wrongdoing by individual police officers, it may not examine the policies and management of the RCMP.

The division of powers has played a role in limiting the authority of provinces to establish public inquiries directed at establishing individual responsibility for acts of a potentially criminal nature. In *Starr v. Houlden*,[60] the Supreme Court found that the "pith and substance" of an Ontario inquiry was alleged criminal wrongdoing by individuals, and that this infringed on the federal government's criminal law power. The Court has since narrowed the holding in *Starr*. In *Consortium Developments (Clearwater) Ltd. v. Sarnia (City)*,[61] the Court rejected an application by a land developer to quash a judicial inquiry initiated by Sarnia City Council into certain land transactions after the police had closed a criminal investigation file on the matter. The Court found that the inquiry was properly directed at the "good government" of the municipality. Even should it turn up misconduct of a possibly criminal nature, the inquiry lacked the power to make criminal findings. Justice Binnie stated that the commissioner's duty to comply with common-law requirements of the duty of fairness were sufficient to protect the interests of the developer. The facts of *Starr*—which included quoting provisions of the *Criminal Code* in that inquiry's terms of reference—were described as unusual.

Public inquiries are bound by the *Charter of Rights and Freedoms* with respect to the exercise of coercive statutory powers, such as the powers to subpoena witnesses or documents. There may be an issue as to whether an inquiry, given its non-adjudicative nature, is subject to the Charter with respect to its fact-finding or recommendation-making functions. In *Blencoe v. British Columbia*,[62] the Supreme Court held that the Charter applies to human rights tribunals as governmental actors. It would seem likely that an inquiry would be viewed similarly, on the basis of the test set out in *Eldridge v. British Columbia*,[63] for entities implementing important government programs or policies. On the issue of the application of the Charter to administrative tribunals and executive agencies, see Chapter 12, The Charter and Administrative Law: Cross-Fertilization or Inconstancy?, by Evan Fox-Decent and Alexander Pless.

---

[58] [1978] 1 S.C.R. 152.

[59] [1979] 1 S.C.R. 218.

[60] *Starr, supra* note 24.

[61] [1998] 3 S.C.R. 3.

[62] *Blencoe v. British Columbia (Human Rights Commission)*, 2000 SCC 44, [2000] 2 S.C.R. 307.

[63] *Eldridge v. British Columbia (Attorney General)*, [1997] 3 S.C.R. 624.

B. Procedural Justice Issues

The status of investigative processes in administrative law is ambiguous. Investigations directed at ascertaining evidence, but not at the determination of legal rights and obligations, are not always subject to common-law rules of fair process. In *Knight v. Indian Head School Division No. 19*,[64] L'Heureux-Dubé J. stated that the question whether a function is final or merely preliminary in nature is a threshold question with respect to the duty of fairness. The most typical example of a "preliminary" function is the investigative stage of a decision-making process. That is, the investigation may be able to be conducted free of procedural obligations, so long as any final determination of legal rights does not occur until the evidence is tested in accordance with due process.

There is little doubt, however, that investigative inquiries are subject to the duty of fairness in administrative law.[65] This follows from three things. First, inquiry statutes authorize inquiries to compel the testimony of witnesses. This extraordinary power exposes witnesses to legal consequences, as well as denying them the right to remain silent in the face of public scrutiny and possible future prosecution. Second, the findings of fact of an inquiry carry with them significant consequences. Inquiry findings may be the closest our society comes to "received truth." Reputations can be made or broken as a result of these findings. Third, public inquiries generally operate like judicial hearings. It is neither difficult nor inappropriate for inquiries to be required to meet standards of fair process.

The particular requirements of fair process in any particular case depend on contextual factors.[66] Courts have frequently held that the investigative nature of public inquiries and the fact that they do not have decision-making power mean that they are subject to relaxed procedural standards and rules of evidence. The question each time is whether this is appropriate in light of the individual interests at stake in a particular inquiry.

The following discussion addresses several issues of fair process that arise frequently in the course of public inquiries.

1. *Inquisitorial Process*

Public inquiries employ an inquisitorial rather than an adversarial approach to adducing evidence. This means that the inquiry commissioners decide what evidence to call rather than any individual parties. The inquiry may receive and act on the advice of a witness or

---

64   [1990] 1 S.C.R. 653.

65   In *Taser International Inc. v. British Columbia (Commissioner)* (*Taser No. 1*), 2010 BCSC 1120, [2010] B.C.J. No. 802 (QL), the manufacturer of Taser weapons sought judicial review against the Dziekanski inquiry headed by Thomas Braidwood on grounds of breach of procedural justice. Justice Sewell of the B.C. Supreme Court addressed the threshold issue in procedural justice briefly, but then concluded, at para. 24:

> My review of the authorities leads me to the conclusion that the courts have readily found a duty to act fairly on the part of investigatory or inquiry tribunals and have focused their analysis on the nature and extent of the duty rather than on whether any such duty exists.

66   See *Baker v. Canada (Minister of Citizenship and Immigration)*, [1999] 2 S.C.R. 817, and generally the discussion in Chapter 5 by Grant Huscroft.

subject of investigation as to what other evidence and other witnesses to call, but is unlikely to cede its authority. A commissioner is charged with the responsibility of conducting a thorough investigation, but must do so in an impartial and non-prosecutorial fashion. Questions as to how to accomplish this task characterize many of the individual issues of fair process that arise in the course of an inquiry's proceedings. These issues will be more acute for inquiries investigating specific acts of alleged misconduct.

Public inquiries will generally produce procedural rules to govern the hearing process at the outset of the inquiry, dealing with matters of calling witnesses and examination and cross-examination, among others. Justice O'Connor established rules for the Arar inquiry that addressed these issues in the following way:

35. In the ordinary course Commission counsel will call and question witnesses who testify at the Inquiry. Counsel for a party may apply to the Commissioner to lead a particular witness' evidence in-chief. If counsel is granted the right to do so, examination shall be confined to the normal rules governing the examination of one's own witness in court proceedings, unless otherwise directed by the Commissioner.

36. Commission counsel have a discretion to refuse to call or present evidence.

(a) Commission counsel will lead the evidence from the witness. Except as otherwise directed by the Commissioner, Commission counsel are entitled to ask both leading and non-leading questions;

(b) Parties will then have an opportunity to cross-examine the witness to the extent of their interest. The order of cross-examination will be determined by the parties and, if they are unable to reach agreement, by the Commissioner;

(c) After cross-examinations, counsel for a witness may then examine the witness. Except as otherwise directed by the Commissioner, counsel for the witness is entitled to ask both leading and non-leading questions;

(d) Commission counsel will have the right to re-examine last.[67]

What is the status in law of an inquiry's published rules? In the *Phillips* case, Cory J. made the general statement that "the nature and the purpose of public inquiries require courts to give a generous interpretation to a commissioner's powers to control their own proceedings."[68]

Although the rules of an inquiry provide useful guidance to all parties and witnesses about how the hearings will unfold, the binding force of an inquiry's rules is questionable. On the one hand, disobedience of the rules might give rise to an exercise by a commissioner of his or her statutory contempt power. On the other, the rules should not be viewed as the last word on procedure before the inquiry. In the absence of an explicit statutory power to make procedural regulations, the rules adopted by an inquiry should be subject to judicial review for compliance with the principles of procedural fairness, either as a general matter or in specific applications.

---

[67] *Supra* note 22, "Rules of Procedure."

[68] *Phillips, supra* note 17 at para. 175.

2. Standing

Standing is the legal concept that defines who has a sufficient interest in proceedings to justify having a participant role in the process.[69] In ordinary legal proceedings, standing is limited to those persons who have a direct interest in the outcome. Standing tends to be an "all or nothing" proposition: a person is either a full participant with responsibility for carrying one side of the legal dispute or not a participant at all. For more on the issue of standing, see Chapter 5 by Grant Huscroft, From Natural Justice to Fairness: Thresholds, Content, and the Role of Judicial Review, and Chapter 7, Access to Administrative Justice and Other Worries, by Lorne Sossin.

The issue of standing in public inquiries is more nuanced. Who are the parties to a public inquiry? Inquiries are generally called in the public interest, with the intention that much of the population has an interest in the outcome. To the extent that an inquiry concerns wrongdoing, individuals who may be found responsible likely have interests at stake that support their right to participate in some or all of the inquiry's proceedings. The same may be true of "victims" of the wrongdoing. In addition, other organizations, such as non-profit societies, who do not have a personal stake in the proceedings but have a long-standing interest and expertise in the area of public policy under scrutiny, may wish to participate in the hearings. Standing can be granted in degrees, both in terms of the scope of participation (that is, whether the person gets to call witnesses, to question and cross-examine witnesses, etc.), and in terms of duration (that is, whether the person has these rights only for some part of the inquiry's hearings, but not for others).

In the Arar inquiry, Justice O'Connor adopted a "substantial and direct interest" test for full party standing. After receiving submissions from persons wishing standing at the inquiry, Justice O'Connor granted full party standing to Maher Arar and the attorney general of Canada, and standing "so far as the evidence affects" their interests to the Ontario Provincial Police, the Ottawa Police Service, and individual RCMP officers. He granted intervener standing to a coalition of non-profit organizations, including the Canadian Council on American-Islamic Relations, the Canadian Arab Federation, and Amnesty International.[70]

In the missing women inquiry, Justice Oppal distinguished between "full participants" and "limited participants." The former, which included families of the suspected victims of Robert Pickton, were those believed to have evidence of a factual nature to provide with respect to the historical events being investigated. They were given the right to access documents, cross-examine all witnesses, and make submissions to the commissioner on any points arising. Limited participants were organizations with strong policy interests but who would be given permission to cross-examine only select witnesses and to make final submissions only.[71]

---

69   In fact, both the British Columbia and Ontario inquiry statutes now refer to standing as "participation" and persons with standing as "participants" at the inquiry.

70   *Supra* note 22, see "Rules of Procedure."

71   See "Ruling on Participation and Funding Recommendations" (5 May 2011), online: Missing Women Commission of Inquiry <http://www.missingwomeninquiry.ca/wp-content/uploads/2011/05/RulingonParticipation andFundingRecommendations.pdf>.

3. Representation by Counsel and Role of Commission Counsel

It is generally accepted that parties to public inquiries may be represented by counsel in the proceedings. Section 12 of the federal *Inquiries Act* makes this a statutory right with respect to persons who are the subject of an investigation:

> The commissioners may allow any person whose conduct is being investigated under this Act, and shall allow any person against whom any charge is made in the course of an investigation, to be represented by counsel.

A more difficult question is whether witnesses called to testify at an inquiry are entitled to be represented by counsel and what role counsel may play. Subject to the requirements of fair process, this is a matter for commissioners to decide depending on the nature of the inquiry and of the evidence being sought. In the Arar inquiry, witnesses were permitted to have their own counsel present during pre-hearing interviews and at the hearing if their interests would not be adequately represented by counsel for a party. Counsel for witnesses were permitted to ask questions of their clients following examination in chief by commission counsel and cross-examination by counsel for parties.

Representation at an inquiry can be expensive given the period of time and amount of documentary material that may be involved. This is a serious barrier to access and participation. The Supreme Court of Canada has recognized a limited right to state-funded legal counsel in matters that implicate the rights of life, liberty, or security of the person protected by s. 7 of the Charter. Given the decision in *Blencoe*, however, the subject of an inquiry likely cannot successfully argue that he or she has a constitutional right to funded counsel.[72] The question of funding for counsel is therefore a decision for government to make on an inquiry-by-inquiry basis. In some instances, governments have provided funding for counsel for parties in the budget of an inquiry and delegated authority to distribute the funds to commissioners. More commonly, inquiry commissioners are asked by government to make recommendations concerning who should receive funding for counsel. Should a recommendation be refused, the inquiry commissioner would be placed in the position of deciding whether it would be fair to continue the proceedings.

Controversy over funding of counsel cast an early shadow over British Columbia's Missing Women Commission of Inquiry. Several groups representing women victims of violence and women living in Vancouver's downtown eastside sought and obtained participant status before the commission. However, the provincial government declined the commissioner's recommendation to fund counsel for those groups. The groups pulled out of the inquiry, which may well have consequences for how the inquiry's work and final report come to be viewed.[73] The groups alleged that the fact police organizations and individual officers would be well represented by government-funded counsel gives them a distinct advantage over unrepresented persons and groups making complaints about police conduct and thereby

---

[72] In *British Columbia (Attorney General) v. Christie*, 2007 SCC 21, [2007] 1 S.C.R. 873, a challenge to the imposition of a provincial tax on legal services, the Supreme Court rejected the argument that the unwritten constitutional principle of the rule of law could serve as a basis for a right to state funding of legal counsel.

[73] See e.g. "U.N. Intervention Sought in Oppal Inquiry," Vancouver Province (7 October 2011), online: <http://www2.canada.com/theprovince/news/story.html?id=dc3f7d95-7308-49af-b2c1-1aaba8237c82>.

render the process unfair. One response of the B.C. government was to say that counsel for the commission had the responsibility to ensure that all participants were treated fairly and to protect participants from any overly aggressive cross-examination by counsel for other participants.

Counsel for a commission of inquiry indeed has a unique role. Although commission counsel takes the lead in adducing evidence before the inquiry and does so in the public interest, he or she does not assume the role of a prosecutor in the proceeding. Rather, counsel works for and is selected by the commissioner. Justice O'Connor, who conducted the Walkerton and Arar inquiries, has described commission counsel as the "alter ego" of the commissioner. Justice O'Connor in fact chose the same lawyer, Paul Cavaluzzo, to act as commission counsel in both inquiries, having clearly established a good working relationship in the Walkerton proceedings. Counsel's responsibilities include advising the commission on matters of legal procedure, preparing the evidence in advance of hearing days, leading most witnesses through their evidence in chief, and increasingly, being a spokesperson for the inquiry and its chair.[74] Counsel must perform these functions in an impartial fashion that does not create an impression that the proceedings are adversarial. In the *Krever Commission* case, the Canadian Red Cross sought a ruling that commission counsel could not participate in drafting the final report because counsel had viewed confidential submissions not introduced into evidence at the inquiry. The Supreme Court of Canada found this objection premature, but agreed that in some circumstances the multiple roles of counsel could lead to an order for disqualification.[75]

4. Notice and Opportunity to Respond

The federal *Inquiry Act* requires that any person about whom a finding of misconduct may be made in a final report must be notified in advance and given an opportunity to respond. Section 13 reads:

> No report shall be made against any person until reasonable notice has been given to the person of the charge of misconduct alleged against him and the person has been allowed full opportunity to be heard in person or by counsel.

Section 13 is a statutory embodiment of the minimal fairness duty to give notice and an opportunity to be heard to persons who may be adversely affected by an inquiry's findings. However, the provision is unclear with respect to what constitutes a "charge of misconduct,"

---

74   Justice O'Connor enumerates six aspects to commission counsel's role. In addition to those just listed, he mentions maintaining communication with parties to the inquiry and participating in drafting the inquiry report. Justice Dennis O'Connor, "The Role of Commission Counsel in Public Inquiries" (2003) 22 Advocates' Soc. J. 17.

75   Cory J. wrote: "This argument too is premature, because there is no indication that the Commissioner intends to rely upon his counsel to draft the final report. ... However, in the unlikely event that the submissions also included material that was not disclosed to the parties, there could well be valid cause for concern. ... If the submissions did contain new, undisclosed and untested evidence, the Commissioner should not seek advice regarding the report from counsel who received the confidential submissions" (*Krever Commission, supra* note 3 at para. 72).

when in the process such notice should be given, and whether a "full opportunity to be heard" includes the calling of further evidence or only the right to make submissions after the evidence is in. In *Krever Commission*, several parties who received s. 13 notices argued that the delivery of notices at the conclusion of the hearing process denied them the opportunity to make full answer and defence. Cory J. disagreed. He pointed out that the statute did not specify any particular period of notice, and that while notices

> should be given as soon as it is feasible, it is unreasonable to insist that the notices of misconduct must always be given early. There will be some inquiries ... where the Commissioner cannot know what the findings may be until the end or very late in the process. So long as adequate time is given to the recipients of the notices to allow them to call the evidence and make the submissions they deem necessary, the late delivery of notices will not constitute unfair procedure.[76]

5. Disclosure

We earlier discussed the compellability of witnesses who face potential criminal prosecution. Closely related to this is the issue of the scope of discovery or disclosure powers of a public inquiry. The very purpose of investigative inquiries seems to support broad powers of discovery. These powers may, however, conflict with competing interests in confidentiality and non-disclosure. Common arguments of this nature include national security, solicitor–client privilege, rights of confidentiality to counselling records, and privacy interests.

In general, public inquiries benefit from the grant of statutory power to compel disclosure. It is up to inquiry commissioners to decide, in each case, what evidence they believe is necessary and relevant to their investigation. A commissioner could always decide not to pursue evidence by means of compulsory power. Where a commissioner issues a subpoena, a recipient who objects to production must make one of the following arguments: (1) the demand for disclosure or its statutory authorization is unconstitutional; (2) the evidence goes to a matter not within the terms of reference of the inquiry; or (3) the statutory authorization is not broad enough to include the particular demand for disclosure in the face of a competing interest. In other words, in light of the statutory power to compel testimony or disclosure, it will rarely be sufficient to argue that the demand is unfair at common law.

In considering the issue of disclosure, it is important to differentiate between disclosure to the inquiry and disclosure by the inquiry to the public. The latter is more a question of what can or must be done in public rather than in closed sessions or *in camera*, and is discussed in the section "Conducting Hearings in Public," below. The issue of disclosure per se goes to the power of the inquiry to obtain evidence, irrespective of claims of confidentiality or privilege.

With respect to handling national security information, Parliament has increasingly placed responsibility in the hands of judges to view information that the federal government claims is subject to a national security privilege, to decide whether in fact it is, and then to decide what part of it is disclosable in legal proceedings. That has been the general approach taken in inquiries looking at national security matters. In the Air India inquiry, commissioner John Major, a former justice of the Supreme Court of Canada, went public with his

---

[76] *Ibid.* at para. 69.

concerns that the inquiry would not be able to accomplish its mandate if the government did not change its position with respect to withholding evidence from the inquiry on national security grounds.

In *McKeigan v. Hickman*,[77] the Supreme Court dealt with the issue of claimed judicial immunity from disclosure. A Nova Scotia public inquiry held into the wrongful murder conviction of Donald Marshall sought to compel testimony and notes concerning the deliberations of the Nova Scotia Court of Appeal at the time when that court had conducted a review of Marshall's conviction. The justices opposed this demand. A majority of the Supreme Court of Canada concluded that, as a matter of judicial independence (a constitutional principle), judges cannot be summoned to answer questions concerning their deliberations. Several of the justices stated that the general language of the province's *Public Inquiries Act* should be read to accord with the power of superior court judges to issue subpoenas and order discovery in civil proceedings, and that the latter power has long been understood to be subject to judicial immunity.

Inquiries dealing with prosecutorial conduct have also raised issues going to immunity and privilege. As noted above, the Inquiry into the Death of Frank Paul led to a ruling by the B.C. Court of Appeal[78] to the effect that because an inquiry is an executive, not a judicial, function, a mandate given it to examine the exercise of prosecutorial discretion does not violate the separation of powers doctrine that underlies a principle of prosecutorial independence. Some of the most important and influential inquiries in recent Canadian history have been those dealing with wrongful convictions.[79] They have examined in detail the internal communications between and among police and prosecution officials.

In the absence of express statutory authority, however, inquiries would not likely be able to compel disclosure of communications falling within solicitor–client privilege. Other privileges, such as doctor–patient and counsellor–client privileges, have generally been viewed as having lesser status. Bryan Schwartz has argued that inquiry statutes should exclude access to counselling records from the purview of inquiries' powers of disclosure.[80]

6. Conducting Hearings in Public

As noted, carrying out the inquiry process in public is one way in which the inquiry achieves its social purposes. One expects that inquiry hearings will be held in public and be reported in the media unless there are strong counterbalancing factors that militate in favour of *in camera* proceedings.

---

77 [1989] 2 S.C.R. 796.

78 *B.C. (A.G., Criminal Justice Branch) v. B.C. (Commission of Inquiry into the Death of Frank Paul)* (2010,) 99 B.C.L.R. (4th) 26 (C.A.).

79 Such inquiries include those into the wrongful convictions of Donald Marshall in Nova Scotia and Guy Paul Morin in Ontario. See the useful discussion of wrongful conviction inquiries in Ratushny, *supra* note 5 at 67-85; see also *Searching for Justice: An Autobiography* (Toronto: Osgoode Society for Legal History, 2005) by Fred Kaufman, Commissioner of Inquiry in the Morin matter.

80 Bryan Schwartz, "Public Inquiries" (1997) 40 Can. Pub. Adm. 72-85.

The Arar inquiry dealt with matters of national security, and it was understood from the outset that parts of the evidence would be received in closed sessions. The terms of reference directed the commissioner to act with discretion in protecting the confidentiality of national security information disclosed to him by government agencies, but still left it to him to rule on those questions.[81] Justice O'Connor addressed the nature of his mandate in ruling on one of several motions dealing with a request for confidentiality:

> The government chose to call a public inquiry, not a private investigation. Implicit in the Terms of Reference is a direction that I maximize the disclosure of information to the public, not just in my report, but during the course of the hearings. The reason for that direction is consistent with what are now broadly accepted as two of the main purposes of public inquiries: to hear the evidence relating to the events in public so that the public can be informed directly about those events, and to provide those who are affected by the events an opportunity to participate in the inquiry process.[82]

The need to receive evidence in secrecy created a serious challenge to the inquiry's credibility, particularly in its early phases when it "disappeared" from public view for weeks and months at a time. Justice O'Connor dealt with this challenge in several ways. First, he provided a public summary of evidence received in closed sessions in September 2004. He granted access to certain confidential material to Mr. Arar for the purpose of preparing his evidence. While Justice O'Connor maintained the confidentiality of evidence and findings, which he concluded were properly protected for national security reasons, he largely succeeded in convincing Mr. Arar, the media, and other observers that the most important facts concerning the events in question had been opened to public scrutiny.

A sequel to the Arar inquiry was the Internal Inquiry into the Actions of Canadian Officials in Relation to Abdullah Almalki, Ahmad Abou-Elmaati and Muayyed Nureddin, conducted by former Supreme Court of Canada Justice Frank Iacobucci (hereafter, "the Iacobucci inquiry"). Justice O'Connor recommended that an inquiry be conducted into the circumstances involving the holding in Syrian custody of these three other Canadian citizens. The Iacobucci inquiry was conducted largely *in camera*, on the basis of extensive evidence that was not disclosed to the individuals concerned, and only partially disclosed to their counsel. One of those counsel, Jasminka Kalajdzic, has written a trenchant critique of the secretiveness of these inquiry proceedings.[83] She writes that although the inquiry's

---

[81] The Arar inquiry's terms of reference (*supra* note 22) stated:

    (k) the Commissioner be directed, in conducting the inquiry, to take all steps necessary to prevent disclosure of information that, if it were disclosed to the public, would, in the opinion of the Commissioner, be injurious to international relations, national defence or national security and, where applicable, to conduct the proceedings in accordance with the following procedures, namely,

        (i) on the request of the Attorney General of Canada, the Commissioner shall receive information in camera and in the absence of any party and their counsel if, in the opinion of the Commissioner, the disclosure of that information would be injurious to international relations, national defence or national security.

[82] Ruling Concerning RCMP Testimony (12 May 2005), online: *supra* note 22, under "Rulings."

[83] Jasminka Kalajdzic, "Outsiders: The Sources and Impact of Secrecy at the Iacobucci Inquiry" (2010) 36 Queen's L.J. 161.

findings largely vindicated the individuals' positions, it failed in meeting the broader purposes for which inquiries are held: informing and educating government and the public,
providing a measure of restorative justice to victims of mistreatment, and the socio-
democratic goal of fostering ethics in government activity. In her view, the lack of visibility
of the inquiry undermined these purposes.

The goal of investigative inquiries may be to bring little-known or unknown facts into
public light, but they are not adversarial proceedings, not should they need to rely on surprise. It is common practice now for commission counsel to interview prospective witnesses
in advance of their public testimony, so that counsel for all sides as well as witnesses will
have a good idea of what will be covered and said in open session. Whether a prospective
witness is entitled to be interviewed in advance or to receive notice of questions to be asked
in open session is a matter of what fairness required in the circumstances. Had an inquiry
commissioner published a rule to this effect, as did Justice O'Connor in the Arar inquiry, a
legitimate expectation of such a process would likely have been created for each witness.

C. Substantive Review

In Canadian administrative law the review of substantive decision making has long been
associated with notions of jurisdiction and the circumstances that justify or limit review by
the courts of findings on the merits made by statutorily delegated delegates. In *Dunsmuir v.
New Brunswick*,[84] the Supreme Court of Canada set a new course in substantive review. It
identified the appropriate approach, a "standard of review analysis," that looked to certain
factors to decide whether review of a decision should be conducted on one of two standards,
correctness or reasonableness. Reasonableness review is a deferential standard in which the
reviewing court allows the decision to stand so long as the court concludes it is supported
by logical and intelligible reasons or falls within a range of reasonable outcomes. Correctness review affords no deference and allows the reviewing court to substitute its view of the
right decision for that of the delegate.[85] Substantive review is relevant to public inquiries in
two principal respects: (1) the inquiry commission's interpretation of its mandate or terms
or reference; and (2) the inquiry's findings and recommendations.

1. Interpretation of Terms of Reference

As earlier stated, the terms of reference established for an inquiry are viewed as the "law of
the inquiry." A commissioner has authority to investigate only those matters identified by
the terms of reference. Like any such statement, however, an inquiry's terms of reference are
subject to interpretation. The commissioner's interpretation of the terms under which he or
she operates is subject to judicial review. The interesting question from the perspective of
substantive review is whether a court should apply a correctness or reasonableness standard
to that interpretation. Depending on the circumstances, a strong case may be made for

---

[84]   2008 SCC 9.

[85]   For detailed discussions of substantive review, the standard of review analysis, and review for reasonableness,
see Chapters 9 and 10 by Audrey Macklin and Sheila Wildeman, respectively.

either. Under the approach set out by the majority in *Dunsmuir*, correctness review may often apply to "issues of law," especially issues of a general nature. The interpretation of an inquiry's terms of reference involves an issue of law—but how general is it?

We can look to certain pre-*Dunsmuir* cases to see how courts have dealt with this issue. In early 2008, the Ontario Court of Appeal rendered judgment on a judicial review application brought by the government of Ontario and several police organizations challenging a ruling by Commissioner Normand Glaude concerning the scope of the inquiry into the handling by various public officials of complaints of child sexual abuse in Cornwall, Ontario over a number of years.[86] The government of Ontario established the inquiry in 2005 with terms of reference reading in part:

2. The Commission shall inquire into and report on the institutional response of the justice system and other public institutions, including the interaction of that response with other public and community sectors, in relation to:

(a) allegations of historical abuse of young people in the Cornwall area, including the policies and practices then in place to respond to such allegations, and

(b) the creation and development of policies and practices that were designed to improve the response to allegations of abuse in order to make recommendations directed to the further improvement of the response in similar circumstances.[87]

Justice Glaude interpreted this mandate as going to the manner in which police in Cornwall had responded to complaints of sexual assault made by minors at any time prior to 2005. The applicants for judicial review argued that the terms of reference limited the inquiry to look into how officials had responded to allegations that a child sex abuse ring existed in Cornwall at a certain limited period. A majority of the Court of Appeal agreed with the applicants and set aside Justice Glaude's ruling on the scope of the inquiry. The majority referred to the commissioner's interpretation of the inquiry's mandate as a "jurisdictional question," declined on that basis to defer to Commissioner Glaude's interpretation of the terms of reference, and found it both incorrect and unreasonable.

In *Stevens v. Canada (Attorney General)*,[88] former federal Conservative Cabinet Minister Sinclair Stevens applied to quash the report of Commissioner William Parker, who had led an inquiry into Stevens's activities while he was in government. Stevens argued that the commissioner had exceeded the jurisdiction given to him by the inquiry's terms of reference. The terms directed that an inquiry and report be made into

whether the Honourable Sinclair M. Stevens was in real or apparent conflict of interest as defined by the Conflict of Interest and Post Employment Code for Public Office Holders and the letter from the Prime Minister [Brian Mulroney] ... of September 5, 1985.[89]

---

86 *Ontario (Provincial Police) v. Cornwall (Public Inquiry)*, 2008 ONCA 33, [2008] O.J. No. 153 (QL).

87 See website for the Cornwall Public Inquiry at <http://www.attorneygeneral.jus.gov.on.ca/inquiries/cornwall/en/index.htm>.

88 2004 FC 1746, [2004] F.C. No. 2116 (O'Keefe J., December 15, 2004) (QL).

89 *Ibid.* at para. 6.

Justice O'Keefe of the Federal Court quashed the inquiry report, which found that Stevens placed himself in a conflict of interest on six occasions, on the basis that the commissioner exceeded his authority by developing his own definition of "conflict of interest" beyond that set out in the code in question. O'Keefe J. did not apply a standard of review analysis, but stated that a court should not adopt an "overly legalistic" approach to reviewing an inquiry's interpretation of its terms of reference, especially where the inquiry is directed at the alleged wrongdoing of a single individual.

The *Cornwall Inquiry* and *Stevens* cases suggest that reviewing courts may take a fairly strict jurisdictional approach, more akin to correctness review, to inquiry commissioner's interpretations of their mandates. However, post-*Dunsmuir* case law from the Supreme Court of Canada has moved in the direction of saying that when tribunals are engaged in interpreting the provisions of their own enabling statutes, they should be accorded deference. In a sense, that is what commissioners do when they interpret their terms of reference. This may point to a more deferential approach in future, at least in instances that do not put individuals' rights at risk.

2. Review of Inquiry Findings

Whether a person who is unhappy with the ultimate findings of fact of an inquiry is able to challenge them in judicial review is an interesting question. In *Dunsmuir* and subsequent cases, the Court has made it clear that fact-based determinations call for reasonableness, or deferential, review. Public inquiries, as we have seen, produce only findings of fact and policy recommendations, not decisions with legal consequences. We expect that inquiry reports would attract deferential review, if indeed they are reviewable at all. This appears to be the case. Following the release of the report and recommendations of the inquiry into the death of Robert Dziekanski at Vancouver airport, the manufacturer of Tasers sought to have the report quashed. The company raised both procedural and substantive grounds, alleging with respect to the latter that there was no evidence on which Commissioner Braidwood could base his findings that the use of conducted energy weapons like the Taser posed some risk of death or serious injury. Justice Sewell ruled that a study commission or phase two inquiry was not exercising a "statutory power of decision," making certain administrative law remedies unavailable. He further concluded that the inquiry's findings met a standard of reasonableness.[90]

Even if an applicant were to succeed in a substantive challenge to an inquiry's findings, questions remain about the nature of the remedies available through judicial review. This issue arose before Reed J. of the Federal Court Trial Division in *Morneault v. Canada*,[91] a case arising from the Somalia inquiry. Lieutenant-Colonel Paul Morneault had been involved in troop training in Canada prior to the troops' deployment to Somalia. The pre-deployment phase ended up being the only one of three time periods in the Somalia mission concerning which the commission of inquiry was able to complete its investigation and

---

90   *Taser International v. British Columbia (Commissioner) (Taser No. 2)*, [2010] B.C.J. No. 1578 at para. 52 (S.C.) (QL).

91   [1998] F.C.J. No. 501 (QL), 1998 CanLII 7647 [*Morneault*].

report, given the termination of the inquiry by the Chrétien government. In its report on this phase, the commissioners made findings of misconduct against Morneault with respect to the inadequacy of the training program. Lieutenant-Colonel Morneault applied to Federal Court to have these findings quashed. Reed J. first had to decide whether the finding of misconduct constituted a reviewable "decision" under s. 2(1) of the *Federal Courts Act*.[92] The respondent argued that mere findings of fact without legal consequences did not constitute a decision. Reed J. disagreed, ruling that the consequences of such findings for an individual's reputation made them a "decision," and thus subject to judicial review. Next, the Court needed to identify the appropriate standard of review for this issue of fact determination. Reed J. concluded that the standard should be patent unreasonableness.[93] Finally, the Court ruled that the commissioners had misconstrued some of the evidence and drawn improper inferences from other evidence, and that their findings of misconduct against Lieutenant-Colonel Morneault were indeed patently unreasonable. With respect to remedy, Reed J. ordered the following:

> What then is the appropriate disposition of his application? The Report has had wide public dissemination. The Commission no longer exists. I have concluded that the appropriate remedy is a declaration by the Court that the Commission's findings of individual misconduct against the applicant set out in chapter 35 of its Report are invalid. Also, as noted, he is entitled to a declaration that the record does not support a conclusion that the two general statements of condemnation found in the Report, identified above, apply to him. Declarations of invalidity will issue accordingly.[94]

A similar order was made by Justice Teitelbaum of the Federal Court of Canada with respect to Jean Chretien's successful judicial review application alleging bias on the part of Commissioner John Gomery in the sponsorship inquiry. Teitelbaum J. ordered that: "the findings in the Phase I Report of the commissioner, dated November 1, 2005, and relating to the Applicant, are set aside."[95] Such an order may provide a degree of solace to an individual who feels wronged by an inquiry's process and report. However, it does not change what was heard and said during the inquiry nor its conclusion. The Canadian public would likely be surprised to learn that the findings of the sponsorship inquiry, at least with respect to the role of the highest government officials, have been "set aside."

III. Public Inquiries and Public Benefit

In his political memoir *My Years as Prime Minister*,[96] former Prime Minister Chrétien engages in a pointed criticism of public inquiries. He defends his decision to shut down the Somalia inquiry in mid-course on the ground that it had become overly long, expensive,

---

[92]   R.S.C. 1985, c. F-7.

[93]   *Morneault, supra* note 91 at para. 59.

[94]   *Ibid.* at para. 114.

[95]   *Chrétien v. Canada, supra* note 55 at judgment para. (a).

[96]   Jean Chrétien, *My Years as Prime Minister* (Toronto: A.A. Knopf Canada, 2007).

and of benefit only to the many lawyers involved. After noting that "I never appointed another commission of inquiry," Mr. Chrétien writes:

> For the opposition parties, calling for a public inquiry is usually an easy way to dig up dirt or keep a hot issue on the front burner after they've exhausted their own supply of facts and questions. For the government, giving in to the calls is often a mechanism to do nothing, to dodge responsibility, or to postpone a controversial decision until after the next election. Very few of these inquiries in my experience have ever been of much use, and those few were valuable only because they didn't turn into television soap operas. ... But it is in the nature of public inquiries to get turned into show trials, kangaroo courts and political entertainment. The rules of evidence don't have to be respected as they are in a court. There's not the same right of due process or even the same process to protect the innocent during the investigation into a possible wrongdoing. Scores of reputations are shattered for no good cause.[97]

Of course, this comment was made in the shadow of the sponsorship inquiry report of Justice Gomery. Nevertheless, Mr. Chrétien's criticism is a good sharp summary of the major concerns about inquiries.

Have Canadian inquiries become overjudicialized and too expensive? Michael Trebilcock and Wendy Austin also asked this question following the Krever inquiry into Canada's blood system in the mid-1990s. The authors noted that the inquiry cost several times what had been budgeted for it, took over three years to complete, and involved the services of over 50 lawyers acting for the parties granted different forms of standing. Canadian public inquiries have indeed become highly lawyered enterprises. This may be an inevitable consequence of having inquiries into specific events with serious consequences in the lives of individuals. The need to respect individual rights is the principal explanation for the takeover of public inquiries by lawyers and judges, and the expenditure of time and money follows from the use of trial-like procedures. If public inquiries are intended in part to provide greater public access to government, it must nevertheless be recognized that this access is now largely filtered through the language and habits of judges and lawyers. To the extent that this is a matter of concern, it should lead to thinking about how the influence of the legal profession can be reduced where it is least needed, in policy inquiries.[98] The division between phase 1 and phase 2 processes might on occasion be helpfully taken one step further, by assigning a judge to the more forensic tasks of event investigation, while naming commissioners with different backgrounds to take the lead on the more consultative and prospective task of making policy proposals.

---

[97]   *Ibid.* at 187-88.

[98]   For a critique of the suitability of a judge to disentangle complicated issues of public administration, see Ruth Hubbard & Gilles Paquet, *Gomery's Blinders and Canadian Federalism* (Ottawa: University of Ottawa Press, 2007). The authors attribute what they view as Justice Gomery's penchant for overemphasizing individual blame for the failed oversight of the sponsorship program to his professional background (*ibid.* at 41-42):

> First, Gomery is a judge. He has been trained to adjudicate and to find guilt or innocence, and he can no more escape from this reality than a turtle can leave its shell. He is neither an organizational design specialist nor an expert in political philosophy or public administration.

However, we have seen that public inquiries have the potential to enhance public accountability in Canada's governing structures. Nowhere has this been more true than with respect to the justice system itself, especially the criminal justice system. The missing women inquiry is only one of many examples of inquiries that have been called to shine light on the actions and decisions of police and Crown officials. Some of the most revealing and important inquiries in Canadian history have been those dealing with wrongful murder convictions, such as those involving Donald Marshall, Guy Paul Morin, and Thomas Sophonow.[99] In Ontario, the Goudge inquiry into the state of pediatric forensic pathology following the revelation that pathologist Charles Smith had testified erroneously in several cases leading to the conviction of innocent persons pointed out numerous problems and needed reforms in the justice system.[100] Those trained in the law are used to thinking that procedural protections afforded in court proceedings, combined with the zealous advocacy promoted by the adversarial system and appellate review, are significant guarantees of fairness and transparency. The fact is, though, that many of the most important things that happen in the justice system take place out of sight of the public, and often under the protection of various immunities and presumptions of good faith that remove them from the scrutiny of the courts themselves. Public inquiries have proven to be an important adjunct to the proper administration of justice. That this is true with respect to one of our society's most open institutions of public authority makes it easier to understand the benefits public inquiries offer to governance in general.

SUGGESTED ADDITIONAL READINGS

BOOKS AND ARTICLES

Manson, Allan, & David Mullan, eds., *Commissions of Inquiry: Praise or Reappraise?* (Toronto: Irwin Law, 2003).

Ratushny, Ed, *The Conduct of Public Inquiries: Law, Policy and Practice* (Toronto: Irwin Law, 2009).

Roach, Kent, "Canadian Public Inquiries and Accountability" in P.C. Stenning, ed. *Accountability for Criminal Justice: Selected Essays* (Toronto: University of Toronto Press, 1995).

Ruel, Simon, *The Law of Public Inquiries in Canada* (Toronto: Carswell, 2010).

Van Harten, Gus, "Truth Before Punishment: A Defence of Public Inquiries" (2003) 29 Queens L.J. 242.

---

[99] See *Report of the Kaufman Commission on Proceedings Involving Guy Paul Morin* (1998), online: Ministry of the Attorney General of Ontario <http://www.attorneygeneral.jus.gov.on.ca/english/about/pubs/morin>; and Manitoba, *The Inquiry Regarding Thomas Sophonow* (2001), online: <http://www.gov.mb.ca/justice/publications/sophonow/toc.html>.

[100] See <http://www.attorneygeneral.jus.gov.on.ca/inquiries/goudge/index.html>.

CASES

B.C. (A.G., Criminal Justice Branch) v. B.C. (Commission of Inquiry into the Death of Frank Paul) (2010), 99 B.C.L.R. (4th) 26 (C.A.).

Canada (Attorney General) v. Canada (Commission of Inquiry on the Blood System), [1997] 3 S.C.R. 440 (Krever commission).

Chrétien v. Canada (Ex-Commissioner, Commission of Inquiry into the Sponsorship Program and Advertising Activities), 2008 FC 802, [2009] 2 F.C.R. 417.

Dixon v. Canada (Commission of Inquiry into the Deployment of Canadian Forces in Somalia), [1997] F.C.J. No. 985 (C.A.) (QL).

Phillips v. Nova Scotia (Commission of Inquiry into the Westray Mine Tragedy), [1995] 2 S.C.R. 97.

COMMISSIONS OF INQUIRY

At least since the late 1990s, commissions of inquiry at both the federal and provincial level have created websites for their proceedings. The websites generally include terms of reference, rules of procedure, rulings made by the commission on standing and other matters, a record of testimony, links to video of public hearings, research reports, and the final reports. This provides a wealth of material for further research into the events and issues studied in the inquiries. Provincial inquiries may be searched under their official names or the names of the inquiry commissioner. Federal inquiries now have their separate websites removed from the Internet at some point after conclusion. The website material is now stored by the Privy Council Office, online: Government of Canada Privy Council Office <http://www.pco .gc.ca/index.asp?doc=archives/topic-sujet-eng.htm&lang=eng&page=information&sub =commissions>.

The site also provides online access to the final reports of all federal inquiries and royal commissions going back to Confederation.

Table of Administrative Boards and Tribunals

Jurisdiction	Name	Legislation
Canada (Federal)	Canada Agricultural Review Tribunal <http://cart-crac.gc.ca/CART-CRAC>	*Canada Agricultural Products Act* (CAPA) (1985) Rules of the Review Tribunal (Agriculture and Agri-Food) (CAPA) *Agriculture and Agri-Food Administrative Monetary Penalties Act* (AA-FAMPA) (1995) Agriculture and Agri-Food Administrative Monetary Penalties Regulations [respecting animals and plants] (AA-FAMPA) Agriculture and Agri-Food Administrative Monetary Regulations respecting the Pest Control Products Act and Regulations (AA-FAMPA) *Health of Animals Act* (HAA) (1990) Health of Animals Regulations (HAA) *Plant Protection Act* (PPA) (1990) Plant Protection Regulations (PPA) *Pest Control Products Act* (PCPA) (2002) Pest Control Products Regulations (PCPA)
	Canadian Artists and Producers Professional Relations Tribunal <http://www.capprt-tcrpap.gc.ca/eic/site/capprt-tcrpap.nsf/eng/home>	*Status of the Artist Act* (SAA) (1992) Canadian Artists and Producers Professional Relations Tribunal Procedural Regulations (SAA)

Jurisdiction	Name	Legislation
Canada (Federal) (continued)	Canadian Forces Grievance Board <http://www.cfgb-cgfc.gc.ca>	*National Defence Act* (NDA) (1985) Canadian Forces Grievance Board Rules of Procedure (Review of a Grievance by Way of a Hearing) (NDA)
	Commission for Public Complaints Against the RCMP <http://www.cpc-cpp.gc.ca>	*Royal Canadian Mounted Police Act* (RCMPA) (1985) Commissioner's Standing Orders (Public Complaints) (RCMPA) Royal Canadian Mounted Police Public Complaints Commission Rules of Practice (RCMPA)
	Hazardous Materials Information Review Commission <http://www.hmirc-ccrmd.gc.ca>	*Hazardous Materials Information Review Act* (HMIRA) (1985) Hazardous Materials Information Review Act Appeal Board Procedures Regulations (HMIRA)
		Hazardous Materials Information Review Regulations (HMIRA) Order Designating the National Capital Region as the Place of the Head Office of the Hazardous Materials Information Review Commission (HMIRA) *Hazardous Products Act* (1985)
	Military Police Complaints Commission of Canada <http://www.mpcc-cppm.gc.ca>	*National Defence Act* (1985)
	National Parole Board <http://pbc-clcc.gc.ca>	*Corrections and Conditional Release Act* (CCRA) (1992) Corrections and Conditional Release Regulations (CCRA) *Criminal Code* (1985) *Criminal Records Act* (1985) *Access to Information Act* (1985) *Privacy Act* (1985) *Canadian Multiculturalism Act* (1985)
	Patented Medicine Prices Review Board <http://www.pmprb-cepmb .gc.ca>	*Patent Act* (1985) Patented Medicines Regulations (*Patent Act*)

Jurisdiction	Name	Legislation
Canada (Federal) (continued)	Pension Appeals Board <http://www.pab-cap.gc.ca/ index-eng.cfm>	*Old Age Security Act* (OASA) (1985) Old Age Security Regulations (OASA) *Canada Pension Plan* (CPP) (1985) Canada Pension Plan Regulations (CPP) Pension Appeals Board Rules of Procedure (Benefits) (CPP) *Pension Benefits Standards Act* (PBSA) (1985) Pension Benefits Standards Regulations (PBSA)
	Public Service Labour Relations Board <http://www.pssrb-crtfp.gc.ca>	*Public Service Labour Relations Act* (PSLRA) (2003) Public Service Labour Relations Board Regulations (PSLRA) P.S.S.R.B. Regulations and Rules of Procedure (PSLRA) *Financial Administration Act* (1985) *Canada Labour Code* (1985) *Canadian Human Rights Act* (1985) *Parliamentary Employment and Staff Relations Act* (PESRA) (1985) PESRA Regulations and Rules of Procedure (PESRA)
	Specific Claims Tribunal Canada <http://www.sct-trp.ca>	*Specific Claims Tribunal Act* (SCTA) (2008) Specific Claims Tribunal Rules of Practice and Procedure (SCTA)
British Columbia	British Columbia Securities Commission <http://www.bcsc.bc.ca>	*Securities Act* (1996) Note: The Commission administers 44 regulations, BC Instruments and National Instruments, all enacted pursuant to the *Securities Act.*
	Building Code Appeal Board <http://www.housing.gov.bc .ca/bcab>	*Local Government Act* (LGA) (1996) British Columbia Building Code Regulation (LGA)
	Community Care and Assisted Living Appeal Board <http://www.ccalab.gov.bc.ca>	*Community Care and Assisted Living Act* (2002)

Jurisdiction	Name	Legislation
British Columbia (continued)	Expropriation Compensation Board <http://www.ecb.gov.bc.ca>	*Expropriation Act* (EA) (1996) Expropriation Act General Regulation (EA) Expropriation Proceeding Cost Regulation (EA) Tariff of Costs Regulation (EA) The Compensation Action Procedure Rule (EA)
	Forest Appeals Commission <http://www.fac.gov.bc.ca>	*Forest Practices Code of British Columbia Act* (FPCBCA) (1996) *Forest and Range Practices Act* (FRPA) (2002) Administrative Orders and Remedies Regulation (FRPA) Administrative Review and Appeal Procedure Regulation (FPCBCA and FRPA) *Forest Act* (1996) *Private Managed Forest Land Act* (2003) *Range Act* (2004) *Wildfire Act* (2004)
	Hospital Appeal Board <http://www.hab.gov.bc.ca>	*Hospital Act* (HA) (1996) Hospital Act Regulation (HA)
	Office of the Information and Privacy Commissioner <http://www.oipc.bc.ca>	Freedom of Information and Protection of Privacy Act (1996) *Personal Information Protection Act* (2003)
	Real Estate Council of British Columbia <http://www.recbc.ca>	*Real Estate Services Act* (RESA) (2004) Real Estate Services Regulation (RESA) *Real Estate Development Marketing Act* (REDMA) (2004) Real Estate Development Marketing Regulation (REDMA)

Jurisdiction	Name	Legislation
Alberta	Agricultural Products Marketing Council Appeal Tribunal <http://www1.agric.gov.ab.ca/general/progserv.nsf/all/pgmsrv109>	*Marketing of Agricultural Products Act* (MAPA) (2000) Review and Appeal Regulation (MAPA)
	Alberta Barley Commission <http://www.albertabarley.com>	*Marketing of Agricultural Products Act* (MAPA) (2000) Alberta Barley Commission Authorization Regulation (MAPA) Alberta Barley Commission Regulation (MAPA) Alberta Barley Plan Regulation (MAPA)
	Alberta College of Medical Diagnostic & Therapeutic Technologists <http://www.acmdtt.com>	*Health Professions Act* (HPA) (2000) Medical Diagnostic and Therapeutic Technologists and Electroneurophysiologists Profession Regulation (HPA)
	Alberta Gaming and Liquor Commission <http://aglc.ca>	*Gaming and Liquor Act* (GLA) (2000) Gaming and Liquor Regulation (GLA) *Criminal Code* (1985) *Tobacco Tax Act* (2000) *Horse Racing Alberta Act* (2000)
	Alberta Irrigation Council <http://www1.agric.gov.ab.ca/$department/deptdocs.nsf/all/irc9440>	*Irrigation Districts Act* (2000)
	Alberta Podiatry Association <http://www.albertapodiatry.com>	*Podiatry Act* (PA) (2000) By-Laws of the Alberta Podiatry Association (PA)

Jurisdiction	Name	Legislation
Alberta (continued)	Environmental Appeals Board <http://www.eab.gov.ab.ca>	*Environmental Protection and Enhancement Act* (EPEA) (2000) Environmental Appeal Board Regulation (EPEA) Environmental Protection and Enhancement (Miscellaneous) Regulation (EPEA) *Water Act* (2000) *Climate Change and Emissions Management Act* (2003) *Government Organization Act* (2000)
	Metis Settlements Appeal Tribunal <http://www.msat.gov.ab.ca>	*Metis Settlements Act* (MSA) (2000) Metis Settlements Land Registry Regulation (MSA) Land Interests Conversion Regulation (MSA) Metis Settlements Subdivision Regulation (MSA)
Saskatchewan	Board of Revenue Commissioners <http://www.gov.sk.ca/BRC>	*Revenue and Financial Services Act* (1983) *Freehold Oil and Gas Production Tax Act* (1982) *Mineral Taxation Act* (1983) *Crown Minerals Act* (1984) *Municipal Employees' Pension Act* (1978) *Cities Act* (2002) *Municipalities Act* (2005) *The Northern Municipalities Act* (2010) The Lloydminster Charter, Alta. Reg. 43/1979 (*City of Lloydminster Act*, SA 2005)
	Denturist Society of Saskatchewan <http://www.saskdenturists.ca>	*Dental Disciplines Act* (1997)
	Registered Psychiatric Nurses of Saskatchewan <http://rpnascom.jumpstartdev.com>	*Registered Psychiatric Nurses Act* (1993)

Jurisdiction	Name	Legislation
Saskatchewan (continued)	Saskatchewan Association of Licensed Practical Nurses <http://www.salpn.com>	*Licensed Practical Nurses Act, 2000*
	Saskatchewan Real Estate Commission <http://www.srec.ca/legis.asp>	*The Real Estate Act* (REA) (1997) Real Estate Regulations (REA)
	Saskatchewan Registered Nurses' Association <http://www.srna.org>	*Registered Nurses Act* (1988)
Manitoba	Automobile Injury Compensation Appeal Commission <http://www.gov.mb.ca/fs/cca/auto/index.html>	*Manitoba Public Insurance Corporation Act* (1987)
	Clean Environment Commission <http://www.cecmanitoba.ca>	*The Environment Act* (TEA) (1988) Participant Assistance Regulation 125/91 (TEA) *The Contaminated Sites Remediation Act* (1996) *The Drinking Water Safety Act* (2004) *The Sustainable Development Act* (1997)
	Manitoba Boxing Commission <http://www.manitobaboxingcommission.com>	*The Boxing Commission Act* (TBCA) (1993) Boxing Regulation (TBCA)
	Manitoba Film Classification Board <http://www.gov.mb.ca/chc/mfcb>	*The Amusements Act* (TAA) (1991-1992) Film Classification and Licensing Regulation (TAA) Manitoba Film Classification Board Forms and Advertising Regulation (TAA)
	Manitoba Horse Racing Commission <http://www.manitobahorsecomm.org>	*The Horse Racing Commission Act* (THRCA) (1991-1992) Horse Racing Commission Regulation 10/91 (THRCA) Racing Days Regulation (THRCA)

Jurisdiction	Name	Legislation
Ontario	Board of Directors of Drugless Therapy – Naturopathy <http://www .boardofnaturopathicmedicine .on.ca>	*Drugless Practitioners Act* (DPA) (1990) *Naturopathy Act, 2007* General (Regulations) (DPA)
	Board of Funeral Services <http://www.funeralboard.com>	*Funeral Directors and Establishments Act* (FDEA) (1990) Composition of Board (Regulations) (FDEA)
	Board of Negotiation (under the *Environmental Protection Act*) <http://www.pas.gov.on.ca/scripts/ en/boardDetails.asp?boardID=754>	*Environmental Protection Act* (EPA) (1990) Note: There are 81 specific environmental regulations enacted pursuant to the EPA.
	Child and Family Services Review Board <http://www.cfsrb.ca>	*Child and Family Services Act* (1990) *Intercountry Adoption Act, 1998* *Education Act* (1990)
	College of Respiratory Therapists of Ontario <http://www.crto.on.ca>	*Respiratory Therapy Act, 1991* (RTA, 1991) *Regulated Health Professions Act, 1991* *Personal Health Information Protection Act, 2004* Professional Misconduct (Regulations) (RTA, 1991) General (Regulations) (RTA, 1991) *Controlled Drugs and Substances Act* (CDSA) (1996) Narcotic Control Regulations (CDSA) *Personal Information Protection and Electronic Documents Act* (2000)
	Conservation Review Board <http://www.crb.gov.on.ca>	*Ontario Heritage Act* (1990)

Jurisdiction	Name	Legislation
Ontario (continued)	Financial Services Tribunal <http://www.fstontario.ca>	*Financial Services Commission of Ontario Act, 1997* *Pension Benefits Act* (1990) *Insurance Act* (1990) *Mortgage Brokerages, Lenders and Administrators Act, 2006* *Loan and Trust Corporations Act* (1990) *Credit Unions and Caisses Populaires Act, 1994* *Co-operative Corporations Act* (1990)
	Health Services Appeal and Review Board <http://www.hsarb.on.ca>	Ministry of Health Appeal and Review Boards Act (1998) Note: Monitors 14 different statutes.
	Landlord and Tenant Board <http://www.ltb.gov.on.ca>	*Residential Tenancies Act, 2006* (RTA, 2006) General (Regulations) (RTA, 2006)
	Ontario Special Education Tribunal <http://www.oset-tedo.ca>	*Education Act* (EA) (1990) Identification and Placement of Exceptional Pupils (Regulations) (EA) *Freedom of Information and Protection of Privacy Act* (1990)
	Tarion Warranty Authority <http://www.tarion.com>	*Ontario New Home Warranties Plan Act* (ONHWPA) (1990) Designation of Corporation (Regulations) (ONHWPA) Terms and Conditions of Registration of Builders and Vendors (Regulations) (ONHWPA) Warranty for Delayed Closing or Delayed Occupancy (Regulations) (ONHWPA) Building Code (Regulations) (*Building Code Act, 1992*)

Jurisdiction	Name	Legislation
Ontario (continued)	Technical Standards and Safety Authority <http://www.tssa.org>	*Technical Standards and Safety Act, 2000* (TSSA, 2000) Amusement Devices (Regulations) (TSSA, 2000) Boilers and Pressure Vessels (Regulations) (TSSA, 2000) Certification and Training of Amusement Device Mechanics (Regulations) (TSSA, 2000) Certification and Training of Elevating Device Mechanics (Regulations) (TSSA, 2000) Certification of Petroleum Equipment Mechanics (Regulations) (TSSA, 2000) Codes and Standards Adopted by Reference (Regulations) (TSSA, 2000) Compressed Gas (Regulations) (TSSA, 2000) Elevating Devices (Regulations) (TSSA, 2000) Fuel Industry Certificates (Regulations) (TSSA, 2000) Fuel Oil (Regulations) (TSSA, 2000) Gaseous Fuels (Regulations) (TSSA, 2000) Liquid Fuels (Regulations) (TSSA, 2000) Oil and Gas Pipeline Systems (Regulations) (TSSA, 2000) Operating Engineers (Regulations) (TSSA, 2000) Propane Storage and Handling (Regulations) (TSSA, 2000) Upholstered and Stuffed Articles (Regulations) (TSSA, 2000)

Jurisdiction	Name	Legislation
Quebec	Chambre des notaires du Québec—Committee on Discipline <http://www.cdnq.org/en/protectionDuPublic/committeeDiscipline.html>	*Notaries Act* (NA) (2000) Règlement sur le Comité d'inspection professionnelle de la Chambre des notaires du Québec, R.R.Q., c. N-3, r. 3 (NA)
	Commission des droits de la personne et des droits de la jeunesse (Human Rights Tribunal) <http://www.justice.gouv.qc.ca/english/tribunaux/trib-droi-a.htm>	Quebec *Charter of Human Rights and Freedoms* (Quebec Charter) (1975) Code of ethics of the members of the Human Rights Tribunal (Quebec Charter) Regulation respecting the procedure for the recruitment and selection of persons apt for designation to the function of arbitrator or appointment to the function of assessor with the Human Rights Tribunal (Quebec Charter) Regulation respecting the handling of complaints and the procedure applicable to the investigations of the Commission des droits de la personne et des droits de la jeunesse (Quebec Charter) Rules of procedure and practice of the Human Rights Tribunal (Quebec Charter)
	Cree Naskapi Commission <http://www.creenaskapicommission.net>	*Loi sur les Cris et les Naskapis du Québec* (LCNQ) (1984) Désignation de la ville d'Ottawa comme le lieu du siège de la Commission crie-naskapie (Regulations) (LCNQ)
	Régie des marchés agricoles et alimentaires du Québec <http://www.rmaaq.gouv.qc.ca>	*An Act respecting the marketing of agricultural, food and fish products* (1990) Note: There are 289 regulations enacted pursuant to this Act currently in force. A further 185 regulations are repealed or spent and no longer in force.

Jurisdiction	Name	Legislation
Quebec (continued)	Tribunal administratif du Québec <http://www.taq.gouv.qc.ca/en>	*Administrative Justice Act* (AJA) (1996) Rules of procedure of the Administrative Tribunal of Quebec (AJA) Code of ethics applicable to the members of the Administrative Tribunal of Quebec (AJA) Regulation respecting the procedure for the recruitment and selection of persons apt for appointment as members of the Administrative Tribunal of Quebec (AJA)
	Tribunal des professions <http://www.justice.gouv.qc.ca/ english/tribunaux/trib-prof-a .htm> <http://www.tribunaux.qc.ca/ Tribunal_professions/index_ professions.html>	*Professional Code* (PC) (1973) Regulation of the Professions Tribunal (PC) Note: There are 654 additional regulations in force pursuant to the *Professional Code*. The Tribunal des professions is the appellate level from the various administrative bodies that apply these regulations at first instance.
New Brunswick	Consumer Advocate for Insurance <http://www.insurance-assurance .ca>	*Consumer Advocate for Insurance Act* (2004) *Insurance Act* (1973)
	Farm Land Identification Appeal Board, New Brunswick Agriculture and Aquaculture <http://www2.gnb.ca/content/gnb /en/services/services_renderer .14296.html>	*Real Property Tax Act* (RPTA) (1988) Farm Land Identification Regulation 84-75 (RPTA)
	New Brunswick Dental Society <http://www.nbdental.com>	*New Brunswick Dental Act, 1985*
Nova Scotia	Adoption Appeal Committee <http://www.gov.ns.ca/exec_ council/abc/pubs/adjudicative/ adopt-appeal.pdf>	*Adoption Information Act* (1996)

Jurisdiction	Name	Legislation
Nova Scotia (continued)	Crop and Livestock Insurance Arbitration Board <http://www.gov.ns.ca/exec_council/abc/pubs/adjudicative/crop&livestk-arbit.pdf>	*Crop and Livestock Insurance Act* (CLIA) (1989) Arbitration Proceedings Regulations (CLIA)
	Dairy Farmers of Nova Scotia organization (previously the Diary Commission) <http://www.dfns.ca>	*Dairy Industry Act* (DIA) (2000) Dairy Farmers of Nova Scotia By-laws (DIA)
	The Disabled Persons Commission (Nova Scotia) <http://www.gov.ns.ca/disa>	*Disabled Persons Commission Act* (1989)
	Elevators and Lifts Appeal Board <http://www.gov.ns.ca/lae/elab> <http://www.gov.ns.ca/exec_council/abc/pubs/adjudicative/Elevators.pdf>	*Elevators and Lifts Act* (ELA) (2002) Elevators and Lifts General Regulations (ELA)
	Freedom of Information and Protection of Privacy Review Office <http://foipop.ns.ca>	*Freedom of Information and Protection of Privacy Act* (FOIPOPA) (1993) Part XX of the *Municipal Government Act* (1998) *Privacy Review Officer Act* (2008) Freedom of Information and Protection of Privacy Regulations (FOIPOPA)
	Pay Equity Commission <http://www.gov.ns.ca/lae/payequity>	*Pay Equity Act* (PEA) (1989) Pay Equity Commission Procedures Regulations (PEA)
	Private Career College Board <http://www.gov.ns.ca/nsarm/gaho/authority.asp?ID=88> <http://www.gov.ns.ca/exec_council/abc/pubs/adjudicative/Private_Career_College.pdf>	*Private Career Colleges Regulation Act* (PCCRA) (1998) Private Career Colleges General Regulations (PCCRA)
	Student Aid Appeal Committee (a.k.a. Student Assistance Higher Appeal Board) <http://studentloans.ednet.ns.ca/content/appeal-boards>	*Student Aid Act* (SAA) (1998) Nova Scotia Student Aid Appeal Committee Regulations (SAA)

Jurisdiction	Name	Legislation
Prince Edward Island	Industrial Relations Council	*Labour Act* (1988)
	Prince Edward Island Social Work Registration Board <http://www.socialworkpei.ca/regisboard.html>	*Social Work Act* (SWA) (1988) Certification Regulations (SWA) Standards and Discipline Regulations (SWA)
	Regulatory and Appeals Commission <http://www.irac.pe.ca>	*Island Regulatory and Appeals Commission Act* (1988)
Newfoundland and Labrador	Income and Employment Support Appeal Board <http://www.hrle.gov.nl.ca/hrle/income-support/appealprocess.html>	*Income and Employment Support Act* (IESA) (2002) Income and Employment Support Regulations (IESA)
	Newfoundland Board of Dispensing Opticians	*Dispensing Opticians Act* (DOA) (2005) Dispensing Opticians Regulations (DOA)
	Royal Newfoundland Constabulary Public Complaints Commission <http://www.justice.gov.nl.ca/rncpcc>	*Royal Newfoundland Constabulary Act* (RNCA) (1992) Royal Newfoundland Constabulary Public Complaints Regulations (RNCA)
Yukon	Social Assistance Review Committee, Yukon Health and Social Services <http://www.hss.gov.yk.ca/sarc.php>	*Social Assistance Act* (SAA) (2002) Social Assistance Regulation (SAA) Social Assistance Review Committee Remuneration Regulation (SAA)
	Yukon Surface Rights Board <http://www.yukonsurfacerights.com>	*Yukon Surface Rights Board Act* (1994) *Placer Mining Act* (2003) *Quartz Mining Act* (2003) Individual Yukon First Nation Final Agreements
	Yukon Utilities Board <http://www.yukonutilitiesboard.yk.ca>	*Public Utilities Act* (2002) Note: There are a dozen regulations and directives issued pursuant to the *Public Utilities Act*, most focused at specific utilities projects.

Jurisdiction	Name	Legislation
Northwest Territories	Aboriginal Languages Revitalization Board	*Official Languages Act* (OLA) (1988) Aboriginal Languages Revitalization Board Regulations (OLA)
	Inuvialuit Environmental Impact Review Board <http://www.eirb.ca>	Inuvialuit Final Agreement (1984)
	Mackenzie Valley Environmental Impact Review Board <http://www.reviewboard.ca>	*Mackenzie Valley Resource Management Act* (MVRMA) (S.C. 1998) Mackenzie Valley Land Use Regulations (MVRMA) *Canadian Environmental Assessment Act* (S.C. 1992)
	Territorial Board of Revision	*Property Assessment and Taxation Act* (1988)
Nunavut	Criminal Code Review Board	*Criminal Code* (1985)
	Discipline Board	*Corrections Act* (1988)
	Nunavut Planning Commission <http://www.nunavut.ca>	Nunavut Land Claims Agreement (1992)
	Water Board <http://www.nunavutwaterboard .org/en/home>	*Nunavut Waters and Nunavut Surface Rights Tribunal Act* (NWNSRTA) (2002) Application of Regulations made under paragraph 33(1)(m) or (n) of the Northwest Territories Waters Act in Nunavut Order (NWNSRTA)

Index